Studies in Ancient Europe

Stuart Piggott, B.Litt., D.Lit.Hum., F.B.A., F.S.A.,
Abercromby Professor of Prehistoric Archaeology, University of Edinburgh.   (Photo: M.J.Murray)

Studies in Ancient Europe

Essays presented to Stuart Piggott

Edited by J. M. Coles and D. D. A. Simpson

Leicester University Press   1968

Designed by Arthur Lockwood

© J. M. Coles and D. D. A. Simpson, 1968

Printed in Great Britain by Western Printing Services Ltd, Bristol
for the Leicester University Press

7185 1079 8   40245

Stuart Piggott became Abercromby Professor of Prehistoric Archaeology in the University of Edinburgh in 1946. Since that date he has instructed and guided the research of many undergraduate and postgraduate students. To these, and to his present students, he dedicated his general survey of European prehistory, *Ancient Europe*. In reciprocation, a number of his former pupils and colleagues in the Department of Archaeology, University of Edinburgh, have prepared a series of essays in his honour. This series in no way forms an official *Festschrift*. It commemorates no significant anniversary nor does it appear, like the aged hag in a Celtic festival, as a sign that the king's powers are waning. It is presented as a mark of respect and affection by former pupils and colleagues who have benefited from Stuart Piggott's scholarship and friendship in the past and who hope to do so for many years to come. The choice of topics presented few problems as Stuart Piggott has ranged widely in his writings over the fields of prehistory and early history, and these essays reflect the breadth of his interest.

January 1967   J.M.C. and D.D.A.S.

Contents

Plates

XV   Palaeo-organology: a musical miscellany
    a. Egeln, Germany; pottery drum (1/9). (Landesmus f. Vorgesch; Halle Saale)
  b–c. Copies of drums from Kralupy and Brozsny (1/9). (National Museum, Prague)
    d. S. England; coin of Tasciovanus
    e. Szájzhalombatta, Hungary; figure with double pipes (2/3)
    f. Ittiri, Sardinia; figure with double pipes (Photo: *Cahiers d'Art*)

XVI   Palaeo-organology: a musical miscellany
    a. Isturitz, France; bone flageolet
    b. Üllö, Hungary; bone flageolet (11/9)
    c. Hradiště, Czechoslovakia; bronze figure with horn (2/3). (National Museum, Prague)
    d. Sutton Hoo, England; reconstruction of a miniature harp
    e. 'Grab des Sangers,' St Severin, Germany; reconstruction of harp

Line illustrations

Abbreviations

A.C.	Archaeologia Cantiana
Arch. Camb.	Archaeologia Cambrensis
Arch.	Archaeologia
Acta. Arch. Hung.	Acta Archaeologica Hungarica
Arch. J.	Archaeological Journal
A.J.A.	American Journal of Archaeology
A.N.L.	Archaeological Newsletter
Arch. Ael.	Archaeologia Aeliana
Ant. J.	Antiquaries Journal
Arch. Rozh.	Archeologické Rozhledy
B.B.C.S.	Bulletin of the Board of Celtic Studies
B.R.G.K.	Bericht der Römisch-Germanischen Kommission
B.S.P.F.	Bulletin de la Société Préhistorique Française
C.A.	Cornish Archaeology
C. and W.	Transactions of the Cumberland and Westmorland Archaeological and Antiquarian Society
D.A.J.	Derbyshire Archaeological Journal
Galpin Soc. J.	The Galpin Society Journal
J.B.A.A.	Journal of the British Archaeological Association
J.C.H.A.S.	Journal of the Cork Historical and Archaeological Society
J.R.H.A.A.I.	Journal of the Royal Historical and Archaeological Association of Ireland
J.R.A.I.	Journal of the Royal Anthropological Institute
J.R.S.A.I.	Journal of the Royal Society of Antiquaries of Ireland
J.R.I.C.	Journal of the Royal Institution of Cornwall
K.S.I.A.	Kratkiye Soobščeniya Instituta Arkheologii
K.S.I.I.M.K.	Kratkiye Soobščeniya Instituta Istorii materialnoyi Kulturi
L.A.A.S.	Lincolnshire Architectual and Archaeological Society Reports and Papers
Mat. Arch.	Materialy Archaeologiczne
Med. Arch.	Medieval Archaeology
M.I.A.	Materialy i Issledovaniya po Arkheologii
Oxon.	Oxoniensia
Pam. Arch.	Pamatky Archeologické
P.D.N.H.	Proceedings of the Dorset Natural History and Archaeological Field Club
P.P.S.	Proceedings of the Prehistoric Society
P.P.S.E.A.	Proceedings of the Prehistoric Society of East Anglia
P.S.A.	Proceedings of the Society of Antiquaries of London
P.S.A.S.	Proceedings of the Society of Antiquaries of Scotland
P.S.I.	Proceedings of the Suffolk Institute of Archaeology and Natural History
P.R.I.A.	Proceedings of the Royal Irish Academy
P.W.C.F.C.	Proceedings of the West Cornwall Field Club
P.Z.N.H.A.S.	Transactions of the Penzance Natural History and Antiquarian Society
S.C.I.V.	Studii şi Cercetari di istorie veche
S.N.M.P.	Sbornik Narodniho Musea v Praze
Sy.A.C.	Surrey Archaeological Collections
Sx.A.C.	Sussex Archaeological Collections

T.D.A.	Transactions of the Devonshire Association
T.D.G.N.H.A.S.	Transactions of the Dumfries and Galloway Natural History and Antiquarian Society
The Lizard	Bulletin of the Lizard Field Club
V.C.H.	Victoria County History
U.J.A.	Ulster Journal of Archaeology
W.A.M.	Wiltshire Archaeological Magazine
W.Z.M.L.U.	Wissenschaftliche Zeitschrift der Martin-Luther Universität Halle-Wittenberg
Y.A.J.	Yorkshire Archaeological Journal

Publisher's Note

Notes and references are printed at the end of each article. The pages on which the notes appear are given, in square brackets, on the headline to each text page.

Ancient man in Europe

John M. Coles

In this essay I have tried to summarize the evidence for the presence of man on the continent of Europe in the earlier part of the Pleistocene, that is, during Villafranchian and early Middle Pleistocene times. As we will see, this evidence is scattered and not always of the most acceptable kind. The survey has been designed to allow comparisons with other areas, and to show the degree of the relationship that must have existed between Europe and, in particular, Africa in these early times. I confine my subject to man in the sense of the genus *Homo*, or in the sense that his presence is attested by evidence of lithic industrial activity. That man as a physical being did not develop indigenously in Europe seems now to be a widely-accepted hypothesis, and I will do no more than state that the evidence for a sub-Saharan origin is strong, as much by virtue of the absence of relevant finds elsewhere as by the presence of a succession of finds on that continent. But the evidence for a tropical African origin of tool-making, of industrial activity, is less conclusive, and it is equally possible that this element of culture arose independently in several areas.

For the European evidence of early man I have selected a certain number of sites that seem to warrant a brief examination, some that demonstrate indisputable evidence for man's presence, others less certainly so, some that may be dated with confidence, a few that are less satisfactory.

Basic to this problem is a chronological framework, whether relative or absolute, within which discoveries of industries and hominids may be encompassed. The last word is deliberately chosen to indicate that it is extremely unlikely that we will be able to use horizontal lines within our chronological sequence, but instead some form of successively overlapping framework seems preferable, particularly so for local sequences based primarily upon glacial deposits.

The Pleistocene succession as it has been established for Europe is based upon several related phenomena, which may here be briefly described under three headings, stratified deposits of glacial or interglacial origin, faunal assemblages, and former ocean levels.

The first attempt to establish a relative chronology for the Pleistocene in Europe was made by Penck and Brückner who worked upon the gravel outwash terraces of the Alps.[1] Four major advances of valley glaciers were recognized, and the names given to this sequence, Günz, Mindel, Riss and Würm, have often been employed in describing Pleistocene sequences elsewhere, a practice which is convenient but illogical, and which has contributed much to the problems of interregional and intercontinental correlations. We are concerned here only with the earlier stages of this sequence. It is important to note that even in the small Alpine area (map, fig. 6), the original fourfold division is not without its own complications. The sequence proposed was based primarily upon outwash gravels of the glacier-fed rivers of Bavaria, and the studies of Penck and Brückner, and later that of Eberl,[2] indicated that both the Günz and the Mindel gravels were bipartite. Eberl demonstrated that five gravel spreads stratigraphically earlier than the Günzian Older Deckenschotter also were of glacial outwash origin; these were called the Donau stages. The 1932 agreement that placed Günz and Mindel within the Lower Pleistocene has been superseded by decisions in 1948 to include the Villafranchian period within this Lower Pleistocene, and by Woldstedt's suggestion in 1958 that the first of Penck and Brückner's glacial stages, Günz, be also included in the Lower Pleistocene.[3] The succeeding Middle Pleistocene period contains the Günz-Mindel and Mindel-Riss interglacials, separated by the extensive Mindel glacial phases.

Of far greater consequence for Europe as a whole were the glaciations of the Scandinavian area.[4] These included not only valley but also piedmont glaciers and ice sheets of tremendous weight and distribution. Smaller ice sheets emanating from Scotland and other British highlands may have been physically connected, but this area must be treated independently because of the absence of preserved morainic deposits continuous between the two regions. Happily a correlation is possible on other criteria.

The ground moraines of northern Europe provide a detailed climatic sequence, although successive ice advances tended to destroy in part the remains of the preceding advance, and only one major moraine (Elster) falls within our compass of the Lower and Middle Pleistocene. It was succeeded by further extensive ice advances, including the Saale. Earlier remains have also been indicated, but at the moment these do not represent unequivocal evidence of pre-Elster glaciations. Important however are other deposits of Lower and Middle Pleistocene age in this northern area, which provide more detailed information about the sequence. Whereas glacial advances depend to a great extent upon purely local physical features, interglacial deposits have been shown to provide opportunities for long-range correlations, and this problem of interregional correlation of local Pleistocene sequences depends to a very great extent upon polleniferous deposits of interglacial origin. Pollen will also distinguish to a certain degree between interglacial deposits, representing for northwestern Europe a climate warmer than that of today, and interstadial deposits, of a cooler and less prolonged nature. From north and western Europe four interglacial periods have been recognized, each with its own characteristic vegetational succession.[5]

The Tiglian interglacial (with abundant *Tsuga*) separates, in Alpine terms, the Donau glacial phases from Günz, the Cromerian interglacial (with rare *Tsuga* and no *Abies*) separates Günz and Mindel, and the Hoxnian interglacial (with abundant late *Abies* and absence of a distinct *Carpinus* stage) lies between Mindel (Elster) and Saale; this important phase is also sometimes called Holsteinian. The fourth interglacial, the Eemian, does not directly concern us here.

The third glacial sequence that may be said to be based upon stratigraphical evidence of glacial deposits is that from Britain. Intensive work on ground moraines, particularly well-preserved in East Anglia, indicates a Pleistocene succession with certain local variations. The ground moraines present are Cromer, Lowestoft, Gipping and a late last glaciation not certainly represented in East Anglia. These four do not, however, fall easily by themselves into line with the Alpine or north European sequence. More important for the problem of early man in Europe are the underlying deposits of the East Anglian series, as found at Cromer and elsewhere. Beneath the Cromer Till lies the Cromer Forest Bed, type site for the Cromerian interglacial, which itself overlies the Crag series, in descending order, Weybourne, Norwich, Red and Coralline.[6] The molluscan fauna contained within these Crags provides some indication of the changes that occurred in water temperatures during their formation, and exhibits differing proportions of cold-preferring and warm-preferring species. The basal Coralline Crag contains a number of present-day Mediterranean forms and practically no Arctic forms, but the Red Crag and Norwich Crag each contain small but generally increasing quantities of Arctic forms; in the Weybourne Crag the Mediterranean species are entirely replaced by Arctic species. A high proportion of the molluscan fauna is extinct and cannot be used as climatic indicators. Also to be noted here is the absence of any pronounced climatic fluctuations within the sequence during the deposition of the Crag sands.

A progressive cooling of the climate is, however, clearly indicated; the junction of Coralline-Red Crag is now accepted as marking the division of Pliocene and Pleistocene, and the increase in arctic species in the Weybourne Crag suggests a correlation with the first full glaciation, a correlation discussed below. The East Anglian succession, therefore, indicates a climatic cooling followed by the Cromerian interglacial, two major phases of glacial action (Cromer and Lowestoft, separated by the Corton Sands of uncertain significance), the Hoxnian polleniferous interglacial deposits and then the Gipping glaciation. The succeeding interglacial deposit, the Ipswichian, correlates with the Eemian of northern Europe.

So far, then, we are able to distinguish varying series of glacial deposits in the three areas, with connecting links provided by the interglacial deposits of East Anglia and northern Europe. Polleniferous remains in the Alpine region are not abundant, but there are indications of a more temperate period separating the Donau glacial phases and the Günz.[7] This should correlate with the Tiglian phase in the north, although there seems little indication of this in the Crag succession of East Anglia. Possibly local land features inhibited the representation in the Crags of relevant faunal remains. In the north there is evidence of a Praetiglian phase, of cold-water mollusca and foraminifera, and a flora with *Fagus* and rare Pliocene forms, which provide indications of a cooling climate such as is generally suggested by the Crag series, and by the Donau stage of the Alps.

It is evident that an understanding of local physical features is necessary if we are to rely entirely upon glacial deposits, and a more complete picture of the events of the earlier Pleistocene will be obtained from polleniferous deposits of interglacial or interstadial character, or from other forms of evidence.

One of these additional forms is palaeontological evidence, which if available in quantity will provide some climatic evidence as well as data for interregional correlations. The elephant, rhinoceros, bear and hyena, and some other forms as well, are most commonly employed for dating purposes. Of these, the elephant provides a complicated evolutionary development in which certain clear divisions are apparent.[8] The interglacial form *Palaeoloxodon*, and the steppe-preferring *Mammuthus*, are well represented in a series of deposits, dated on independent geological grounds, and may therefore be employed as correlating factors.

From *Archidiskodon* (*Elephas*) *meridionalis* and *A. planifrons* in Lower Pleistocene times there emerged a *Palaeoloxodon* (*Elephas*) lineage, containing varying specific forms of *antiquus* in Cromerian, Hoxnian and Eemian times, and a *Mammuthus* lineage with two main specific forms, *trogontherii* and *primigenius*, and varying intermediate and sub-specific forms. *M. trogontherii* is characteristic of Mindel times but earlier and later forms of this species are known from the preceding and succeeding glaciations respectively. *M. primigenius* in its typical form appears only in the last glaciation. Hyenas are also commonly used to provide chronological indications in the Pleistocene. *Crocuta crocuta*, for instance, appears in Europe not before Mindel times.[9] Both Zeuner and van der Vlerk have provided lists of those mammals which seem to be best suited for dating purposes.[10] Attempts, however, to use European faunal assemblages in other continental areas, such as Africa, are liable to cause confusion, because different climatic and environmental conditions in the south favoured not only different genera and species but also produced conditions for survival unmatched in the north.[11]

Although large mammals such as these may be successfully used in establishing a broad chronological framework, generally they are tolerant of quite considerable climatic variations and are therefore of little value in any attempt at a more detailed framework. In central Europe, the work by Kretzoi has recently succeeded in producing a well-stratified faunal sequence.[12] The Lower Pleistocene stage, called the Villanyian, is characterized by a developing dominance of steppe elements; the *Mimomys* species of vole is characteristic in the microfauna, while the macrofauna is of Kretzoi's Valdarno type. Kretzoi considers that a distinct cooling of climate occurred at the end of this period. The Middle Pleistocene stage, called the Biharian, is marked by the appearance of modern vole genera (*Microtus*, *Pitymys* and others) and may be divided into a number of sub-phases, representing the temperate period of the Cromerian interglacial, an arctic Tarkö phase, followed by a temperate Vértesszöllös phase and ending with a further arctic phase. The two arctic phases are correlated with Mindel I and Mindel II. Kretzoi and Vertes consider that sufficient comparable micromammalian fauna may be identified in Europe and in Asia to allow firm correlation between sites.

The evidence, however, most susceptible towards intercontinental correlations is that of ocean levels, levels which fluctuated widely throughout the Pleistocene because of glacial eustasy. Only in areas where local uplift or decline of the land was absent may such traces of former sea levels be employed in this way. The basic study of Pleistocene beaches was carried out by de Lamothe in north Africa, and by Depéret on the north Mediterranean shores.[13] The fact that the raised beaches in these areas range from several hundred metres to only a few metres above present sea level must indicate a progressive Pleistocene elevation of the land unconnected with glacial phenomena or local instabilities. The explanation of this convenient feature is perhaps more likely to be a continual expansion of the earth,[14] thereby increasing the potential capacity of the ocean basins, than isostatic uplift of the continents through the loss by erosion of an average 100 m. per million years.[15] This fact, that shore-lines are preserved at varying levels, means that a sequence of high interglacial or interstadial seas of Pleistocene age can be determined. The relative heights of these sea levels are approximately 200 m. (Calabrian), 100 m. (Sicilian), 60 m. (Milazzian), 30–45 m. (Tyrrhenian), 15–18 m., 6–8 m., and 2–4 m. (Main, Late and Epi-Monastirian, respectively). Associated fauna have provided some indications of specific dates for these former high seas. In Italy, foraminifera in late Pliocene deposits suggest an increasingly cool climate, associated with a lowering of the ocean levels prior to the first Pleistocene high sea of approximately 200 m. Blanc has argued that the presence of a northern form, *Cyprina islandica*, in the 200 m. shore-line demonstrates the survival of one cold-preferring form in the warmer phase following the Acquatraversan regression at the beginning of Pleistocene times.[16] The fauna of the Sicilian phase of high seas, and that of the Milazzian, contains a few northern species, again perhaps survivals from regression phases, but the Tyrrhenian fauna includes no northern forms and introduces a new warm fauna containing the tropical *Strombus bubonius*, which continues through the Monastirian stages of 15–18 m. and 6–8 m. The terminology of these high sea level deposits has been confused through conflicting usage of the original names, but the relative heights are agreed.

There is, of course, less evidence of the regression phases, during glacial times, but it appears that the regression between the 60 m. and 30–45 m. sea levels (the Romanian Regression) was of considerable magnitude, not only in the actual fall of the sea but also in the major faunal changes both of marine molluscs and of continental mammals.[17] The regressions of the sea during glacial periods are represented in Italy not only by the Acquatraversan phase but also by a regression following the temperate Calabrian stage, marked by erosion in the Tiber valley and by polleniferous deposits with *Pinus*, *Abies* and *Picea* as well as by solifluction. This phase is called the Cassian glaciation, and should be representative of the Günz glaciation, and the Weybourne Crag of East Anglia. A succeeding glacial episode, the Flaminian, is also represented by a *Pinus* and *Abies* zone, northerly molluscan fauna and soliflucted material. Volcanic activity in the area of Torre in Pietra indicates that the Flaminian glaciation succeeded the Milazzian phase of high seas, and may therefore be correlated with the Romanian Regression.[18]

Correlations between glacial deposits and high shore-lines have been attempted on many occasions; of these, only the Main Monastirian level is generally accepted as being certainly assignable to a specific phase, in this case the last interglacial. The precise positions of succeeding and preceding high levels are less certain, but recent work has demonstrated with a high degree of probability that the 30–45 m. sea is of the Hoxnian interglacial. Less certain is the correlation of the 60 m. sea with the immediately pre-Elster interstadial, or Mindel interstadial. If accepted, then the 100 m. sea should correlate with the Cromerian, and the Calabrian sea level of 200 m. then may represent a pre-Günz warm phase in the Lower Pleistocene.[19]

From glacial features we know of the existence of the Günz glaciation and the pre-Günz Donau glacial stages, separated by temperate Tiglian deposits. We know from the East Anglian Crags that a progressive cooling of climate is indicated from the Red Crag through to the Günz-correlated Weybourne Crag, with little indication of the Tiglian warmer phase. Nor do the deposits contemporaneous with the Acquatraversan glacial phase in Italy indicate a marked change from Pliocene to initial Pleistocene times, although the later Cassian phase, of Günz age, shows marked climatic cooling, probably contemporary with a late stage of the Villanyian faunal stage in Hungary, wherein there is also indication of a distinct cooling of the climate. A subsidiary element in this is obtained by palaeotemperature curves for parts of the Pleistocene, which, in so far as they can be assumed to correlate with glacial and interglacial phases, show not a uniform series of undulations representing the major continental climatic phases, but a complex series of major and minor fluctuations. Emiliani's reconstruction of a palaeotemperature curve for the Middle and Late Pleistocene,[20] with absolute dates based upon extrapolation from radiocarbon and protoactinium/thorium determinations, is now a better basis for our understanding of Pleistocene events on a world-wide scale than is the traditional glacial sequence; but for the continent of Europe with which we are concerned, the local glacial and interglacial episodes are meaningful.

A tentative correlation of some of these lines of evidence, for the Lower and Middle Pleistocene, might appear as follows:

Period	Glacial and interglacial phases	Mediterranean sea levels	Fauna
Middle Pleistocene	Hoxnian, Holsteinian	Tyrrhenian, 30–45 m.	*Strombus bubonius*
	Lowestoft, Mindel II, Elster, Flaminian	Romanian Regression	
		Milazzian, 60 m.	Biharian
	Cromer, Mindel I	Regression	
	Cromerian	Sicilian, 100 m.	
Lower Pleistocene	Weybourne, Günz, Cassian	Regression	
	Crags, Donau-Günz, Tiglian	Calabrian, 200 m.	Villanyian
	Red Crag, Donau, Praetiglian	Regression	
Pliocene	Corraline, Astian		

This now brings us to a stage where we may look for the first traces of man's activities in Europe. There are at the moment of writing two distinct sets of evidence, one concerned with 'pre-Crag man' and his claimed representations in the Lower Pleistocene series of East Anglia, the other a well-established series of sites that indicate occupation of wide areas in Europe within early Middle Pleistocene times. I have chosen to describe some of East Anglian evidence because it seems to me unjust to dismiss all this material without some consideration. Our knowledge about natural fracturing agencies, in other parts of the world, provides a sufficient cautionary element.[21]

The evidence for the existence of man in East Anglia in 'pre-Crag' times is intimately associated with the research of J. Reid Moir, who stands as the champion of a number of archaeologists of the earlier part of this century. It is not necessary here to go into the detailed problems of stratigraphical correlations, because it is possible to select a few sites whose geological age is not in question. What is in question is the evidence for human activity at these sites. This involves us at once in a definition of tool-making as practised in early times. It is, of course, obvious that not all flakes exhibiting cones and bulbs of percussion are thereby of human manufacture. Natural agencies for the flaking by percussion and pressure are many and varied, and include storm beaches and river-beds, rock falls and glacial pressures. In addition, such natural actions are also capable of applying 'secondary retouch' to previously fractured flint and stone. In general, an absence of what to our minds would be a logical application of this trimming is apparent in these naturally-affected flakes, but this is not always the case and seemingly logical 'implements' can be found in quite impossible early geological contexts, or, rarely, in modern beach and river gravels.

To insist that rigorous rules must be complied with before any stone objects are accepted as of deliberate manufacture is a proper and scientific approach to the problem of recognition, but the very nature of the evidence for the earliest traces of tool production makes it extremely difficult to formulate such rules. Three laws have been advanced from time to time, requirements that must be fulfilled before an object may be considered as a tool, (1) that the object conforms to a set and regular pattern, (2) that it is found in unequivocable association with other manifestations of man's activities, whether settlement or burial, or chipping or killing site, (3) that it itself shows signs of flaking from two or three directions at right angles to one another. Natural agencies will tend to flake in one direction only, if the stone is held in place, or in multi-directions, if the stone is being tumbled about. Ideally, recognized implements should conform to all three rules above, but in practice it is unnecessary for objects clearly in traditional styles, such as forms of handaxe, or prepared-core flakes, to be associated with other evidence of man's presence. Yet at the earliest level of controlled tool-making, traditions of pattern and technique will be only weakly developed and here the rule of association becomes paramount. Unfortunately, the first group of evidence considered here about early man in Europe lacks these vital associations.

The East Anglian evidence for early tool-manufacturing comes from a variety of sites and geological positions, but the latter may, I think, be effectively reduced to five. The terms used in the past to describe the flints from these sites include eolith, pre-Crag, and Cromerian, but in this essay I propose to disregard these names. The Cromerian flints, for example, need not be associated with the Cromerian interglacial period, nor are they necessarily from Cromer itself, and the pre-Crag flints are in certain cases found within the Crag sands. The word eolith has had such a variety of connotations that it has come to mean, in most cases, non-humanly struck flints.

The geological position of the stone objects in question may be simply stated. The earliest are reported from the basal portion of the Red Crag, where they are found as rolled and derived flints. On this basis these objects are of the initial phase of the Pleistocene period. High within the Red Crag, further and more prolific flint assemblages are reported. Of later age are assemblages, including the test specimen rostro-carinate, from a basal stony deposit of the Norwich Crag. Two assemblages are reported as contemporary with the Cromer Forest Bed, an uncertain group from the lower Freshwater bed, and a different form perhaps to be associated with the upper Freshwater bed.

The geological age of these stone assemblages is not in much doubt, but their verity as tools remains a considerable problem. The rolled flints from the detritus bed at the base of the Red Crag, found at Bramford near Ipswich,[22] are for the most part flaked from varying directions upon both dorsal and ventral surfaces, but there is one object superficially of handaxe form, with thirteen flake scars upon one face, and twelve upon the other (fig. 1, 1). These scars appear to have been directed from a multiplicity of positions on the edges, and are sufficiently elongated to overlap at the centre of one face, producing thereby a triangular-sectioned 'tool.'

Stratigraphically later are assemblages recovered from the '16 Foot Level' (below the surface) at Foxhall Hall, near Ipswich, by Reid Moir in 1919–20.[23] The Red Crag sand deposits here were interrupted in their upper portion by a sand-with-gravel intercalated between thin darker deposits with shell-casts, bones and flints. Above and below were horizontally stratified clean sand deposits, showing no evidence of natural agencies sufficient to flake the flints found sporadically in the two dark layers. Moir presumed that the latter represented temporary land surfaces covered by encroaching waters of the Crag sea. The flints from the dark bands are patinated white, but some darker-patinated flints are also present. Again there are a number of struck flakes with little or irregular secondary flaking, associated with one or two bifacially-flaked objects and others which appear to exhibit flake scars leading up to a point (fig. 1, 2–4). The geological position of the Foxhall assemblage, if undisturbed, suggests that there was no natural agency present that could have produced such flaking, and the apparently unrolled fresh nature of the flints suggests that these have not been transported. The claimed association of a human jawbone with these flints caused considerable controversy in the later nineteenth century.

The stone bed at the base of the Norwich Crag, from which other flint assemblages were recovered, represents a further stage of the Lower Pleistocene Crags.[24] At Thorpe in Norfolk, beneath approximately 25 feet of mainly horizontally-stratified deposits of clays, sands and gravels, the Stone Bed was one foot thick, and consisted of flints in clayey-sand with abundant shells preserved *in situ* and unbroken. Many slender flint nodules were also undamaged. The flaked flints recovered proved to represent only 5% of the total of flints, and many of these Thorpe flakes were believed to exhibit deliberate flaking. The flakes include irregular forms with even retouch along one or two edges. Most important, however, is a large 'hand-axe,' bifacially-flaked with cortex remaining on parts of both surfaces, and with quite straight edges (fig. 2, 1). This implement is in fresh condition, and it is unlikely that it could have survived transport in this state. It is said to have been found during Sainty's investigations, embedded with a fallen boulder of the Stone Bed, at Whitlingham, site of the 'test specimen,' which is described below.

Two sites formerly believed to have been contemporary with the upper Crag series are the famous 'workshop-sites' at Cromer and East Runton, Norfolk. Both sites were worked by Reid Moir from 1920, and a large quantity of fractured flints was recovered. The sites lay on the foreshore, and Moir believed that the occupation had taken place on the Stone Bed, and that it should therefore extend in places under the cliffs at Cromer.[25] Of the immense quantities of flints available, only a small proportion were flaked, and Moir believed, rightly it seems, that wave-action could not have caused this fracturing. Most of the flaked pieces were irregular, but a few straight-edged retouched flakes occurred (fig. 2, 2). Moir examined other areas of foreshore, to serve as a check on natural flaking in the exposures, and claimed that

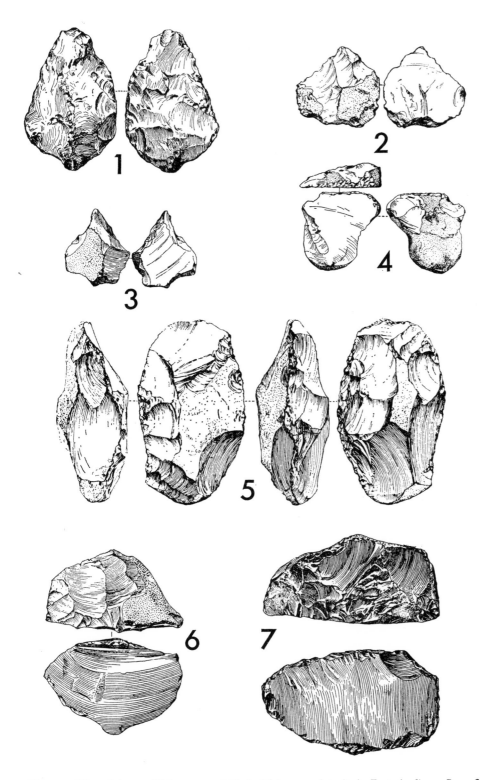

Figure 1. Flints from pre-Pleistocene and Early Pleistocene deposits in East Anglia. 1, Bramford, Suffolk, England. 2–4, Foxhall, Suffolk, England. 5, Sidestrand, Norfolk, England. 6, Grays, Essex; below Eocene beds. 7, Whitlingham, Norfolk, England; rostro-carinate. (1–5, after Moir; 6–7, after Oakley) 1/2

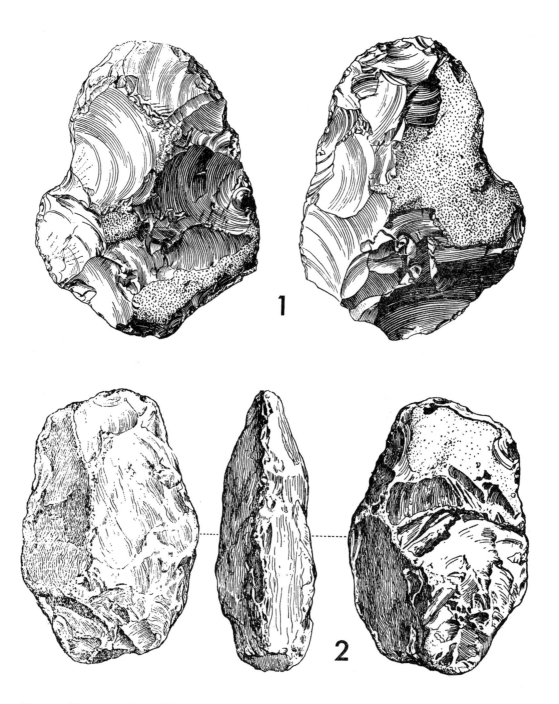

Figure 2. Flints from Early Pleistocene deposits in Norfolk. 1, Whitlingham, Norfolk, England. 2, Cromer, Norfolk, England. (1–2, after Moir) 1/2

there were no struck flakes outside his 'workshop-sites,' which had yielded both fractured flakes and cores.[26] These sites, however, are not generally accepted as showing any sign of man's activity; the flint deposit is believed to occur only on the foreshore, and not to extend under the Cromer Forest Bed in the cliffs at Cromer. The flints are clearly eroded from the chalk which underlies the present shingle beach. Their fracturing in isolated areas of the foreshore is discussed below.

The last deposit to be noted here is at Sidestrand, Norfolk, where a boulder clay, apparently the Cromer Till, yielded an undoubted handaxe,[27] although its precise typological character is subject to some uncertainty (fig. 1, 5). It is believed to have been transported by glacial action from the upper part of the Cromer Forest Bed.

The controversy that developed in scientific publications about the authenticity of many of these assemblages as human work led to extravagant claims on both sides. One of the first of these statements was made in the publication of the Norfolk test specimen of the rostro-carinate series, from the Stone Bed, which was published by Sir Ray Lankester in 1914, following his more extensive publication in 1912.[28] Lankester prefaced his description with the words that in his judgment 'it is not possible for anyone acquainted with flint-workmanship and also with the non-human fracture of flint to maintain that it is even in a remote degree possible that the sculpturing of this Norwich test flint was produced by other than human agency.' His description was full and was accompanied by drawings and photographs, showing that approximately 40 flakes had been removed from various angles and positions around the flint, consisting of two cleaving fractures, a group of large conchoidal flakings, and a third group of smaller flakings directed upon specific parts, particularly the beaked portion (fig. 1, 7). The general comparison with the series of rostro-carinates collected together by Lankester in his 1912 paper is worthy of note.

Lankester's belief in the artificial manufacture of rostro-carinates was strongly criticized by F. N. Haward in 1919, who advanced entirely natural agencies as the fabricator of this object, and of Moir's 'Cromerian.'[29] This prompted Moir to make a number of pointed remarks backed by some strong evidence of the precise geological deposits in which his 'industries' had been discovered.[30] A. S. Barnes also severely criticized Haward's work, and sharp exchanges took place in the pages of the *Proceedings of the Prehistoric Society of East Anglia*.[31]

A more scholarly attack on the authenticity of the 'industries' was made by S. Hazzledine Warren in 1921, who claimed that mechanical movement of flint upon flint under pressure produced flaking comparable to that seen on not only the Kentish eoliths but also the rostro-carinates (fig. 1, 6) and other Crag assemblages.[32] Warren based his argument upon his observations of fractured flints in Eocene deposits in Essex, and upon experiments.[33] Moir and Barnes defended themselves vigorously, and claimed that natural pressure flaking could easily be distinguished from the edge-flaking on the Kentish eoliths and on the Crag series. The naturally-produced specimens claimed by Warren to be of rostro-carinate form from the Essex gravels were said to be entirely different.[34] An International Commission, established to examine the question, was overwhelmingly in support of Moir's conclusions, that the flints from the base of the Red Crag near Ipswich were in undisturbed strata, and that some of the flaking was indubitably of artificial origin.[35] Warren however did not retire from the field but reiterated his contention that the circumstances of flaking by entirely natural means were so varied that there could be no doubt that all the eoliths and Crag flints had been naturally fractured.[36] Barnes and Moir replied in their usual fashion, and the controversy continued for a number of years.[37]

In 1932 T. D. Kendrick outlined some of the different viewpoints, and came down strongly in support of Moir, not so much on the geological problems involved as on the character of some of the flints.[38] He believed, not only for Moir's flints but also for other 'eolithic industries,' that 'many of them are to be regarded as "probably artifacts," while there are one or two (in the British Museum) . . . that I feel certain *are* man's handiwork.' One of the final statements was made by Warren in 1948 in an address to the Geological section of the Southwestern Union of Scientific Societies.[39] He believed that the Crags as a whole represent a series of offshore sands, and that the stone beds which are found at the base of a number of the Crag sands are not beach deposits but are the result of slow submarine erosion of the Chalk. In this he followed Clement Reid, who considered that the forming beach was pushed forward with the encroachment of the sea upon the land, leaving behind a more or less bare surface of basic rock, with, in places, flint beds exposed through this erosion and left on top of the marine platform. The abundance of marine shells in places would be expected, and the occurrence of animal bone might be explained as fluviatile-derived or as drifted material. Warren considered that it was unlikely to suppose that the basement beds of flint were ever elevated sufficiently to form a land surface, as the extent of the marine Crag sands is considerable, and there is no evidence of a series of emergence and submergence. The question of actual land surfaces was never thoroughly examined by Moir or his associates. Warren believed that the density of the flaked flints over the Crag platforms reached as much as 50% in places. He agreed with Moir in considering that, at the present day, wave action was not an effective process in the fracturing of flint in a way comparable to that seen on Moir's Crag specimens, but tried to find some other natural process that could have flaked the submarine flints exposed by erosion of that Chalk. Warren concluded that during the formation of the Crag deposits, the area must have been subject to the arrival of icebergs from the north. Such ice, grounding near the shores of the Crag sea, might well have caused the pressure-crushing and striation of the flints exposed on the seabed. These arguments, apart from being practically the last word in the controversy, also neatly disposed of many of the points made by Moir about the differences between sea action fractures and his 'implements,' and allowed the exposure and deposition of fragile marine shells amidst the ice-fractured stone beds.

That, however, the scientific world did not see fit to accept either side without considerable uncertainty must account for the quite remarkable inattention that this East Anglian problem has received since the days of active controversy. I suspect that Warren's arguments may well be correct in basic detail and, if so, then there remains only one positive source of support for Moir's views, that some flints from a few deposits are in themselves so shaped that by no conceivable means could they have been so formed by nature alone. Unfortunately, the natural processes that were at work upon the flints are not observable today in precisely comparable circumstances, so that an element of doubt must remain, but we might select, without excuse for this subjective attitude, several flints for a last time. On inspecting both the published finds, which in all cases seem to have been the flints most favourable to the theory of human workmanship, and some of the actual specimens, I believe that only two flints are worthy of more careful examination, apart from the undoubted handaxe apparently from the Cromer Till at Sidestrand in Norfolk. Nothing yet seen from the foreshore deposits at Cromer and East Runton can be accepted, nor, in my opinion, can the rostro-carinates be shown to represent human activity; the quantity of flake scars is not as important as the quality.

There remain two flints to consider, one apparently from the Stone Bed at the base of the Norwich Crag, at Whitlingham. On the face of it, this object is convincing as a handaxe (fig. 2, 1). Unfortunately, it was not discovered *in situ* but lay with fallen material at the foot of a tall section. Moir believed this was associated with Stone Bed material, but the section consisted of eroded chalk with embedded flints underlying the Stone Bed and Crag sands capped by glacial gravels. It is possible that this object came from the till and not from the Stone Bed although Sainty and Moir claimed it was definitely from the latter. The second flint was found at the base of the Red Crag at Bramford in Suffolk and its stratigraphical horizon is not in doubt. It lay in the Detritus Bed in London Clay and was sealed by Crag sands. It is reminiscent of Chellean axes with triangular sections, but is considerably rolled; although it bears some 25 flake scars, and has lost all its cortex, the irregular nature of the object itself is not convincing (fig. 1, 1).

Lastly, the flints from the 16 Foot Level at Foxhall are worthy of note again, because they, and they alone, were stratified in such a position as to make their presence and fracturing *in situ* under the conditions envisaged by Warren most unlikely. The flints are in fresh condition, and were not at all common in the two black bands within the Red Crag sands, where natural pressures are not likely to have been operational with effect. The bands may represent temporary periods of land exposure during a general marine phase in this area. The source of the flints is unknown, unless eroded on the landward side and brought by fluvial action upon the sands; nothing in the stratigraphy indicates such action. The fact that little flint was observed in the intervening coprolite bed at Foxhall makes it the more likely that there may well have been artificial agencies at work here. Unfortunately, however, few of the flints found by Moir are convincing; a number are small flakes little over one inch in length, others are larger with edge flaking (fig. 1, 2–4). One or two are bifacially retouched.

Nevertheless, it must be borne in mind that a number of the flakes from a site such as Vértesszöllös (see below) might also not have been accepted as demonstrating human workmanship if they had not been found on an undoubted working floor, in association with other human activities. As far as Foxhall is concerned, the presence of the jawbone, quite clearly *Homo sapiens*, suggests disturbance of some sort. Perhaps local landslip has occurred, bringing an upper Crag deposit on top of a recent land surface which itself overlay Crag sands *in situ*.

Recent brief considerations given to these flint assemblages from and beneath the Crags include acceptance of the existence of artificial flaking on some of the flints, by Leakey and Burkitt for instance,[40] a non-committal statement by Breuil and Lantier,[41] and rejection of all, by Oakley and others.[42] Although Oakley goes so far as to say that 'the chipping in some cases suggests intelligent design,' he believes that none can be accepted without some reserve. Howell dismisses all of this material[43] by stating that 'the angles of fracture and the nature of the flake removal . . . fall outside the range of variation of specimens known otherwise to be of human manufacture,' but this is surely not a valid basis for rejection, particularly in view of the variability of known industries of the Lower and early Middle Pleistocene throughout the Old World.

We might summarize by pointing out that, in view of the evidence of early man in north Africa and in southern Europe, there is nothing basically startling about the presence of human industries in East Anglia at the beginning of the Middle Pleistocene. The axe from Sidestrand, if it is, in fact, a palaeolithic tool and not a neolithic rough-out in an erosion pocket, suggests that man was present during the Cromerian interglacial period, or early in Mindel times. This would not be out of step with the evidence for man's presence in Europe, discussed below, during these periods, but the character of the handaxe is rather surprising. But even more surprising would be the existence of a handaxe tradition encompassing the Whitlingham axe in the Norwich Crag phase, of pre-Günzian age, which at the moment would seem radically out of step with our evidence for early man, and early industries, in both Africa and Europe. The evidence for humanly-struck flints at Foxhall, certainly the most puzzling of all the East Anglian sites, if accepted would extend back to the earliest Villa-franchian, and would indicate that an enormous gap in our evidence for early man existed, if we were to maintain our belief in an African origin. The Foxhall flints do not exhibit any element of a handaxe tradition, and this at least is in keeping with the evidence of a pre-handaxe tradition in Europe, involving flakes and choppers, and perhaps involving the term Abbevillian as well.

A fair comment on the East Anglian material would, I think, be concerned to point out that the typology of the claimed implements was not necessarily outside the range of variation known from humanly-worked industries in Europe and Africa, but that we have very little information about the natural flaking processes available in East Anglia in early Pleistocene times, some of which might well have been capable of producing flaked flints including bifacially-worked 'handaxes'; no natural sources are known today which could do this under observation. Our greatly augmented evidence about the chronology of early tool-making in other parts of the world continues, however, to suggest how extraordinary it would be if the East Anglian Crag industries were of human manufacture. Perhaps future discoveries will remove this particular chronological difficulty.

I turn now to the second group of evidence, one which fortunately does not involve us in such problems of authenticity and rivalry. At the moment of writing, the earliest known human remains from Europe are represented by a single jaw from the Mauer Sands near Heidelberg.[44] The site lies in an abandoned meander of the Neckar river, and the fluvatile sands were later covered by extensive loessic deposits. The date of the jawbone depends upon the geological sequence and the associated fauna. On the basis of the number of loesses, Soergel believed that the sands could not be later than the Mindel I–Mindel II interstadial, and might be earlier.[45] The fauna suggested to Zeuner that the Mauer Sands were not likely to be as early as the Cromerian interglacial.[46] The assemblage included an early form of *Palaeoloxodon antiquus, Dicerorhinus etruscus, Hippopotamus* sp., *Cervus elaphus, Bison priscus,* and *Homo heidelbergensis.* The last-named is probably allied to the *Homo erectus* group, although there is still some disagreement.[47] Recent work on rodent fauna in central Europe has prompted Kretzoi and Vértes to place Mauer in their stage C of the Biharian sequence, in the Cromerian interglacial. Oakley supports this dating on the basis of the early form of elephant which contrasts with Mindel's *Mammuthus trogontherii*, and of the absence of *Crocuta crocuta*, a hyena introduced into Europe not before the beginning of Mindel times.[48]

Although these views hold that the Mauer jaw is of Cromerian age, Rust's attempts to associate it with a lithic industry have met with little success. Rust claimed to have found stone tools at Mauer and elsewhere in contemporary sites of northern Germany.[49] The stones from the jaw site were recovered from the base of the Grafenrain sandpit and from overlying gravels; the latter correlate with the actual horizon from which the jaw was extracted. The claimed tools are on sandstone, and some are fresh, others severely rolled. The publication of these in detail, with various sub-groups, has met with little acceptance, but the claim by some reviewers of the book that they are unacceptable because they do not conform to clear-cut tool types is surely unjust. Industries of this date may have been unstandardized to an overwhelming degree. Nevertheless, Rust presented no evidence that these sandstone objects were different from naturally-fractured rocks in corresponding geological formations.

A site that provides acceptable evidence of an industry of fossil man in early middle Pleistocene Europe is Vértesszöllös.[50] Vértesszöllös lies some 50 km. to the northwest of Budapest in the Atáler valley, a former tributary of the Danube. The site itself consists of a stratified sequence of calcareous muds and loessic elements with travertines. Geologically this series indicates the end of a warm period and the onset of colder loess-forming conditions, but the rich fauna enables a more precise date to be assigned. The fauna belongs to stage E of the Biharian stage, that is, a slightly warmer phase between D and F. We might recall here that the Mauer fauna is considered to belong to stage C, in late Cromerian times, and Vértesszöllös is best interpreted as falling within the Mindel interstadial and Mindel II (Elster). The relative decrease in numbers of *Pitymys arvalidens*, and the increase of *Microtus conjungens*, from the base of the fossiliferous deposits upwards, point to a deteriorating climate. Five separate industrial horizons have been discovered at Vértesszöllös, two in the travertine and lime mud of the lower complex, two in the overlying loessic deposits and one in upper lime muds. Although this physical separation must indicate a considerable period of time, the five industries are remarkably alike in general character.

Represented in these levels are actual working floors, with unrolled quartzite and other stone tools, cores and waste flakes, fragments of animal bones including burnt bone, and traces of hearths. The lithic industry is mainly on pebbles, some on limestone boulders, and about half are of quartzite with the remainder of flint, chert and radiolarite. Cortex remains on most of the tools, which average only 24 mm. in length and have rather irregular retouch forming denticulated edges (fig. 3, 1–4). The industry as a whole belongs to the Buda pebble industries of the immediate area. A similar association of Upper Biharian mammalian fauna and a pebble-tool industry on flint and quartzite occurred at the Varhegy of Buda. In the lowest industrial horizon at Vértesszöllös there have been found hominid teeth and fragments of occipital bone, which have been described as *Homo erectus* or *Homo* sp. Man, therefore, with an unspecialized non-handaxe lithic tradition, was present in this part of central Europe by later Mindel times. Possible analogous material from Czechoslovakia, and reported pebble tools from the River Dirjov in Rumania (map, fig. 6), cannot unfortunately be dated

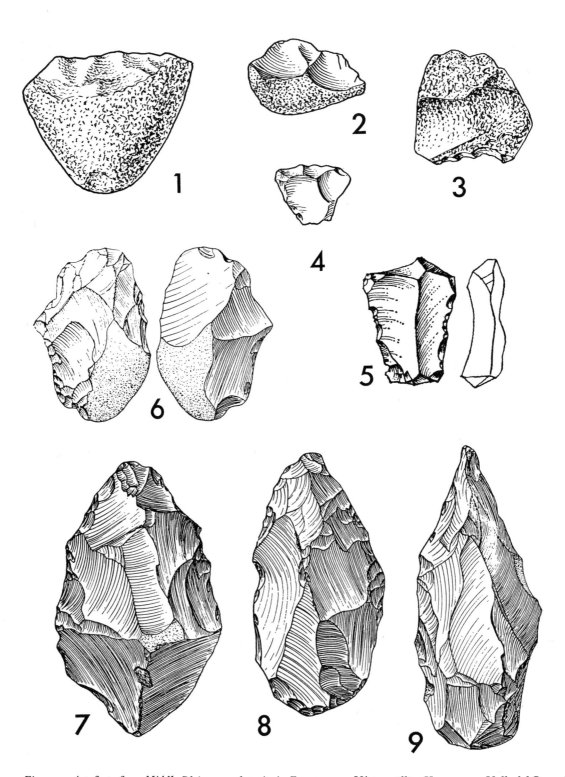

Figure 3. Artefacts from Middle Pleistocene deposits in Europe. 1–4, Vértesszöllös, Hungary. 5, Valle del Correchio, Emilia, Italy. 6–9, Abbeville, France. (1–4, after Kretzoi and Vertes; 5, after Leonardi; 6–9, after Bordes) 1/2

with any degree of certainty. Similarly, there seems no justification for the reported presence of Chellean handaxe industries in European Russia. Flake industries from the Kuban basin, and along the Dnieper, are also undated.

An occupation in Italy contemporary with Vértesszöllös is, however, suggested by a find in the Valchetta Cartoni, Rome, where flakes have been found underneath the earliest volcanic tuffs from the Sabatino group of volcanoes.[51] The volcanic activity of this group began during a cold period, and, at Torre in Pietra, Milazzian deposits apparently underlie the first tuffs. At other exposures, the early tuffs are intercalated in peat deposits with pine and silver-fir, or stratified with cold-preferring mollusca and fauna. The flakes, of an unspecialized character, are thus probably of Mindel II age. Flakes recovered from a terrace of the Rio Correchio valley may represent a similar industry (fig. 3, 5), although they occur with handaxes of 'Abbevillian' and Acheulean forms. In England, it is unlikely that Clactonian flakes from the lower gravels at Swanscombe are as early as the Valchetta Cartoni flakes, although the striations on some of the former may indicate original deposition during late Mindel times.[52]

In France any discussion of early man must refer to the river terraces of the Somme. These formations have been the subject of many studies by geologists and archaeologists since the beginning of this century but the essential information we require comes from reports and collections made in the last decade of the nineteenth century by G. d'Ault de Mesnil at the Porte du Bois suburb of Abbeville. Breuil and Koslowski recorded the details of other significant exposures along the Somme,[53] basing their conclusions on reinterpretations of the work of another pioneer, V. Commont. The Upper Middle terrace, the bench of which lies at 42–5 m. above the floor of the buried channel below the terrace exposure, has been linked with a sea level of 57–8 m. above that of the present day according to de Lamothe, who employed the levels of the highest fluviatile deposit on each terrace exposure. This terrace was well represented by sections at Abbeville (Carrière Carpentier) and at St Acheul (C. Fréville). On the bench, cut by an erosion phase of the river, lies a series of gravels, the basal portion apparently of coarse angular material with coombe rock, and this solifluction merges with less angular gravel and sands of fluviatile origin, capped by horizontally-bedded sandy calcareous silts, probably indicating the former existence of a shallow marsh on a meander of the river. The faunal remains associated with the silts and marl have been reinterpreted on several occasions, but there seems to be general agreement that it contained *Palaeoloxodon trogontherii* and *P. antiquus*, the latter perhaps an archaic form with *Archidiskodon meridionalis* affinities, *Dicerorhinus etruscus*, *Equus stenonis*, *Sus scrofa*, *Hippopotamus* sp., *Cervus elaphus*, *Machairodus latidens* and other forms. The assemblage clearly belongs to the Cromerian faunal phase. An unrolled industry containing archaic (Abbevillian) handaxes was associated with this fauna (fig. 3, 6–9) and this provides the only evidence of associated handaxe industry and Cromerian fauna known at the present day in Europe. The Cromerian faunal stage, however, does not necessarily signify a Cromerian interglacial age, as it has been shown recently that much of this fauna survived well into Mindel times. The silts of the implementiferous deposit may in fact belong to a restricted series stratigraphically between the Upper Middle and the Lower High Terrace, but their dating remains as above.

Above the first fluviatile series is an erosional disconformity to be correlated probably with the Romanian Regression, overlain by a second partly fluviatile deposit, mainly of sands and containing a more developed industry and more evolved fauna. The latter includes *Palaeoloxodon antiquus*, *Bos*, *Equus*, *Dicerorhinus* (*merckii*) *kirchbergensis*, *Hippopotamus*, and the industry is in the Acheulean tradition. These gravels are, in fact, a part of the Lower Middle Terrace deposits which overlapped on to the eroded surface of the Upper Middle Terrace. They are overlain by Older Loess, and are evidently of the Mindel-Riss interglacial. According to de Lamothe, the top of the first fluviatile series graded into a sea level of 57–8 m., a height which is correlated with the Milazzian or Sicilian II sea, and such a sea is now considered to represent a Mindel I–Mindel II interstadial sea. The evidence of the Somme terraces, then, is that man's occupation of this area took place at least as early as the Mindel interstadial.

There is some slight evidence that industrial activity was being carried on in the area before this date.[54] At Montières, some 40 km. away, a High Terrace series has been recognized, consisting of two deposits, a Lower High Terrace 50–5 m. above the river channel, and an Upper High Terrace at 61–6 m. The latter deposit is made up of silts conformably overlying an ancient soil which itself rests upon coarse calcareous gravels. These gravels, believed to represent a cold period in the history of the river system, have yielded a number of flint flakes which were lying near or at the top of this deposit. The flints include a large natural flake with secondary flaking (fig. 4, 4) and a group which lay close together and were altered by the action of fire. The excavators believed that this site indicates occupation by man in the Eburonian phase during the Günz glaciation.

Industrial material probably contemporary with the Abbevillian of the Somme is reported from other river gravels in France. The Pleistocene river channel at Mainxe-Tilloux in the Charente, for example, has been believed to date by its fauna to Mindel times or earlier.[55] The bed of the ancient channel lies some 10–12 m. above the present Charente, and its filling rises to 14–24 m. above the river. The associated fauna was originally identified by Boule as including *Archidiskodon meridionalis*, *Palaeoloxodon antiquus* and *Mammuthus primigenius*, but later studies apparently suggested that *M. trogontherii* was present and not *M. primigenius*. The cultural material consisted of rolled 'Abbevillian' and less-rolled Acheulean handaxes with many flakes. A cordiform axe and disc were also associated. The site requires further study and confirmation.

In the Garonne valley, a series of terraces with glacio-fluvial gravels and associated industrial material may also indicate human occupation before the Great Interglacial.[56] The industry contained within some of these gravels is on quartz and quartzite (fig. 4, 1–3). A terrace deposit 80 m. above the river is said to contain rolled fractured stones, including bifacial handaxe forms. Below this, at heights approximately 55–60 m. above the river, are further sloped and eroded gravel spreads with a few unrolled handaxes deep in coarse gravel, and many rolled specimens within the upper levels. Breuil claimed that this terrace was connected with Mindel moraines.

In the Alpes Maritimes, the cave of Vallonnet has recently been investigated.[57] The cave lies just over 100 m. above sea level, and its basal filling consists of marine deposits laid down during the Sicilian (108 m.) transgression. The abundant littoral fauna includes *Gryphaea virleti* and the tropical *G. cucullata*, as well as *Patella ferruginea*. The marine deposit was eventually overlain by terrestrial sediments containing a quantity of mammalian fauna and some stone tools. The upper part of these deposits exhibits frost fracturing. The fauna

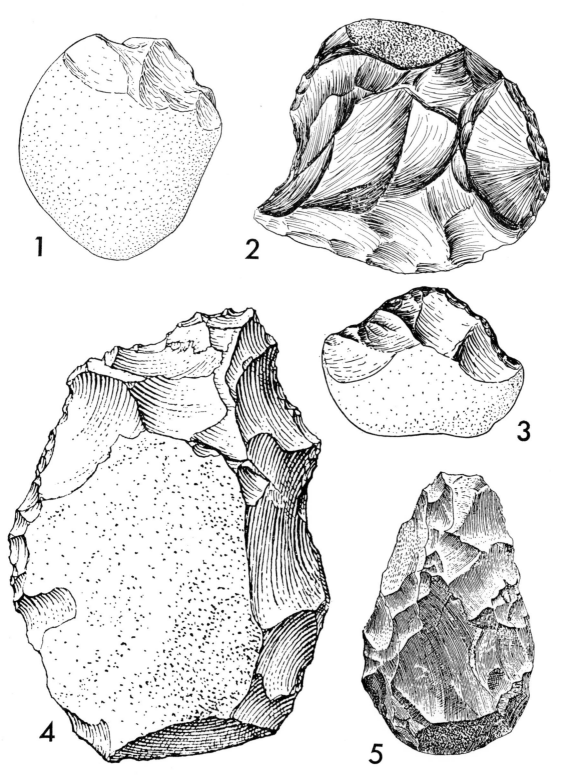

Figure 4. Artefacts from Early and Middle Pleistocene deposits in western Europe. 1–3, Mondavezan, Haute-Garonne, France. 4, Montières, France. 5, Torralba, Spain. (1–3, after Breuil and Meroc; 4, after Agache and Bourdier; 5, after Müller-Karpe) 1/2

contains a bovid, *Leptobos etruscus* and the brown bear, *Ursus* cf. *arctos*, as well as smaller quantities of *Dicerorhinus etruscus*, *Archidiskodon meridionalis*, and *Equus* cf. *stenonis*. The industry, on limestone, quartzite and flint, is sparse, containing several flakes with edge fractures, and a few pebbles with flakes removed from end or side (fig. 5, 1–2). The occupation has been dated to late Villafranchian times, on the basis of the fauna and the geology.

Probably of a later age is the human occupation reported from the Escale cave, Bouches-du-Rhône.[58] Details are rather sparse, but apparently the cave sediments contain a fauna with both Villafranchian and Middle Pleistocene elements, including *Ursos* cf. *deningeri*, *Machairodus* sp., *Dicerorhinus* cf. *kirchbergensis*, *Crocuta brunea*, *Canis etruscus* var. *arnensis* and *Acinonyx pardinensis*. On geological grounds a cold climatic period is indicated, and it has been suggested that the occupation took place in Mindel I times. Only a few limestone flakes have been recovered, but a number of hearths up to one metre in diameter are reported, with ash and wood charcoal.

In Portugal, the evidence of early man is obtained from high-level raised beaches with contained pebble industries.[59] A well-marked fossil beach, at heights varying from 20 to 35 m., may represent the Tyrrhenian sea, and thus higher exposures would logically be of greater antiquity. Unfortunately only this Tyrrhenian beach is well preserved, and traces of Milazzian and Sicilian deposits are sparse. Nevertheless, fractured pebbles are reported from both of these earlier beaches, quartzite pebbles with two or three flake scars at one end (fig. 5, 9), as well as some flakes and one true biface from Açafora at the higher level. These sites and objects require further research, but their potential correlation with north African raised beach evidence is of the utmost importance.

Another southwest European site worthy of mention here is the palaeolithic site of Torralba, which lies some 156 km. northeast of Madrid at an altitude of over 1100 m.[60] On the basis of palaeontology, geology and palynology, the occupation here may be dated to a period of cool climate during late Elster times. Various occupation levels, extending in thickness to over 3 m., were discovered within a series of sands, gravels and marls, divided by two erosional phases. The climate in general was cooler and wetter than that of today, but a number of minor oscillations occurred. The occupation seems to have taken place first in a cold moist phase, succeeded by a temperate interval and finally by a return to cool moist conditions. Pinewoods were the dominant trees at all times in this marginal periglacial area. Occupation had ceased by the time moist, temperate conditions returned, and this was succeeded by a very cold phase. There follows, at Torralba, the development of Terra Fucsa soil which has been correlated with the Great Interglacial. Geologically the occupation seems therefore to belong to a later stage in pre-Mindel-Riss times, in late Elster. The fauna recovered from the occupied butchery sites is predominantly *Palaeoloxodon antiquus*, with *Equus caballus*, *Cervus elaphus* and *Bos primigenius*. The industrial material used for killing and dismembering large game includes handaxes (fig. 4, 5), cleavers and many flake tools, made on quartzite, flint and limestone. Bone, ivory and wooden objects have also been recovered, as well as some evidence of fire.

A number of other sites could be mentioned here, sites that have some claim to be included in a pre-Great Interglacial group, but doubts remain about either the detailed stratigraphy or the finds. The Hanborough terrace of the upper Thames, with a temperate fauna and a trace

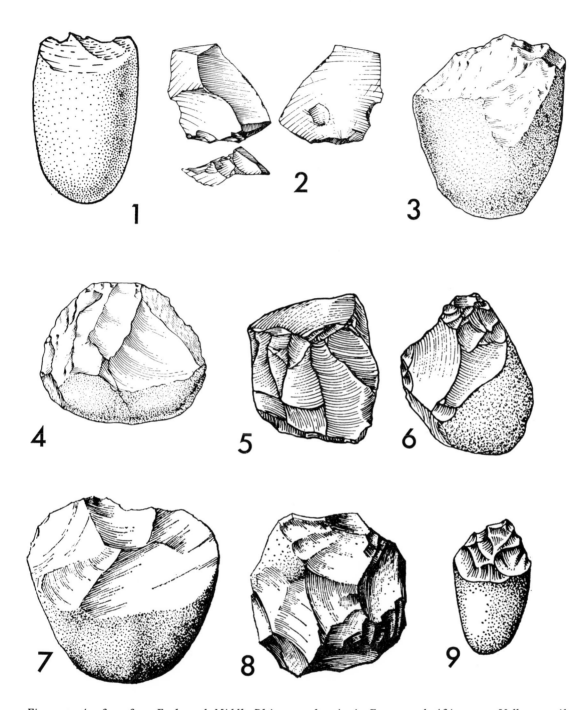

Figure 5. Artefacts from Early and Middle Pleistocene deposits in Europe and Africa. 1–2, Vallonnet, Alpes-Maritimes. 3–4, Olduvai Gorge, Tanzania. 5–6, Ain Hanech, Algeria. 7–8, Tardiguet-er-Rahla, Morocco. 9, Magoito, Portugal. (1–2, after de Lumley; 3–4, after Leakey; 5–6, after Balout; 7–8, after Biberson; 9, after Breuil and Zbyszewski) 1/2

of an early Acheulean axe tradition, may be of Great Interglacial age, although there has been some support for an earlier date. Similarly, the fluviatile gravels at Dartford Heath, with rolled typologically-early handaxes, have been said to belong to a complex of deposits earlier than the Swanscombe gravels, but this is now doubtful. In England there are, in fact, no river terrace deposits that can be correlated with the Upper Middle Terrace of the Somme, although there is one riverine implementiferous deposit for which claims of a pre-Great Interglacial age have been advanced. I refer to the Caversham Channel, an ancient course of the Thames between Caversham and Henley.[61] The channel was cut through pre-existing gravel deposits at a time when the Thames flowed to the northeast, through a gap at Finchley, and is filled with fluviatile gravels. The top of these gravels lies at a height of about 160 feet above present sea level. No significant faunal remains have been recovered from the gravels, but a great number of flint implements, both handaxes and flakes, have been found in varying states of preservation, fresh to rolled, throughout most of the gravels,. At Caversham, a bluff separates the channel deposits from the gravels of the Boyn Hill terrace complex, and although it has been claimed that industrially the artifacts from the two deposits suggest contemporaneity, this seems improbable on the basis of general stratigraphy. Zeuner believed that altimetrically the gravels flowed into a sea level of the order of 60 m. above that of today, and well above that of the Boyn Hill and Swanscombe gravels. Whether or not this may be correlated with the Milazzian sea, it will still be difficult to interpret the industrial material in terms of internal homogeneity and chronological relationship with the gravels. Nevertheless, the Caversham Channel provides a hint of human occupation in pre-Mindel-Riss times; that this should be so is not surprising in view of the Sidestrand, Norfolk, axe which if of palaeolithic age may be of Mindel I or even Cromerian age.

Up to this point we have been able to demonstrate that man was present in parts of Europe well before the Great Interglacial, with industrial activity claimed from Villafranchian deposits; there is no doubt that man was present, during Mindel times, in Spain, Britain, France and Hungary, with the distributional gap in central Europe filled by the earlier Heidelberg jaw. The traditions present were varied, from the pebble and flake industries of Hungary, Italy and the west, to handaxe industries, with or without cleavers, apparently restricted to western Europe.

From these beginnings, industrial development during the Great Interglacial seems to have accelerated, so that by the end of this period there is evidence of not only flake traditions and handaxe traditions, but also the emergence of the prepared core technique from the Acheulean. It is not the purpose of this essay to examine these industries, but the distribution of finds dating to the Mindel-Riss, although more dense, is still effectively restricted to the initial settled areas, in general terms. Finds of fossil man of this period are also sparse, with Swanscombe and Steinheim as the principal members.

It is of interest now to bring forward another source of knowledge, the evidence from other areas which may have initiated and stimulated cultural developments in Europe. The absence of finds of early Middle Pleistocene age from the Balkans and eastern Europe has generally been interpreted as indicating that the initial colonization of the continent of Europe came from north Africa, and that southwest Asia played no part in this earliest of movements. I do not consider that this case is closed because of the ample evidence that man as a tool-making animal was present as far east as China and Malaya in early Middle Pleistocene times, in the Chou-k'ou-tien and Tampanian industries, and that man in the *Homo erectus* pattern was known as far east as Java at the same time. Unless we accept the idea of separate evolution into similar forms, we must accept the view that man, as *Homo erectus* or as an earlier form, somehow made his way over much of the habitable area of the Old World before or in early Middle Pleistocene times. The finds of *Homo erectus* in east Africa and north Africa, in Europe and in the Far East point to obvious areas in which we should expect to find similar traces. One of these areas is southwest Asia, where the Ubeidiyeh remains may well hold a key, both morphologically and industrially, to our understanding of the source of the occupation in the Bükk mountains of Hungary (map, fig. 6).[62] The lower level at Ubeidiyeh has yielded industrial remains comparable in general character to those from Ain

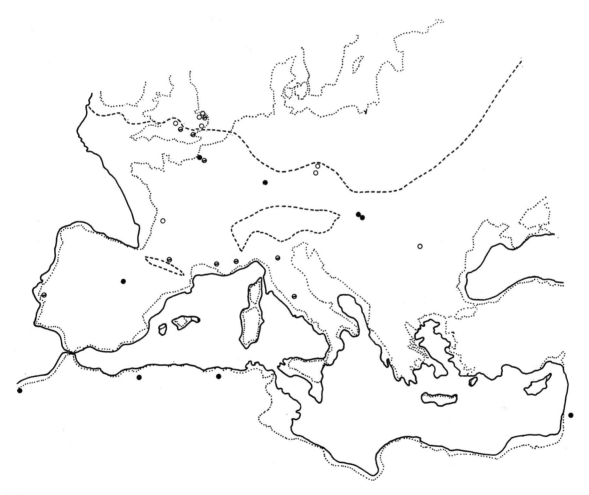

Figure 6. The distribution of finds of fossil man and industries in Europe claimed to be of pre-Great Interglacial age. The dashed lines indicate the approximate limits of ice, and the solid lines indicate the approximate coastline, during the Mindel glacial period. Solid circles: finds certain. Halved circles: finds probable, but without adequate dating evidence or human association. Open circles: finds unlikely (England), or without acceptable dating evidence (Continent).

Hanech in Algeria (see below), with spheroids and choppers. Rolled river pebbles were flaked at one end or along one edge. Handaxes of primitive type are reported from the upper level. The faunal spectrum is said to contain both Villafranchian and later elements, as well as a few teeth and skull fragments of *Homo erectus*. We should therefore not neglect the possibility that it was from this area that penetration into eastern Europe took place, perhaps along the same natural passages that later peoples utilized.

But the claims of northwest Africa as a primary source for west European penetration in early Middle Pleistocene times are not to be denied, because here there is an unrivalled sequence of industries set within a clear geological framework.[63] The Lower and Middle Pleistocene sites that have been discovered in recent years appear to provide evidence for a developing series of stone tool-manufacture from, typologically, pre-Oldowan stages into developed Acheulean handaxe industries, and at the moment the northwest African 'Pebble Culture ancienne' represents perhaps the first recognizable indusrty in the world (fig. 5, 7–8). The Moroccan sites of Tardiguet-er-Rahla and the Carrière Déprez at Casablanca are dated through raised beach deposits to a pre-Günz or inter-Günz period. The succeeding 'Pebble Culture évoluée' appears to correlate typologically with the Oldowan of east Africa, and is dated to Biberson's Salétien climatic phase and the Sicilian I sea level. This may be of Cromerian age in northern terms. There follows a long series of handaxe industries, from a Marifien (Milazzian) marine phase which may be of the Mindel interstadial, on to the final interglacial. The Sidi Abderrahman complex in Morocco provides convincing evidence that the Acheulean tradition was present as early as Mindel times.

This sequence for the Atlantic coast of northwest Africa is not as completely known elsewhere in north Africa, but there is no doubt that both the handaxe tradition, and man in the *Homo erectus* pattern, were present in the Mediterranean coastal region early in the Middle Pleistocene, at Ternifine in Algeria for example. Biberson believes this site is of early Mindel age. Earlier than this site, on the basis of associated fauna, is the industry from Ain Hanech, near St Arnaud, Algeria.[64] The fauna includes *Archidiskodon* cf. *meridionalis*, *A. planifrons*, *Stylohipparion libycum* and *Libytherium maurusium*. Although few would now claim a Pliocene aspect to this fauna (*Archidiskodon*, for instance, surviving into the Middle Pleistocene in parts of Africa), nevertheless there is little doubt that this assemblage as a whole is earlier than that from Ternifine and Lake Karar, the industries from which exhibit considerable common elements. The cultural material from Ain Hanech includes globular cores, and possibly handaxes (fig. 5, 5–6).

Correlations with sub-Saharan Africa are at the moment difficult to make with any degree of certainty. Although the view that the climatic sequence of pluvials was the equivalent of the glacial sequence in northern latitudes continues to be supported, there are sufficient imponderables to make any theoretical considerations on the basis of simple climatic episodes hazardous and in many cases unproductive. The growing acceptance of the view, for instance, that the Mindel glaciation was a complex event involving not only two distinct glacial advances in some areas, but that these were separated by a sea level of the order of 57–8 m. above that of the present day as represented by raised beach formations, suggests that such a glaciation should be represented by more than a single pluvial deposit such as is said to be present at Olduvai Gorge in the middle and upper Bed II, if we are talking of equivalent quadripartite sequences. On the other hand, the meteorological view that the last two pluvials, the Kanjeran and the Gamblian, were in fact phases of a single pluvial, does not make glacial correlations any less difficult, and on industrial grounds, if Olduvai Bed I is to be considered as of the Kageran pluvial (and the Mindel glaciation), then east Africa at any rate would lose its vital interest as a potential source of tool-making. The same theory, however, also involved the existence of six glacial maxima, and three pluvials, with a correlation-supposition that would place the Kageran in a pre-Donau cold phase. In view of difficulties with the evidence from polleniferous interglacial deposits in Europe, Oakley has suggested another line of reasoning, as yet unexplored fully, but which might lead to a correlation of three pluvials with three interglacials. This problem remains insoluble at the moment, but the evidence of sea levels and fauna from northwest Africa and east Africa, respectively, demonstrates the existence of tool-making in a general period in late Villafranchian times in both these areas.

Typologically the 'Pebble Culture ancienne' of Morocco appears more primitive than the earliest recognizable industry of east Africa, the Oldowan (fig. 5, 3-4), which is matched in its bidirectional flaking by the northwest African 'Pebble Culture évoluée.' Geologically the latter has been dated to the Günz glaciation, but a substage later seems equally as reasonable. Our knowledge of the makers of these tools is regrettably imperfect, for it is only in east Africa that fossil remains have been found in association with industrial material. At Olduvai Gorge, some half-dozen finds of fossil man have been recovered from late Villafranchian deposits, with at least three finds of *Homo* sp. in middle and upper Bed II, of early Middle Pleistocene age.[65] The several finds of *Australopithecinae* in Beds I and II are not included in the above figures. The view that Villafranchian *Homo habilis*, known only from tropical Africa, is antecedent to the widespread *Homo erectus* of the Middle Pleistocene, suggests that east Africa may not yet have yielded its earliest evidence for the emergence of tool-making in Villafranchian times.

The evidence seems to suggest that man as a tool-making animal was present in both east and northwest Africa in late Villafranchian times. During this time his industrial tradition involved the fabrication of tools on pebbles and flakes, and there are grounds for believing that this tradition was introduced into Europe and into southwest Asia. The European evidence is rather imprecise, but there is no doubt that industrial activity involving flakes and pebbles or choppers was established in Europe early in Middle Pleistocene times. It may be that there was a dual source for these European industries, from northwest Africa and from southwest Asia (fig. 6). There is less uncertainty about the evidence that, at a later stage in man's industrial development, the African handaxe tradition was introduced into Europe, supplanting the earlier tradition only in the west. These developments, and contemporary events in southern Asia, which in total indicate the occupation by *Homo erectus* of much of the habitable Old World well before late Middle Pleistocene times, represent to my mind one of the first great achievements of mankind.

Acknowledgements: My thanks are extended to Dr Kenneth Oakley for discussions on the problem of eoliths.

Notes

1. Penck and Brückner, *Die Alpen im Eiszeitalter* (1909)
2. Eberl, *Die Eiszeitenfolge im nördlichen Alpenvorland* (1930)
3. Woldstedt, *Das Eiszeitalter* II (1958)
4. Woldstedt, *op. cit.*
5. Oakley, *Frameworks for Dating Fossil Man* (1964) 28–32, 102–3 with refs.
6. *P.P.S.* III (1937)
7. *Inst. Lombardo di Sci. e Lett.* LXXXIII (1950) 1
8. Oakley, *op. cit.* 33
9. *Commentationes Biol. Soc. Sci. Fennica* XXIV, No. 3 (1962) 1
10. Zeuner, *The Pleistocene Period* (1959); van der Vlerk and Florschütz, *Nederland in het Ijstijdvak* (1950)
11. *South African J. Sci.* LIX (1963) 340
12. Summary, *Current Anthropology* VI (1965) 78
13. de Lamothe, *Mem. Soc. Géol. Fr.* (4) I (1911); Depéret, *Bull. Soc. Géol. France* (4) VI (1906); *Comptes Rendus des Séances de l'Academie des Sciences, Paris* 167 (1918) 418
14. *Nature* 194 (1962) 521
15. *Quaternaria* I (1954) 55
16. *Quaternaria* IV (1957) 95
17. *Quaternaria* II (1955) 109; Zeuner, *op. cit.* 285
18. *Quaternaria* II (1955) 187; IV (1957) 95
19. Oakley, *op. cit.* 50
20. *Journal of Geology* LXIII (1955) 538; LXVI (1958) 264; *Science* 154 (1966) 851
21. Breuil and Lantier, *The Men of the Old Stone Age* (1965) 44; *P.P.S.* XXIV (1958) 64
22. *P.P.S.E.A.* III (1920) 411
23. *P.P.S.E.A.* III (1920) 390
24. *P.P.S.E.A.* VI (1929) 57
25. *J.R.A.I.* LI (1921) 385; LV (1925) 311
26. *P.P.S.E.A.* V (1928) 274
27. *Ant. J.* III (1923) 135
28. Lankester, *Royal Anthropological Institute Occ. Paper* 4 (1914); *Phil. Trans. Roy. Soc. Lond.* (B) 202 (1912) 283
29. *P.P.S.E.A.* III (1920) 118
30. *P.P.S.E.A.* III (1920) 158
31. *P.P.S.E.A.* III (1920) 259, 448, 458
32. *Quarterly Journal of the Geological Society* LXXVI (1921) 238
33. *J.R.A.I.* XLIV (1914) 412
34. *Man* (1923) No. 32
35. *Revue Anth.* XXXIII (1923) 53
36. *Man* (1922) No. 53; (1923) No. 51
37. *Man* (1923) No. 74
38. Kendrick and Hawkes, *Archaeology in England and Wales, 1914–1931* (1932) 5
39. *The South-eastern Naturalist and Antiquary* LIII (1948) 48
40. Leakey, *Adam's Ancestors* (1953) 68; Burkitt, *The Old Stone Age* (1963) 112
41. Breuil and Lantier, *op. cit.*
42. Oakley, *Man the Toolmaker* (1961)
43. *American Anthropologist* LXVIII, No. 2, pt. 2 (1966) 89
44. *Current Anthropology* I (1960) 199; *Jahrb. d. Römisch-Germanischen Zentralmuseums Mainz* XI (1964) 15
45. *Paläontologische Zeitschrift* X (1928) 217; XV (1933) 322
46. Zeuner, *op. cit.* 99, 318
47. Day, *Guide to Fossil Man* (1965) 65; *Discovery* (June 1964)
48. Oakley, *op. cit.* 37
49. Rust, *Artefakte aus der Zeit des Homo heidelbergensis in Süd- und Norddeutschland* (1956)
50. *Current Anthropology* VI (1965) 74; *Nature* 208 (1965) 205; *Antiquity* XXXIX (1965) 303; *American Anthropologist* LXVIII, No. 2, pt. 2 (1966) 36

51. *Quaternaria* IV (1957) 95; *Riv. di Antropologia* XXXI (1936)
52. Oakley, *op. cit.* 140
53. *L'Anthropologie* XLI (1931) 449; XLII (1932) 27, 291; *P.P.S.* V (1939) 33
54. *Comptes Rendus des Séances de l'Academie des Sciences, Paris* 248 (1959) 439
55. *L'Anthropologie* VI (1895) 497
56. *Préhistoire* XI (1905) 1
57. *Comptes Rendus des Séances de l'Academie des Sciences, Paris* 256 (1963) 4261; *Bull. du Musée d'Anthropologie préhistorique de Monaco* X (1963) 5
58. *Comptes Rendus des Séances de l'Academie des Sciences, Paris* 256 (1963) 1136
59. *Comunicações dos Serviços Geológicos de Portugal* XXIII (1942)
60. *Excavaciones arquelogicas en España* X (1963); *American Anthropologist* LXVIII, No. 2, pt. 2 (1966) 111; Butzer, *Environment and Archaeology* (1964) 366
61. *P.P.S.* XIV (1948) 126; *P.P.S.* XXVII (1961) 1; see *P.P.S.* XXX (1964) 257-8, for typologically early industry from Fordwich, Kent
62. *South African J. Sci.* LIX (1963) 77; Stekelis, *Archaeological Excavations at 'Ubeidiyah, 1960-63* (1966)
63. Biberson, *Le Paléolithique inferieur du Maroc Atlantique* (1961)
64. Müller-Karpe, *Handbuch der Vorgeschichte* I (1966)
65. *South African Arch. Bull.* XX (1965) 167

A preliminary study of the early neolithic and latest mesolithic blade industries in southeast and central Europe

Ruth Tringham

The purpose of this article is to outline the general relationships between the earliest agricultural communities of central Europe, represented by the Linear Pottery culture, and the preceding and contemporary hunting/fishing communities on their periphery. This has special relevance in the question of whether the Linear Pottery cultures (Danubian I) represent an acculturation by the indigenous mesolithic hunting/fishing population of the middle Danube basin to the agricultural and associated techniques of the early neolithic communities of the Balkan peninsula, or whether they represent an actual colonization of agriculturalists from the lower to the middle part of the Danube basin.

The three most important elements which the earliest agricultural communities of temperate central Europe have in common with the contemporary communities of the Mediterranean woodlands of southeast Europe, represented by the Starčevo/Karanovo I/Criş/Körös group of cultures, are the forms and decoration of their pottery, the agricultural techniques and economy, and the macrolithic flint blade industry and polished stone implements; these features are intrusive when they appear in the early neolithic culture of central Europe (Linear Pottery cultures), and yet they are basic elements of the earlier neolithic cultures of southeast Europe.

Because of the limited space available, the study, in this case, has been made on a basis of one of these elements: the flint blade and, to a certain extent, the polished stone industry of the earliest agricultural communities of central and southeast Europe; in order to emphasize the close similarity of the early neolithic blade industries of these two areas, they have been compared to the markedly different microlithic blade and trapeze industries of the preceding and partly contemporary 'mesolithic' and 'aceramic neolithic' cultures.

In each area the latest mesolithic blade industries have been compared with the earliest neolithic blade industries; for this reason, the industries of only the earlier phases of the Linear Pottery cultures of each region have been considered, and the later neolithic blade industries of southeast Europe, including those of the Vinča/Veselinovo, Boian, Gumelniţa, Cucuteni/Tripolye cultures have not been discussed.

The study has necessarily been made on a relatively superficial basis, since very few of the implements used in the analysis have been examined for working traces under a microscope.

No doubt if the same method as that employed with so much success by Korobkova in central Asia could be applied to the early neolithic blade industries of southeast and central Europe, rather more detailed and positive evidence could be supplied for the conclusions discussed at the end of the paper.[1]

The distribution of microlithic elements in the blade industries of Europe and the Near East

The tendency towards microlithic implements, including geometric forms such as lunates, trapezes and triangles, seen in the Near East in the mesolithic (terminal food-gathering), 'proto-neolithic' and 'early pre-pottery neolithic' (incipient and early cultivating and domesticating) cultures, is not necessarily an indication of economic or cultural degeneration; as Semenov has pointed out, they can represent a technological advance, for the small blades were used compositely in the manufacture of a much wider range of tools than could be designed from a single flint blade; these included long, straight or curved tools, with a constant long-lasting degree of sharpness down the whole length of the cutting edge.[2]

In southeast Europe, microlithic elements appear consistently in the mesolithic industries of Greece, Bulgaria and Rumania, and, to a certain extent, Yugoslavia. So far, there is very little evidence from Carbon-14 or palaeobotanical analysis to indicate the chronological position of these industries in relation to the similar industries of southwest Asia.

In Greece, a predominantly microlithic industry is associated, presumably at a rather later date than in southwest Asia, with an incipient agricultural economy, for which there is the direct evidence of carbonized cereal grains and bones of domesticated animals; the 'preceramic neolithic' culture occurs in the basal layers of a number of 'tell' settlements, especially in Thessaly, as at Argissa, Arapi and Gremnos, and Sesklo and Sufli.[3]

The excavation of a predominantly microlithic blade industry with evidence for incipient cultivation and domestication of animals in Thessaly has prompted an outburst of discoveries of similar aceramic or preceramic neolithic cultures in Yugoslavia, Bulgaria, Rumania, and even as far as Slovakia.[4] Even though there may be no direct evidence for domestication or cultivation, it seems to be frequently understood that the occurrence of a microlithic industry *ipso facto* should be associated with the initial stages in the development of an agricultural economy in these regions.

The sites which have been claimed as representing a 'preceramic neolithic' culture are almost exclusively limited to coastal areas such as the Dobrogea, or the foothills of mountain ranges, especially the Carpathians. They have very rarely been claimed in the large river valleys which were settled by communities with a comparatively developed agricultural economy, represented by the Karanovo I/Starčevo/Körös/Criş group of cultures; and there is certainly no evidence for any such 'preceramic neolithic' culture in the basal layers of any of the tell settlements of these areas.

In Yugoslavia, very little research has been made into the cultures which immediately preceded those of the earliest agriculturalists; however, at least two centres of a 'mesolithic,' although not predominantly microlithic, industry have been distinguished: one in the foothills of the Montenegran mountains of southwest Yugoslavia, and the other in the foothills of the Alps in Slovenia in northwest Yugoslavia.

The most important site of the Montenegran centre (fig. 7, 1) is the stratified cave-site of Crvena Stijena.[5] Above thick Middle and Upper Palaeolithic layers, there are four post-Palaeolithic layers of interest in this study: IVb2, IVb1, IVa, and III. Layer IVb represents an impoverishment in the blade industry of the preceding late palaeolithic industry, with predominantly long blades, but some implements of almost microlithic dimensions; however a great development is seen in the bone implements of this period.

Layer IVa, regarded by the excavator as late mesolithic, shows an industry which is obviously derived from that of IVb, but with a much greater range in the type and function of the implements; although the implements are small none could be described as truly microlithic, and certainly not geometric. Because of the possible indirect evidence for incipient sheep-breeding in the apparently deliberate selection of animals, seen among the animal bones of this layer, it was soon claimed that Crvena Stijena IVa represented an 'aceramic neolithic' culture.[6] Recently, however, it has been questioned whether there is, in fact, any such indirect evidence, and it seems more likely that the material of this layer represents a late mesolithic community existing on the periphery of the area of agricultural colonization, probably at a period preceding this colonization.[7]

The flint blade implements of layer III are clearly developed from those of layer IVa, with an increase in longer blades; they are associated, however, with rough, poorly baked pottery, decorated with the impressions of cardium shells, finger-nails etc. Similar pottery and associated blade implements have been excavated in south Bosnia at the cave-site of Zelena Pećina, layer III,[8] and on the Adriatic coast, as at Smilčić, near Zadar,[9] and the islands of Cres and Krk,[10] and at Gudnja near Dubrovnik. It is unlikely, from the stratigraphical evidence on these sites, that the impressed ware occurred earlier than the settlements in the river valleys of east Yugoslavia which have material of the Starčevo culture; this is supported by Carbon-14 dates from Italian impressed ware sites to which the Smilčić impressed ware has been compared:[11] Grotta Piccioni, 4286 ± 130 B.C. (Pi 46) and Penne di Pescara, 4618 ± 135 B.C. (Pi 101).[12] There is very little evidence for the economy of the sites with cardial impressed ware, although there is direct evidence for fishing on the coastal sites; it seems probable that this, along with hunting, provided the basic subsistence, rather than agriculture.

In Bulgaria, microlithic implements have been excavated from two sites in the Bulgarian Dobrudža, at Dikilitaš (Pobiti Kamani) and Gebedže; both are a few kilometres from the Black Sea coast at Varna.[13] Neither site has produced any positive evidence for the basic economy, or the relative chronological position of the industry; the industry itself, although microlithic, does not include any deliberately geometric forms.

North of these sites, however, in the Rumanian Dobrogea (Dobrudža) (fig. 7, III), a similar microlithic blade industry has been excavated in the stratified cave-site of La Adam, near Constanţa. The industry has great similarities with the so-called 'Tardenoisian' of the Crimea, further along the Black Sea coast.[14] It has been shown that the microlithic industry of La Adam was associated with possible evidence for an early deliberate selection of sheep/goats, which could be interpreted as incipient domestication; in other words the layer may represent a 'preceramic neolithic' culture.[15]

It has generally been assumed that, since this material with its associated evidence for incipient domestication is stratified below a 'pre-Hamangia horizon with Cardial Impressed ware,' it is very much earlier than the early agricultural settlements of the Danube basin, represented in Rumania by the Criş culture.

At La Adam, above the Cardial Impressed ware, is a layer with material of the Hamangia culture, which has been dated from material at Hamangia itself: Hamangia 3930±70 B.C. (Grn 1986).[16] The majority of Carbon-14 dates for the Karanovo I and Starčevo cultures are from 1000 to 500 years earlier; there is, in fact, no evidence that the Cardial Impressed ware or the 'aceramic neolithic' layers at La Adam were necessarily earlier than the settlements of the Karanovo I/Starčevo/Criş cultures and the introduction of a developed agricultural economy in the river basins of the Balkan peninsula. It is just as likely that the population of the Dobrogea was essentially peripheral to the main agricultural colonization, and that its economy was based on hunting and fishing, with a slight development of sheep domestication.

Similar evidence of a population on the periphery of the early Criş culture area, with a blade industry with a strong microlithic element, and evidence for a certain amount of animal domestication (in this case, pig) has been excavated on the Dniester (fig. 7, v) at the site of Soroki (Trifautski).[17]

In the foothills of the Carpathians, a number of sites have been claimed as having a 'preceramic neolithic' culture.[18] For example, at Dîrţu in the foothills of the Ceahlău range in Rumanian Moldavia, and Băile Herculane on the southern edge of the Carpathians in southwest Rumania (fig. 7, IV, VI), where blade industries of a predominantly microlithic nature were excavated; since on neither of these sites was there any evidence for the domestication of animals among the bone material, the claim that they represent a 'preceramic neolithic' culture has generally been refuted.[19]

In northwest Rumania, on the terraces of the upper Criş river as at Valea lui Mihai (material unpublished in Oradea museum), and the dune area of the upper Tisza river (fig. 7, VII), as at Ciumeşti, reg. Maramureş,[20] a predominantly microlithic industry, including a high proportion of obsidian implements, and a large number of geometric forms, has been excavated; the blade industry occurs on some sites with early neolithic pottery, sometimes with definite evidence for a basically agricultural economy, and on other sites without any pottery. It was suggested that this was evidence for an 'aceramic neolithic' culture, at a period preceding the early neolithic settlements;[21] it is more likely, however, that the fluctuating presence of pottery and/or evidence for an agricultural economy, may represent the differences to be expected among a population on the periphery of the main centre of agricultural

Figure 7. Distribution of the Earliest Agricultural Settlements in central and southeast Europe. (Stippled area : land over 500 metres.)

Key to the centres of mesolithic settlement :

I Montenegro (Crvena Stijena)	*VII Ciumeşti*	*XIII N. Germany*
II Slovenia	*VIII W. Ukraine/S.E. Poland*	*XIV N. Switzerland/*
III Dobrogea	*IX Czech/Moravian uplands*	*S.W. Germany*
IV Ceahlău	*X S. Bohemia/E. Bavaria*	*XV Low Countries*
V Bug-Dniester culture	*XI Saxo-Thuringia*	*XVI S. Slovakia*
VI Băile Herculane	*XII Central Poland*	*XVII Argissa (Thessaly)*

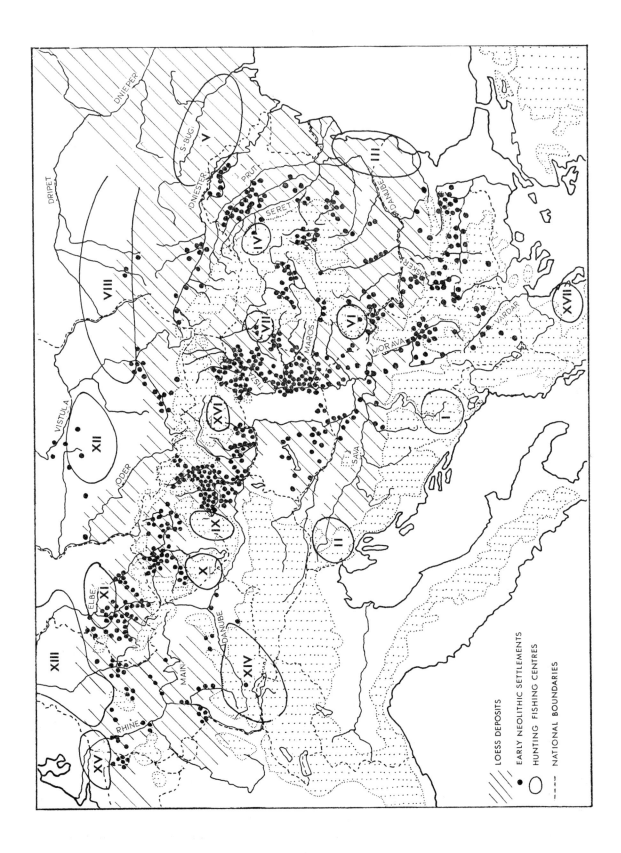

settlement, or that on some sites the sherds have been dispersed or disintegrated through strong wind and sand action.

Apart from the microlithic flint and obsidian industries which occur sporadically on the limestone hills and dune areas in the foothills of the Carpathians in northeast Hungary and southeast Slovakia, which bear a strong resemblance to the industries of Ciumeşti, there is almost no evidence for mesolithic settlement in the basin of the Tisza river.

North of the Carpathians, there are centres of mesolithic settlement with microlithic industries along many of the large river valleys of the Ukraine (fig. 7, VIII), such as the upper Dnieper/Desna basin, the lower Dnieper, middle Dniester etc.[22] A centre with a similar industry to that of the upper Dnieper, as seen at Kudlayevka, has been discovered in the mesolithic settlements on the loess along the upper Vistula river in southeast Poland; the industry, as seen at such sites as Grzybowa Gora,[23] Nowy Mlyn, Marcinkowo etc.,[24] is basically a microlithic one, with non-geometric forms predominating, although geometric forms such as trapezes and lunates clearly increase in frequency in the later mesolithic settlements.[25] A similar industry occurs in settlements in the foothills on the southern edge of the Carpathians in Czechoslovakia (northern Moravia/northwestern Slovakia).

There are scattered settlements of a hunting/fishing population with a microlithic blade industry in the Czech-Moravian uplands (fig. 7, IX) and their extension in north Austria, and in the south Moravian karst country. In this region, again, the geometric forms among the implements are almost entirely absent.[26]

The Czech/Moravian uplands are not a naturally fertile area, and were never settled by agriculturalists with the Linear Pottery culture; nor was the large sandy area of south Bohemia/east Bavaria (fig. 7, X). This region, however, was the centre of an important area of mesolithic settlement, represented by such sites as Tašovice, Souš and the stratified cave-site of Ensdorf;[27] the microlithic blade industry of these sites is more similar to the southwest German late mesolithic industry, in that it contains many more implements with a regular geometric form, especially trapezes and triangles.

In north Bohemia, in the upper valley of the Elbe, on sites distributed especially along riverbanks, by lakes, and on dunes, but avoiding the loess basins, a microlithic non-geometric industry has been excavated.[28] A very similar industry has been excavated on sites a little further down the Elbe in Thuringia (fig. 7, XI); the sites are again limited to sand-dunes.[29] There is no evidence from radiocarbon or palaeobotanical analysis for the chronological position of these sites in relation to the early agricultural settlements, which are distributed on the loess deposits of the Elbe basin, a relatively short distance away. Although it is possible that the two populations were partly contemporary, and although many claims have been made for evidence of contact between the two,[30] it is unlikely that the comparatively sparse hunting/fishing population had any effect in this region on the large innovating agricultural population.

On the sand-dunes of central and north Poland, between Poznan and Warszawa (fig. 7, XII), was a large centre of mesolithic population with a microlithic blade industry containing a higher proportion of geometric implements than either the upper Elbe or the southeast Polish centres.

The settlements of hunting/fishing populations with a predominantly microlithic blade industry in the western part of temperate Europe[31] are distinguished by having frequently produced evidence from radiocarbon and palaeobotanical samples. Thus it is possible to see their chronological position in relation to that of the early neolithic settlements in temperate Europe.

From the centre of blade and trapeze industries in north Africa, Iberia and south France, a series of midden sites situated along the Muge river in south Portugal has produced Carbon-14 dates between 5750 and 4150 B.C. (fig. 8). The samples for the analysis were taken from a level in the middens with a microlithic blade industry, stratified below a level with the same flint industry but which was associated with coarse impressed pottery.

The stratified cave and open mesolithic sites of the centres in northeastern France and southwestern Germany/north Switzerland (fig. 7, XIV) show, in the later mesolithic levels (Tardenoisian industry), a development of smaller lighter microlithic blades with an increase in regular-geometric forms such as trapezes, crescents etc.[32] In the latest aceramic level on many of the sites of these regions, the geometric microlithic industry is associated with direct evidence for domestication of animals; this fact, at one time, caused murmurs of an expansion of a 'preceramic neolithic' or 'protoneolithic' culture from southeast Europe, preceding the Starčevo/Körös and Linear Pottery cultures;[33] from recent radiocarbon and palaeobotanical evidence, however, it would seem that the latest 'Tardenoisian' levels were contemporary with the latest stages of the Linear Pottery culture and the post-Linear Pottery neolithic cultures (fig. 8), when agricultural techniques had been practised in the large river basins of temperate Europe for almost a thousand years.

The most complete evidence from radiocarbon and palaeobotanical analysis has been collected from the stratified cave site of Birsmatten (Basisgrotte) on the northern edge of the Swiss Juras.[34]

Birsmatten (Basisgrotte)	Radiocarbon analysis	Pollen analysis
Layer 5 (Early Sauveterrian)	5510±160 B.C. (B 238) ⎫	End zone VI
Layer 4 (Late Sauveterrian)	5720±120 B.C. (B 237) ⎬	to mid-zone VIIa
Layer 3 (Sauveterrian/Tardenoisian transition)	5020±120 B.C. (B 236) ⎭	i.e. 6800–4000 B.C.
Layer 2 (Early Tardenoisian (II))	3360±240 B.C. (B 235) ⎫	
	5530±200 B.C. (B 241) ⎪	Late zone VIIa
Layer 1 (Late Tardenoisian (III))	3400±120 B.C. (B 234) ⎬	to early zone VIIb
	5250±600 B.C. (B 240) ⎭	i.e. 4000–3000 B.C.

Samples B 241 and B 240 were taken from unburnt bone and are therefore regarded as less reliable.

Interesting evidence for the chronological relationship between the mesolithic population of southwest Germany and the early neolithic population represented by the Linear Pottery culture, has recently been excavated at the stratified site of Lauterach, near Ehingen, 20 km. north of the Federsee, on the upper Danube.[35] A lower layer, referred to as late mesolithic, contains a microlithic blade industry but with no trapezes, and is probably similar to the earlier mesolithic layers of Birsmatten and Weilersteusslingen. Above this was a layer containing sherds of the middle phase of the Linear Pottery culture, dated in the Low Countries to

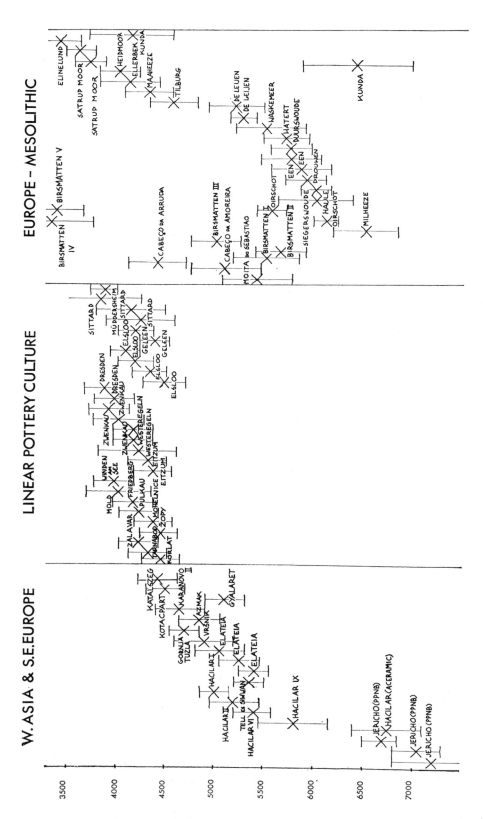

Figure 8. Evidence for absolute chronology from radiocarbon samples, at two standard deviations.

c. 4100–3900.[36] The pottery is associated with a poor blade industry when compared with that of the preceding layer and compared with that of the contemporary Linear Pottery settlements of northwest Germany; it consists of scrapers, and blades with irregular retouching down one or both edges; there is no mention of microliths. Nor is there any mention of direct evidence for an agricultural economy, but rather for a predominance of hunting and fishing.

The blade and trapeze industries of the Low Countries centred on the highland plateau of Belgium and the sandy areas of Belgium and Holland, have been dated by pollen analysis to the pollen zones VI (Late Boreal) and VIIa (Atlantic).[37] Carbon-14 evidence also dates the sites to 6500–4000 B.C. (fig. 8), although Bohmers does not regard any of the microlithic industries in the Low Countries as later than 5500 B.C.; he has suggested that the samples which show a later date than this are likely to have been contaminated.

Although it is possible that the population with the microlithic blade and trapeze industries may have been partly contemporary with those represented by the Linear Pottery culture, their distribution patterns are mutually exclusive, and, from the typology of the implements themselves, there seems to have been no effective contact between the two.[38]

The blade industry and polished stone implements associated with the
earliest agricultural communities in southeast Europe

With the further development of the agricultural economy and techniques in the Near East, associated with the beginning of the manufacture of pottery, a basic change may be observed in the associated blade implements; this change is seen for example at Jericho in the Pre-Pottery Neolithic B level, accompanying the earliest direct evidence on this site for the domestication of animals and the cultivation of plants; it consists primarily in a predominance of macrolithic over microlithic forms, especially relatively long sickle blades, borers and tanged arrowheads.

The macrolithic blade industry becomes even more apparent with the development of the 'later neolithic' and 'early chalcolithic' cultures, as seen in the Hassuna and Samarra cultures of Iraq, and in the relevant layers at Hacilar and Çatal Hüyük in Anatolia *etc.*, when the microlithic elements completely disappeared from the blade industry, and the macrolithic blades were frequently accompanied by polished stone axe/adzes.

The development and predominance of the macrolithic blades, especially the blades with an area of 'sickle-gloss,' must represent a new set of functions and a predominance of these functions over those performed by the microlithic blades. It is clear that the occupations associated with these implements are to be connected with the changing basic economy, expressed also in the animal bone and plant evidence, a development from intensive collecting and hunting to the deliberate production of food; as the agricultural economy developed, the implements connected with hunting and gathering, which can be recognized by their working-traces, gradually disappeared, and those connected with cultivation and domestication developed and were constantly elaborated to keep up with the evolving economy.[39]

All this is very obvious, that flint and other stone implements are as important as other aspects of the material culture in providing a fully comprehensive picture of any prehistoric community, especially the relationships between two cultures with different basic economies. Yet it is surprising how often it is neglected to give details and adequate illustrations of the blade and polished stone industries from the sites of the early neolithic cultures in southeast and central Europe, as well as Anatolia and the Near East.

Thus, along with monochrome and then painted pottery, the introduction of a developed agricultural economy and techniques, and settlements forming 'tells,' macrolithic 'sickle' and other blades and polished stone axe/adzes may also be added to the intrusive neolithic material culture in Greece, Bulgaria and Yugoslavia as seen in the Early and Middle Neolithic cultures of Greece, and the Karanovo I and Starčevo cultures.

Stone implements, except for the flat polished stone trapezoid axe/adzes, have rarely been recorded in reports of the Greek neolithic sites; an exception is the site of Nea Nikomedea in Greek Macedonia, where the blade industry shows great similarities to the other early neolithic blade industries in west Asia and southeast Europe (fig. 9, 1–14); the implements include short 3–4 cm. blades with a glossy area diagonally across one corner, longer 4–6 cm. blades with shallow retouching down one or both edges, small scrapers etc.[40]

In the material culture of the Karanovo I culture, excavated at the base levels of many of the tell settlements in south Bulgaria, the flint blade industry shows the same forms as in Greece and Anatolia (fig. 9, 23–32). These include short 3–4 cm. blades with a diagonal area of gloss across one corner of the blade; on at least two sites, Karanovo and Azmak, curved antler sickle handles, 25–30 cm. long, have been found (fig. 9, 23, 32);[41] on the example from Karanovo, the short blades were still partly adhering to the slot in the handle. There also occur longer (4–7 cm.) blades, with shallow retouching down the complete length of one or both edges, and with the bulb of percussion incorporated into one end of the implement; from a superficial examination of these longer blades, from the absence of a glossy area on almost all of them, it is likely that they served as an all-purpose cutting/scraping instrument.

In the cave-sites of north-central Bulgaria, e.g., Loveč and Devetaki,[42] although a hiatus and complete break with any palaeolithic traditions of the preceding layers is apparent, the flint blade industry of the early neolithic layer is richer than in the settlements of the Marica valley and Sofia basin, probably because of the abundance of local flint and a slightly different economy. In the valleys and lowland plains, however, it is obvious from their greater frequency that the polished stone trapezoid axe/adzes, 6–12 cm. long, with a flat rectangular cross-section were the main working tools (fig. 9, 28, 30). In fact, it is likely that they remain the main working tools of the early neolithic colonists in southeast and central Europe.[43]

The blade industry associated with the Starčevo culture of eastern Yugoslavia and its extension in the Banat area of northeast Yugoslavia and southwest Rumania has usually been

Figure 9. Blade and polished stone industries from Early Neolithic sites in southeast Europe.
1–14 : Nea Nikomedea, N. Greece (after Rodden, 1962) 2/3
15–18 : Vršnik, Macedonia, Yugoslavia (Štip Museum) 1/1
19–22 : Gračanica (Gladnica), S. Serbia, Yugoslavia (Priština Museum) 1/1 ; 22 : 1/2
23–28 : Karanovo, S. Bulgaria (after Georgiev, 1954) 24–7 : 1/1
29–32 : Azmak, S. Bulgaria (Stara Zagora Museum ; 32 after Georgiev, 1958) 29, 31 : 1/1 ; 30 : 13 cm.; 32 : 30 cm.
33–5 : Nosa (Gyongypart), N. Serbia, Yugoslavia (Subotica Museum) 1/1
36–40 : Leţ, E. Transilvania, Rumania (Sf. Gheorghe Museum) 1/1
41–8 : Kopancs (Kovacs), S.E. Hungary (Hódmezővásárhely Museum) 1/1

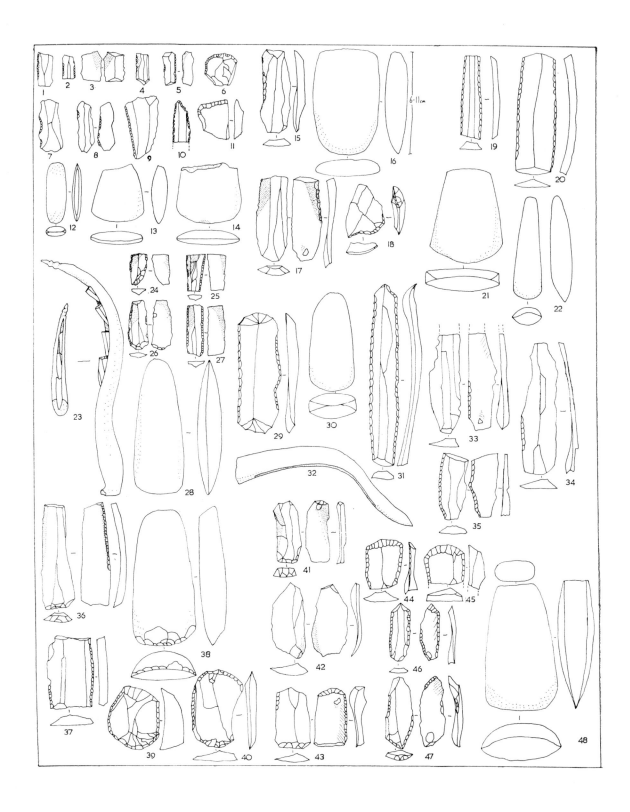

dismissed in a few sentences as being unimportant. Nevertheless, it does form a definite part of the material culture, and a certain number of blades occur on every site; the majority are long (4–7 cm.) blades with shallow, or more rarely steep, retouching down one or both edges, and nearly always with the bulb of percussion retained, leaving one bulbous end, perhaps to facilitate hafting into a bone or wooden handle, as the working traces would suggest (fig. 9, 19, 20, 33–5). Some of these longer blades show traces of 'sickle-gloss' in a diagonal area across one corner, almost invariably at the end opposite that with the retained bulb of percussion (fig. 9, 15, 17). Pointed blades with steep retouching on both faces also occur, especially in the more southern sites, and short end scrapers. However, as in the Karanovo I culture, the polished stone trapezoid axe/adzes with a flat rectangular, or slightly plano-convex cross-section (fig. 9, 16, 21), are of rather greater importance.[44]

The stone industry of the Criş culture of Moldavia (northeastern Rumania) is very similar to that of the Karanovo I culture, consisting of long blades with shallow retouching, smaller blades, 3–4 cm. long, with only one corner retouched, and flat trapezoid polished stone axe/adzes. However, on these sites, such as Perieni, where material of the Criş culture is stratified below that of the later Linear Pottery culture, there also occurs a more rectangular, longer, narrower type of polished stone axe/adze, with a thicker more oval cross-section.[45] This implement becomes comparatively common in the stone industry of the Moldavian Linear Pottery culture, and it may offer possible further proof that the Moldavian Criş culture represents the latest expansion of the agriculturalists with this culture, as is also shown, to a certain extent in their pottery, and by the difference in their economy, which has a pre-dominance of cattle among the domesticated animals, instead of sheep.[46]

The Criş culture of Transylvania (central Rumania), as seen for example at Leţ, shows similar forms among the blade implements, which are produced in obsidian as well as flint. These include longer blades often with the end opposite the bulb of percussion chipped into a rounded point (fig. 9, 36–7), smaller 3–4 cm. blades with a diagonal area of 'sickle-gloss' across one corner. The polished stone axe/adzes tend to be less trapezoid and narrower than in Yugoslavia and Bulgaria, although the cross-profile is still flat or slightly plano-convex (fig. 9, 39–40).

The polished stone axe/adzes of the Körös culture of southeast Hungary include short wide trapezoid implements with a flat cross-profile, as in the Starčevo and Karanovo I cultures (fig. 9, 48), and longer narrower implements, also trapezoid, but with a more plano-convex cross-profile. Blade implements, although certainly less numerous on the sites than polished stone implements, are present on every site. The majority examined from the sites of Kopancs (Kovacs tanya) and (Zsoldos tanya) were blades 3–5 cm. long; those with little or no retouch-ing on the edges had a diagonal glossy area across one corner of the blade on the end opposite that with the retained bulb of percussion (fig. 9, 41–2); those with regular shallow retouching down one edge had scratches all down the same edge on the under side at an angle of approximately 45° to it (fig. 9, 43, 46–7); there were also small short scrapers (fig. 9, 44–5) (material in Hódmezövásarhély Museum).

The blade and polished stone industries associated with the earliest agricultural communities in temperate Europe, represented by the Linear Pottery cultures

As with the introduction of agricultural and ceramic techniques, the blade and polished stone industries represent a complete transference of the southeast European neolithic types to temperate Europe, with a certain amount of regional variation and adaptation especially in the peripheral areas of the culture. There seems to have been very little internal development in the blade industry throughout the evolution of the culture, but it is possible to see an increase in importance of blades in the material culture, especially in the 'classic' phase of the culture.

In the early phase of the Linear Pottery culture as seen in the centre of settlement on the Great Hungarian Plain (Alföld) of east Hungary, the blade implements, as in the Körös culture immediately to the south, are comparatively rare, and are most commonly produced from obsidian. The majority of the blades are small, 3–5 cm. long, with shallow retouching down one edge, or part of it, or, very rarely, down both edges (fig. 10, 1–7). The typical polished stone axe/adzes of the early Linear Pottery culture of this region are the short trapezoid implements, 5–10 cm. long, with a flat rectangular cross-section, as in the Körös, Starčevo, and Karanovo I cultures.

In the northeast corner of the Alföldi, on the dune settlements of northwest Rumania, the blade industry associated with pottery of the early Linear Pottery culture, including painted pottery, is much richer and contains a large number of microliths, including trapezes. This blade industry, as seen at Ciumeşti,[47] is also found on dune and terrace sites in the same region, as mentioned above, but without associated pottery (fig. 10, 18–31). The industry associated with the Linear Pottery sherds, consisting of 90% obsidian implements, and 10% flint, is not exclusively microlithic; of the total number of 2930 implements, 83% are microlithic, that is smaller than 3·5 cm., and 17% are 3·5–7 cm. long. The small percentage of longer blades consists of blades with retouching down one or both edges (fig. 10, 18–24). There are also one or two examples of the short trapezoid polished stone axe/adzes, with a flat cross-profile (fig. 10, 16).[48]

The low limestone mountains, known as the Bükk mountains, in northeast Hungary/southeast Slovakia provided a great source of obsidian for the blade industries of the surrounding neolithic settlements. In the settlements in caves and open sites in the mountains themselves, the blade industries associated with the early phase of the Linear Pottery culture, as seen at Kőlyuk, Aggtelek, and Istállóskő (material in Miskolc Museum), are almost exclusively obsidian (fig. 10, 10, 14, 15). The obsidian blades are identical to those seen in the Alföldi settlements; apart from the obsidian blades, there occur longer blades of flint, 4–7 cm. long, with retouching down one or both edges, and often on the end opposite that with the retained bulb of percussion (fig. 10, 11, 13); a few showed a glossy area across one corner, but this was a comparatively rare feature (fig. 10, 9). There is certainly no true microlithic element in the blade industry of this region. Polished stone tools of this early phase of the culture were predominantly small trapezoid axe/adzes with a flat rectangular cross-profile (fig. 10, 8), although longer narrower examples with a more plano-convex cross-profile do occur (fig. 10, 12).

In the central area of the Linear Pottery culture, that is in the middle basin of the Danube valley, even in the earliest phase of the culture, a great increase in the manufacture of flint implements is evident, compared with those of east and northeast Hungary, and the Körös culture *etc.* In west Hungary from an examination of the blade industry of Bicske (Galagonashégy) and Felsöszentistvan (material in Székesfehérvár Museum), Zalavár (material in the National Museum, Budapest, unpublished), and Keszthely at the western end of Lake Balaton (material in Keszthely Museum), it is possible to see that the blades vary from 3–7 cm. in length, and that 'sickle-gloss' occurs on blades of all lengths, although mostly on those under 4·5 cm. (fig. 10, 32–5); when the gloss appears, it is in a diagonal area across one corner, often on both surfaces, almost invariably on the end opposite to that with the retained bulb of percussion. Most blades are elaborated by shallow retouching on one or both edges, often on both surfaces. It is interesting to note that in association with the new features of 'sickle-gloss' on long blades and on both surfaces, there occurs the feature of diagonal scratches often within the glossy area, or at least on the same surface. It is possible that this reflects slightly different methods or functions for the blades which, in other respects, are identical to those of the early neolithic cultures of southeast Europe.

The polished stone implements of the west Hungarian and central area of the early Linear Pottery culture consist of the short trapezoid axe/adzes 6–10 cm. long with a flat rectangular cross-section, as well as a few examples of the longer narrower axe/adzes with a more plano-convex cross-section. The true 'shoe-last' axe/adzes do not occur until the middle phase of the Linear Pottery cultures. Vencl in his study of the polished stone implements of the Linear Pottery culture,[49] and their function as the most important working implements,[50] has worked out a chronological classification of the axe/adzes: the flat trapezoid axe/adzes remain unchanged throughout the evolution of the Linear Pottery cultures; the long rectangular axe/adzes, however, which appear in the early phase of the culture with a comparatively low

Figure 10. Blade and polished stone industries from Early Neolithic sites in central Europe.
1–4: Tiszavasvári (Keresztfál), E. Hungary (from N. Kalicz, Inst. of Arch. Budapest) 1/1
5–7: Hortobagy (Faluvéghalom), E. Hungary (Debrecen Museum), obsidian. 1/1
8–12: Istállóskő, N.E. Hungary (Miskolc Museum) 10, obsidian. 8–11: 1/1; 12: 1/2
13–15: Kölyuk, N.E. Hungary (Miskolc Museum) 14, 15, obsidian. 1/1
16–32: Ciumeşti, N.W. Rumania (Beria IX: 16–20; Beria I: 21–21) (after Păunescu, 1963) 16: 1/2; 17–32: 1/1
32–5: Keszthely, W. Hungary (Keszthely Museum) 1/1
36–9: Žopy, S. Moravia, ČSSR. (from R. Tichý, Inst. of Arch., Brno) 1/1
40–1: Velatice, S. Moravia, ČSSR. (Moravske Museum, Brno) 1/1
42–6: Mohelnice, N.W. Moravia, ČSSR. (after Tichý, 1962) 1/1
47–8: Kateřinka, N. Moravia, ČSSR. (Opava Museum) 1/1
49–51: Bylany, E. Bohemia, ČSSR. (from B. Soudský, Inst. of Arch. Praha) 1/1
52–5: Nerkewitz, Thuringia, DDR. (after Behm-Blancke, 1963) 1/1
56–64: Glăvăneşti Vechi, Moldavia, Rumania (from E. Zaharia, Inst. of Arch. Bucureşti) 1/1
65–8: Floreşti, Moldavian SSR. (after Passek and Chernush, 1963) 1/2
69–72: Nezviska, W. Ukraine SSR. (after Chernush, M.I.A. 102 Moskva (1962)) 1/2
73–5: Giebultow, S.E. Poland (after Dzieduszycka, Mat. Arch. I (1959) 23–43) 1/1
76–7: Sandomierz, S.E. Poland (after Burchard, Mat. Arch. II (1960) 5–9) 1/1
78–81: Müddersheim, N.W. Germany (after Schietzel, 1965) 1/1
82–4: Sittard, S. Holland (after Bohmers and Bruijn, 1959) 1/1
85: Geleen, S. Holland (after Bohmers and Bruijn, 1959) 1/1

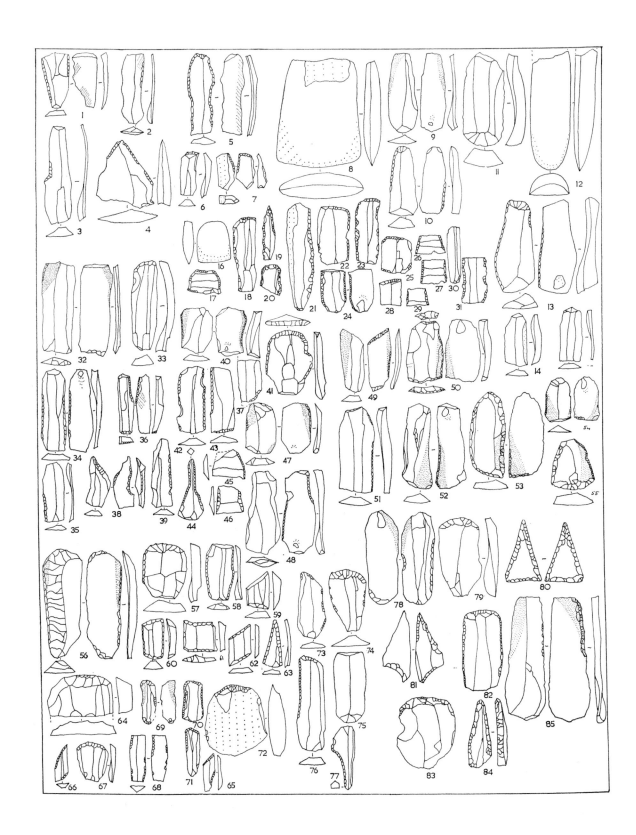

plano-convex cross-section, gradually develop along with other aspects of the culture, so that the back of the axe/adze becomes higher and the implement narrower until the form known as the 'shoe-last' axe/adze, and seen also in the Vinča-Tordoš culture,[51] was evolved.

In the central loess basin of Czechoslovakia (Moravia and southwestern Slovakia), in the settlements of the earlier phases of the Linear Pottery culture there occurs an almost identical material culture to that of the west Hungarian settlements. The blades examined from the site of Žopy in south Moravia are predominantly irregular, 3–5 cm. long and with very little evidence for 'sickle-gloss'; only part of one edge is ever retouched, and this sometimes shows oblique scratches (fig. 10, 36–9)[52] (material in the Institute of Archaeology, Brno).

The blade industry from other Linear Pottery sites in south Moravia, associated with slightly later stages in the evolution of the pottery, generally includes short blades 2·5–4 cm., occasionally with a glossy area across one corner (fig. 10, 40), longer 4–6 cm. blades with very little retouch on the edges, and small round scrapers (fig. 10, 41).

In north Moravia the same long blades, 3–5 cm., prevail, with retouching down one or both edges, and the bulb of percussion retained (fig. 10, 42–3); 'sickle-gloss' occurs on many of the smaller blades, especially on those of 3 cm. and shorter, in a diagonal area across one corner. Among the blades from the site of Mohelnice, there were two or three blades shaped into a long narrow borer at one end (fig. 10, 44); the nearest analogy for these is in the late Palaeolithic 'Magdalenian' industry of Czechoslovakia; in the same pit there were one or two microlithic trapezes (fig. 10, 45–6); this has been interpreted as not only a mesolithic, but also an upper Palaeolithic survival in the neolithic blade industry;[53] it seems inconceivable, however, that one type of implement as distinctive as this could represent a continuing tradition for 9000 years with no examples in the intervening period. It is more likely that the sporadic 'Magdalenian' borers found in early Linear Pottery sites, such as Mohelnice and Bylany, either represent the re-use of palaeolithic implements, or the completely independent manufacture of neolithic implements whose function caused them to resemble the palaeolithic implements.

In the upper Oder valley in the area near the Polish/Czech border, where the Oder has made a gap in the mountains, there is an important series of sites of the middle phase of the Linear Pottery culture, centred on the modern town of Opava; these sites testify to the probable original route of expansion of the early agriculturalists into south Poland from north Moravia; in Poland the sites are distributed on the upper Oder and thence along the upper Vistula river. Although so close to the rich centre of mesolithic settlement with its microlithic blade industry mentioned above, the flint industry of the Linear Pottery settlements of the upper Oder has no traces of microlithic elements, and does not differ from those of the contemporary Linear Pottery settlements of south Moravia and west Hungary, except that it is, if anything, slightly richer, and obsidian occurs frequently (fig. 10, 47–8) (material in Opava Museum and the branch of the Institute of Archaeology in Opava).

In Bohemia, the dense settlement by the early agriculturalists follows the loess deposits, in the basin of the upper Elbe river. The site of Bylany, which is the most important excavated settlement of this region and of the whole Linear Pottery culture, has been excavated systematically for the last 12 years, so that it is possible to tell exactly from which pits the blades came and with which pottery and therefore with which stage in the evolution of the culture each blade is associated. Using this information, and from an analysis of the blades of this site and other sites of the culture in Bohemia, it is clear that the blade industry of this region is rather richer than that of the settlements further east. The blades are generally long, 4–6 cm., with shallow retouching on one or both edges, and the bulb of percussion retained; the blades with 'sickle-gloss' across one corner, however, are predominantly shorter, approximately 3·5 cm. long, with the bulb of percussion less frequently retained (fig. 10, 49–51). Although the blade industry is richer, it is clear that the main working tool is still the polished stone axe/adze.[54]

The blade industry of the Linear Pottery settlements of Saxony and Thuringia, the regions covering the loess basins of the upper Saale and middle Elbe valleys, has been analysed by Behm-Blancke on a basis of the material from settlements predominantly of the middle phases of the culture;[55] he has classified the blades with 'sickle-gloss' into four groups, to show that there was more than one way of hafting the blades into the sickle handles, or of cutting the cereal stalks; the first two groups were hafted diagonally into the handle, with the result that the 'sickle-gloss' covers a diagonal area across the righthand corner (fig. 10, 52–4); the hafted end was either unworked, or only roughly retouched; often the bulb of percussion was incorporated in the hafted end, or less frequently in the cutting end; the cutting end was either roughly retouched or unworked. The second group is distinguished by having a rounded or obliquely angled cutting end, which is more frequently finely retouched; the third group also has a diagonal area of 'sickle-gloss,' but they are shorter broader blades, and the bulb of percussion is invariably incorporated into the hafted end (fig. 10, 55). These three groups are also produced, but much more rarely, with the area of 'sickle-gloss' in the left-hand corner. The fourth group includes similar long narrow blades, but they were hafted with the long edge parallel to the handle, so that the glossy area is in a band parallel to the cutting edge; the bulb of percussion was often incorporated into one of the non-hafted ends, the other end being roughly retouched.

These groups, except for the rarer fourth group, may all be found in the settlements of the Linear Pottery culture in Bohemia, and in west Germany and the Low Countries. Microlithic elements are absent from the blade industry of the Linear Pottery settlements of Saxony and Thuringia, as they are from those of Czechoslovakia, although one or two examples of geometric microliths occur sporadically, as at the settlement from the late phase of the culture at Zwenkau (Harth), near Leipzig.[56]

In the western part of continental temperate Europe, the upper valleys of the Danube and Rhine rivers and the lower valley of the Rhine were comparatively densely populated by a hunting/fishing population during the Late Boreal/Atlantic period (pollen zones VI/VIIa), with a geometric microlithic blade industry. In the expansion of the agricultural communities represented by the Linear Pottery cultures, especially in the middle and later phase, which by pollen analysis and Carbon-14 dating took place during the later Atlantic period, c. 4000 B.C., it is possible that there was a certain amount of contact and acculturation between the two populations.

In Bavaria, where the mesolithic flint industry of such sites as Ensdorf was essentially a geometric microlithic one, the scattered settlements of the Linear Pottery culture along the upper Danube, such as Alburg, show no geometric or microlithic elements in their blade industry;[57] the blades are 3–5 cm. long with retouching down one or both edges.

The upper Rhine and upper Danube valleys do not appear to have been settled by agriculturalists with the Linear Pottery culture, except sporadically as at Lauterach, mentioned above, probably because of the lack of suitable loess deposits.

On the loess deposits of the middle Rhine valley, the Linear Pottery settlement was much denser, especially in the Köln district. The earliest large excavation of a Linear Pottery settlement took place at Köln (Lindenthal). A much better example of the rich flint blade industry of the middle Rhine Linear Pottery settlements is the recently excavated site of Müddersheim, also on a loess terrace above the Rhine at Köln, with pottery of the middle and later phases of the culture.[58] As at Bylany, the exact location of each blade and polished stone implement has been recorded. The same inventory of the Linear Pottery culture blade industry as in Czechoslovakia and east Germany appears at Müddersheim, including 55 blades with 'sickle-gloss,' the majority of which are between 4–6 cm. long, longer than the majority of examples in Czechoslovakia (fig. 10, 78); crescent-shaped and wider blades with 'sickle-gloss' also occur, although these are completely absent from the settlements further east. Also the area of 'sickle-gloss' is at a much shallower angle to the cutting edge of the blade, and tends to run much further down the length of the blade than in the central European examples.

There are 24 polished stone axe/adzes from Müddersheim, 6 of which are the wide trapezoid type with a flat rectangular cross-section, and 18 of which are the true 'shoe-last' type, narrower and more rectangular with a high-backed plano-convex cross-section.

The two really new features in this inventory are the 9 large discoid scrapers and the 37 arrowheads. The arrowheads are symmetrical and asymmetrical triangles, with an average length of 3 cm. (fig. 10, 80–1); most are touched only along the edges, but four examples have retouching on the surface. Microlithic elements in the industry are so scarce as to be almost insignificant: there are six examples of true microlithic points, one example of a trapeze, and one example of a transverse arrowhead.

It is possible that the appearance of the triangular arrowheads and the large discoid scrapers, and the relatively scarce occurrence of the polished stone axe/adzes, are to be connected with new features in the basic economy of the settlements of this area, as indicated by the animal bone evidence from Müddersheim.[59] Bones of wild animals, especially aurochs, and to a certain extent wild pig, make up 28·8% of the bone material and 46% of the total number of individuals; thus, of the total number of individual animals represented in Müddersheim, only half are those of domestic animals, whereas from the analysis at Bylany in Czechoslovakia there was not a single bone of a wild animal.[60] Of the domestic animals at Müddersheim, 66·5% were cattle, and 20·7% were of pig, whereas at Bylany 80% were cattle, and 20% consisted of sheep, goat and pig.

The flint blade industry of the Linear Pottery settlements of the Low Countries in the region known as Limburg is even richer than that of the Köln district to the east.[61] The industry consists of basically the same types as at Müddersheim, including triangular arrowheads and large discoid scrapers; the blades with 'sickle-gloss' were longer than those of Müddersheim, having an average length of 5–7 cm. and width of 2 cm., with 'sickle-gloss' sometimes extending down the whole length of the blade (fig. 10, 85). As in northwest Germany, the rectangular narrow 'shoe-last' axe/adzes predominate over the flat trapezoid type, but even then their occurrence was not very frequent.

Although the forms of the arrowheads, and some of the end-scrapers and borers may have their prototypes in the 'Tardenoisian' of the Low Countries and northwest Germany, those of the Linear Pottery culture are quite distinct from the mesolithic implements, and not in the least microlithic. It would seem that the occurrence of geometric blades in the Linear Pottery culture of the Low Countries and northwest Germany does not represent an acculturation by the local mesolithic population, so much as a possible cultural borrowing, or slight adaptation by the intrusive agricultural population. As mentioned above, Carbon-14 evidence would suggest that the two populations were partly contemporary (fig. 8), but their distribution patterns are mutually exclusive.

The Linear Pottery settlements in Poland represent an expansion of the agriculturalists from northeast Moravia via the upper Oder gap; they are distributed on the loess deposits of the upper Oder and upper Vistula valleys. The flint blade industry is associated with pottery of the middle phase in the evolution of the culture. In this south Polish region, the blade industry consists predominantly of long blades with an average length of 3·5–5 cm., retouched down one edge, or very rarely down both edges, and occasionally at one end (fig. 10, 73, 75–6); it is assumed that some of these were sickle blades, although it is impossible to prove this without examination for working traces. There are wide blades retouched at one end which may, for the sake of convenience, be referred to as end-scrapers (fig. 10, 74); these appear as a large percentage of the whole inventory, as in the Linear Pottery sites of the Low Countries. As in north Moravia, obsidian implements form an important part of the blade industry of these settlements. Microlithic elements in the blade industry of this region are completely absent; trapezes and blunted-back blades, typical of the south Polish mesolithic sites, do not occur on the Linear Pottery settlements. Polished stone implements of the south Polish sites included especially the longer rectangular 'shoe-last' axe/adzes, with a high-backed plano-convex cross-section.

In the sporadic Linear Pottery settlements of central Poland, such as Chełmża, features which may indicate contact with the local mesolithic population do occur, including transverse arrowheads and blunted-back blades;[62] but the examples are so isolated that it is very difficult to make any conclusive statements as to the degree of contact or acculturation.

In the U.S.S.R., the Linear Pottery settlements are centred on the middle and upper basin of the river Dniester in the Ukraine S.S.R., and its tributary the Reut in the Moldavian S.S.R.[63] The settlement highest up the Dniester is Kotovane, near the watershed between the Dniester and the river San which is a tributary of the upper Vistula in southeast Poland. It seems extremely likely, from the similarity of the 'notenkopf' decoration of the pottery of the Ukraine sites to that of the south Polish sites, that the route of expansion of the early agriculturalists represented by the middle phase of the Linear Pottery culture was from the upper Vistula and down the Dniester river.

The blade and polished stone industry associated with the Linear Pottery of the Dniester and Reut is intrusive and very similar to that associated with the same pottery in south Poland and Moravia; the blades are predominantly 4–6 cm. long, with shallow retouching only on part of one edge or at one end, in the majority of cases at the end furthest away from that with the retained bulb of percussion (fig. 10, 68–71). There are also a large number of wide long blades with retouching at one end, which might be interpreted as end-scrapers.

The polished stone implements consist predominantly of the long narrow rectangular axe/adzes with a triangular or almost square cross-section; the flat trapezoid type are very rare.

It would seem from the evidence of recent excavations on the middle Dniester and southern Bug rivers, that the Linear Pottery communities were not the earliest agriculturalists in the middle Dniester basin. There is a series of stratified sites on the lowest terraces of the Dniester and southern Bug in which a culture known as the southern Bug or Bug-Dniester culture has recently been distinguished.[64] On the basis of stratigraphical evidence, five phases of the culture have been recognized. The first three consecutive phases, known as Skibinitz, Sokoletz and Petčora, are grouped together as Early Southern Bug; recently, Sulimirski has pointed out, after further examination of the stratigraphical evidence, that no two Early Southern Bug phases ever appear stratified on the same site, and that it seems likely that the three Early Southern Bug 'phases' are, in fact, three local facies of the Early Southern Bug culture.[65]

On several sites, such as Zankivtsy, a layer in which pottery is absent occurs below the Early Southern Bug culture layer. The blade industry of this layer is a mixed one consisting of blades 2–10 cm. long, including end-scrapers and geometric microliths such as trapezes. The economy associated with this layer is one based on hunting and fishing except at the most western of the sites so far excavated, Soroki (Trifautski I and II) on the Dniester in the Moldavian S.S.R., where on both sites the aceramic culture layer has produced blades with sickle working traces, and the bones of domestic pig.[66]

The pottery of the early Bug-Dniester, or southern Bug culture, is associated with an almost identical blade industry to that of the aceramic layers; the pottery itself is generally soft, poorly baked ware with pointed bases and decorated all over by rows of tiny incisions, impression *etc*. In the more western sites of the culture, however, especially in the Petčora group, this pottery is often accompanied by pottery of a better quality with many features such as flat bottoms, low pedestals or sharply angled bi-conical profiles which connect it with the Criş culture of the Prut and Seret rivers further west in Rumanian Moldavia.[67] The economy associated with the material of the early Bug-Dniester culture is again that based on hunting and fishing, but at the Soroki sites, although hunting and fishing seem to have predominated, there is evidence for 'sickle-gloss' on one or two of the blades, and there are bones of domesticated cattle, as in the Moldavian Criş sites.[68]

The middle phase of the Bug-Dniester culture, known as the Samtčin phase, shows a continuation in the local blade industry consisting of predominantly macrolithic end-scrapers and geometric microlithic blades, and a continuation in the development in the local style of pottery. In some of the more northwestern sites of the culture, such as Basikov Ostrov, imported sherds from the Linear Pottery settlements of the upper Dniester occur in association with the local ware.[69]

The analysis of the animal bone material from Soroki has not yet been published in detail, so that it is not yet possible to see if the various animals occur in the same proportions as those on the Linear Pottery settlements of the Ukraine and Moldavia. At Soroki, in association with material of the middle phase of the culture, only domesticated cattle are mentioned, and the other animals are wild. In the Linear Pottery settlements of the Dniester, Reut, Prut and Seret valleys, wild animal bones form a much higher proportion of the whole, as on the western periphery in Germany and the Low Countries, than they do in central Europe.[70] Among the domestic animals, cattle form 50–60% of the individual animals, and pig 30%. Pig, red deer, and aurochs were among the most important wild animals.

It is interesting to note, in this context, the occurrence of geometric microliths, including trapezes and triangles, on the Linear Pottery settlements of the Moldavian S.S.R. and Rumanian Moldavia, such as Floreşti (fig. 10, 66), on the Reut,[71] and Glăvăneşti Vechi in Rumanian Moldavia (fig. 10, 59–63) (material in the Institute of Archaeology, Bucureşti). It seems very likely that, in the case of the Moldavian Linear Pottery settlements, there was a certain amount of adaptation to different physical conditions, and of contact and acculturation with the population in the surrounding areas whose economy was based to a very great extent on hunting and fishing, and whose blade industry included a large proportion of geometric microliths.

From this rather selective analysis of the blade and polished stone industries of the late mesolithic and early neolithic settlements of southeast and temperate Europe, it is possible to draw several conclusions:

1. In western Asia, the settlements associated with evidence for incipient agriculture, and known as 'protoneolithic,' have produced microlithic blade industries, often including geometric forms; e.g., Karim Shahir in northern Iraq, and the 'Natufian' and 'PPNA' layers at Jericho. A similar industry may be seen in Greece, also in connection with evidence for incipient agriculture; e.g., the basal layer at Argissa in Thessaly. The approximate date of these industries is 9000–7500 B.C.

2. In southeast Europe, north of Greece, there are similar microlithic blade industries, although not necessarily including geometric forms; these are especially located in mountain and sand-dune areas. These sites, along with the macrolithic industry of Crvena Stijena IVa in Yugoslavia, have been claimed as 'pre-pottery neolithic' settlements, as at Argissa. There is evidence for intensified collecting and hunting, but no direct evidence for incipient agriculture on any of these sites, except La Adam and Soroki, which have not been proved conclusively to be earlier than the main expansion of agriculturalists in the Danube basin.

3. In temperate Europe, settlements of a hunting/fishing population with a microlithic blade industry are distributed on low sandy hills and dunes; that is, with a distribution pattern quite exclusive of the loess basins, except in southeast Poland (fig. 7). These industries have been dated in the western part of temperate Europe by pollen analysis to zones VI (Late Boreal) and VIIa (Atlantic), and by the Carbon-14 method to between 7000 and 3500 B.C. (fig. 8). There is no evidence for incipient agriculture from these sites until the last stages in their development, that is at a time when they would have been contemporary with and on the periphery of the early agricultural population on the loess basins of temperate Europe.

4. The earliest productive agricultural communities of west Asia are associated with a macrolithic blade industry in which small blades with an area of 'sickle-gloss' occur, also with a polished stone industry consisting especially of trapezoid axe/adzes with a flat rectangular cross-section; e.g., Jericho (PPNB) and Hacilar (aceramic), c. 7000–6700 B.C.

The industry evolves with the developed agricultural economy, and the appearance of monochrome and then painted pottery; *e.g.*, Çatal Hüyük, Hacilar VI–I, Hassuna etc., *c.* 6000–5000 B.C.

5. The macrolithic blade and polished stone industry appears with the earliest direct evidence for a developed agricultural economy, and with monochrome and then painted pottery in Greece, Bulgaria and east Yugoslavia, in sites of the Proto-Sesklo, Sesklo, Karanovo I, and Starčevo cultures *c.* 5000–4500 B.C.; the same industry appears in the settlements of the Criş and Körös cultures in southeast Hungary and Rumania.

6. The same blade and polished stone industry expands with the agricultural economy and appears on the sites of the Linear Pottery culture distributed on the loess deposits of Hungary, Czechoslovakia, Austria and east Germany, *c.* 4600–4000 B.C. As the Linear Pottery cultures evolved in this area there was very little change in the blade or polished stone industry, except that the 'shoe-last' axe/adzes with a high-backed plano-convex cross-section predominated in the later phases; there was no evidence for contact with any peripheral mesolithic population.

7. The western periphery of the Linear Pottery cultures, represented by the settlements in northwest Germany and the Low Countries, show basically the same blade and polished stone industry, just as the economy was still basically agricultural; however, it is possible to see definite new features such as triangular arrowheads and discoid scrapers, and the importance of wide end-scrapers; a slight change in the economy is also evident in an increase in the importance of hunting (or at least in the killing of wild animals, especially aurochs), and a lesser predominance of domestic cattle with a growing importance in domestic pig. This may be interpreted as acculturation by the local hunting/fishing population, but it is more likely to represent further adaptation by the intrusive agriculturalists, 4100–3800 B.C.

8. The eastern periphery of the Linear Pottery cultures represented by the settlements in south Poland, and the upper valleys of the rivers Dniester and Reut, Prut and Seret, has a very similar blade and polished stone industry to that of the middle phase of the culture in Moravia, except that there is a high frequency of wide long end-scrapers and a relatively frequent occurrence of geometric microlithic blades, although this latter feature is limited to the Moldavian settlements. As with the western peripheral area, the economy of the settlements of the eastern periphery is slightly different from that of central Europe, with an increase in the number of wild animals represented, and an increase in the importance of the domestic pig, although cattle still predominated among the domesticated animals. It is likely that the microliths in this case represent some contact with the Bug-Dniester culture, but it is very unlikely that the Linear Pottery settlements themselves represent acculturation by the local mesolithic population on the upper Dniester.

Several hypotheses for contact between mesolithic and neolithic populations in central and east Europe have been put forward, based principally on material from settlements in Czechoslovakia and Germany;[72] these involve seeing mesolithic elements in the Linear Pottery culture blade industry, or neolithic elements in the latest mesolithic microlithic industry. However, as Vencl has pointed out, many of the implements, such as trapezes and notched microlithic blades, which Mazalek has claimed are mesolithic elements in neolithic sites, come, in fact, from surface collections and are, therefore, not truly valid.[73]

Also, if one might venture an opinion, it is the generalities which make up the basis of the interpretation of prehistoric communities, not the exceptions, especially where stone industries are concerned, so that one trapezoid microlith on one or even several Linear Pottery sites in Moravia, out of a total of at least 500 sites, need not necessarily be interpreted as contact with a microlithic-producing mesolithic population.

The other group of hypotheses which it is hoped this study has, to a certain extent, disproved, are those which suggest that the neolithic cultures of Europe north of the Danube river are the result of acculturation to the agricultural and ceramic techniques of the more advanced innovating communities further down the Danube by the local hunting/fishing mesolithic population of the middle Danube basin, or even that they are the result of the independent autochthonous development of agriculture and pottery-manufacture by the mesolithic population.[74]

It has been shown that the hunting/fishing mesolithic population in temperate Europe was, in almost every case, absent from the areas settled by the earliest agricultural communities (fig. 7), and that although they may have been, to a certain extent, contemporary, as is shown by pollen analysis and Carbon-14 evidence (fig. 8), the distribution patterns of the mesolithic and Linear Pottery culture sites is mutually exclusive, the former limited to mountain and sand-dune districts, the latter to the loess basins of the large river valleys. In addition to this, the blade industry, as well as other features of the Linear Pottery culture, shows a complete break with the microlithic blade and trapeze industries of the mesolithic cultures in temperate Europe. Thus, there is hardly any evidence for contact between the two populations, let alone acculturation.

Appendix. Details of the Carbon-14 samples used in the study (fig. 8). All dates B.C.

Western Asia

Jericho PPNB	7220±200 BM 115	(*Radiocarbon* V (1963) 83)
,,	7075±110 Grn 963	,,
,,	6708±101 P 381	,,
Hacilar (aceramic)	6750±180 BM 127	(*Radiocarbon* V (1963) 108)
Hacilar IX (beg. late neolithic)	5380±94 P 314	(*Radiocarbon* IV (1962) 149)
,,　　VII (late/middle neolithic)	5820±180 BM 125	(*Radiocarbon* V (1963) 108)
,,　　VI (end late neolithic)	5390±85 P 313a	(*Radiocarbon* IV (1962) 145)
,,　　II (early chalcol.)	5210±134 P 316	,,
,,　　Ia (end early chalcol.)	5030±121 P 315	,,
Tell-es-Siwwan (cf. Hassuna)	5349±86 P 856	(*Radiocarbon* VII (1965) 190)

Southeast Europe

Elateia (early neolithic)	5400±90 Grn 3037	(*Radiocarbon* V (1963) 183)
,,　　　　,,	5240±100 Grn 3041	,,
,,　(middle neolithic)	5080±130 Grn 3502	,,
Vršnik (Starčevo)	4915±150	(Milojčić, *Germania* XXXVI (1958) 414)
Gornja Tuzla (Starčevo)	4690±75 Grn 2059	(*Radiocarbon* V (1963) 183)

Azmak (Karanovo I)	4808±100 Bln 267	(*Radiocarbon* VIII (1966))
Karanovo (Karanovo II)	av. 4676±115 Bln 201, 234, 152	,,
Gyálaret (Körös)	5140±100 Bln 75	(*Radiocarbon* VI (1964) 315)
Kotacpart ,,	4500±100 Bln 115	,,
Katalszeg	4420±100 Bln 86	,,

Central Europe (Linear Pottery Cultures)

Korlát (N.E. Hungary)	4490±100 Bln 119	,,
Tarnabod (E. Hungary)	4330±100 Bln 123	,,
Zalavár (W. Hungary)	4230±100 Bln 87	,,
Mohelnice (Moravia, ČSSR)	4395±100 Bln 102	,,
Žopy ,,	4480±100 Bln 57	,,
Mold (Austria)	4040±160 Bln 58	,,
Pulkau ,,	4265±100 Bln 83	,,
Winden am See (Austria)	3990±100 Bln 55	,,
Eitzum (Thuringia, DDR)	4360±200 Bln 51	,,
,, ,,	4430±210 H 1487/985	(Quitta, *Praehistorische Zeitschrift* XXXVIII (1960))
Westeregeln (Saxo-Thurin., DDR)	4190±100 Bln 92	(*Radiocarbon* VI (1964) 316)
,, ,,	4250±200 Grn 223	,,
Dresden (Nickern) ,,	3995±100 Bln 73	,,
,, ,,	3865±100 Bln 77	,,
Zwenkau (Harth) ,,	3950±100 Bln 66	
,, ,,	4210±70 Grn 1581	(*Radiocarbon* V (1963))
,, ,,	3820±120 K 555	(*Radiocarbon* II (1960))
Friedburg (Bavaria, DBR)	4170±100 Bln 56	(*Radiocarbon* VI (1964) 310)
Wittislingen ,,	4080±110 Grn 265	(Milojčić, *Germania* XXXVI(1958))
Müddersheim (Rheinland, DBR)	4190±90 H ?	(Schietzel (1965) 126)
Geleen (S. Holland)	4412±70 Grn 995	(*Science 128* (1958)
,, ,,	4217±70 Grn 996	,,
Elsloo ,,	4200±70 Grn 2160	(*Radiocarbon* V (1963) 176)
,, ,,	4370±90 Grn 2159	,,
,, ,,	4320±85 Grn 2164	,,
,, ,,	4105±80 Grn 2884	,,
Sittard ,,	3835±210 Grn 422	(*Science 127* (1958))
,, ,,	4145±160 Grn 320	,,

Mesolithic temperate Europe

Moita do Sebastiâo (S. Portugal)	5400±350 Sa 16	(*Radiocarbon* VI (1964) 245)
Cabeço da Amoreira ,,	5080±350 Sa 195	(*Radiocarbon* VII (1965) 238)
Cabeço da Arruda ,,	4480±300 Sa 197	,,
Birsmatten (Basisgrotte) (Switzerland) 5	5510±160 B 238	(Bandi (1964) 88)
Birsmatten (Basisgrotte) (Switzerland) 4	5720±120 B 237	,,
Birsmatten (Basisgrotte) (Switzerland) 3	5020±120 B 236	,,
Birsmatten (Basisgrotte) (Switzerland) 2	3360±240 B 235	,,
Birsmatten (Basisgrotte) (Switzerland) 1	3400±120 B 234	,,
Milheeze (Low Countries)	6550±160 Grn 2318	(*Radiocarbon* V (1963) 170)
Oirschot ,,	6080±60 Grn 1659	,,
,, ,,	5550±70 Grn 1510	,,

de Leijen (Low Countries)	5280±65 Grn 1683	(Bohmers and Wouters (1956) 35–8)
,, ,,	5200±140 Grn 685	,,
Haule ,,	6012±370 C 627	,,
Tilburg (Labe) ,,	4550±120 Grn 1597	,,
Maaheeze ,,	4280±115 Grn ?	,,
Een ,,	5840±120 Grn 1505	(*Science 128* (1958) 1553)
,, ,,	5765±120 Grn 1508	,,
Siegerswoude (Low Countries)	6000±80 Grn 1509	(*Science 128* (1958) 1553)
Drouwen ,,	5905±100 Grn 1513	,,
Duurswoude ,,	5750±70 Grn 1173	(*Radiocarbon* V (1963) 169)
Hatert ,,	5720±110 Grn 1602	,,
Waskemeer ,,	5500±140 Grn 615	(*Science 127* (1958) 134)
Ellerbek (Schleswig-Holstein, DBR)	4105±200 Y 440	(*Science 126* (1957) 911)
Heidmoor ,,	3985±100 Y 162	,,
Satrup Moor ,,	3735±70 Y 160	,,
,, ,,	3665±50 Y 471	,,
Elinelund (S. Sweden)	3360±210 U 48	(*Radiocarbon* I (1959) 97)
Kunda (Estonia SSR)	4050±210 Ta 16	(*Arctic Anthropology* III (1965))
,, ,,	6375±280 Ta 14	,,

Notes

1. *Arkheologiya i Estestvenniye Nauki* (1965) 193–5
2. Semenov, *Prehistoric Technology* (1964) 63
3. *Germania* XXXVIII (1960) 320; Milojčić, *Die deutschen Ausgrabungen auf der Argissa – Magula in Thessalien* (1962) 1–26; *Thessalike* I (1958) 70–86
4. Soudský, *Bylany : osada nejstarších zemědělcu z mladši doby kamenné* (1966) 15–18
5. *Glasnik Zemaljskog Muzeja*, Sarajevo XIII (1958) 21–42
6. *S.C.I.V.* IX, 1 (1958) 91
7. *S.C.I.V.* X, 2 (1959) 230–5
8. *Glasnik Zemaljskog Muzeja*, Sarajevo XII (1957) 80
9. *Diadora* I (1960) 5–26
10. *Arheološki Radove i Rasprave* II (1962) 175–212
11. *Diadora* I (1960) 5–26
12. *Radiocarbon* III (1961) 100
13. *Studia in Honorem Akad. D. Dečev* (1958) 360
14. *K.S.I.I.M.K.* LIV (1954) 62–70; *Sovětskaya Arkheologiya* V (1940)
15. *Zeitschrift für Tierzuchtung und Zuchtungbiologie* LXXVI (1962) 282–320
16. *Radiocarbon* V (1963)
17. *K.S.I.A.* Moskva CV (1965) 86
18. *Omagiu lui Constantin Daicoviciu* (1960) 21–8
19. *S.C.I.V.* X, 2 (1959) 221–35
20. *Dacia* VII (1963) 477–83, 467–75
21. D. Berciu in a paper given at Edinburgh, 1 March 1965
22. *Sovětskaya Arkheologiya* XXI (1954) 38–51
23. *Mat. Arch.* VI (1965) 5–33
24. Jazdzewski, *Poland* (1965) 57
25. *Mat. Arch.* VI (1965) 12–13
26. *XIV sjezd pro mineralogii a geologii*, Brno (1963) 155; *Archaeologica Austriaca* XII (1953) 9–18
27. *Arch. Rozh.* XVIII (1966) 67–71; Barrière, *Les Civilisations tardenoisiennes en Europe occidentale* (1956) 285–7
28. *Arch. Rozh.* XVI (1964) 9
29. *Alt-Thüringen* V (1961) 18–75

30. *Alt-Thüringen* II (1957) 46; *Anthropozoikum* III (1953) 203–34
31. *P.P.S.* XXIV (1958) 24–42
32. *P.P.S.* XXIV (1958) 32–3; Barrière, *op. cit.* 115–24; *Festschrift für Pieter Goessler* (1954) 113–32
33. *P.P.S.* XXIV (1958) 33, 42
34. Bandi, *Birsmatten-Basisgrotte* (1964) 86–8
35. Taute in *Second Atlantic Colloquium*, Groningen (1964)
36. *Radiocarbon* V (1963) 176
37. *Palaeohistoria* V (1956) 36–7
38. Bohmers in *Second Atlantic Colloquium*, Groningen (1964)
39. *S.N.M.P.* XIV, 1–2 (1960) 2
40. *P.P.S.* XXVIII (1962) 267
41. *Studia in Honorem Akad. D. Dečev* (1958) 369–87
42. Mikov and Džambazov, *Devetaškata Peštera* (1960)
43. *S.N.M.P.* XIV, 1–2 (1960) 3
44. Garašanin, *Starčevačka Kultura* (1954) 48–9
45. *Acta Arch. Hung.* IX (1959) 53–68
46. *Acta Archaeologica Carpathica* I (1959) 173–84
47. *Dacia* VII (1963) 467–75, 477–83
48. *ibid.* 478
49. *S.N.M.P.* XIV, 1–2 (1960) 1–43
50. *Arch. Rozh.* XIII (1961) 678–93
51. Garasanin, *Hronologija Vinčanske Grupa* (1951) 46
52. *Pam. Arch.* LIII (1962) 268
53. *ibid.* 268–77
54. *S.N.M.P.* XIV, 1–2 (1960) 1–43
55. *Alt-Thüringen* VI (1962–3) 107–8
56. *Alt-Thüringen* II (1957) 46–7
57. *Wiener Prähistorische Zeitschrift* XXVIII (1941) 10
58. Schietzel, *Müddersheim : eine Ansiedlung der jüngeren Bandkeramik in Rheinland* (1965) 45–65
59. *ibid.* 115–23
60. Soudský, *op. cit.* 63
61. *Palaeohistoria* VI–VII (1958–9) 183–211
62. Jazdzewski, *op. cit.* 67
63. *Arkheologiya SSSR* B I–II (1963)
64. *K.S.I.A.* Kiev XII (1962) 23–4; *Atti del Congresso Internazionale*, Roma (1962) 128–30
65. Sulimirski, *Prehistoric Russia* (in press) chapter III
66. *K.S.I.A.* Moskva CV (1965) 86
67. *Acta Arch. Hung.* IX (1959) 66
68. *K.S.I.A.* Moskva CV (1965) 87
69. *Arkheologiya SSSR* B I–II (1963) 13
70. *ibid.* 31–2; *Materiale* Bucuresti VIII (1962) 262
71. *Arkheologiya SSSR* B I–II (1963) 22–30
72. *Mannus* XXV (1933) 255; *Alt-Thüringen* II (1957) 27–47; *Anthropozoikum* III (1953) 203–34; *Wiener Prähistorische Zeitschrift* XXVIII (1941) 1–20
73. *S.N.M.P.* XIV 1–2 (1960) 63–72
74. Schliz, *Das steinzeitliche Dorf : Grossgartach* (1901); *A.J.A.* LXI (1957) 61; *Starinar* IX–X (1959) 11–16; (ed.) Braidwood, *Courses towards Urban Civilization* (1962) 213

Some aspects of ovicaprid and pig breeding in neolithic Europe

Jacqueline Murray

One of the main distinctions between the neolithic period and the preceding mesolithic was the method by which food was obtained. During the mesolithic period hunting, fishing and gathering of plants were the sole means of procuring food, whereas with the advent of the neolithic, agriculture was evolved. There are three main animals upon which the economy was based, namely cattle, ovicaprids and pigs, and two plants, wheat and barley. The material considered in this paper is taken from a postgraduate thesis, shortly to be submitted to the University of Edinburgh. Further details of the economy of the sites and cultures mentioned here are to be found in this reference. It should also be mentioned that the material available varies a great deal. Some sites are extremely well documented, and both descriptions of the animals bred and their statistical importance are provided. At the majority of sites, however, such information is not given, and at others it may be stated that a certain animal is the basis of the economy but the statistics upon which this conclusion is made are unavailable.

Neolithic communities can be divided into three animal-breeding groups; those which had their subsistence-economics centred upon cattle breeding, those which were based upon ovicaprid breeding, and those to which pigs were of more importance. The best-documented early neolithic community is that of the Linear Pottery culture. Here the evidence shows that cattle and wheat were the chief constituents in the economy. This culture brought the knowledge of agriculture to the greater part of central Europe, spreading it from Hungary in the southeast to Holland and Denmark in the northwest. A large proportion of the subsequent cultures in central and western Europe follow this agricultural tradition, but there are some which do not do so, namely the cultures which bred more ovicaprids or pigs than they did cattle.

Sheep and goat were domesticated earlier than cattle or pig, and the earliest neolithic communities in the Near East and southeast Europe concentrated upon the breeding of these animals. Cattle then became of greater significance, and at a later stage of the neolithic sheep and goat become once more of prime importance to the economy. In other areas the pig supersedes the ox as the basic domestic animal. It is these pig-breeding and late ovicaprid-breeding cultures that are discussed in this paper (see map, fig. 14).

The chief pig involved in domestication in Europe is the large wild European pig *Sus scrofa ferus*, which can be seen in most zoos today. The pig found in Greece is slightly different, being both smaller and more slender than its central European counterpart. This pig bears many similarities to the wild pig of southeast Asia, known as *Sus vitattus*. Recently domesti-cated pigs, *Sus scrofa domesticus*, differ only a little from the wild prototypes, the most obvious changes occurring in the foreshortening of the tusks and jaws. This produces a shorter snout and smaller teeth. The animals also become a little smaller in size. As breeding progresses these characteristics of domestication become emphasized. The turbary pig *Sus palustris* is considerably smaller than *Sus scrofa ferus*, with shorter jaws, limbs and body and a more slender appearance. The jaw measurements show an overall reduction of between 1-in-14 to 1-in-5.[1]

The European domestic goat, *Capra hircus*, is descended from the bezoar goat *Capra aegagrus*, which has large scimitar-shaped horns and is found in the Near East. As early domestication progressed the goat became smaller, as did the pig, and this is shown most clearly by the reduction in size of the horns. Eventually these may become very small, perhaps three or four inches high, straight and pointed.

The moufflon and the urial are the main species of sheep concerned in sheep domestication in this context. Both are found in the Near East and the former occurs on some Mediterranean islands. They are robust animals with large outswept horns which lie in the form of an open spiral. Domestication reduces the size of these horns as well as that of the rest of the body. The shape of the horns also changes to an arc of a circle rather than an open spiral. Turbary sheep are smaller still and the horns become small, erect and goat-like.

The pig-breeding cultures are considered first. These consist of the Sesklo, early Salcuṭa, Tripolye A and Horgen cultures. The site which illustrates the economy of the Sesklo culture best is that of Otzaki.[2] This culture has been divided into an early and late phase, and as is seen from figs. 11a and 11b pigs are the dominant feature in the economy in both cases. These pigs are small in size and for the most part fall within the range of variation of the turbary pig. There are also a few bones of a more primitive-looking pig which probably represents recent local domestication of the indigenous small boar. Pigs are also present at Argissa, but too few bones were found to evaluate the relative importance of the domestic animals.[3]

The only evidence from the Salcuṭa culture comes from the type-site of Salcuṭa.[4] No exact statistics were available but Berciu says that pigs were the dominant feature in the economy of the Salcuṭa I–IIc period. They then decrease in importance, but for the culture as a whole they are still more common than either cattle or ovicaprids.

Nearly 8,000 bones were identified at the Tripolye A site of Luka-Vrublevetskaia, and so an excellent impression of the economy of this site is obtained.[5] Pigs are seen to be nearly twice as frequent as any of the other domestic animals (see fig. 11c). Comparative measurements between these pigs and various known breeds show the pigs bred at Luka-Vrublevetskaia fall within the range of the turbary breed. Pigs are again the most frequent animal found at Lenkoutsa, and they account for over half of the domestic stock.[6]

Two sites of the Horgen culture yielded a sufficient number of bones for a statistical analysis to be carried out. The turbary pig is seen to be the basic domestic animal at Auvernier III[7] (fig. 11d), and at St Aubin III[8] (fig. 11e). A particularly large quantity of osteological remains were identified at the last site, where pigs are substantially more numerous than cattle.

The Sesklo, Salcuṭa, Tripolye A and Horgen cultures clearly have a similar economy. The first culture may be dated to between 5200 and 4300 B.C., the second to 3700 to 3200 B.C.,

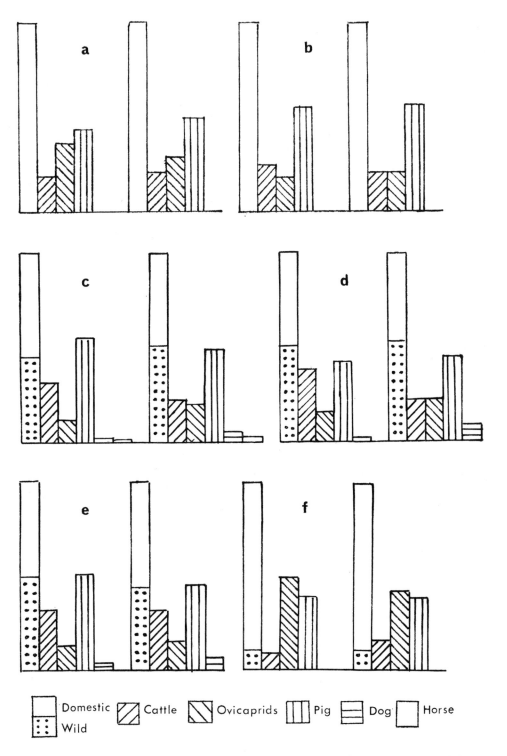

Domestic / Wild   Cattle   Ovicaprids   Pig   Dog   Horse

Figure 11. Histograms showing the relative proportions of animals represented at neolithic sites. In each pair of histograms, the left portion represents the relative percentages of bones, the right portion the relative minimum numbers of animals, at each site. Scale : 1 mm.= 2%.
a. Otzaki (early) ; b. Otzaki (late) ; c. Luka-Vrublevetskaia ; d. Auvernier III ; e. St Aubin ; f. Arapi.

the third to 3800 to 3500 B.C. and the last to 2700 to 2300 B.C. by means of radiocarbon dating. In order to see if this common factor is coincidental or the result of other cultural contact, it is necessary to consider some of the characteristics of these cultures.

The pottery of the Sesklo culture consists usually of fine red burnished ware, which occasionally bears black and white rectilinear patterns. The flame design is also typical of this pottery. In northern Greece these vessels might have red designs on a white slip background. The general impressions of these pots is that they are extremely fine and delicately made. The pottery of the Salcuţa culture is somewhat different. Very little red or white painted ware occurs, but graphite painting, rustication and wave impressions are more common. The Tripolye culture is characterized by pots of sophisticated form and design. Elaborate curvilinear geometric designs are painted in two or occasionally three colours on many different shapes of pots. The basic colour is red or white, and the patterns are outlined either by channelled grooves, red, black or white paint. The Horgen pottery represents a complete contrast to that of Tripolye. It is coarse, badly baked and has no painted decoration. Both splayed and round-based pots occur. Hence it appears that these four cultures all have a different form of pottery.

There is not so much difference in the stone industry. Stone vases occur in the Sesklo culture, which is otherwise a macrolithic blade industry, and long blades are found at Salcuţa sites in addition to the traditional Boian stone work and adzes. Perforated axes occur at Horgen sites.

Hunting was of varied importance. It remained relatively unimportant during both the Sesklo and Salcuţa cultures, but during Tripolye A and Horgen it accounted for between two-fifths and half of the food supply, as the osteological evidence shows (figs. 11a–c).

From the above discussion it may be concluded that these cultures do not show any overall agreement in their pottery, stone industry or in the importance of hunting. Hence their similar economy cannot be connected to any of these factors. There may however have been some common geographical or climatic factor. It is known that wild boar were to be found in large quantities in the surrounding countryside, so that their exploitation would have been comparatively easy, and their domestication may have proved easier to accomplish than that of the aurochs.

In order to shed light upon the evolution of these pig farmers it is necessary to analyse in detail the animal domestication of the Linear Pottery culture. This culture can be divided into three main phases, early, mid and late. In all stages cattle are the main domestic animal, but there is a difference in the importance of ovicaprids and pigs in the late stage to that of the preceding two stages. This late stage is characterized by 'Stichbandkeramik,' or the filled-in band style of ornamentation on the pottery. To illustrate this difference a few sites of the early and mid phases will be compared to those of the late phase. There are unfortunately only a small number of sites at which both reliable statistics and the phase of occupation are known. The early and mid sites considered are Barleben-Schweinemästerei A, Cochstedt, Halle-Trotha, Köthen Geuz and Tröbsdorf;[9] and the late sites are composed of Barleben-Schweinemästerei B, Magdeburg-Prester, Müddersheim and Traian.[10] As can be seen from figs. 12a and 12b ovicaprids are considerably more important than pigs during the early and mid phases. During the last phase however this situation is reversed. Therefore, as the Linear Pottery

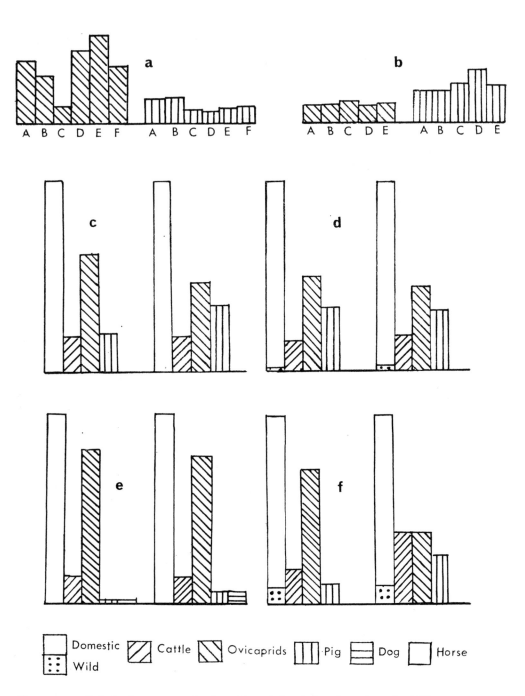

Figure 12. a. Relative importance of ovicaprids and pigs during the early and middle phases of the Linear Pottery Culture. A. Barleben-Schweinemästerei; B. Cochstedt; C. Halle-Trotha; D. Kothen Geuz; E. Trobsdorf; F. average.
b. Relative importance of ovicaprids and pigs during the late Linear Pottery Culture. A. Barleben-Schweine-mästerei; B. Magdeburg-Prester; C. Müddersheim; D. Traian; E. average.
c-f. Histograms showing the relative importance of animals represented at neolithic sites. In each pair of histograms, the left portion represents the relative percentage of bones, the right portion the relative minimum numbers of animals, at each site. Scale: 1 mm. = 2%.
c. Argissa; d. Otzaki; e. Gimel; f. La Paillade.

culture progressed, the importance of pig breeding increased, and that of sheep and goat declined. It is probable that this increase in pig breeding was a natural adaptation to the local surroundings which supported many wild boar. Also pigs cannot be successfully bred by mobile communities, but thrive in a stable environment. This suggests that towards the end of the Linear Pottery culture some sedentary communities had emerged, and that the people of the Sesklo, Salcuţa, Tripolye A and Horgen cultures did not travel over large distances.

The ovicaprid-breeding cultures are now considered. These include the Dimini, Salcuţa IIc, Cernavoda, Tripolye Cii, Baden, Swiss Corded Ware and French Copper Age cultures.

The sites of Arapi, Argissa and Otzaki[11] all illustrate the economy of the Dimini culture. As is seen from figs. 11f, 12c and 12d sheep and goat were the basic domestic animal at all three sites. Most of these animals were of medium-size, although considerable variation on either side of this mean has been observed. One horn core found at Otzaki was exceptionally robust.[12]

The only evidence for phase IIc of the Salcuţa culture comes from the type site itself. Berciu[13] reports that sheep and goat are the main domestic animal, but the extent to which they exceed the other animals is not known. Many horn cores of goat are recorded. Berciu also reports that the economy of the Cernavoda culture was based upon ovicaprid breeding, but no further details were available.

The site at which most bones could be identified during the Tripolye Cii culture was that of Usatovo.[14] Of the five thousand bones identified, more than half belonged to sheep. The basic animal appears to have been the turbary breed of sheep (fig. 13a). The site of Gorodsk belongs to this period also, but most of the bones found were of horse. Sheep were less frequent than cattle, but since far fewer bones were identified, this is not as representative as the results from Usatovo.[15] Childe also mentions a late site at which sheep were the main domestic animal.[16]

Osteological remains from a Baden context in Hungary have been examined by Bőkőnyi.[17] The two settlements of this culture with a statistical analysis of the bones are Budapest-Andor utca and Szekely-Zoldteltk. At both sites ovicaprids are more frequent than both cattle and pigs (figs. 13b and c). The breed of sheep and goat could not be identified. Ovicaprids are also the most important animal at the Austrian site of Ossarn.[18]

The general impression of the agriculture of the Corded Ware sites in Switzerland is not uniform. Sheep and goat are the main domestic animal at the sites of Auvernier[19] (fig. 13e), and Baldegg[20] (fig. 13d), but both cattle and pigs are more important at Utoquai.[21] The turbary sheep was the main breed, but there were also bones of the large Copper sheep. This last animal is very similar to the moufflon in appearance, and also occurs at the Danish Middle Neolithic site of Bundsø[22] and probably at Stora Karslo in Sweden.[23] Both of these finds can be linked with the expansion of the Single Grave Complex.

Four sites of the French Copper Age have had a detailed analysis of their osteological remains. These are Anis-2-Hortus, Bergerie neuf, Gimel and La Paillade.[24] In all cases sheep and goat are the main domestic animals, and the breed of sheep has been ascertained as turbary (figs. 12e–f, 13f–g). Sheep are more numerous than goats.

One of the main difficulties facing cultures which had their economy centred upon the breeding of sheep and goat, rather than on cattle or pig, would be the problem of obtaining

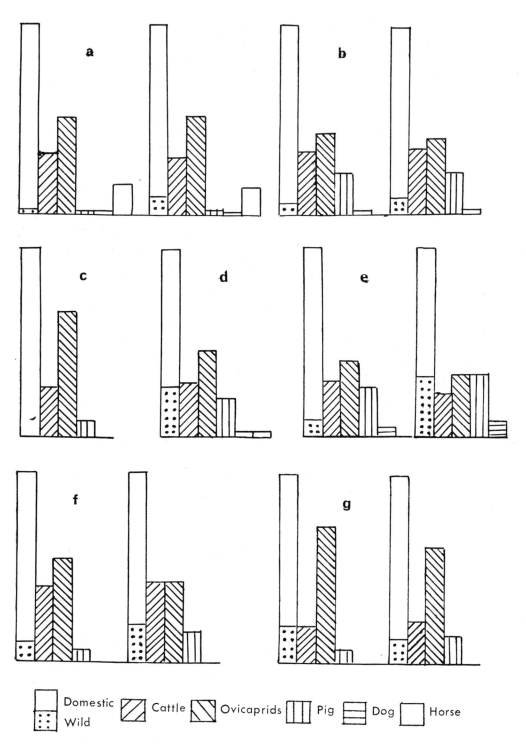

Figure 13. Histograms showing the relative proportions of animals represented at neolithic sites. In each pair of histograms, the left portion represents the relative percentages of bones, the right portion the relative minimum numbers of animals, at each site. Scale: 1 mm. = 2%.
a. Usatova; b. Budapest-Andor utca; c. Szekely-Zoldteltk; d. Baldegg; e. Auvernier II; f. Anis-2-Hortus; g. Bergerie neuf.

new stock. In Europe it was impossible for the communities to go and domesticate the wild animals themselves, so that either the old stock would have to be improved without external means, or these animals would have to be obtained by trade from the Near East. These animals are likely to be close to the wild ancestors. Such animals are only known with certainty from one of the six cultures considered. This is the Swiss Corded Ware culture where the Copper sheep has been identified. Apart from its occurrence at Utoquai, mentioned above, this sheep is also known from Greng.[25] One exceptionally large sheep is also recorded at Otzaki in a Dimini context.[26] There has been no detailed investigation of the sheep of the Salcuţa IIc or Cernavoda cultures.

The Dimini culture represents a complete break with the preceding Sesklo culture, as its pottery, stone work and agriculture show. Its pottery is inferior in quality to that of Sesklo and has painted decoration with spiral and meander patterns. Occasionally it is tricoloured. The patterns are usually white, black or incised on a buff, brown or red ground. It bears some similarity to the Gumelniţa culture to the north, and so may be linked indirectly with the Salcuţa culture. However the main difference between the Gumelniţa and Salcuţa culture lies in the pottery so that no direct contact between the Salcuţa and Dimini cultures can be established. The Tripolye pottery is discussed above. The pottery of the Baden culture is characterized by channelled decoration, and has distinctive ribbon handles to its jugs, which rise above the level of the rim. The Swiss Corded Ware pottery is again different and consists of long necked beakers and amphorae which are richly decorated with cord impressions over their upper portion. Both plain and decorated pots occur at the French Copper Age sites considered by Josien. The pottery at Gimel and La Paillade consists of plain ware as well as pots which are decorated with incised chevrons, channelled decoration or diamond-shaped reliefs.

As is apparent there is no overall agreement on the distinctive pots produced by these individual cultures. Some cultures are characterized by painted ware and others by plain ware. Channelled decoration, or grooved ware, is found at sites of the Baden culture as well as those of the French Copper Age and at some Tripolye sites. Occasional cord impressions occur at some Tripolye Cii sites, for instance Usatovo, which connects this culture with that of the Swiss Corded Ware.

The stone industry of all these cultures is similar to those of the earlier neolithic, with a few new features appearing. Perforated axes are found for the first time in Greece in a Dimini context, long blades are found in Salcuţa IIc, and battle-axes at the Swiss Corded Ware sites.

One feature common to all these cultures is the occurrence of copper. Both copper and gold occur in small quantities at Dimini, Salcuţa IIc and Tripolye Cii sites. Copper is the more common of the two. Objects include copper celts and small ring pendants of gold in the Dimini culture, copper axes and adzes and gold ring pendants in the Salcuţa and Cernavoda cultures. Little metal is found in the Tripolye culture before the Cii phase, and the forms at this stage include copper axes, daggers with a midrib on one face only, and small rings and spirals in copper and silver.

A small amount of gold is also found. By the time the Baden culture had developed, large copper axe/adzes had evolved, and at this stage copper neck rings occur for the first time in Hungary and Austria. This culture is particularly rich in finds of copper. Axes, rhomboid and triangular daggers have been found at Swiss Corded Ware sites. Daggers occur in southern France, and there are also occasional gold objects.

However it must be emphasized that the occurrence of metal in the various cultures mentioned does not imply that these objects were manufactured by the communities themselves. With the exception of the Baden culture, it is much more probable that the copper or gold trinkets, the daggers and axes, were the result of trade with long-established metal-producing societies. Such societies are to be found in the Near East. It is also in this area that the wild sheep and goat are to be found.

Hence it appears that some of the Dimini, Salcuţa IIc, Tripolye Cii, Cernavoda, Baden, Swiss Corded Ware and French Copper Age cultures have certain elements in common. There is no basic agreement in the pottery, but cord impressions and channelled decoration are common to some cultures. However this connection cannot be regarded as being very strong. The most obvious link between these cultures lies in the rise of the trade in metals.

The isotopic dating of these cultures is of great interest. The Dimini culture may be placed at around 4200–3600 B.C., Salcuţa IIc to between 3500 and 3300 B.C., Cernavoda to 3200–3000 B.C., Tripolye Cii to 3100–2900 B.C., the Baden culture to 3200–2900 B.C. The approximate dates of the Swiss Corded Ware sites are thought to be 2800–2200 B.C. and those of the French Copper Age as 2600–2100 B.C. When the time-span of these cultures is mapped over their known area of distribution a clear wave of influence is seen to spread from Greece through eastern and central Europe as far west as France (fig. 14). This illustrates the spread of the ovicaprid-breeding cultures over Europe. Their origin must be placed somewhere in the Near East, but as yet there is not sufficient evidence from that area to enable the location to be determined. They must, however, have evolved there by the fifth millennium.

To summarize, the following conclusions have been made. During the earlier neolithic period in central Europe pig breeding is seen to have increased, whilst that of sheep and goat declined. The outcome of this was the evolution of certain cultures which had their economy centred upon pig breeding. No other apparent connection between these cultures has been observed. During the late neolithic or copper age ovicaprids became the main domestic animal of several cultures. These cultures may be linked with the spread of trade in copper and gold over Europe. There is a clear expansion of these ovicaprid-breeding cultures from Greece through eastern and central Europe to France within the period 4200–2100 B.C. Their origin must be placed in the Near East, probably in the fifth millennium, and they are closely connected with some long-established metal-trading societies.

Notes

1. *M.I.A.* XXXVIII (1953) 411–58; Rütimeyer, *Die fauna der pfahlbauten in der Schweiz* (1861)
2. *B.R.G.K.* XXXVI (1955) 1–51; Boessneck in Milojčić, *Die deutschen Ausgrabungen auf der Argissa Magula in Thessaliens* I (1962)
3. Boessneck in Milojčić, *op. cit.*
4. Berciu, 'Contributii la problemele Neoliticului in Rumania' in *Lumina noilor Cercetari* (1961)
5. *M.I.A.* XXXVIII (1953) 411–58
6. *M.I.A.* LXXXIV (1961) 1 ff.

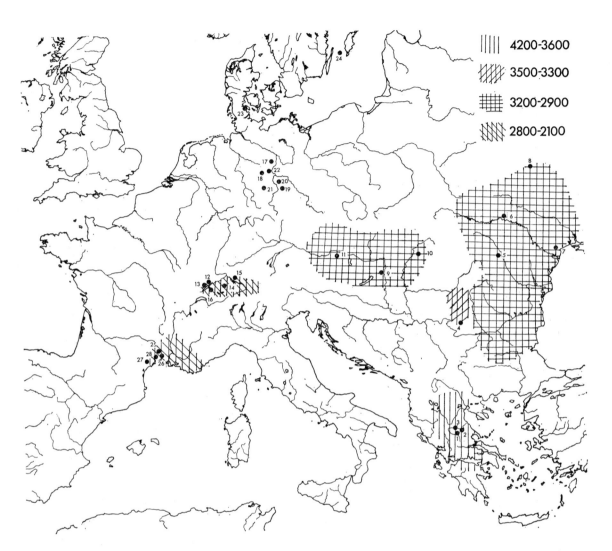

Figure 14. Spread of Ovicaprid Breeding Cultures over Europe, divided on the basis of absolute age (B.C.).
Sites mentioned in the text : 1. Otzaki ; 2. Argissa ; 3. Arapi ; 4. Salcuta ; 5. Traian ; 6. Luka-Vrublevetskaia ;
7. Usatovo ; 8. Gorodsk ; 9. Budapest–Andor utca ; 10. Szekely-Zoldteltk ; 11. Ossarn ; 12. Auvernier ;
13. St Aubin ; 14. Baldegg ; 15. Utoquai ; 16. Greng ; 17. Barleben-Schweinemästerei ; 18. Cochstedt ;
19. Halle-Trotha ; 20. Köthen Geuz ; 21. Tröbsdorf ; 22. Magdeburg-Prester ; 23. Bundsø ; 24. Stora Karslo ;
25. Anis-2-Hortus ; 26. Bergerie neuf ; 27. Gimel ; 28. La Paillade.

7. *Archives des Sciences physiques et naturelles* (1932) 101–5
8. *Archives des Sciences physiques et naturelles* (1930) 83–6
9. Muller, 'Die Haustiere der Mitteldentschen Bandkeramiker', *Deutsche Akademie der Wissenschaften zu Berlin* XVII (1964) 1 ff.
10. *ibid.*, Schietzel, 'Műddersheim—Eine Ansiedlung der jungeren Bandkeramik in Rheinland', *Fundamenta* I (1965) 1 ff.; *Materiale si Cercetari Arheologice* VIII (1962) 261
11. *B.R.G.K.* XXXVI (1955) 1–51; Boessneck in Milojčić, *op. cit.*
12. *ibid.*
13. Berciu, *op. cit.*
14. *Arch' Pam' Ukr' SSR'* IV (1952) 124-130; Hančar, 'Das fferd in prăhistorischen Frűhhistorische Zeit', *Wiener Beitrage zur Kulturgeschichte und Linguistik* IX (1956) 1 ff.
15. *ibid.*
16. Childe, *The Dawn of European Civilization* (1957)
17. *Acta Arch. Hung.* XI (1959) 39–97
18. *Eiszeit und Urgeschichte* V (1928) 60–120
19. *Archives des Sciences physiques et naturelles* (1932) 101–5
20. *Naturforsch. Ges. Zurick* LXXXV (1940) 59–70
21. *Rev. Suisse de Zool.* (1932) 531–768
22. Degerbøl in *Aarbøger f. Nord. Oldkynd. og. Hist.* (1939) 99 ff.
23. *Acta Zoologica* (1926) 123–217
24. *B.S.P.F.* LIV (1957) 94–102, 757–62
25. *Naturforsch. Ges. Bern* (1883) 1–99
26. Boessneck in Milojčić, *op. cit.*

Old mortality: some aspects of burial and population in neolithic England

R. J. C. Atkinson

Sir Thomas Browne's 'sad and sepulchral Pitchers, which have no joyful voices, silently expressing old mortality, the ruines of forgotten times' symbolize the preoccupation of many prehistorians with death and burial. In this essay I have tried to use the evidence of neolithic burial in England as a means of investigating the problem of neolithic population, which on many occasions in the last twenty years I have discussed *inter pocula* with Stuart Piggott. Here I have attempted to formulate the main parameters of the problem in quantitative terms, and thereby to reduce, if only marginally, the area of speculation. I offer him the results, however inconclusive, in gratitude and friendship, as a footnote to chapters II–V of his *Neolithic Cultures of the British Isles*.

Future historians of British archaeology will undoubtedly give special emphasis to *Neolithic Cultures*, not merely as a brilliant and comprehensive synthesis of knowledge and interpretation, but also as an illustration of the influence of a definitive work upon the historical development of archaeological thinking. The concept of 'models of the past' is one which Piggott himself has introduced to archaeologists[1] as an explanation (indeed, as itself a model) of the way in which they think about their subject, and of the constraints which are imposed, for the time being, upon their interpretations by the current climate of thought. He will be the first to agree that, by an historical accident, *Neolithic Cultures* has served to perpetuate a particular 'model of the past' beyond its natural span of life.

It so happens that *Neolithic Cultures* was completed, though not published, precisely when the chronological model of later British prehistory had reached its maximum contraction, and just before the development of gas-counting techniques of radiocarbon dating had begun to yield neolithic dates of enhanced reliability and in increasing numbers. It is difficult, and surprising, now to recall that in the spring of 1951, when *Neolithic Cultures* was completed, only two relevant dates were available, for Ehenside Tarn and for Aubrey Hole 32 at Stonehenge.[2] Within the framework of the chronological and cultural model then current, it was legitimate to suppose that both these contexts 'should on archaeological grounds be broadly contemporary.' Accordingly the Ehenside Tarn date (3014 B.C. ±300) was regarded as suspect, since it was about a millennium earlier than the current model would allow; and in his chronological table, so presciently labelled 'provisional,' Piggott gave for the duration of the primary neolithic cultures of the lowland zone of England a period of little more than 250 years, starting around 2000 B.C. In this he did no more than to give precision to the orthodoxy of the day.

But already by the time that reviews of *Neolithic Cultures* appeared, new radiocarbon dates from Europe required the raising of this initial date by up to half a millennium;[3] yet even as late as 1959 I find, to my present surprise, that I was putting it no earlier than 2400 B.C.[4] In the meantime, the very short chronology of the early 1950s had become widely disseminated and accepted, not least through its use on the explanatory notices erected at neolithic monuments in the care of the Ministry of Works, which are only now being revised.

Today, though we still lack all but a small fraction of the radiocarbon dates required for a detailed chronology of the British neolithic period, we have enough to show beyond reasonable doubt that its duration must be four or five times the allowance originally made by Piggott, with a starting date not later than 3000 B.C. There is indeed some irony in the realization that the two radiocarbon dates available in 1951 estimated very fairly the duration of the period, as we now see it.

In the last few years we have come to accept without question the expansion of the neolithic chronology which radiocarbon dates require; but we have perhaps been slower to accept the implications of this necessary expansion in human and cultural terms. Though the time-scale has been extended, the amount of archaeological material to be fitted within it remains the same. That is to say, the same amount of human activity must now be spread out, as it were, over a period four or five times longer than we previously supposed.

The alteration of the time-scale thus requires a reassessment of our whole view of the nature of neolithic life and culture in Britain, and of the processes whereby patterns of behaviour were conserved or were changed over the course of time. If it can be shown that certain customary activities, such as the building of earthen long barrows, persisted throughout the neolithic period, two conclusions follow from the lengthening of that period. First, any estimate of the rate of cultural change, or of the strength of the forces resisting change, must be proportionately altered, simply because the period of persistence is by that much the longer. Second, the conditions in which a particular cultural practice could successfully be transmitted over a wide expanse of space and time would be proportionately more difficult to overcome, because at any one instant the size and the number of individual human groups will have been smaller, and the opportunities for contact between them fewer, than we had previously envisaged.

The lengthening of the time-scale of our neolithic communities thus necessarily alters our view of their cultural history and development in geometric, not arithmetic, proportion. This is particularly relevant to Piggott's own very illuminating concept of innovating and conserving societies in prehistory.[5] Both terms are relative, in that they require prior definition of the time-scale involved, and a prior estimate, so far as the evidence allows, of the size and density of the population within which innovations can be adopted and diffused, or traditional practices preserved.

In this context it seems worth while to explore the possibilities of arriving at an estimate of neolithic population through the medium of neolithic burials, but within a deliberately restricted field. I have intentionally confined this inquiry to the 'primary neolithic' material of lowland England (that is, to the Windmill Hill and Severn-Cotswold groups defined by Piggott) because these alone appear to provide an acceptable basis for hypothesis. For the secondary neolithic cultures the evidence is mainly in the form of artifacts rather than structures, and burials are rare.[6] In the highland zone, though there is no lack of burials in chambered tombs, the methods of estimating a population from its burials cannot be applied with any confidence, partly because of the multiplicity of tomb-types, partly because of the ruined and robbed condition of so many of them, and not least because of the chronological uncertainties involved.

In what follows, therefore, I have used as a basis for estimation the burials which have been recorded from the 'earthen' or 'unchambered' long barrows of Piggott's Windmill Hill group, and from chambered tombs of the Severn-Cotswold type. Apart from a very few neolithic burials beneath round barrows,[7] these constitute the sepulchral evidence for the population of lowand England, which for present purposes may be taken as the area lying to the south and east of a line drawn from Scarborough through Gloucester to the coast at Lyme Regis, on the Devon-Dorset border. In calculation, I have not hesitated to use approximations, because the uncertainties of the data and the assumptions alike make it impossible to achieve precision.

Concerning these burials, four questions arise. First, how many burial sites are now known? Second, how many are there likely to have been originally? Third, how many burials did they contain in the aggregate, and on the average? Fourth, what fraction of the total contemporary population *may* these burials represent?

For the area concerned the numbers of unchambered long barrows still surviving, or recorded but since obliterated, are listed by counties in Table 1. This table excludes long barrows so described in the literature cited, but known or suspected to be chambered; and those stated by the author (usually Mr L. V. Grinsell) to be doubtful. The figures given are therefore minima; but the addition of the doubtful examples would not increase the total by more than a few per cent.

Table 1

County	Long barrows	Sites with recorded burials	Number of burials
Yorkshire	25	5	61
Lincolnshire	11	1	8
Norfolk	3		
Bedfordshire	5		
Hertfordshire	1		
Kent	1		
Surrey	1		
Sussex	13		
Hampshire	30	2	16
Berkshire	4	1	14
Wiltshire	80	23	146
Dorset	41	3	9
Somerset	14		
Totals	229	35	254

It seems unlikely that further fieldwork will significantly increase the numbers listed. In Wiltshire, the county with the densest concentration of long barrows, Mr Grinsell's intensive survey,[8] aided by air-photographs, yielded only four new discoveries (Bishops Cannings 92, Broad Chalke 11, Collingbourne Ducis 23 and Ramsbury 1), of which the third is doubtful and the fourth had hitherto been identified as a round barrow.

The number of long barrows destroyed without trace or record is necessarily unknown, but is again likely to be small. Unlike many small round barrows and other earthworks of low relief, long barrows are large enough, and more particularly high enough, to have resisted successfully the erosive effects of cultivation, at least until the recent introduction of mechanized farming and deep ploughing. On the river gravels, where almost all earthworks have been obliterated by prolonged tillage, the crop marks for which this type of terrain is particularly favourable have not so far revealed any new long barrow sites, in spite of the widespread discoveries of other neolithic monuments, such as cursuses.[9] It is assumed below, therefore, that the original number of earthen long barrows built in lowland England did not exceed 250.

To estimate the number of individuals buried in the aggregate in these long barrows, we have to rely on 35 excavated sites for which there are adequate records, which are summarized in columns 3 and 4 of Table 1. In many instances the minimal character of these figures is clear. For the Skendleby long barrow, for instance, Cave[10] records the presence, besides eight identifiable individuals, of additional complete and incomplete bones representing an unknown number of other persons. Where the human remains are disarticulated, incomplete and disordered, as is commonly the case, it is inherently likely that the excavator will have underestimated, perhaps seriously, the number of separate bodies. At Fussell's Lodge, for example, Mr Ashbee's estimate at the time of excavation (15–19) differs by a factor of about three from the figure given by Dr D. R. Brothwell (53–7) after laboratory examination.[11] It should be remembered, however, that one of the principal excavators of long barrows, John Thurnam, was a practising doctor of medicine; and that another, Canon Greenwell, enjoyed the collaboration from time to time of one of the leading anatomists of the day, Professor George Rolleston.

The figures for recorded burials given in Table 1 are reproduced in fig. 15a as a histogram of grouped frequencies. The arithmetic mean for the number of burials per barrow is about seven; but this is perhaps unduly inflated by the inclusion of the abnormally large number found at a single site, Fussell's Lodge. If this is excluded, the mean falls to about six. On this basis, the aggregate number of persons buried in an estimated 250 long barrows, throughout the neolithic period, will have been in the range 1500–3000, according to the allowance made for underestimation of numbers from disarticulated and disordered bones.

The minimum period during which earthen long barrows were built in lowland England may be estimated at about ten centuries. For the upper chronological limit we have the radiocarbon date from Fussell's Lodge of 3230 B.C. ±150.[12] The chances of the real date being later than 3000 B.C. are about 1 in 17. For the lower limit we may use the evidence of the Beaker sherds found in the chalk rubble mound of the Skendleby long barrow.[13] It seems difficult to avoid the conclusion that these were incorporated in the mound during its construction, which can hardly have taken place, therefore, earlier than 2000 B.C.

These figures suggest, it seems, that on the average throughout the neolithic period no more than two or three individuals were buried each year in a long barrow. If we assume a crude death rate of 40 per 1000 per annum (excluding infant mortality),[14] then we may expect this number of deaths to have occurred annually, on the average, in a population of between 40 and 75 persons, excluding infants.

This estimate rests, however, on the obviously false assumption that the 'long barrow population' remained static throughout the neolithic period. It is more realistic to assume a pattern of exponential growth, which can be justified here on two principal grounds. First, the food-producing economy introduced by the neolithic immigrants permitted the accumulation of a food surplus, in the form of stored grain and live meat, and thus increased the chances of survival, and therefore the reproductive capacity, of individual families. Second, the impact upon the natural environment both of primitive, slash-and-burn agriculture and of controlled, and thus locally concentrated, grazing must itself have produced an exponential change in the environment, through the clearance of forest, which created conditions favourable for further agricultural exploitation.

It is unfortunate that the chalk and limestone formations, on which neolithic activity was

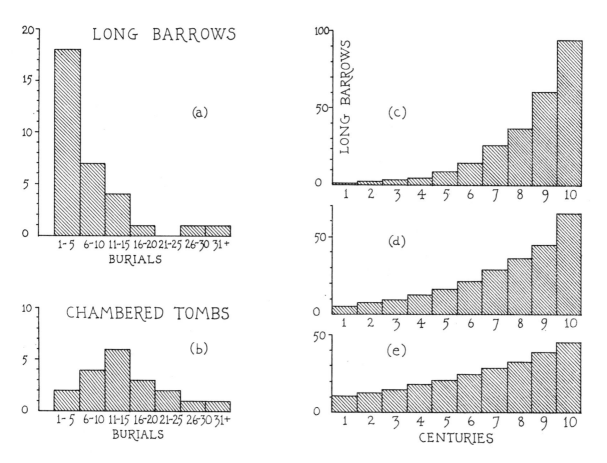

Figure 15. a, b. Grouped frequencies of occurrence of burials in long barrows and Severn-Cotswold tombs, for England only. c–e. Theoretical time-distributions for the building of 250 long barrows.

concentrated, are inimical to the preservation of fossil pollen, so that we have no direct evidence for the early vegetational history of these areas of primary settlement. Nonetheless, it seems safe to assume that these calcareous uplands presented to the neolithic immigrants an almost continuous cover of high forest, the replacement of which by open grassland is an entirely man-made phenomenon.[15] The decline in elm pollen, associated in England, as elsewhere in Europe, with the neolithic colonization, is indeed the strongest evidence for the contemporary existence of widespread forest, and the relative absence of open grassland; for under these conditions the leaves and bark of forest trees would provide the main source of fodder. It need not be supposed that the use of such fodder was confined to the elm alone, for it seems possible that the intermittent and irregular flowering of this tree may have rendered it more vulnerable than other deciduous species to persistent exploitation in this way.

The process of forest clearance is initiated by burning, and maintained by grazing. Grain will be sown on the area cleared by fire for five to ten years continuously, until the fertility of the soil is depleted so far that clearance of a fresh area becomes necessary. However, the plots initially cleared for tillage, and now abandoned, will remain available for grazing, so that regeneration of the natural forest will be prevented. The growth of spiny shrubs, resistant to grazing, such as blackthorn, hawthorn, bramble and holly, will certainly take place; but these are very vulnerable to a second clearance by fire.

In this way a single family, growing grain on some ten acres at a time, can in the course of a century convert up to a third of a square mile of forest to relatively open scrub and grassland; and in so doing they will provide favourable conditions for the establishment of at least one other family in the area thus converted. In fact, however, the rate of conversion is probably higher than this, because grazing alone will eventually reduce woodland, particularly through the rooting activities of pigs and the gnawing of bark by goats, which combine to prevent the replacement of old trees by young saplings.

For these reasons it seems safe to assume an approximately exponential increase of the 'long barrow population' of England during the neolithic period. Three theoretical models of this increase are presented in figs. 15c–15e, in terms of the numbers of long barrows likely to have been built in each of the centuries from 3000 to 2000 B.C. The histograms are derived from exponential growth-curves of the form $y = ae^{bx}$, where x is the elapsed time, the constant a gives the initial number of barrows built (*i.e.*, is related to the assumed size of the initial immigrant group), and the constant b satisfies the condition that the total number of barrows built throughout the period shall be 250. The initial number of barrows assumed is respectively one, five and ten.

These theoretical models are of course much oversimplified, in that they take no account of any subsequent immigrations, and allow only for a sudden cessation of long barrow building at the end of the period concerned. Only the accumulation of a long series of radiocarbon dates for long barrows will make it possible to decide which model, if any, approximates to the truth. Meanwhile, however, it should be noted that on this theoretical basis the maximum number of barrows built in any one century (the last) would be respectively about 95, 65 and 45. If we assume an average of six burials per barrow, and a crude death rate of 40 per 1000, excluding infants, we arrive at a maximum 'long barrow population' of between

70 and 140. *Ex hypothesi*, the population during any earlier century will have been even smaller.

At first sight these figures are so small that one is inclined to reject them as a tenable estimate of the total 'long barrow population,' and to conclude that only a fraction, say one-tenth, of the contemporary population was accorded the distinction of burial in a long barrow. This may well be true; though it is clear that there is no means of estimating what proportion of a given community received this special treatment. Before adopting this inconclusive conclusion, however, it is perhaps worth examining a little further the hypothesis that long barrow burials may represent an entire population.

Ever since Pitt-Rivers' excavation of Wor Barrow[16] it has been recognized that burials in long barrows occur in varying states of articulation, preservation and completeness, and may thus be assumed to represent people whose deaths occurred over a span of time, and whose remains were stored, above or below ground, over varying periods, until the decision was made to bury them collectively beneath a long barrow. This view has more recently been confirmed by the detailed study of the burials at Skendleby,[17] Wayland's Smithy I[18] and Fussell's Lodge.[19] It is likely, therefore, that the building of a long barrow was the terminal stage in a funerary ritual which lasted over an extended period of time.

If so, we must suppose that some particular event determined the moment in time at which a barrow was to be built, and a group of bodies transferred from some place of temporary storage to their final resting place; and since there appears, at least in the better-attested cases, to be at least one body which was buried more or less entire, and thus presumably not long after death, it is tempting to assume that the determining event was the death of an individual of special importance, perhaps, indeed, the leader for the time being of the community concerned, whether it be a single family or an aggregation of families forming a clan or tribe. If, as hitherto, we assume a crude death rate of 40 per 1000 for those who survive infancy, then the mean lifespan of an individual will be 25 years, and the interval between the deaths of successive leaders of a community will not, on the average, exceed this period and may well be shorter. Thus a given community would be expected to build a long barrow at least four times in a century. If the average period of time represented by a single long barrow is 25 years, and if the average number of deaths in that period is six, the size of the community necessary to give that number of deaths is also six – in other words, a single family.

The outcome of this line of reasoning, admittedly highly speculative, is that an earthen long barrow *could* have been the burial place of the dead of a single family over a period of a single generation. At any rate this hypothesis seems tenable for the majority of these monuments, in which the number of recorded burials does not exceed 15. It is less easy to support where the number of burials is large, as at Fussell's Lodge; and it is inapplicable to the few long barrows which appear to be cenotaphs.

Where the burials are relatively numerous, it may be that they were accumulated over a longer period of time than was customary elsewhere; but the evidence for timber enclosures beneath a number of long barrows suggests again that the period of accumulation did not exceed about one generation. Such enclosures occur at Wor Barrow,[20] Skendleby,[21] Nutbane,[22] Fussell's Lodge,[23] East Heslerton,[24] and probably at Willerby Wold,[25] Kilham,[26]

Westow[27] and Hanging Grimston;[28] and they can plausibly be related to the practice of storing the bodies of the dead. Yet their timber uprights, apparently unprotected from the weather, can hardly have had a useful life of more than half a century; and where, as at Fussell's Lodge, they served subsequently as the retaining wall for a massive chalk mound, their period of previous use was probably substantially shorter. The burials found on this site thus probably represent deaths at a mean frequency of about two per annum, or a population, excluding infants, of about 50 people.

It is noticeable, however, that the proportion of children buried at Fussell's Lodge is unusually high, and that there is evidence for pathological conditions which *may* be attributable to malnutrition or an ill-balanced diet.[29] It may be, therefore, that this particular community had an abnormally high death-rate and was in fact substantially smaller than the estimate given above.

At the other end of the scale, a few long barrows appear to have contained no burials at all. The best-attested example is that on Thickthorn Down in Dorset,[30] where animal bones were well preserved but no human bones were found, even though the mound was completely excavated. More recently, two long barrows near Avebury (Bishops Cannings 76 and Avebury 68) have been comprehensively excavated by Dr Isobel Smith and Dr John Evans respectively, with a similar negative result. The significance of these apparent cenotaphs is far from clear; but their rare occurrence need not upset the tentative calculations made above.

It may be objected that if a long barrow is the tomb of a single family, the labour required to build it is beyond the capacity of so small a group. For the largest long barrows, ranging up to 400 feet in length, this is obviously true; but it is not necessarily true for more normal examples. The mound at Fussell's Lodge, for instance, which is rather above the mean size of Wessex long barrows, would have required about 5000 man-hours for its construction,[31] or four months' work for six people. For an enterprise undertaken, perhaps, only once in a generation this is by no means impossible. For the larger barrows, for the causewayed camps, and above all for major works of civil engineering such as the two parts of the Dorset Cursus,[32] we must in any case assume that a number of families combined to work together, often for long periods. Indeed, whatever the size of the contemporary population, it must have been through such communal activities that the social coherence of individual groups found its expression, and customary practices were transmitted from one generation to another over wide reaches of space and time.

The foregoing argument contains far too many unverifiable assumptions to allow it to be pressed to any firm conclusion. I have tried to show, however, that it is *possible* that British long barrows were the burial places of individual families. It remains to be seen whether the development of techniques for the blood-grouping of ancient bones will throw any light on this tentative hypothesis.[33]

The second principal group of neolithic burials in lowland Britain is that from chambered tombs, mainly of the Severn-Cotswold type. After exclusion of doubtful sites, their distribution by counties is as follows: Gloucestershire 70,[34] Wiltshire 20,[35] Oxfordshire 7,[36] Dorset 7,[37] Somerset 7,[38] Berkshire 1 (Wayland's Smithy II), Herefordshire 1.[36] To this number of 113 a further 15% should perhaps be added for sites unrecognized or totally destroyed, to give an estimated original total of 130.

The numbers of recorded burials have already been tabulated by Piggott.[39] For the strictly lowland area here considered, 126 burials in five Welsh sites (Ffostyll South, Parc Cwm, Pen y Wyrlod, Tinkinswood and Ty Isaf) should be subtracted, and at least 40 burials added for the four intact chambers at West Kennet,[40] to give a total of at least 293 burials from 19 excavated sites. The grouped frequency distribution of these, with a mean of about 15, is shown in fig. 15b. As for long barrows, these figures must be regarded as minima, because the disordered and disarticulated state of the remains has almost certainly led to underestimation of the number of individuals present.

The mean number of burials per tomb is about two-and-a-half times larger than for earthen long barrows, and probably reflects a longer period of use. A stone-built burial chamber can be reopened for each successive interment, and its effective life is limited in practice only by its structural stability. There is thus no reason why it should not have been used over a period of many generations; and indeed for the West Kennet tomb Piggott has suggested use over not less than a millennium.[41]

It is unfortunately not possible at present to estimate with any confidence the period during which chambered tombs were constructed and used in lowland England. We have only one radiocarbon date, of 2820 B.C. ± 130, for Wayland's Smithy II,[42] and apart from the secondary occurrence of Beaker sherds on a few sites, there is nothing to tell us how long their construction continued. It would be rash, therefore, to attempt even a tentative estimate of the rate of growth of the 'chambered tomb population.' It is clear, however, that the total number of individuals thus buried is likely to have been about 2000, or rather more than the minimum estimate for burials in earthen long barrows.

It remains to be considered whether the average chambered tomb, containing about 15 burials, could have served as a family vault. If we assume the same crude death rate as before, then a family of six people, of assumed constant size, will experience 15 deaths in a little more than 60 years. This seems too short a period for the use of structures whose potential life was clearly far longer; and even where the number of burials greatly exceeds the average, as at West Kennet, the period of use calculated on this basis is still less than two centuries, a result quite incompatible with the chronological evidence from the site itself.

It seems likely also that the labour required to build a chambered tomb, particularly on Cotswold limestone, was considerably greater than for a long barrow on the chalk. The mean size of both types of structure is very similar; but the materials used differ considerably in weight. Chalk rubble weighs about 70 lb. per cu. ft., and for the building of a long barrow is generally derived from an adjacent quarry-ditch, so that the average distance of transport does not usually exceed about 50 feet. The coarse limestone rubble used for the cairns of Severn-Cotswold tombs, on the other hand, weighs about 160 lb. per cu. ft., and has to be quarried and transported over a much greater distance; nor can it be broken up directly with antler picks, as chalk can be, at any rate near the surface. In addition, account must be taken of the labour of transporting and erecting the components of the burial chamber itself; though the effort involved here may have been matched, in at least some long barrows, by that required for the felling, transport and erection of massive and numerous timbers. It seems reasonable to guess, however, that the man-hours needed for the building of a Cotswold tomb were at least three times as great as for a chalk long barrow of the same size, and by that much less within the compass of a single family.

On balance, therefore, I incline to the view that chambered tombs in lowland England were used for the burial of selected members of the population only, and not for the population at large. This is perhaps supported by the marked disparity in the numbers of identified male and female burials, which is too large to be accounted for satisfactorily by sampling errors.

This conclusion necessarily requires that the bodies of some, and perhaps the majority, of the dead were habitually disposed of in a way which has left no archaeological trace. There is no difficulty in this supposition. We have for many years accepted, tacitly at least, that with minor exceptions the population of the greater part of the British Iron Age does not appear in the funerary record; and where, for that matter, are the burials of our Late Bronze Age?

The greater part of this essay consists, as I am well aware, of speculation and surmise, yielding no decisive conclusion. Yet if the prehistorian is to substantiate his claim that he studies human societies through their material remains, he must attempt to define the basic characteristics of those societies by whatever means he can. As Sir Thomas Browne said, in another archaeological context, 'To make the dead to live . . . and discourse of humane fragments . . . is not impertinent to our profession.'

Notes

1. Piggott, *Approach to Archaeology* (1959) 3–6
2. Piggott, *Neolithic Cultures of the British Isles* (1954) 380
3. *P.P.S.* XX (1954) 115–17
4. Atkinson, *Stonehenge and Avebury* (1959) 4, 11
5. Piggott, *Ancient Europe* (1965) 17
6. Piggott, *Neolithic Cultures of the British Isles* (1954) 302–64
7. Piggott, *op. cit.* 64, 111–12
8. *Victoria County History of Wiltshire* I, pt. 1 (1957) 137–46
9. Royal Commission on Historical Monuments (England), *A Matter of Time* (1960) 24–7
10. *Arch.* LXXXV (1935) 90–5
11. *Arch.* C (1966) 53
12. *loc. cit.* 27
13. *Arch.* LXXXV (1935) 53
14. Atkinson, Piggott, and Sandars, *Excavations at Dorchester, Oxon.* I (1951) 77–8
15. Godwin, *History of the British Flora* (1956) 331–9
16. Pitt-Rivers, *Excavations in Cranborne Chase* IV (1898) 58–100
17. See above, n. 10
18. *Antiquity* XXXIX (1965) 126–33
19. *Arch.* C (1966) 8–14, 29–32, 37–42, 48–63
20. See above, n. 16
21. *Arch.* LXXXV (1935) 46–50
22. *P.P.S.* XXV (1959) 20–4, 32–4
23. *Arch.* C (1966) 6–7
24. *Antiquity* XXXIX (1965) 49–52
25. *P.P.S.* XXIX (1963) 173–205
26. Greenwell, *British Barrows* (1877) 553–6. Recently re-excavated by Mr T. G. Manby
27. Greenwell, *op. cit.* 494–5
28. Mortimer, *Forty Years' Researches* (1905) 102–5
29. *Arch.* C (1966) 53–5
30. *P.P.S.* II (1936) 77–96

31. *Arch.* C (1966) 35
32. *Antiquity* XXIX (1955) 4–9
33. Brothwell and Higgs (ed.), *Science in Archaeology* (1963) 437–64
34. *Trans. Bristol & Gloucestershire Arch. Soc.* LXXIX (1960) 68–96
35. See above, n. 8
36. Crawford, *Long Barrows of the Cotswolds* (1925) 147–66
37. Grinsell, *Dorset Barrows* (1959) 24
38. Dobson, *Archaeology of Somerset* (1931) 47–57
39. Piggott, *Neolithic Cultures of the British Isles* (1954) 140
40. Piggott, *The West Kennet Long Barrow* (1962) 24–6, 79–89
41. Piggott, *op. cit.* 78
42. *Antiquity* XXXIX (1965) 132

Easterton of Roseisle:
a forgotten site in Moray

Iain C. Walker

The neolithic on the Laigh of Moray is represented chiefly by the pottery from the site of Easterton of Roseisle[1] in Duffus parish, Moray, three miles south-southeast of Burghead (fig. 16a and b.) When Graham Callander published his paper on Scottish neolithic pottery in 1929, he was apparently never aware of all the reports on the site;[2] he refers to what was in fact the second of four reports, which together with a letter from Canon Greenwell to Hugh Young, the excavator of the site, cover an extensive but subsequently totally forgotten series of discoveries in the area.

The purpose of this paper is to synthesize Young's reports, which are masterpieces of diffuse, at times incoherent, writing, with a woeful lack of vital detail, a geographical description incomprehensible to anyone unfamiliar with the district, and an extremely individualistic interpretation.[3] If at this late date relatively little can be made from these reports, perhaps their reappearance will stimulate interest in determining whether a major excavation of the former lake bed adjacent to the site might be justified.

Hugh W. Young was at one time harbourmaster at Burghead, and an indefatigable antiquarian some of whose collection is now in the National Museum of Antiquities of Scotland, and the British Museum. Though his reports on Roseisle are poor, Young was an above-average archaeologist for his time, to judge by his work on the murus gallicus fort at Burghead.[4,5]

The nineteenth-century reports

He began his first report by mentioning the discovery of great quantities of bone turned up, and ploughed almost to bits, in May 1894, about 1000 yards west-southwest of the Easterton of Roseisle farmhouse[6] (Nat. Grid NJ 139649). He then casually mentioned, implying the discovery was already well known, that on the shores of the former Loch Spynie and opposite a knoll which had once been an island, had been found hearths, many of them with their stones fused by heat. Each one, he noted, was some distance from the next, except at the east end of the bay 'where there had been rows of dwellings covering a considerable space' (fig. 17a). No evidence of structures is mentioned; doubtless he referred to dwellings because he assumed each hearth had originally been in some form of hut. Among the hearths were 'some curious artificially shaped stones, more or less pyramidal in form, broad and flat underneath, and pointed at the top,' which he suggested were rubbers. These he said he had seen; also found, but not further described, were 'one or two pieces of pottery of an early type'; it is not clear whether he had seen these. Numerous shells, chiefly oyster and mussel, were also found.

Returning to the great concentration of bone which was about 60 yards from the isolated hearths at the head of what he called the old bay, he said he was informed of the discovery too late to do other than piece together what information he could. There seemed to have been a mass grave measuring about 50 yards by 30, bounded by an earthen wall and with a clay partition across it, the purpose of which Young could not explain, unless it was a division between two races or the two sexes. All the skeletons appeared to have been those of adults, though they included young and old: they lay on their backs orientated north–south, almost touching each other. He could find no undamaged skulls, but thought one was that of a woman. Some, he implies most, were dolichocephalic and of average thickness, with prominent brow-ridges and well-developed mastoid processes. Others, however, were brachycephalic and extremely thick-walled, one piece having a surviving thickness of $\frac{3}{8}$ in. The teeth in some cases were worn down almost to the roots, and in many cases the enamel on the outside was longer than the centre of the tooth. Young claimed this was a common phenomenon among primitive races past and present.

All over the field, stone implements – axes, flint arrowheads, scrapers, and other objects – were found. Most occurred in an area about 40 yards away (fig. 17a), but many scrapers and worked flints were found among the

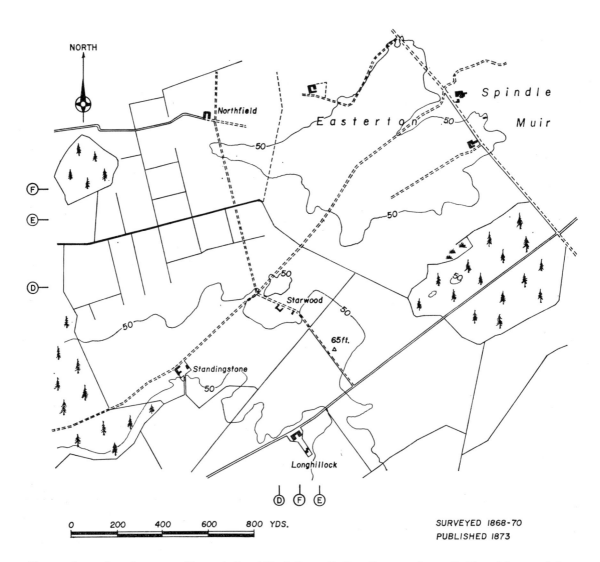

Figure 16. a, Location maps. Sites: A. Longhillock farm; B. Standingstone farm; C. Site of Starwood farm; D. Kill hillock: Young's Starwood ridge; E. Site of farm cottages on part of area of Young's discoveries; also possible site of former bay of Loch Spynie; F. Alternative possible site of former bay of Loch Spynie (reproduced with the sanction of the Controller of Her Majesty's Stationery Office).

bones, and Young thought they might have been buried with them. In the same field, Mr Dawson, tenant of the farm, found a 'most peculiar . . . hammer stone' which Young said was almost identical to one found in palaeolithic levels at Wolvercote, near Oxford.[7] The other axes found, 'six or seven in number,' were, he said, very handsome and finely polished.

The field was examined after harvest by the Rev. Mr M'Kewan of Dyke, another well-known local antiquary, and the tenant Dawson, Young being absent. A succession of furrows about ten feet apart were ploughed in order to localize the area, and to quote M'Kewan's letter to Young 'the spade was then used.' By this time most of the bones had gone, but two bodies were found in their original positions. The skull of one had been only slightly damaged by the plough, but part of it was little more than coloured matter, and the top disintegrated while attempts were made to measure it; it exhibited heavy brow-ridges and was compared to those in Huxley and Laing's *Prehistoric Burials at Keiss in Caithness*. The bones lay out to a length of six feet.[8] M'Kewan noted with interest how well the stains of the body were marked in the sand.

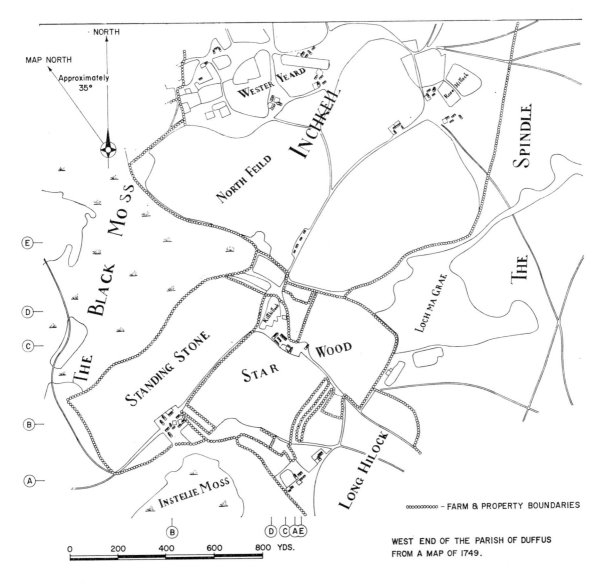

Figure 16. b.

Dawson then took M'Kewan to a spot about 80 yards southwest of the place where the bones had been found, where some time before the plough had struck a stone; digging revealed a cist (fig. 17e). The first-noted stone was over three feet high by two feet broad, the other sides of the cist being some two feet lower; M'Kewan considered that it was the grave of the leader of the men buried nearby. The cist, of which a picture is published, was of large slabs, rough construction, and unusual shape; and Dawson, completing the work, found ten or twelve oval and round white beach stones, and two sharp sandstones which he thought might be axes. He thought the grave had contained two bodies in 'sitting' posture, or two skulls with the ashes of the bones. There was, he says, evidence for bodies at both ends and there were two spots of black ashes. The cist was orientated north–south, and from the scale given must have had an internal length of about four feet two inches. Dawson also added a note on the clay baulk across the mass grave which he had presumably reinvestigated: originally, he said, it had been twelve to eighteen inches wide and was (now, one infers) eight inches deep. The clay, he continued, seemed to have been brought from a point 30 yards off.

Young, summing up, said that as there must have been several hundred skeletons at least, a battle or massacre must have taken place, backing his opinion by reference to the flint arrowheads and stone axes; and there the matter rested until the following spring (1895) when Dawson informed Young that the winter rains had cleared the sides of the still-open cist, revealing carvings on one of the slabs (fig. 17d, left). These, which proved the slab to be a Pictish symbol-stone, were very rough and uneven, and Young considered they had been made by a sharp flint or stone instrument, not a metal one. The two sandstone objects in the grave he identified as beach pebbles with marks of usage at both ends; he also found some flint scrapers nearby. Stressing the lack of metal objects, even on the surrounding land, and the general crudeness of the cist and its grave-goods (if such they were), Young suggested that the cist might be older than the mass grave, though he inclined to consider them contemporary.

The symbol-stone was removed, revealing on the other side carvings in a much superior style (fig. 17d, right) which Young compared to the slabs with the carved bulls discovered at various times during that century at Burghead,[9] though again he considered it quite possible that the carvings were made with a flint. Under this slab was a very rough granite or quartz axe. The bottom of the cist was roughly paved with small stones four to six inches long. No lid was found, but it was recalled that a year or two before a large stone had been removed from the spot.

The report ended with a polite note from the editor, J. Romilly Allen, saying in effect that he was not responsible for contributors' opinions, and noting that many symbol-stones were directly associated with Christian remains, and 'only two' with apparently pagan burials.

Young's next report is that which deals with the sites which we now know from the pottery to be neolithic;[10] it covered work done in the autumn of 1895. Dawson had noted three different spots on his land with pieces of 'ancient pottery' on the surface, and it was decided to excavate these areas; but apparently only one, about 200 yards north of the cist, was investigated. Close to the surface a well-made rubbing-stone of millstone grit was found, and also a pounder with abraded ends. About a foot deeper the diggers came on two stone-lined pits eighteen inches apart dug into the firm, white sand. They were about five feet in diameter at the top and nearly five feet deep, with rounded egg-shaped bottoms. They were full of wood ash and pieces of charcoal; the stones had been reddened by fire, and the large quartz ones could be crushed to powder by the hand. The pottery was found in the ash and continued all the way to the bottom of the pit. In one of the pits a fine spear- or arrow-head, coloured by heat, was found inside a piece of pottery. All the vessels were broken, and the bottoms had rotted away so that it was impossible to reconstruct any one pot entirely; however, Young judged from the curve of the rim and the sides of the vessels that they must have had a diameter of sixteen inches and a depth of eight inches. He reckoned there must have been at least five and perhaps as many as eight in each pit.

He divided the pottery into three kinds: (1) the thin, very hard and well-fired pottery, with shallow vertical groovings inside and out, made by either the finger or a wood or bone spatula. These vessels, Young said, were made from pounded clay with crushed iron pyrites, and were full of small glittering specks. (2) 'Cinerary urns' of great size, with very thick, coarse, badly-fired, rotten and porous walls. These had flat or very slightly rounded bases and were made from clay, crushed shells and broken quartz. (3) Pottery 'exactly corresponding with that found in the Oban cave recently excavated.' This too was made from clay, crushed shells and broken quartz.

As to the use of the pits, he put forward three alternatives – (1) that they had been kilns; (2) that they had been cooking places after the style of the Australian aborigines; and (3) that they had been used for cremation, 'perhaps the very place where the bodies in the cist had been burnt.' Though the first two were possible, Young decided on the third explanation, because at the bottom of (apparently) each pit lay large lumps of fatty matter, the adipocere, he said, of the burnt flesh. Not a fragment of bone was found, the heat, according to Young, being too intense for it to survive. It was impossible to say whether all the ashes of the bodies had been removed. The pottery, he wrote, 'filled a good-sized box' and there was also a fine stone anvil about eight inches all round, with a surface smooth as glass and slightly hollowed on the top. Young sent some of the pottery to Romilly Allen, who was unable to find any close parallels in the British Museum collections, but felt satisfied that the pieces were of 'no known Bronze Age pottery, nor Roman, Saxon, nor Mediaeval.' He said, however, that there was in the British Museum a 'small sepulchral urn' from Milborne St Andrew's, Dorset, which had horizontal smoothings on it and that this idea was characteristic of prehistoric pottery from Germany. The shape, he hazarded, with unconscious accuracy, was paralleled among the pottery from White-park Bay, Co. Antrim, and Dundrum Bay, Co. Down.

Meanwhile, Young had also found parallels, noting two fluted rim sherds in the National Museum in Edinburgh, from Achnacree, Argyll, and identifying his third class of pottery with that from the Oban cave. In the Industrial Museum (now the Royal Scottish Museum) he found an urn from Prussia with some vertical markings, and on consulting *The Bone Caves of Ojcow* by Ferdinand Romer, found illustrated a similarly marked piece which had been dug up in the cave at Ferzmanowice along with, so it was averred, the remains of cave bear, mammoth and the like. The same book illustrated a bone object with two perforated holes and rows of cup marks: a similar steatite object two inches long by one and a half inches broad was found in the field at Roseisle. This seems identifiable with an object now in Burghead Museum. Young considered it was half of a bead mould, but thought that the Polish object was unlikely to be one as its holes were smaller. To Young all this seemed to add weight to Romilly Allen's Germanic parallels, but in fact Romilly Allen, noting the proximity of the site to the former sea, had suggested that the remains probably belonged to the same tradition ('race') as the similarly-shaped vessels he had noted on the Irish coast.

After mentioning that 'a bone spear point or large pin' had also been found (where is not stated, nor is a further description given) Young concluded, perhaps conscious of his controversial dating of the cist and its symbol-stone, with a renewed defence of its antiquity.[11] The much-weathered face which had formed the inner side of the slab when used as part of the cist was older, he said – possibly very much older – than the perfectly preserved bird and fish on the other side. (This is irrelevant, however: the outer side of the slab could hardly have been carved subsequently to the building of the cist.) Noting that the handle of the mirror had been partly broken off, he suggested this had been done to square off that end for the carving of the bird on the other side, and deduced that the latter was the later face.

In a letter to Young, Canon Greenwell noted that the pottery was very similar to that in the chamber of a large cairn he had excavated at Kilmartin, Argyll, and also to that in a similar chamber in an unspecified part of Argyll dug by the late Dr Angus Smith.[12] Kilmartin having produced a secondary Beaker burial, Greenwell agreed with Young in his conclusion as to the date of the pottery, but he did not believe that the pits had ever held a burial after cremation (Young, however, never suggested this). As to the use of the pits, he could offer no explanation, but he noted that all of the very large number of cremations he had dug had never failed to yield some evidence of bone. On the subject of the cist, he tactfully suggested a date more in keeping with what was known about symbol-stones.

Young's third report on the site was prefaced by a reply to Greenwell in which he defended his dating of the cist:[13] cists, he said, certainly belonged to the Bronze Age in England but in Scotland he believed them to be mainly Stone Age – he referred to those at Keiss, Caithness, and noted that while stone and flint objects had been found in cists he had never heard of a bronze weapon with an urn. He believed that the Stone Age in Scotland had lasted far into the Iron Age and even into the Christian era, and seriously doubted a true Bronze Age. All the bronze weapons in the National Museum in Edinburgh, he says, would not equip 50 men, and the whole northeast of Scotland from the Spey to Caithness had so few bronzes that they could almost be counted on one's fingers. For unspecified reasons he excluded the Hebrides from this generalization. Leaf-shaped swords were of Etruscan pattern and probably imported from Italy; spearheads and javelins were of either Greek or Roman pattern. Iron ore, he averred, was so plentiful in the Spey valley that bronze would be a superfluity in Moray; at Roseisle he found several lumps of fine-quality iron ore along with worked flints, which seemed to have been used as strike-a-lights. This remarkable reorientation of Scottish prehistory concludes: 'I am writing this paper far from the aid of authorities and books, and I am aware that these views are an innovation on accepted theory, but they are founded on facts.'

He then goes on to describe new finds: Dawson, while ploughing 'the highest point of the farm . . . discovered charcoal in trenches' and made an 'exact drawing' for Young (fig. 17c). The area thus covered measured 60 yards by 50. (Young never mentioned the two smaller areas on the plan, nor did he specify what the rectangle

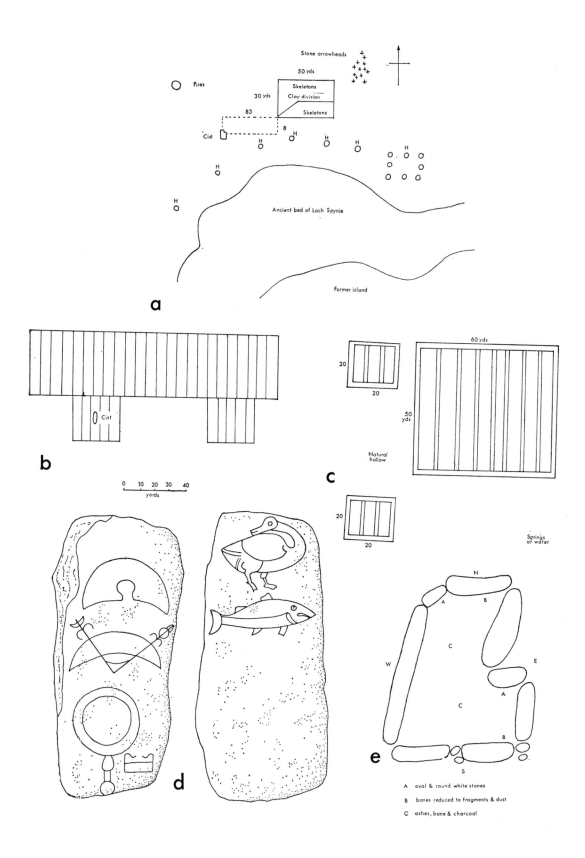

delimited by broken lines in the middle of the large area is.) The spaces between what had probably, he said, been double rows of piles, were nine feet 'apart' (wide) and the spaces filled with charcoal three feet wide. This he concluded was probably a platform with huts or stores on it used in times of flood by those who normally dwelt on the lakeside.

The site stood 'at a little higher elevation' than the next discovery he made, which was about 400 yards west of the symbol-stone cist, and was on the south side of a small ridge called Starwood, where burnt oats were noted in a rabbit hole. On excavation, a pit was discovered, of which he published a photograph: it was about ten feet wide at the top by nine feet, four feet square at the bottom, and five and a half feet deep, built of rough boulders and separated from the hard natural sand by a clay backing. Young remarked it looked like an arch reversed. The bottom was paved with large stones, and the pit was filled with burnt oats and wood – mostly oak, though some seemed to be hazel or birch – which he interpreted as evidence of the burning down of a large wooden building. 'The age of the work was fixed by the state of the wood which was almost identical with black bog oak below the burnt surface.' The working of the wood was similar to that of the very early lake dwellings; presumably he means the wooden platforms previously described. The structure apparently erected over this pit was of pointed stakes driven into the ground, supported by cross-beams with rough log floors fixed to them by wooden pins driven through bored holes. He gave drawings (scaleless) of uprights, cross-beams, floor beams and pins. The holes, he asserted, had not been made by any metal tools; they were wider at one end than the other and had probably been burnt out; no early metal tool could have made such a perfectly smooth and polished hole.

The deposits in the pit were four layers of burnt oats and three or four of burnt wood. The fire, Young said, had burnt down the pit, as six inches of burnt oats lay on the floor with no wood ashes beneath. Few old kilns, he said, could dry more than a quarter of corn at a time, yet here there had been fifty quarters or more. The layering of the pit, he suggested, was caused by the structure having four levels for drying grain. Although the wall of the structure had fallen away on the side facing the loch he thought he could trace an entrance near the bottom and wondered if this might have been some kind of grain elevator. Less than 50 yards away Dawson had found a cist with a paved bottom and a few bones in it, but nothing else; the whole ridge, he said, was covered with worked flint.

Young now had second thoughts on the two pits previously described as cremation pits, noting that the lower stones of these pits were not marked by heat and that therefore the fire had burnt from the top downwards. He thus thought they must be storage pits. He compared the superstructure to the storehouses on piles used by the Lapps for storing grain. He noted with regret that no midden had been found, and that as the place had been 'thoroughly examined' it was unlikely that anything further would be discovered. 'The true story of the race of people whose remains have been found will never now be known, but the end had been a terrible tragedy. Some superior race had swooped down on them, not to plunder, but to destroy. A massacre on a grand scale, a hurried burial, the firing of their poor dwellings and stores, the destruction of their corn, and the wreck of everything adds one more pitiable story to the annals of the human race, one more tragedy to the records of time.'

However, two years later another report appeared.[14] In it Young modified his conclusions and divided the complex into two distinct periods. The cists (by this time he had four), the hearths, the symbol-stone, the most primitive of the stone weapons, and 'the early pottery' were, he said, the earliest; later were the mass grave, the granary, the wooden platforms, and perhaps the finer arrowheads and polished stone weapons. He refused to commit himself on placing the storage pits (his former cremation pits).

He suggested that the time between the periods might well be considerable; the proof he produced from a new discovery on the site, the only place where there was some suggestion of relative dating. In the summer of 1897, following a long dry spring and westerly gales, immense quantities of sand were blown off the land, revealing, on an unspecified part of the site, an enormous burnt structure of wood 160 yards long by 40 wide, with two other erections 'near this' (fig. 17b).

Beneath this was a cist, four feet by two, which contained several pieces of bones, flints, various kinds of hammer stones, and one round ball of polished stone one inch in diameter. The floor of the cist was roughly

Figure 17. Plans. a. Young's sketch plan of the 1894 discoveries; b. Burnt wooden structure discovered in 1897; c. Dawson's plan of the 'lake dwellings' discovered in 1895; d. Pictish symbol stone forming part of the cist, discovered in 1895; e. Plan of cist marked on a.

paved. How far below the platform the cist was is not stated, but Young and Dawson were convinced that the builders of the platform had known nothing of the cist.

With this evidence Young regrouped the sites in his two periods. (Presumably his line of thought was that since in this particular case a cist appeared to be definitely earlier than the wooden structure, all the cists, and therefore the symbol-stone, were earlier than all the wooden structures; his ideas on the stone and flint objects are presumably based on a rough typology). Altogether there were four cists discovered: even if this includes that with the symbol-stone there is still one cist which Young never described. All were roughly paved, but their stones differed in size. The pottery on the level of the enormous burnt platform was of a 'different and superior style': it was red, of pure clay, well made, and glazed. The position of this structure in relation to the previous finds is never given.

'A short way off, also at the same level,' was a kitchen midden of shells and bits of bone and 'sundry other remains all much decayed and worn.' The shells were mostly buckies, a few limpets and cockles – there were no mussels. Young, alleging that cockles preferred fresher water than mussels and flourished best at mouths of rivers, mentioned in this connection the legend that the Findhorn once flowed east into Loch Spynie, the traditional course having along it stones which were river-worn, not sea-worn – Young said the difference is considerable.[15] Returning to the wooden structure, he said there was no evidence of piles, merely long lines of charcoal and small pieces of burnt wood. Numerous worked flints, including a saw and many scrapers, were found.

Thus ends the series of reports on the great Easterton of Roseisle mystery. It is clear that Young threw together the information as and when it came to him, and made little attempt to synthesize it, although he did attempt, sometimes correctly, to search for parallels and interpretations. Now, 70 years later, there is little that can be done except list the structures found, discuss them, try and fit the pottery into its prehistoric background, and hope that at some future date excavation may yet reveal something more of this site.

Interpretation

There are nine major sites in the entire complex: the lakeside hearths, the mass burial, the concentration of flints, the cist with the symbol-stone, the pits with the neolithic pottery, the granary pit, the so-called lake dwellings, the platform with the cist beneath, and the shell midden.

1. The lakeside hearths, mentioned so casually in the first report, are perhaps the most interesting of the hitherto overlooked finds. Though nothing more is known about them than the presence amongst them of rubbers and 'one or two pieces of pottery of an early type' it is tempting to suggest that this site represents a settlement such as that discovered at Ehenside Tarn in 1870.[16] Unfortunately, it is impossible to establish what connections, if any, these hearths had with the pits containing the undoubtedly neolithic pottery.

Although it is dangerous to try to interpret Young's remarks, they do imply, provided he actually saw the 'early' pottery, that the neolithic pottery found in the pits was different, and perhaps, if by 'early' he meant crudely made, of better manufacture. There still remains enough pottery from Ehenside Tarn to indicate that there were both carinated bowls of Grimston type ware and coarser bowls of Peterborough ware.

That the hearths with their pottery may have belonged to the same settlement as the pits with theirs is therefore possible, although we have to assume that the association of the 'one or two pieces of pottery' with the hearths is valid and not the result of ploughing or other disturbance.

2. It is hard to make constructive comments on the mass burial: flints were so common over the whole area that their occurrence among the skeletons, especially after the area had been ploughed, cannot be taken as significant. The meaning of the term 'earthen wall' which is said to have enclosed the pit is not clear, but the presence of the clay dividing wall and the laying of the estimated hundreds of skeletons on their backs orientated north–south and almost touching each other certainly implies a definite burial (as opposed to the direct result of a massacre, or to a plague pit), yet the description does not resemble that of a burial ground. If the burials were as regular as is implied, this might suggest that they were all substantially of one period: this would certainly suggest some considerable calamity, but were this the case one might have expected at least a local legend to have survived.

In Burghead Museum there is a box of bones, among which fragments of two skulls and several pieces of longbones, hip-joints, and vertebrae are readily identifiable: two pieces of flint, one a brick-red projectile point, are labelled as having been found with the skeletons. None of the bones has been studied by an anatomist.

3. The concentration of flints suggests extensive occupation, or at least a large working area. Some half-dozen similar sites (one centred on NJ 275627) were uncovered in the Meft area of Urquart parish, Moray, three miles east of Elgin, in the 1870s by another well-known local antiquary, the Rev. James Morrison of Urquart.[17,18] Urquart is rich in neolithic and Early Bronze Age finds, and at one place a gale removed the topsoil, revealing 'thousands' of flints, including barbed, lozenge- and leaf-shaped projectile points, a few blocks and cores and many amorphous pieces, as well as a polished stone axe. Flint is scarce in Scotland: the source nearest to Moray and the only major source in Scotland, is in the Buchan district of northeast Aberdeenshire.[19,20] However, there are deposits of flint nodules on the Culbin Sands, eight miles west of Roseisle: a geologist's theory held that the nodules were rafted by floating ice from a now-submerged cretaceous outcrop in the North Sea.[21] Other deposits along the south shore of Moray Firth include beach pebbles of flint at Boyndie Bay, immediately west of Banff,[22] and flint concentrations at Meft and Roseisle.[23] The Buchan flint beds have never been studied, but objects made from its characteristic red flint occur along the south shore of Moray Firth, and as far north as Freswick Sands, north of Wick.[24] There is a small flint outcrop near Delgaty Castle, two miles east of Turriff, Banffshire, though according to Scott[25] there is no evidence that it was worked in prehistoric times.

Most of the Roseisle specimens appear to have been lost, and those now in Burghead Museum are almost all unlocalized: Young illustrated a selection of stone objects[26] and those of flint include a very large hollow-based projectile point, an equally big barbed-and-tanged one, and what may be an equally big leaf-shaped one. Smaller examples of these types, and of lozenge-shaped ones, are also shown, as are two polished stone axes. There were in 1960 at Burghead Museum three unprovenanced stone axes, two apparently of greenstone, as well as an abraded quartz hammerstone and what is probably part of another, both labelled as coming from the site. None of these has been analysed.

The variety of flint types suggests that occupation included diverse traditions, including neolithic, but there is no indication as to how much time they cover.

4. The cist incorporating the Pictish symbol-stone cannot antedate the symbol-stone which

belongs to Romilly Allen's Class I.[27] Stevenson would date the earlier side of this stone (fig. 17d, left) to *c.* A.D. 700 and the later side to the following generation or even less;[28] Thomas would move Stevenson's commencing date for Class I stones from A.D. 650 to the fifth century A.D.[29] The cist and burials must follow whichever date is chosen; however, cremations are presumably pagan, and the presence in the cist of white stones suggests the persistence of a tradition dating from the arrival of the Clava Cairn builders perhaps 2500 years earlier, and ultimately to a more general passage-grave tradition.[30] The earlier side has its symbols in pecked lines without much attempt at subsequent smoothing, a technique used in the cup marks common in the area, while the later side is apparently incised. The use of a slab for successive carvings, and its final use as part of a grave can be paralleled elsewhere:[31] at both Birsay, Orkney, with a cremation and at Dunrobin, Sutherland, with a double burial and what may have been an iron spearhead; a slab appears to have been reused in graves of the Viking period. The disposition of the goose and fish on the later side and the defacing and weathering of the part that would have been visible on the other side (the mirror and comb) suggest that latterly the slab was an earth-fast vertical. The extent of the carvings and the weathering (on this side only) on the earlier side suggest the stone once either lay horizontally or was originally taller and had the second face to leeward.

5. The next site is that with the pits containing the neolithic pottery. As this site is already partly known, discussion of it and its pottery will be deferred until later.

6. The next site is the granary pit: in the Hunterian Museum, University of Glasgow, there is a box of oats from the site, in the Henderson Bishop Collection, he having obtained it from the Rev. James M'Kewan of Dyke. Dr Berrie of the Department of Botany in the University confirmed the identification. Most of the husks were missing, due either to accidental charring or deliberate roasting.[32] Oats and rye probably originated as weeds of cultivation associated with wheat and barley, and while oats were possibly cultivated as early as the Michelsberg culture,[33] the normal view is that oats and rye were cultivated as crops in their own right only following the worsening climate of Sub-Atlantic times. Neither is recorded from prehistoric Britain.[34,35]

The dimensions, shape, and position in a hillside support the belief that the pit was a granary. Further, if any sense can be attached to Young's remark about the bog oak below the burnt surface it could refer to the loose, open platform of wood on top of the stone foundation over which drawn straw was laid as a bed for the grain, which was then laid three to four inches deep, although no straw is mentioned. His six inches of oats at the bottom with no burnt wood beneath, however, fits the rest of the evidence. As for the pegging of cross-beams to verticals a barn built over the granary is probable; but such construction practice was still used in Scotland last century. The earliest unambiguous evidence for a corn-drying kiln in Scotland is in the late twelfth century.

Young describes the site as being on the south side of Starwood ridge, and 400 yards 'west' (south) of the symbol-stone cist: this ridge is the 'former island in Loch Spynie' on fig. 17a. Just south of the southwest end of the ridge lay the now-vanished hamlet of Starwood. This was in existence by 1662[36] and in 1888 the land was amalgamated with Standingstone farm to the west with part going to Roseisle: in 1892 the farmhouse (NJ 139646) was vacant[37] and if it was dismantled soon after, Young, first coming to the site in 1894, possibly never knew of it. Thus he probably excavated part of the Starwood farm complex, which would explain the well-preserved wood. (Dawson only farmed Easterton from 1892 to 1898.) Regarding the amount of oats in the granary, a good average yield on the Laigh early last century was about four quarters an acre;[38] the granary's contents might thus represent a twelve-acre crop for one season. In 1749 Starwood farm was just over 60 Scots acres (76 Imperial acres).

7. There is too little information on Young's so-called lake dwellings to enable much to be made of them. However, he specifically mentioned that the huge wooden structure discovered later was not of pile construction, so perhaps his assertion that the 'lake dwellings' were thus constructed may be accepted. If these remains were indeed vertical posts, they may have supported a platform, perhaps for hay-drying; but they could alternately be the remains of pens or folds, although something 60 by 50 yards is extremely large. The site of these finds is not clear; but if the granary pit, than which it is 'a little higher,' is a mistake for the pits with neolithic pottery, the site can be reconciled with its being at the highest part of the farm, in other words north of the area in fig. 17a.

8. The wooden structure 166 by 40 yards is never located, but such a huge affair may have been in the general area of the other wooden structures discussed previously; it certainly could not have been on Starwood ridge. The red, well-fired pottery made of a 'different and superior style' of glazed pure clay sounds like medieval pottery, though it is difficult to believe that Young could not have recognized this had it been the case. However, an association of medieval pottery with the structure is not necessarily significant, as the area must have been ploughed.

9. The neighbouring shell-midden is not described in any datable terms. In the same area in Urquart where the great deposits of worked flint noted earlier were discovered[39,40] shell-middens with cinders but no datable objects were found, which could well be prehistoric; but many of the Culbin Sands shell-middens are medieval.[41]

The complex which Young excavated covered sites from the third millennium B.C. to as late as the nineteenth century A.D.: the neolithic pottery discussed below is third millennium B.C., the lakeside hearths are probably of the same general period, and the flint concentrations appear to be both neolithic and Bronze Age. The symbol-stone and associated cist date to the first millennium A.D. while the granary must be medieval or later, and could be as late as the nineteenth century.

The writer has dealt elsewhere with the early geographical background, so it will suffice here to say that Young's reference to the area being adjacent to the former shore of Loch Spynie is substantially correct.[42] The loch as late as 1793 extended well towards the Roseisle area; and in 1749 there was still a loch to the northwest. Geological surveys indicate that the Burghead-Covesea area must once have been substantially an island with the sea passing through Roseisle to Spynie and local legends agree with this. The Roseisle neolithic settlement may have been one by coastal voyagers taking the lee side of the Burghead-Covesea island and finding a sunny southern exposure to grow their corn. An imprint of Naked Barley was noted on one fluted, carinated sherd from the site.[43] The fertility of the Laigh and the geniality of its climate have been proverbial for centuries. Roseisle is midway between Elgin and Forres: the former has an average rainfall of 26 inches and a mean average temperature of 49° F., the latter, 25 inches and 46° F. The whole coastline boasts the most sunshine in Britain[44] and in neolithic times the climate would have been markedly drier and milder than now. Pollen analyses in the former lake bed by the site might be rewarding.

The neolithic pottery came from the two stone-lined pits which Young first took to be cremation pits but later identified as storage pits. The latter identification may well be correct, and, interestingly, shows that Young was prepared to change his opinion when considering new evidence. These pits have parallels with those under a great number of 'mossy-looking' patches found all over apparently the same eight-acre field in Urquart covered in flints and referred to previously. These latter pits contained ashes and burnt wood fragments; some had flints, and burnt stones, and there were occasional bits of pottery, some decorated. Morrison presented the National Museum with a large collection of material, including pottery, from this site[45] (subsequently lost; identified and published about 75 years later).[46] It includes six sherds, three decorated. Two of the latter have vertical grooves made either by a fingernail or a thin blunted splint of wood while the third has a metopic motif and can be identified as an example of Unstan ware. It is conceivable that the vertical grooves reflect fluting, but the pottery, while not thick or coarse, is not in the same class as the Roseisle Class I material. The clay includes occasional specks of golden mica. With the exception of a tiny unpublished scrap of neolithic-looking pottery from the Culbin Sands in the Hunterian,[47] Meft and Roseisle are the only known sites with neolithic pottery on the Laigh.

Young's three classes of pottery, however, cause problems, particularly as much material has been lost. His first class is the pottery which is now virtually all that survives, the high-quality fluted ware of Piggott's type G.[48] This pottery has not been analysed: it may contain iron pyrites, but the glittering specks to which Young referred appear to be golden mica.

The second class, coarse, badly-fired, with rotten and porous walls, made of clay, crushed shells, and quartz, and with flat or slightly rounded bases, cannot now be identified. Fragments of a coarse ware showing similar bases came from the upper levels of Lyles Hill cairn, but was never found in a datable context.[49]

The third class 'exactly corresponding with that found in the Oban cave recently excavated' and apparently also of clay, crushed shell and broken quartz, causes problems. Young must refer to the Gas Works Cave, the only one of several excavated at this time which yielded pottery.[50] As Lacaille pointed out,[51] if this pottery is really associated with the broadly Obanian material also found in the cave the occupation must be later than true Obanian: the cave's pottery comprises four pieces which fit together to make a small portion of the rim (with marked internal bevel) and upper body of a pink-coloured, Bronze Age-looking pot made of fine clay and backed by very coarse grit, and it would appear from the original report that this was all that was found. It is unlike any surviving material from Roseisle.

Apart from one small fragment, triangular in section, brick red in colour, and with a smooth, waxy surface; and several pieces of what appear to be a genuine Cinerary Urn, all at Burghead, there do appear to be two types of pottery presumably from the site in addition to the well-known type. One type (fig. 18e), represented by one fragment in Edinburgh and one at Burghead, is made of a very pure clay, grey in colour, with a very flat, totally unsplayed rim and a slightly outward-curved profile beneath. The other type (fig. 18a) is again represented by only two fragments, one each at Edinburgh and Burghead. This pottery is coarse with a great deal of mica backing, has a Bronze Age look about its firing, and under its irregular rim are holes, rectangular in cross-section, made from the inside out by a sliver of wood or something similar. The hole in the body on the sherd illustrated is hour-glass-shaped, apparently drilled from both sides, suggesting a sizeable diameter for the pot. Presumably it served either to bind a crack or to stop a crack 'running' further.

No convincing parallels to these two types have been found, and holes under the rim are not a common decoration. Anderson noted pottery from the round cairn at Camster, Caithness, with 'holes, about the diameter of an ordinary goose-quill . . . bored in it at intervals, immediately under the lip';[52] but the rest of his description made it clear that this pottery is superior to the type at Roseisle. This pottery apparently did not have mica: he mentioned pottery at Ormiegill and Camster with mica, and a long-necked beaker from Yarrows which had so much mica that he described it as 'probably to add a glittering beauty to the sombre receptacle of the ashes of the dead.' He noted micaceous clay did not exist in the district. Newbiggin[53] noted mica backing in Grimston-Heslerton ware and it occurs in some sherds from Glenluce, Wigtown, one representing a carinated bowl.[54] As work on neolithic pottery in southern England has shown the presence of backing that could only have come from the Highland Zone, probably Cornwall, work along these lines on Scottish material, although possibly of less value because the area is already in the Highland Zone, might be profitable.

Before discussing the Easterton Class I neolithic pottery it is necessary to sketch in the background both in its Scottish context and in its broader setting and to summarize some of the widely differing views currently held; that the Scottish neolithic is in need of a major reappraisal is best indicated by the fact that the only published corpus of pottery available for study is still Callander's paper of 1929.[55]

Radiocarbon dates from the British Isles suggest our neolithic had commenced by 3000 B.C.[56] It is only very recently, however, that absolute dates have been available for Scotland; dates from a Clyde-Carlingford tomb on Arran indicate a third millennium floruit,[57,58] and dates indicate the same millennium from a barrow in Perthshire.[59]

Not all disputes regarding the British neolithic revolve round the new chronology. In 1951 Piggott,[60] while doubting that Roseisle was a destroyed long cairn as Childe[61] had suggested, regarded the scattering of long barrow-like structures and the sporadic finds of open-mouth carinated bowls on the east coast north of Yorkshire as far as the Moray Firth as probable representatives of a movement from Yorkshire. At the same time, he suggested a larger movement from Yorkshire to Ulster, represented by the Grimston ware-derived Lyles Hill ware of the latter area.[62]

However, Atkinson suggested that in fact the movement might be from Ulster to Yorkshire,[63] and Case suggested an origin in the region of the Tagus estuary in Portugal for the carinated bowl tradition, spreading to Ireland, thence to England and finally, if necessary, to the Michelsberg culture of Germany.[64]

Subsequently, Atkinson, adding to the number of long barrow-like structures known in eastern Scotland and also to the scattered finds of shouldered bowls in that area, maintained

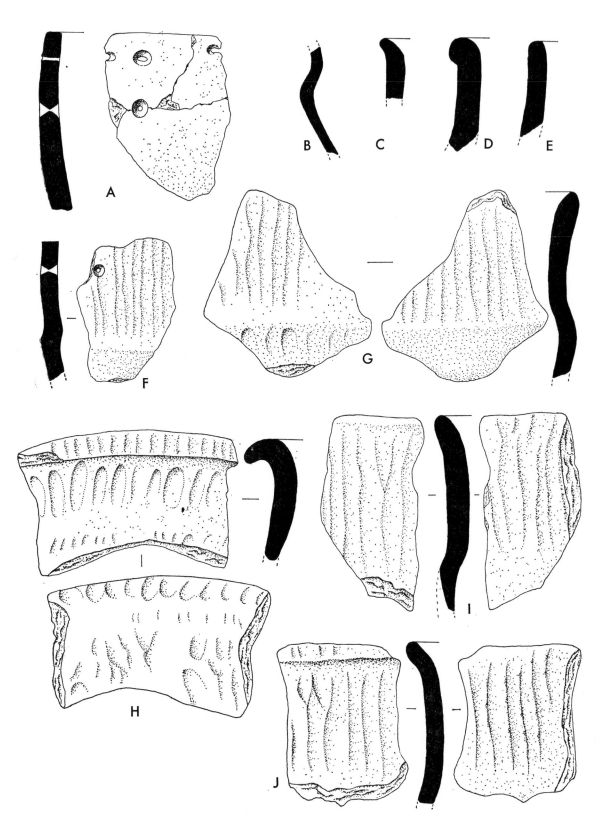

Figure 18. Pottery from Easterton of Roseisle (1/2).
A-F : Burghead Museum; G–J : from Reliquary and Illustrated Arch. *II (1895) 39–44.*

that it was possible to derive the neolithic settlement in eastern Scotland from two sources, one coming north up the coast from Yorkshire, the other coming ultimately from the same area, but immediately from Ulster.[65] In this regard, he differentiated between bowls of Piggott's types D and E, and type G: the former were predominant in Lyles Hill ware, the latter in Grimston ware. He also noted that the characteristic finger-tip fluting on Lyles Hill ware occurs on the body of the pot as well as on the rim, and sometimes inside the neck as well, while that on Grimston ware is confined to the rim.

Corcoran did not feel that valid distinctions could be made between the various forms of these shouldered bowls and suggested that their origin should be sought in a settlement in the Irish Sea area by people using such bowls, or possibly that this bowl form evolved along the Atlantic route or even in the southern Irish Sea area.[66]

The Clyde-Carlingford culture of Piggott[67] bears on these problems in two aspects: first because of its connection with Lyles Hill ware, and secondly because it has been suggested that long barrows may be the ultimate degeneration of Clyde-Carlingford chambered tombs. Recent studies by Corcoran[68] and de Valéra[69,70] have provoked a number of review articles[71-3] and two points have become quite clear: the terminology used to describe chambered tombs is as confused as ever, and the origins, and even the components, of the Clyde-Carlingford 'culture' are even more confused.

If the origin of fluted bowls is confused, that of Clyde-Carlingford tombs is far more so. Piggott believed in a fundamentally westwards expansion from the Clyde estuary across Ulster;[74] Corcoran felt the Carlingford elements progressed eastwards but were independent of, though sharing a common ancestry with, Clyde elements; de Valéra wanted a west to east progression, with long barrows perhaps the ultimate evolution. Case felt his study of Irish neolithic pottery agreed better with de Valéra's views than those of Piggott and Corcoran.[75]

Yet some understanding of the Clyde-Carlingford culture is necessary for a study of Lyles Hill ware. That the two are coexistent neither in time nor extent is not disputed: in Ulster the pottery occurs in all typological variants of the tombs, but in Scotland occurs only sporadically, and Piggott in 1954 could list its occurrence in tombs only at Cairnholy I, where it occurred in the latest phase of the tomb's use.[76]

The recent re-excavation of Monamore chambered tomb on Arran found a single rim sherd of fluted Lyles Hill ware in the upper part of the forecourt deposits, also implying only a late appearance of this pottery in terms of the Clyde-Carlingford tombs.[77] The radiocarbon dates from this excavation gave 3160 ± 110 B.C. (Q. 675) for a deposit later (although by how much is not certain) than the construction, and 2240 ± 110 B.C. (Q. 676) for a deposit apparently immediately predating the blocking pavement of the forecourt. Thus the sherd of Lyles Hill ware should date to 2500–2000 B.C., while the tomb itself might have been built 750 years earlier. The remarkable longevity implied by these dates agrees with that deduced from the pottery found at West Kennet,[78] so that we must regard our chambered tombs as being at least as enduring in their use as any church and churchyard in the Christian era.

Scott was undoubtedly correct when he noted 'that to explain the Clyde-Carlingford culture in Ireland merely as a west to east, or an east to west, movement, with Scottish cairns commencing or concluding the series, is greatly to oversimplify the problem.'[79] The time is past when we can postulate great movements of apparently unified peoples heading Mormon-like over the far horizon, their tomb types and pottery steadily degenerating as they went: this is like Abercromby's Beaker folk moving 'about 50 miles in each generation or about 5 miles every three years.'[80] If we can have a Beaker reflux movement there is no reason why we should not have the same complexities in our chambered tombs, and the occurrence of radiocarbon dates of pre-3000 B.C. from widely scattered sites in England and Ireland (and now from Scotland) indicate an initial rapid spread of the neolithic.[81] It would be unwise to be dogmatic on the grounds of one Scottish Clyde-Carlingford date, but it is difficult to accept that a tomb with a likely construction date of before 3000 B.C. as being late in any typological sequence.

In the light of these dates, the idea that the British neolithic commenced in Wessex and spread north and west is no longer tenable: dates for neolithic occupation either directly evidenced or deduced from pollen analysis suggest a widespread neolithic settlement over the northern half of Ireland by 3000 B.C., and there are no dates from southern England, or indeed England as a whole, which indicate any earlier, or even as early, an occupation.[82] Piggott in 1951 argued that Grimston ware could most plausibly be derived from the Whitehawk ware of Sussex; and that from Yorkshire the carinated bowl tradition continued to Ulster: he gave reasons why this sequence was to be preferred to the opposite, that is, a spread from Ulster to Yorkshire, but in view of dates now available, the former alternative should be restudied. Here future dates from Yorkshire sites will prove vital.[83] However, it seems more plausible to ascribe the instances of fluted decoration in southern England to influences coming south from Yorkshire than to suppose that in some manner only those in the south who made carinated bowls and used fluted decoration moved north: there is virtually a complete lack of decoration other than fluting on Grimston ware[84] and it seems both unlikely and uncharitable to suggest that all those who used fluting on their carinated bowls in southern England were banished to the Yorkshire Wolds.

Thus while Case's Tagus to Michelsburg suggestion[85] with a progressive increase in the variety and extent of decoration from Ireland to southern England 'is greatly to oversimplify the problem,' the central part may be quite valid. In his study of Irish neolithic pottery, Case[86] shows that fluted decoration is common on the third of his styles of pottery, the Lyles Hill style, but rare in the two preceding styles, Dunmurry and Ballymarlagh, and in the succeeding style, Limerick (Lough Gur I/Ia): using the dates available for the Irish neolithic he gives this style a floruit of c. 2750 B.C. to c. 2000 B.C.

The earliest dates for Grimston ware must await radiocarbon analyses, and it would be unwise to attempt to pinpoint the departure of the Grimston ware settlers from Ulster, but on this hypothesis it should be prior to the appearance in southern England of carinated bowls and the occasional fluting found on sherds, for example at Abingdon,[87-8] Windmill Hill,[89] Whitehawk and Maiden Bower.[90] Possibly the idea of stripes either transversely or diagonally across the rim, for example at Abingdon, retains a vestige of this tradition. At two Welsh Severn-Cotswold chambered tombs, Ty Isaf and Parc le Breos Cwm, faint finger-made rippling occurred on some rims,[91] but these may reflect influence from the Irish Sea area rather than from southern England.

It would be safer and more honest to admit that long barrows present an unsolved problem: if we accept the radiocarbon date for the Fussell's Lodge long barrow (BM 134; 3230±180

B.C.),[92] then long barrows belong to the earliest phases of our neolithic, and not only is de Valéra's suggestion of their origin from Clyde-Carlingford tombs refuted, but the dual, if not the multiple, nature of our neolithic is implicitly admitted, for they can scarcely come from the same immediate source as the earliest neolithic settlers in Ireland who had certainly arrived by that time. However, this date, and that for the Nutbane long barrow, have been questioned,[93-4] as has that of 3760±300 B.C. (Sa 96) for the long barrow at Carnac, Brittany,[95] although a recent radiocarbon reading for an antler in the primary silt of the Windmill Hill long barrow gives 3240±150 B.C. (BM 180).

Henshall[96] tentatively grouped the eleven known long barrows in northeast Scotland together as her Balnagowan group and tended to Childe's suggestion[97] that they have connections with the Orkney-Cromarty tombs of Sutherland and Caithness: in particular she suggested that some at least of the Orkney-Cromarty long cairns may never have been chambered, as a number, though severely robbed of covering material, still reveal no chambers.

Relatively little is going to be solved without a great deal more excavation and radiocarbon dating: it is extremely unlikely that long barrows will be as easily disposed of as typological equations might suggest, nor is it likely for that matter that carinated bowls can be disposed of with similar suggestions. Long barrows are found from Poland to Spain and any analogies other than the broadest and most tentative are likely to be of little practical value. What has to be determined is whether there is anything more in common to these structures than size and shape.

With all this as a background, it is difficult to set the Roseisle material in any detailed setting. The most important diagnostic trait of the pottery is its fingertip fluting: this appears, on all the surviving fragments seen by the writer in the National Museum and Burghead Museum, to occur on the rim and upper inside of the vessels, and on the outside to extend below the carination. These are features common to Lyles Hill ware, while the fluting on Grimston ware is confined to the rim and sometimes the upper inside. However, most of the surviving profiles and rims (an unfortunately small proportion of the surviving material as much of it comprises small and amorphous pieces) seem to fit Piggott's type G, which is a form much more common among Grimston ware than Lyles Hill ware, where club and other types of rim are also more common than the hook or simpler rims of Grimston ware. Both Newbiggin and Evans noted the relative scarcity of true fingertip fluting in their studies: the surviving material from Roseisle contains no examples of the rippling so common at Lyles Hill and although the weathered surface of many of the Roseisle sherds makes precise observations difficult, they do appear to be genuinely fluted, either with the width of a finger or less, but do not have deep, narrow, grooves.

It must be emphasized that the apparently isolated position of Roseisle relative to Yorkshire and Ulster, the two nearest sources for its pottery, is largely illusory, particularly in the case of connections with Ulster. There were extremely close connections via the Great Glen between Ulster and northeast Scotland in the Early Bronze Age, and again in the Late Bronze Age:[98-100] indeed when the former ceased, the area became a backwater. Again, in the early Christian period the route was used by missionaries from Ireland. In neolithic times this route was used to trade porcellanite (Group IX axes) from Tievebulliagh Hill, Co. Antrim, and Rathlin Island to northeast Scotland:[101-3] at least four come from Urquart parish, Moray. The route was also used by the Clava Cairn builders coming from the Irish Sea route.[104] However, connections with Yorkshire, if not proven for the neolithic, certainly seem to have existed in Early Bronze Age times: a Food Vessel from Banffshire belongs to a small class which seems to have had its centre in the Yorkshire-Lincolnshire area, and a Cinerary Urn from the same county, an Enlarged Food Vessel, has skeuomorphic groove-stops recalling Yorkshire types.[105]

It can thus be seen that the origins of the Roseisle material cannot be stated with absolute certainty, but the weight of evidence inclines the writer to the view that the material is Lyles Hill ware. This occurs on the Solway Firth, in the Firth of Clyde and Argyll area, and in northeast Scotland.

The first two areas have obvious geographical connections with Ulster, and northeast Scotland, as already indicated, must be regarded as just as close by reason of the Great Glen. Even the apparently isolated find from a possible Clyde-Carlingford tomb in Perthshire can be set against the distribution of these tombs or at least the routes by which they spread from the Clyde by way of Loch Lomond.[106] However, the exact chronological or stratigraphic position of many of these finds is in a number of cases far from clear: at Cairnholy I and Monamore scientific excavation has indicated that at these sites at least Lyles Hill ware arrived at the end of the tombs' use; and at East Finnercy, Atkinson[107] found a single sherd of cord-zoned Beaker included with a deliberate deposit of neolithic pottery, almost all of it Lyles Hill ware, indicating that the deposit can scarcely date to before *c.* 2200 B.C. at the earliest. All this would suggest that Lyles Hill ware appears rather late in Scotland, during the half-millennium prior to 2000 B.C. Henshall[108] noted Lyles Hill ware rims, two at least from an apparently primary position, among the material excavated at the Recumbent Stone Circle at Loanhead of Daviot, Aberdeenshire, and these monuments seem to date from at least Beaker times, though they are badly in need of a detailed study.[109]

However, some at least of the fluted Lyles Hill ware listed by Atkinson[110] in southwest Scotland seem to be rather the reflection of the fluting tradition on the Beacharra ware found in the Scottish series of the Clyde-Carlingford tombs; and if this is the case it not only emphasizes dichotomy between the distribution of Lyles Hill ware and Clyde-Carlingford tombs but also suggests that finds of 'classic' Lyles Hill ware in Scotland may belong to a different settlement pattern, and thus possibly to a different period. The Roseisle material could be the result of a direct movement from Ulster up the Great Glen, not necessarily as late as reflections of Lyles Hill ware traditions implicit in the appearance of fluting on sherds from Clyde-Carlingford tombs in southwest Scotland. That Roseisle may not have been totally isolated is suggested by the fluted Lyles Hill ware sherd found in Strath Spey at the foot of a power pylon.[111] Firm morainic mounds, or apparent morainic mounds, would be an obvious place to erect pylons and it may be that a barrow was unwittingly used. With the exception of the Clava Cairn builders, who appear to have delighted in settling areas uninviting to later peoples and who must have come from Strath Nairn across Strath Dearn and Slochd, Strath Spey south of Knockando bears no evidence of neolithic or Bronze Age occupation save for one isolated bronze axe;[112] but a possible long cairn has been noted recently at Glenbanchor, 1½ miles west of Newtonmore.[113] Fresh fieldwork in Strath Spey, untouched since the work of Cash over 50 years ago,[114] might reveal more early occupation.

Since the halcyon days 60 to 90 years ago when the local societies and antiquarians collected and recorded finds, little archaeological work has been done on the south shore of the Moray Firth: the prehistoric material now in the museums at Inverness, Forres, Burghead, Elgin, and Banff nearly all came during this period. With the refounding of the Inverness Scientific Society and Field Club, and the emergence of the Banffshire Society, perhaps interest will again be aroused. Perhaps, too, excavations to modern standards will be done in the area. The long barrow at Longman Hill near Banff,[115] the unique murus gallicus fort at Burghead,[116] the Culbin Sands with an occupation stretching at least from Early Bronze Age times until the end of the seventeenth century A.D., and the site of Easterton of Roseisle itself are all of the first importance. Their excavation would yield results important far beyond the Laigh of Moray.

Acknowledgments: I wish to thank the editors and Mr Stevenson and Miss Henshall of the National Museum of Antiquities of Scotland who have assisted me with information for this article, originally part of my M.A. thesis. For specific information I should also like to thank Mr I. H. Adams, Scottish Record Office; Dr J. T. Andrews, Physical Geography Division, Department of Mines and Technical Surveys, Ottawa; Professor R. J. C. Atkinson; Dr A. H. Clarke, Jr., National Museum of Canada, Ottawa; Mr S. E. Durno and Mr R. Grant, Macaulay Institute for Soil Research, Aberdeen; Mr A. Fenton, National Museum of Antiquities of Scotland; Dr D. R. Hughes, National Museum of Canada, Ottawa; Mr E. MacKie, Hunterian Museum, Glasgow; Mr S. Willy, Ordanance Survey, Edinburgh; Miss A. Young, National Library, Edinburgh; and the Misses Young, Edinburgh, daughters of Hugh W. Young.

Notes

1. In this report the name is abbreviated to 'Roseisle'
2. *P.S.A.S.* LXIII (1928–9) 29–98
3. They were originally refused by *P.S.A.S.*, probably for this reason
4. *op. cit.* XXV (1890–1) 68, 435–47
5. *op. cit.* XXVII (1892–3) 86–91
6. *Reliquary & Illust. Arch.* I (1894) 142–50; 124–5
7. *Antiquary* XXX (July–December 1894) 148–52
8. Presumably less when articulated, *cf.* Brothwell, *Digging Up Bones* (1963) 171
9. Romilly Allen, *The Early Christian Monuments of Scotland* (1903) III, 118–24
10. *Reliquary & Illust. Arch.* II (1895) 39–44
11. Anderson's *Scotland in Early Christian Times* (second series) had been published in 1871, 24 years previously
12. *Reliquary & Illust. Arch.* II (1895) 120–1
13. *ibid.* 237–41
14. *op. cit.* IV (1897) 49–51
15. Cockles (*Cardium edule*) can live in marginally fresher water than mussels (*Mytilus edulis*) but the difference is negligible. However, cockles burrow in sand and mud while mussels attach themselves to rocks, which may be what was at the back of Young's mind. Regarding river- and sea-worn boulders, the difference between them is small enough to make it unlikely that Young could have been able to identify them
16. *Arch.* XLVI, pt. II (1874) 273–92
17. *Trans. Inverness Scientific Soc. & Field Club* II (1880–3) 37
18. *P.S.A.S.* IX (1870–2) 250–63
19. *P.P.S.* XVII (1951) 40–2; 70 fig. 1

20. *A.N.L.* IV, 10 (1952) 145–6
21. *Geog. J.* XC (1937) 500 n. 2
22. *P.P.S.* XVII (1951) 40, but spelt 'Boyndlie'
23. *Cf.* Morrison's remark about the tradition of a harbour at the foot of the Hill of Kinnairdie (probably Meft Hill) with *The Northern Scot Christmas Number 1966*: 25
24. *P.P.S.* XVII (1951) 40
25. *loc. cit.*
26. *Reliquary & Illust. Arch.* I (1894) 144–5
27. For further descriptions of this stone see *P.S.A.S.* XXIX (1894–5) 449–53; Romilly Allen, *op. cit.* III, 124–6, Pl. XV, but reference to findspot as Spindle Muir (immediately northeast of Easterton of Roseisle) is erroneous; and *P.S.A.S.* LXVIII (1933–4) 55
28. In conversation; for general statement see chapter V in (ed.) Wainwright, *The Problem of the Picts* (1955)
29. *Arch. J.* CXVIII (1961) 40–7
30. *P.S.A.S.* XCVI (1962–3) 94–5, 106
31. *op. cit.* XCII (1958–9) 36
32. The only other possibility was rye but this has no hairs on the kernel, and some of the kernels in this sample did. Hunterian Museum catalogue number of oats B.1951.995, labelled 'from the ancient granary at Easterton of Roseisle, 1896'
33. De Laet, *The Low Countries* (1958) 79
34. Clark, *Prehistoric Europe : The Economic Basis* (1952) 109
35. Cole, *The Neolithic Revolution* (1959) 16
36. *New Statistical Account* XIII, 38 of Elgin Section; written 1835, published 1845
37. *loc. cit.*
38. Leslie, *General View of the Agriculture in the Counties of Nairn and Moray* (1811) 180
39. *Trans. Inverness Scientific Soc. & Field Club* II (1880–3) 37
40. *P.S.A.S.* IX (1870–2) 250–63
41. *op. cit.* XXV (1890–1) 484–511, esp. 488–90, 491, 492
42. *The Northern Scot Christmas Number 1966*: 25, 27–8
43. Jessen and Helbaek, *Cereals in Great Britain and Ireland in Prehistoric and Early Historic Times* (1944) 18
44. Matheson, *Moray and Nairn* (1915)
45. *P.S.A.S.* IX (1870–2) 241–2
46. *op. cit.* LXXX (1945–6) 141–3
47. Catalogue Number B.1951.986 in Henderson Bishop Collection, probably from M'Kewan of Dyke
48. *Arch. J.* LXXXVIII (1931) 67–158
49. Evans, *Lyles Hill* (1955) 32, 43–6
50. *P.S.A.S.* XXIX (1894–5) 417–18
51. Lacaille, *The Stone Age in Scotland* (1954) 210
52. *Memoirs read before the Anthrop. Soc. London* II (1865–6) 226–56
53. *P.P.S.* III (1937) 189
54. *P.S.A.S.* XCVII (1963–4) 42, 60, Class 1, No. 2, 61; Miss MacInnes suggests the use of mica backing is a Yorkshire trait occurring there, in Scotland and the Isle of Man, but not in Ireland
55. *P.S.A.S.* LXIII (1928–9) 29–98
56. *Antiquity,* XXXIX (1965) 45–8, *cf.* Piggott, *Ancient Europe* (1965) chapter 2
57. *Antiquity* XXXVIII (1964) 53–4
58. *P.S.A.S.* XCVII (1963–4) 1–34
59. *P.P.S.* XXXI (1965) 34–57
60. Piggott, *Neolithic Cultures* 170 n.1, 271, 272, 113–14
61. Childe, *The Prehistory of Scotland* (1935) 51
62. Piggott, *op. cit.* (1954) 120–1, 182
63. *A.N.L.* VI, 1 (1955) 14
64. *Ant. J.* XXXVI (1956) 11–30
65. Atkinson, in (ed.) Piggott, *The Prehistoric Peoples of Scotland* (1962) 11–16
66. *P.P.S.* XXVI (1960) 134–5, 136
67. Piggott, *op. cit.* (1954) *passim,* esp. chapter VI
68. *P.P.S.* XXVI (1960) 98–148

69. *P.R.I.A.* (C) LX (1960) 9–140
70. *P.P.S.* XXVII (1961) 234–52
71. *ibid.* 353–5
72. *Studia Hibernica* I (1961) 228–32
73. *Antiquity* XXXVI (1962) 97–101
74. Piggott, *op. cit.* (1954) 181
75. *P.P.S.* XXVII (1961) 174–233; for further discussion of the neolithic see *Antiquity* XXXVI (1962) 212–16
76. Piggott, *op. cit.* (1954) 170
77. *P.S.A.S.* XCVII (1963–4) 1–34
78. Piggott, *The West Kennet Long Barrow, Excavations 1955–56* (1962) 68–78
79. *Antiquity* XXXVI (1962) 98
80. Abercromby, *A Study of the Bronze Age Pottery of Great Britain and Ireland* (1912) I, 86
81. *Antiquity* XXXVI (1962) 22
82. *loc. cit.*
83. Piggott, *op. cit.* (1954) 116, 117; Willerby and Seamer long barrows both have radiocarbon dates centred on 3000–3100 B.C. (*J. Cork Hist. and Arch. Soc.* LXXI (1966)) 11, 12
84. *P.P.S.* III (1937) 189–216
85. *Ant. J.* XXXVI (1956) 11–30
86. *P.P.S.* XXVII (1961) 174–233
87. *Ant. J.* VII (1927) 455
88. *op. cit.* VIII (1928) 474
89. *op. cit.* XXXVI (1956) 26
90. *Arch. J.* LXXXVIII (1931) 67–158
91. Piggott, *op. cit.* (1954) 144
92. *Antiquity* XXXVIII (1964) 139–40
93. *P.P.S.* XXXI (1965) 71
94. *Antiquity* XXXVI (1962) 215
95. *ibid.* 140; *op. cit.* XC (1966) 299
96. Henshall, *The Chambered Tombs of Scotland* (1963) I, 40–4
97. Childe, *The Prehistory of Scotland* (1935) 51
98. *P.S.A.S.* XCIV (1960–1) 317–20
99. *P.S.A.S.* XCVIII (1964–5) forthcoming
100. *Univ. Edin. Dept. of Arch., 13th Ann. Rep.* (1960–1) 6–9
101. *U.J.A.* XV (1952) 31–60
102. (ed.) Piggott, *op. cit.* (1962) 19 n. 3
103. Unpublished map in National Museum of Antiquities of Scotland, Edinburgh
104. *P.S.A.S.* XCVI (1962–3) 87–106
105. *op. cit.* XCIV (1960–1) 320
106. *P.S.A.S.* XCII (1958–9) 72–3, fig. 2
107. (ed.) Piggott, *op. cit.* (1962) 18–19
108. Henshall, *op. cit.* I, 39
109. *P.S.A.S.* XCVI (1962–3) 97–100
110. (ed.) Piggott, *op. cit.* (1962) 15 fig. 2, 34–5
111. *P.S.A.S.* LXXI (1936–7) 367, found on the east side of the Spey between Grantown-on-Spey and Newtonmore; all but 3½ miles of the course of the powerline between the two places is on the east side of the river. The sherd is known only from a drawing
112. *P.S.A.S.* XCVI (1962–3), *cf.* 88 fig. 1 and 90 fig. 2
113. Henshall, *op. cit.* I, 378
114. *P.S.A.S.* XL (1905–6) 245–54; XLIV (1909–10) 189–203
115. Henshall, *op. cit.* I, 390 and refs.
116. *P.S.A.S.* IV (1860–2) 321–69; XXV (1890–1) 68, 435–47; XXVIII (1892–3) 86–91

The stone implement trade in third-millennium Scotland

P. R. Ritchie

The study of implement petrology in Scotland dates back to 1917 at least, and perhaps to an even earlier date. This present paper is not intended as a full account, but rather as a survey of what has been done and of future possibilities. Professor Piggott introduced me to this inquiry as an extension of the work in which he had participated as a member of the Sub-Committee of the Southwestern Group of Museums and Art Galleries on the Petrological Identification of Stone Axes. It was felt unnecessary to create a separate Scottish Committee since it was intended that the inquiry should concentrate on the collections of the National Museum of Antiquities of Scotland which are representative of the country as a whole. Subsequently it has been confirmed that this is indeed the case; inspection of implements in other collections has simply increased the density of distribution patterns and has not led to any radical change in them.

After obtaining reference material from the principal known sources the whole axe collection was examined macroscopically. Axes which appeared to belong to known factories were grouped together. Initially, thin-section examination was limited to axes of presumed Group IX from the known sources at Tievebulliagh and Rathlin Island in the north of Ireland. Whilst the work was in progress two likely sources of material for axes within Scotland were noticed and these are briefly described here. Subsequently, in the Hunterian Museum of the University of Glasgow, attention was drawn to sources of material which acted as a substitute for flint and these are also described.

Since then, petrographic studies have been continued on the collections in the Hunterian Museum and in Dumfries Museum by Livens and Holgate,[1] and more recently by MacKie and Holgate.[2] The axe collection of Dundee City Museum and Art Gallery is at present being examined by Coutts and Whyte. There have also been a number of separate identifications carried out by the Geological Survey of axes of Group VI origin[3] and some finds have been examined by the Sub-Committee of the South-Western Group.[4]

Implements of Rhum bloodstone

Bloodstone as a material for prehistoric implements in Scotland is first mentioned in the report by Clark appended to Scott's paper on the cave at Rudh'an Dunain in Skye.[5] Harker, who examined some of the finds, picked out certain pieces as being of bloodstone from a locality on the island of Rhum. More recently, pieces were noticed among the collections from

Figure 19. Distribution map of northwest Scotland, with finds of Rhum bloodstone. Square : source.

RHUM

Ardnamurchan in the Hunterian Museum and the identifications were confirmed by sectioning.

In the Geological Survey Memoir on 'The Small Isles of Inverness-shire' the material is described as occurring on the upper part of Creag nan Stairdean. This is a hill, 1273 feet high, which lies on the most westerly part of Rhum at the point where the southwest and northwest coasts meet. Although this name appears on the six-inch Geological Survey map it has now been dropped and the present edition of the Ordnance Survey six-inch map carries the name 'Bloodstone Hill' (the site is NG 315007). The Memoir notes[6] that the principal occurrence is a solid band about nine inches thick, not far below the summit on the northern face of the hill. At that date (1902–3) the outcrop was covered but pieces of bloodstone could be obtained from that level and from the screes below. At one time it was worked as an ornamental stone and the six-inch map marks the site of an old quarry.

Although Harker describes the hand-specimen as of a deep-green colour with spots of blood-red the specimens from Bloodstone Hill in the geological collections of the Hunterian Museum show some variation and some pieces are quite pale in colour. Harker's description of the rock in thin section was '. . . a field mottled with light-green and colourless portions, sharply separated. The colourless are chalcedony with a finely-tufted quasi-spherulitic structure. The light-green substance has the form of clusters of little spherules, partly coalescing; but no radiate structure is apparent, and the substance is sensibly isotropic. This green colouring-matter of the bloodstone seems to be the same which occasionally occupies some of the flat amygdaloidal cavities in the mugearite, and it is identified by Heddle as celadonite . . . The red spots in the bloodstone are perhaps connected with the oxidation of pyrites, minute crystals of which, in a partly altered state, are visible in a thin slice. Many specimens again contain little brown patches which are globular aggregates of chalybite, tending to become oxidized.'[7]

Pieces of this material have been found amongst the stone industries from Risga in Loch Sunart, at Drynan Bay on the north side of the Ardnamurchan Peninsula, and at Redpoint, Loch Torridon, as well as at both the cave and the chambered cairn at Rudh'an Dunain in Skye. The finds from Redpoint have not been sectioned and Gray has a cautionary word about a possible occurrence of this mineral in the parish of Gairloch.[8]

The content of the Ardnamurchan mesolithic industries has been described by Lacaille and his fig. 5 no. 4 is one of the pieces of bloodstone.[9] Since waste material is found on these sites this must be a case of people going to Rhum for material and afterwards working it into artefacts on their normal domestic sites. Direct dating evidence is lacking, although a date just before 3000 B.C. would seem reasonable for these late mesolithic people. At Risga there seem to have been two occupations, the earlier with barbed points of Obanian type and socketed antler mattocks comparable with the well-known find from Meiklewood in the Carse of Stirling. By analogy with the north of Europe these finds would fit with the date suggested. However, there is a later occupation at Risga characterized by pottery and flint knives such as those from the Arran chambered cairns. At the cave at Rudh'an Dunain[10] the worked stone was associated with Beaker (but disturbance was noted by the excavator) and this is confirmed by events at the adjacent chambered cairn,[11] where the 'roughly shaped point of dark green chert' from the Beaker stratum is, in fact, a piece of bloodstone. Whilst we cannot then be

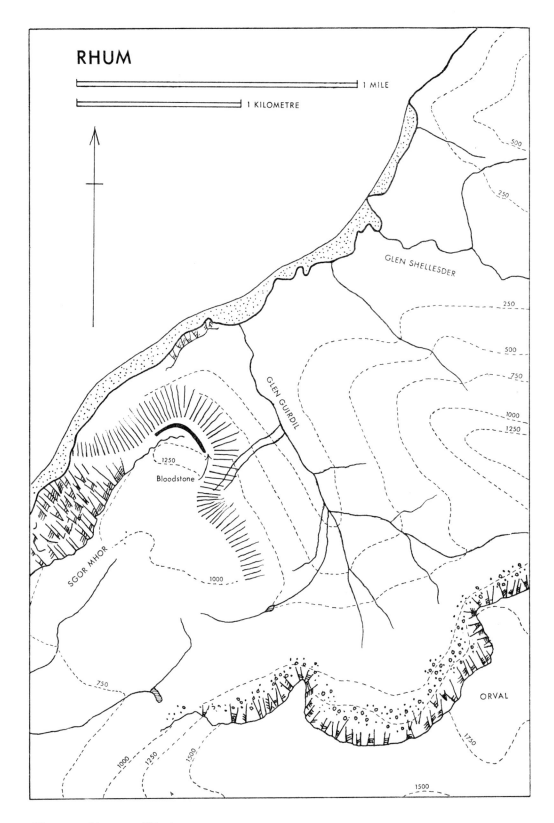

Figure 20. Site map of bloodstone.

certain of the starting date for the exploitation of bloodstone, we can say that its use continued into the early part of the second millennium B.C. and the appearance of Beaker pottery.

Implements of Arran pitchstone

One of the earliest cases of petrographic scrutiny must be that of the pitchstone of Arran. Its presence at Shewalton, on the mainland opposite Arran, was noted by John Smith in 1897.[12] In a paper of his own on the use and distribution of pitchstone Mann commented that Smith was a pioneer of the microscopic study of that rock but there is nothing to show that the microscopic work was extended to archaeological finds. Mann was joined by Scott who examined his finds in thin section and pointed out that the pitchstone flake and core from Dunagoil could not have come from either Bute or the Corriegills district but were more likely to have originated from the outcrop near Brodick sometimes known as the Invercloy pitchstone.

These pitchstones were well known to late nineteenth-century petrographers and were figured in colour in Teall's *British Petrography* as well as being discussed in a number of papers. Probably because of their striking appearance in thin section the pitchstones of the Corriegills/Clauchlands district became best known and, in his series of papers on the chambered tombs of Arran and Bute, Bryce repeatedly refers to the finding of Corriegills pitchstone. There is no evidence in his writings to show that these finds were subjected to any geological examination and a macroscopic study of the pieces in the National Museum of Antiquities shows that a number of different pitchstones are probably represented amongst the finds.

Following Mann's recognition of occurrences outside Arran this material was noticed on a number of occasions between the Wars and there are numerous references to surface finds being made in the east of Scotland.

With the further recognition of the value of petrographic studies the finds made during postwar excavations were submitted to the Geological Survey and a series of identifications were made under the microscope which confirmed the presence of Arran material from the chambered cairn of Cairnholy I and from sites in the east of Scotland as far north as Fife.

Although he knew that the material was used for the manufacture of implements Bryce was puzzled by the nature of the pieces which turned up in his excavations and commented that 'In every situation save Monyquil, flakes or fragments of the greenish mineral identified as Corriegills pitchstone were found, and similar flakes were found in the Tormore cists last year. . . . No implement or object made of this mineral has been seen, yet these broken fragments or flakes can hardly be regarded as stones occurring incidentally in the soil.'[13] MacKie, too, noticed that in his re-excavation of Monamore 'none of the pitchstone fragments were even broken artefacts.' Of the 128 fragments which he found, only four were clearly struck flakes and the remainder were shattered lumps of various sizes. He felt that only waste material was scattered in the forecourt of the cairn.[14]

Since there are numerous outcrops of pitchstone throughout the island, and since the movement of ice during glaciation was from north to south, there would seem to be a case for the natural occurrence of pitchstone in the soil despite Bryce's comment. This was a point which had not been overlooked by Mann.[15] On re-examination there are found to be struck flakes from each of Bryce's excavations with the exception of Giants' Graves, Whiting Bay, from whence come three fairly large but unworked lumps of porphyritic green pitchstone. Whilst pitchstone fragments are to be found occurring naturally in the soil as mentioned by Mann and confirmed in MacKie's Monamore excavation their appearance in the Arran tombs is due to human intervention and puts them in line with the finds from Cairnholy I, Brackley and Beacharra as well as Glecknabae and Michael's Grave in Bute.

Throughout, the aim was to produce blades and flakes as counterparts of tools in flint and

Figure 21. Distribution map of finds of Arran pitchstone. Squares : sectioned finds. Triangle : Schoolhouse outcrop.

there are some good small cores and blades, particularly from the Luce Sands. As with the use of bloodstone, so it is difficult to find an initial date for this exploitation. It is found with late mesolithic industries, as at Ballantrae,[16] but for firm dating we must turn to the chambered cairns. Two radiocarbon dates were obtained for the layer which contained the pitchstone at Monamore. The earlier date was 3160±110 B.C. and the later 2240±110 B.C.[17] MacKie had noted the possibility that the carbon might be considered to have come from a pre-existing domestic site and thrown in with the blocking. The same argument could be applied to the fragments of pitchstone and presumably we must consider that the later of the two dates is the correct one for the formation of the layer. The flakes from Cairnholy I belonged to the period of use of the cairn but the flake from the Beacharra cairn was considered by Scott to come from the original ground level.[18]

At Brackley in Kintyre the pitchstone finds were associated with a cremation burial which was also accompanied by parts of at least two jet necklaces, a plano-convex knife, and an incomplete food vessel.[19] Another possible late occurrence is that at Cowdenbeath where a flake was picked up during the examination of a cemetery containing six cinerary urns.[20] It was not directly associated with any of these and may merely have been a stray find as was the case at Scotstarvit.[21] On the other hand one cannot help remarking that pitchstone was also found at another Fife cremation cemetery – that at Brackmont Mill. Like the bloodstone from Rhum we can only say that the initial exploitation of pitchstone is connected with hunter–fisher groups of the mesolithic and that its use continued into the early part of the second millennium B.C. or even rather later.

The Arran pitchstones can be divided into two main groups, those from the Corriegills district which are generally non-porphyritic and are characterized by the presence of plumose and arborescent groups of microlites, and the other types which carry phenocrysts in varying quantities and are sub-divided according to the nature of these.

The best-known pitchstones are those from the Corriegills district in which the glassy base is crowded with pleochroic green needles, scopulites and arborescent groupings. These had been identified as hornblende by Harker[22] but recently Tilley has pointed out that clinopyroxene is more frequent than descriptions suggest and that biotite with its chlorite pseudomorphs is a common constituent. He identifies the main elements of the tree-like growths as hornblende, with the feathery fringes as minute plates of biotite. The scopulites are plates of biotite fringed at their edges by fine diverging plates of the same mineral.[23]

The only possible working site which has been mentioned is that which figures in Mann's paper.[24] It was seen on an outcrop of pitchstone near the Brodick Schoolhouse and is presumably the occurrence known to geologists as the Schoolhouse or Invercloy pitchstone. It is exposed at the back of the Schoolhouse, and in Stronach Wood where it runs for about 350 yards in a roughly west–southwest direction. Macroscopically it is dark green, almost black, with phenocrysts of felspar and olivine occurring in bands. Some bands are almost free of these. Scott considered that the finds from Dunagoil in Bute had probably originated here.

Axes of Irish porcellanite

When originally this work started with the examination of the axes of Group IX (the porcellanite from Tievebulliagh and Brockley in Co. Antrim), copies of the list of identifications were placed in the National Museum of Antiquities and sent to the Council for British Archaeology. However, no map of this distribution has been published and fig. 22 now shows the plot of these identifications supplemented by those published by Livens.[25] Since the original list was compiled more axes which are likely to be of Group IX origin have come into the national collection but have not been sectioned. These are not plotted on this map; their distribution merely reinforces that which is shown.

There is a remarkable concentration in the northeast, particularly in Aberdeenshire, and it is a great pity that precise locations are not available for the six axes which are catalogued simply as 'Aberdeenshire.' In this northeastern district seventeen axes of Irish origin were identified and another six have subsequently been added. Outside this area the only other concentration is in the region of the Clyde Estuary around which another nine axes are scattered. Amongst the axes in the Kelvingrove and National Museums are another six, unsectioned, which will add to the density of the distribution pattern between Loch Fyne and Glasgow.

The remaining 25 finds are widely scattered throughout the country. In Campbeltown Museum a few unsectioned axes look as though they would add to the pattern in Kintyre but it is surprising to see the complete lack of imports in south Ayrshire and Galloway. The only confirmed Group IX axe from the south, from Kirkpatrick-Durham in Kirkcudbrightshire, lies to the east of the area in which chambered cairns are concentrated. Since Jope commented in similar terms[26] a few axes have appeared in Stranraer Museum. There is little doubt that sectioning would confirm the Group IX origin of these. Unfortunately most of the axes are unlocalized, but since they were presented by Stair Estates they are probably from the district. Of particular interest are two roughouts; one, which has not been sectioned, is a recent acquisition in the Edinburgh collection and comes from Machrie in Arran; the other, from Southend in Kintyre, has been confirmed by sectioning.

For dating evidence we must look outside Scotland. Only one piece, that from Eilean an Tighe, has come from an excavation.[27] The axe from Giants' Graves has been said by Livens to be a doubtful association. Piggott has discussed the dating of the trade in axes as a whole.[28] He felt that the working of the Group IX rock and its distribution must be fitted into his second phase of factory exploitation in the middle to late third millennium. An argument for an earlier date depended on the working-floors being sealed by a peat of the Zone VIIa–VIIb transition, implying a beginning for this industry before the end of the fourth millennium, but Piggott wondered if this might not be simply an 'agricultural' horizon of later date. Tievebulliagh axes had been found at Newferry on the River Bann. A radiocarbon date for one of the hearths of 3330 ± 170 B.C. might bear out the palaeobotanical evidence from Tievebulliagh, but the hearth from which this was done was not one which produced an axe.[29] Otherwise the attributions from Irish sites are to Zone VIIb, as at Cushendun and Island MacHugh, but in this latter case Hartley pointed out that whilst the stone was of the same type as that from Tievebulliagh it was not identical with it.[30]

Connections between northeast Scotland and Ulster were noticed by Atkinson who discussed the colonization of the area by people using Lyles Hill ware.[31] His thesis is supported by the manner in which the Group IX finds cluster in the northeast, and at two of the localities which he mentions as having settlements, Urquhart in Elginshire and Whitemoss

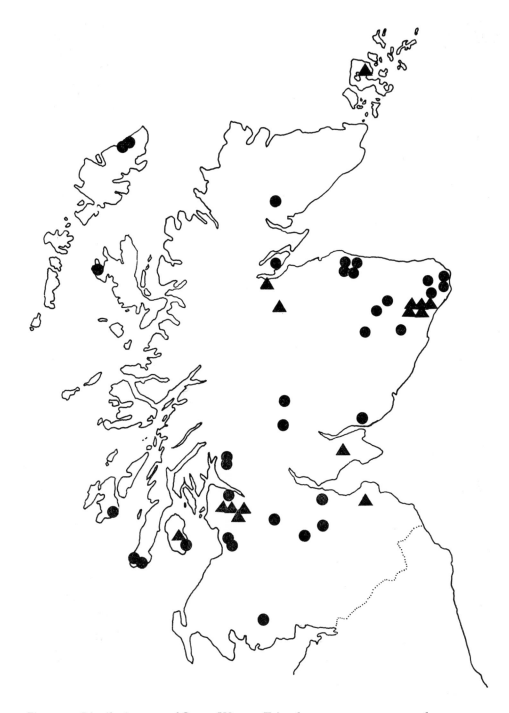

Figure 22. Distribution map of Group IX axes. Triangles : county provenance only.

(Bishopton), Renfrewshire, Group IX axes have been confirmed. Indeed his map of the distribution of Lyles Hill ware is very similar to that of Group IX axes but it must be remembered that this was done before Case's study of Irish pottery. However, the concentration of axes around the Clyde, the finds from Loch Lomond and from central Perthshire combine to suggest that a riverine route through the Central Highlands might be considered to be equally as possible as his Great Glen route. Another point worthy of notice is the presence of these axes in the Hebrides.

In his discussion of foreign connections in the Irish neolithic Case wrote, 'This style [*i.e.,* Lyles Hill ware] has sufficiently marked individuality to suggest a true expansion-phase as the correct explanation for such foreign resemblances as at . . . Nether Largie and Achnacree, Argyllshire, and Glecknabae, Bute. The expansion may have been trade in Antrim flint.'[32] Might we not rather write 'The expansion may have been trade in Antrim axes'?

The Creag na Caillich hornfels

The discovery of a working-site near Killin in Perthshire is due to Dr Poore who, during the course of botanical work, noticed a piece of rock whose appearance suggested to him that it might have been humanly worked. He sought the assistance of the late Dr A. M. Cockburn who showed the find to me. There was no doubt that it had been deliberately flaked. A search has since been made of the area and this has produced further finds. The site lies on the south face of Creag na Caillich, the western member of the three hills which group together to form a large corry (Coire Fionn Lairige) to the north-northeast of Killin. From the south end of Loch Tay the ground rises steeply northwards to about 1400 feet and is composed of rocks of the Dalradian metamorphic assemblage. The Loch Tay Limestone at the foot of the hill is followed upwards by garnetiferous mica schists – the Ben Lui schists of Highland geologists. Above about 1500 feet the Geological Survey have mapped the ground as being made up of clay-slate phyllite, including calcareous sericite schist, and with some bands of quartzite. These are the Ben Lawers schists. After the initial steep slope the ground rises more gently from 1400 feet for the next 600–800 feet to form a platform from which rise the hills on the northern margin of the valley.

The succession is inverted; the Loch Tay Limestone which lies at the foot of the hill is actually at a higher stratigraphic level than the phyllites at the summit. Within the latter formation occur bands of grey-green indurated rock of very fine grain. One of these bands outcrops at an altitude of about 2500 feet on the south face of Creag na Caillich and appears to have been used as a source of raw material for implements.

A ridge projects southwards from the main mass of the hill at a height of about 2000 feet. Between this ridge and the rocky south face a saddle is covered with peat through which the rock is occasionally seen. At the present time the peat is being eroded and forms hags with their faces generally aligned in an east–west direction. In the most northerly of these peat hags flakes of deeply weathered hornfels have been picked up at intervals over the last twelve years. During this period the face of the peat has receded and the flakes, found originally at the base of the peat, are now occurring at a higher level, suggesting that this is material which has come from a position higher up on the slope. This might have happened at any time in antiquity and is certainly happening at the present time. However, six squamous flakes were

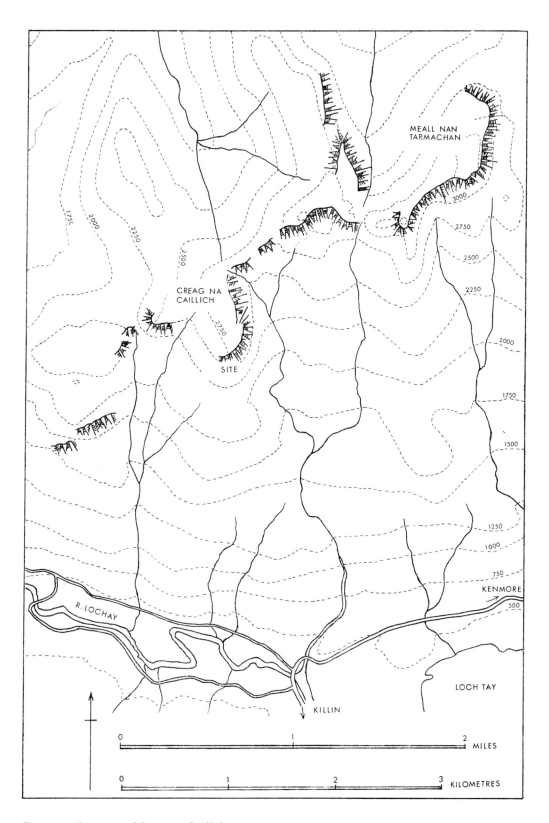

Figure 23. Site map of Creag na Caillich.

found together at one point in the peat as though they represented the debris from the initial dressing of a roughout and it may be that dressing to shape was carried out on the saddle as well as higher up the slope.

From the saddle the flakes can be traced back up the slope in impermanent water-courses and by digging into the turf. About halfway up the south face two distinct small areas of scree are seen. The eastern and more distinct of these is formed of moderately sized blocks and no waste material was seen amongst it. To the west of this is a very small area of scree, pale in colour, resting at a very steep angle, and made up of material which is being washed down through a cleft in the rock from a terrace higher up. This scree is made up of pieces about the size of a human fist or less, and on it lie flakes which appear to be workshop waste. A few possible roughouts have also been recovered.

Higher up is an outcrop of hornfels against which a narrow terrace has been formed. This is now grass-covered but search in the holes in the turf produced more flakes. No hornfels of this nature was seen further up on the south face or on the hill slopes to the north. Large blocky scree is found at the foot of the east face of the hill. Search in this area fourteen years ago produced no waste although it was noticed that the strongly-banded green rock closely resembled that of a number of axes in the National Museum of Antiquities. It would be worthwhile looking again in this area, probably at a rather higher level where there is more small material.

Although axes which look from the nature of the banding as though they might have originated from this exposure have been seen, no attempt has been made to suggest possible distributions. This is certainly a case for thin section work since it is very easy to confuse this material in hand-specimen with that of the Borrowdale Volcanics from the Lake District. A very small chip removed from an axe from Abernethy was examined under the microscope and showed near identity with a section from the original roughout from Creag na Caillich. In view of the variation to be expected in this particular rock type there is little doubt that this axe originated there.

The distribution which has been suggested for Group VI axes should be used with caution.[33] It would be better only to consider those which have been checked in thin section since confusion is possible.

At the present time the detailed petrography of this rock is still being worked out and this, together with a description of the finds, will have to form the substance of another paper.

The Shetland riebeckite felsite

Amongst the stone implements of the Shetland archipelago two types are distinctive and contrast with finds from other regions of the British Isles. Adzes are found as well as axes, and polished stone knives of thin section and oval or kidney outline are found in quantities. The latter are so distinctive that the term 'Shetland knife' has been applied to them, although they are also known as flensing knives because of their shape. There does not seem to be anything in the associated finds to bear out this latter attribution. Examples of all of these are known to have been made from a distinctive rock type which has been studied by Phemister[34] who also comments on the use of the stone for prehistoric implements. The rock has often been called 'Uyea porphyry' and it has been said that it occurs only on the Beorgs of Uyea, a boulder-

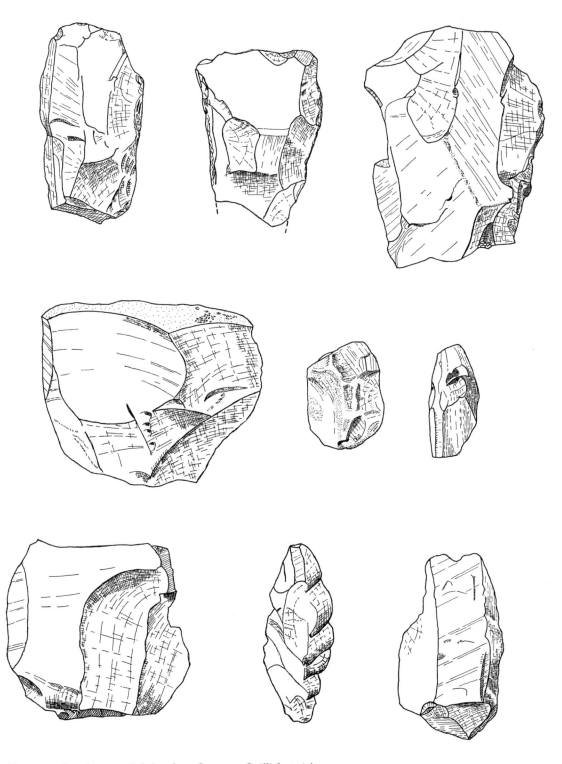

Figure 24. Roughouts and flakes from Creag na Caillich. (1/2)

strewn slope in the northern part of the parish of Northmaven. Its distribution, however, is not as restricted as this.

Thanks to the series of excavations carried out by Calder on Stone Age houses in the Shetlands we now know something of the background of these implements. Apart from a find at Jarlshof none of these tools had previously been found in any sort of archaeological context.

At Jarlshof a knife was found in Dwelling I, the oldest in the group excavated by Curle. The dwelling was built over a shell midden which Hamilton found to be identical with that at the base of the Midden II series. From this midden came quartz tools, mainly scrapers, core and flake tools, slate axes, discs and rings, grain rubbers and a trough quern. The most important object from this midden was the bone plaque found at the base of the thin sand layer intercalated between Midden IIA and Midden IIB. In its form it has been compared with the girdle-plates from Västerbjers and Scandinavian passage graves although the decoration relates rather to the ornament of Iberian schist plaques. With the trough quern, whose appearance on the western seaboard of Europe is coupled with the coming of passage graves, this suggests a relationship between the earliest Jarlshof and the builders of chambered tombs.[35] Another piece of riebeckite felsite (not mentioned in the report) from Jarlshof was found in a position corresponding stratigraphically to Curle's Bronze Age Village I.

Following on these associations it is no surprise to find two broken knives at the Stanydale temple.[36] Another five fragments are listed in the finds from the house at Ness of Gruting.[37] One of these was a piece of a knife, another possibly from an unfinished knife. An adze was also amongst the finds as was another at the Benie Hoose in Whalsay.[38] The Benie Hoose provided a scraper of riebeckite felsite which had been made from a broken polished implement. The finds from these houses are generally similar and in her report on the finds Miss Henshall suggests that, apart from Jarlshof and Wiltrow, connections are to be looked for with the builders of the chambered tombs and contacts with the makers of Beakers and Food Vessels. In view of her suggestion that we ought to look to the Hebrides, rather than to Orkney, for chambered tomb connections, it is worth noting that one of the few implements found outside Shetland and likely to be of this material has come from Orkney. It has not been sectioned but it is obviously desirable that this should be done. A terminal date for the use of this rock is difficult to find. An axe with strongly splayed edge must be a copy of one in metal and at Clickhimin fragments of knife were recovered from a domestic context dated to about 500 B.C.[39]

The distribution of these implements lies almost entirely within the Shetland Islands and scrutiny of the distribution of the knives shows that it corresponds with Calder's distribution map of houses,[40] although it must be remembered that he has written cautionary words about the likely incompleteness of his map. So far, no thorough study has been made of axes and adzes likely to emanate from this source but a number of occurrences outside Shetland have been seen during the course of the work and obviously these ought to be checked by sectioning. Two adzes in the Bishop Collection in the Hunterian Museum come respectively from Leslie in Aberdeenshire, and from Selkirk. In the same collection is an axe which may be of this material and which is labelled Houlland, Stenness, Orkney. In the collection of the Kelvingrove Museum in Glasgow there is a knife which was found in Lanarkshire, and an axe from Nisbet Farm, Pencaitland in East Lothian, also looks as though it should come from

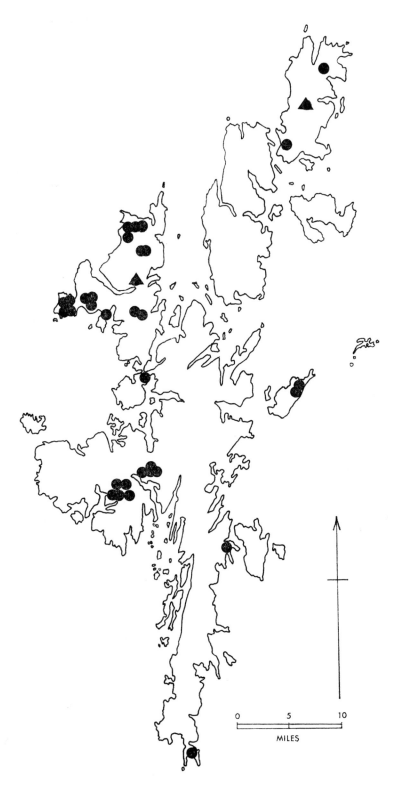

Figure 25. Flat stone knives of riebeckite felsite in Shetland. Triangle : only district known.

Shetland. Although it has been claimed from macroscopic examination that the cushion macehead from Knock in Lewis is made of riebeckite felsite[41] the present writer feels that the really distinctive diagnostic characteristics are not present and that sectioning is essential before any comment is made about the material. Another cushion macehead from Fife has similarly been claimed to stem from this source.

The source of the riebeckite felsite has been known for some time and Scott and Calder have published[42] a description of a working-site on the Beorgs of Uyea to the west of the Mill Loch (N.G.R. HU 327901). This took the form of a gallery constructed underground against the side of one of the dykes of felsite. It was about ten feet long, of variable width, and lintelled over. On the floor there was an accumulation of rock chippings, cores, hammer stones and a rubbing stone which had been re-used as an anvil. The gallery was, in effect, a short trench dug against the dyke which had been quarried and undercut. The only other factory at which actual quarrying has been proved is that of Mynydd Rhiw.[43] In that case the opencast working was of a slightly different nature. Lacaille has discussed the working properties of a Shetland porphyry but it is not clear if he was dealing with this particular rock.[44]

In his description of the characteristic type[45] Phemister notes that the spherulites range in size from 1 mm. to 1 cm. in diameter, but in some of the knives they are even larger and show concentric zoning. Although the specimens which I have so far seen from the working gallery are both spherulitic and porphyritic the structures are smaller, and it seems that some, at any rate, of the knives have probably been made of material from another outcrop.

The dykes which provide this material outcrop in the area of the mainland to the north of Ronas Voe. The distribution extends from Roga Field in the south to Calder's Head and North Hill on the north coast of the mainland and is restricted to a narrow belt about one and a half miles wide. All of the dykes run in a generally north–south direction and range in width from about 2 to 30 feet. Composite dykes are frequent. Dykes of other rock-types occur both within this zone as well as outside it.

Phemister points out that there is a wide range of types, ranging at one end from a non-porphyritic homogeneous rock of fairly deep blue to dove-grey and stone-grey colour, through non-porphyritic spherulitic types to the other end-member of the series which is both porphyritic and spherulitic with pink or red phenocrysts of felspar, clear quartz and deep blue spherules set in a silver-grey ground sprinkled with blue.

In thin section the first type shows prismatic grains of micropegmatite and granular quartz with slender prisms of riebeckite distributed throughout. Aegirine is usually present as a subordinate constituent in stout subhedral prisms. The porphyritic spherulitic types contain idiomorphic phenocrysts of quartz and felspar, although mutual interference is seen in cumulophyric aggregates. The quartz crystals show some corrosion. The felspars are twinned according to the Carlsbad and Baveno laws with an optic axial angle near to 90° and a Beta of 1·523. Phemister identifies the felspar as a soda-orthoclase. There are rare phenocrysts of clear soda-sanidine of small 2V. The groundmass is made up of micropegmatite spherulites cemented by clear granular quartz with stout hypidiomorphic prisms of alkali-felspar. Riebeckite in fine needles with occasional aegirine radiates from the centre of the spherulites to produce the blue spots which are conspicuous in the hand-specimen. Alkali-felspar is also present and presents crystal outlines to all the other minerals.

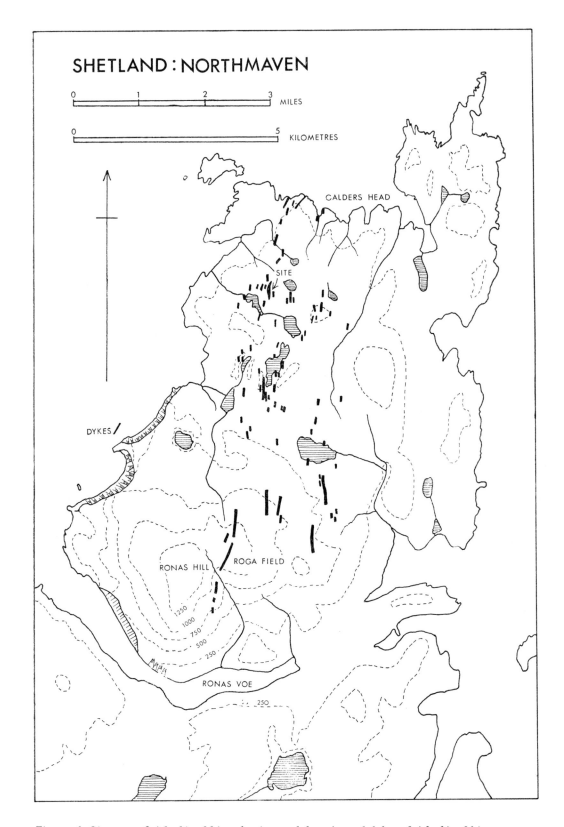

Figure 26. Site map of riebeckite felsite, showing workshop site and dykes of riebeckite felsite.

In conducting this work some points have emerged which may seem obvious but which do not seem to have been stated anywhere else. These are really concerned with the difficulty of enlisting petrological aid and the need to avoid burdening petrologists with work which is not likely to produce worthwhile archaeological results.

The examination of axes which appear macroscopically to stand on their own, as far as material is concerned, is felt to be unwarranted at the present time unless there is some special reason for this examination. It is better to tackle the problem systematically by studying any collection as a whole, picking out those axes which are of like material, and then placing known groups at the beginning of the work. With this approach there is an immediate and worthwhile accretion of knowledge without any need for the search for a source which is the really time-consuming part of the inquiry. Following the examination of groups from known sources comes the determination of grouped axes whose source is unknown. In this case the effort spent by the petrologist on trying to trace the outcrop is really worthwhile.

Although some use has been made of macroscopic examination in the compilation of the present paper this has been done to show where problems exist and to indicate the lines on which future work might be carried out. Confirmatory sectioning must be regarded as essential and the labelling of unsectioned axes with Group identifications is something to be strongly deprecated. In some cases, where the rock possesses really good diagnostic features, macroscopic attributions made by petrologists may be justified; made by the unskilled they are not, and there is always the danger that these identifications may creep into literature.

In Scotland it would be well worthwhile completing the distribution pattern of Group IX implements by examining specimens from other collections. On the whole, the axes are easily recognized in the hand and there should not be great difficulty in selecting those which ought to be sectioned. The obvious blank in our knowledge lies in the fact that an implement of this material has only once been found in Scotland during an excavation. Any Group IX axe from an excavation is clearly worth sectioning and the most likely place for these to be found is in the examination of monuments in Aberdeenshire and other northeastern counties. Any association which would allow of radiocarbon dating is of importance not only to Scotland but to the country as a whole.

This comment also holds good for the Shetland source where no absolute dates are available. It should be possible to obtain this from excavated sites in Shetland itself. The important point which requires clarification is the extent to which these implements were sent outside the archipelago. This is also likely to have a bearing on the relationships of the Shetland neolithic which are still obscure.

Examination of fine-grained greenstone axes needs special consideration. If the working site at Creag na Caillich was producing axes then it is likely to be difficult on first inspection to distinguish these from others coming from the Lake District. It may be that the latter can be recognized on the basis of typology allied with material, but clearly any distribution based only on macroscopic examination must be viewed with caution.

Concentration on these particular problems should provide good evidence in relatively little time to form the basis for archaeological discussion. Thereafter the problems associated with any other groups which emerge in Scotland can be tackled.

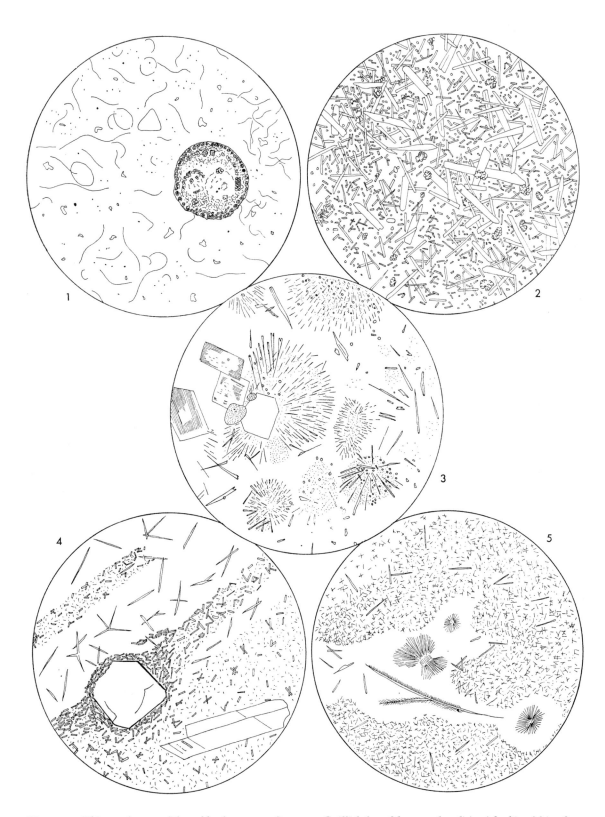

Figure 27. Thin sections. 1. Rhum bloodstone; 2. Creag na Caillich hornfels; 3. spheralitic riebeckite felsite from Beorgs of Uyea; 4. Pitchstone of Tormore/Glen Shurig type; 5. Pitchstone of Corriegills type.

Notes

1. Livens, *P.S.A.S.* XCII (1958–9) 56–70
2. Council for British Archaeology, Report No. 16 for year ended 30 June 1966, 20
3. Piggott, *Neolithic Communities of the British Isles* (1954) 295 n. 1
4. Evens, Grinsell, Piggott and Wallis, *P.P.S.* XXVIII (1962) 209–66
5. Scott, *P.S.A.S.* LXVIII (1933–4) 200–23
6. Harker, *Geology of the Small Isles of Inverness-shire* (1908) 134
7. Harker, *ibid.*
8. Gray, *P.S.A.S.* XCIII (1959–60) 236–7
9. Lacaille, *Archaeologia* XCIV (1951) 103–39
10. Scott, *P.S.A.S.* LXVIII (1933–4) 222–3
11. Scott, *P.S.A.S.* LXVI (1931–2) 199
12. Smith, *Prehistoric Man in Ayrshire* (1897) 116
13. Bryce, *P.S.A.S.* XXXVII (1902–3) 64
14. MacKie, *P.S.A.S.* XCVII (1963–4) 1–34
15. Mann, *P.S.A.S.* LII (1917–18) 140
16. Lacaille, *P.S.A.S.* LXXIX (1944–5) 86
17. MacKie, *op. cit.* (1964) 12
18. Scott, *P.P.S.* XXX (1964) 147
19. Scott, *P.S.A.S.* LXXXIX (1955–6) 38
20. Lacaille, *P.S.A.S.* LXV (1930–1) 268
21. Items BN 417 and BN 418 in the collection of the National Museum of Antiquities of Scotland
22. Tyrell, *The Geology of Arran* (1928) 224 ff.
23. Tilley, *Geol. Mag.* 94 (1957) 329–33
24. Mann, *op. cit.* (1918) 144
25. Livens, *op. cit.* (1959) 66
26. Jope, *U.J.A.* XV (1952) 31–55
27. Scott, *P.S.A.S.* LXXXV (1950–1) 36
28. Evens, Grinsell, Piggott and Wallis, *op. cit.* (1962) 233–7
29. *Radiocarbon* 3 (1961) 26–38
30. Davies, *Excavations at Island MacHugh* (1950) 22
31. Piggott (ed.), *The Prehistoric Peoples of Scotland* (1962) 11 ff.
32. Case, *U.J.A.* 26 (1963) 8
33. Piggott, *op. cit.* (1954) 295
34. Phemister, *Mineral. Mag.* XXIX (1950) 359–73
35. Hamilton, *Excavations at Jarlshof, Shetland* (1956) 16, 26
36. Calder, *P.S.A.S.* LXXXIV (1949–50) 196
37. Calder, *P.S.A.S.* LXXXIX (1955–6) 391–2
38. Calder, *P.S.A.S.* XCIV (1960–1) 42
39. Hamilton, *Excavations at Clickhimin, Shetland* (in press)
40. Calder, *P.S.A.S.* XCVI (1962–3) fig. 15
41. Gibson, *P.S.A.S.* LXXVIII (1943–4) 16–25
42. Scott and Calder, *P.S.A.S.* LXXXVI (1951–2) 174–7
43. Houlder, *P.P.S.* XXVII (1961) 108–43
44. Lacaille, *Trans. Glasgow Arch. Soc.*, n.s. IX (1940) 313–41
45. Phemister, *op. cit.* (1950) 362–4

Jet sliders in late neolithic Britain

Isla McInnes

Jet sliders form a small and distinctive group of objects which have been described as *late neolithic*[1] and *of the Early Bronze Age*.[2] There are seventeen jet sliders in Great Britain with a distribution which extends from Dorset to Skye (fig. 28). They are not found in Ireland or on the Continent, nor is there any indication of the existence of similar objects in a different medium. Jet sliders are therefore a purely British phenomenon.

Of the seventeen examples of jet slider known (see catalogue), four are stray finds, Wiltshire, Basildon, Berkshire, Skye, and Wigtownshire (?); four come from round barrows, Handley Down 26, Dorset, Aldro 177, Riggs 16 and Painsthorpe 118, Yorkshire; two come from the same sub-megalithic tomb, Gop Cave, Flintshire; one from a chambered tomb of Clyde-Solway type, Beacharra, Argyll; one from a cist, Hambleton Moor, Yorkshire, one from a burial enclosed by a double ring ditch, Linch Hill, Stanton Harcourt, Oxfordshire, and one from a long barrow, Giants' Hills, Skendelby, Lincolnshire. The three remaining examples come from circumstances which are somewhat similar. The finds from Newbury, Berkshire, Balgone, East Lothian and Glinzier, Dumfriesshire, were all made in peat deposits and Newbury and Balgone were associated with animal bones. In addition there were human bones at Balgone. It is tempting to suggest that these finds represent deliberate deposition, perhaps burials, especially in view of the animal bones with the burial in Painsthorpe 118, but this is precluded by the reference to cave bear among the bones at Newbury.

There are two further objects of jet which should perhaps be mentioned. These are both stray finds; they come from Scawton, Yorkshire[3] and Hallmyre, Newmains, Peeblesshire[4] (fig. 29, 15). Both of these objects, however, have circular openings in the centre and they are much cruder in manufacture than any of the sliders previously mentioned. In addition they both have grooved ornament.

It is possible to classify jet sliders into two groups. The first group consists of those sliders in which the width is greater than half the length. The four sliders from Linch Hill, Wiltshire (?), Aldro 177 and Hambleton Moor form this group. The central opening is wide and has rounded ends. The upper and lower faces of these sliders are concave to a greater degree than is general in Group II. The sliders in Group I are smaller than those of Group II. In Group II the central opening is sometimes pointed at the ends and the concavity of the upper and lower faces may be absent. However, as will be shown, these groups do not appear to have any cultural significance and it seems likely that the shape of the sliders was to a great degree dictated by the shape of the raw jet from which they were fashioned.

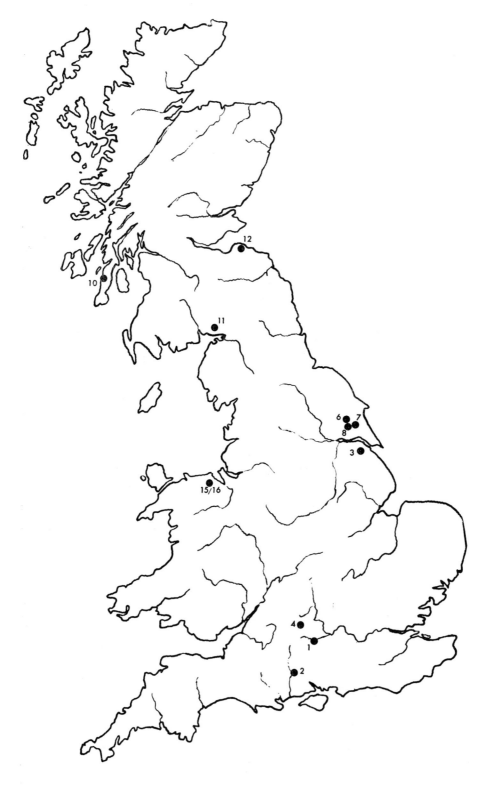

Figure 28. Distribution of jet sliders: only those sliders which have definite findspots are included.

When Pitt-Rivers excavated Handley Down 26 he found the jet object against the hip of the skeleton. When Painsthorpe 118 had been excavated previously the jet link had been found close to the pelvis of the skeleton. Pitt-Rivers suggested that although the use of the object did not appear to be very clear, 'the fact of two of them having been found on, or close to, the hip made it probable that it was used with a belt or sash',[5] the assumption being that the bodies had been buried fully clothed. From these two discoveries the jet objects now discussed have come to be known as *belt-sliders*. The writer has only examined nine of these sliders but has been unable to find evidence of wear on the inner edge of the central opening such as would be produced by the rubbing of a belt. On the contrary there is a tendency for this edge to be definitely sharp, particularly on the highly polished sliders such as that from Hambleton Moor. The sliders from Giants' Hills, Glinzier, Balgone and Wigtownshire (?) clearly show crude cutting marks on the central perforation, marks which any wear could be expected to remove. If these objects are indeed belt sliders they cannot have been worn for any period of time before deposition.

The circumstances in which these jet sliders have been found have already been mentioned, but the cultural significance of these circumstances is not at all clear. In Yorkshire, round barrows are not infrequently associated with purely neolithic material,[6] although over the rest of the country the introduction of the round barrow is a phenomenon connected with the coming of beakers.[7] The tomb at Gop Cave is classified as sub-megalithic[8] but the variety of grave-goods found in chambered tombs in Britain has shown that such tombs were connected with a variety of cultures over a period of time and the presence of sliders in a tomb does not connect the objects with a specific culture. The ring burial at Linch Hill, Stanton Harcourt, is one of a number of such burials in the vicinity which can be shown to belong to Beaker, Wessex and later cultures.[9] Unchambered long barrows are generally regarded as essentially neolithic features[10] but at Giants' Hills the jet slider is not connected with the building or use of the structure. One is therefore left with the associations to find a clue to the cultural significance of jet sliders.

The association of Peterborough pottery with the sliders at Gop Cave, Flintshire has been much mentioned.[11] Unfortunately the excavation report is not at all clear. There is no ambiguity regarding the association of the sliders with a polished flint knife; the report specifically states that these objects were found together. But of the pottery the only mention is that sherds of pottery were found in the burial chamber with fourteen bodies. The number of bodies suggests that the tomb was likely to have been used over a period of time (*viz.*, West Kennet, 40 bodies)[12] and there is the possibility that the pottery and jet sliders were deposited at different times. The skewer pin from Gop Cave[13] came from a later excavation than the jet sliders and the polished flint knife. The skewer pin is mentioned as coming from a black habitation layer but it is not possible to correlate this layer with the findings of the earlier excavation.[14]

At Handley Down 26 the evidence is more convincing. There the Peterborough pottery, of Mortlake type, was found in the make-up of the barrow and in the silting of the ditch. Although pottery did not occur in the grave itself it is likely to be contemporary with it. It is possible that the pottery represents a surface scatter which was incorporated into the barrow mound and that it antedates the erection of the barrow; but the mass of the barrow material

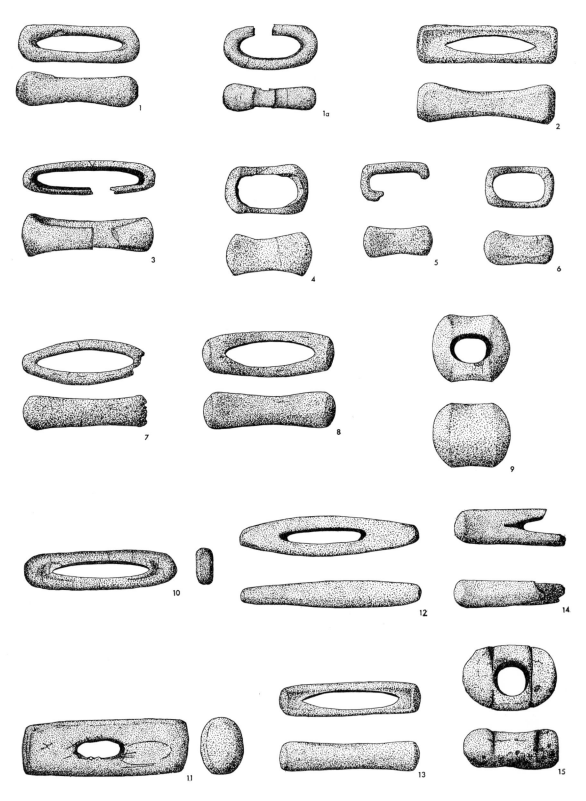

Figure 29. Jet sliders. 1. Newbury. 1a. Basildon, Berkshire. 2. Handley Down (after Pitt-Rivers). 3. Giants'
Hills. 4. Linch Hill (after Grimes). 5. Wiltshire? (after Simpson). 6. Aldro. 7. Riggs. 8. Painsthorpe. 9.
Hambledon Moor. 10. Beacharra. 11. Glinzier. 12. Balgone. 13. Skye. 14. Wigtonshire? 15. Hallmyre. (1/2)

must have come from the surrounding quarry ditches and the condition of the sherds themselves does not suggest exposure on the surface for any length of time.

There can be no doubt, however, about the association of the sliders at Gop Cave and Linch Hill with polished flint knives. Atkinson has drawn attention to the similarity between the flake knife from Aldro 177 and the polished knife from Linch Hill.[15] The flake knife from Aldro 177 was found *near* to the jet slider and although one cannot say that these finds are associated the presence of the flake knife in the same barrow as the jet slider may be significant. Atkinson likens this knife and that from Linch Hill to a knife from Dorchester and points to the occurrence of such knives with skewer pins and their neolithic contexts. Piggott also has pointed out the occurrence of polished flint knives in specifically neolithic contexts such as Duggleby Howe and Seamer, Yorkshire and Liff's Lowe, Derbyshire.[16] Piggott therefore included polished flint knives, and jet sliders, in his Dorchester culture which he regarded not as a single entity but rather as an aspect of his late neolithic cultures in general. Little can be added to Piggott's assessment of the cultural significance of jet sliders except to stress that they are a British phenomenon and that they occur in contexts which are culturally neolithic.

The importance of the date of jet sliders has recently been emphasized by Scott,[17] but the conditions of discovery of the sliders have made their dating a complex problem. As has already been shown the sliders do not come from readily datable sites and only two are clearly associated. Polished flint knives, although occurring in neolithic contexts, can also be shown to be contemporary with beakers. At Windmill Hill, Wiltshire, a polished flint knife came from Outer Ditch I at a level which also contained Mortlake, Rinyo Clacton and beaker sherds.[18] Three further polished flake implements, one with a serrated edge similar to that from Liff's Lowe,[19] came from similar levels on the causewayed camp. On the West Kennet Avenue occupation site, Wiltshire three polished flint knives occurred and, although Peterborough pottery preponderated, both Rinyo Clacton and beaker pottery were present.[20]

A date contemporary with beakers for polished flint knives and therefore for jet sliders would, of course, be in accord with the evidence from Giants' Hills, Skendelby, Lincolnshire where the jet slider came from a level in the ditch fill which the excavator equated with that of a beaker hearth.[21] There was also beaker pottery in the primary silt of the ditch. What, therefore, of the evidence from Linch Hill? There the two ditches enclosing the burial with the jet slider and the polished flint knife were cut into by a grave surrounded by its own ditch; this grave contained an inhumation accompanied by a beaker, seven barbed and tanged arrowheads and a bone pendant. Grimes, however, points out that the quantity of silting in the double ditches does not really give any indication of the time lapse between the two burials[22] and this time lapse could be fairly short.

No mention has been made of the types of beakers involved but at the time of writing the publication of Clarke's corpus of British beakers[23] is still awaited and it seems unwise to invoke a beaker classification which by the time of publication will have been superseded.

Jet sliders vary considerably in appearance but they form a distinctive type. They are found on a variety of types of site and their distribution is scattered. The relative rarity of jet sliders suggests that they were made for only a short period of time. The only site from which comes clear indication of contemporaneity between beakers and jet sliders is Giants' Hills, Lincolnshire. This site is complex in character but the existence of weathered beaker sherds in the mound indicates that the mound cannot be pre-beaker. Therefore the jet slider, which comes from the upper levels of the ditch filling, must belong to a phase some time after the arrival of beakers in Lincolnshire. It has generally come to be accepted that the arrival of beakers in Britain occurred some time in the first quarter of the second millennium.[24] A date in the second quarter of the second millennium is now suggested for the short life of jet sliders.

CATALOGUE

England

1. Newbury, Berkshire (fig. 29, 1)
Jet slider found 4 miles from Newbury 8 ft. below the surface in a bed of peat 16 ft. deep. With the slider were bones of red and roe deer and cave bear.
Length 9·3 cm.; width 1·9 cm. Highly polished
P.S.A. IV (1867–70) 521
Journal Br. Arch. Assoc. XVI (1860) 323
1a. Basildon, Berkshire (fig. 29, 1a)
Jet slider found on dump beside towpath of Thames Conservancy dredgings.
Length 5 cm.; width 2·4 cm.
Berks. Arch. J. LXI (1963–4) 99

2. Handley Down 26, Dorset (fig. 29, 2)
Jet slider found at the hip of a crouched skeleton beneath a round barrow. This burial, 8 ft. off-centre, and a central fragmentary inhumation were regarded by Pitt-Rivers as primary. The barrow was surrounded by an irregular ditch 40 ft. in diameter which was broken by a causeway on the west side. Peterborough pottery occurred in the mound and in the ditch. Beaker also occurred in the ditch, but at a higher level.
Length 7·7 cm.; width 1·9 cm. Highly polished
Pitt-Rivers, *Excavations in Cranborne Chase* IV (1898) 140

3. Giants' Hills Long Barrow, Skendelby, Lincolnshire (fig 29, 3)
Jet slider found in the upper levels of the ditch of the long barrow at a level which is equated with a beaker hearth. Beaker also occurred in the primary silting of the ditch and in the mound of the barrow.
Length 7·1 cm.; width 1·9 cm. (distorted). The edges of the central opening very crudely gouged out and unfinished
Arch. LXXXV (1936) 37–106

4. Linch Hill, Stanton Harcourt, Oxfordshire (fig. 29, 4)
Jet slider found associated with a polished flint knife accompanying a crouched skeleton in a pit at the centre of a double ring ditch. A secondary burial pit surrounded by its own ditch cut into the first double ditch. The secondary burial consisted of a crouched inhumation accompanied by a beaker, a bone pendant and seven barbed and tanged arrowheads.
Length 4·6 cm.; width 2·7 cm.
Grimes, *Excavations on Defence Sites* (1960) 154–64

5. Wiltshire (?) (fig. 29, 5)
Site unknown
Length 3·85 cm.; width 2·05 cm.
Annable and Simpson, *Cat. of the Neolithic and Bronze Age Collections in Devizes Museum* (1964) No. 131

6. Aldro 177, Yorkshire (fig. 29, 6)
Jet slider found in a quantity of dark soil about 12 in. below the surface of a round barrow. Close by was a barbed and tanged arrowhead and a small flint knife. The centre of the barrow had previously been examined by the Yorkshire Antiquarian Club and no grave was found; near the centre at the base of the barrow were the disturbed remains of two inhumations.
Length 3·85 cm.; width 2·25 cm.
Mortimer, *Forty Years' Researches* (1905) 73

7. Riggs 16, Yorkshire (fig. 29, 7)
Jet slider found nearly level with the old turf line 2 ft. south of centre beneath a round barrow. On the old turf line at the centre was a crouched inhumation of a child.
Length 7 cm.; width 1·4 cm. Highly polished
Mortimer, *Forty Years, Researches* (1905) 177

8. Painsthorpe 118, Yorkshire (fig. 29, 8)
Jet slider found near the left hip of a crouched inhumation at the base of a round barrow. There were also animal bones in the grave, which Mortimer regarded as primary. The barrow also contained a number of cremations and Food Vessel and Cinerary urn secondary burials.
Length 7·1 cm.; width 2·35 cm.
Mortimer, *Forty Years' Researches* (1905) 125–8
Arch. XLIII (1870) 315
Greenwell, *British Barrows* (1877) fig. 6

9. Hambleton Moor, N.R. Yorkshire (fig. 29, 9)
The discovery of this object is not clearly recorded. It is labelled and recorded (B.M. 82.3–23.41) as having been found in a cist with an iron spearhead. The spearhead is Anglo-Saxon. The locality of this find is also uncertain.
Length 4·15 cm.; width 3·35 cm. Highly polished
Elgee, *Early Man in North-east Yorkshire* (1930) 112

Scotland

10. Beacharra, Argyll (fig. 29, 10)
Jet slider found in the final blocking of the burial chamber of a tomb of Clyde-Solway type. In the tomb was Beacharra pottery, some of typologically late form.
Length 8·475 cm.; width 2·25 cm.
P.S.A.S. XXXVI (1901–2) 102–9
P.P.S. XXX (1964) 134–58

11. Glinzier, Dumfriesshire (fig. 29, 11)
Jet slider found, not later than 1783, 4 or 5 ft. deep in a very solid peat moss beside the Glinzier Burn, about midway between Overtown of Glinzier and Glinzier Beck Knowe, near Canonbie. (Information from Mr J. G. Scott.)
Length 9·3 cm.; width 3·175 cm. Outside brilliantly polished but central opening roughly cut and incomplete.
Unpublished; in private possession

12. Balgone, near North Berwick, East Lothian (fig. 29, 12)
Jet slider found with a number of animal and human bones deeply embedded in peat. 'Several of the animal bones appear to have been formed into cutting implements.'
Length 7·6 cm.; width 2·55 cm. Lacking final polish; cutting marks clearly visible
P.S.A.S. VI (1864–6) 107–8
P.S.A.S. L (1915–16) 221; described as from Berwickshire

13. Skye, Inverness-shire (fig. 29, 13)
Stray find of jet slider.
Length 7·6 cm.; width 1·8 cm. Highly polished
Arch. XLIII (1870)
Wilson, *Prehistoric Annals of Scotland* (1863) 441

14. Wigtownshire (?) (fig. 29, 14)
Jet slider from a collection from Castle Kennedy. Find spot unknown.
Length 6·7 cm.; width 1·9 cm. (fragment only). Highly polished outside, but central perforation clearly shows marks of cutting
Unpublished

Wales

15 and 16. Gop Cave, Flintshire (fig. 29, 15)
Two jet sliders found associated with a polished flint knife in a sub-megalithic tomb. Part of the cave was walled off to form a burial chamber which contained fourteen skeletons and fragments of Peterborough-type pottery. A later excavation of the site (1920; unpublished) produced a fragment of a skewer pin, a leaf-shaped arrowhead, scrapers and various worked flints.
Length 5·45 cm.; width 2·25 cm.
Length 7 cm.; width 2·9 cm.
Arch. J. LVIII (1901) 322–41
Arch. Camb. XC (1935) 194–200

Acknowledgments: The writer wishes to express her thanks to Miss A. Henshall for the drawing of the Beacharra slider, Mr J. G. Scott for the drawing of the Glinzier slider, Mr N. Thomas for the drawing of the Newbury slider.

Notes

1. Piggott, *Neolithic Cultures of the British Isles* (1954)
2. *Arch.* LXXXV (1936) 37–106
3. Elgee, *Early Man in North-east Yorkshire* (1930) 112, Pl. XVIII, fig. 3
4. *P.S.A.S.* L (1915–16) 221
5. Pitt-Rivers, *Excavations in Cranborne Chase* IV (1898) 140
6. Piggott, *op. cit.* 111
7. Ashbee, *Bronze Age Round Barrow in Great Britain* (1960) 15
8. Daniel, *Prehistoric Chamber Tombs of England and Wales* (1950) 46
9. Grimes, *Excavations on Defence Sites* I (1960) 144
10. Piggott, *op. cit.* 50
11. Piggott, *op. cit.* 311; Atkinson, Piggott and Sandars, *Excavations at Dorchester, Oxon.* I (1951) 72
12. Piggott, *The West Kennet Long Barrow* (1962) 24
13. Atkinson, Piggott and Sandars, *op. cit.* 143
14. Grimes, *Prehistory of Wales* (1951) 152
15. Atkinson, Piggott and Sandars, *op. cit.* 72
16. Piggott, *op. cit.* (1954) 359
17. *P.P.S.* XXX (1964) 158
18. Smith, *Windmill Hill and Avebury* (1965) 105
19. Bateman, *Vestiges of the Antiquities of Derbyshire* (1848)
20. Smith, *op. cit.* 241
21. *Arch.* LXXXV (1936) 104
22. Grimes, *op. cit.* (1960) 163
23. *P.P.S.* XXXII (1966) 367
24. (ed.) Foster and Alcock, *Culture and Environment* (1963) 163

Stone mace-heads and the latest
neolithic cultures of the British Isles

Fiona Roe

The term 'mace-head' is one that has come into use comparatively recently, having gradually replaced the older expression 'stone hammer' or 'hammer-head,' and it is now standard practice to describe as mace-heads all those stone implements with shaftholes that do not have a cutting edge. However, a detailed terminology has never been laid down for the different types of mace-head, nor has a complete survey of the material been published since Sir John Evans first listed the examples known to him in 1897.[1]

It was Reginald Smith in 1911 who first gave names to individual types such as the *cushion* and *pestle* classes,[2] and he drew attention to the morphological resemblances between perforated antler mace-heads and those made of flint and stone. Smith suggested that these implements were intended for ceremonial use, introducing the term 'mace-head' to describe them.[3]

A notable advance in the study of mace-heads was made by W. G. Gibson, who gave a full definition of the cushion type.[4] These implements do not closely resemble cushions, but the name has become assimilated into the literature, so that it is convenient to retain it. Another group of mace-heads, those which are *egg-shaped*, was discussed by Eliot Curwen in 1941.[5] In 1946 H. H. Coghlan and L. F. Chitty, in their combined note, distinguished between implements with a *curvilinear* outline and those of *angled* outline.[6] As recently as 1954, in his book *The Neolithic Cultures of the British Isles*, Professor Piggott made an important contribution to the study of mace-heads by drawing attention to the associations they have with his secondary neolithic cultures.[7] The numerous references to his book throughout this paper show the solid foundations upon which it has been possible to build new work.

The present need is for a clear system of terminology with which mace-heads may be described. The necessity for a comprehensive survey was emphasized recently, when it was found impossible to specify particular types of mace-head in the list of stone implements examined for petrological determination by the Southwestern Group of Museums and Art Galleries. To quote from their report, 'In view of the difficulties in classification, the term "mace" has been set in inverted commas.'[8] Now, some 70 years after the second edition of *Ancient Stone Implements* appeared, it is hardly too soon to consider what exactly we mean by a mace-head, what sub-groups it may be possible to distinguish, and how they fit into the palimpsest that is the prehistoric sequence in Britain. The first part of this paper is concerned with the typology of mace-heads; the second part takes account of the contexts in which some of them have been found.

The first step must be to define the implements under consideration. Whereas an axe-hammer, battle-axe or adze has a cutting edge, a mace-head is distinguished by the absence of a blade of any kind, being instead convex in shape at either end. A further detail is the occurrence of the point of maximum breadth nearer to one end of the implement, while the hole, which is typically cylindrical or near-cylindrical in shape, is placed invariably nearer the other, narrower end. The few exceptions to this asymmetrical form are the well-known mace-heads from Early Bronze Age burials in barrows, which constitute more individual types. Those from Bush Barrow[9] and Towthorpe[10] have a centrally placed hole, while that from Clandon[11] has only a slot for the shaft. It may not in fact be a mace-head. Piggott has used the term 'sceptre' for the Bush Barrow and Clandon examples.[12]

The definition of a mace-head, as given above, does not, purposefully, include those implements that are often called 'pebble mace-heads.' These consist simply of pebbles, often of quartzite, modified only by a hole of hour-glass shape through the centre. Pebbles utilized in this way were selected, as far as possible, for their regular outline, with the maximum breadth falling in the centre, in line with the hole, resulting in a form very different from that of the implements described above. They are less thick in relation to their breadth than are true mace-heads. Such 'pebble mace-heads' often exhibit marks of battering at either end, as if they had been used as hammer tools of some kind. This seems to be borne out by the traces of wear sometimes found within the hole, where the narrowest part may be polished, as though by a haft. These features are not found on the mace-heads described above. The cultural connections of the pebble implements are different too. W. F. Rankine has shown that in southeastern England they occur in mesolithic contexts,[13] although it is possible to show that others are later in date than this. Since a rather different aspect of prehistoric culture seems to be represented by these small hammer tools, it would seem wise to name them accordingly; the name '*pebble-hammer*' is suggested, so that the term '*mace-head*' may be retained for the more sophisticated forms.

If pebble-hammers are eliminated from the material under consideration, and the Early Bronze Age examples are set aside, there remain some 275 mace-heads that can be divided without difficulty into three main groups, all sharing common characteristics. Most notable is the fact that the hole is always placed approximately two-fifths of the length distant from the narrower end. Other factors are the smoothly prepared surface of each mace-head that has escaped serious weathering, and the carefully judged shape and proportions.

The first of the three groups is that comprising all *cushion* mace-heads. These are readily recognizable, being long and slender in marked contrast to the more pear-shaped form of other mace-heads. Gibson has given a detailed description of their basic characteristics[14] and the ranges of measurements within which they fall. Rather more than 50 specimens have now been traced, together with about a dozen possible prototype forms. However, the presentation of a corpus, and a fuller discussion of these implements, some of which are the most perfectly made of all mace-heads, must await further treatment, and meanwhile the present paper is concerned with the other two mace-head groups.

These are based on the valid distinction made by H. H. Coghlan and L. F. Chitty between *curvilinear* and *angled* mace-heads.[15] This is a concept that can be applied successfully to those mace-heads generally described as being of the 'pestle' type. While they are all of much the same size and proportions, it can be observed that some have an entirely rounded outline, while others have an undoubted angular shape. Those which are fully rounded or curvilinear tend to be pear-shaped or egg-shaped in outline, so that the term '*Ovoid*' mace-heads seems suitable (fig. 30, A, B, C; fig. 32). The more pestle-shaped mace-heads in this group merge gradually into more squat forms that correspond with Curwen's egg-shaped mace-heads (fig. 32, 1–5). The term '*Pestle*' mace-head has been retained for the angular forms (fig. 30, D, E; fig. 33), described correctly by Sir John Evans as 'quasi-conical' or 'a frustum of a cone with convex ends.'[16] It was Evans who first noticed the Ovoid types, pointing out how they are intermediate in form between the Pestle mace-heads proper on the one hand, and, on the other, the egg-shaped forms, but this distinction has never been followed up.

In most cases it is easy enough to tell whether a specimen should be assigned to the Ovoid or Pestle variety, but inevitably there are examples when an implement appears as though it could belong to either. It was therefore necessary to discover what the differences between Ovoid and Pestle meant in metrical terms, and so to subject all the mace-heads under discussion to a detailed metrical analysis.

Only 105 mace-heads could be used for this purpose, since, of the 210 implements so far recorded that fall into these two categories, no less than 62 are broken across the hole, so that only half or less now remains, while a further number are damaged so that they are not suitable for detailed measurement. Also excluded from the analysis were mace-heads made from nodules of flint with a natural hole, since the shape of these depends to some extent on the form of the nodule that was used. A further two specimens appear to be made of pottery.

An examination of the basic measurements and proportions of both Ovoid and Pestle mace-heads serves only to show how little they vary from one another, being remarkably standardized in their dimensions and the ratios or indices that can be obtained from them. The means for length (L), maximum breadth (B), maximum depth (D), and the diameter of the hole (H), measured as illustrated (fig. 30, B), compare well, differing only in the fact that the Pestle mace-heads are, on average, rather less broad and thick. (The figures are given in Appendix I.) This point is reflected in the ratios breadth : length (B/L), depth : length (D/L) and depth : breadth (D/B); the Pestle mace-heads have slightly lower values. The position of the hole, indicated by the ratio Li/L, is virtually the same in both classes, varying neither with shape nor size.

It is with a more detailed examination of the proportions of Ovoid and Pestle mace-heads that the differences between them become apparent. Altogether some 1040 measurements were taken, and 1248 ratios calculated, so that the most useful results could be selected from the data then available. The position of the maximum breadth can be expressed by the ratio L_2/L, where L_2 is the distance between the point of maximum breadth and the broader end of the implement (fig. 30, A, C, D, E). All true Pestle mace-heads have the greatest breadth close to the wider end of the implement, giving low measurements for L_2 (fig. 30, D, E), and correspondingly low values for L_2/L. With the Ovoid mace-heads, the greatest breadth is considerably nearer to the hole (fig. 30, A, C), with correspondingly higher values for L_2/L. (The figures are given in Appendix I.) All the values for L_2/L, when plotted as a histogram (fig. 30, F), give an apparently bi-modal distribution. It was found that the position of the maximum depth, expressed by L_3/L, followed the same rule, but to a less great extent. (See

Appendix I.) So it is in terms of values for L2/L that the difference between Ovoid and Pestle mace-heads can best be demonstrated.

However, as mentioned above, Pestle mace-heads have on average a less great thickness in relation to length (expressed by D/L) than those of Ovoid type; the Ovoid mace-heads, though, possess a wider range of values for D/L. These points are brought out by plotting the values for L2/L against those for D/L on a scatter diagram (fig. 31). The two main classes fall into two separate areas.

The next question that arises is whether these two mace-head classes can be sub-divided in any way. With the Pestle mace-heads there are no obvious variations that can be demonstrated metrically; the emphasis is rather on the homogeneity of the group. An observation that can be made subjectively however, is that some of these mace-heads, as seen in plan, have a *concave*, waisted outline, with the minimum breadth falling in line with the hole (fig. 30, E; fig. 33, 8–14), while others have an outline that is slightly *convex* or almost straight-sided, and

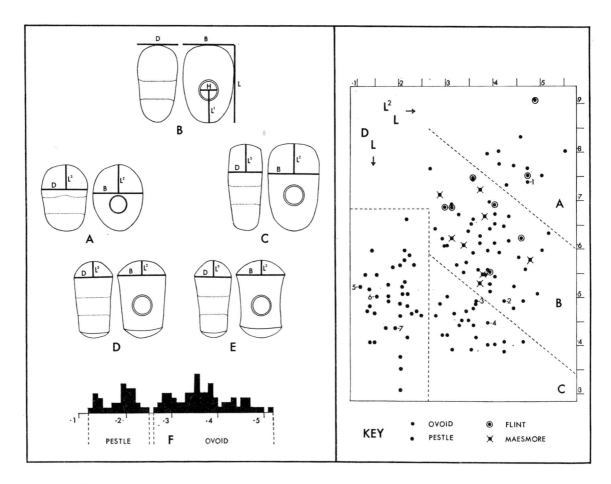

Figure 30. Ovoid and Pestle Mace-heads drawn according to the means for the different groups.
A, B, C: Ovoid Mace-heads; D, E: Pestle Mace-heads; F, Histogram, L2/L. (1/4)
Figure 31. Scatter diagram, D/L : L2/L.
Associated Mace-heads: 1. Garrowby Wold; 2. Stonehenge; 3, Tormore; 4. Ormiegill; 5. Taversoe Tuick; 6 Doune; 7. Isbister.

the minimum breadth at the narrower end (fig. 30, D; fig. 33, 1–7). When these two groups are mapped, it can be seen that the concave type occurs for the most part in Scotland, with a number from Shetland and Orkney (fig. 34), while the more convex variety has a more southern distribution, with a number that have been found in the Thames, although a few are known from Scotland, including Orkney. Appropriate names for these sub-groups would seem to be the '*Orkney*' and '*Thames*' types respectively.

In considering the Ovoid mace-heads, a point that is immediately apparent from the scatter diagram is that they are much more numerous than the Pestle variety, and with a wider range of shapes. Those with the highest values for both D/L and L2/L, at the top of the diagram, are the most squat, egg-shaped forms (fig. 30, A); at the other end of the scale come more elongated specimens, quite different in appearance (fig. 30, C), while the majority of the Ovoid mace-heads fall between these two extremes (fig. 30, B). Thus three sub-divisions seem possible. These have been made of necessity in an arbitrary fashion, indicated by the dotted lines drawn across the scatter diagram.

The first division has been named the 'Ovoid A' group, and includes mace-heads shaped not unlike large hens' eggs, such as those of Curwen's egg-shaped type (fig. 32, 1–5). It can be seen that, although not common, they are all very much alike. They can be further defined by the fact that they are all shorter than average, and proportionally both broader and thicker. (The figures are given in Appendix II.)

These egg-shaped examples merge into the second, middle group, 'Ovoid B' (fig. 32, 6–17). These are all generally standard in shape and size, with means that correspond with those given for all Ovoid mace-heads, though the specimen from Stonehenge (fig. 32, 16) is unusually small.

Thirdly come mace-heads that are more elongated in shape, the 'Ovoid C' group (fig. 32, 18–25). These are less thick than average, and often longer as well. An example from Kirkwhelpington, Northumberland is 5·4 inches in length, though well proportioned.

These three sub-divisions enable the Ovoid mace-heads to be considered in a more detailed perspective. For instance, it can be seen that the mace-heads of naturally perforated flint, of which eight complete examples have been recorded, belong to the Ovoid A and B groups only (fig. 31; fig. 32, 9). Such mace-heads have been recovered largely from the Thames in the London area (fig. 34). Some have been barely modified from their original form, while others have been partly polished and flaked into the correct shape.[17] The flaking is often neatly done in a manner that is reminiscent of the ornamentation of the faceted stone mace-heads,[18] of which the example from Maesmore is perhaps the best known[19] (fig. 37). Other faceted mace-heads come from Quarnford, Staffordshire[20] (fig. 38), Airdens, Sutherland[21] (fig. 35, A), and Urquhart, Moray[22] (fig. 35, B). All appear to be made of light-coloured flint, with holes that are artificially made. These four implements have an ovoid, rounded outline, as seen in plan, but are more angular in profile, with flattened surfaces on the top and bottom, and a characteristic *squared* section. They compare closely with one another in metrical terms, and may be regarded as a sub-division of the Ovoid B group.

There are another four mace-heads that compare well with the examples in this '*Maesmore*' group, both in general outline and squared section, though none is ornamented. These come from Laverstock, Wiltshire,[23] Mold Rural, Flintshire,[24] Tinwald, Dumfriesshire[25] (fig. 36, B)

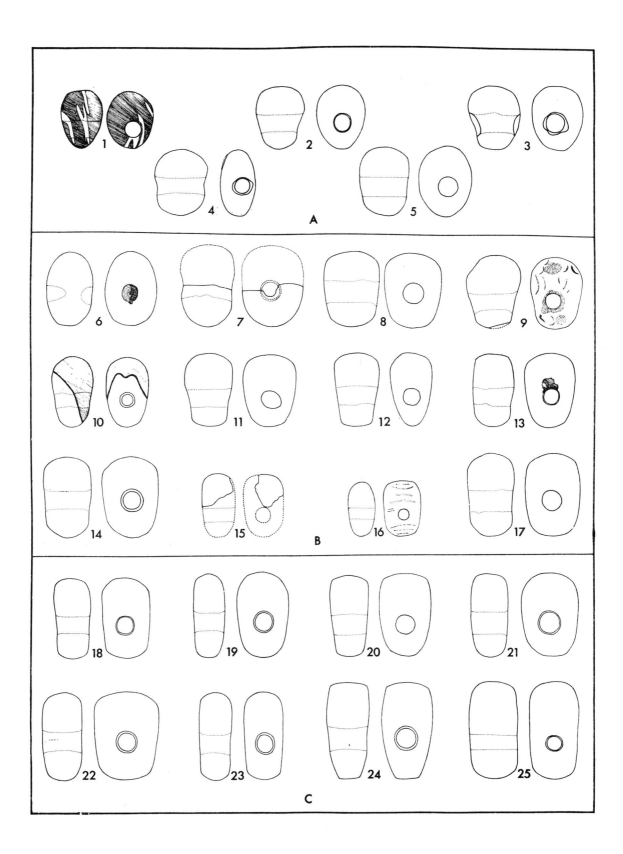

and White Hill, Rafford, Moray[26] (fig. 36, A). They are made of quartzite or sandstone, no doubt chosen in the three latter examples for the attractive red colouring of the stone. (See also fig. 32, 1, 10, 13, and fig. 33, 9.)

A final mace-head which may be assigned to this small but interesting Maesmore group is a fragment from the Upper levels at Windmill Hill.[27] This has been previously assigned to the cushion type,[28] which indeed it appears at a first glance to resemble. However, if reconstructed, it would be somewhat broader than is usual for such implements. In addition, the side has a greater degree of curvature than is found on cushion mace-heads, while the section shows a squared corner, offering a strong suggestion that it should belong to the Maesmore group. This Windmill Hill mace-head is the only one so far recorded as being made of Group VII rock. It is interesting that two of the examples in the Maesmore group are provenanced from north Wales, an area where mace-head finds are not abundant (fig. 34).

The matter of reconstructing mace-heads is considerably more important than one might expect, since there are no less than four fragmentary examples, discussed below in the light of their associations, which have come from domestic sites, while other broken ones are made of Grouped rocks, useful for dating purposes on account of the associations they have elsewhere. As already mentioned, a large number of mace-heads survive only in part; altogether some 29·6% are not complete. By comparison, only 16·7% of battle-axes are mere broken halves. The implication would seem to be that some, at least, of the mace-heads were broken intentionally. It was J. G. Callander who first noticed the large proportion of broken mace-heads from Orkney,[29] and here damaged specimens account for 75% of the 24 Ovoid and Pestle specimens from the archipelago. However, even excluding the Orkadian examples, there are still some 23·7% of broken mace-heads from the rest of Britain.

While an intimate knowledge of a large number of mace-heads is valuable for the purposes of reconstruction, the tables of means given in the appendices are also essential. In particular, use can be made of Li/L, which varies very little, to determine the approximate length of a fragment. If it is the broader end of a mace-head that survives, the ratio L2/B will indicate whether it is of the Pestle or Ovoid variety, though the distinction is less exact than that obtained from L2/L. The mace-head reconstructions included on figs. 32 and 33 have been drawn as far as possible within one standard deviation of the means for Pestle or Ovoid mace-heads, as appropriate.

The half mace-head from Cam (see below) is slightly broader and thicker than average, but seems to belong within the Ovoid B group (fig. 32, 7), though it cannot be far removed from those of Ovoid A type. It can be compared with an example from Gordon, Berwickshire

Figure 32. Ovoid Mace-heads (1/4).
A. 1. Friston, Sussex; 2. Faldingworth, Lincs.; 3. Wigtownshire; 4. Longtown, Cumberland; 5. Garrowby Wold, E.R. Yorks.
B. 6. West Linton, Peebles; 7. Cam, Glos.; 8. Gordon, Berwicks.; 9. River Thames, Windsor; 10. St Andrews, Fife; 11. Hotham, E.R. Yorks.; 12, Ipswich, Suffolk; 13. Breadsall, Derby; 14. Methlick, Aberdeens.; 15. Rinyo, Orkney; 16. Stonehenge, Wilts.; 17. Low Burnham, Lincs.
C. 18. Sound of Harris, Inverness.; 19. Chirnside, Berwicks.; 20. Tormore, Arran; 21. Auchterless, Aberdeens.; 22. Fyvie, Aberdeens.; 23. Dunscore, Dumfries; 24. Ormiegill, Caithness; 25. Legsby, Lincs.

(fig. 32, 8), and one thought to come from Shefford, Berkshire.[30] The hour-glass-shaped hole is very narrow, and it seems that the mace-head broke in two before this was completed.

From Skara Brae and Rinyo come two small fragments, and the reconstruction of these can only be of a tentative nature. That from the former site (fig. 33, 6) appears to belong to the Pestle variety, and is not unlike one from Henley (fig. 33, 7). The Rinyo fragment (fig. 32, 15) seems to be part of a small Ovoid mace-head.

The first part of this paper ends with details about the holes of mace-heads, and the ways in which they were made. A feature that is unknown on stone implements with shaftholes, save on mace-heads of the Ovoid and Pestle varieties, is an internal widening of the hole. This occurs on some 39·2%, usually, though not invariably, being found towards the wider end of the implement. Eliot Curwen[31] observed this phenomenon within the hole of the mace-head from Friston, Sussex (fig. 32, 1), but otherwise this is a detail that seems to have escaped notice.

A practical explanation is hard to find. However, mace-heads of antler, which seem likely precursors for those made of stone, have holes that are internally hollowed in the same way, the reason being perhaps connected with the fact that the cancellous tissue is softer in the area through which the shafthole passes. These antler mace-heads will be discussed further below in connection with the associations in which they have been found.

It is interesting that the mace-heads with the highest incidence of internal hollowing of the hole (see Appendix II) are those in the Maesmore group. It has long been realized that there must be some relationship between the faceted stone mace-heads and ones made of antler with similar decoration, of which well-known examples have been found in the Thames at Teddington,[32] and at Liff's Low, Derbyshire,[33] while others have been found in the Thames.[34] On the other hand, the mace-head types with the lowest incidence of internal concavity of the hole are the Ovoid C and Orkney Pestle groups, both of which would appear to be late on typological grounds.

Disregarding the feature of internal concavity, the holes of Ovoid and Pestle mace-heads are for the most part straight-sided, or at least approximately cylindrical, sometimes with slightly widened ends, while a small proportion are gently waisted. (See Appendix II.) The mean minimum diameter is around three-quarters of an inch, a size which compares well with the holes of battle-axes. The holes of Pestle mace-heads tend to be more exactly straight than those of the Ovoid variety, a fact which probably has chronological connotations. It would seem likely that those of a precise cylindrical shape were made with a metal, tubular borer,[35] and others too that are less exactly made, though no evidence survives in proof of this. A straight-sided but funnel-shaped hole, seen for instance on the Doune mace-head (fig. 33, 10), would have been caused by an excessive use of sand with the metal borer.[36] Such few unfinished holes as survive suggest rather that they were made by a pecking and grinding process, being conical in shape (fig. 32, 6), so evidently less advanced methods of boring were also used. It is among the mace-heads of Cushion type, which are probably later than the Ovoid and Pestle types, that the most perfectly made cylindrical holes are to be found.

In considering the various contexts in which mace-heads have been found, and the cultural connections which these would seem to imply, one difficulty already encountered is that the four mace-heads from non-funerary contexts are all fragmentary, while another is the paucity of direct associations, the majority requiring treatment of a most generalized nature. Where the potential associated finds are many and varied, attention will be drawn to those most useful for making wider comparisons. The actual finds of mace-heads in meaningful contexts are so few that they may be considered individually.

1. Ovoid A. BARROW C 69, GARROWBY WOLD, E.R. YORKSHIRE[37] (fig. 32, 5)
This mace-head was mistakenly recorded by Mortimer as 'a portion of an egg-shaped hammer,' for it is complete. It came from the barrow material, and should therefore be not later than the latest additions to it, while more probably it may antedate the barrow construction. The primary burials included three inhumations associated with Food Vessels; two cinerary urns contained secondary cremations. The mace-head itself is made of Group XVIII quartz dolerite from the Whin Sill area, which was used also for making battle-axes of all kinds.[38]

2. Ovoid B. LOWER KNAPP FARM, CAM, GLOUCESTERSHIRE[39] (fig. 32, 7)
This mace-head, of which only half now remains, was found in one of two pits, both of which yielded sherds which, Dr Isobel Smith kindly informs me, can be classified as Fengate Ware. The other finds from these pits consisted of pieces of burnt daub, two small flint flakes, various rock fragments, and animal bones, mostly of domestic animals.

3. Ovoid B? RINYO, ROUSAY, ORKNEY[40] (fig. 32, 15)
A mace-head fragment was found before Childe's excavations had started, in the doorway of chamber G. Though not entirely a secure stratification, this should relegate it to the third phase of occupation at the site, Rinyo II. To the same phase belongs a Late Northern British beaker, approximating to a late version of a Short Necked beaker, according to the recent analysis by D. L. Clarke.[41] Other finds from the site, besides the pottery, are well known, and include a polished edge flint knife, a flint fabricator, small button scrapers, and small sub-triangular stone axe blades.

4. Ovoid B, Maesmore group. WINDMILL HILL, AVEBURY, WILTSHIRE[42]
A third fragmentary mace-head from a non-funerary context comes from the Upper levels of the Inner ditch at Windmill Hill. Finds which should be broadly contemporary with this mace-head have wide cultural affinities. Pottery from the Upper levels includes late neolithic wares of the Mortlake, Fengate and Rinyo-Clacton styles; beaker sherds are mainly of the Long Necked variety, Developed and Final Southern British types according to the new terminology.[43] The flint work that goes with this pottery has been divided by Isobel Smith into three groups, comprising beaker types, late neolithic types, and those that do not belong obviously to either of these groups. Among the two latter groups are included transverse arrowheads, tools with polished edges, fabricators, partly polished adzes, plano-convex knives and serrated flakes or saws.[44] Noteworthy from the bone and antler industries is part of a bone pin with a lateral loop that belongs to Piggott's Rinyo-Clacton type ii.[45]
　The mace-head itself has added interest as it is made of Group VII stone from Graig Lwyd. Other grouped rocks that occur in the Upper levels include Groups I, VI and XIII.[46]

5. Ovoid B. STONEHENGE, WILTSHIRE[47] (fig. 32, 16)
The mace-head from Stonehenge was found with one of a number of cremations on the inner side of the bank. These form part of a cremation cemetery discovered by Col. Hawley in the 1920s, scattered in the bank and ditch. This cemetery, together with the Aubrey Holes, has been assigned to the first phase of the monument. Finds associated with these cremations include four Rinyo-Clacton type i skewer pins, flint fabricators, and a cup of Rinyo-Clacton type, while a sherd of Rinyo-Clacton ware, found at the bottom of the ditch, also belongs to Stonehenge I. Chips of Prescelly stone, along with beaker sherds, both of which have been assigned to the second phase of the monument, first appear in the secondary ditch silt, about halfway up. The beaker sherds have been classified by Clarke as belonging to his Developed Southern British type, approximating to Long Necked beakers.[48] Some of the cremations from the ditch, the exact position of which was never recorded, appear to have been at this level or even higher, so that some at least must belong to Stonehenge II. Also attributed to this phase is part of an axe made of Group I greenstone.[49]

6. Ovoid C. TORMORE CISTS, MAUCHRIE MOOR, ARRAN, BUTE[50] (fig. 32, 20)
The Tormore mace-head came from the north chamber of a Clyde-Carlingford tomb. In the same chamber were found a polished edge knife, two plano-convex flint knives, and a sherd of Rinyo-Clacton pottery.

7. Ovoid C. ORMIEGILL, ULBSTER, CAITHNESS[51] (fig. 32, 24)
This mace-head is of a slightly aberrant shape, with the narrower end flattened rather than rounded. It was found embedded in the floor of a short-horned cairn of Camster type. Though it cannot be directly linked with any of the other finds from this chambered tomb, it may be noted that these include three transverse arrowheads and part of a polished edge knife.

8. Pestle, Thames type? SKARA BRAE, ORKNEY[52] (fig. 33, 6)
The fragmentary mace-head from Skara Brae came as a loose find from the site before Childe's excavations, but, as Piggott has already stated, there seems no reason to disassociate it from some phase of the occupation.[53] Of the many and varied objects that come from this settlement, those with wider connotations, besides the pottery, include a polished edge flint knife, small button scrapers, stone axes, an antler mace-head or haft and bone pins of distinctive types.

9. Pestle, Orkney type. ISBISTER, S. RONALDSAY, ORKNEY[54] (fig. 33, 12)
This finely made mace-head was found as part of a cache in the cairn material of a chambered tomb of derivative Camster type. With it were three small, triangular stone axes and a polished knife of pink chert. A V-bored jet button was found near them.

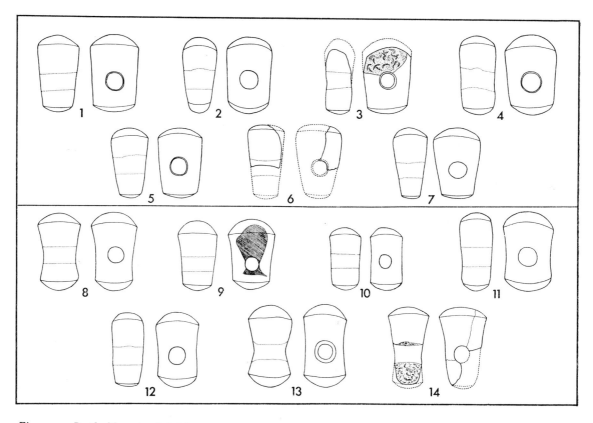

Figure 33. Pestle Mace-heads (1/4).
Thames type : 1. Thames, Richmond, Surrey; 2. Cold Ash, Berkshire; 3. Newport, Pembrokeshire; 4. Isle of Rum, Inverness; 5. Thames, Kingston, Surrey; 6. Skara Brae, Orkney; 7. Thames, Henley, Berks.
Orkney type : 8. Scotland? 9. Castleton, Derby; 10. Doune, Perthshire; 11. Culloden, Nairn: 12. Isbister, Orkney; 13. Lunnasting, Shetland; 14. Taversoe Tuick, Orkney.

10. Pestle, Orkney type. TAVERSOE TUICK, ROUSAY, ORKNEY[55] (fig. 33, 14)
The fourth Scottish chambered tomb in which a mace-head has been found belongs to Audrey Henshall's Bookan type. As at Ormiegill, the mace-head cannot be directly related with any of the other finds from the tomb. The quantities of Unstan ware should probably belong to earlier deposits. Among the finds of probable later date are fragments of an undecorated 'beaker-like vessel.' Of interest is a knife of approximate plano-convex form, and made of the same pink chert that was used for a knife at Isbister.[56] A group of grey shale beads resemble ones from Yarrows, where they are presumed to be of beaker date, being found with a vessel, now lost, with twisted cord decoration.[57]

11. Pestle, Orkney type. GLENHEAD FARM, DOUNE, PERTHSHIRE[58] (fig. 33, 10)
This mace-head is small and neatly made from veined black and white stone. It was associated with a Yorkshire Vase Food Vessel, both being found in a cist under a cairn.

To these associations may be added a further four mace-heads recorded to date made of the Cornish Group I greenstone, and one made of Group XIII Prescelly stone. This is a Thames Pestle mace-head (fig. 33, 3) found not far from the source of the material, at Newport, Pembrokeshire.[59] One of the Group I mace-heads, from Purlogue, Shropshire,[60] is of the Ovoid variety, and though damaged, it seems to be of the Ovoid C type. The other three specimens are all Pestle mace-heads of the Thames variety, one a complete example from Cold Ash, Berkshire[61] (fig. 33, 2), the second a fragment from Santon Warren West, Norfolk,[62] apparently very like that from Cold Ash, while the third is a broken half with secondary cup marks from Deptford, Wylye, Wiltshire.[63] It is not certain whether this last example originally had a shafthole; it may have been no more than an implement of pestle shape, similar to one also made of Group I rock from the barrow material at Collingbourne Ducis G.10, where the primary burial was a cremation with an antler mace-head or hammer.[64]

With all these 'associated' finds, certain recurrent themes may be detected; from them may be devised a 'Mace-head Complex,' with a hard core consisting of the objects or petrological materials appearing most frequently in mace-head contexts.

Mace-heads occur most often as grave-goods, in Scotland the most common rite being that of deposition in chambered tombs, which, in three cases out of four, belong to the Orkney-Cromarty group.

The pottery most frequently associated with mace-heads is that included under the heading of 'Rinyo-Clacton' or 'Grooved Ware,' which is probably contemporary in five instances. Fengate Ware is present at two sites. The best guide to the contemporaneity of the Mace-head Complex with the later part of the beaker cultures is the Late Northern British beaker from Rinyo. According to the recent valuable work by D. L. Clarke, this should not be far removed in date from the Developed Southern British Beaker in the ditch filling at Stonehenge,[65] and it is Developed and Final Southern Beaker that are present in quantity in the Upper levels at Windmill Hill. The V-bored button from Isbister should also belong to the later part of the beaker cultures.[66]

Turning to flint and stone industries, the most striking feature is the use of Group I greenstone, both for mace-heads and for the fragments of stone axes found at Windmill Hill and Stonehenge. Group XIII preselite, used for one mace-head, is also recorded from the same two sites.

Flint knives with polished edges are known from five mace-head sites; only that from Tormore is directly associated, but the knife of pink chert from Isbister appears to be an analogous type. Only at Tormore are plano-convex knives directly associated, while others come from Windmill Hill, and the implement of pink chert at Taversoe Tuick seems to belong to the same category. Common though less distinctive are flint fabricators, often of the variety with a lozenge-shaped section. Transverse arrowheads are recorded only from Windmill Hill and Ormiegill. The small triangular axes from Isbister compare well with ones from Skara Brae and Rinyo.

Pins of bone or antler are significant. Skewer pins of type i were found with cremations at Stonehenge, and part of a type ii pin came from Windmill Hill. Both types occurred at Skara Brae.

Having defined a Mace-head Complex so far as this is possible, it is useful to take a wider look at some of the basic components within it. First may be considered sites, other than those already mentioned, that have produced Rinyo-Clacton pottery. Some 90 findspots are now known to the writer, double the number recorded by Piggott in 1954.[67] Clearly this additional material calls for a detailed survey, and a reconsideration of the different pottery styles, so that at present only comments of a general nature can be made. Nothing will be said of possible differences between northern and southern provinces within the Rinyo-Clacton culture. The basic distribution pattern has not altered, with 72% of the finds from southeastern England, a few from Yorkshire, and a scatter in southern Scotland, as well as the Orkadian sites. Considering that much of northern England and Scotland consists of Highland areas, and that finds of both Rinyo-Clacton pottery and mace-heads are confined to Lowland areas, the two distributions do not compare altogether unfavourably, excepting in Aberdeenshire, an area especially rich in mace-heads, but lacking in pottery finds. However, it is difficult to judge to what extent the known distribution of Rinyo-Clacton ware is the reflection of the poor survival capacity of this pottery. As Isobel Smith has pointed out, 'This soft, friable ware is extremely perishable, and the sherds that have chanced to survive may represent only a fraction of the original deposits' (at Windmill Hill).[68]

It would be premature to attempt a detailed analysis of the finds associated with this pottery, but it can be shown that these correspond broadly with the main elements of the Mace-head Complex. There is evidence for the presence of beaker wares of different varieties at many of the sites producing Rinyo-Clacton pottery, but only rarely can it be demonstrated that they are closely contemporary. Recent excavations at West Overton barrow G.6b have suggested that a specific style of Rinyo-Clacton ware was a little earlier than the Developed Southern (Long Necked) beaker that accompanied the primary burial.[69] Further north, recent excavations at Green Low, Derbyshire, have revealed Rinyo-Clacton ware in association with beaker sherds reported to be probably of Maritime type, which would correspond with Clarke's early European Bell Beaker group.[70] At Beacon Hill, Flamborough, a sherd of Rinyo-Clacton ware also appeared to be contemporary with European Bell Beaker, as well as the All Over Cord (Cord Zoned) version, again suggesting an early date.[71] In the chambered tomb of Unival, a 'Rinyo I' dish was considered to be earlier than an undecorated beaker of early type, belonging to the All Over Cord or European Bell Beaker groups.[72]

Associations such as these give a possible range of about 600 years for the use of Rinyo-Clacton pottery. However, the beaker finds within the Mace-head Complex, such as they are, seem to suggest that this complex belongs only to the *later* part of the beaker cultures. In the

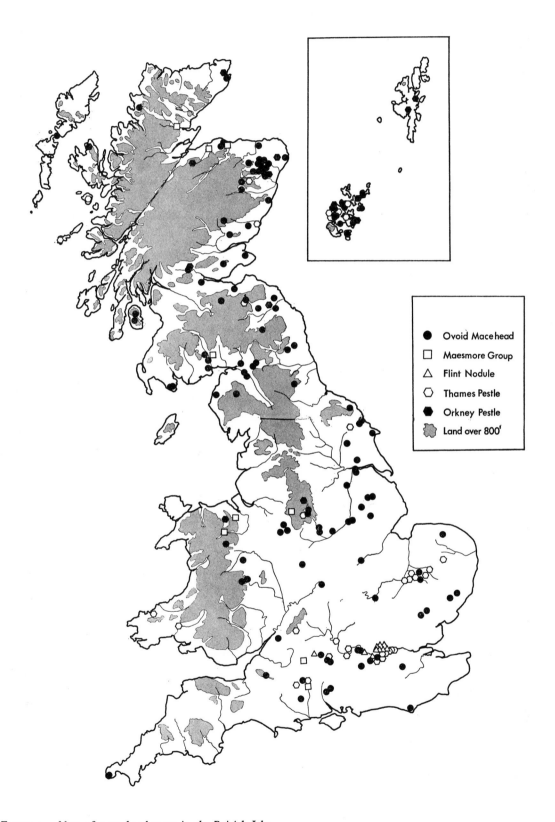

Figure 34. Map of mace-head types in the British Isles.

same way, while Rinyo-Clacton pottery is known in loose association with Mortlake ware, notably at Orton Longueville,[73] Edingthorpe and Icklingham (two sherds),[74] this pottery style does not, from the evidence available, form part of the Mace-head Complex. Fengate ware on the other hand, which is firmly associated with a mace-head at Cam, has been found with Rinyo-Clacton pottery also at Icklingham, and again at Lawford, Essex,[75] and West Overton, Wiltshire,[76] and this ware should be of a generally later date than that of the Mortlake style.[77] A Mortlake bowl from Pit 12 at Grimes Graves has a carbon date of 1870 ± 150 (B.M.97).[78]

Petrological associations with Rinyo-Clacton ware include only one find with Langdale stone, at Beacon Hill, Flamborough,[79] while Graig Lwyd stone is associated at Woodlands,[80] and at the occupation site on the West Kennet Avenue.[81] Group I greenstone has been recorded to date from Woodhenge,[82] Lion Point, Clacton,[83] and Poundbury, Dorset.[84]

The flintwork found with Rinyo-Clacton pottery is that characteristic of Piggott's secondary neolithic cultures, and includes polished edge knives, plano-convex knives, transverse arrow-heads, fabricators, serrated flakes, and flakes made from partly polished flint axes. Dr Isobel Smith has noted in her thesis that among the flint implements associated with Peterborough ware in southeastern England 'there is not a single association with a type defined by Piggott as Secondary Neolithic,' while outside this area such associations are rare, though some occur with typologically late pottery,[85] as at Gop Cave.[86]

Thus there seems to be a distinction between finds associated with Peterborough pottery, and those found with Rinyo-Clacton ware and mace-heads, though the Fengate pottery style seems to be common to both divisions.

Skewer pins, of the types that occur three times within the Mace-head Complex, have already been listed,[87] and only one addition can be made, the tip of a pin, possibly of this type, from the occupation site on the West Kennet Avenue, where it was associated with Rinyo-Clacton, Beaker and Peterborough sherds.[88] A skewer pin of type i was associated with the mace-head from cremation 21 at Dorchester Site II, along with a flint fabricator.[89] This mace-head has been omitted so far from the discussion, since on statistical grounds it appears to relate more closely to the Cushion type than to the Ovoid variety, having a very low depth: breadth index. It can be described as a 'proto-cushion' mace-head. It is striking how similar the context of this mace-head is to that of the one found at Stonehenge, as they both come from cremation cemeteries in monuments of henge type, with contemporary bone pins and closely comparable flint fabricators.

Skewer pins are also known to be contemporary with mace-heads of antler, as shown below. Another noteworthy occurrence is at Cairnpapple, where two type i skewer pins were found with cremations of the first phase of the monument, contemporary with Langdale and Graig Lwyd stone,[90] and earlier than Northern British/North Rhine and Developed Northern (Short Necked) beakers.[91]

It is also instructive to examine the contexts of the finds so far recorded of stone of Groups I, VI, VII and XIII. Group VI has partly Middle Neolithic associations; it was found, for instance, in the Lower levels at Windmill Hill,[92] and its use seems, from the evidence available, to have little connection with the Mace-head Complex. It is found, as already mentioned, with Rinyo-Clacton and beaker wares at Beacon Hill, and with skewer pins and

Graig Lwyd stone at Cairnpapple. At North Deighton there are loose associations with Group VII stone, a polished edge flint knife, and Peterborough pottery of the Ebbsfleet and Mortlake varieties.[93] All these associations should antedate the Mace-head Complex. At Windmill Hill, where Langdale stone also occurs in the Upper levels, no precise dating can be attempted. However, distribution maps show concentrations of Langdale axes in the Lake District and southern Scotland,[94] where a number of Ovoid mace-heads have also been found (fig. 34), so that the possibility of some connection between the two need not be discounted.

The use of Group VII augite granophyre too goes back to the Middle Neolithic; sites probably attributable to this period have been recorded in Wales not far from the factory.[95] Carbon-14 dates that can be related to axes from Upware, of c. 2700–2200 B.C.,[96] and from Shapwick Heath, of 2580±130 (Q.430)[97] are in agreement with such finds. Associations of a general nature with Mortlake and Western Neolithic pottery are known from Bryn yr Hen Bobl,[98] and with Ebbsfleet and Mortlake wares at North Deighton. Belonging to a later date probably is the mace-head of Group VII rock from Windmill Hill, where there is a date from the Upper levels of 1540±150 (B.M.-75). Group VII is also recorded from Cairnpapple, at Woodlands with Rinyo-Clacton pottery, and from the West Kennet occupation site.

By contrast, the first use of Group I greenstone need not be earlier than the Late Neolithic. Apart from the finds of actual mace-heads, and its occurrence at Windmill Hill and Stonehenge, it has been found three times in association with Rinyo-Clacton pottery, while an axe from the West Kennet Avenue comes probably from the occupation site there.[99] Group I was also used for making battle-axes, specifically of the earlier types (Stages II and III), which elsewhere are associated with Long Necked or Southern Beakers, and Food Vessels; a Group I rubber was included in the grave-goods with the battle-axe burials at Upton Lovell barrow 2a.[100]

Group XIII preselite has been recorded less widely. Besides its use for a Pestle mace-head, and at Stonehenge, and the find in the Upper levels at Windmill Hill, three early (Stage II) battle-axes made of it have so far been identified, giving the same links with Beakers and Food Vessels as for Group I.

Before considering whether it may be possible to make chronological deductions with regard to a mace-head series, attention must be paid to the mace-heads of antler. These are few in number, their discovery being limited almost entirely to finds from barrows and rivers, and in particular the Thames, so that no real evidence for their original distribution pattern is available. A number belong to a distinct type, in which the lower, burr or crown end of the antler is utilized, with the brow tine removed. It is suggested that this variety should be known as 'Crown' antler mace-heads. Points to observe are that these implements, like those of stone, are wider towards one end, and have the hole placed rather nearer the other (narrower) end. They also have a greater breadth than thickness. There seems to be a resemblance between the burr end of an antler mace-head, and the shaped end of a Pestle mace-head, while there is reason to suppose that the concave-sided form of the Orkney Pestle mace-heads could have been inspired from the same source.

A complete survey of Crown antler mace-heads has not been attempted, but it can be noted that in general principles they compare well with the stone examples, though tending to be larger, and with a greater breadth relative to length and depth. There is also the connection

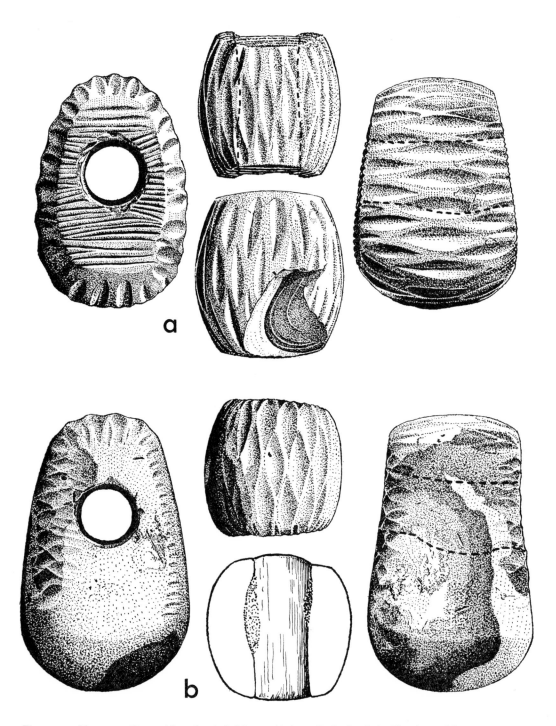

Figure 35. Maesmore Group Mace-heads (1/1). a. Airdens, Sutherland. b. Urquhart, Moray.

between the ornamented mace-heads of the Maesmore group and those made of antler decorated with a similar lattice-work of lozenges. Another possible shared trait, consisting of internal hollowing of the hole, has already been suggested.

Table 1 gives the finds recorded in direct association with, or else demonstrably broadly contemporary with, various Crown antler mace-heads from inhumation burials in barrows. These were included in his Dorchester Culture by Professor Piggott, who has discussed the finds in greater detail.[101]

Table 1

	Barrow, round or oval	Inhumation	Flint axe	Polished edge knife	Plano-convex knife	Lozenge arrowhead	Transverse arrowhead	Leaf-shaped arrowhead	Boars' tusks	Skewer pins type i	Skewer pins type ii	Yorkshire Neolithic Pottery	Beaker sherds	Food Vessel sherds	Miscellaneous pottery	Cremations
Ayton E. Field, Seamer Moor, N.R.Yorks.	×	?	×	×	×	×			×							
Howe Hill, Duggleby, E.R.Yorks.	×	×	×	○		×	○		○	○	○	?				○
Cowlam barrow lvii, E.R.Yorks.	×	×						○	○	?		○	○	○		
Liff's Low, Biggin, Derby	×	×	×	×					×						×	
Crosby Garrett, barrow clxxiv, Westmorland	×	×							○	?	○					○
Cop Heap Hill, Warminster, Wilts.	×	×	×													?

× = direct association ○ = probably contemporary ? = uncertain association

The various objects recorded in this table may be divided into two groups. First are articles included in the Mace-head Complex: skewer pins, and flint implements such as polished edge knives, plano-convex knives and transverse arrowheads. In two instances, cremations, after the manner of those at Stonehenge and Dorchester, are present. The second group consists of finds that are more distinctive of these particular grave-groups, such as the chipped and polished flint axes, and the lozenge-shaped arrowheads. Boars' tusks frequently occur, twice in direct association.

The flint axes from these burials are similar to ones from the battle-axe graves at Upton Lovell, which also produced boars' tusks and a rubber made of Group I greenstone. The distinctive lozenge-shaped arrowheads have closest affinities with those of leaf-shaped form. Others are known from barrow 18 at Towthorpe, where they are associated with inhumations and bowls of Heslerton ware,[102] while one example comes from the Lower levels at Windmill Hill.[103]

The pottery that is contemporary with these antler mace-heads is not distinctive. The bowl of Heslerton ware from Duggleby is lost, and may never have come from the barrow.[104] The sherds from Cowlam are not specifically associated, while the vessel from Liff's Low is without parallels elsewhere, though Piggott originally suggested it had possible Peterborough affinities.[105]

More recent discoveries, of a non-funerary nature, are more helpful. At Northton, Harris, an antler mace-head, almost identical to that from Warminster, came from the lower occupation layer, where it was associated with pottery similar to Unstan and Hebridean neolithic wares. In a later level, separated by a sterile layer of sand, were sherds of Necked Beakers and an Irish Bowl Food Vessel.[106] Another antler mace-head of the same type, from Attenborough, Nottinghamshire,[107] was discovered in a gravel pit, which also produced, though not in recorded positions, sherds of Mortlake ware, a Langdale axe, a perforated adze and a polished flint axe. In spite of the lack of evidence, it seems quite plausible that these objects should be associated.

The first group of finds linked with Crown antler mace-heads suggests some contemporaneity with the mace-heads of stone, further substantiated by the link between the ornamentation of the Liff's Low mace-head, and those in the Maesmore group. It seems possible, however, that the lozenge-shaped arrowheads and also the Northton find could be earlier than the Mace-head Complex. Northton invites comparison with Rinyo, where sherds of Unstan type were primary to or contemporary with the first, main phase of occupation.[108] Not all skewer pins need be as late as the Mace-head Complex; those at Cairnpapple were primary to Northern beakers of early types that would be likely to antedate, for instance, the Northern beaker from Rinyo.

While mace-heads of antler seem, on the whole, to be earlier than mace-heads of stone, small pendants of pestle shape seem rather to tie in with those stone mace-heads that are probably the latest forms. Ovoid types (nearest in shape to the Ovoid C group) are barely represented among these pendants, save a few examples from Boyne tombs, where they occur with others of pestle form.[109] Boyne art has been linked with decoration on a sherd from Skara Brae, and bone pins from the same site compare with some of those from the Boyne tombs.[110] A recent find of a shale pendant at West Overton G.6b[111] compares well with Orkney Pestle mace-heads. It was thought by the excavators to have been lost possibly during the construction of the mound, making it contemporary with the Developed Southern beaker from the primary burial. Other pendants, from 'Wessex Culture' graves at Wilsford G.8 and Cressingham,[112] are shaped more like the Thames Pestle type. At Wilsford the finds include an Aldbourne cup, a form of pottery often considered to have developed from Rinyo-Clacton ware. These two grave-groups can be linked culturally with those including mace-heads from Bush Barrow and Towthorpe.

In the present state of knowledge concerning the later part of the neolithic period, it is not possible to draw detailed chronological conclusions about the stone mace-heads under discussion. It seems unlikely that the period during which the Ovoid and Pestle varieties were made occupied any great length of time – perhaps 150 years at the most. This factor, and the nature of the associations themselves, make it impossible to state with certainty that any one group is earlier than another. Possible chronological differences may, however, be considered as follows.

Typological development

Technological considerations seem to be relevant. It can be seen that the Pestle mace-heads are on the whole more finely made, of a more sophisticated shape, and with a higher percentage of straight bored holes than Ovoid mace-heads, indicating that the Pestle type may on the whole be later in date.

It has been suggested above that the internal widening sometimes found within the shaft-holes of stone mace-heads can be connected with similar features on antler examples, and these seem to be at least partly earlier than those made of stone. Internal widening of the hole, then, should be an early feature. It is found most frequently with the Maesmore group, also linked to the antler mace-heads by the faceted decoration, and among mace-heads of Ovoid A type. It is common among Ovoid B and Thames Pestle mace-heads, but rare with the Ovoid C and Orkney Pestle types. Therefore, considering the evidence from the holes alone, the Ovoid A and Maesmore groups could be the earliest, Ovoid B mace-heads might be expected to be intermediate, and the latest groups would be the Ovoid C and Pestle types. The Orkney group could be regarded on typological grounds as the most evolved of the Pestle mace-heads, and morphologically these are the furthest removed from the Ovoid A group.

The Ovoid C mace-heads, typically longer, and with a lower length : depth index than the other Ovoid examples, seem to be at least in part the progenitors of the Cushion mace-heads, which could evolve from a number of 'proto-cushion' mace-heads, such as that from Dorchester Site II. Pending a more detailed discussion of the Cushion mace-head group, and their very limited associations, it may be stated that they do seem to be mainly later than both the Ovoid and the Pestle varieties, possessing a very high degree of craftsmanship, and having very exactly bored straight holes, with no examples of internal widening.

Mace-heads made of materials other than stone

The mace-heads made from flint nodules are restricted to the Ovoid A and B groups, where they are also equated with the Maesmore group, the inference being that they may also be early. Some of these are roughly faceted after the manner of the Maesmore group. There are also two mace-heads that appear to be made of pottery, one, from Longtown, Cumberland, of Ovoid A form (fig. 32, 4), the other, from Winchester,[113] belonging to the Ovoid B group. Thus apparently early mace-heads are made of diverse materials: antler, flint nodules, and pottery, as well as stone and flint with artificial shaftholes. Their manufacture must have been connected with some specific requirement calling for the use of a hafted implement possessing a partly spherical surface. One could deduce that although at first antler was found to be a suitable material, it was eventually replaced by the general use of stone, which should of course have been more durable. Unlike battle-axes, which seem everywhere to have been objects of prestige, mace-heads seem at first, at any rate, to have fulfilled some definite purpose. The uses for which they were made, however, are less easy to infer.

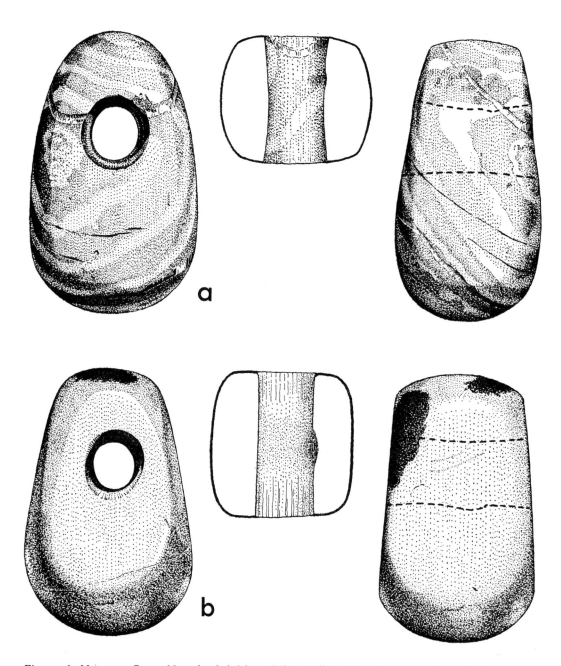

Figure 36. Maesmore Group Mace-heads (1/1). a. White Hill, Rafford, Moray. b. Tinwald, Dumfries.

Associations and dating

The associated mace-heads may now be examined in the light of the considerations on typology. A recent view of the origins of the Rinyo-Clacton ware from southeastern England is that taken by Clarke, who suggests a possible derivation from Fengate and Southern British (Long Necked) beaker traditions. Clarke states that the domestic site at Lawford in Essex has produced pottery that integrates the shapes and techniques of both Fengate and Rinyo-Clacton wares.[114] This being so, the mace-head from Cam, reconstructed as being of Ovoid B type, though not far removed from Ovoid A, should be among the earliest mace-heads in the south. Smith would date the Cam pottery to within a century of 1600 B.C.[115] At Windmill Hill a fragmentary mace-head from the Maesmore group is, broadly speaking,

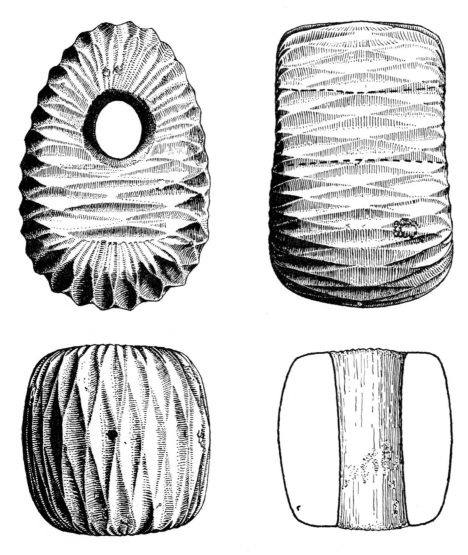

Figure 37. Maesmore Group Mace-heads (1/1). Maesmore, Corwen, Merioneth.

contemporary with Fengate ware, though of course other pottery forms are also present, including Rinyo-Clacton sherds and other items that have been included in the Mace-head Complex. The Upper levels at this site have a carbon date of 1540±150 (B.M.-75). At Stonehenge the Ovoid B mace-head is probably earlier than the use of Presely stone in Phase II of the monument. The mace-head made of this stone, of Thames Pestle type, from Newport, Pembrokeshire, represents a further stage in mace-head morphology, being typologically more developed than the Stonehenge specimen.

In the north, the fragmentary mace-head from Rinyo, probably of Ovoid B type, is loosely contemporary with a Late Northern (Short Necked) beaker, which would be dated by Clarke to rather after 1600 B.C.,[116] and this again should be an early type of mace-head. Indeed, Orkney, with a high density of mace-heads of all kinds, would seem a suitable place of origin, though mace-heads of seemingly early kinds have a wide distribution. The closely comparable decorated Maesmore group mace-heads have been found as far apart as north Wales and Sutherland.

The two mace-heads from Stonehenge and Tormore, which border the Ovoid B and C groups (fig. 31), also compare well metrically, though differing in size. The Stonehenge mace-head is made of hornblendic gneiss, which, though it may originate in Brittany, could also have come from Scotland.[117]

The four mace-heads from Scottish chambered tombs cannot be dated with any precision. There does, however, seem reason to suppose that they all belong to secondary deposits. Carbon dates available for Clyde-Carlingford tombs, and for the Lyles Hill ware found with them, indicate a generally pre-beaker date,[118] while at East Finnercy, Aberdeenshire, Lyles Hill pottery is associated with All Over Cord beaker,[119] which too would antedate the Tormore grave-group.

A. S. Henshall has shown that a number of Orkney-Cromarty tombs had beaker sherds in primary positions (Carn Glas, Kilcoy S., Lower Dounreay),[120] but in each case the beakers are of the earliest types,[121] giving a date in the region of 2000 B.C., while such mace-head/beaker correlations as are available are with altogether later types of beaker. As yet the only carbon date for Unstan ware comes from Northton (Gak-848: 4100±140 B.C.), but pottery of Unstan type is earlier than, or perhaps contemporary with, Rinyo I pottery at Rinyo, and one would expect a date for it a little *later* than the floruit of Lyles Hill ware, and at any rate *earlier* than the Mace-head Complex.

The absence of Rinyo-Clacton pottery from chambered tombs is conspicuous; it is found only at Tormore and Unival in the north, but much of the pottery originally found in the Orkney-Cromarty tombs does not survive.[122] Other objects included in the Mace-head Complex have, however, been recorded from these tombs besides the mace-heads themselves, both flintwork such as polished edge and plano-convex knives, fabricators and transverse arrowheads, along with small triangular stone axes and a bone skewer pin.[123] Such evidence would seem to argue the continued use of the tombs in this area by the makers of Rinyo-Clacton pottery, who could reasonably be expected to be at least in part the descendants of the makers of Unstan wares, and the builders of the tombs.

The Orkney Pestle mace-head from Doune, of the same type as those from Isbister and Taversoe Tuick, is associated with a Yorkshire Vase Food Vessel, a type known to be at least partly contemporary with both Northern and Southern beakers. One would therefore expect it to be of a date little removed from the mace-heads with later beaker/Rinyo-Clacton associations, though probably later than the Cam mace-head, which would fit well with the other conclusions so far made about dating. The only dates available for such Food Vessels as yet, of 1750 ± 150 B.C. (B.M.-210) and 1490 ± 150 B.C. (B.M.-178), come from Harland Edge, Derbyshire.[124]

Petrology

A distinction can be made between those mace-heads linked, albeit tenuously, with Groups

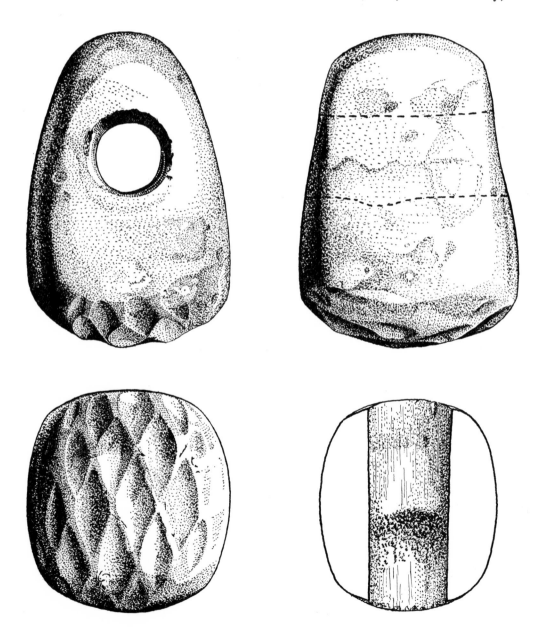

Figure 38. Maesmore Group Mace-heads (1/1). Quarnford, Staffs.

VI and VII, and those connected with Groups I and XIII. It has already been shown that the earliest use of Groups VI and VII goes back to the Middle Neolithic; the axe-factories appear to have been abandoned by the Early Bronze Age. It is a mace-head of early type that is made of Graig Lwyd stone at Windmill Hill (where Langdale stone is probably also contemporary), and it is Ovoid mace-heads only that are distributed in the lowland areas to the north of Great Langdale.

Groups I and XIII have no links with the Middle Neolithic, but are known from Early Bronze Age contexts. In terms of mace-heads, one Ovoid C specimen is made of Group I greenstone, while four Thames Pestle mace-heads are made of this material or of preselite. At Stonehenge, the mace-head of Ovoid B type probably belongs to the first phase, while Groups I and XIII have been recorded from the second phase. So the petrological evidence seems to tie in with the conclusions already reached, with the kinds of rock that were in use first being connected with the earlier mace-heads, while later mace-heads can be linked with materials known to have been in use at a later date.

Relations with battle-axes

Groups I and XIII are known also to have been used for making battle-axes, of early, although probably not the earliest types, since no Stage I examples are represented. Thus mace-heads and earlier battle-axes must be broadly contemporary, especially as Prescelly stone is thought only to have been in use for a limited period.[125] Evidently the manufacture of mace-heads, which were perhaps eventually intended to be ornamental rather than functional, was abandoned in favour of the later varieties of battle-axe, such as the Codford St Peter group, and the Northern and Southern Variants, all of which are known in association with cinerary urns.[126]

Battle-axes from Stages I and II are sometimes associated with Southern (Long Necked) beakers.[127] An early grave-group is that from Garton Slack, where a Stage I battle-axe was found with a Primary Southern beaker.[128] It cannot clearly be shown that any of the mace-heads under discussion antedate such a grave-group. It can therefore be postulated that the technique of making stone mace-heads with near-straight shaftholes (as opposed to the hour-glass holes of pebble-hammers) may have been acquired from such beaker sources. Comment has already been made on the fact that the holes of mace-heads are very similar in size to those of battle-axes. The positioning of the holes of these two classes of implements can also be compared closely; a mean of 0·44 has been obtained for the index Li/L from a sample number of battle-axes.[129]

The makers of the first British battle-axes, as shown by their associations, had strong beaker connections; two Stage I battle-axes, from Ratfyn[130] and Woodhenge,[131] came from contexts where Rinyo-Clacton wares were present, but in neither case can the exact relationship, if any, be established. The makers of mace-heads, by contrast, seem to have been indigenous neolithic folk, who soon ended the working of Langdale and Graig Lwyd stone, which were more suitable for polished stone axes, in favour of other materials more amenable to the boring of shaftholes. Group XVIII quartz dolerite, of which the mace-head from Garrowby is made, was used almost exclusively for implements with shaftholes, mainly axe-hammers, and battle-axes of all kinds, though with an emphasis on the earlier varieties.[132] So it is to the makers of battle-axes in Britain that one must look for the inspiration that caused the makers of antler mace-heads to adopt a new technology and translate their implements into stone.

Much of the detail that has been omitted in this paper, together with a corpus and further work on the types of mace-head not included here, will be found in the writer's thesis, and it is hoped that a full corpus will eventually be published. Meanwhile, the aim has been to present some new ideas on the typology of certain kinds of mace-head; to relate these mace-heads, as far as the evidence permits, with a particular range of pottery styles and artefacts, and to show that such pottery and artefacts also occur with one another when not associated with mace-heads, so limiting the implements under discussion to a particular sphere of British prehistory.

It gives particular pleasure to have been able to write this paper for dedication to Stuart Piggott, who has done so much work on this period.

Acknowledgments: The illustrations of mace-heads in figs. 35–38 were drawn for the National Museum of Antiquities, Edinburgh, by Mr J. A. Brown, and are reproduced here by permission of the Museum, which retains the copyright.

I am grateful to Dr D. L. Clarke for permission to use material, in advance of publication, from his thesis 'The Origin and Development of British Beaker Pottery.' This is to be published under the same title by the Cambridge University Press late in 1967, with the same corpus numbers for the pottery that have been quoted here.

I am grateful to the following museums, which have provided material for illustration in this paper: Ashmolean Museum of Art and Archaeology, Oxford; Bristol City Museum; British Museum; Carlisle Museum and Art Gallery; Derby Museum and Art Gallery; Dumfries Burgh Museum; Forres, Falconer Museum; Glasgow Art Gallery and Museum, Kelvingrove; Hull Museums; Hunterian Museum, Glasgow University; Ipswich Museum; Lewes, Barbican House Museum; Lincoln City and County Museum; National Museum of Antiquities of Scotland, Edinburgh; National Museum of Wales, Cardiff; Newbury Borough Museum; Reading Museum and Art Gallery; Salisbury, South Wiltshire and Blackmore Museum; Sheffield City Museum.

Appendix I. Table of means

	Ovoid (71)	Pestle (34)
L	3·24 in.$\pm$·5 in.	3·21 in.$\pm$·3 in.
B	2·17 in.$\pm$·3 in.	2·05 in.$\pm$·2 in.
D	1·86 in.$\pm$·3 in.	1·6 in.$\pm$·26 in.
H	$\frac{3}{4}$ in.$\pm\frac{1}{8}$ in.	$\frac{23}{32}$ in.$\pm\frac{3}{32}$ in.
B/L	·676$\pm$·08	·63$\pm$·04
D/L	·581$\pm$·11	·49$\pm$·07
D/B	·86$\pm$·12	·79$\pm$·12
Li/L	·41$\pm$·04	·426$\pm$·03
L2/L	·375$\pm$·06	·19$\pm$·03
L3/L	·33$\pm$·06	·21$\pm$·06
L2/B	·56$\pm$·1	·3$\pm$·05

Appendix II. Table of means and percentages

Total: 105	Maesmore group (8)	Ovoid A (8)	Ovoid B (35)	Ovoid C (20)	Thames Pestle (21)	Orkney Pestle (13)
L	2·97 in.	2·75 in.	3·2 in.	3·6 in.	3·22 in.	3·2 in.
B	1·93 in.	2·15 in.	2·2 in.	2·19 in.	2·06 in.	2·02 in.
D	1·85 in.	2·1 in.	1·9 in.	1·62 in.	1·63 in.	1·57 in.
B/L	·64	·79	·69	·61	·641	·627
D/L	·624	·77	·6	·447	·506	·488
D/B	·97	·99	·87	·74	·777	·782
L2/L	·365	·446	·38	·34	·189	·195
L3/L	·283	·37	·33	·33	·21	·221
Internal hollowing of hole	71·5%	62·5%	40·6%	17·7%	50%	20%
Straight or nearly straight hole	86%	87·5%	75%	70·6%	100%	93%

Notes

1. Evans, *Ancient Stone Implements*, second edition (1897) 221–7
2. *British Museum : A Guide to the Antiquities of the Stone Age*, second edition (1911) 122
3. *Arch.* LXIX (1917–18) 6–8
4. *P.S.A.S.* LXVIII (1933–4) 431; LXXVIII (1943–4) 16–25
5. *Ant. J.* XXI (1941) 337
6. *Man*, XLVI (1946) No. 105, 125
7. Piggott, *Neolithic Cultures of the British Isles* (1954) chapter XI
8. *P.P.S.* XXVIII (1962) 242
9. Hoare, *South Wiltshire*, I (1812) 202–5, Pl. XXVII, 3
10. Mortimer, *Forty Years' Researches . . .* (1905) 6, fig. 9
11. *P.D.N.H.* LVIII (1936) 18–24, Pl. IIIa. I am grateful to Miss S. Gerloff for her comments on this 'mace-head'.
12. *P.P.S.* IV (1938) 87
13. *P.P.S.* XV (1949) 70; Rankine, *The Mesolithic of Southern Britain* (1956) 29; *P.P.S.* XXVI (1960) 252, fig. 6, 5
14. *P.S.A.S.* LXXVIII (1943–4) 16–25
15. *Man* XLVI (1946) No. 105, 125
16. Evans, *op. cit.* 223–4
17. *Trans. East Riding Ant. Soc.* XXIII (1920) 49, fig. 3b; *Arch. J.* LXXXVI (1929) 80, Pl. VIII, A2; Annable and Simpson, *Guide Catalogue of the Neolithic and Bronze Age Collections in Devizes Museum* (1964) 37, No. 41
18. *P.S.A.S.* XLIII (1908–9) 377–84
19. *P.S.A.S.* VI (1864–6) 42
20. *P.S.A.S.* XLIII (1908–9) 383, fig. 4
21. *ibid.* 380, fig. 2
22. *P.S.A.S.* IX (1870–1) 258, Pl. XXI, fig. 1
23. *Salisbury and South Wiltshire Museum Annual Report* (1958–9) 16, Pl. 1
24. Grimes, *The Prehistory of Wales* (1951) 171, No. 363, Pl. IV, 5
25. *P.S.A.S.* XXII (1887–8) 374
26. *P.S.A.S.* XXII (1887–8) 353

27. Smith, *Windmill Hill and Avebury* (1965) 113, fig. 51, S.9
28. *P.P.S.* XXVIII (1962) 243, No. 1
29. *P.S.A.S.* LXV (1930–1) 91
30. *Trans. Newbury District F.C.* VIII, No. 4 (1946) 285, fig. 3
31. *Ant. J.* XXI (1941) 337
32. *Arch.* LXIX (1917–18) 7, fig. 7
33. Bateman, *Vestiges of the Antiquities of Derbyshire* (1848) 41–3
34. *Arch.* LXIX (1917–18) 6, figs. 5, 6; *Arch. J.* LXXXVI (1929) 80, Pl. VIII, A1
35. *J.C.H.A. Soc.* LX (1955) 103
36. *ibid.*
37. Mortimer, *op. cit.* 138–40, fig. 373
38. *P.P.S.* XXXII (1966) 245
39. Information from I. F. Smith, in a letter. Report pending for *Trans. Bristol & Gloucester A.S.*
40. *P.S.A.S.* LXXIII (1938–9) 6–31
41. Clarke, Ph.D. thesis, 'The Origin and Development of British Beaker Pottery' (Cambridge, 1964) Corpus No. 1734. See also forthcoming book with the same title (Cambridge University Press, 1967) and report of the second Atlantic Symposium at Groningen, 1964 (Spring, 1967)
42. Smith, *op. cit.* 113, fig. 51, S.9
43. Smith, *op. cit.* 11 and 74–82; Clarke, *op. cit.* Corpus Nos. 1055–60
44. Smith, *op. cit.* 103–9
45. Smith, *op. cit.* 129, fig. 55
46. Smith, *op. cit.* 113–14
47. *Ant. J.* VI (1926) 2; Atkinson, *Stonehenge* (1960) 28–9, 88–91
48. Clarke, *op. cit.* Corpus No. 1047
49. *P.P.S.* XXVIII (1962) 261, No. 947; Atkinson, *op. cit.* 206
50. *P.S.A.S.* XXXVI (1901–2) 95–102
51. Henshall, *The Chambered Tombs of Scotland*, 1 (1963) 284
52. Childe, *Skara Brae* (1931) 112
53. Piggott, *op. cit.* 331
54. Henshall, *op. cit.* 205
55. Henshall, *op. cit.* 234
56. Henshall, *op. cit.* 111–12
57. Piggott, *op. cit.* 253
58. Anderson, *Scotland in Pagan Times* (1886) 83
59. *B.B.C.S.* XX (1962–4) 165–7, fig. 1
60. (ed.) Foster and Alcock, *Culture and Environment* (1963) 186
61. *P.P.S.* XXVIII (1962) 247, No. 241
62. *P.P.S.* XVII (1951) 145, No. 242, fig. 6
63. *P.P.S.* XXVIII (1962) 256, No. 717
64. *W.A.M.* X (1867) 94–7; *P.P.S.* XXVIII (1962) 248, No. 291
65. Clarke, *op. cit.* I, 492
66. (ed.) Foster and Alcock, *op. cit.* 76–7
67. Piggott, *op. cit.* 386, Appendix C, fig. 48
68. Smith, *op. cit.* 78
69. *P.P.S.* XXXII (1966) 122–55; Clarke, *op. cit.* Corpus No. 1131
70. *D.A.J.* LXXXV (1965) 1–24
71. *Y.A.J.* XLI (1964) 191–202; Clarke, *op. cit.* Corpus Nos. 1276–8
72. *P.S.A.S.* LXXXII (1947–8) 1–47; Clarke, *op. cit.* I, 144, Corpus No. 1671
73. *Arch. J.* LXXXVIII (1931) 151; Smith, Ph.D. thesis 'The Decorative Art of Neolithic Ceramics in S.E. England and its Relations' (London, 1956) list of finds in vol. II
74. Smith, *op. cit.* (1956) list of finds in vol. II
75. Clarke, *op. cit.* I, 698
76. *P.P.S.* XXXII (1966) 122–55
77. Smith, *op. cit.* (1956)
78. *P.P.S.* XXXI (1965) 72

79. *Y.A.J.* XLI (1964) 191–202
80. *W.A.M.* LII (1947–8) 290–1
81. Smith, *op. cit.* (1965) 214
82. *P.P.S.* XXVIII (1962) 259, No. 837
83. *P.P.S.* XXVIII (1962) 260, No. 892; Smith, *op. cit.* (1956) list of finds in vol. II
84. Information from I. F. Smith; report intended for *P.D.N.H.* by C. Green
85. Smith, *op. cit.* (1956) I, 119
86. Piggott, *op. cit.* 307
87. Atkinson, Piggott and Sandars, *Excavations at Dorchester, Oxon.* (1951) 142–4
88. Smith, *op. cit.* (1965) 213, 234; fig. 79, B.23
89. Atkinson, Piggott and Sandars, *op. cit.* 115, fig. 31
90. *P.S.A.S.* LXXXII (1947–8) 101–6
91. Clarke, *op. cit.* Corpus Nos. 1790–2
92. Smith, *op. cit.* (1965) 113
93. *P.S.A.S.* LXXXII (1947–8) 103; Smith, *op. cit.* (1956) 80, 104
94. Piggott, *op. cit.* (1954) fig. 45; *P.S.A.S.* XCII (1958–9) 57–64, fig. 1
95. Piggott, *op. cit.* 292–3
96. *P.P.S.* XXXI (1965) 72
97. *P.P.S.* XXXIX (1963) 26
98. Piggott, *op. cit.* (1954) 292; *Arch.* LXXXV (1936) 269–70; Smith, *op. cit.* (1956) I, 98
99. Smith, *op. cit.* (1965) 234
100. *P.P.S.* XXXII (1966) 199–245
101. Piggott, *op. cit.* 355–8
102. Mortimer, *op. cit.* 9–10, figs. 16, 21
103. Smith, *op. cit.* (1965), fig. 45, F.78
104. *P.P.S.* III (1937) 206
105. *Arch. J.* LXXXVIII (1931) 130–3, fig. 20
106. *Antiquity* XL (1966) 137–9, and information from D. D. A. Simpson
107. *Ant. J.* XXXVIII (1958) 87–9, fig. 1
108. Piggott, *op. cit.* 327–8
109. Piggott, *op. cit.* 205, fig. 32, 17–23
110. Piggott, *op. cit.* 217, 220
111. *P.P.S.* XXXII (1966) 126, fig. 4, 1
112. *P.P.S.* IV (1938) 52–106
113. *P.P.S.* XXVIII (1962) 245, No. 125
114. Clarke, *op. cit.* I, 698
115. Information from I. F. Smith
116. Clarke, Information circulated at the Second Atlantic Colloquium, Groningen, April 6–11, 1964, p. 16
117. Information from Salisbury Museum
118. *Antiquity* XXXIV (1960) 112, 113; *Antiquity* XXXVIII (1964) 52; *P.P.S.* XXXI (1965) 34–57
119. *P.P.S.* XXXI (1965) 46
120. Henshall, *op. cit.* I, 112–13
121. Clarke, *op. cit.* Corpus Nos. 1757–8, 1750–6, 1611–12
122. Piggott, *op. cit.* 248
123. Piggott, *op. cit.* 250–2; Henshall, *op. cit.* I
124. *D.A.J.* LXXXVI (1966) 39
125. *P.P.S.* XXVIII (1962) 236
126. *P.P.S.* XXXII (1966) 224–7
127. *ibid.* 219–22
128. Clarke, *op. cit.* Corpus No. 1296; Mortimer, *op. cit.* 209
129. *P.P.S.* XXXII (1966) 203
130. *W.A.M.* XLVII (1935–7) 57, fig. 3
131. Cunnington, *Woodhenge* (1929) 148, Pl. 40
132. *P.P.S.* XXVIII (1962) 224; *P.P.S.* XXXII (1966) 245

Scottish dagger graves

A. S. Henshall

Among his many writings Professor Piggott has given us two essential papers on the British Early Bronze Age, both largely based on a study of the graves, firstly in Wessex and recently in the rest of the country.[1] One day in 1965 I had the opportunity of examining with him the daggers in the collection of the National Museum of Antiquities of Scotland, and I now have pleasure in offering him the paper which he then suggested I should prepare. My purpose is to provide a corpus of the graves in succession to the lists of Anderson, Childe and Scott,[2] and to record the results of a re-examination of all the existing blades. The small knives with straight-ended hilts, and the lost blades of uncertain form, have been omitted.

It is convenient to begin with the blades of more complex form, those with mid-ribs and cast grooves. It may be noted that in Scotland ogival daggers, characteristic of the second phase of the Wessex culture in south England,[3] do not appear as grave-goods. The unusual blades from Craigscorry and Gilchorn are badly damaged, but they seem to have been long and triangular. The Craigscorry dagger has on either side of the mid-rib a wide groove which fades away near the tip. The form is similar to the dagger from a Wessex I grave at Cressingham, Norfolk,[4] but it continues to appear on knife blades from later Wessex II graves such as Wilsford, Wiltshire.[5] A Scottish blade apparently of this type was found with a cremation at Campbeltown, Argyll.[6] The peculiarity of the Craigscorry blade is the narrow groove in the thickened outer part of the blade, dying away well above the tip. With the dagger there were found a plano-convex knife and a barbed-and-tanged arrowhead.

The Gilchorn dagger may be nearer the ogival type, having a broad mid-rib with a diamond-shaped section in the upper part; the faint narrow moulding outside the mid-rib is suggestive of such blades as those from Winterbourne Stoke, Wiltshire, or West Cranmore, Somerset.[7] With this dagger was found a most unusual small tanged blade. It is very delicate and beautifully made, with a low mid-rib, a groove on each side, and chased lines. The Gilchorn burial was primary to collared urns, one of which held a glass bead of the eighteenth Dynasty (1580–1344 B.C., but probably fifteenth century), and a notched bronze blade.[8]

The blade from Bishopmill, once thought of as a halberd,[9] has a relatively wide mid-rib but the rest of the blade is flat. The form, and in particular the shallow Ω recess at the base of the hilt, and the chased lines halfway between the mid-rib and the edges, relate it to the earliest mid-rib daggers from Wessex culture graves, such as those from Bush Barrow or the Wilsford grave already mentioned.[10] But the Bishopmill blade is rather more developed than these, having a mid-rib rather wider in proportion to the blade and a careful bevel at the top of the

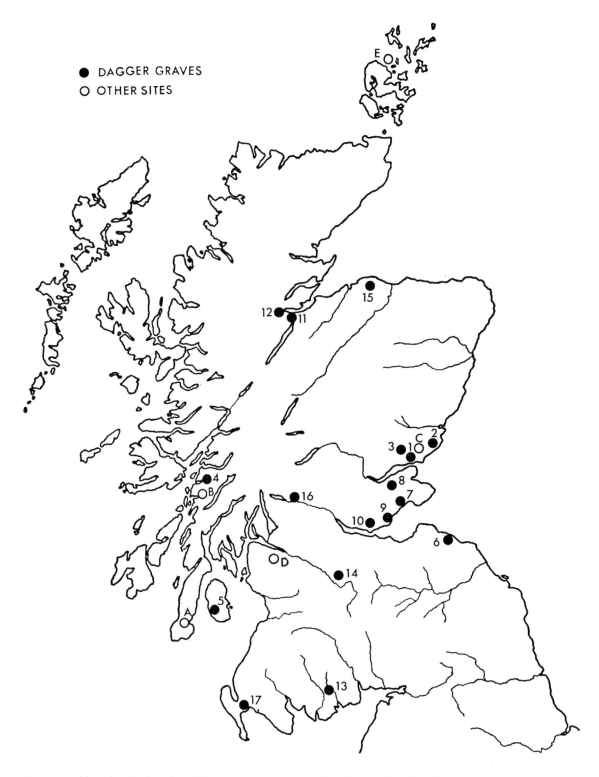

Figure 39. Map showing location of the dagger graves and other sites mentioned in the text.

mid-rib. The pendant semicircles can be paralleled on the later ogival daggers from Arreton Down, Isle of Wight, and Gurvagh, Co. Derry.[11] The blade, then, may be contemporary with the earlier part of Wessex II.

Two blades, from Law of Mauldslie and Auchterhouse, have narrower mid-ribs than the foregoing blades, and no incised lines. The Auchterhouse mid-rib is triple-reeded, a feature found only on blades from Teddington, Middlesex, Reaverhill, Northumberland, and Ireland.[12] These two Scottish daggers may also be compared in a general way with the Wessex I mid-rib daggers, and we may note the northern extension of that type into Yorkshire.[13] The straight heel and the groups of three rivets on the Auchterhouse blade are particularly reminiscent of the six-rivet Wessex daggers. Another Scottish dagger, from Blackwaterfoot, has three delicate spaced ribs. The closest British parallel is a blade from Cambridge, with rather heavier ribs and a slightly ogival outline.[14] The form of the heel of the Blackwaterfoot blade is curious, having two rivets in angular shoulders with a fish-tail tang between, a form otherwise only known on the flat dagger from Skateraw.

The Auchterhouse and Blackwaterfoot daggers, and the flat dagger from Cleigh, are decorated by lines of punched dots, as is also the Cambridge blade (Pl. I, c, d). This decoration relates the daggers to those few objects with lines of dots (generally used to emphasize contours) which include the armlets from the Masterton grave. It also connects the daggers with objects having areas of pointillé decoration as have many Wessex II ogival daggers, and the Arreton Down type of tanged spearhead.[15] An interesting lost blade from Winterbourne Monkton 34c, Dorset, pointillé decorated, apparently had three ribs similar to the Blackwaterfoot blade,[16] and later development of this form can be seen on the Arreton Down and Gavel Moss, Renfrewshire, daggers.[17]

We may, then, link together a group of Scottish daggers which are likely to be close together in date: the two mid-rib daggers from Law of Mauldslie and Auchterhouse; the dot-decorated daggers from Auchterhouse, Blackwaterfoot and Cleigh, and the plain flat dagger from Masterton; the curiously formed two-riveted daggers from Blackwaterfoot and Skateraw, and one may note that the Masterton dagger is the only other known to have had only two rivets. The Blackwaterfoot and Skateraw daggers are also linked by their gold pommel-mounts, which brings the Collessie flat dagger within the group as it has the only other Scottish example. The three mounts are almost identical. The rivets in this group of daggers are all large, with diameters of 1 cm. or more, except for Masterton and the unusual triple rivets on the Auchterhouse blade.

A date about the middle of the Wessex culture seems to be indicated on the grounds of form and decoration. Associated finds must also be considered. The only other pommel-mount, from Topped Mountain, Co. Fermanagh, was with an E-type Food Vessel,[18] a form of pot which has been shown by Simpson to equate chronologically with the Wessex culture.[19] Less informative, another possible pommel-mount, from Monikie, Angus (perhaps more likely to have been an armlet), was also with a Food Vessel.[20] The gold pommel-cover from a Wessex I grave at Ridgeway, Dorset, provides a partial parallel for our pommel-mounts, but the comparison with the small ribbed ring from a Wessex I grave at Cressingham, Norfolk, is less satisfactory.[21]

The flat dagger from Masterton was associated with a small blade, jet necklace and a pair of bronze armlets. This grave-group has been compared with a pair of similar armlets and a necklace (made up from two or three jet spacer-plate necklaces) from a grave at Melfort, Argyll.[22] The relatively early appearance of penannular bronze strip armlets in Britain is indicated by the association with a Long Necked Beaker at Knipton, Leicestershire.[23] The Masterton armlets are of this form but have the distinction of repoussé decoration. The Melfort armlets also have repoussé decoration, but were made as cylinders, as were also two lost gold armlets. The first of these, from Lisnakill, Co. Waterford, found in a grave with a pot which from the description can hardly be anything other than a Food Vessel, provides a very close parallel to the Masterton armlets. The other, from Cuxwold, Lincolnshire, has plain ribs outlined by rows of dots.[24] The rarity of the repoussé technique in the Early Bronze Age has led to comparisons between the Melfort armlets and the Mold cape, a piece of infinitely more elaborate design and higher relief, with implications for an unnaturally late date for the armlets, spacer-plate jet necklaces and certain Food Vessels.[25] But the strip of bronze with repoussé lentoid bosses in the Migdale, Sutherland, hoard,[26] very similar to the Melfort decoration, links the armlets with a range of Early Bronze Age metal types. There is also the association at Melfort with a spacer-plate necklace. While the difficulties in dating the amber spacer-plates remain unresolved,[27] a useful pointer is the constant decoration of the jet spacer-plates in the pointillé art style of the Aldbourne cups and ogival daggers and spear-heads, for which a date in the fifteenth century is required. If the Melfort armlets are somewhat later than the Masterton armlets, then it may be significant that the Melfort necklace had spacer-plates whilst the handsome five-string Masterton necklace did not.

If these various considerations are sound, a date in the early to mid-fifteenth century may be suggested for this group of Scottish daggers, which includes two flat daggers of Piggott's class II.[28] It may be noted that the Collessie and Auchterhouse daggers were with cremations, and that the former was secondary to two beakers.

The remaining flat daggers are mainly shorter than the daggers which have been discussed. Also, with the exception of Ashgrove, their rivet diameters are distinctly smaller, 0·5–0·7 cm. Two of the daggers, Ashgrove and Cairn Greg, were associated with late incised, beakers and the Kirkcaldy dagger is likely to be contemporary with the similar beaker and V-bored jet buttons in an adjacent woman's grave.[29] A date contemporary with the early Wessex culture in the sixteenth century, or possibly starting earlier, seems likely for this group of daggers, as already argued by Professor Piggott.

The Scottish flat daggers have triangular blades with slightly convex edges, and three fairly large rivets. The central rivet is in a notch which may nearly encircle the rivet: there is no certain example of a blade with three rivet holes. The lower edge of the hilt is recessed in either a V or an Ω shape, there being eight of the former to four of the latter, or nine to seven if all the daggers are counted. The V-shaped recess is a north British variant[30] which appears early, and the two forms of recess have no chronological significance: the Ω recess is used on the latest daggers of all.

The blades of the 'flat' daggers, with the exception of that from Kirkcaldy, are not truly flat but are just perceptibly convex in cross-section. In long section they thin in both directions from the maximum thickness just below the edge of the hilt; the Cleigh blade, for instance, thins gradually from a maximum of 2·6 mm. to 1·5 mm. at the tip, and it thins

I Scottish dagger graves

a. Details of armlet from Masterton, Fife, showing repoussé ribs outlined by punched dots.
b. Upper part of dagger from Drumlanrick, Perthshire, showing cut-marks where the lower edge of the hilt has been.
c. Upper part of dagger from Cleigh, Argyll, showing punched dots at cut-marks at lower edge of hilt.
d. Upper part of dagger from Blackwaterfoot, Arran, showing ribs outlined with punched dots and (in the centre) dots at lower edge of vanished hilt.
(National Museum of Antiquities of Scotland; about 4/3)

Gold bowls from (*top*) Gonnebek, Holstein; (*middle and bottom*) Ebberswalde, near Berlin.

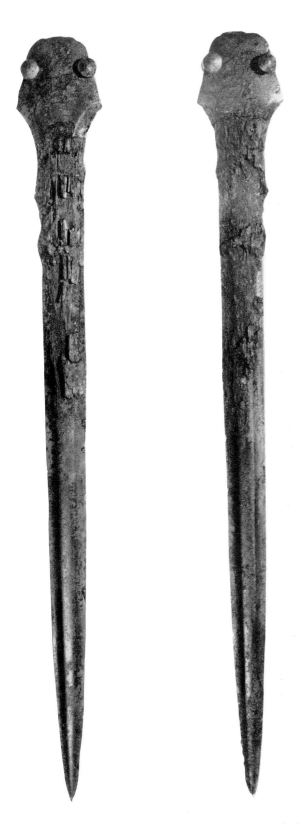

Rapier from West Row, Suffolk. (Photo: L. P. Morley)

b. Palmersheim, Kr. Euskirchen, FB 12. Site FB 8.

a. Vernich, Kr. Euskirchen, FS 34. Site FS 33.

b. Kleinbüllesheim, Kr. Euskirchen, GG 15. Site EZ 21.

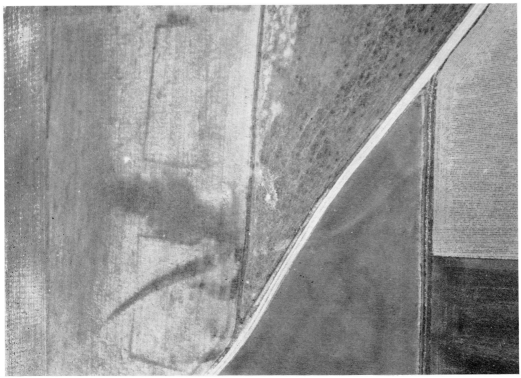

a. Wichterich, Kr. Euskirchen, GG 45. Site GF 82.

Top: Auchenbaddie. *Bottom:* Castle Newe.
(Top photo: National Museum of Antiquities of Scotland)

Top: Glamis, Angus. *Bottom:* Achavrail, Sutherland.
(Photos: National Museum of Antiquities of Scotland)

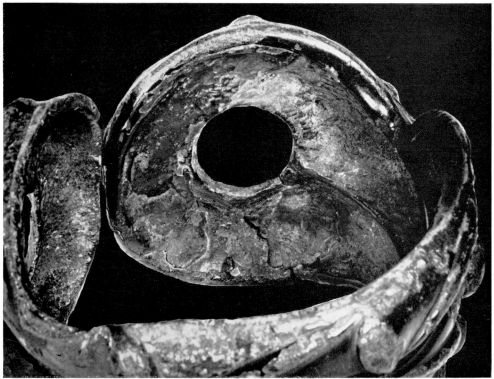

Newry, Co. Down. (Photo: National Museum of Ireland)

Detail of enamelling on armlets from Castle Newe (*top*) and Pitkelloney.

Top : Pitkelloney. *Below :* details.

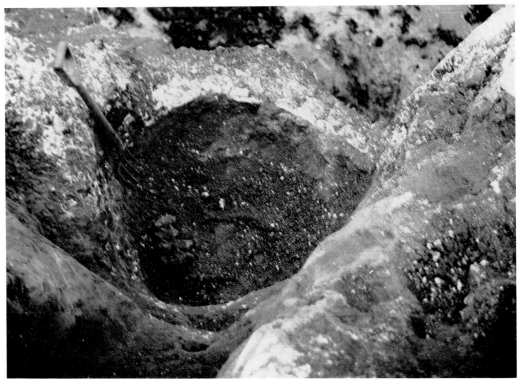

Top: Ipswich shafts 1 and 2 partly exposed.
Bottom: Birchington shaft during excavation with bones *in situ.*

Pottery vessels from the Sandwich shaft.
Height of vessels: *top left*, 14 in., *top right*, 5 in., *bottom*, 5 in.

Top: Ford Down: diameter of rim 20·3 cm.
Bottom: Wilton: diameter of rim 27·6 cm.
(Salisbury and South Wiltshire Museum)

a. Sakatova, Russia; bone pan-pipes.
b. Certosa di Bologna, Italy; detail of bronze *situla* (1/1). (Photo: Thames & Hudson Ltd)

a. Egeln, Germany; pottery drum (1/9). (Landesmus f. Vorgesch; Halle Saale)
b. Kralupy, Bohemia; pottery drum (1/9). (National Museum, Prague)
c. Copies of drums from Kralupy and Brozsny (1/9). (National Museum, Prague)
d. S. England; coin of Tasciovanus.
e. Szájzhalombatta, Hungary; figure with double pipes (2/3).
f. Ittiri, Sardinia; figure with double pipes. (Photo: *Cahiers d'Art*)

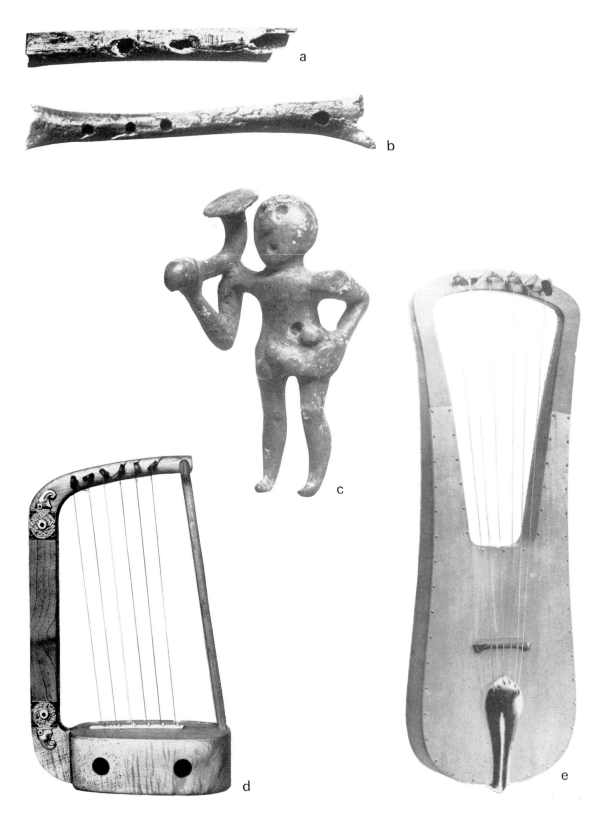

a. Isturitz, France; bone flageolet.
b. Üllö, Hungary; bone flageolet (11/9).
c. Hradiště, Czechoslovakia; bronze figure with horn (2/3). (National Museum, Prague)
d. Sutton Hoo, England; reconstruction of a miniature harp.
e. 'Grab des Sangers', St Severin, Germany; reconstruction of harp.

rapidly to 1·3 mm. at the top edge. The bevels along the edges, where they survive, are very regular, and the surface of the blade has been polished to a high gloss. Sometimes striations from an abrasive are still visible underneath the hilt, and a few blades bear cut marks made when trimming the edge of the hilt (Pl. I, b). The condition of the surface of the blades, and their bevels, differentiate these daggers from those not found in graves. The grave daggers appear to be perfect examples of highest quality, whereas those from Wasbister and Auchnacree,[31] neither from graves, are working tools with hammered surfaces and much-whetted edges.

Some new details have emerged from a re-examination of the daggers. In the five cases where remains of the hilt were examined the material is horn. But all three reasonably intact hilts are different. At Ashgrove the ivory pommel survived. It is the normal 'trough' type with a socket in the base and transverse peg-holes; a considerable number are known in England.[32] These pommels fitted on to a tang projecting from the top of the hilt. A solid horn hilt with such a tang survives on the Wasbister dagger, together with one of the wooden pegs. But the Ashgrove hilt was made of two horn plates with a central wooden plate, an arrangement which required the unusual feature, sometimes found in England, of extra rivets to secure the upper parts of the hilt. The form of the gold pommel-mounts shows that they covered rigid cores, probably of wood, which fitted between two parts of the hilt, for the flanges at their upper and lower edges were not meant to be seen. There can be little doubt that the mounts fitted between the hilt and the pommel, presumably with the tang passing through the core. On the gold casing of a pommel from barrow 7, Ridgeway, Dorset, they are represented by the ribbed lower part of the object.[33] It is tempting to suggest that the pommel-mounts are skeuomorphs of bindings used instead of rivets on composite hilts. The third hilt, from Auchterhouse, was cut entirely from a horn, without a separate pommel.

Dr A. S. Clarke has shown exactly how the Auchterhouse hilt was cut, with neat economy, from a horn, and how the remaining lower edge of the horn was made into a mount for the top of the sheath.[34] His hypothetical reconstruction was confirmed by studying the Kirkcaldy find where the sheath and horn mount have survived fairly intact. Vestiges of the same arrangement can be seen on some Wiltshire daggers.[35]

Four Scottish daggers had remains of sheaths of animal skin (technically 'leather' implies tanning, and it is unknown if these were tanned), and the two capable of being examined were different. The Kirkcaldy sheath is quite simple, with a side seam, but the Ashgrove sheath had sewn ribs running lengthwise. The sheaths found on English daggers have mainly been of wood,[36] and the Gilchorn and Collessie sheaths had a wood foundation below the animal skin. The Gilchorn sheath seems to have had a carefully shaped upper edge designed to fit against the lower edge of the hilt.

Finally, we may note the types of grave in which the burials were made. With four exceptions, all the bodies had been placed crouched in short cists, all but one built below ground in pits. The cists tend to be more massive than the average late neolithic or Early Bronze Age cist, and the joints were often luted with clay. Two exceptions, Craigscorry and Bishopmill, had the burial in a long cist. Full-length burials, though unusual, are known in late Beaker and post-Beaker times in England, and the few Scottish examples include the Melfort grave already mentioned.[37] The two other exceptions were the double cist at Auchterhouse which was partly above ground, and the pit without cist at Collessie. These two graves held the only cremations associated with the daggers, though the Craigscorry skeleton seems to have been partly burnt. Another point is that the Auchterhouse cremation was under a turf mound. As far as is known turf barrows are unusual in Scotland and a southern influence is suggested. The enlargement of the mound with cairn material might be a capping or an extension for an undiscovered secondary burial.[38] Of the other graves, seven were under cairns, all recorded as very large. While it is natural to assume that the dagger graves were primary this need not be so. Only the Cairn Greg cist is actually recorded as being in the centre of the cairn, though it is implied that the Gilchorn cist was also: the Collessie cremation was undoubtedly secondary to two beaker burials.

The careful sealing of some cists has allowed fragments of organic material to survive. Traces of hide were found at Bishopmill, Ashgrove and Masterton, and evidence of foliage, moss and fragrant flowers at Ashgrove and Kirkcaldy. These may, of course, have been commonly included with the body, only to survive in exceptional circumstances. Plant remains have been occasionally noted in England.[39]

LIST OF DAGGERS AND ASSOCIATED OBJECTS
Additional measurements are given in the table on p. 193

1. CAIRN GREG, LINLATHEN, ANGUS

Dagger blade[40] (fig. 40). It was last recorded in existence in 1878. The blade, which is of the usual shape with slight curvature of the sides, has been about 5 in. [12·6 cm.] in length, and 2 in. [5 cm.] wide at the butt end. It bears the mark of the handle, and has been fastened by three rivets' 1·25 cm. long. The careful drawing of 1878 shows that the rivets were small. The hilt appears to have had a V-shaped lower edge.

Beaker[41] (fig. 40; 63.34 in Dundee Museum and Art Gallery). It is a rather irregular pot of coarse ware, with a concave neck and well-marked shoulder. The fabric is fairly hard, buff coloured with a reddish tinge. The rather irregular decoration is incised with strokes of varying depth.

The burial.[42] Cairn Greg lies 2½ miles north of Broughty Ferry, on rising ground on the north side of the Firth of Tay (NO 466337). The cairn, opened in 1834, was described as 'a large heap of stones' in 1842.[43] The central cist, measuring 4 ft. 10 in. by 2 ft. 9 in. by 2 ft. 10 in. deep, rested on ground level. The joints were luted with clay. The large capstone, 7 ft. by 4 ft. 6 in., was separated from an upper capstone by a foot-thick layer of soil. In the cist were the beaker and dagger. Piece of a Pictish symbol-stone was said to have been found between the capstones.

2. GILCHORN, ANGUS

Dagger blade (fig. 44, a EQ 227 in the National Museum of Antiquities of Scotland). It is now in three pieces and greatly corroded, the existing length being 13·7 cm. None of the original edges survives, but at the upper end a fragment of the hilt shows the form of its lower edge with a shallow Ω-shaped recess. The wide mid-rib tends in the upper part to be diamond-shaped in cross-section, but becomes rounded lower down. The maximum thickness is about 6 mm. Outside the mid-rib there has been a very shallow groove, with a slight thickening before the blade thins to the edge.

The sheath. When the blade was discovered 'a considerable portion of a wooden sheath' adhered to it.[44] Fragments of wood remain near the tip, and also immediately below the hilt where they show that the top of the sheath was shaped to complement the form of the lower edge of the hilt, for the wood extends into the omega recess. Between the hilt and the sheath there is a regular gap, 1 mm. wide, filled with a pale brown substance.

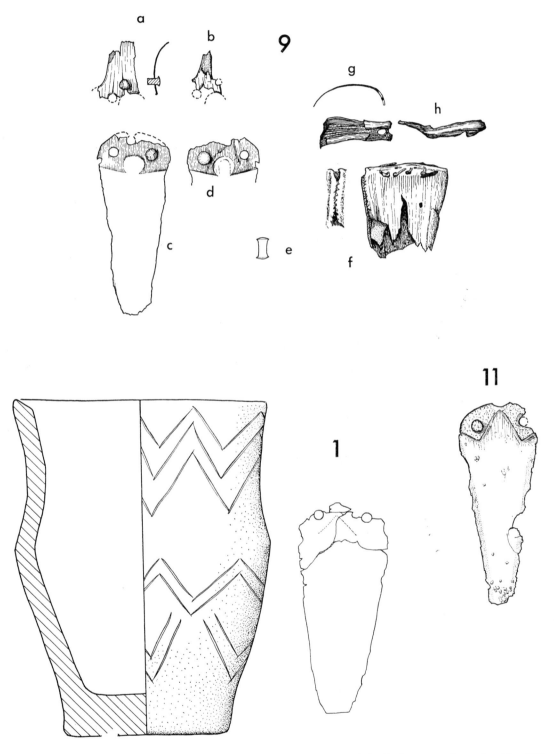

Figure 40. 1. Cairn Greg, Angus; 9. Kirkcaldy, Fife (a. fragment of hilt; b. fragment of opposite side of hilt; c. blade; d. upper part of opposite side of blade; e. loose rivet; f. sheath with detail of seam; g–h. hilt mount); 11. Bught Park, Inverness. 1/2

This was analysed by Dr H. McKerrell, who concluded that it was a wax/resin material. The likeliest explanation is that it derives from treatment of the blade at the time it came to the museum. A detached piece of the sheath consists of wood on one side, and animal skin retaining its fibres on the other side. The sheath was therefore of wood covered by hide.

Small blade (fig. 44, b; EQ 228). Six fragments of a delicate tanged blade survive. Its original length has been at least 11 cm. There is a mid-rib, 2·8 mm. thick, and a groove near the cutting edge. Just inside the groove are two traced lines. The surface is glossy, but under magnification shows a mass of lengthwise striations. The mouldings are very regular and crisp.

The burial.[45] The site was in agricultural land four miles north of Arbroath (NO 651483). A cairn of stones and earth, about 30 ft. in diameter and 3 ft. high, was investigated in 1891. The surface below the cairn was thickly covered by fragments of burnt wood. There was a more or less central pit, 6 ft. by 3 ft. and 3 ft. deep, in which the fragments of the blades were found. The pit filling seemed to be disturbed, and it was suggested that it had once held the cist, 5 ft. long by 2 ft. deep, which had been found beneath a cairn in the immediate neighbourhood about 1808. In 1891 two secondary collared urns, containing two incense cups, a glass bead and a bronze blade, and cremations, were found; to these may be added the three urns and one incense cup found in 1808.

3. HILL OF WEST MAINS, AUCHTERHOUSE, ANGUS

Dagger blade[46] (fig. 43; EQ 255 in the National Museum of Antiquities of Scotland). It measures 16·4 cm. long by 6·6 cm. across the heel, and retains six rivets. There are also three loose rivets. The blade is in fairly good condition except at the tip, but most of the surface is covered by a layer of oxide. Down each face there is a triple-reeded mid-rib, tapering towards the point and fading away at the heel. Tiny punched dots flank the mid-rib; they are rather irregularly spaced, about twelve per cm. There is also a very faint line of dots down the grooves of the mid-rib, only just visible in one area. Except for the mid-rib the blade appears to be flat.

The heel of the dagger is angular with a straight upper edge. The rivets are still firmly in place, their length varying from 0·9 cm. at the outer end to 1·2 cm. at the inner end, graduated to coincide with the cross-section of the hilt. Around the rivets are remains of the hilt, and the form of the lower edge, with the small Ω-shaped recess enclosing the top of the mid-rib, is clear on one face.

The hilt. This survives as two separate badly warped and shrunken horn plates, the lower edge broken through a group of three rivet holes. The inner faces of the plates have a smooth surface with a dusty appearance except for the two upper corners where there is clean oblique ridging.

Dr Clarke has concluded that the hilt was cut in one piece from the end of an ox horn, the upper part or pommel being solid, the rest being in two layers, the smooth inner surface being the interior surface against the horn core.[47]

In plan the hilt-plates narrow for the grip from a somewhat expanded end, and widen sharply to cover the heel of the blade. It seems unlikely that there has been much lengthwise shrinkage, as the reconstruction using the existing length (6·5 cm. if straight, from the centre of the rivet holes) brings the hilt to almost the same length as that on the Ashgrove dagger. When found, the length was given as 3½ to 3¾ in. [8·7–9·5 cm.] but it is uncertain how the measurement was taken. The shrinkage in width appears to have been much greater, as might be expected across the grain of the horn. The hilt is said to have measured 1⅛ in. [2·9 cm.] across when found; if the measurement was taken across the upper end a loss of a third is indicated. A comparison of the rivet holes with the thickness of the loose rivets also indicates a loss of between a third and a quarter in width. A loss of about a third in thickness is shown by comparing the plates with the length of the rivets. The dagger and hilt has been reconstructed in fig. 43, 3 d.

Sheath-mount (fig. 43, 3 e–f). Besides the hilt, there are also some pieces of horn preserved with the dagger, which in the original report were assumed to be part of the sheath. They have now been joined together to form three main pieces, leaving a few fragments. One piece (*e*) is almost intact, lacking only one corner. It is warped, but if flat would measure 5·7 by 1·7 cm. The centre portion is 2 mm. thick, but the ends are rebated leaving them 1 mm. thick from which they thin away to the outer ends. Through each of the thin end-portions is a pair of holes in line lengthwise, 3 mm. in diameter. The holes of one pair are 1·5 mm., the other 5 mm., apart. On either side of the inner of each pair of holes there is a much smaller hole, about 1 mm. in diameter, and in two of these there remains a tiny bone or ivory peg. Both pegs have what appears to be the original straight-cut end surviving on the outer side.

Another piece (*f*) retains an intact end which in dimensions and arrangement of the holes almost exactly reverses the arrangement of the ends of piece *e*. In one of the smaller holes is an intact bone peg 4 mm. long. The other end of piece *f* is broken and from the inner large hole it has split lengthwise and warped apart. On the assumption that no horn is missing from the inner edges of the split, the piece can be said to have widened from 1·7 cm. at the intact end to 2·45 cm. at the broken end. The maximum thickness is 1 mm. The other pieces and fragments are featureless. The largest measures 2·45 by 3·4 cm., and may have been larger for none of the edges is certainly original.

In the original report[48] a tiny 'rivet or pin of ivory' was noted among the finds. Presumably this was another peg similar to those remaining in the horn plates.

A minute fragment of black substance adhered to each face of piece *e*. This was examined by Dr M. L. Ryder, who reported that both were almost certainly animal skin, but no hair remains survived to allow precise identification.

When examining these pieces Clarke made a tentative reconstruction of the sheath in which they formed the strengthening mount at the top. The key to the reconstruction is piece *e*. Even after warping one end of *e* so nearly mirrors the end of *f* that it is reasonable to suppose they overlapped and that the ends of *e* were rebated for this purpose. Clarke assumed that the other pieces formed a continuous band, widening at the front to at least 2·5 cm. wide (fig. 43, 3 h, g, based on Clarke's drawings). The tiny pegs are presumed to have held the pieces of horn together. The larger holes, for which no pegs were found, may have been used for a cord or thong which attached the sheath to a belt.

The outer surfaces of *e* and *f* are slightly ribbed lengthwise, which might suggest that they had been cut longitudinally from the horn. However, Clarke points out that the very base of a horn bears horizontal growth ridges. One of the most satisfactory aspects of Clarke's experiments is that almost all of a horn was used for the dagger, the small strip left at the base after cutting out the hilt being just what was needed for the sheath-mount as reconstructed by him.

The burial.[49] The Hill of West Mains rises to 950 ft., about seven miles north-northwest of Dundee (NO 315376). It is crowned by a cairn, which, at the time of the excavations in 1897, was about 63 ft. in diameter and 5 ft. 6 in. high, but formerly had been higher. In the centre of the cairn was a double cist, the two long sides each composed of one slab. The slabs were set into the subsoil which was only 4 to 5 in. deep. The cist was luted with clay, and the capstones were covered by a 3 in. layer of clay. Around the cist was a rough wall of stones. The cist and wall were covered by a mound about 20 or 30 ft. in diameter, probably made of turves, containing broken pieces of quartz and quantities of 'wood ashes.' This mound was edged by a kerb of large stones, 3 ft. high. The whole was covered by the cairn edged by a kerb of smaller stones.

The cist was divided into two compartments by a transverse slab, and was covered by six capstones. The larger compartment measured 2 ft. by 2 ft. 2 in., and was 2 ft. deep. In it were two heaps of partly burnt bones, not necessarily representing more than one body, and the dagger. The smaller compartment contained only a thoroughly burnt cremation.

On top of the stone 'wall' surrounding the cist were two bronze objects, each placed between two flat slabs. 'Both were so much decayed as to exist only as a vivid green powder.' One was about 10 cm. long and 1·3 cm. or less in width; the other 'was more leaf-shaped,' about 7·5 cm. in length.

4. CLEIGH, LOCH NELL, ARGYLL

Dagger blade[50] (fig. 42; Pl. 1, c; DI 1 in the National Museum of Antiquities of Scotland). It is in good condition with a fine green patina, though one face is obscured by dirt and accretions. The inner edges of the bevels remain, so only a little has been lost from the edges of the blade. It measures 12·6 cm. long by 5·4 cm. wide. The blade is unusual in being just perceptibly convex in long section as well as in cross-section. Three rivets remain in position, two loose and one rigid. The central rivet is in a notch which encircles about two-thirds of its circumference. The mark left by the lower edge of the hilt is very clear on both faces showing an Ω-shaped recess. Last vestiges of the hilt remain as a paper-thin substance with vertical graining. On one face, immediately below the edge of the hilt, there is a line of punched dots, fairly evenly spaced with about ten per cm. Fine multiple cut and scratch marks can also be seen, mainly just below the dots in the recess. On the other face neither dots nor cut marks are visible at present.

The rigid rivet is the best preserved, measuring 1·2 cm. across the head, and 0·9 cm. through the shank. In profile it can be seen that the heads of the rivets slant slightly to be flush with the surface of the vanished hilt

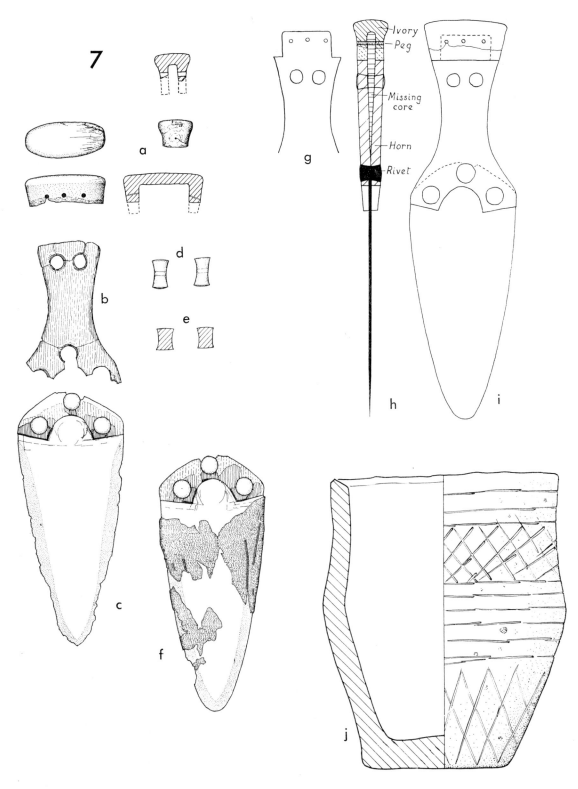

Figure 41. Ashgrove, Fife; a. pommel; b. hilt-plate; c. bronze blade; d. rivets from top of hilt; e. sections through side and central rivets in the blade; f. opposite side of blade with remains of sheath; g. plan of missing core of hilt; h. reconstruction of section and plan of dagger; j. the beaker. 1/2

which has increased slightly in thickness from its lower edge; the rivets therefore vary from 1 cm. to 1·25 cm. long.

The burial.[51] A cairn formerly existed in the valley pasture between inland Loch Nell and tidal Loch Feochan only a mile away, less than 3 miles south of Oban (NM 880263). The site was examined in 1872, by which time only the base of the cairn survived 'encircled by standing stones' (probably a kerb or spaced peristalith), and the cist it had covered had been exposed. The cist was 2 ft. deep, and one side was formed of natural rock. Though it had been opened previously, fragments of bone were found, and the dagger which was in an undisturbed corner.

5. BLACKWATERFOOT, ARRAN, COUNTY OF BUTE

Dagger blade[52] (fig. 42; Pl. 1, d; EQ 268 in the National Museum of Antiquities of Scotland). It is much corroded, damaged down both edges, and broken in two. The existing length is 22·8 cm., and the width 6·4 cm. On each face of the blade are three delicate ribs, slightly tapering in width and thickness towards the point, and fading away in the area covered by the hilt. The total thickness through the ribs is only 2·95 mm. Except for the ribs the blade is flat, 2 mm. thick, but thinning towards the top edge. The form of the heel is unusual. Two rivets are set in the angular shoulders which are formed by a deep notch leaving a central fish-tail tang. The upper edge of the tang is damaged, but it is unlikely that more than a fraction is missing. Otherwise, the edges of the heel are original, very crisp, with a narrow bevel. The surface of the area under the hilt is covered by very fine lengthwise striations. The W-shaped base of the hilt can be traced by variations in the corrosion, and is delineated by a row of tiny dots, partly visible on both faces. The ribs are also outlined by dots, spaced ten to thirteen per cm.

Although the rivets are damaged it can be seen that the heads are at a slight angle to be flush with the slightly convex cross-section of the vanished hilt. The rivets are 0·7–0·9 cm. long.

Gold pommel-mount. Made of sheet gold, it is now in two pieces and greatly distorted, but the curve of one end appears to be undamaged. It measures 0·5–0·6 cm. wide, and was probably about 4·1 cm. long. In profile the sides are slightly tapering, and they are decorated with six ribs divided by five grooves. The mount is made with rough flanges at the upper and lower edges in exactly the same way as that from Skateraw where its features are more clearly visible.

The burial. A very large cairn formerly stood at Blackwaterfoot, in low-lying agricultural land near the shore in the southwest part of the island of Arran (NR 898281). In 1772 it was described as a 'stupendous cairn, a hundred and fourteen feet over, and of a vast height.'[53] By 1861 it had already been partly robbed, and many 'stone coffins' were said to have been found in it.[54] Only the base of the cairn, a few feet high, remained when further robbing in 1900 exposed a cist which was empty except for the dagger. The cist was very well made, measuring 4 ft. 3 in. by 2 ft. 4 in., and 2 ft. 6 in. deep. The capstone was said to have measured 7 ft. by 5 ft.[55]

6. SKATERAW, DUNBAR, EAST LOTHIAN

Dagger blade[56] (fig. 42; EQ 237 in the National Museum of Antiquities of Scotland). It is almost entirely covered by a layer of corrosion, which is especially thick just inside the long edges. This might suggest that it incorporates the remains of a sheath with vertical ribs such as that on the Ashgrove dagger. Except that the blade is broken in half it is little damaged but for the loss of part of one edge. It measures 14·8 cm. long by 5·5 cm. wide. The unusual form of the heel is like that of the Blackwaterfoot dagger, with a central tang (apparently intact) and a rivet in each of the angular shoulders. Around the rivets are the last remains of the hilt, now completely oxidized. The W-shaped lower edge of the hilt is clearly visible. The rivet-heads, now much damaged, are about 1·05 cm. in diameter.

Gold pommel-mount (EQ 238). It is made of sheet gold decorated by four ribs divided by three grooves. It has been cut into two pieces and so is slightly distorted, now appearing more circular than the original form which seems to have been a somewhat pointed oval measuring about 3·6–3·8 cm. by 2·5 cm. It is slightly tapering in profile, and is 0·82 cm. deep. The outer surface is worn smooth. Along the top and bottom the sheet is turned in as flanges, and these flanges are unworn with roughly cut inner edges. In places the metal has been 'pleated' and beaten almost flat to reduce the diameter of the flange on the curve.

The burial.[57] An 'immense cairn' in a field on the farm of Skateraw, near the coast three and a half miles southeast of Dunbar (about NT 7375), was removed some time between 1806 and 1814. 'There was found at the bottom of the pile a large stone measuring 9 ft. in length, 5 ft. in width, and nearly 3 ft. in thickness. Beneath it was a grave, the sides composed of four slabs neatly fitted together.' In the cist were remains of a skeleton, with the dagger at one side and 'pieces of a substance resembling fragments of a blue glass bottle' near the feet.

7. ASHGROVE, METHILHILL, FIFE[58]

Dagger blade (fig. 41; in Kirkcaldy Museum and Art Gallery). It is in good condition except for the very edge, but even this was perfect when it was found. In the heel of the blade are three rivets, the centre one placed in a notch which encircles about two-thirds of its circumference. The lower edge of the hilt, still in place on the blade, is slightly convex with a semicircular recess. Immediately below the hilt both faces of the blade are marked by a number of fine cut marks, presumably the result of trimming the edge of the hilt. One set of marks is 0·3 cm. below the present end of the hilt and form an Ω-shaped recess, indicating that the original end of the hilt was longer and of this form. The blade has been re-hafted, or the hilt trimmed back, apparently on two occasions. The rivets are 1 cm. long.

The hilt. When the dagger was excavated the remains of the hilt were still attached. It had been constructed of two horn plates between which there must have been a third plate (totally decayed and probably of wood) with a tang at the top on to which the pommel had been fitted.

The hilt-plates were attached to the blade by the three rivets still in place in the blade, and two more rivets held the horn plates and centre plate together just below the pommel. Around each rivet hole the horn plates are marked by part of a ring of tiny radial nicks, less than 1 mm. long, with about fifty-four in a complete circle. Possibly these marks are ornamental, or possibly they were formed by the overlapping edge of a punch used in hammering the rivets.

The original length of the hilt-plates was 8 cm. In plan their sides are gently concave. At the lower end they were 0·4 to 0·45 cm. thick (fragments of this thickness remaining round the lower rivets), and increased slightly to 0·6 cm. at the upper end (indicated by the corrosion variation on the shanks of the loose rivets).

The two loose rivets which held the upper ends of the plates are 1·4–1·45 cm. long.

The missing centre plate extended from the blade up into the socket of the pommel. At the bottom it was as thin as the blade, but increased to a thickness of 0·25 cm. at the upper rivets (indicated by the corrosion of the rivet shanks) and to 0·5 cm. inside the pommel.

The pommel is of ivory, almost certainly from the tooth of a sperm whale. The high gloss only survives in places, and the lower edge has decayed completely for it is evident that another 0·7 cm. is required to bring the curve of the sides of the pommel in line with the curve of the sides of the hilt-plates. The rectangular socket in the lower edge of the pommel was to receive the tang from the centre plate of the hilt. Three holes bored straight through the pommel were for pins which held the pommel in place; the pins had completely disappeared, so they also were probably of wood.

The sheath. On the blade were the last traces of the sheath, so degraded that it could only be identified as some kind of animal skin. Running down the sheath there were five lines of sewing forming tiny ribs. The thread had decayed completely, but under magnification lines of tiny holes and the impressions of the threads lying across the ribs could be seen. The sewing had been a very fine and regular whipping with about eighteen stitches per cm. Two ribs were near each edge and one down the centre. There did not appear to be any seam down the edge of the sheath.

The beaker (fig. 41, j). It is a crudely made slightly biconical vessel of coarse ware with a thin slip partly covering the grits. The vessel is buff coloured except for a crumbly red patch probably due to secondary burning. The decoration is deeply but roughly incised.

The burial. The site is about a mile from the north shore of the Firth of Forth, in gently undulating agricultural land (NT 352999). A cist was discovered during building operations in 1963. The top of the coverstone was 2 ft. or more below ground level. This stone measured 6 ft. 7 in. by 5 ft. 3 in. The cist was carefully built and the joints were luted with clay. It measured 2 ft. 7½ in. by 2 ft. 3 in. by 2 ft. 7 in. deep.

The skeleton lay crouched on the left side. The sex was probably male, and the wear on the teeth suggested the age was about fifty-five years.

Over the skeleton and the cist floor was a thin deposit of black crumbly matter, which formed a deep deposit in front of the chest. On examination this deposit was found to be plant remains, amongst which were fragments

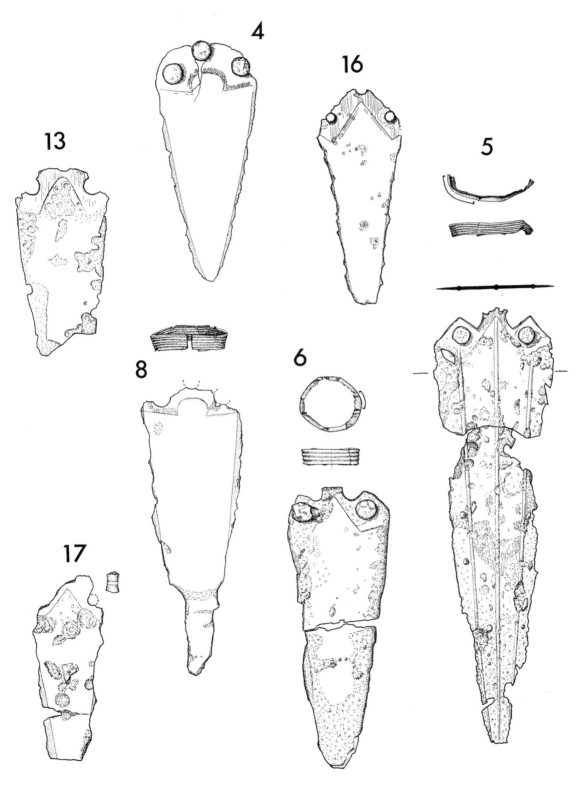

Figure 42. 4. Cleigh, Argyll; 5. Blackwaterfoot, Co. of Bute; 6. Skateraw, East Lothian; 8. Collessie, Fife; 13. Carlochan Cairn, Kirkcudbrightshire; 16. Drumlanrick, Perthshire; 17. Dunragit, Wigtownshire. (Black line outside pommel-mounts of 5 and 6 indicates portion not distorted.) 1/2

of birch, cross-leaved heath, rush, moss, and fairly abundant sphagnum moss. A 'stick' lying over the upper part of the body was a fern rhizome. In addition, pollens of twenty-three species were identified. With the exception of a high proportion of lime and meadowsweet, the pollens convey 'an impression of open plant communities affected by agricultural activity.' The high proportion of lime and meadowsweet might be explained by a flowering bunch of these plants being deliberately included with the burial. Both plants are noted for their fragrance, and bloom in July and August.

Some animal fibres found on the hilt plates were identified as bovine, possibly from the aurochs.

8. GASK HILL, COLLESSIE, FIFE

Dagger blade[59] (fig. 42; EQ 62 in the National Museum of Antiquities of Scotland). The metal is greatly decayed and all the edges are damaged, but much of the original glossy surface remains. From the illustration made at the time of discovery it can be seen that the blade has convex edges. The inner edge of the bevels down the sides remains in places. The blade is now 15·3 cm. long by 5·3 cm. wide. At the heel parts of two rivet holes and a notch (or three rivet holes) remain, 1 cm. in diameter with slightly bevelled edges. The Ω-shaped notch in the lower edge of the hilt is clearly marked by colour variation and by a number of very fine cut marks in the surface.

Gold pommel-mount (EQ 53). It is almost identical to that found at Blackwaterfoot. It is now greatly distorted and broken in two, but it was drawn at the time of its discovery when it still seems to have been intact. It was originally oblong with rounded ends, and slightly tapering in profile. It is 0·7 cm. wide, and originally was about 4 cm. long. It is decorated with six ridges separated by five grooves. The edges are very similar to the other specimens, with roughly cut flanges and 'pleating.'

The sheath. In the excavation report Anderson describes the organic remains visible on the blade when it was found. 'When I examined the blade with a pocket magnifying glass immediately after it was taken up, the appearance of woody structure was quite distinctly visible in patches.' Other patches, forming an upper layer, consisted of masses of straight fibres attached to tiny fragments of a black substance which appeared to be leather. Anderson ended his description by saying, 'I have little doubt that we have here the remains of the sheath of wood, covered with hide, having its hair outward.' A specimen preserved in the Museum has been examined and proves to be ox hair.[60]

The burial.[61] A very large cairn, about 120 ft. in diameter and 14 ft. high, known as Gask Hill, stood beside the public road just southeast of the village of Collessie in central Fife (NO 288131). It was partly excavated in 1876–7. The primary structure on the site seems to have been a cairn, about 60 ft. in diameter, edged by a kerb of sandstone slabs set on edge, 3 ft. to 4 ft. high, traced for about one-third of the circumference. They were set in gravel, with a bank of gravel against their inner faces. Within the kerb the ground was covered by clay, with burnt patches, in which 'the black ashes and charcoal of wood might be taken up in handfuls.' Roughly in the centre of this cairn was a cist, built on ground level. It was 4 ft. 6 in. long by 3 ft. wide, and 1 ft. 3 in. high. In the cist were the last remnants of an inhumation and a Bell Beaker. About 8 ft. from the cist, but at a depth of 6 ft. below the ground surface, a Short Necked Beaker was found, in pieces, 'imbedded among the gravel, which was discoloured by ashes and charcoal.'

About 23 ft. from the cist, and roughly in the line of the kerb which was not found in this part of the cairn, there were 'three or four stones of large size placed against each other on the ground level.' Beneath these, at a depth of 4 ft., was a deposit of burnt bones, covering an area about 3 ft. by 4 ft. and about 1 in. deep, and among the bones was the dagger and pommel-mount. The cairn was enlarged so that the kerb lay eccentrically within it, probably when this last burial was made.

9. KIRKCALDY, FIFE

Dagger blade[62] (fig. 40 j; in Kirkcaldy Museum and Art Gallery). The blade is now in poor condition, having lost most of the edge and tip. The surface tends to flake away, but where well preserved it is glossy. The present length is 9·6 cm., the width 3·85 cm.; a small part of the bevel of the original edge remains. The blade appears to be flat, only 1·2 mm. thick. The heel of the blade is somewhat angular, and the three rivets have been unevenly spaced. One rivet remains in place, the other two (one broken) are loose. The best preserved measures 1·2 cm. long, and has a domed head. Remains of the hilt still adhere to the blade, and the lower edge of the hilt with its Ω-shaped recess is clear. On one side of the blade the area inside the recess bears faint scratch marks in the form of an inverted U.

The hilt. Two small pieces of horn (recently identified by Clarke), now badly warped and shrunk, and some tiny fragments, survive. Piece *a* is from the lower edge on the side of the blade which is fully drawn. The piece retains the central rivet (lacking its head on the under side), half the left rivet hole, and part of the original edge round the recess and down the left side. On the inner face an oxide stain and faint impression indicate the position of the upper edge of the blade. The central rivet was evidently in an almost closed notch as shown by the dotted line on the drawing of the blade. It can be shown that the piece has lost at least a quarter in lateral shrinkage.

Piece *b* is from the lower left corner of the opposite face. It retains about a third of the central rivet hole, a fragment of the left rivet hole, and part of the original edges of the recess and left side.

The sheath and mount. The upper part of the sheath survives. It is made of two layers of animal skin,[63] the lining being a thinner lighter-coloured skin. When found, the dagger was rammed down so that the upper part of the blade and two lower rivets were below its upper edge. The outer layer is made of one piece of skin, joined by a side seam, now mainly sprung apart, but still held for a short distance by a fine 'gut' drawing the edges together by under-and-over stitches, about 10 per cm. The lining is fragmentary, but can be seen to have a seam running down the centre of one face. At the top of the sheath two thin layers, presumably skin, lie between the sheath and the lining, but as they do not appear to project any distance down the sheath they are probably only strips used to strengthen the upper edge. Inside the lining round the top are a few fibres, either remains of sewing or perhaps of fabric.

At the back of the sheath, near the top edge, are four holes through which two thongs are threaded. One thong passes through the outer holes, and inside the sheath passes straight across between the sheath and its lining, covering the other thong which emerges from the centre holes. All the thongs have broken close to the outer face. Just below the top of the sheath are some smaller holes, two near the centre and two near the seam, one of the latter retaining an end of fine sewing 'gut.' These holes might be connected with attaching the lining, but there are no holes on the front of the sheath

Two strips of horn, *g* and *h*, have formed a mount round the top of the sheath. Piece *g* would measure 5·2 cm. long if straight; it is 1 cm. across the narrower end where both original edges survive, and widens to 1·5 cm. at the other end. Piece *h*, which retains only its upper edge, would be 5·3 cm. long if straight.

Part of one surface of piece *g* has split away. In the narrow end is a hole measuring 0·55 cm. by 0·3 cm., and part of another. When described in 1943 some fragments of thong remained in the holes. The dagger has left an impression on a piece of skin on which it lay, and in 1966 a small fragment of piece *h* was found adhering in the groove which represents the top of the sheath. Near it is a layer of horn flaked from the outer surface of piece *g*. These three clues allow only one reconstruction of the sheath-mount. The hole must fit over the left thong as drawn with piece *g* curving round the left edge with its defective surface outside. Piece *h* belongs to the other side with its narrow tip representing the part of the mount over the two right thongs. Only about 1 cm. is missing from the front face, and only the ends with their perforations from the back face. It is evident that the mount widened towards the front to a breadth of nearly 2 cm.

The skin. The piece, featureless with no original edges, measures 6·4 cm. by 8·2 cm., and consists of two layers. On the concave side the impression of the dagger, and especially of the sheath-mount, is clear. On the other side the skin is drawn into a number of folds which ran up the hilt. These folds do not appear on the concave face, so the two layers appear to have been separate. The purpose of the skin is uncertain, but, from the evidence noted below, it is more likely to have been clothing than a cover or a bag. In 1943 fabric was seen adhering to the skin, and 'was certainly woven from a vegetable fibre, but its exact nature could not be decided.' No trace of this remains.

Plant remains. On the convex side of the skin, and on the front face of the sheath, there are fragments of leaves adhering. The presence of leaves on the side of the sheath which had lain against the clean side of the leather is noteworthy, especially as they extend to the top edge which was originally covered by the mount. The explanation is probably that during decay the mount sprung apart at the join and the leather sheath and dagger fell away into a position in contact with the leaves. It is unlikely to have moved if the skin had been part of a bag, and it is unlikely that it would have been in contact with the leaves if the skin had been a covering of the floor or of the body.

The leaves were examined by Mrs C. Dickson, Department of Botany, University of Cambridge. At least three leaves have been tentatively identified as Rubiaceae, *Galium odoratum* (Sweet Woodruff) being the most likely species on morphological grounds. Sweet Woodruff is a fragrant plant both flowering or dried. Another leaf is certainly from one of the two native species of oak.

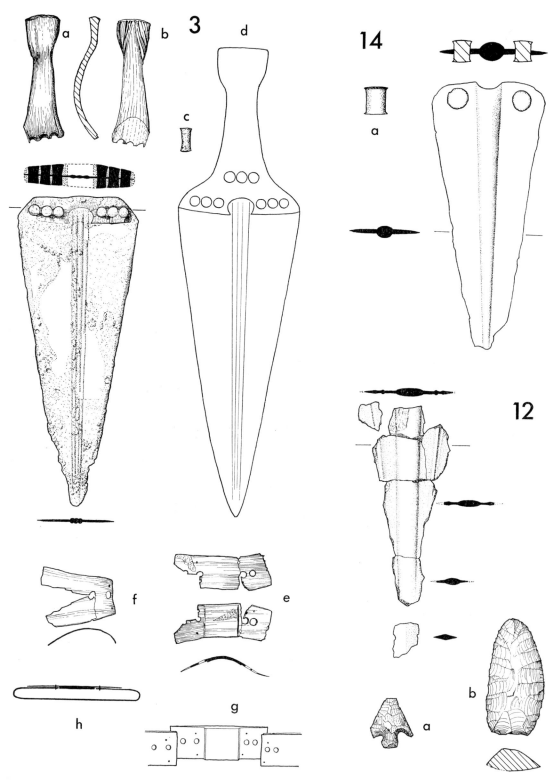

Figure 43. 3. Auchterhouse, Angus (a, b. outside and inside of hilt; c. one of loose rivets; d. reconstruction; e. piece of sheath-mount; f. end fragment of sheath-mount; g-h. reconstruction of sheath-mount); 12. Craigs-corry, Inverness. (a. arrowhead; b. knife); 14. Law of Mauldslie, Lanarkshire (a. loose rivet). 1/2

The burial.[64] The cist containing the burial was found in 1931 when excavating the site of the abattoir at Kirkcaldy (NT 272916). The badly decayed skeleton was male, about fifty years old.[65] Four or five feet away a second cist was found containing a richly furnished woman's grave. The two cists are assumed to be contemporary.

10. MASTERTON, FIFE[66]

Dagger blade (fig. 44; EQ 640 in the National Museum of Antiquities of Scotland). Much of the surface of the blade is pitted with corrosion, and the edges are damaged. However, little appears to be missing from the heel and the original form appears to have been rounded with only two rivets. The edges of the rivet holes are bevelled, and the more complete is not accurately circular. The V-shaped form of the lower edge of the hilt is clearly marked on both faces by difference in corrosion, and, on the face drawn, by the upper limit of dark staining. Multiple cut-marks are just visible along the edge of the staining, but are hardly distinguishable on the poor surface of the other side. The blade is 13·4 cm. long by 5·2 cm. wide. In one place the original sharp edge is preserved showing that the original bevel was 0·65 cm. wide. Only one damaged rivet was recovered, measuring 1 cm. long.

During excavation the hilt was visible on the floor of the cist as a black mass; the minute fragments recovered were identified as decomposed horn.

Jet necklace (EQ 642). It was found with most of the beads lying in the order in which they had been strung. There were sixty-seven fusiform beads, ninety-one small disc beads, and a triangular toggle for fastening. The fusiform beads had been strung in five rows, and were more or less graduated having the larger beads in the centre. The disc beads were placed at the ends of the strings. When reassembled it was clear that the necklace was not long enough to encircle the neck, and each string must have continued for at least 5 cm. before being attached to the toggle; the toggle was in fact found separated from the beads. Most of the fusiform beads show signs of wear.

Bronze blade (EQ 641). Only the centre portion was recovered. It is very delicate with sharp edges, only 1·2 mm. thick. A small wood or horn handle with a knob end, greatly decayed, was found near the armlets and presumably belonged to the blade which had been disturbed before the excavation.

Pair of bronze armlets (EQ 639). They are represented only by pieces and fragments. The armlets were 3·5 cm. wide and 7·5 cm. in diameter. They were made from a curved strip of sheet metal, for one end-piece survives. The end is cut, slightly convex, and has three small rivets. The rivets are very short, not allowing for another layer of metal, and it seems likely that they attached the armlet to a thin layer of leather or cloth. The edges of the armlets were neatened and strengthened by being turned in.

The quality of the workmanship is high. Where uncorroded the surface has a high gloss. The decoration is very carefully and accurately carried out. There are four ribs running round the armlets, and the edges are slightly everted. In the hollow between the edges and the two outer ribs is a row of transverse punched lines. The two inner ribs swell into pairs of low points, six in the circumference, and are outlined by a row of punched dots. (Pl.I, a)

Hide. Over much of the floor of the cist there was a black stain, and where there had been contact with metal some fibres were preserved. The fibres were probably from a European bison or aurochs. The stain presumably represents a hide which had been laid on the floor of the cist.

The burial. The site, accidentally exposed in 1961, was in undulating agricultural land just over 2 miles north of the shore of the Firth of Forth, between Inverkeithing and Dunfermline (NT 121845).

The carefully built cist was unusually large, orientated east-northeast–west-southwest. It was made of five well-fitting sandstone slabs (one long side having two slabs). Internally it measured 5 ft. 3 in. long by 3 ft. 2 in. wide and 2 ft. 9 in. deep. It was covered by two very large capstones with 6 in. of earthy gravel between them. All the joints had been freely luted with clay. The cist had been built in a pit a little over 5 ft. deep from the surface. At each lower corner a lump of clay spread fan-wise over the floor. In the northwest and southwest corners they covered an empty post-hole. It is likely that the two posts had supported the west stone during the construction of the cist, and were later withdrawn.

The remains of the armlets, the small blade and the necklace were near the northeast corner, and the dagger was against the south side about halfway along. The only human remains were some tiny fragments of oxide-impregnated bone inside the armlets and over the dagger, and the crowns of some teeth near the beads. The grave-goods suggest a double burial, of a man and a woman; the unusual size of the cist has been noted. The position of the objects at the east end of the cist suggests that the woman lay crouched on her right side facing northwest or west with her hands in front of her face. The teeth indicated an age of about twenty-five years at the time of death.

11. BUGHT PARK, INVERNESS[67]

Dagger blade (fig. 40; in Inverness Public Museum). The blade is in fair condition, pieces having broken away from the edges and tip. Much of the original glossy surface remains though pitted in places by corrosion. The blade measures 10·6 cm. long by 4·25 cm. wide. The heel of the blade is damaged at one side. It is clear that there were only two rivet holes, and that a third rivet rested in a notch in the top of the blade. One rivet remains firmly in place. It is 0·72 cm. long, the shank being markedly concave in profile. At the top of the blade, just below the edge of the hilt, the surface is covered with many fine lengthwise striations which fade away lower down; they are also just visible in the area covered by the hilt. These give the impression that the blade was rubbed down by abrasive but polished after hafting. The hilt has left a thin olive green deposit where it covered the blade, and the W-shaped lower edge is clearly visible. Just below and parallel to the edge there are fine cut marks.

Atkinson, who examined the dagger soon after finding, noted 'minute traces of black substance adhering to the surviving rivet which suggested the possible use of resin as a glue.'

The burial. A cist was found in the Queen's Park, Bught, in September 1954, when removing a tree. The site is a gravel terrace less than a quarter of a mile from the northwest bank of the River Ness (NH 656437). The cist had been built in a pit 6 ft. deep, and the space between the cist and side of the pit had been packed with stones. The cist was constructed of slabs set on edge with walling on their upper edges giving a total depth of 3 ft. 4 in. Internally the cist measured 4 ft. 4 in. by 2 ft. 3 in., orientated east-northeast–west-southwest. The joints were luted with clay and the floor was covered with clay: no earth had fallen into the cist. It was covered by two overlapping capstones. The skeleton was of a man about fifty years of age.

12. CRAIGSCORRY, INVERNESS-SHIRE

The blade[68] (fig. 43; EQ 366 in the National Museum of Antiquities of Scotland). Fragments survive of a dagger with a mid-rib, maximum thickness about 5 mm. Outside the mid-rib there is a wide tapering hollow which dies away near the tip. On the upper part of the blade, where the thicker portion outside of the hollow is wider, there is a tapering cast groove which dies away about halfway down the blade. Near the tip the distinct mid-rib disappears and the blade becomes diamond-shaped in cross-section.

The flints (EQ 367–8). A damaged barbed-and-tanged arrowhead, and a rather thick plano-convex knife, are both burnt.

The burial.[69] The grave, found in 1925, was on a rugged hillside 2 miles southwest of Beauly (NH 503452). A capstone lay at ground level. The grave was oval, 7 ft. long by 4 ft. wide. It was rock-cut with an average depth of 2 ft., but the walls were built up with rough masonry. It contained a partly burnt skeleton, the burnt flints and the unburnt dagger.

13. CARLOCHAN CAIRN, CROSSMICHAEL, KIRKCUDBRIGHTSHIRE

Dagger blade[70] (fig. 42; DI 3 in the National Museum of Antiquities of Scotland). It is much damaged and lacks the point. Much of the surface has flaked away, but where remaining it has a high gloss, the whole covered by a green patina. Where the hilt-plate has protected the surface this is well preserved and bears many lengthwise striations. The heel is damaged, but half of two rivet holes remain, and a small part of a third hole or notch. The holes are not accurately circular, they have bevelled edges, and are about 0·9 cm. in diameter. The lower edge of the hilt has been V-shaped, very clear in the corrosion difference of the face drawn, but less clear on the other face. On this face a lightly incised line is visible just below one side of the V. None of the original edges of the blade survives, but a short length of the inner edge of the bevel remains along one side of the face not drawn. The blade now measures 9·8 by 5 cm.

The burial.[71] Carlochan Cairn, which was said to have been the largest in Galloway, was removed in 1776. It stood on the top of a small hill, in agricultural land, 3 miles north of Castle Douglas (NX 757674). 'In the

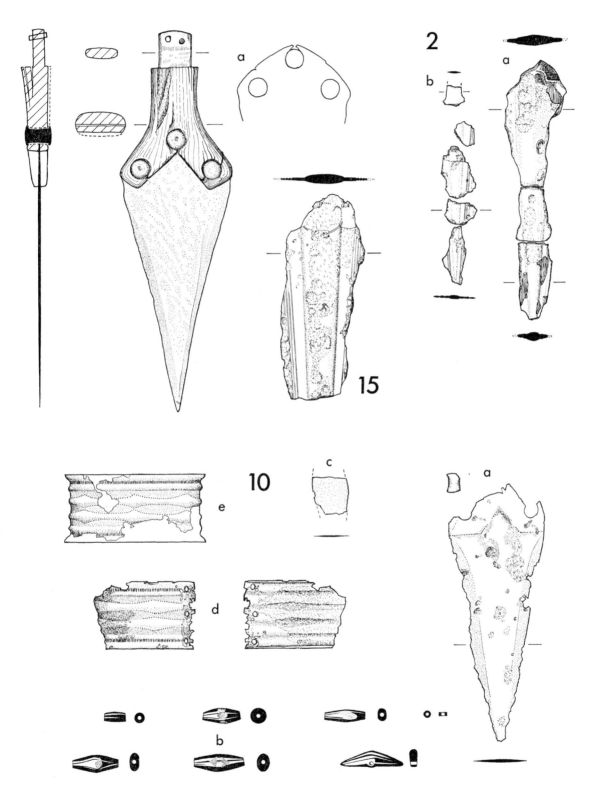

Figure 44. Top left, Wasbister, Orkney (a. top of blade from an X-ray photograph); 2. Gilchorn, Angus (a. tanged blade); 10. Masterton, Fife (a. dagger; b. beads from complete necklace; c. bronze blade; d. end of armlet, outside and inside; e. reconstruction of armlet); 15. Bishopmill, Moray. 1/2

middle of this cairn, at the bottom, was found a coffin, composed of large stones, but there were no bones in it.' The dagger was found with 'a round pin of the same material,' presumably a rivet. The silver armlet and amber bead later said to have been associated with this burial are in fact Viking, and are recorded as coming from another cairn in the same district.[72]

14. LAW OF MAULDSLIE, CARLUKE, LANARKSHIRE

Dagger blade[73] (fig. 43). It is only known from a note and drawing made at the time of discovery. It was 13·3 cm. long, but the tip was damaged. Down the centre of the blade was a mid-rib, rounded in section. Two large rivets remained in position, and a third larger rivet found loose had presumably rested in the notch in the top edge of the blade. The rivets were 1·3 cm. long with expanded heads.

The burial.[74] A cist was found in 1866 at the highest point of the Law of Mauldslie, 1½ miles west-northwest of Carluke (NS 821514). The huge capstone was 2 ft. below ground level. The cist measured 3 ft. 4 in. by 1 ft. 8 in., by 2 ft. 3 in. deep. It contained a crouched skeleton and the dagger.

15. BISHOPMILL, ELGIN, MORAY[75]

Dagger blade (fig. 44; 1888.1 in the Elgin Society Museum). Only a fragment of the upper part of the blade survives lacking all edges, but rivet holes remained in 1881. It now measures 10·8 cm. by 4·2 cm., and is in poor condition. There is a wide mid-rib, about 6 mm. thick, outside which the blade bears four narrow traced grooves. At the top the mid-rib dies away, and the edge of the bevel is marked by a double incised semicircle. Difference in the corrosion shows the form of the lower edge of the hilt with an Ω-shaped recess.

The burial. The site, now built over, was in a field on the outskirts of Elgin (about NJ 220637). The burial, found in 1864, was in a cist, 6 ft. long, 3 ft. wide in the centre but tapering to 1 ft. wide at each end. Besides the dagger there were 'portions of a skin, apparently that of an ox, on which the hair remained.' As no bones were seen the body was probably unburnt.

FLANDERS MOSS, WASBISTER, ORKNEY[76]

Dagger blade (fig. 44, top left; B.1914.317 in the Hunterian Museum, Glasgow). The blade is well preserved, the surface having a slightly uneven 'hammered' appearance, and the bevelled edges are slightly concave as if from whetting. Above the bevel and below the hilt there is a distinct contraction of the edges. Three rivets hold the hilt in place. An X-ray photograph has revealed that the upper edge of the blade is rounded and that the central rivet is in a notch which almost encircles it. The rivet heads are rather irregular and dimpled from hammering; the two outer rivets are 1·2 cm. long, the central one is 1·35 cm. long.

The hilt. This is of horn, very well preserved, made of one piece split from the base for about half its length; the blade has been inserted between the two layers. At the base the hilt is 0·6 cm. thick, but a tendency to laminate in the upper part prevents accurate measurements. The uppermost part of the hilt is in the form of a tang 2 cm. long, 1·8 cm. wide and 0·6 cm. thick. Near its upper edge are two transverse holes which retained wooden pegs when found, but one of these has since disappeared. This tang is evidently for the attachment of a pommel, presumably of bone. The pommel can hardly have been less than 2·5 cm. long, giving a total length to the dagger of 20·5 cm.

The circumstances of finding. The dagger was found during peat cutting in 1905.

16. DRUMLANRICK, CALLANDER, PERTHSHIRE[77]

Dagger blade (fig. 42; Pl. I, b; DI 2 in the National Museum of Antiquities of Scotland). It is in fairly good condition, covered by a dark green patina, with only small spots of corrosion. All the edges are damaged, but the inner edges of the bevels remain. The blade measures 11·4 cm long by 4·6 cm. wide. Much of the surface retains a high gloss, which extends over the area which was covered by the hilt, though this area bears numerous very fine lengthwise striations. Damage to the heel of the blade has allowed the centre rivet to fall away, and it is uncertain whether it was in a rivet hole or a notch. The V-shaped edge of the hilt is indicated by a slight change in the colour of the patina, and by a number of fine cuts or scratch marks below the lower edge.

The two surviving rivets, still in position, are 0·95 cm. long.

The burial. An old label records that the dagger was found in a cist in September 1870. Drumlanrick is the former name of Lendrick Lodge, near the north shore of Loch Venachar (about NN 549064).

17. DUNRAGIT, GLENLUCE, WIGTOWNSHIRE

Dagger blade (fig. 42; DI 7 in the National Museum of Antiquities of Scotland). The surface is covered by a green patina, with much corrosion on one face. All the edges are damaged, and in the heel only part of one rivet hole survives. The blade now measures 9·6 cm. by 3·7 cm. The V-shaped lower edge of the hilt is clearly visible in the colour variation of the patina on both faces. The surface of the blade retains a high gloss in places, but the area under the hilt is covered by very fine lengthwise striations, some of which extend beyond the edge of the hilt. In places along both sides of both faces the inner edge of the bevel is visible.

The three loose rivets are much damaged, the best preserved measuring 1·1 cm. long. A difference in corrosion round the shank shows where the rivet has been lying against the blade or the hilt-plates.

The burial.[78] The blade was found before 1931, 7 ft. below the surface of the gravel pit at Dunragit Station (NX 145576), 'between two large stones, with some ashes.' Presumably it had been in a wrecked cist.

	Estimated original length of blade	Maximum thickness of blade, excluding mid-rib	Diameter of rivet heads	Form of hilt end	Decoration	Mid-rib	Gold pommel-mounts	Burial rite	Grave	Clay luting	Associated finds
1. Cairn Greg	12·6	–	0·5	V	–	–	–	?I	Cist under cairn	*	Beaker
2. Gilchorn	20·0	–	–	Ω	–	Yes	–	?I	?Cist under cairn	–	Bronze blade
3. Auchterhouse	17·5	1·85	0·6	Ω	Dots	Yes	–	Partly C	Cist under composite barrow/cairn	*	–
4. Cleigh	13	2·6	1·2	Ω	Dots	–	–	I	Cist under cairn	–	–
5. Blackwaterfoot	24·8	2·0	0·95	V	Dots	3 ribs	Yes	?I	Cist under cairn	–	–
6. Skateraw	14·8	–	1·1	V	–	–	Yes	I	Cist under cairn	–	–
7. Ashgrove	13·6	2·25	0·95	Ω	–	–	–	I	Cist	*	Beaker
8. Collessie	17·5	2·2	over 1·0	Ω	–	–	Yes	C	Pit, secondary in cairn	–	–
9. Kirkcaldy	10·5	1·2	0·7	Ω	–	–	–	I	Cist	–	–
10. Masterton	14·5	2·35	0·9	V	–	–	–	I	Cist	*	Bronze armlets, Bronze blade, jet beads
11. Bught Park	11·7	–	0·7	V	–	–	–	I	Cist	*	–
12. Craigscorry	–	–	–	–	–	Yes	–	Partly C	Long cist	–	Arrowhead, flint knife
13. Carlochan	14·5	2·3	over 0·9	V	–	–	–	?I	Cist under cairn	–	–
14. Law of Mauldslie	16·0	–	1·3	–	–	Yes	–	I	Cist	–	–
15. Bishopmill	over 19	–	–	Ω	Traced lines	Yes	–	?I	Long cist	–	–
Flanders Moss	15·2	1·65	1·1	V	–	–	–	Not in grave		–	–
16. Drumlanrick	13·0	1·9	0·7	V	–	–	–	–	Cist	–	–
17. Dunragit	12·5	3·1	0·7	V	–	–	–	–	?Cist	–	–

Measurements in cm. except thickness of blade in mm. Italics where measurements approximate.

I = Inhumation   C = Cremation

Acknowledgments: I am especially indebted to Dr A. S. Clarke of the Royal Scottish Museum, Edinburgh, for allowing me to use his work on the hilts and sheath-mounts before publication. My thanks are also due to Mr R. B. K. Stevenson for discussion and advice, and to Dr A. S. Robertson, Mr W. Hood and Mr R. Milne for permission to examine daggers in their care in the Hunterian Museum, Glasgow, the Museum and Art Gallery, Kirkcaldy, and the Public Museum, Inverness, and to Mrs C. Dickson, Department of Botany, University of Cambridge, for examining the plant remains from the Ashgrove and Kirkcaldy graves, and to Mr S. Willy, Archaeology Division, Ordnance Survey, for providing the map references.

Notes

1. 'The Early Bronze Age in Wessex,' *P.P.S.* IV (1938) 52–106; 'Abercromby and After,' in (ed.) Foster and Alcock, *Culture and Environment* (1963) 53–91

2. *P.S.A.S.* XII (1876–8) 439–56; Anderson, *Scotland in Pagan Times* I (1886) 3–14; Childe, *Scotland Before the Scots* (1946) 121–2; *P.P.S.* XVII (1951) 72

3. *Inst. of Arch., 10th Ann. Rep.* (1954) 37–62

4. *Arch.* XLIII (1871) 454

5. Annable and Simpson, *Guide Catalogue of the Neolithic and Bronze Age Collections in Devizes Museum* (1964) No. 165; also 229, 374 etc.

6. To be fully published by J. G. Scott; in Inveraray Castle

7. Annable and Simpson, *op. cit.*, No. 220; *Arch.* XLIII (1871) Pl. XXXV, 2

8. (ed.) Piggott, *The Prehistoric Peoples of Scotland* (1962) 99; or about 1400 B.C., *British Museum Quarterly* XXXI (1967) 114

9. *Arch.* LXXXVI (1936) 312; Childe, *The Prehistory of Scotland* (1935) 100; Childe, *op. cit.* (1946) 119

10. Illustrated *P.P.S.* IV (1938) 63, 86; Annable and Simpson, *op. cit.* Nos. 170, 164

11. *P.P.S.* XXIX (1963) 286, Pl. XXVII; *Inst. of Arch., 10th Ann. Rep.* (1954) fig. 1, 4

12. *Arch. J.* XIII (1856) 305; *Arch. Ael.* XLIII (1965) 65–75; *Inventaria Arch.* GB28

13. *Inst. of Arch., 10th Ann. Rep.* (1954) 55

14. Evans, *Ancient Bronze Implements* (1881) 243–4, fig. 304

15. Listed and illustrated *P.P.S.* XXIX (1963) 406–11, 419–21

16. *ibid.* 409, but best illus. Warne, *Celtic Tumuli* (1866) Pl. 10, D

17. *Inventaria Arch.* GB28

18. *P.R.I.A.* IV (1896–8), 653; *Bericht über den V Internationalen Kongress, Hamburg, 1958* (1961) 285

19. *T.D.G.N.H.A.S.* XLII (1965) 26–9

20. *P.S.A.S.* II (1854–7) 447

21. *P.D.N.H.* LVIII (1936) 24; Cressingham, *P.P.S.* IV (1938) 93

22. *Inventaria Arch.* GB25

23. *ibid.* GB20

24. Lisnakill, Soc. Ant. Lond. MS. *Primaeval Antiquities* I, f. 55, and *Minutes*, 20 February 1755 (it is hoped to publish this soon); *Arch. J.* XC (1933) 143; I am indebted to Professor Piggott for these references

25. *Inventaria Arch.* GB25, 26

26. *ibid.* GB26

27. *ibid.* GB25; *Antiquity* XXXIII (1959) 292–5; *T.D.G.N.H.A.S.* XLII (1965) 31–2

28. (ed.) Foster and Alcock, *op. cit.* 84

29. *Inventaria Arch.* GB32

30. *P.S.A.S.* LXXXVIII (1954–6) 9–10

31. Wasbister, in present paper; Auchnacree, *Inventaria Arch.* GB27

32. Ashbee, *The Bronze Age Round Barrow in Britain* (1960) 100, 102; Evans, *op. cit.* 227–31. Hilts listed in *P.P.S.* XXIII (1957) 164–5

33. *P.D.N.H.* LVIII (1936) 24, Pl. V, 1; illus. Ashbee, *op. cit.* fig. 30

34. Clarke, forthcoming paper

35. Annable and Simpson, *op. cit.* Nos. 159, 194, pls.

36. Ashbee, *op. cit.* 103

37. (ed.) Foster and Alcock, *op. cit.* 77; Scottish list, Childe, *op. cit.* (1946) 119, needs revision
38. Ashbee, *op. cit.* 47–50
39. *Inventaria Arch.* GB19; *W.A.M.* XLV (1930–2) 435, 440
40. *P.S.A.S.* XII (1876–8) 448–9, 455; Anderson, *op. cit.* 11–12
41. *ibid.*; *P.S.A.S.* LXVIII (1933–4) 154
42. *P.S.A.S.* VI (1864–6) 98–103; XII (1876–8) 448, 455; Anderson, *op. cit.*; Stuart, *Sculptured Stones of Scotland*, II (1867) 54–5; Childe, *Scotland Before the Scots* (1946) 121
43. *New Statistical Account* XI (1845) 546
44. *P.S.A.S.* XXV (1890–1) 460
45. *op. cit.* 447–63; Childe, *op. cit.* (1946), 119, 122; (ed.) Piggott, *op. cit.* (1962) 99; *P.P.S.* XXII (1956) 83
46. *P.S.A.S.* XXXII (1897–8) 210–12; Childe, *op. cit.* (1935) 99; Childe, *op. cit.* (1946) 122; *Inst. of Arch., 10th Ann. Rep.* (1954) 56
47. Forthcoming paper by Dr A. S. Clarke on the organic remains of the Scottish daggers
48. *P.S.A.S.* XXXII (1897–8) 211
49. *ibid.* 205–20; Childe, *op. cit.* (1935) 109; Childe, *op. cit.* (1946) 120
50. *P.S.A.S.* X (1872–4) 84–5; XII (1876–8) 454–5; Anderson, *op. cit.* 12–13; Evans, *op. cit.* 239; Childe, *op. cit.* (1946) 121
51. *P.S.A.S.* X (1872–4) 84; XII (1876–8) 448–9; Anderson, *op. cit.*; Smith, *Loch Etive and the Sons of Uisnach* (1885) 248–9
52. *P.S.A.S.* XXXVI (1901–2) 120; LVII (1922–3) 129, 131; (ed.) Balfour, *The Book of Arran* (1910) 109–11; Childe, *op. cit.* (1935) 99; Childe, *op. cit.* (1946) 120, 122; *Inst. of Arch., 10th Ann. Rep.* (1954) 47, 56
53. Pennant, *A Tour in Scotland* II (1776) 208
54. M'Arthur, *The Antiquities of Arran* (1861) 29; *New Statistical Account* V (1845) 53
55. *P.S.A.S.* XXXVI (1901–2) 117–19; Balfour, *op. cit.*
56. *P.S.A.S.* XXVII (1892–3) 7–8; Childe, *op. cit.* (1946) 119, 121; *Inst. of Arch., 10th Ann. Rep.* (1954) 56
57. *P.S.A.S.* XXVII (1892–3) 7–8
58. *P.S.A.S.* XCVII (1963–4) 166–79
59. *P.S.A.S.* XII (1876–8) 451–3; LVII (1922–3) 129, 131; Anderson, *op. cit.* 8–10; *Inst. of Arch., 10th Ann. Rep.* (1954) 38, 56
60. *P.S.A.S.* XCVII (1963–4) 175
61. *P.S.A.S.* XII (1876–8) 439–45; Anderson, *op. cit.* 3–8; *New Statistical Account* IX (1845) 28; Childe, *op. cit.* (1946) 121
62. *P.S.A.S.* LXXVIII (1943–4) 112–13; Childe, *op. cit.* (1946) 121
63. *P.S.A.S.* XCVII (1963–4) 176
64. *ibid.* LXXVIII (1943–4) 109–10
65. Unpublished report by Dr T. R. Murphy, Department of Anatomy, University of St Andrews
66. *P.S.A.S.* XCVI (1962–3) 145–54
67. *P.S.A.S.* LXXXVIII (1954–6) 7–10
68. *P.S.A.S.* LIX (1924–5) 205; LXXVIII (1943–4) 138
69. *P.S.A.S.* LIX (1924–5) 204–8; Childe, *op. cit.* (1946) 119
70. *P.S.A.S.* XII (1876–8) 454; *T.D.G.N.H.A.S.* XLII (1965) 70–1
71. *ibid.*; *Account of the Institution and Progress of the Society of Antiquaries of Scotland* pt. II (1784) 55; Wilson, *Prehistoric Annals of Scotland* (1863) 394; Royal Commission on Ancient and Historical Monuments, *Inventory of Kirkcudbrightshire* (1914) 82; Childe, *op. cit.* (1946) 121
72. *T.D.G.N.H.A.S.* XIV (1926–8) 290, but see *P.S.A.S.* X (1872–4) 586 and (ed.) Shetelig, *Viking Antiquities* II (1940) 109; *Account of the Institution, op. cit.*
73. *P.S.A.S.* XCV (1961–2) 307; Society of Antiquaries of Scotland *MS.* 634.
74. *P.S.A.S.* VII (1866–8) 440–1; XII (1876–8) 456; Childe, *op. cit.* (1946) 122
75. Stuart, *op. cit.* XCVI; Childe, *op. cit.* (1935) 100; Childe, *op. cit.* (1946) 119; *P.S.A.S.* XII (1876–8) 456; XXII (1887–8) 342
76. *P.S.A.S.* XLII (1907–8) 74–7
77. *ibid.* XII (1876–8) 456; Anderson, *op. cit.* 13; Childe, *op. cit.* (1946) 121
78. *P.S.A.S.* LXVI (1931–2) 19; Childe, *op. cit.* (1946) 122; *T.D.G.N.H.A.S.* XLII (1965) 71

Food Vessels: associations and chronology

D. D. A. Simpson

In an important paper published in 1962 entitled 'Abercromby and After'[1] Professor Piggott reviewed the evidence for the dating of the British beaker groups which he subtitled 'The Early Bronze Age outside Wessex.' This brief review is offered as a complement to Professor Piggott's work and summarizes the much scantier evidence for the associations and dating of another aspect of the Early Bronze Age outside Wessex.

No attempt will be made to discuss the classification and origins of the great variety of pottery which has been included under the term Food Vessel. Here the problems of association and dating will be considered under the three major and generally accepted categories of Yorkshire Vase, Irish Bowl and Type E or Irish Vase Food Vessel.

Yorkshire Vase

Miss Kitson Clark long ago demonstrated the contemporaneity of vessels with and without stops, both perforated and unperforated.[2] There appears to be a similar contemporaneity among the various groups of Yorkshire Vase which can be distinguished both in terms of form and decoration.[3] The chronological implications, therefore, such as they are, may be taken as referring to the series as a whole. The associations may be discussed under the categories of personal ornaments, weapons and tools, and dress fasteners. Only a single radiocarbon date exists for a Food Vessel in Britain. This is from a grave at Harland Edge, Derbyshire, which contained two Yorkshire Vases and a cremation. Charcoal from the grave yielded a date of 1490±90 B.C. (B.M.178).[4]

The most spectacular and chronologically important group in the category of personal ornaments are the space-plate necklaces of jet, copies of the amber forms of the Wessex Culture, associated with Vase Food Vessels at Lunanhead,[5] Pitreuchy,[6] Kellas[7] and Tealing,[8] Angus, Blinmill, Aberdeenshire,[9] High Cocklaw, Berwick,[10] and Kyloe, Northumberland.[11] Similar associations occurred in three other cases where the pot is too fragmentary to classify within the Food Vessel series or has since been lost.[12] Simpler necklaces or token deposits of disc beads of shale or jet have been recorded with Food Vessels from Hartington, Derbyshire,[13] Garton Slack 75[14] (fig. 46, 2) and Weaverthorpe XLIV,[15] Yorkshire, Balmerino, Fife,[16] Scalpsie Bay, Bute,[17] and Embo, Sutherland.[18] Such necklaces are known from Beaker contexts but survive at least into the period of the first phase of the Wessex Culture.[19] The bone cylinder beads decorated with lozenge patterns from Folkton LXXI[20] (fig. 45, 5) are paralleled by a group of similarly ornamented bone discs found with a cremation and a small bronze knife dagger in Hoare's barrow 20 at Lake, Wiltshire,[21] and by a further bone disc from the lower Beaker midden at Northton, Harris.[22] At Ratho, Midlothian, a vase was associated with a bronze D-sectioned ring.[23] In Britain, this is a purely Scottish type, associated with a Bowl Food Vessel at Kinneff, Kincardineshire,[24] a Short-Necked Beaker at Crawfurd, Lanarkshire,[25] and an unaccompanied cremation at Stobo, Peebleshire,[26] and in the metalwork hoards of Auchnacree, Angus, the Maidens, Ayrshire, and Migdale, Sutherland.[27] Professor Piggott has compared such armlets with the more massive C-shaped bracelets of the later phase of Reinecke A, and therefore contemporary with Wessex I.[28] A tentative equation with Wessex may also exist in the segmented jet cylinder from Garton Slack 153[29] (fig. 45, 2), a possible copy of a segmented faience bead. A similar segmented bone cylinder was found with a Yorkshire Vase at Corrandrum, Co. Galway[30] (fig. 49, 7) in association with two plano-convex flint knives. The excavator suggested that it was the head of a segmented or ribbed pin with Iberian affinities, but it could perhaps be more reasonably interpreted again as a copy of a faience bead.

The only other ornaments with Food Vessels are pairs of bronze earrings from Garton Slack C53[31] (fig. 45, 2) and Goodmanham CXV[32] (fig. 45, 1), of simple strip type at the former site and corrugated at the latter. The Goodmanham pair appears to be related to the basket earring series recently studied by Butler.[33] Corrugations occur on basket earrings from Periediwanic and Stublo, Poland[34] and Schonfeld, Silesia[35] and suggest a source for the type in the contemporary multi-strand wire earrings[36] which sometimes occur in the same hoards, although corrugations are known on basket-type earrings from Troy.[37] In northern and central Europe, basket earrings and related ornaments fall into the period of late Beakers and Únětice, equivalent to the first phase of the Wessex Culture in southern Britain.

In the category of tools and weapons, the most frequent association and the only object recorded in any number with Vase Food Vessels is the plano-convex flint knife (fig. 45, 6), which form is to be distinguished from a simpler blade knife with a marked keel on its upper surface and retouched only along the edges (fig. 45, 6); these are also found with Food Vessels and with other ceramic and non-ceramic associations.[38] In 1932 Clark demonstrated the predominantly Food Vessel associations of plano-convex knives.[39] To his list of 24 knives with Food Vessels, one can now add a further 19 specimens. Of this total, 37 are associated with Yorkshire vases, including, interestingly, two of the few Yorkshire Vase forms in Ireland[40] (fig. 49, 7). Four other knives were found with Irish Vases and two with Irish Bowl Food Vessels, one of the latter significantly bearing stops, a characteristic of the Yorkshire Vase series.[41] These small knives look rather like female equipment although in fact they are equally distributed between the sexes in graves. The skeletal evidence from Food Vessel graves also shows that one cannot interpret such burials as the female element in a culture, as has recently been suggested.[42] There are approximately equal numbers of adult males and females, and these are outnumbered by the bodies of children, as one might expect in a primitive society with a high infant mortality rate. Plano-convex knives are of course known from other contexts. Longworth, for example, lists five with Primary Series collared urns[43] and they are also known from megalithic tombs of the Clyde-Carlingford series;[44] but the high percentage of Food Vessel associations and specifically Yorkshire Vase Food Vessels suggests that these knives are to be considered an integral part of the material culture of this

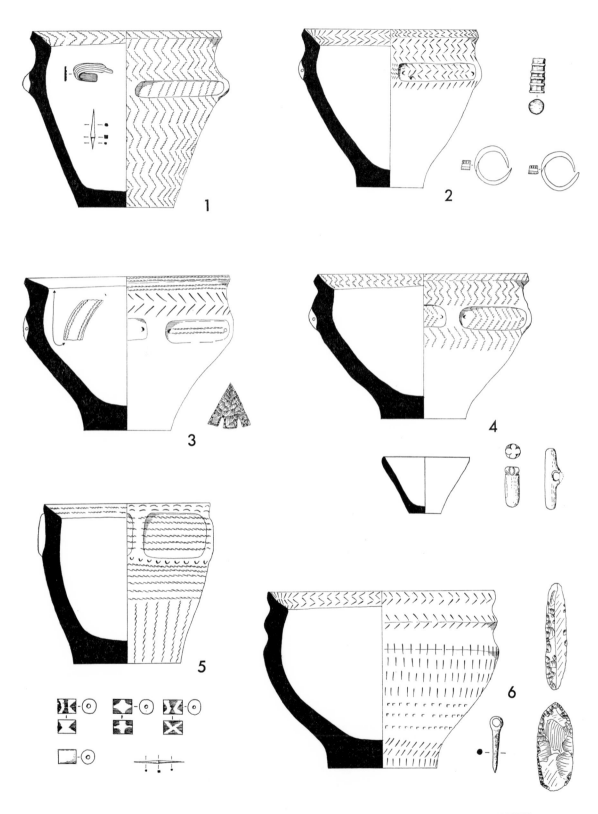

Figure 45. Food Vessel grave groups. 1. Goodmanham CXV. 2. Garton Slack 153. 3. Rudstone LXIII.
4. Garton Slack C62. 5. Folkton LXXI. 6. Wharram Percy 47. (1/3)

group. The association of five knives with Primary Series collared urns, which Longworth would largely equate with Wessex I and II, and of a knife with a Wessex I dagger in a grave without pottery at Towthorpe 139[45] are useful chronological indicators. If the association of a plano-convex knife with two segmented bone beads and a tanged bronze Class I razor in a barrow near Pickering is a valid one, this would add a further century to the life of the type.[46]

Only two bronze daggers are associated with Vase Food Vessels. Both are small and simple types, the example from Amble, Northumberland,[47] originally having three tiny rivets, and that from Kilmaho, Argyll two.[48] On the Continent such small knives first appear in Reinecke A1 contexts, but have a long life, appearing in Britain for example in female graves of Wessex I and II.[49] Battle-axes of Mrs Roe's Calais Wold type,[50] whose contexts are Long Necked Beaker and Wessex I, occurred with vessels at Calais Wold, Yorkshire, and Doune, Perthshire (fig. 46, 1); and a Woodhenge type axe[51] with Necked Beaker associations was found with a Food Vessel at Little Gonerby, Lincolnshire.

The remaining metal associations are bronze or copper awls. Of the nine recorded examples two are too fragmentary to classify, and the remainder include examples of the three main awl types found in Britain. From Garrowby 101,[52] Garton Slack 75[53] (fig. 46, 2) and Kilmaho, Argyll[54] come examples of the type with double point, having a wholly square section or the tang square. This form is widely distributed both in time and space in Europe, going back to Early Minoan times and is found in Bell Beaker contexts in Spain and central Europe.[55] In Britain, the associations range from Bell Beaker to Wessex I.[56] The second form, associated with Food Vessels at Goodmanham CXV[57] and Folkton LXXI[58] (fig. 45, 5), is again double pointed with an expanded and square-sectioned centre. This is a Rhineland-North German type, found in Britain in Bell and Necked Beaker graves.[59] The final awl type is single pointed with a flattened tang, and has been recorded with Vase Food Vessels at Rudstone LXII[60] (fig. 46, 4) and Life Hill 294.[61] The form appears to be a purely insular development and none of the associations imply a date earlier than the Wessex Culture.

Both the occurrence of awls and plano-convex knives imply the treating and preparation of skins, and the existence of leather clothing is borne out to some extent by the discovery of buttons and toggles with Food Vessels; and by the fragmentary remains of such clothing in Doddington CLXXXIX, Northumberland.[62] Three conical V-bored buttons occur in Food Vessel contexts; a pair in jet from Great Tosson, Northumberland,[63] and single examples in bone and fired clay from Folkton LXXI[64] and Garton Slack 40[65] respectively. More interesting are the bone toggles with perforated side loop from Driffield C38[66] (fig. 46, 3) and Garton Slack C62[67] (fig. 45, 4). Piggott has compared these with a looped crescentic bone object from a cist at Letham Quarry, Perthshire, also containing an inhumation and bronze riveted dagger.[68] An exact parallel from Iberia is provided by the bone toggle accompanying a Cord Zoned Bell Beaker from Filomena, Castellion.[69] A number of bone pins of simple form might be interpreted as ornaments, tools or dress fasteners, but one example at least, with a carefully polished shank and expanded perforated head, from Wharram Percy 47[70] (fig. 45, 6) must fall into the latter category. Similar polished pins were found with an unaccompanied cremation at Aldro 109[71] and with a cremation and bone belt hook in Slingsby CXLV.[72] The latter object is known from Wessex Culture contexts, the only closely datable association being from a barrow on Arreton Down, Isle of Wight, with a transitional Wessex I/II dagger.[73] The polished pins too have Wessex Culture parallels, and, like the metal forms which they copy, should also belong to the second phase of the culture.[74] Such pins are also known from late Únětice contexts on the Continent.[75]

Among these associations, those of any datable value suggest a broad contemporaneity with the Wessex Culture, and this is supported by the stratigraphical relationship between Food Vessels and other ceramic types.

Food Vessels were contemporary with Short Necked Beakers at Hawkhill, Northumberland[76] and Edington Mill, Berwick.[77] In four other cases, Towthorpe 21,[78] Painsthorpe 4,[79] Garrowby 104[80] and Garton Slack 75[81] Food Vessels occurred in the upper fill of large pit graves, at the bottom of which were burials accompanied by Long Necked Beakers. Presumably no great interval of time elapsed between the successive deposition of burials in these graves, although it is interesting that the stratigraphical position of Beakers and Food Vessels in a single grave is never reversed.

Food Vessels were secondary to a Bell Beaker at Ferry Fryston 161[82] and to Short Necked Beakers at Goodmanham CXIV,[83] Rudstone LXII,[84] Driffield 138[85] and Borrow Nook,[86] Yorkshire and to Long Necked Beakers at Folkton CCXLII,[87] Rudstone LXIII,[88] Acklam 204,[89] Aldro 116,[90] Garton Slack 37[91] and to an anomalous Beaker at Hastings Hill, Durham.[92]

The relationships with collared urns may be summarized as follows: contemporary with

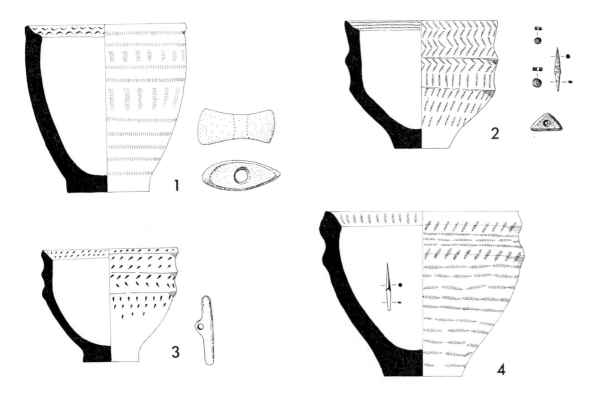

Figure 46. Food Vessel grave groups. 1. Doune, Perthshire. 2. Garton Slack 75. 3. Rudstone CXXXVIII. 4. Rudstone LXII. (1/3)

Primary Series vessels at Folkton LXX, Sherburn XII, Ford CLXXXVII and Caythorpe, Lincolnshire;[93] Primary Series vessels were secondary to Food Vessels in Painsthorpe 98, Staxton, Willerby 38, Weaponess 1, East Ayton, a barrow near Pickering[94] and Harland Edge, Derbyshire.[95] A Food Vessel was contemporary with a later collared urn at Riggs C42a,[96] and in Goodmanham 114[97] a similar urn was secondary to the Food Vessel burial. The only other useful relationships are at Towthorpe 233, where a Food Vessel burial was secondary to an inhumation with a Wessex I dagger,[98] at Hutton Buscel CLII, where a similar dagger was secondary to the Food Vessel burial;[99] and, finally, at Llandyfnan, Anglesey, where the Food Vessel was contemporary with an Enlarged Food Vessel containing two bronze flanged axes and a dagger related to the Bush Barrow series.[100]

Although one can no longer accept the chest-of-drawers Beaker-Food Vessel-Collared Urn sequence, and the evidence cited above indicates a considerable degree of chronological overlap, it is still curious that no Food Vessel has been found in a barrow stratigraphically earlier than a Beaker, and no collared urn in a similar relationship to a Food Vessel.

A final approach to the problem of dating is through burial rites. Associations, distribution and typological considerations would suggest that the chalk wolds of the East Riding of Yorkshire are a primary area for the development of the Yorkshire Vase series. In this area, inhumation burial predominates over cremation in a ratio of approximately 10 : 1. In the North Riding, the percentage of cremation burial increases, and this increase continues as one moves north and west (figs. 47–8). Whether this geographical distinction also has chronological significance is uncertain in view of the rarity of closely datable associations as a control, but the similar northerly and westerly distribution of typologically developed split herringbone and debased herringbone ornamented vessels within the large series of pots decorated with an all-over herringbone design, suggests that it may.

The evidence of stratigraphy and association, however, indicate a general contemporaneity with the two phases of the Wessex Culture. There is no evidence for an earlier development of the Yorkshire Vase, nor of its survival after 1400 B.C., although this cannot be argued too closely, in view of the paucity of datable associations with any pottery in Britain in the post-Wessex Bronze Age.

Irish Bowls

There are even fewer useful associations with Irish Bowls than with the Yorkshire Vase type. The two plano-convex knife associations have already been mentioned. Flanagan has shown that the Croghan Erin, Co. West Meath, dagger, related to the Bush Barrow series, was not in fact associated with the Food Vessel sherds.[101] This leaves the small knife dagger from Corky, Co. Antrim (fig. 49, 4)[102] and a fragmentary dagger distorted by heat from Carrickinab, Co. Down.[103] The Corky dagger has a W-shaped hilt outline and two small rivets. Such daggers appear to be a purely insular development, and, in view of their association in two cases with ribbed gold pommel mounts, are probably contemporary with the first phase of the Wessex Culture. No rivet holes survive on the Carrickinab specimen, but the remaining small rivet suggests that it is a similar form.

At Killicarney, Co. Cavan[104] (fig. 49, 3), the bowl and a cremation burial were accompanied by a ground stone axe and a bone belt fastener consisting of a plate with two hooks worked from it on one face. A similar bone belt fastener with a single hook was associated with a collared urn in the Brackmont Mill cemetery, Fife;[105] an unlocated example from Wiltshire is preserved in Devizes Museum,[106] and the most famous member of the group is the sheet gold covering for such a fastener from Bush Barrow, Wiltshire which provides a useful chronological indicator for the series.[107] The recent suggestion that the hook and plate of the Bush Barrow piece should be regarded as two separate and detachable elements in a belt fastener is difficult to accept in view of the existence of the single-piece objects in bone to which the Bush Barrow specimen is clearly related.[108]

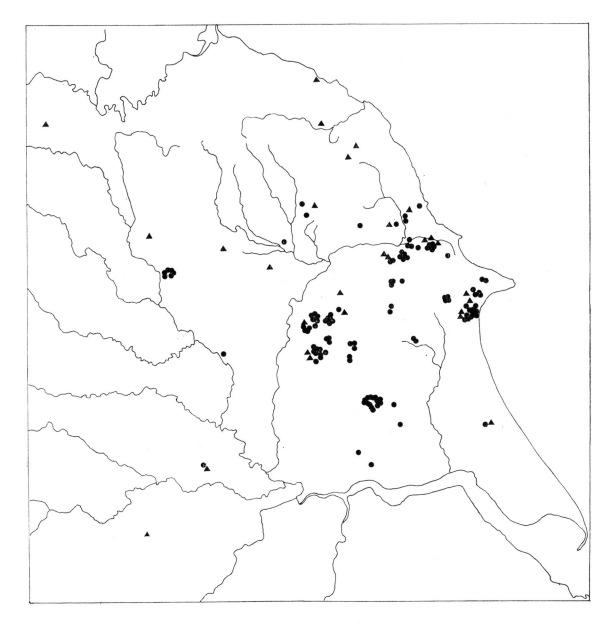

Figure 47. Food Vessel burials in Yorkshire : ● *inhumation,* ▲ *cremation.*

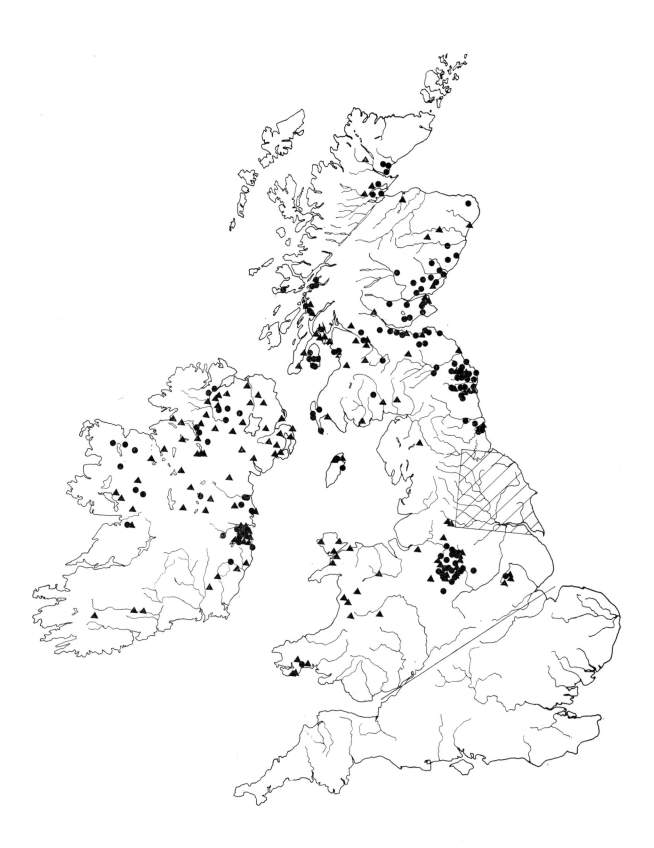

Figure 48. Food Vessel burials : ● *inhumation,* ▲ *cremation.*

In addition to the ground stone axe from Killicarney, similar axes are associated with bowls at Cookestown, Co. Tyrone[109] (fig. 49, 2) and Rathbarron, Co. Sligo[110] (fig. 49, 5), at the latter site with a ground stone disc similar to shale examples from massive cists at Auchnacloich and Stittenham, Inverness-shire.[111] Although one cannot date such axes closely, they are an essentially neolithic tool which does not survive long in the Single Grave period.

Among ornaments, the most frequent associations are of necklaces of shale or jet beads. In two cases, Kingquharrie, Angus[112] and Mountstuart, Bute[113] these are of space-plate form with fusiform beads. Professor Piggott has suggested that these jet copies of the Wessex amber necklaces are likely to belong to the phase immediately following or overlapping with the final phase of that culture. This argument was based in part on the association of a jet space-plate necklace with a pair of armlets with lenticular boss ornament from Melfort, Argyll.[114] The lenticular bosses on these armlets were compared to the decoration on the Mold ornament, which in turn may be equated with metalwork of Montelius II in northern Europe. Henshall[115] has pointed out however in publishing a similar bossed armlet from Masterton, Fife that such decoration occurs in Scotland with earlier associations, and the occurrence of a jet space plate from a necklace of the type under discussion at Kerguévarec, Finistère[116] in a stone chamber beneath a round barrow, accompanied by three flat axes, five daggers and 24 barb-and-tang arrowheads of Giot's first phase of Armorican barrow cultures (contemporary with Wessex I), implies an early date for the beginning of the jet space-plate necklace series. In two other cases, Bunbrosna, Co. West Meath[117] and Ballybrew, Co. Wicklow,[118] fusiform jet beads of the type associated with such necklaces were found, but these also occur in Bowl Food Vessel graves with the simpler disc beads at Old Bridge, Co. Meath[119] and Glamis, Angus,[120] so their presence cannot be taken to indicate a space-plate necklace. At Brownhead, Arran[121] and Gemmel, Argyll[122] disc beads only occurred. The latter form are known from Beaker contexts, but continued to be deposited in graves of the first phase of the Wessex Culture. The remaining ornaments consist of two pairs of bronze D-sectioned rings of the type discussed above from Kinneff, Kincardine[123] and Lug na Curran, Co. Leix.[124] At the latter site there were also 'two little links of beads of some mineral substance of bluish colour and highly polished.' These objects have not been preserved, but from their description must have been segmented faience beads. The polished shank of a bone pin from Labbamolaga, Co. Cork[125] is again probably a copy of a metal form, and the bone ring pendant from the same grave appears to be related to pendants such as that from Stanton Harcourt, Oxon.,[126] found with a Bell Beaker and occurring in northern Europe in late Passage Grave and Corded Ware contexts.[127]

Relationships with other ceramic forms are also few. A bowl was secondary to an inhumation with a Long Necked Beaker at Merdyn Gwynne, Anglesey;[128] sherds of bowls were associated with those of Beakers and Class I and II ware at Lough Gur, Co. Limerick[129] and with Necked Beaker sherds beneath a barrow at Swarkeston, Derbyshire.[130] Bowls were associated with collared urns at five Irish sites and secondary to a cordoned urn at Gort-corbies, Co. Tyrone.[131]

None of this evidence need imply a date earlier than c. 1650 B.C. and the grave-goods, although few, suggest that the forms are again broadly contemporary with the Wessex Culture. In the absence of closely datable associations to indicate any internal stylistic

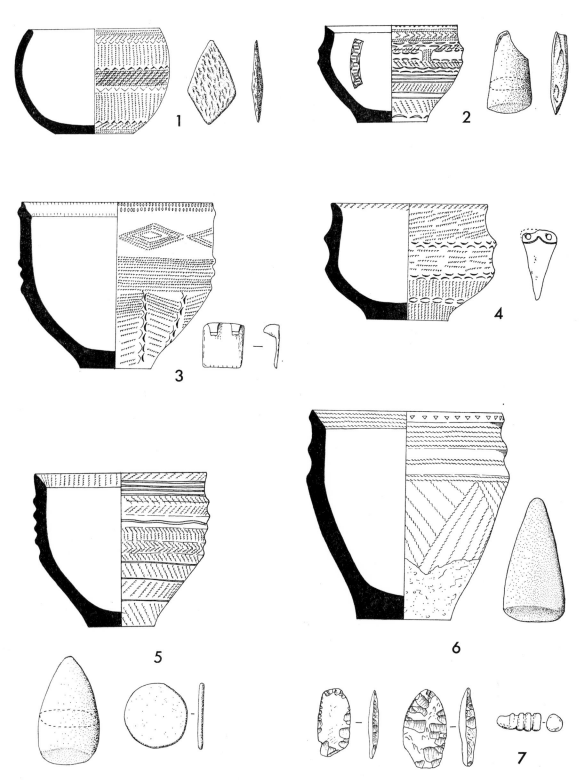

Figure 49. Food Vessel grave groups. 1. Omagh, Co. Tyrone. 2. Cookestown, Co. Tyrone. 3. Killicarney, Co. Cavan. 4. Corky, Co. Antrim. 5. Rathbarron, Co. Sligo. 6. Craignish, Argyll. 7. Corrandrum, Co. Galway. (1/3)

development, any attempt at typology is no more than an exercise. A series can however be built up based on ornamental motifs (fig. 50). Two main forms are recognizable in the profile of Irish Bowls. One group consists of smooth profiled vessels, in some cases with a medial constriction. The second main category is of ridged bowls, in which class would come Young's Tripartite Bowl Food Vessels, although there is no stylistic or other evidence to suggest that these are a distinct group, provided with one or as many as six ridges or carinations. This distinction of form appears justified, in view of the differing motifs occurring with the two main groups and of the differing frequency of the use of motifs in the two categories. Both groups include vessels decorated with a repeating horizontal pattern which is the dominant type in ridged bowls, but extremely rare in the smooth profiled form. Conjoined lozenge or panelled patterns, frequently reserved, are also shared. Peculiar to the ridged form are chevron ornamented vessels and to the smooth bowls vertical line or grooved ornament. From these ornamental groups, a series can be built up with vessels decorated with lozenge and chevron patterns at the head. From this stage, development could take the form of multiplication of the bands of decoration, producing an all-over repeating pattern; or the conjoined lozenges might become separate panels. At the end of the series would be those vessels in which the panels have become vertically attenuated, producing pots with vertical lines or grooves. It is this final form which has been compared to the gold bowls of Montelius II/III of northern Europe, first by Menghin,[132] later supported by Childe.[133] The bowls in question are those from Gonnebeck, Holstein, Langendorf, Pomerania and Ebberswalde, near Berlin (Pl. II).[134] The flaring rims, rows of bosses, rope ornament and concentric circular patterns, typical of the Nordic Bronze Age, are quite unlike anything on an Irish Bowl Food Vessel. All the metal vessels admittedly have a star or cruciform pattern on their bases, but such a feature is widespread in European Bronze Age pottery and metal vessels, and the inspiration for such bowls is more likely to be southeastern and ultimately Mycenaean rather than Irish. Finally, if one rejects the late dating of the Melfort armlets and the associated space-plate necklace, then there is no other evidence to indicate survival of the bowl form after 1400 B.C., while the disc beads with the vertically grooved bowl from Gemmel imply a date in the previous century.

Irish Vases

With this group of Food Vessels there are only four useful associations. Of these, the best known is the Bush Barrow type dagger with corrugated pommel mount from Topped Mountain, Co. Fermanagh.[135] Another early association is a thin butted ground stone axe from Craignish, Argyll[136] (fig. 49, 6). The other two associations are of faience beads; a bead of two segments, compared with one from the Fosse Temple at Lachish dated 1450-1400 B.C. by Stone,[137] and a second example from Llangwym, Denbigh,[138] which has not been spectro-scopically examined but is likely to fall within the same chronological bracket.

The two early associations of Wessex I dagger and stone axe accompanied inhumation burials, while the Wessex II beads were buried with cremations in cist graves. It is possible therefore that in this group one can use burial rite in relative dating. Nine inhumation burials are recorded and 25 cremations, 18 of these being in cist graves, as were all the inhumations. The remaining seven cremations were contained in pots, which become cinerary urns, and

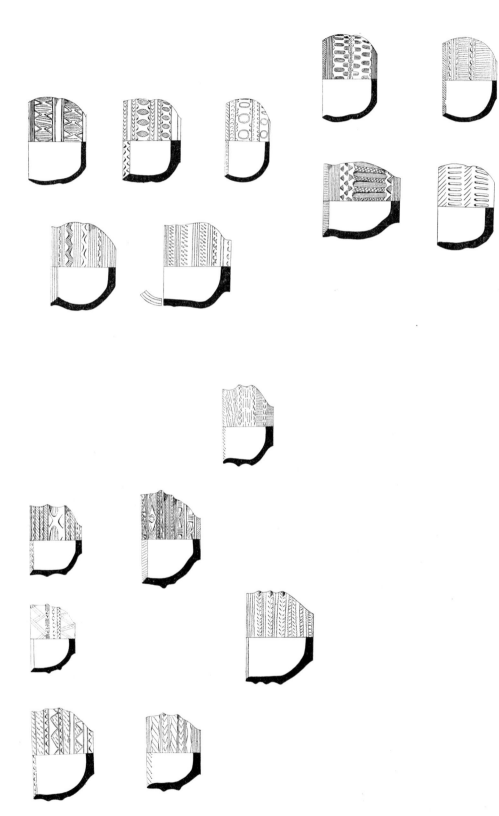

Figure 50. Typological development of Irish Bowls.

these were buried in simple pit graves. They could then be the final graves in the series, although one cannot say how late they are in view of the total absence of grave-goods in this latter category of burial.

From this brief survey of grave-goods and barrow stratigraphy two general conclusions may be drawn. First, the datable associations indicate a general contemporaneity with the two phases of the Wessex Culture, currently dated 1650–1400 B.C. Secondly, and more obviously, there is a general absence of consistently recurring grave-goods. The only association which is found in any number with Food Vessels is the plano-convex flint knife, with vessels of the Yorkshire Vase series, and this is the only object which one can ascribe to a Food Vessel 'Culture.' Many of the other infrequent associations look like female equipment, but this is belied in a number of cases by the skeletal evidence. None of these objects can be said to be elements of a culture, in the way that archers' equipment is associated with certain Beaker groups for example, but appear simply as products manufactured and traded in Britain in the sixteenth and fifteenth centuries B.C. which might be purchased by one of a series of culturally interrelated groups rather as were the ground stone axes of an earlier period.

Notes

1. In (ed.) Foster and Alcock, *Culture and Environment* (1962) 53–91
2. *Arch. J.* XCIV (1937) 43–63
3. Simpson, 'The Food Vessel Cultures of the British Isles,' lecture delivered to the Prehistoric Society, January 1967
4. *D.A.J.* LXXXVI (1966) 31–53
5. *P.S.A.S.* XII (1877–8) 288
6. *P.S.A.S.* XLI (1906–7) 65
7. *P.S.A.S.* XXIV (1889–90) 9
8. *P.S.A.S.* XIV (1879–80) 260
9. *P.S.A.S.* VI (1864–6) 203
10. *P.S.A.S.* LXIII (1928–9) 370
11. *Arch. Ael.* 3rd ser. V (1928) 26
12. Bogheadly, Kincardine: *P.S.A.S.* VI (1864–6) 88; Brechin, Angus: *P.S.A.S.* LXVIII (1933–4) 412; Newport, Fife: *P.S.A.S.* VIII (1868–70) 411
13. Turner, *Ancient Remains near Buxton* (1899) XXV, fig. 2
14. Mortimer, *Forty Years' Researches in the British and Saxon Burial Mounds of E. Yorks.* (1905) 222–4
15. Greenwell, *British Barrows* (1877) 197–8
16. *P.S.A.S.* XXXVI (1901–2) 645
17. *P.S.A.S.* XXXVIII (1903–4) 52–6
18. *P.S.A.S.* XC (1956–7) 225–7
19. *e.g.* Preshute G1 (a): Annable and Simpson, *Guide Catalogue to the Neolithic and Bronze Age Collections in Devizes Museum* (1964) 101, No. 203
20. Greenwell, *op. cit.* 276
21. Hoare, *Ancient Wiltshire* I (1810) 212, Pl. xxxi
22. *Antiquity* XL (1966) 137
23. *P.S.A.S.* LVIII (1922–3) 130
24. *Inventaria Arch.* GB34
25. *P.S.A.S.* LXVIII (1933–4) 185
26. *P.S.A.S.* II (1854–7) 272
27. *Inventaria Arch.* GB26, 27 and 31
28. *op. cit.* GB27

29. Mortimer, *op. cit.* 218
30. *Journ. Galway Arch. & Hist. Soc.* XVI (1935) 125–33
31. Mortimer, *op. cit.* 218
32. Greenwell, *op. cit.* 324
33. *Palaeohistoria* V (1956) 59–72
34. *Praehistorische Zeitschrift* XXV (1934) 191, Taf. 2
35. *Altschlesien* I (1926) 76, Taf. 8
36. *Romische-Germanische Forschungen* III (1929) Taf. 12
37. Aberg, *Chronologie* III (1932) 129, Abb. 233
38. Atkinson, Piggott and Sandars, *Excavations at Dorchester, Oxon.* I (1951) 72
39. *Ant. J.* XII (1932) 158–62
40. Corrandrum, Co. Galway; Ballywilliam, Co. Down
41. *U.J.A.* XV (1952) 61–4
42. Ashbee, *The Bronze Age Round Barrow in Britain* (1960) 138
43. *P.P.S.* XXVII (1961) 304–6
44. Piggott, *Neolithic Cultures of the British Isles* (1954) 175
45. Mortimer, *op. cit.* 5–6
46. Elgee, *Early Man in N.E. Yorks.* (1930) 80
47. *Arch.* LII (1890) 67
48. Information from Mr J. G. Scott, Kelvingrove Museum, Glasgow
49. Annable and Simpson, *op. cit.* 101, No. 210; 102, No. 219
50. *P.P.S.* XXXII (1966) 207
51. *ibid.* 206
52. Mortimer, *op. cit.* 136
53. *ibid.* 222
54. Information from Mr J. G. Scott
55. Leisner, G. and V., *Die megalithgräber der Iberischen Halbinsel: Der Westen* (1956) 525
56. Annable and Simpson, *op. cit.* 101, Nos. 205–7
57. Greenwell, *op. cit.* 324
58. *ibid.* 274
59. *P.P.S.* XXXII (1966) 130, fig. 3, 5
60. Greenwell, *op. cit.* 234–45
61. Mortimer, *op. cit.* 203–4
62. Greenwell, *op. cit.* 411
63. *A History of Northumberland* XV (1939) 53, Pl. I, 5
64. Greenwell, *op. cit.* 274
65. Mortimer, *op. cit.* 229
66. *ibid.* 272
67. *ibid.* 213
68. *P.P.S.* XXIV (1958) 228
69. *B.R.G.K.* (1937–8) 8
70. Mortimer, *op. cit.* 45
71. *ibid.* 58
72. Greenwell, *op. cit.* 352
73. *P.P.S.* XXVI (1960) 273, fig. 5a
74. Annable and Simpson, *op. cit.* 98, No. 160
75. Billig, *Die Aunjetitzer Kultur in Sachen, Katalog* (1958) 177, Abb. 109
76. *Arch. Ael.* 2nd ser. III (1859) 36
77. *R.C.A.H.M. Berwick.* (1909) No. xxxii
78. Mortimer, *op. cit.* 11
79. *ibid.* 113
80. *ibid.* 134
81. *ibid.* 222
82. Greenwell, *op. cit.* 371
83. *ibid.* 323

84. *ibid.* 234
85. Mortimer, *op. cit.* 271
86. *Y.A.J.* XXI (1911) 214
87. *Arch.* LII (1890) 10–12
88. Greenwell, *op. cit.* 245
89. Mortimer, *op. cit.* 86
90. *ibid.* 54
91. *ibid.* 209
92. *Arch. Ael.* 3rd ser. XI (1914) 146–50
93. *P.P.S.* XXVII (1961) 283
94. *ibid.* 283
95. *D.A.J.*, LXXVI (1966) 39
96. Mortimer, *op. cit.* 174
97. *ibid.* 169
98. *ibid.* 6
99. Greenwell, *op. cit.* 357
100. *B.B.C.S.* XVII (1957) 210
101. *V Internationaler Kongress fur vor- und frühgeschichte, Hamburg* (1961) 284
102. *U.J.A.* I (1895) 98
103. Unpublished, Ulster Museum, Belfast
104. *J.R.H.A.A.I.*, 4th ser. V (1879–82) 191–2
105. *P.S.A.S.* LXXVI (1941–2) 86
106. Annable and Simpson, *op. cit.* 108, No. 331
107. *ibid.* 99
108. *W.A.M.* LXI (1966) 8
109. Ulster Museum, Belfast
110. Nat. Mus. Ireland, Dublin
111. *P.S.A.S.* LVI (1921–2) 18; *Trans. Gaelic Soc. Inverness* XII (1885–6) 333
112. Unpublished: Sunderland Museum
113. *P.S.A.S.* XXXVIII (1903–4) 63–9
114. *Inventaria Arch.* GB25
115. *P.S.A.S.* XCVI (1962–3) 145 ff.
116. *P.P.S.* V (1939) 193–5
117. *P.R.I.A.* XL (1931–2) 308
118. *P.R.I.A.* XLIII (1935–7) 255
119. *P.R.I.A.* III (1845–7) 747–50
120. *P.S.A.S.* LXXXV (1950–1) 46
121. *P.S.A.S.* XXXVI (1901–2) 120–2
122. Unpublished: Fort William Mus.
123. *Inventaria Arch.* GB34
124. *J.R.S.A.I.* XV (1879) 446
125. *J.C.H.A.S.* LV (1950) 15
126. Grimes, *Excavations on Defence Sites* (1960) 161, fig. 67
127. Sprockoff, *Die Nordische Megalithkultur* (1938) Taf. 63, 2
128. *Arch. Camb.* VIII (1908) 219
129. *P.R.I.A.* LVI (1953–4) 341
130. *D.A.J.* LXXX (1960) 29
131. *J.R.S.A.I.* LXXVII (1947) 5–11
132. *Altschlesien* V (1934) 188
133. *American Anthrop.* XXXIX (1937) 13
134. *Ausgrabungen und Funde* III (1958) 217, Abb. 37; 226, Abb. 44
135. Coffey, *Bronze Age in Ireland* (1913) 56, fig. 55
136. Nat. Mus., Edinburgh
137. *J.R.S.A.I.* LXXXII (1953) 50–6
138. *B.B.C.S.* XVII (1957) 227

Fenland rapiers

Bridget A. V. Trump

An important find has recently been made at West Row, near Mildenhall in Suffolk, a rapier with the remains of its wooden scabbard still adhering to the blade (Pl. III). No scabbard has before been found with any British Middle Bronze Age weapon, though it is said of a dirk found at New Bilton, near Rugby, that patches of corrosion on the blade show traces of hair, probably from the lining of a sheath of hide.[1] The wood, which has been studied and treated in the Museum of Archaeology and Ethnology, Cambridge, is hazel. Unfortunately there is not much of it left, though there are patches on both sides of the blade. Presumably two pieces of wood were bound together with strips of sheet bronze or leather. Surprisingly, there is no trace of the hilt, not even a hilt mark; perhaps that was not made of wood but of horn, like those from Shower and Galbally in Ireland, the only surviving British rapier hilts. Conditions favourable to the preservation of wood might well be too acid for horn or bone. The find was made by a farmer working a field on the north bank of the river Lark, opposite the junction of the Lee brook.

The blade of this rapier is well preserved. The two rivets are held not in rivet holes but in notches in the sides of the butt. This feature, combined with the smooth cross-section of the blade, which lacks any central arris, shows that it belongs to my Lisburn class.[2] In spite of being named after an Irish find, this form was probably developed in the Thames valley in the present area of London, where 28 examples have been found. Nineteen are now known from the Fens. The West Row rapier is larger than any of the others, being 41·5 cm. long, the next longest being only 36·6 cm. Nor does it resemble any of them particularly closely. It retains both its rivets, and only two other rivets survive among the 138 Lisburn weapons from the British Isles. This is mere chance, but a more truly distinctive feature of this West Row rapier is the way in which the rivets are set well down the sides of the butt. Four other weapons also show this feature, three of which, interestingly enough, were found in the same locality, two from West Row itself and one from Mildenhall, the fourth being the rapier in the Downham Fen hoard. One of the West Row rapiers, however, is of the Barnes-Corrib class. This class has the same blade form, but the rivets are set in holes instead of notches. Four such similar weapons from one small area provide as good evidence as one could hope for of local manufacture. The same area has also produced a good many palstaves and at least one basal-looped spearhead. It may also be noted that a T-shaped bronze anvil came from West Row. It is 10 cm. across the top and looks more likely to have been used for bronze than gold working.

GROUP I

That there was a flourishing bronze industry in the Fenlands during all stages of the Middle Bronze Age is suggested by the number of finds. The weapons mentioned so far all belong to my Group III, which dates from the eleventh century B.C. There are, from the other end of the period (*i.e.*, 1400–1200 B.C.), sixteen weapons which I assign to my Group I. This was the time of experiment, when British smiths, stimulated by ideas coming across the North Sea, were developing their own distinctive forms of rapier. Since a feature of Group I weapons is their very indeterminateness, it is impossible to be sure that some of these sixteen are not late and degenerate, instead of early and primitive, since none of them has any associations. All the Fenland examples have more or less trapeze-shaped butts and two rivet holes, except for a small dirk from Burwell which has three rivets in a straight line; this is unique.

Several Early Bronze Age daggers have been found in or near the Fens. Evans shows one from Cambridge and mentions others.[3] There is one from a grave-group at Chippenham near Newmarket, only about three miles from the Fen edge, and another grave with Wessex-type gold, amber and a dagger at Little Cressingham, Norfolk, about ten miles from the Fens.[4] So a certain amount of Wessex culture influence was felt in these parts. This would explain how the blade of a weapon like the one illustrated (fig. 51, 5), again from West Row, has the graceful, slightly ogival lines of a Wessex dagger. The trapeze-shaped butt with two rivet holes is, however, a Tumulus Bronze form which developed in the Middle Rhine area and spread down the river. So British Middle Bronze Age weapons, whether made near the Fens, the Thames valley or in Ireland, all show a fusion of native and intrusive traditions.

GROUP II

Group I weapons are not divided into classes. There are, however, four classes in Group II, all the weapons in which have a marked arris down the centre of the blade. Group II belongs to the middle phase of the Middle Bronze Age (*i.e.*, the twelfth century B.C.), the time of the flowering of the British rapier industry. In my original work on these rapiers I distinguished a Wandsworth from a Chatteris class as variants of the normal trapeze-butt rapier of this Group. Wandsworth came almost exclusively from the London area, with a few which I claimed to be able to recognize as of Thames valley manufacture from other regions. Chatteris took in all the remaining trapeze-butt rapiers, including those from Ireland as well as the Fens. One feature of the Wandsworth class was the sharply projecting shoulders between the sides of the butt and the top of the blade (fig. 53, 1), but not all the finds from the London area have this. The rapier from Chatteris has the sides of its butt nearer vertical, and therefore a much less abrupt transition into the blade. I now prefer to combine the two into one Wandsworth-Chatteris class, merely noting that the sharp shoulders are much commoner in the Thames area than elsewhere.

This has some bearing on Fenland rapiers, because two of them, one from Cambridge, the other from Horningsea, have sharp, indeed in the Cambridge specimen exaggerated, shoulders (fig. 53, 2). Whether these were made locally or brought by some means from London is an open question. There are only ten other weapons of this type from the Fens to compare (or contrast) with these two, while there are 28 from the London area. The Cambridge and Horningsea rapiers are particularly fine and large, having strongly moulded blades with a

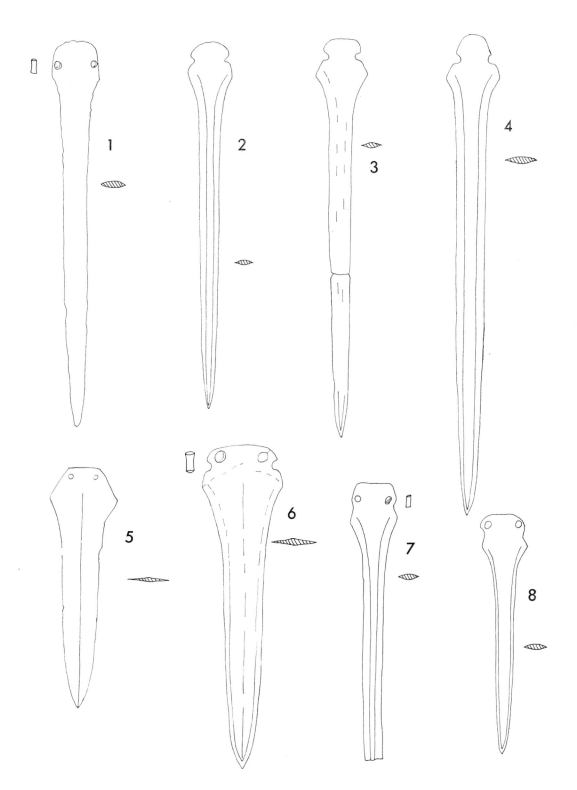

Figure 51. 1. Barnes-Corrib class dirk from West Row, Suffolk. 2. Lisburn class dirk from West Row. 3. Lisburn class dirk from Mildenhall, Suffolk. 4. Lisburn class rapier from the Downham Fen hoard, Cambs. 5. Group 1 dagger from Cook's Drove, West Row. 6. Mortlake class dirk from Mildenhall. 7. Barnes-Corrib class dirk from Toome, Co. Antrim. 8. Barnes-Corrib class dagger from South Kyme, Lincs. (1/3)

marked arris. A high proportion of the Thames rapiers are similarly elegant, but the same can also be said of the Thetford class rapiers and these are taken to be local products.

The Thetford class is distinguished by having its two rivets set in cast penannular notches at the top corners of the butt, instead of in punched rivet holes. It is named after the weapon figured by Evans and now in the Ashmolean.[5] Eleven other examples have been found in the Fen area, and two more from East Anglia were almost certainly made in the Fens. In fact the vicinity of the southern Fens was the only place in England where this form appears to have been manufactured, since there are only two from the London area, usually so prolific. Two others from southeast England are probably from the Fens, while those from southwest England, Wales and Scotland were more likely made in Ireland. This form was produced in Ireland also, since thirteen specimens are known from there. In fact it seems to have been a popular form for Irish merchants to hawk round western Britain since two hoards, Talaton, Devon, and Drumcoltran, Dumfriesshire contained six and twelve weapons respectively of the Thetford class alone. Thirteen is, however, a relatively small number of finds for the whole of Ireland, and it seems likely that this form was invented by Fen bronze-smiths.

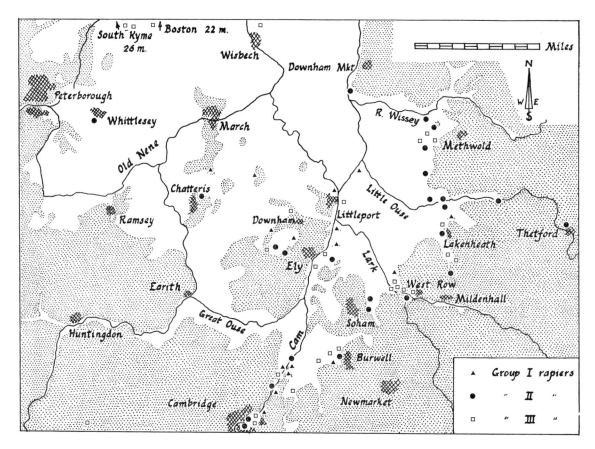

Figure 52. Distribution map. Fen peat and alluvium are left white : stippling indicates other soils.

Several of the Fen rapiers are particularly fine and large. That from Feltwell, though sadly corroded, is 65·7 cm. long and a well-preserved find from Undley Fen is 51·5 cm. long. The average length is about 36 cm. A feature of the class is that the blade is sharply ridged, with moulding and arris well defined, making it suitable for a thrusting blow only (fig. 53, 3).

The Mortlake class clearly originated in the London area as several Group I prototypes have been found for it there. It is distinguished by having two rivets in holes and two notches for additional rivets or lashing in the side of the butt. The corners of the butt are rounded. The blade is broad and fairly flat in cross-section, with the moulding close to the edge and not very marked. The three Fen finds are so true to form as shown by the eleven examples from the Thames valley that one is prompted to think they came from there. Their broad flat blades (fig. 51, 6) are very different from the tapering ridged blades of the Wandsworth-Chatteris and Thetford class rapiers which we can be fairly certain were made here, and there are no Group I finds from the Fens of this type. Ireland has produced only seven Mortlake weapons and traded none to Scotland or western England and Wales. These seven do not look like exports from England, having narrower, more tapering blades than the Thames weapons, but obviously the form never became popular in Ireland.

Irish smiths, however, were solely responsible for producing weapons belonging to the Keelogue class. The characteristics of this class are a broad heavy blade with an arris but no cast moulding. The butt has rounded shoulders and near-vertical sides. The rivets tend to be rather long and slim. There are twenty examples from Ireland, and plenty of Group I prototypes there. Twelve have been found in the rest of the British Isles, mostly from western districts, but there is one from the Fens and six from the Thames. The Fenland example is from Wilton Bridge near Lakenheath, Suffolk. It is similar to Irish specimens, and there is little doubt that it originated there (fig. 53, 4–5).

There is one other rapier which must have been imported into the Fens, and that is the one found at Isleham. This weapon, now regrettably corroded, is decorated with groups of lightly engraved lines which converge well above the tip of the blade. The lines start, not at the rivet holes, as on other British Early and Middle Bronze Age weapons, but on the sides of the butt, which on one side appear to be indented at that point. There were originally two rivet holes (now broken) and also two small notches in the top to the butt (fig. 54, 1). This is not a British form. The decoration in fact shows clearly that this weapon was made in northern France. Coutil shows a very similar weapon from the Seine at Les Andelys.[6] Two other grooved French rapiers reached England. There is a very corroded one in the Layton Collection, and a fine one displayed in the British Museum from the Thames at Surbiton, Surrey. This, like Isleham, has an asymmetric butt, there being one notch on one side and two indentations on the other. Though only 41·2 cm. long it is broad and massive, and in form and decoration it is very like a giant blade from Plougrescant, Côtes du Nord. A weapon considerably smaller found at Kimberley in Norfolk is illustrated by Greenwell.[7] This has a trapeze-shaped butt with no rivet holes at all. The blade is decorated with single lines of reeding running from the sides of the butt and converging almost at the tip. The interesting thing about this weapon is that there are ricasso notches at the top of the blade, showing that it was made after the introduction of swords. Greenwell compares Kimberley with the monstrous blade from Beaune, Côte d'Or, which is 68 cm. long and 16 cm. across the butt; Kimberley is about

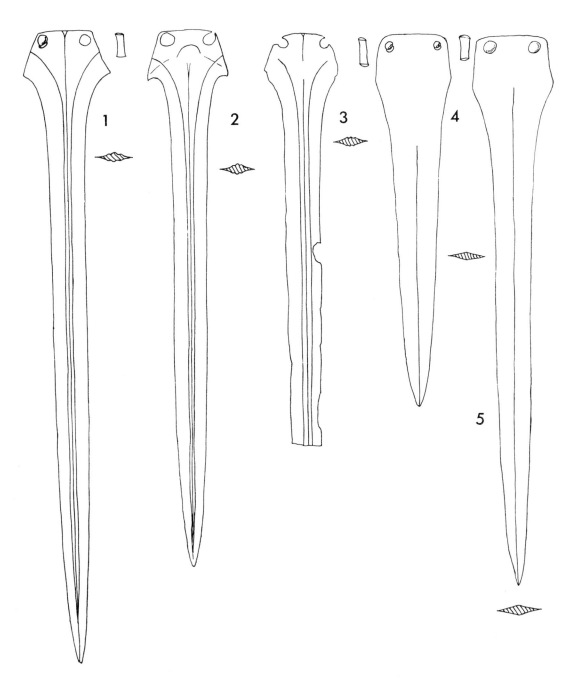

Figure 53. 1. Wandsworth-Chatteris class rapier from Hammersmith. 2. Wandsworth-Chatteris class rapier from Cambridge. 3. Thetford class rapier from Waterbeach, Cambs. 4. Keelogue class dirk from Fethard, Co. Tipperary. 5. Keelogue class rapier from Wilton Bridge, Suffolk. (1/3)

32 cm. long. Beaune likewise has ricasso notches and no rivet holes. For ornament there is a flat-topped ridge starting at the sides of the butt and converging halfway down the blade. The Beaune rapier certainly was never intended for fighting: far too big and heavy and impossible to haft, it is totally blunt and obviously always has been. The Surbiton rapier also looks rather a parade weapon, but the one from Isleham could have dealt a dangerous stab.

GROUP III

In my third group of British rapiers, which belongs to the eleventh century B.C., all the weapons lack any arris, though moulding is usually apparent. The blades do not taper much, and, having a smooth cross-section, are reasonably well adapted for slashing. In England there are only two classes as I wish now to combine Barnes and Corrib into one, in the same way as with the Wandsworth and Chatteris classes of Group II, so as to have a single class for all late rapiers with two rivets in holes. What distinguishes these weapons from those of Group II, apart from their blade form, is that the sides of the butt are now almost vertical, instead of sloping outwards, making the angle between butt and blade less marked. Why this change was made is a mystery. It is in fact a retrograde step, as a narrow butt makes for a less steady blade than a broad one.

There are only five examples from the Cambridge-Ely Fens. One from West Row has already been mentioned. A find from Suffolk was probably made in the Fens, as it resembles a dirk from Cambridge, though the latter has an anomalous hump in the top of its butt. A rapier from Boston, Lincolnshire, however, is more likely to be of Irish manufacture, though the butt is so broken as to make any ascription uncertain. The two weapons found together at South Kyme, Lincolnshire, are certainly Irish. The Barnes-Corrib one is unusual in having indentations like a Lisburn butt, as well as two rivet holes (fig. 51, 8). A dirk from the Bann at Toome, Co. Antrim, is very similar (fig. 51, 7). The Lisburn dirk from South Kyme is poorly preserved and indeterminate. Though this area of Lincolnshire is geographically part of the Fens it seems to have had no contact with the bronze workshops of the southern Fens in the Middle Bronze Age.

The Lisburn class has already been discussed in connection with the West Row rapier. It is only with this late class of rapier that there are any associated finds in this area. The well-known Downham Fen hoard contains a particularly fine Lisburn rapier (fig. 51, 4), a socketed sickle and a looped palstave.[8] All these objects can be dated to the eleventh century B.C.

There is another hoard containing rapiers which is of considerable interest. It was found in the neighbourhood of Eriswell, a village near Mildenhall, Suffolk.[9] A ploughman found a 'sword,' an awl and a Lisburn rapier and dirk (fig. 54, 3–6) together in a layer of dark soil full of burnt flints. Three yards north of these was found a mass of partly melted bronze which contained a heavy hook and crumpled fragments of a sheet bronze vessel. It is not certain that these were associated with the weapons, but it seems likely. The 'sword' is a hybrid between true swords and Rixheim rapiers which developed in the Seine basin.[10] Rixheim rapiers were centred on south Germany but there are also three on the Seine and one found in Belgium.[11] They have, usually, three slim rivets in a pointed butt and a straight-sided blade with milled ricasso at the top. Eriswell is typical as to outline, though somewhat broader, but has four notches and then two rivets in holes below. I know of no other weapon with exactly this

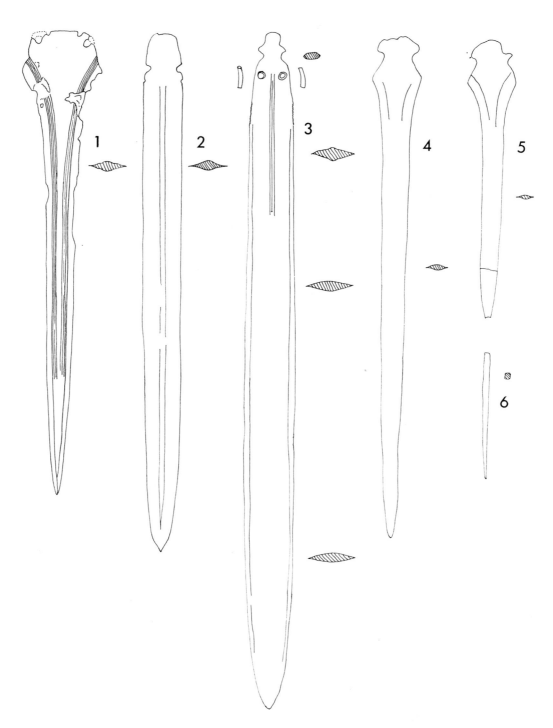

Figure 54. 1. Grooved rapier from Isleham, Cambs. 2. Rapier sword from Methwold, Norfolk. 3. Rapier sword from the Eriswell hoard, Suffolk. 4. Lisburn rapier from the Eriswell hoard. 5. Lisburn dirk from the Eriswell hoard. 6. Awl from the Eriswell hoard. (1/3)

arrangement, but Déchelette shows a rapier with six rivets from Villeneuve St George,[12] and there are at least six weapons with similar blades and four notches from the Seine basin. Perhaps the closest match is one from Amiens figured by Coutil.[13] His drawings do not show ricasso, but this rapier-sword probably has it. One other weapon of this four-notch type but without ricasso has been found in Britain, and that, interestingly enough, close by, at Methwold, Norfolk. This has two notches well down from the top of the butt and two small ones immediately below. The blade is parallel sided most of its length, which is 40·3 cm. (fig. 54, 2). It is comparable to a weapon from Épinal. It is probable that the Eriswell and Methwold weapons were made in France. Two weapons with similar blades and four rivets in holes have been found in the Thames at Kingston and Lambeth, and another in Ireland. All these rather curious weapons are imports from France. The Lisburn rapiers from Eriswell are, however, of local manufacture. They are somewhat unusual in that the top of their butts is highly domed and there is no lower lip to the notches (fig. 54, 4–5). Two other rapiers both found near Ely are very similar. Since it seems likely that all the weapons in the Eriswell hoard were about to be melted down by a Late Bronze Age scrap merchant but were for some reason spared, their exact contemporaneity is not proved by this association. But other evidence suggests that they were made at about the same date since Rixheim rapiers are of the eleventh century on the Continent, and Lisburn the same in the British Isles. That rapier-swords belong to the end of the Middle Bronze Age and not the Late Bronze Age is shown by the hoard from Pennavern, Rosnöen, Finisterre which contains one with four notches and another with four rivets in holes.[14] It also contains a leaf-shaped spearhead, a Class II razor and a socketed hammer.

Distribution

The distribution map shows that there are no finds of rapiers at all from the central Fens, at the head of the Wash and around Spalding (fig. 52). A large part of this area may still have been covered by a marine transgression which took place in neolithic times.[15] There is one find of a Group III dirk from near Wisbech, but this is an outlier, being about thirteen miles north of the nearest find, a Group I weapon from the Chatteris district. The nearest Group III find is at Methwold, sixteen miles southeast. There is another outlier from near Peterborough, a fine Wandsworth-Chatteris rapier found at Whittlesey. This is ten miles northwest of the nearest Group II find, which is at Chatteris. The concentrations of finds are around Ely, up the Cam as far as Cambridge, all along the southern margin of the Fens, and up the eastern edge as far as Methwold. Between Cambridge and Methwold the Fen is bordered by a strip of land consisting first of chalk and then of the sandy soil of the Breckland. It is along this strip that the Icknield Way runs, southwest to Wessex along the chalk and northeast to the Norfolk coast. These light soils would have been open country favourable to pastoralists, such as the Middle Bronze Age folk seem to have been. Between Cambridge and Peterborough the Fen margins were heavily wooded at that time,[16] which explains why there are no finds from the Ouse in the Earith-St Neots direction apart from one Lisburn dirk from Croxton Park, four miles east of St Neots. Apparently the Fen islands, in spite of consisting of clay like the forested regions, were inhabited or at least visited. The Downham Fen hoard, so clearly one man's possessions, suggests this, together with the numerous single finds from the vicinity of the islands. On the distribution map all the symbols are drawn on the actual Fen, since even when this is not stated, the good condition of the majority shows they must have lain in wet ground. One wonders how they came to be there in such numbers. The Chatteris rapier is stated to have been found inside a dug-out canoe.[17] Were all these weapons, 65 of them, lost in boating accidents? Or did men come down from the higher ground in order to cast offerings into the dark pools and sluggish rivers of the Fens to appease spirits they believed to reside there?

Reluctant as one is to invoke 'ritual' explanations, this does seem the one best fitted to the facts. For one thing it would help to explain why finds of rapiers are so numerous from the southern Fens and so sparse from the rest of England apart from the Thames at London (where 129 rapiers are known) if only the deities of certain meres and rivers demanded the sacrifice of rapiers. Men wishing to appease these deities may have come considerable distances in order to cast their cherished weapons into the waters. The distribution of rapiers in use was probably much more even over the country as a whole than the distribution of finds suggests. The majority were probably melted down later, as the evidence of Eriswell and several other Late Bronze Age hoards, Wallington for example,[18] suggests. Rapiers were not put with burials, and settlements (apart from the house at Gwithian)[19] have yet to be found, so it is those cast out as offerings which form the bulk of the finds we know today, the remainder surviving purely by chance after being lost or hidden.

The offering theory also explains why the majority are single finds, unassociated with other artifacts, structures or burials. The cult was obviously quite unorganized, as nowhere from the Britain of this period is there a site such as La Tène where hundreds of bronzes are found in a small area. If the Fenland rapiers, together with the scores of palstaves and looped spearheads found in the same area, are taken as a vast scattered votive deposit, brought together from the whole of southeast England, it makes it less difficult to accept the non-local origins which have been suggested for some of the finds: the Wandsworth-Chatteris rapiers from Cambridge and Horningsea and the three Mortlake weapons made in the Thames valley, the Keelogue rapier from Wilton Bridge made in Ireland, the decorated rapier from Isleham and the two rapier swords from Eriswell and Methwold made in northern France. On the other hand there does seem to have been a local bronze industry, almost certainly up on the dry ground rather than in the Fens themselves. The evidence for this has been discussed particularly in connection with the West Row rapiers and the Thetford class. This industry, founded by descendants of Beaker folk who flourished on the chalk and Breckland,[20] was in a strategic position both to trade with East Anglia and southwest along the Icknield Way route, and also to receive influences from across the North Sea. With Thetford rapiers in particular the bronze-smiths of this area produced some of the most elegant blades this country has ever seen.

Acknowledgments: I wish to thank the following people: John Coles for providing drawings of the Eriswell hoard; my husband for drawing the distribution map; Mary Cra'ster of the Museum of Archaeology and Ethnology, Cambridge, for solving scores of minor problems; Barbara Green of Norwich Castle Museum and Mr Edwardson of the Moyses Hall Museum, Bury St Edmunds, for helping me to study the rapiers in their charge; and Mr S. Ford and Mr F. Curtiss for allowing me to examine their private collections; last but not least Professor Stuart Piggott for having directed my attention to the subject of rapiers and for guiding my original research.

CATALOGUE

(Abbreviations: F: fragment only; B.M.: British Museum; Cambridge: University Museum of Archaeology and Ethnology.)

Findspot	Length in cm.	Museum
GROUP I		
Burwell Fen, Cambs.	21·7	Ashmolean 1927 2344
Cambridge Fens	25·1	„ 1927 2352
Waterbeach Fen, Cambs.	20 F	„ — —
Downham Hill, Coveney, Cambs.	28·5	Cambridge 22558
Ely Fens	20·8	„ 22.561
Horningsea, Cambs.	17·5	„ 32.221
Littleport, Cambs.	25·2	„ 59.414
Manea, Isle of Ely	23 F	„ 83.176 A
Padnal Fen, Prickwillow, Ely	30·9	„ 49.694
Fen Ditton, Cambs.	19·6 F	B.M. WG 2066
Littleport, Cambs.	20	„ WG 2065
Waterbeach, Cambs.	17	„ WG 2072
Ely, Cambs.	17	King's Lynn Museum
Lakenheath, Suffolk	19	Ipswich Museum 1934 76 16
Wimblington, Cambs.	27	Wisbech Museum
West Row, Suffolk	19·2	Mr S. Ford, West Row
GROUP II		
Wandsworth-Chatteris Class		
Chatteris, Cambs.	38·9	Ashmolean 1927 2353
Catsholm, Methwold, Norfolk	35	B.M. WG 2067
Burwell, Cambs.	31	Cambridge 2 4247
Cambridge (fig. 4, 2)	42·8	„ 29 185
Horningsea, Cambs.	35	„ 32 219
Ely Fens	22·8	„ 22 560 CA
Brandon, Suffolk	38·1	„ 23 1563
Whittlesey, Cambs.	34·3	Peterborough Museum L665
Methwold Fen, Norfolk	30	Mr F. Curtiss, Feltwell
Hockwold-cum-Wilton, Suffolk	49·5	Norwich Castle Museum 346.958 (8)
Thetford Class		
Thetford, Norfolk	44·8 F	Ashmolean 1927 2524
Cambridge	41·6	Cambridge 97 72
Ely	39	„ 22 557
Feltwell, Norfolk	65·7	„ FB 232
Soham Fen, Cambs.	18·2	„ —
Soham, Cambs.	26·4 F	„ 99 327
Waterbeach, Cambs. (fig. 4, 3)	32·7	„ 83 162
Wilton Bridge, Suffolk	31	„ 47 D1
Undley Fen, Suffolk	51·5	Bury St Edmunds F.27
Downham Market area, Norfolk	39·5	Norwich Castle Loan 1965.3
Catsholm, Methwold, Norfolk	37·2	„ „ cast

Findspot	Length in cm.	Museum
Mortlake Class		
Cambridgeshire	34·7	Cambridge 54 300 A
Mildenhall, Suffolk (fig. 2, 2)	25·8	,, FB 228
Quavney, Cambs.	29·5	,, 22 559 CA
Keelogue Class		
Wilton Bridge, Suffolk (fig. 4, 5)	43·6	Cambridge 46 412
Grooved Rapier		
Isleham Fen, Cambs. (fig. 5, 1)	36·7	Cambridge 22 555

GROUP III

Findspot	Length in cm.	Museum
Barnes-Corrib Class		
Burwell Fen, Cambs.	16·1	Ashmolean 1927 2343
Boston, Lincs.	37·9 F	B.M. 52 5–18–1
Whiteplot, Methwold, Norfolk	27·4 F	,, WG 2071
Wilton Bridge, Suffolk	29	Cambridge 46 413
Cambridge	34·6	St Albans Museum
West Row, Suffolk (fig. 1, 1)	30·5	Bury St Edmunds F.28
South Kyme, Lincs. (fig. 2, 3)	19·2	Alnwick Castle Museum 241
Lisburn Class		
Isle of Ely	33	B.M. 1910 12–10 1
Methwold, Norfolk	22·2	,, WG 2076
West Row, Suffolk (Pl. I)	41·5	Bury St Edmunds F.169
,, ,, ,, (fig. 1, 2)	29	,, ,, ,, —
Burwell, Cambs.	18·8	Cambridge 28 516
Croxton Park, Cambs.	32·4	,, 29 517
Downham Fen, Cambs. (fig. 1, 4)	39·5	,, PB 135 87 164
Horningsea, Cambs.	6 F	,, 34 881
Littleport, Cambs.	16·2	,, 59 416
Mildenhall, Suffolk (fig. 1, 3)	31·7	,, 83 163 A
Quy Fen, Cambs.	25	,, 83 164 A
Reach, Cambs.	17	,, 27 604
Stuntney, Cambs.	31·5	,, FB 231
Undley, Suffolk	14·2	,, FB 230
Eriswell, Suffolk (fig. 5, 5)	22·5	Elveden Estate Museum
,, ,, (fig. 5, 4)	39·2	,, ,, ,,
Ely, Cambs.	36·6	King's Lynn Museum
Cambridge	35	Pitt-Rivers Museum, Farnham
South Kyme, Lincs.	26·9	Alnwick Castle No. 240
Undley, Suffolk	17	Mr S. Ford, West Row
Walsoken, Norfolk	34·8	Wisbech Museum
Rapier-Swords		
Eriswell, Suffolk (fig. 5, 3)	53·7	Elveden Estate Museum
Methwold, Norfolk (fig. 5, 2)	40·3	Cambridge 33 505

Notes

1. *P.S.A.* (2) IV (1868–70) 50
2. *P.P.S.* XXVIII (1962) 91
3. Evans, *Ancient Bronze Implements of Great Britain and Ireland* (1881) 245, fig. 304
4. *P.P.S.* IV (1938) 92
5. Evans, *op. cit.* fig. 316
6. Coutil, 'Poignards, Rapières et Épées de l'Âge du Bronze.' Extrait de *L'Homme Préhistorique* (1926–8) Pl. IX
7. *Arch.* LVIII, pt. I (1912) 3
8. Fox, *Archaeology of the Cambridge Region* (1923) Pl. VIII
9. *Ant. J.* XXXV (1955) 218
10. *P.P.S.* XXVIII (1962) 93
11. *Mainzer Zeitschrift* XXIX (1934) 58, Abb. 1
12. Déchelette, *Manuel d'Archaeologie* I (1908) fig. 62, 5
13. Coutil, *op. cit.* Pl. III
14. Giot, *Brittany* (1960) 153, fig. 46
15. Fox, *op. cit.* XXII
16. Fox, *op. cit.* 13
17. Evans, *op. cit.* 250
18. *P.P.S.* XXVIII (1962) 92
19. *P.P.S.* XXIV (1958) 214
20. Fox, *op. cit.* 13

Iron Age enclosures in the Cologne Basin

Irwin Scollar

Some years ago K. V. Decker and the author published a brief survey of the then known square Iron Age burial enclosures in the Rhineland.[1] At that time a few dozen examples had been found by ground survey and about a hundred more had been discovered from the air during 1960–61. A complete list of the air discoveries, along with illustrations, was published subsequently by the writer in a more comprehensive fashion.[2] Five further years of aerial exploration in the Rhineland have so modified the picture that it seems useful to revise it.

Published information on the distribution of late Iron Age sites in the Rhineland is not extensive.[3] Two dissertations,[4] unpublished as of late 1966, substantially aid in understanding the material from the southern part of the region that is, in the Hunsrück and Eifel mountains, both north and south of the Moselle. For the Cologne Basin and the lower Rhine valley, no general study exists or is in preparation at this time. Detailed fieldwork carried out during the last five years in a few counties in the last-named areas has shown that the number of late Iron Age sites far exceeds anything previously expected, with some 50 examples now known through important surface sherd scatters.[5] Aerial photography has been able to add almost another 50 sites which can probably be attributed to the period in question. Thus, even though the material north of the Ahr is not well published, a pattern of pre-Roman Iron Age occupation of some extent is beginning to emerge.

Aerial sites can be assigned to a particular period only if their forms are singular enough. Settlements, seen only as conglomerations of pits and ditches, cannot be dated without ground survey and excavation. Graves, on the other hand, are often sufficiently distinctive in themselves to allow of immediate identification. As the previously mentioned studies have shown, square enclosures are quite common for the burials and sacred places of the late Iron Age in the southern part of the Rhineland. In 1962 it was thought that the type did not exist north of the Neuwied Basin. This was shown in the distribution map accompanying the survey first mentioned.

The dry spring and summer of 1962 and 1964 resulted in a series of new sites being found on the borders of the Loess area of the Cologne Basin. Normally the Loess is too water-retentive to allow for good contrast in crop sites even in the driest year.[6] However sometimes the Loess lies thinly on the gravel ridges of the higher Rhine terraces and, in these areas, a dry spring and early summer will permit good results to be obtained. Between 1962 and 1966, 59 rectangular and square enclosures at 47 different locations had been found in the small area included in Kreis Bonn, Düren and Euskirchen. This distribution seems to be determined solely by the geological phenomenon mentioned and is presumably not character-istic of the true distribution of the monument types. In the southern region along both sides of the Moselle, conditions are somewhat better and the aerial distribution is probably somewhat more characteristic, though still not equal to the true pattern.

As shown in the distribution map (fig. 55), the sites presented here seem to be related to those found along the edge of the Loess in the unpublished field survey of settlements. The field survey, which is complete in only a few counties, has discovered Iron Age settlement in a broad east–west band from the Dutch border north of Aachen right to the Rhine. Had geological conditions been more suitable, it seems likely that the distribution of square or rectangular enclosures would also follow that of the settlements, instead of being restricted to only a part of it.

The sites in the Cologne Basin are more varied in form than their neighbours in the south. The Moselle group, to give the southern branch a convenient name, is characterized by almost perfectly square enclosures from 10 to 40 m. on a side, sometimes with a central barrow, occasionally with bank external to the ditch, often occurring in groups of up to seven or eight closely spaced and aligned units and, in a few instances, even joined to one another. The northern, or Cologne Basin, group contains a number of different types. These are shown in Pl. IV and V. Site FS 33 (Pl. IV, a) shows an example identical in proportion and size with those of the Moselle group. Fourteen of the examples are of this type. In Pl. IV, b, a variant, site FB 8, is shown in which the proportions are rectangular with side lengths roughly in the ratio of three to two. This type can be definitely identified in 24 instances. A third type, if it is a true type and not simply a distortion due to errors in laying out examples of the second type, is shown in Pl. V, a, of site GF 82. Here, the monuments are usually a bit larger than those just mentioned and are roughly trapezoidal in shape. They tend to occur in pairs or groups of up to three. This variant can be identified in thirteen instances. The remaining examples are too fragmentary to classify.

The rather unsatisfactory knowledge of the chronological position of the Moselle group of enclosures was summarized previously.[7] The Cologne Basin group is represented only by crop sites whose existence was not even suspected prior to aerial exploration. Only two sites have been excavated. The results, published by L. H. Barfield,[8] give us an end date for the square type, judging from the early Imperial material found in the ditch filling. Lack of finds in the centre of the two excavated enclosures is surely due to the destruction of the ancient surface through ploughing and erosion. Unfortunately, this condition is likely to prevail in the majority of air-discovered sites. Another chronological indication for the Cologne Basin types is given in three instances where square or rectangular enclosures can be seen to cut the ditches of ploughed-out circular barrows. Plate V, b of site EZ 21 presents the clearest example of this type of 'aerial stratigraphy.' In site FA 52 (not shown) the circular ditch is cut by a rectangular type, while FI 1 (also not illustrated) is similar to EZ 21. In four other instances, the square or rectangular types are found in close proximity to circular barrows. Circular ditched barrows are known, where they have survived and have been excavated, to begin in the late Beaker period and to continue well down into the middle of the late Iron Age (Niederrheinische Grabhügel Kultur). Most belong to the last-named culture. The air photo 'stratified' examples are, in the absence of excavation, not too helpful. However, they tend to

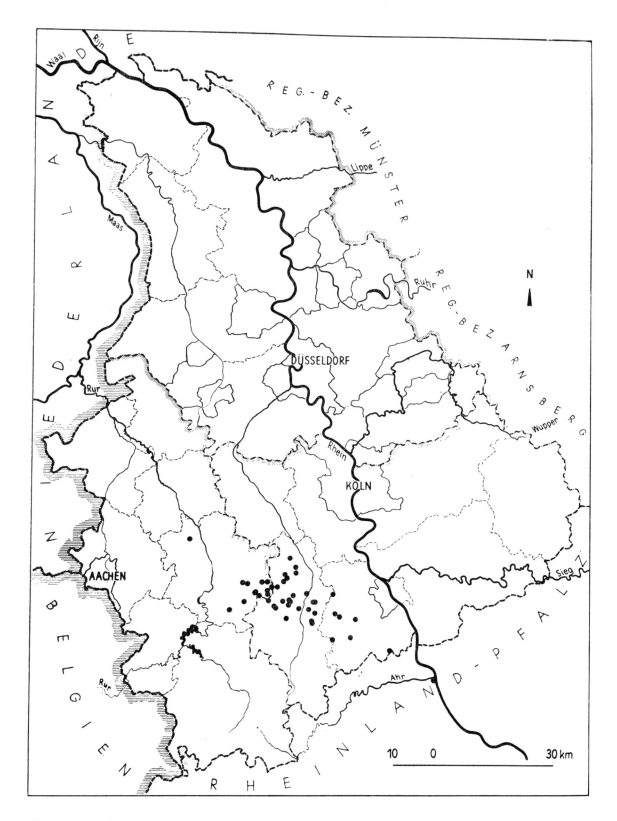

Figure 55. Distribution map of Iron Age sites in the Cologne basin.

suggest that the square and rectangular enclosures are final Iron Age in date, like their fellows in the Moselle group and elsewhere.

Comparable enclosures have been noted in a number of countries.[9] Examples found in Champagne and similar finds which have been reported from the Ardennes are the nearest neighbours in type to those of the Moselle group. The Cologne Basin finds present a number of singularities which seem to have no direct parallels. Enclosures of rectangular and trapezoidal shape are known in Bavaria in considerable number, but these are usually much larger than those which have been discussed up to now.[10] Six very large enclosures, up to 150 m. side length, have been found during aerial survey of the Cologne Basin. None are known from the Moselle region. Three of these are associated with round barrows and one is partly overlaid by a large cemetery of unknown date. The sides of these big enclosures are rather irregular, sometimes even slightly rounded, though the corners are well-marked near right angles. One enclosure with slightly rounded corners contains a clearly visible Gallo-Roman peristyle temple. It is possible that these larger enclosures had a cult character similar to that usually attributed to their Bavarian counterparts. Their relationship, if any, with the smaller enclosures of the Cologne Basin is not understood.

The value of aerial photography for obtaining data about field monuments has been enthusiastically advocated in the last few decades. The Cologne Basin contains some of the richest agricultural soil in northern Europe and certainly has one of the densest concentrations of sites from Bandkeramik onwards. Modern occupation is also intense, and there are practically no vestiges of the past surviving above ground. It is scarcely surprising that systematic aerial exploration should produce a whole new group of sites under favourable geological conditions. But this very situation points to some of the limitations of the aerial method: distributions are a reflection of the local geology suited to crop sites rather than to cultural or geographical conditions; destruction of the ancient land surface by modern agriculture, wind erosion etc. often prevents the recovery of finds on air sites; difficulties in chronology exist due to absence of finds and lack of large numbers of stratified sites; it is necessary to concentrate on types of sites with identifiable shapes to the detriment of those whose forms or features cannot be well determined from the air. Aerial survey presents a biased sample of the data, the bias determined largely by natural conditions. It would seem advisable not to add to this the additional bias of a forced or exaggerated interpretation. It is hoped that excavation of a number of the sites newly found will help in providing answers to some of the basic questions which these discoveries have raised.

REGISTER OF SITES

Location	Air photo archive number	Coordinates (Gauss)	Appearance
Kreis Ahrweiler			
Sinzig	FG 13	25.89.76×56.02.20	Two fragments
Kreis Bonn			
Buschhoven	EG 26	25.69.60×56.15.94	One small square
Fritzdorf	EJ 76	25.77.92×56.08.41	One fragment
Miel	DF 17	25.65.61×56.16.70	One square
Ollheim	FI 1	25.64.30×56.17.38	One small square cutting circular barrow, two more circular barrows nearby
Rheinbach	Z 2	25.68.34×56.11.66	One trapezoidal
Kreis Euskirchen			
Erp	DY 14	25.51.97×56.25.39	One rectangular, two circular barrows nearby
Erp	EA 5	25.52.63×56.26.15	One small rectangular
Erp	EE 56	25.52.20×56.26.95	One fragment with adjacent circular barrow
Frauenberg	EW 1	25.52.34×56.16.50	One trapezoidal, two circular barrows nearby
Grossbüllesheim	SBP 20	25.59.63×56.17.62	One rectangular
Kleinbüllesheim	EZ 21	25.58.86×56.15.67	One square cutting a circular barrow (Pl. V, b photo GG 15 shown)
Kleinbüllesheim	EZ 33	25.58.97×56.15.17	Two fragments and one circular barrow
Lechenich	EE 46	25.54.95×56.27.39	One trapezoidal
Lechenich	FM 45	25.53.30×56.30.92	One rectangular
Lechenich	FS 64	25.54.78×56.28.78	One rectangular
Lommersum	Z 27	25.59.12×56.20.32	One trapezoidal
Lommersum	GL 28	25.59.38×56.20.30	One trapezoidal
Lommersum	66/3	25.55.68×56.18.72	One large trapezoidal, irregular
Metternich	FS 1	25.64.08×56.22.12	One rectangular
Niederberg	GI 15	25.54.10×56.21.86	One square
Oberelvenich	BD 45	25.49.53×56.19.64	One fragment
Oberelvenich	88/5	25.49.90×56.18.90	Three rectangular
Palmersheim	FB 8	25.63.84×56.11.20	One rectangular (Pl. IV, b FB 12 shown)
Vernich	FS 33	25.57.65×56.22.32	One square (Pl. IV, a FS 34 shown)
Vernich	FS 38	25.57.36×56.22.50	One trapezoid, one square, one fragment
Wichterich	GF 72	25.53.28×56.20.74	Four rectangular, two intersecting each other
Wichterich	GF 82	25.51.64×56.20.38	Two trapezoidal (Pl. V, a GG 45 shown)
Wichterich	GM 24	25.53.31×56.20.50	One square
Wichterich	SCK 6	25.52.90×56.19.74	One rectangular
Weiler i.d. Ebene	EF 9	25.50.14×56.24.09	One rectangular fragment
Wüschheim	FI 38	25.58.03×56.18.50	One square

Location	Air Photo archive number	Coordinates (Gauss)	Appearance
Kreis Düren			
Disternich	EJ 39	25.48.90×56.24.02	One square
Disternich	FU 1	25.47.70×56.23.22	One rectangular
Disternich	FZ 76	25.48.12×56.22.32	One rectangular
Disternich	70/6	25.47.80×56.23.40	One rectangular, one trapezoidal
Froitzheim	GA 29	25.42.26×56.20.37	One rectangular
Ginnick	Q 8	25.38.59×56.18.73	One trapezoidal, large, irregular
Gladbach	FA 62	25.43.05×56.24.73	One rectangular
Kelz	FA 52	25.41.74×56.25.27	One rectangular cutting, two circular barrows
Müddersheim	FA 25	25.47.88×56.25.10	One small square
Müddersheim	GD 26	25.46.64×56.25.16	One trapezoidal
Pier	FB 46	25.29.02×56.35.80	One square
Sievernich	DE 9	25.44.80×56.22.70	One square
Sievernich	DE 16	25.44.90×56.22.85	One square, one rectangular (see *Bonner Jahrbücher* CLXV (1965) 165–76)
Sievernich	EV 26	25.45.88×56.21.63	One rectangular
Sievernich	FZ 84	25.48.24×56.20.68	One trapezoidal with one round corner

Notes

1. *Antiquity* XXXVI (1962) 175–8
2. Scollar, *Archäologie aus der Luft* (1965) Pls. 4–14 and pp. 51–5
3. K. Tackenberg, Fundkarten zur Vorgeschichte der Rheinprovinz. Beiheft 2, *Bonner Jahrbücher* (1954)
4. By K. V. Decker, Univ. Mainz, and G. Joachim, Univ. Marburg
5. Information from H. J. Driehaus, Rheinisches Landesmuseum
6. *Colloque International d'Archéologie Aérienne* (1964) 39–47
7. *Antiquity* XXXVI (1962) 175–8
8. *Bonner Jahrbücher* CLXV (1965) 165–76
9. *Ant. J.* XLI (1961) 44 ff.
10. Schwarz, *Atlas der Spätkeltischen Viereckschanzen Bayerns* (1959)

Massive armlets
in the North British Iron Age

Morna Simpson

This discussion of an armlet type peculiar to the Iron Age in northeast Scotland is an expanded excerpt from a doctoral thesis, submitted to Edinburgh University in 1966. To Professor Piggott, therefore, its contents will come as no surprise; and for resting upon these dubious and tarnished laurels, I must apologize with humility. If nothing else, however, the essay will serve to emphasize his own contribution to the sphere of Early Iron Age metalwork.

The descriptive title 'massive armlets' is proposed for self-explanatory reasons; as further definition, it is enough to say that all are penannular in shape, with expanded and centrally perforated terminals for the insertion, in some cases at least, of circular, enamelled plaques. Diagrammatic illustrations of all save the Irish example are provided (figs. 57–61). In these, each armlet has been unrolled, so to speak, and drawn to a uniform and arbitrary size.

The 20 or possibly 21 massive armlets known to me are listed at the end of this article, together with basic measurements, details of present localities and major references. Of this number, five (Belhelvie, Glamis, Stichill and the Tillychetly pair) are totally lost, although the first and third mentioned were probably identical to still-extant examples, while the second is represented by an admirable plaster cast. A further three (from Aboyne) are in a private collection and have been examined at second hand only – that is, from casts; and my information on the lone Irish specimen rests solely on photographs (Pl. VIII).

All subsequent studies have owed a great debt to the pioneer work of J. A. Smith, whose collation of the material was read to the Society of Antiquaries of Scotland in 1879, finally published in the Society's *Proceedings* for 1880–1,[1] and supplemented by a note in the 1882–3 volume.[2] Previous investigation had been confined to brief donation and discovery notes and to meagre mention by Wilson in his *Prehistoric Annals of Scotland*.[3] From this sound beginning, the Iron Age date of massive armlets was never in question. Anderson's study of 1883[4] adds little to the information proffered by Smith, but some time later,[5] we have this author to thank for his disentanglement of find spots and identities. Evans' comparison of the armlet decoration with that on the Æsica brooch[6] was far in advance of his time; however, it was not until 1933 that Leeds[7] fitted them into the national scheme of artistic development in the Iron Age. The latest illumination has been provided by Professor Piggott[8] and by Stevenson.[9] My only excuse for raking over this much-published material is the presentation of fresh opinions in the realms of technology and stylistic analysis.

I am greatly indebted to Mr Mancini, bronze founder of Fountainhall, Edinburgh, for his contribution to the first category. He wishes me to state that, given the complexities of the subject, plus a lack of facilities for microscopic examination, some of his conclusions must be little more than inspired guesses; to the uninitiated, they are nevertheless welcome and exciting.

All the armlets are of tin bronze, the alloy varying considerably. Thus, a sample taken from the Stanhope specimen revealed it to be 'true' bronze; one of the Aboyne pair on the other hand incorporated 4·41% lead and 1·4% zinc, and the other as much as 9·13% zinc (Nat. Mus. Edin. FA21 and FA22 respectively). Both these last ingredients were beginning to appear in alloys as early as the Late Bronze Age, the former intentionally, the latter accidentally;[10] yet it must be admitted that widespread and conscious inclusion of zinc is a feature of Roman metallurgy.

The armlets are sturdy castings, executed by the 'cire perdue' method. No two specimens have yet proved identical, despite a tendency to occur in pairs; however, should mass production be envisaged, a flat wooden template with a sunken 'negative' of the surface pattern could have allowed for the execution of any number of identical wax models, upon which penannular shape could then be imposed by the application of gentle heat and pressure. On the other hand, at least some of the armlets appear to have been cast flat and subsequently curved by a process of annealing, hammering and quenching. It must be admitted that massive armlets provide direct evidence for neither a wooden template nor the process of flat casting, but the closely related bracelet type called 'spiral snake,' and in particular that representative from Pitalpin, Angus,[11] does just that; the impression of wood graining is still visible in its spinal recess – whose 'kerbschnitt' filling, by the way, is far more suited to a wooden than to a metal medium; and clamp bruises, connected with the process of coiling after casting, are to be detected towards both ends.

If flat then, the clay mould would be laid decorative face downwards, so that the metal could flow into the ornamental cavities while at its most molten. In connection with the actual pouring of the cast, Mancini would attribute a certain slurring of decoration to the use of excessively hot metal and the resultant glazing of the clay mould interior. Most clues to the mechanics of casting have been removed; for instance, the position of the gate is not clear; however, two pin-like stumps upon the Bunrannoch armlet may be the remains of vents.

An interesting question is posed by the Glamis armlet (Pl. VII, top and fig. 60), formed as it is of three juxtaposed but separated bars of flattened oval section (the central bar continued about the terminal voids to form the two flanking ones). Such a shape would be most easily arrived at by casting three separate units and then joining them together, perhaps by the process of 'burning on.' This technique is displayed not only by the chapes of a Group III scabbard from the River Tweed at Carham[12] and a Group IV scabbard from Mortonhall, Midlothian,[13] but also, with more relevance, by the famous snake armlet from the Culbin Sands, Morayshire.[14] In this last instance, the junction was strengthened in a workmanlike fashion by the excision of two rebates on the opposing segments to be joined, by the drilling of bell-mouthed holes immediately behind each rebate, and by the pouring of metal into these features as well as into the actual point of juncture itself. This sawn and drilled keying was so successful that discoloration alone reveals its position today. Unfortunately, we shall never know for certain whether this technique was used in the manufacture of the Glamis armlet; we can only suspect, for, in the only comparable pieces (Pitkelloney, Pl. X), a similar juxtaposition of bars has been reached by solid casting as a single unit and subsequent splitting of the thin web of metal between each pair of strands.

Despite the skill displayed, much post-casting consolidation has been necessary in most armlets. Some of this is simple; a ragged excess of metal at one edge of the Belhelvie specimen has been merely folded on to the undersurface and beaten flat. Much is extremely complex and best exemplified by the armlet from Auchenbadie (Pl. VI, top), both of whose terminals apparently showed a tendency to crack just above their perforations. Large uneven sections including two lenticular bosses have been entirely replaced. Internally, a mass of globules of run on metal reveal the crude method of repair, but careful camouflage has reduced exterior traces to fine hair cracks and almost imperceptible changes in metal coloration. The replaced edges of one terminal have been further consolidated by pins which have torn away from their seating; while, on the other terminal, there are both marginal rivet holes, now unoccupied, and large flush rivets which pass through the run on metal of the undersurface. Armlets from Aboyne, Belhelvie, Bunrannoch and Newry (Pl. VIII, bottom) tell a scarcely less complex tale; the remainder display only minor flaws such as air bubbles, metal failure at the summit of high-relief adornment and a sponge-like pitting which, I am told, results from insufficient cooking of the clay mould to expel trapped moisture before the actual casting process. The curious removal, by the way, of a slice from each end of the Stichill armlet must remain a mystery; perhaps these segments were faultily cast, removed and replaced; but the single rivet which alone remains in each case seems hardly sufficient for the task of attachment; moreover, each slanting cut is smooth and 'complete' in appearance.

The two pairs of armlets from Castle Newe and Pitkelloney alone retain the red and yellow diaphragms for which also the single specimens from Auchenbadie and Belhelvie bear definite and the Glamis plaster cast doubtful evidence (Pl. IX). This champlevé enamel, distorted by heat, has been laid upon sheet bronze which, in the case of the Castle Newe examples, was further mounted on iron discs of slightly larger diameter. Each colourful panel rests upon a thin ledge provided on the circumference of the aperture and is overlaid by a fragile repoussé frame of half-tubular section, convex upwards, and secured by four countersunk rivets which pass through to the underlying ledge. A cast frame is substituted in the case of the Auchenbadie armlet, but the arrangement of flush rivets is otherwise similar; their protrusion for 3–4 mm. from the underside reveals the thickness of the diaphragms they once served to attach.

Attention must be drawn to an extraordinary structural feature of the Pitkelloney armlets. The split grooves which separate each pair of contiguous bars have been overlaid by two bronze wires of rectangular section at their ends and U-section, concave upwards, in their middle stretches; from the back of each wire, at the point where it abuts on to the terminal apertures, a small oval loop emerges to pass through to the back of the armlet, there to be filled by a short length of transverse bar, partly recessed into the armlet and thus forming a T-shaped anchorage (Pl. X, middle). The remaining free ends of wire are merely folded in hook-like fashion to the armlets' undersurface; but before this final fixture, equal lengths of three-quarter-sectioned, beaten tubing, their convex upper surface neatly ribbed, were threaded over the wire. This irrational mode of construction may explain certain features on three other armlets; for instance, there is a small recess at the base of each terminal perforation of the Achavrail specimen (Pl. VII, bottom and fig. 60, a) which may be a rebate for the insertion of a now missing wire with tubular channel ornament in Pitkelloney fashion; while on the undersurfaces of the Castle Newe pair, patches of rust suggest that each enamelled diaphragm may have been secured by means of a Pitkelloney-like 'T' strut, straddling the underside of each terminal to clip over its margin at two opposing points where small excisions were provided for that very purpose (Pl. VI, bottom and fig. 58, b).

As already mentioned, there is a tendency for massive armlets to occur in pairs, whose appearance is very similar, though never identical. The realization that the Pitkelloney pair, between them, weigh 7 lb. 7¼ oz. calls for a discussion of their actual use. It must surely be assumed that they were intended to adorn limbs – whether animate or inanimate is the question. There are several facts to support the theory of human adornment. Firstly, a small amount of wear is visible on the interior of armlets from Seafield and Stanhope. Then again, the dimensions are not totally improbable; the average maximum measurement, taken internally, falls between 10·2 cm. and 11·5 cm.; width across the back can be as narrow as 3·8 cm. or as broad as 9·2 cm., but most lie between 5 cm. and 7·5 cm. Even the largest could be envisaged (albeit with some difficulty) clasped around a muscular arm with, for some measure of comfort and additional bulk, a thick garment between metal and flesh. It has been suggested that they could just as easily adorn the calves, but two rather frivolous objections seem to demolish this theory; worn as a pair by anyone not suffering from excessive bowleggedness, they would result in an undignified gait and ludicrous clanking noise, and, should either slip from its position below the knee, the resultant damage to foot and ankle can well be imagined. The arguments against human use need not apply to such moderate versions as those from Aboyne and Glamis, Perth, Stichill and even from Belhelvie, Seafield and Stanhope; but they become vociferous for the remainder. None of the larger examples displays any sign of internal wear; the rubbed appearance of their protuberances could be explained by modern handling. Most persuasive of all is the total disregard for weight evidenced by the crude patching of Auchenbadie and the iron fitments of Pitkelloney. Is it a flight of fancy to imagine these armlets upon representations of local gods? Never common, they do exist, and Scotland has a representative in the Ballachulish figure.[15] It must be confessed that the precise age of this find is not known; yet the recent discovery at the source of the River Seine of 190 such wooden statues makes a first-century date perfectly feasible.[16]

It is of course quite reasonable to select the best of both arguments. One thing is certain – their very size plus the links of form and design existing between massive armlets on the one hand and ring torcs on the other reveal their importance to the community responsible for their existence, whether social, political or magico-religious. (I cannot seriously entertain – nor, I think, did he – Smith's comparison with armlets of 'the African Mitoos which apparently have no other object than to make a single combat as effective as possible'; it conjures up a fascinating scene!)

With one exception, from Newry, Co. Down, massive armlets are exclusively Scottish (see fig. 56). Their findspots range along the east coast from Peebleshire and Roxburgh in the south to Sutherland in the north with a strong emphasis on Perthshire and Angus (eight

Figure 56. Distribution map of massive armlets.

examples) and a secondary concentration in Aberdeenshire (five examples). This is precisely the territory later to be described as Pictish, but, as Wainwright warns,[17] there is no literary support for the projection of the title beyond the year A.D. 297 when it was first mentioned in a panegyric by Eumenius. We can merely ascribe the manufacture of massive armlets to proto-Pictish tribes under the group name of Caledonii – in the sense used by Dio Cassius, that is – and perhaps to that other amalgam, the Maeatae.[18]

Dating is a problem. The chronological range of souterrains is too long to be of much help, although Wainwright suspected a peak of popularity in the second century A.D. A denarius of Nerva (A.D. 96–8) was unearthed close by the findspot of the Castle Newe armlets, although not actually with them, and this is virtually our only clue. Hoards are by no means a decisive help. The Bunrannoch armlet was accompanied by some 'small articles all in a vessel of some kind which was broken to pieces at the time of finding'; the only survivor is a spiral snake bracelet of somewhat degenerate appearance.[19] Eight ornaments of this type are known, all save one being Scottish finds of predominantly eastern distribution with, excluding the example under discussion, three from Angus,[20] one from Moray,[21] an outlier from the island of Skye[22] and one without location.[23] Unfortunately, one half of the known number consists of stray or unlocated finds, so that attention must be focused on (1) a specimen from Hurley Hawkin which came from one of several rectangular huts erected against the internal wall of a broch, amongst whose small finds were sherds of late first-century Roman ware; (2) another from the souterrain of West Grange of Conan which contained sherds of Roman amphorae; and (3) the probable prototype for the series, from the Belgic burial of Snailwell, Cambridgeshire,[24] whose additional grave-goods indicate a date within a year or two of A.D. 43. We are thus equipped with a date for the type's commencement; while it is unnecessary (although perfectly feasible) to extend its popularity beyond the second century A.D.

The Stanhope hoard included a Roman patera about whose date neither Bosanquet[25] nor Curle[26] would commit himself, beyond a general tendency to favour the second century; Nierhaus[27] favours the middle of this century or even the early years of the succeeding one. The remainder of the hoard comprises two ovoid horse-trappings of indefinite purpose; their degenerate appearance would seem to make them later than comparable pieces from the Stanwick hoard, itself attributed to the third quarter of the first century A.D.;[28] and from Corbridge, Northumberland, where a single example occurred in a Flavio-Trajanic context.[29]

The Stichill armlet or armlets may have been associated with a well-known bronze collar.[30] Five others have been found, predominantly in the south and southwest.[31] The specimen from Portland Island is said to have lain in a stone coffin with a pear-shaped, bead-rim pot of dark, smooth-faced ware, a second-century Samian ware platter and a riveted bronze knife of Late Bronze Age type; apart from this curious association, there are no chronological clues; we are therefore forced to rely on stylistic analysis. The Stichill collar is post-Conquest, for its cast strip decoration must surely emulate the spacer plates of Roman multistrand necklaces, such as that included in the Æsica hoard.[32] Its applied frontal panels are in die-stamped repoussé and therefore conform to Fox's 'casket ornament' series, whose greatest popularity seems to fall in the mid-late first century A.D.; and the motif is even more helpful. A sinuous variant of Leeds' 'swash N,' it is to be encountered on the enamelled tops of a series of seal boxes from Chesters, Northumberland, Lincoln and the unspecified 'north';[33]

also from Humby, Lincolnshire, and Castle Hill, Nottinghamshire;[34] while most of their associations are unrecorded, the last example returns a firmly Flavian date.

Upon this flimsy chronological support, we may suspect that the massive armlet series has its roots in the latter part of the first century A.D. and that the succeeding hundred years likely saw its floruit. Thomas has recognized armlet portrayals on Pictish stones of his Class 1;[35] but it is not necessary to stretch our small group of objects to span four centuries. In such symbols, a conscious antiquarianism is only to be expected, in view of the recent interpretation put upon them.[36]

With the paucity of our legitimate dating evidence in mind, deductions based on stylistic considerations cannot but better the scene. I shall attempt to deal first with points of difference and similarity within the group, before considering it in the wider scope of British Iron Age metalwork. In both cases, I shall have to make several unashamed presumptions about the decorative and formal development, which, in less desperate situations, would be justly frowned upon.

Massive armlets fall into two categories according to their form. To these, Smith gave the titles 'oval' and 'folded'; they will be retained here at the risk of referring occasionally to 'Smith's ovals' – a phrase more reminiscent of dog biscuits. The oval type of armlet is symmetrical in both outline and decorative detail; there are twelve examples. Three of the seven folded armlets are executed as a series of linked and contiguous strands (as already mentioned), while the remainder retain a reminiscence of this origin in the asymmetry of their shape and decoration (the arrangement is impossible to define briefly; a glance at the drawings will illuminate the situation).

The two armlet shapes are closely related. Terminal outline is virtually identical, while the decorative layout scarcely varies. When viewed as a flattened diagram, the form assumed by folded armlets seems illogical, and there is considerable puzzlement about the treatment of the 'loose' ends; therefore, one must commence by assuming (1) that oval and folded armlets overlap in their dating and that (2) should one form be a little earlier in its beginnings than the other, this forerunner is most likely to be oval.

The argument may seem obvious, but it serves to draw attention to a worrying feature of certain oval examples – namely an irregular, yet smooth indentation of the armlet edge at one side only, behind one or both terminals. This is particularly noticeable in the three from Aboyne (fig. 57, a and b) and the remaining specimen from Stichill (fig. 59, c); faint traces are visible also on Belhelvie (fig. 58, a) and Stanhope (fig. 58, c). It could be postulated that this feature is a recollection of 'folded' arrangement, incorporated in skeuomorphic fashion in the oval form, which would therefore be later; but there are alternative and better explanations. For one thing, these scallops do not occur at two diametrically opposed points on the hoop edge, as one might reasonably expect. In fact, only the Aboyne pair displays two such features on the one armlet, and they are both at the same side. Symmetry of outline could have been damaged by excessive paring of the model; or, if cast flat, this is precisely the area in which one would expect weaknesses to appear during annealing, and over-enthusiastic removal of a cracked margin could result in just such an indentation. It is therefore impossible to place any weight of argument on this problematic feature. One further explanation is wear; this would necessitate a revision of the long-accepted armlet interpretation and is no solution.

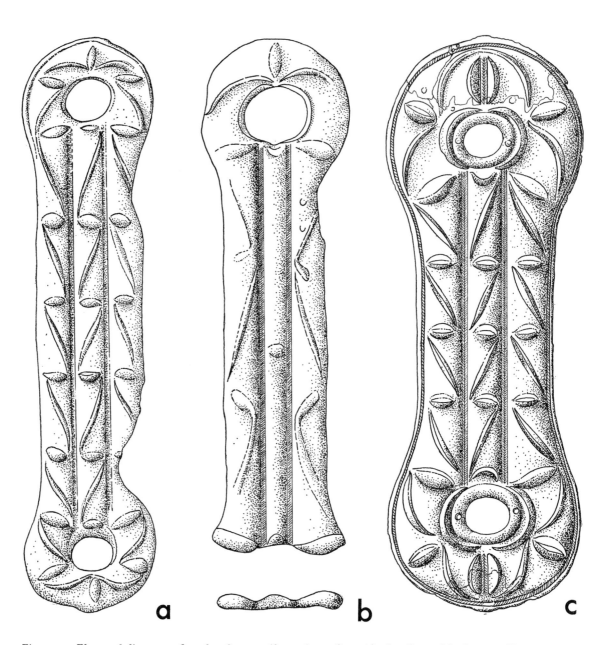

Figure 57. Flattened diagrams of armlets from a. Aboyne (one of a pair); b. Aboyne (single example); c. Auchenbadie.

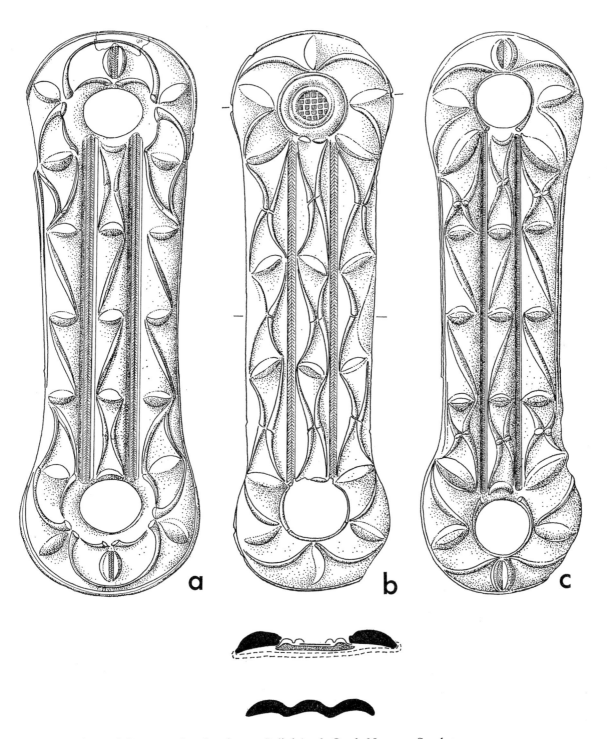

Figure 58. Flattened diagrams of armlets from a. Belhelvie; b. Castle Newe; c. Stanhope.

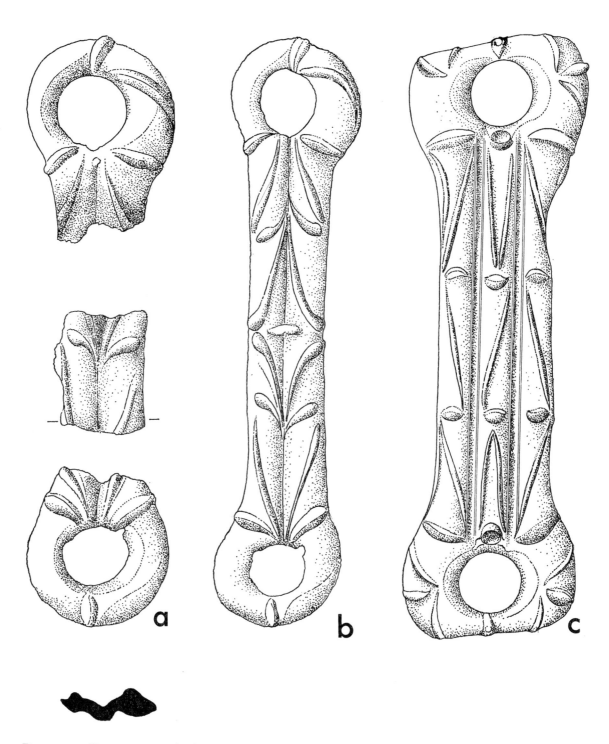

Figure 59. a. Fragmentary armlet from (?) Perth vicinity ; b. conjectural flattened diagram of a ; c. Stichill

The next set of assumptions to be proffered and tested is again concerned with the most superficial features of armlet decoration. Given that (1) meticulous craftsmanship, reasonably subtle and low relief and the actual presence of or evidence for enamel insets are likely to be early characteristics; while (2) slovenly craftsmanship and/or excessively three-dimensional treatment, misunderstood motifs and absence of colour may indicate later work; then in what order do the armlets at our disposal arrange themselves? Amongst the oval series, only the Castle Newe pair (fig. 58, b) fits category (1), but Belhelvie and Stanhope lack only evidence for the enamel diaphragms. The Stichill armlet lacks subtlety of surface treatment, but otherwise leans towards the specimens already mentioned. On the other hand, armlets from Auchen-badie (fig. 57, c) Aboyne and 'Perth vicinity' (fig. 57, a and b) conform with the characteristics classed as (2), although the first-mentioned was originally provided with enamelling. The late relegation of the last two is affirmed by omission of adornment on the central panel of the single Aboyne example and by omission of the actual panel itself in the case of the 'Perth' one. Turning to the folded series, the representative from Glamis plus the Pitkelloney pair are clearly the best candidates for our early group, more especially when it is realized that they alone retain actual structural proof of the separation of their various hoop strands. Newry occupies a middle position, with careful execution and enamelling to qualify for an early date, and high relief to lead on to the later series of Achavrail (fig. 60, a), Bunrannoch (fig. 60, b) and Seafield (fig. 61, c) – none of which, however, looks as late as the oval specimen from 'Perth'.

If the scene be widened a little to permit comparison with the clearly related carnyx mouth from Deskford, Banff,[37] and spiral snake bracelet from the Culbin Sands (fig. 62), then the position becomes less perilous. Compare the framework surrounding the eye sockets of both boar and snake interpretations.[38] Each is a linked arrangement of 'slender trumpet' motifs (fig. 63, e), and, taken out of context, both can be paralleled in botanical guise by detail on a fragment of 'casket ornament' found in Pit LVIII at the Roman fort of Newstead (fig. 63, n) – there accompanied by 'early' pottery and Flavian coins.[39]

By such tortuous means, the proposed sequence of armlet construction becomes less ephemeral; thus, 'slender trumpets' are employed on the terminals of the sole surviving Belhelvie armlet, where they are even grouped and juxtaposed in a similar manner. Less clearly, slender trumpet formations encircle the apertures of Castle Newe and Stanhope; but none appears on oval armlets which we have suspected of a later date; nor upon any folded armlet, which is a further clue to their slightly later inception. A second important feature of the Belhelvie, Castle Newe and Stanhope armlets is the 'saltire' (fig. 63, b), formed by the juxtaposition of two centrally jointed or 'broken-backed' curves (in Leeds' definition). Symmetrized, this motif defines the bumps on the spine of the Culbin Sands snake. Its 'early' date is supported by an absence on the Auchenbadie, Aboyne and 'Perth' armlets, and yet it does occur on the 'early' folded versions from Glamis, Pitkelloney and Newry, thus support-ing their qualifications for a position towards the beginning of the stylistic sequence. The use of 'keeled diagonals' (fig. 63, f) on the back panel may be merely a simplification of saltire layout; already used in conjunction with saltires on the earliest representatives of both oval and folded groups, its rigid application as the sole motif is characteristic of 'later' specimens such as Stichill and Auchenbadie of the former series and Achavrail and Bunrannoch of the latter. Its curious transformation into golfclub-like trails (fig. 63, g) on the Aboyne single example and on 'Perth' and Seafield must surely be a degenerate and late development.

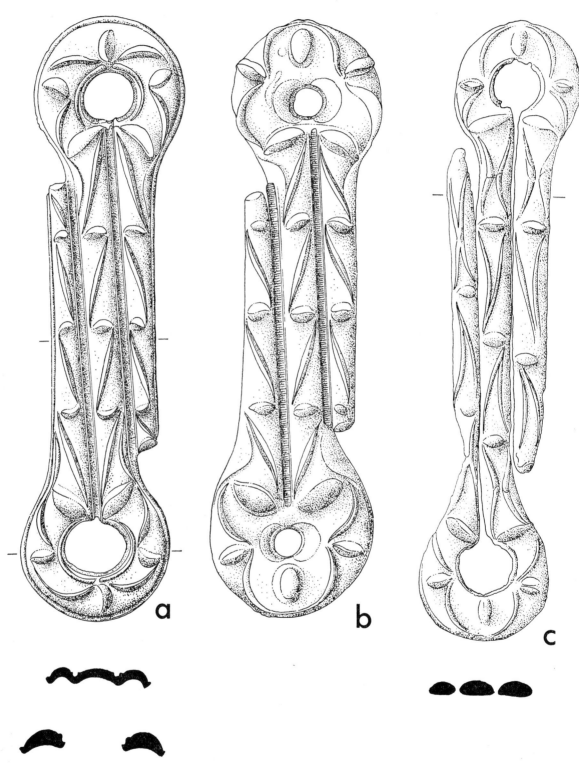

Figure 60. Flattened diagrams of armlets from a. Achavrail; b. Bunrannoch; c. Glamis.

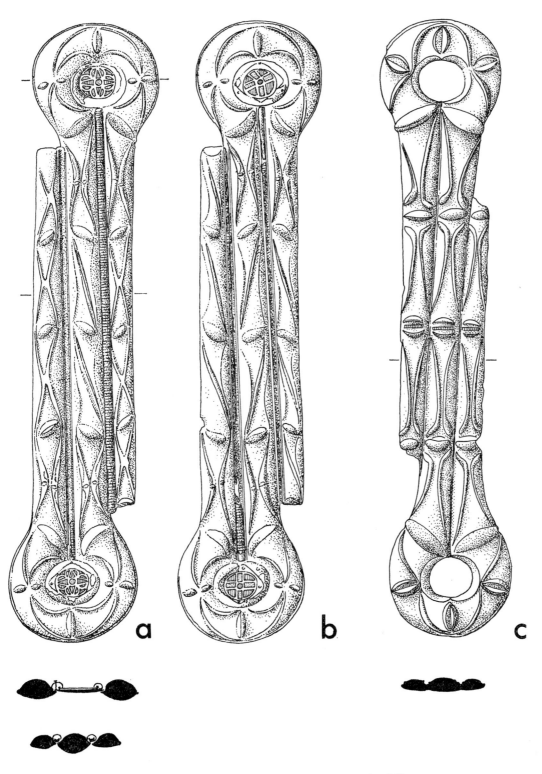

Figure 61. Flattened diagrams of armlets from a and b. Pitkelloney; c. Seafield.

The discussion has been largely conjectural. There may be false assumptions, such as the interpretation of poor craftsmanship as the deterioration of design due to the passage of time. Certainly, there are anomalies; the slender trumpets of Belhelvie would seem to declare its prime of place in the sequence, and yet, doubt is shed upon this by its saltire and keeled diagonal features, so inferior to the adornment of the Castle Newe armlets. A salutary warning is sounded by one of the Pitkelloney pair, on which saltires of Belhelvie- or Stanhope-like appearance occur side by side with versions of a stick-like malformation that cries out for relegation to the last stages of the series. Yet our sequence must contain some element of truth if only because, in its present state, it cannot be reversed so that the last becomes chronologically first. If anything, its merit lies in the identification of 'early' motifs, for analogies to which the more southerly metalwork may now be sifted.

As an origin for the form assumed by massive armlets is highly conjectural, it is most fairly regarded as one facet of stylistic analysis. It was Professor Piggott who first drew attention to the formal links between oval armlets and ring terminal torcs, such as the famous electrum specimen from Hoard E at Snettisham.[40] Members of both groups share penannular shape and expanded and rounded terminals with central perforations. The main difference lies in the hoop construction, but, even here, the longitudinal channelling and keeled diagonals of oval armlets could be envisaged as a cast reflection of the multistrand twists of such torcs. That these were available for emulation in Scotland is proved by the Shaw Hill torc terminal;[41] and the link becomes less strange when viewed against the mounting evidence for metalwork contacts between Scotland and south England.[42]

An additional ingredient is required to account for the pseudo-spiral construction of folded armlets, and this is proffered by spiral snake armlets, perhaps yet another contribution from the south, as already mentioned. It is to be noted that the early folded armlets come from precisely that area which has been most productive of spiral snake bracelets. Also, the Bunrannoch hoard contained both a massive armlet of folded type and a spiral snake armlet; unfortunately, both look 'late' in their respective sequences.

Turning to decorative layout and to the mode of its expression, one's immediate reaction is to class massive armlets as an alien development, unaccountable within the framework of British Early Iron Age art as it is known at present; and yet this is not so. The only novelty is that of scale, and one is led to marvel rather at the Celtic genius for limitless variation on a very few decorative themes. Take, for instance, the terminals of the Stanhope armlet. Given a sub-oval area with a central focus, the designer has produced a decorative solution which differs little from that on the Torrs pony cap,[43] the Battersea shield's end roundels[44] or the crescentic terret from Richborough, Kent,[45] although, in each case, the mode of expression is totally different. The basic inspiration is Fox's lyre palmette unit; it is doubtful whether the manufacturers of massive armlets possessed even the vaguest notion of that source.

We may pass directly to a search for comparable motifs in more southerly metalwork. Closest parallels for the 'swag and drop' unit (fig. 63, a) just mentioned can be found on 'casket ornament,' in particular its most northerly representatives such as the Balmaclellan mirror[46] and even the Æsica brooch (fig. 63, k), whose cast execution is not compatible with the casket ornament' series, but whose decorative quirks nevertheless render it a convincing member.[47] Even closer is cast detail on the Group IV sword pommels from Brough-under-Stainmore, Westmorland[48] and Worton, Lancashire (fig. 63, p).[49]

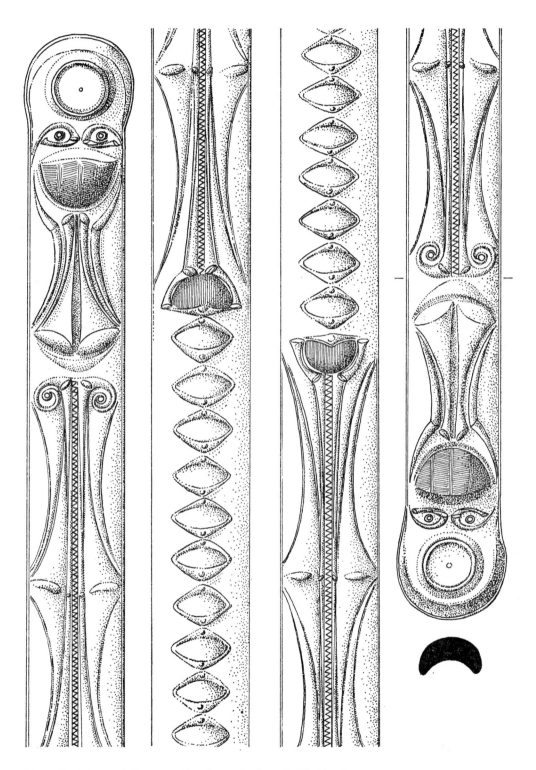

Figure 62. Flattened diagrams of snake armlet from Culbin Sands.

The 'saltire,' in that symmetrical variant displayed on the central panel of the Belhelvie armlet, occurs in repoussé upon the strap loops of certain scabbards, again belonging to Piggott's Group IV.[50] Its sinuous variant, as portrayed *par excellence* by the Castle Newe pair, is inextricably related to the 'swash N' motif. A shorthand version may be found on a terret of Leeds' Type 6 from Great Chesters or Benwell, Northumberland[51] and on a late first/second-century mount from Traprain, East Lothian;[52] and the applied panel at the mouth of the Mortonhall scabbard is nothing but a sinuous saltire, disguised by trumpet coil tips (fig. 63, q). The debased variant of Pitkelloney is not present in more southerly repertoire; only the spinal detail of the Pitalpin snake armlet is strictly relevant.

'Broken-back S coils' are present on the Castle Newe, Belhelvie, Glamis and Pitkelloney armlets. Being the voids created by linked saltires of the sinuous type (fig. 63, c), they are not immediately recognizable; yet, they are motifs in their own right, and are well known from north English and Lowland Scottish products; for instance, the Mortonhall scabbard displays a single unit, with trumpet coil additions (fig. 63, q), while the beaded torc from Lochar Moss, Dumfries bears a linked chain of similar motifs.[53] On a less exalted scale, one of the bowls from the second-century hoard of Lamberton Moor, Berwickshire was originally repaired by means of a patch of broken-back S coil outline, now discernible only as an area of discoloration.[54] Finally, what are dragonesque brooches if they are not zoomorphosed broken-back scrolls (fig. 63, 1 and m)?[55]

From actual motifs and their southern parallels, we may now turn to the modes of their expression. On the 'earlier' armlets, differential modelling of each ovoid bump – one side crisply defined, the other gradually emerging from the metal surface (fig. 63, d) – reveals that we are dealing with a massive trumpet moulding, whose roundel, in the Llyn Cerrig definition,[56] has vanished, whose trumpet is the adjacent panel of background and whose dome alone is immediately recognizable. It is small wonder that this subtlety rapidly disappeared, so that by the Auchenbadie and Seafield stage, little trace of trumpet coil inspiration remains. The massive quality of treatment is best foreshadowed by the Group III scabbard chape from Hounslow, Berwickshire[57] and is shared significantly by two 'belt plates' or 'strap junctions' from Drumashie, Inverness-shire[58] and York Railway Station[59] (fig. 63, o) respectively. A third, commonly thought to be represented by a cast in the collection of the Society of Antiquaries of London, may never have existed, as its measurements tally so exactly with those of the York specimen that it may be merely a restoration of this fragmentary find.[60] I suspect that the English example is closer to its place of manufacture than the Scottish, for, accompanying this last, and unique to the north, was a square-headed dressfastener, known to have been popular in the military zone of Britain during Hadrianic and Antonine times.[61]

Much of the massive armlet decoration is executed in terms of the 'slender trumpet.' It will be sufficient to indicate this motif's appearance in embryonic form on, say, the Bugthorpe scabbard chape[62] or the gold bracelet from Hoard E at Snettisham.[63] It is more important to stress its employment in 'casket ornament' – for example, on strip from Rodborough, Gloucestershire,[64] on a shaped panel from Gayton Thorpe, Norfolk[65] and, of course, on the fragment from Newstead. Cast versions are available also – on a fragmentary horse trapping from the Stanwick hoard,[66] on the Æsica brooch and its relative from Tre'r Ceiri, Caernarvonshire;[67] most of all, upon the dragonesque brooch from Lakenheath, Suffolk[68] (fig. 63, m).

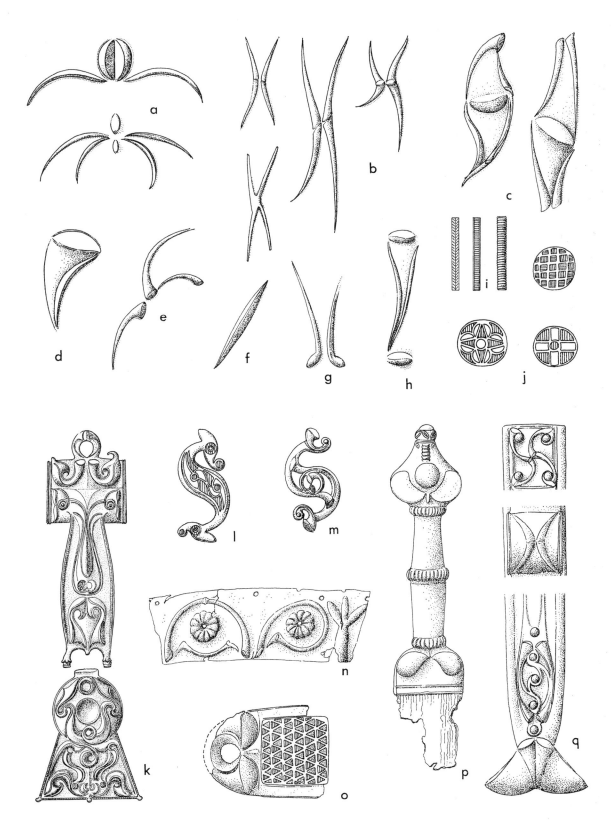

Figure 63. 'Grammar' of motifs relevant to massive armlets.

Indeed, the central roundel of this last displays an unusual juxtaposition of slender trumpet domes, which can be paralleled precisely beneath each enamelled roundel of the Castle Newe armlets.

A characteristic of massive armlet decoration is the keeled effect of many of its motifs, such as the diagonal ribbons of the back or the oval frames surrounding the terminal apertures. This crested treatment is shared once more by the Lakenheath and Æsica brooches; also by the Trawsfynnyd tankard holdfast.[69] The Stanwick horse mask is even closer;[70] admittedly, the crested effect is less emphatic; but bisect the muzzle about a longitudinal axis and what does one find? – an arrangement of linked ribbons, converging on a split vesica which is precisely comparable with a unit of decoration upon the Glamis folded armlet (fig. 63, h).

Channel detail is present on many, though not all, of the massive armlets (fig. 63, i). The convex ribbing of Pitkelloney is unique, approached only by cast detail on the Worton sword pommel. Ladder incision, as displayed by Bunrannoch and Newry, is of course nothing but milling on a large scale, for which analogies are easily available – on terrets from Muircleugh, Berwickshire[71] and Newstead;[72] on the scabbard from Sadberge; and on beaded torcs from Carlisle[73] and Stanwix,[74] Cumberland. Feathering on the Castle Newe and Auchenbadie specimens is akin to detail on the Brough pommel and Group IV scabbard from Embleton, Cumberland.[75]

The enamelled diaphragms of Castle Newe and Pitkelloney bring our stylistic summary to a close (fig. 63, j). Whatever the chronological significance of a combination of red and yellow enamel in the south,[76] it can have little meaning in the north; however, the four-petalled arrangement of Pitkelloney is closely comparable with that on terrets of Leeds' Group 6 from the Icenian hoard of Saham Toney, Norfolk.[77] The chequer pattern of Castle Newe is nothing but an expansion of the tabbard layout on similar terrets from Fremington Hagg, North Riding of Yorkshire[78] and Traprain;[79] but studs on the Group IV sword hilt from Thorpe, East Riding of Yorkshire[80] and, of course, the Drumashie dressfastener are even closer.

By now, the alien appearance of massive armlets should have dwindled. Their greatest debt is to Brigantia, and may even include a certain largeness of treatment. Lowland Scotland would seem to be less important; stylistically relevant material from its confines, such as the Mortonhall scabbard and Lochar Moss torc, may well be Brigantian imports; while there is no trace in massive armlet decoration of the 'petal-boss' unit, so well represented at Newstead and Traprain. The debt to Icenian culture is vague, frequently secondhand but nonetheless real. And to complete the complex scene, there are even tenuous links with Ireland. Surprisingly, the bonework from Lough Crew, Co. Meath[81] provides engraved analogies not only for the slender trumpet,[82] but also for the sinuous saltire,[83] the paired and opposed trumpet domes of Castle Newe,[84] the broken-back S unit[85] and even for the more elaborate of the diaphragms of the Pitkelloney armlets.[86] The relationship between the Lough Crew slips and massive armlets must be a cousinly rather than a parental one, the product of a common inspiration, perhaps as far back as the Snettisham/Broighter stage, upon which an ever-increasing debt to Brigantia was superimposed in the first century A.D. Irish evidence for this last is provided not only by actual imports, such as the Lambay Island beaded torc, 'casket ornament' and scabbard mounts,[87] Ballymoney mirror handle[88] and Antrim terret;[89] but also by a common decorative atmosphere. This should explain the similarity between coils on the Irish dished plates[90] and the Stanwick human masks,[91] between surface modelling on the Bann disc[92] and the rear portion of the Stichill collar; between the zoomorphic detail on the Bann disc and Petrie Crown[93] and the British range of dragonesque brooches.

To summarize, stylistic comparisons to the massive armlet decoration emphasize the period A.D. 50–150. The Deskford carnyx fragment and Culbin Sands bracelet, obvious precursors, reduce this possible time span at its lower end; the upper is purely arbitrary. We emerge with no new information as to the precise place of manufacture and no absolutely conclusive dating; but, it is hoped, with a revised mental picture of the proto-Picts. Buchan's uncouth dwellers on the Scarts o' the Muneraw are melting into the mists of romanticism. Instead, we can dimly detect a series of interrelated tribes, fully aware of artistic and, no doubt, political developments in the south; perhaps even harbouring fugitive craftsmen from that area and benefiting from their miraculous skills. Granted, foreign influences may have arrived in northeast Scotland as an aftermath of the Agricolan penetration; however, in view of the stylistic analysis above, it is safe to assume some measure of infiltration before this date, perhaps as a direct result of the revolts of Boudicca and Venutius.

Catalogue of massive armlets

ABOYNE, PERTHSHIRE   Present paper: fig. 57, a
Internal diameters: 10·2–7·8 cm. and 10·8–8·3 cm. respectively
Number: one pair   Location: Inveraray Castle
Major reference: *P.S.A.S.* XV (1880–1) 335–6, 358, fig. 29

ABOYNE, PERTHSHIRE   Present paper: fig. 57, b
Maximum width: 7·6 cm. (approximate)
Number: one   Location: Inveraray Castle
Major reference: *ibid.* 335–6, 355–61, 360, fig. 30

ACHAVRAIL, ROGART, SUTHERLAND   Present paper: Pl. VII, bottom and fig. 60, a
Internal diameter: 10 cm.   Width at back: 6 cm.
Number: one   Location: Dunrobin Castle
Major reference: *P.S.A.S.* XXXVIII (1903–4) 266, 267, fig. 6

AUCHENBADIE (Mains of), ALVAH, BANFF   Present paper: Pl. VI, top and fig. 57, c
Internal diameter: 11·5–9·2 cm.   Maximum width: 13·5 cm.
Number: one   Location: Nat. Mus. Edin. FA 15
Major reference: *P.S.A.S.* XV (1880–1) 327–9, figs. 8–9

BELHELVIE (or DRUMSIDE), ABERDEENSHIRE   Present paper: fig. 58, a
Internal diameter: 10·7–8·4 cm.   Maximum width: 11·4 cm.
Number: one pair, one lost   Location: Nat. Mus. Edin. FA 16
Major reference: *ibid.* 333–5, figs. 14–15

BUNRANNOCH, SCHIEHALLION, PERTHSHIRE   Present paper: fig. 60, b
Internal diameter: 10·1–8·9 cm.   Maximum width: 7·6 cm.
Number: one   Location: Nat. Mus. Edin. FA 18
Major reference: *ibid.* 337–40, figs. 17–18

CASTLE NEWE, STRATHDON, ABERDEENSHIRE
Maximum internal diameter: 11·5 cm.
Number: one pair
Major reference: *ibid.* 330–1, fig. 10

Present paper: Pl. VI, bottom and fig. 58, b
Maximum width: 12·5 cm.
Location: Brit. Mus. 1946.4–2.2

GLAMIS (vicinity of), ANGUS
Maximum diameter: 10·8 cm.
Number: one

Major reference: *P.S.A.S.* XVII (1882–3) 90–2

Present paper: Pl. VII, top and fig. 60, c
Maximum width: 6·4 cm. (approximate)
Location: mislaid; originally in collection of the
Earl of Strathmore. Cast in Nat. Mus. Edin. FA 74

NEWRY, County DOWN
Internal diameter: 11·8–9·2 cm.
Number: one
Major reference: *P.S.A.S.* XV (1880–1) 362–3, fig. 31

Present paper: Pl. VIII
Maximum width: 9 cm.
Location: Nat. Mus. Ireland

PERTH? (vicinity of), PERTHSHIRE
Diameter: 10·2 cm. (approximate)
Number: one
Major reference: *P.S.A.S.* XXXVI (1901–2) 15

Present paper: fig. 59, a and b
Maximum width: 6 cm.
Location: Perth Mus. 139

PITKELLONEY, MUTHILL, PERTHSHIRE
Maximum internal diameters: 10·9 and 11·4 cm.
respectively
Number: one pair
Major reference: Smith, *Guide to Early Iron Age Antiquities Brit. Mus.* 2nd ed. (1925) 155–6, fig. 186

Present paper: Pl. X and fig. 61, a and b
Maximum width: 8·3 cm.

Location: Brit. Mus. 38.7–14.3

SEAFIELD TOWER, KINGHORN, FIFE
Maximum diameter: 13·2–11·9 cm.
Number: one
Major reference: *P.S.A.S.* XV (1880–1) 342–4, 343, fig. 21

Present paper: fig. 61, c
Maximum width: 6·8 cm.
Location: Nat. Mus. Edin. FA 19

STANHOPE, STOBO, PEEBLESHIRE
Maximum internal diameter: 11·4 cm.
Number: one
Major reference: *ibid.* 317–19

Present paper: fig. 58, c
Maximum width: 10·4 cm.
Location: Nat. Mus. Edin. FA 25

STICHILL or STICHEL, ROXBURGHSHIRE
Maximum diameter: 11·4 cm.
Number: ? one pair, one lost
Major reference: *ibid.* 336, fig. 16 (wrongly attributed)

Present paper: fig. 59, c
Maximum width: 8·2 cm.
Location: Nat. Mus. Edin. FA 17

TILLYCHETLY, ALFORD, ABERDEENSHIRE
Number: one pair
Major reference: *P.S.A.S.* IV (1860–2) 385

Present paper: not illustrated
Location: lost

Notes

1. 316–63
2. 90–2
3. (1863) 139–40
4. *Scotland in Pagan Times: the Iron Age* 140–56

5. *P.S.A.S.* XXXVIII (1903–4) 460–6
6. *Arch.* LV (1896) 179–94
7. *Celtic Art in the British Isles down to A.D. 700* 126–36
8. *Ant. J.* XXXIX (1959) 19–32
9. In Rivet ed., *The Iron Age in North Britain* (1966) 31–2
10. Tylecote, *Metallurgy in Archaeology* (1962) 51
11. *P.S.A.S.* XV (1880–1) 348–9 and fig. 25
12. *P.P.S.* XVI (1950) 7, fig. 2, 4
13. *ibid.* 18, fig. 9, 3A, B
14. *P.S.A.S.* XV (1880–1) 345, fig. 22
15. *ibid.* 158–78
16. *Rev. Arch. de l'est et du Centre-est.* XIV, fasc. 1–3 (1964) 7–53
17. Wainwright ed., *The Problem of the Picts* (1956) 2–3
18. *ibid.* 52–3
19. *P.S.A.S.* XXXVIII (1903–4) 460–1 and fig. 1
20. Hurley Hawkin; *Disc. & Excn.: Scotland 1961* (1962) 5. Pitalpin; *P.S.A.S.* XV (1880–1) 348–9 and fig. 25.
    West Grange of Conan; *ibid.* 350, fig. 27
21. Culbin Sands; *ibid.* 345, fig. 22
22. Duntulm; *Ill. Lond. News* (April 1953) 580
23. *P.S.A.S.* XV (1880–1) 349, fig. 27
24. *C.A.S.* XLVII (1953) 25–37
25. *P.S.A.S.* LXII (1927–8) 246–54
26. *P.S.A.S.* LXVI (1931–2) 301
27. Stevenson in Rivet ed., *The Iron Age in North Britain* (1966) 43, n. 93
28. *P.P.S.* XXVIII (1962) 40, fig. 5, Nos. 11–13 and 41, fig. 6, No. 15
29. Unpublished: Corbridge Mus.
30. *Arch.* XCVI (1955) Pl. LXXXV, b
31. Llandyssul, Card.; Grimes, *Prehistory of Wales* (1951) Pl. XVIII. Portland Island, Dorset; Smith, *Guide to
    Early Iron Age Antiquities Brit. Mus.* (1925) 2nd ed. 150. Trenoweth, Cornwall; *Arch.* XVI (1805) 137–8
    and Pl. X. Weymouth, Dorset; Smith, *op. cit.* 151. Wraxall, Som.; Appendix to *Arch.* LIV (1892) 495–6
    and Pl. XLVIII
32. *P.S.A. Newcastle* VI (1893–4) 241
33. *Préhistoire II* (1933) 144, fig. 46, Nos. 1, 6 and 4
34. Oswald, *Pamphlet of the City of Nottingham Art G. & Mus.: Nottingham Castle* (1927) 28, fig. 2 and
    Pl. VI, 7
35. *Arch. J.* CXX (1964) 57, No. 32
36. *ibid.* 31–97
37. *Ant. J.* XXXIX (1959) 19–32
38. Or human? See Stevenson in Rivet ed., *The Iron Age in North Britain* (1966) 32
39. Curle, *A Roman Frontier Post and its People* (1911) 303 and Pl. LXXV, 5
40. *P.P.S.* XX (1954) 27–86
41. *P.S.A.S.* XCI (1957–8) 112–16 and Pl. XI, 4
42. *P.S.A.S.* LXXXVII (1952–3) 1–50
43. *Arch.* XCVI (1955) 197–235
44. Fox, *Pattern and Purpose: a Survey of Early Celtic Art in Britain* (1958) Pl. 17
45. Bushe-Fox, *4th Report on the Excns. on the Site of the Roman Fort at Richborough* (1949) Pl. 1, 2
46. *Arch. Camb.* C (1949) 28–9, fig. 4 and Pl. 11
47. *Arch.* LV (1896) 179–94 and 187, fig. 9
48. *Cumb. & Westm. Trans.* ns. XXXVII (1937) 67–71
49. *V.C.H. Lancs.* 1, pt. 4 (1920) 247, fig. 30
50. Cotterdale, N.R. Yorks.; *P.P.S.* XVI (1950) 18, fig. 9, 2A–D. Mortonhall, Midlothian; *ibid.* 18, fig. 9,
    3A and B. Sadberge, Durham; *ibid.* 19, fig. 10, 1A and B
51. Unpublished: University Mus., Newcastle
52. *P.S.A.S.* LXXXIX (1955–6) 192, No. 327
53. *Arch.* XXXIV (1852) 83–7

54. *P.S.A.S.* XXXIX (1904–5) 371–2
55. *Ant. J.* XXXI (1951) 32–44
56. Fox, *A Find of the Early Iron Age from Llyn Cerrig Bach, Anglesey* (1946) 48–51
57. *P.P.S.* XVI (1950) 13, fig. 7, 3
58. *P.S.A.S.* LVIII (1923–4) 11–13
59. Fox (1958) *op. cit.* Pl. 52, c
60. Allen, *Celtic Art in Pagan and Christian Times* (1904) Pl. opp. 17
61. Gillam in Richmond ed., *Roman and Native in North Britain* (1958) 79–90
62. *P.P.S.* XVI (1950) Pl. III
63. Fox, *op. cit.* (1958) 45, fig. 32
64. Smith (1925) *op. cit.* 146, fig. 169
65. Unpublished: King's Lynn Mus.
66. *P.P.S.* XXVIII (1962) 48, fig. 11, No. 82
67. Fox (1958) *op. cit.* Pl. 41, d
68. *ibid.* Pl. 41, b
69. *ibid.* Pl. 64
70. *P.P.S.* XXVIII (1962) Pl. V
71. *P.S.A.S.* LV (1920–1) 17–19
72. Curle, *A Roman Frontier Post and its People* (1911) Pl. LXXV, 2
73. *P.S.A.* 2nd ser. VIII (1879–81) 534–5
74. *Arch. Ael.* 4th ser. XIX (1941) 23–5
75. *P.P.S.* XVI (1950) 19, fig. 10, 2A–C
76. *Préhistoire* II (1933) 118
77. *V.C.H. Norfolk* I, opp. 273
78. Unpublished: York Mus.
79. *P.S.A.S.* LXXXIX (1955–6) 195, No. 355 and Pl. XIV
80. *P.P.S.* XVI (1950) 19, fig. 10, 3
81. *J.R.S.A.I.* LV (1925) 15–29
82. *ibid.* 17, fig. 3; 18, figs. 5 and 7; 20, fig. 12 etc.; *also J.R.S.A.I.* XXVI (1896) 257–8
83. *J.R.S.A.I.* LV (1925) 19, fig. 10
84. *ibid.* 19, fig. 9; 25, fig. 54
85. *ibid.* 24, fig. 20
86. *ibid.* 25, fig. 43
87. *P.R.I.A.* XXXVIII (1928–9) 240–6
88. *U.J.A.* XVI (1954) 92–6
89. *U.J.A.* XIII (1950) 57, fig. 1, 3
90. *e.g.*, Piggott and Daniel, *A Picture Book of Ancient British Art* (1951) No. 48
91. *P.P.S.* XXVIII (1962) Pl. V
92. *U.J.A.* III (1940) 27–30
93. *Arch.* XLVII (1883) 472–8

Shafts, pits, wells –
sanctuaries of the Belgic Britons?

Anne Ross

The evidence for Iron Age religious cults and their antecedents in Europe generally is not plentiful and, owing to paucity of reliable documentation, extremely difficult to interpret. Progress has been made during this century, however, in the spheres of both linguistic research and field investigation, and it is becoming increasingly evident that much material is extant and awaits recognition for what it is, and for correct assessment.

One of the drawbacks in the wider appreciation of the religious practices of the pagan Celts has been the apparent lack of temples, that is, of structures given over entirely to cult purposes. This scarcity of temples built in Mediterranean fashion, and the fact that they only finally appear under the aegis of the Roman Empire, has led to the conclusion that the Celts worshipped their deities in natural contexts alone, on hilltops, in sacred groves of trees, beside ancestral burial mounds, or adjacent to some sacred spring. To a certain extent this is correct, and worship undoubtedly did regularly take place in such situations, with a crude stone pillar or slab, perhaps, serving as the focal point for ritual in which a holy tree and a venerated spring frequently played a part. The evidence, however, suggests that actual structures were also involved. The *bruidne*, the hostelries of the early Irish tales,[1] in which much of a transparently mythological nature allegedly took place, may well correspond to the type of small building, rectangular or circular, found in Britain and Europe, in some of which objects of a clear votive significance have been found. Many such places, no doubt, have yet to be recognized as sanctuaries; and a considerable rethinking of many excavated sites as well as a careful eye to future field investigation are essential if any progress in the sphere of Iron Age religious practices is to be made.

The purpose of this paper is to consider a class of structure the ritual nature of which has only begun to be appreciated and accepted in this country, and in connection with which much reassessing and research remain to be done. These are the shafts, pits and wells, which are as varied and complex as they are numerous, and in some of which the evidence of religious associations is clear and dramatic while in others it can only be inferred. In Britain, these manifest themselves even as early as the end of the third millennium B.C.; and they continued to be made and used, later perhaps for purely mundane purposes, into the medieval period. It would appear to be a straightforward task to treat these structures as three separate manifestations of the same religious beliefs and habits; but they are in fact much too closely interconnected for such a segregation into types to be valid. A shaft of over 120 feet in depth, for example, may also be a well; and many pits seem to have begun their existence as wells which had subsequently dried up, or where digging had been abandoned before water-level was reached. Some of the most spectacular ritual shafts in Britain are extremely deep and narrow, and do not contain a well; but, like the Swanwick shaft,[2] they may have a depth of only some 24 feet, or even less. A comparatively shallow pit may yield contents of an identical kind and arrangement to those of a deep shaft, and so demonstrate their basic affinity and function. For the purposes of Celtic religion, therefore, the three groups of structures can be shown to have a single significance; but this fact by no means answers all the questions or overcomes the various problems encountered in studying them.

The most dramatic structures of all are the narrow circular shafts, often attaining a very considerable depth, the structure and the contents of which suggest beliefs of a powerful nature about which we can now do little more than speculate. Allied to these are the ritual pits in which objects have been arranged in such a manner as to suggest deliberate order and purpose, or in which hoards of material occur which cannot be easily explained in practical terms. If we accept that the three types of structure have a more or less identical ritual connotation, then we must seek for reasons which may have governed the choice of structure in any given region. This may have depended upon such a factor as the geology of the locality, as well as upon tribal preference. No one would be likely to attempt to sink a deep shaft through Lewisian gneiss, for example; and if no suitable spring were to occur at a place in some way distinguished for its religious associations, then a sacred pit would no doubt serve equally well. Again, in the chalk regions where all three structures occur, it may be that the deepest and most impressive shafts were connected with the ritual of the aristocracy and the priests who presided over the rites, while the more humble pits and wells may have been of an essentially local character, the cult spots of some lesser Iron Age landlord and his dependants. All these possibilities must be kept in mind while examining the evidence for such sacred offering places.

One of the many problems to be met with in this study is what to include and what to reject. We must recognize from the outset that people used wells for the everyday purpose of obtaining water from them; and that the detritus that sometimes gathered when a well ceased to be used for water is by no means invariably of a votive nature. Pits were dug both for rubbish and for corn storage, as far as we can gather; and, as much of the material thrown into votive pits was put there in a haphazard and unordered manner, it is no easy matter to separate one from the other in many instances, although in some it is obvious. Deep shafts were sunk in the chalk and clay for a variety of purposes, such as the mining of flint and chalk, and dene-holes and man-made caves abound in Kent and Essex.[3] Where we find traces of human activity in the form of pottery and bones in shafts and other excavations, it can by no means be taken for granted that these activities were necessarily of a religious nature. Moreover, some extremely deep shafts were sunk even in recent times simply to obtain a water supply; A. C. Smith's remarks about this are useful. Writing about the parish of Yatesbury, in Wiltshire, in the latter part of the last century, he says, 'For the most part our wells provide ample supplies of excellent water; they are very deep, never less than 60, oftener 80 feet, sometimes – as in the case of the rectory well – 120 feet, and even – in the case of a well I had occasion to sink for a cottage on the glebe – 140 feet.'[4] That certain of the shafts at least were sunk for the purpose of obtaining water must therefore not be forgotten, although an original or a secondary association may have been present. Wells in, for example, the Isle of Skye, which were widely resorted to for healing and fertility purposes until the end of the last century at least, can be seen today in use on crofts as ordinary domestic wells. Only the name (which is often descriptive of function, such as Fertility Well, or Toothache Well) and the oral traditions which still circulate amongst the old people bear testimony to once-powerful belief in the inherent virtues of the water.

Appreciation of the ritual importance of certain shafts began in France with the researches of Baudry and Ballereau,[5] the term 'puits funéraires' being applied to such structures. A recent publication by Schwarz[6] has comprehensively documented the evidence for ritual shafts in Europe, and this work should be used for comparison with the material found in the British Isles. Piggott[7] and Ashbee[8] have drawn attention to the nature of the Bronze Age shafts at Swanwick, Hampshire, and Normanton Down (Wilsford), Wiltshire. Ashbee has cited comparable structures at Maumbury Rings, Dorset, and Dorchester on Thames, Oxfordshire; and there can be no doubt that the British shafts and pits which we will consider here, with their clear Belgic affinities, have a well-attested ancestry in Bronze Age, Hallstatt and La Tène Europe. This must be seen to have an unmistakable significance when the origins of Celtic religion and the Druidic priesthood are in question.

It is unfortunate that many shafts and pits were revealed during the construction of railways in the nineteenth century because, thorough although several of the investigations of such structures were, they were essentially restricted by lack of modern scientific methods and equipment, and many of the questions we should seek answers for today were not asked. Many examples must have been destroyed without record, or even without having been observed; but fortunately there are likely to be an unknown number still awaiting discovery, and with the knowledge and increasing understanding we now have of such sites, these are likely to receive the full care and attention they warrant. The first person to excavate a ritual shaft in this country and to recognize its true significance was J. P. T. Burchell,[9] and the greatest credit is due to him both for his perspicacity in recognizing the importance of what he was investigating and his care while carrying out the work; and for his subsequent caution once he was aware of the religious nature of the shafts. His discoveries, added to those of the French scholars, gave a lead to subsequent research, and enabled the significance of much that had been passed over as deposits of rubbish, pure and simple, to be properly appreciated.

Because of the, at present, almost insurmountable difficulty of keeping shafts, pits and wells in separate categories, the material to be discussed has been arranged alphabetically according to location, and treated together. The common factors are listed in the Appendix under the same alphabetical arrangement. After the ensuing description of the structures there is a discussion of the most striking features that emerge, and some suggested interpretations and parallels. Only shafts, pits and wells which seem to be of clear ritual importance have been included. No doubt there are some which should not have been included; and there are surely some which should have been included but, because the arrangement of the contents or the unsatisfactory nature of the excavation reports leaves uncertainty as to the true purpose of the structures, it has been thought best to exclude them from the list. The study is by no means exhaustive, and it is certain that published accounts of many more examples of each kind have yet to be brought to light and investigated.

In the alphabetical list which follows diameter or section and depth are given if mentioned in the original record.

SHAFTS, PITS, WELLS

ARDLEIGH, Essex[10]
Situation   Gravel pit.
Diameter   At least 5 ft.
Depth   11 ft.
Character and Contents   A hollowed-out oak trunk 3 ft. in diameter, packed inside with clay and surrounded with clay 1 ft. thick, was inserted into the pit. When the clay both inside and outside the trunk was stripped many Roman potsherds were found. The clay in the interior of the trunk appeared to have been packed in deliberately. For more than 2 ft. down, clay mixed with sherds of Roman pottery and about six pieces of pulpy matter. Below this a layer of red-brown soil, on top of which a base of Samian ware. In this soil a large quantity of animal bones and parts of antlers. No deer bones were found. A horse's skull, bones of a young horse. The bones were curiously decayed and there was a large quantity of ferrous sulphate present, indicative of organic matter.

ARMSLEY, Hampshire[11]
Situation   In a garden, one mile below Breamore Mill.
Diameter   No measurement recorded.
Depth   7 ft.
Character and Contents   All the relics found in the well belong to the Roman period. At a depth of about 5 ft. in dark-coloured mud, which was full of sticks, there were many animal bones but few sherds. Also in this layer were two complete thumb pots, a wooden head 8 in. high, and carpentered wood. At 5 ft. 6 in. were the top edge of a wooden board and stakes; large blocks of stone marked the circular outline of the well. Within this circle was the same stiff mud containing sticks, a horse's skull, a vase, fragments of a sandal. Eight coins dating between A.D. 68–305 were found, lead and bronze fragments, iron shears, a knife with a bone handle, nails, tools, etc. Broken quern stones, whetstones, burnt stones, lumps of white clay, burnt flints, etc. Several pieces of sawn wood, horn cores, antlers, teeth and a total of 146 bone fragments were recovered.

ASHILL, Norfolk[12]
Situation   A square enclosure of 10 acres with rounded angles, formed by a ditch, having within it a second enclosure also formed by a ditch; 100 ft. between the two. Within the northeast angle between the two ditches were formerly traces of foundations. In 1870, within the inner enclosure two shafts and a pit were found.
Section   Shaft 1, 3 ft. 6 in. square.
Depth   Shaft 1, 40 ft.; shaft 2, 22 ft., but abandoned while under construction; pit, about 5 ft.
Character and Contents   Noticeable paths were found leading to the site. *Shaft 1* lined with oaken planks. From the top of the woodwork, 6 ft. below the surface, to 19 ft. down, the contents were miscellaneous; at 4 ft. pottery, charcoal, ox and deer bones, a wicker basket. At 8 ft. sherds, including Samian; ox, deer, pig bones; at 10 ft. Samian ware, wall plaster, socketed iron knife, whetstone; at 15 ft. sherds, oak staves, pig and deer bones, oyster and mussel shells. At 19 ft. the deposit changed. More or less perfect urns were found placed in layers in a symmetrical manner, and continued to be so placed down to the bottom, embedded in leaves of hazel and nuts, the nuts in the upper layers being more mature than those in the lower layers. A bronze bow-shaped fibula, an iron implement (? key). At 24 ft. to 26 ft. more urns symmetrically placed as before, the lower layers in oak and hazel leaves. At 30 ft. urns set as before, a boar's tusk, pieces of antler. At 32 ft. another layer of urns and leaves, with large stones over them. At 33 ft. Samian ware, a bucket with iron handle, neck of amphora, part of a quern stone, etc. At 34 ft. urns, over them stones showing traces of fire. Some of the urns had bands of sedge round them; some were cased in basket work. At 40 ft. the haunch-bone of a deer. The bottom of the shaft was paved with flints. In all about 100 urns were found of which more than fifty were perfect and many very beautiful.

Shaft 2 lined for only a few feet. Contained a bottle, two urns, two smooth stones, a skull of *Bos longifrons* and some antlers of red deer. The bottom was of flints.

Pit. Sherds; skull of a goat; pig, ox and deer bones.

ASHTEAD, Surrey[13]

Situation Two shafts found at an old disused chalk quarry, about 1933.

Diameter No information.

Depth *Shaft 1* had for the most part been removed before the report was written, the upper 15 ft. apparently before the seventeenth century, leaving only a few feet. *Shaft 2* about 9 ft.

Character and Contents *Shaft 1*, filling mixed with charcoal, sherds, bone chips. The pottery dated to the Bronze Age/Iron Age transition period, and may be compared with some of that from All Cannings Cross. *Shaft 2* contained clean dug chalk, small sherds and pieces of bone.

ASTHALL, Oxfordshire[14]

Situation At a Roman site.

Diameter *Well 1*, 5 ft. 6 in.; *well 2*, 4 ft. 6 in.; *pit*, 5 ft. by 2 ft. 6 in.

Depth *Well 1*, 11 ft. 6 in.; *well 2*, 9 ft. 6 in.; *pit*, 4 ft.

Character and Contents *Well 1* was roughly circular; there was no water, and no revetting. The bottom was paved with flat stones. In the first 3 ft. pottery sherds in which fourth-century types prevail. At 3 ft. 6 in. mass of debris from a Roman wall that had been built over the mouth of the well. At 5 ft. 6 in. to 8 ft. 6 in. numerous sherds of mid-second-century to third-century date and some wall debris. Next, a layer devoid of sherds in which were the skeletons of five terrier-type dogs, a horse's jawbone, and many other animal bones. At 10 ft. to 11 ft. 6 in. a first-century brooch, and the better part of a coarse grey-black hand-made pot of a Belgic type, and other sherds.

Well 2 contained Belgic pottery at the bottom, later pottery above this.

The *pit* contained much pottery from the first century on the bottom to the fourth century near the top; bronze and bone pins; iron objects including the broken haft of a knife; and fragments of charcoal.

In 1955 two small objects were recovered from the site, which emphasized its cult nature. These are a small jug handle in bronze in the shape of a swan, the ends of the rim-splays being in the form of bird heads; and a model axe, like those from Woodeaton and elsewhere.

AYLESFORD, Kent[15]

Situation In a quarry; a Belgic cemetery consisting of many pits, some entirely filled with clean flints. One or two seem to be of particular relevance here.

Diameter *Pit 1*, 8 ft.

Depth *Pit 1*, 12 to 15 ft.; *pit 2*, 3 ft. 6 in.

Character and Contents *Pit 1* was found near the middle of the quarry. It was entirely filled with animal bones.

Pit 2, in which the famous bucket was found, was circular; the sides and the bottom had been coated with the kind of chalky compound which occurs so frequently in ritual shafts.

BAR HILL, Dunbartonshire[16]

Situation In the courtyard of the *praetorium* of the Roman fort on the Antonine Wall.

Diameter Maximum of 4 ft.

Depth 43 ft.

Character and Contents The well was found to have been deliberately filled up, the upper stratum consisting of building material. At 12 ft., a capital, and lower down more capitals, and bases, and a fragment of an inscribed tablet. Lower again more fragments of the tablet, and pieces of oak. At 33 ft. an inscribed altar, red deer antler, a coin, pieces of squared oak some of which were 9 ft. long, and many objects of iron. At 38 ft. was a huge amphora, broken, containing a bag of tools and a collection of iron objects. Then deer antlers and hoofs; shoulder-blades of ox and sheep, oyster shells, a quantity of hazel nuts, and hawthorn twigs.

There were also nine pits. One contained amongst other things a chariot wheel; two were circular, perhaps started as wells and then abandoned for this purpose.

BEDFORD, Bedfordshire[17]

Situation In a brickyard on the north side of Bedford

Diameter 'Funnel-shaped,' but no measurements given.

Depth From 4 to 5 ft.

Character and Contents   Over 50 pits, bearing a close similarity to each other, were found at a depth of some 6 ft. from the surface. The infillings were found to contain quantities of charcoal, burnt stones and bones of ox, horse, deer and perhaps wolf, most of them burnt. Fragments of what was described as coarse pottery, but no complete vessels, were found. Several flint flakes, some apparently worked, were found among the potsherds.

BEKESBOURNE, Kent[18] (fig. 66)

Situation   Discovered during railway construction; 6½ miles west of the SANDWICH shaft.
Section   3 ft 3 in. square.
Depth   Shaft 12 ft. deep found 13 ft. below surface; so total depth of this shaft (shaft 1) presumably originally 25 ft. The shaft, which had been sunk in sandy loam, was lined by a four-sided structure of oak, covered with oak planks, and filled with large flints. Towards the bottom of the shaft was a single Romano-British urn, protected by large flints. Beneath this urn was a layer of flints; and beneath this five urns of similar age containing probably calcined bones, the mouth of one covered with a piece of burnt clay. Of these urns, one was placed centrally and one in each corner of the shaft. Beneath the urns was a flat piece of stone which covered the saucer-shaped bottom of the shaft and was kept in place by six pegs of chestnut wood. A circle of horses' teeth was arranged on the upper surface of the stone.

   Shaft 2, which had no timber lining, was located nearby. It was filled with flint nodules in which, at a depth of about 15 ft. below the surface, two or three urns and a large amphora were found.

BERTHA, Perthshire[19]

Situation   On the (? left) bank of the River Almond.
Diameter   No measurement recorded.
Depth   About 18 ft.
Character and Contents   Eight pits were discovered in the eighteenth century and noted by Pennant. The discovery resulted from a large urn being seen projecting from the riverbank. The soil filling the pits was of a dark colour which contrasted with that of the bank. The pits stood about 10 ft. apart, and one or more vessels were found at the bottom of each. All the vessels appear to have contained ashes, mixed, in one instance, with charred pieces of oak. It appeared that when the pits were dug the urn or urns had been placed at the bottom and the pit then filled with dark alluvial soil which had been tightly pressed down. In 1774 a two-handled urn resting on a tablet of brick was found at the bottom of one of the shafts. Nearby lay the remains of a helmet, a socketed spearhead and, beneath these, an oblong bar of lead.

BIDDENHAM, Bedfordshire[20] (fig. 64)

Situation   Found in 1857 when workmen were digging for gravel in a field about 300 yd. from the River Ouse, on Lord Dynevor's property. No trace of any building or other structure was noticed in the vicinity.
Diameter   2 ft. 9 in.
Depth   37 ft.
Character and Contents   The shaft was originally excavated to a width of about 8 ft., and then steined up to a uniform diameter of 2 ft. 9 in. At different depths were found an altar slab; a human skeleton; a mutilated statue; a broken stone slab incised with the representation of a crane; fragments of about fifty Roman urns; pebbles; and the bones of horse, ox, dogs, pig and fox.

BIRCHINGTON, Kent[21] (fig. 66; Pl. XI, bottom)

Situation   On the shore at Minnis Bay. Excavation work had to be carried out between tides.
Diameter   2 ft. 7 in.
Depth   32 ft.
Character and Contents   Circular shaft, having for the first 21 ft. footholds cut in the chalk. The infilling for the first 27 ft. contained remains of ox and horse, and a few pieces of Romano-British pottery. At 27 ft. the shaft was almost filled from side to side by a roughly circular piece of sandstone some 4 in. thick pierced with a central hole. At 30 ft. a horse's skull, some bones and a few pieces of oak were found. The last 18 in. of the shaft contained a deposit of several hundred unopened oyster shells.

   At a distance of about 7 yd. northwest of the shaft what was described as a 'Romano-British pit dwelling' was found.

BOSSENS, ST ERTH, Cornwall[22]
Situation   Found in 1756 by a farmer in the northwest corner of a sub-rectangular earthwork.
Diameter   No measurement given.
Depth   36 ft.
Character and Contents   Perpendicular shaft with holes up the sides like the Bedfordshire shafts. At 18 ft. a metal patera dedicated to Mars was found (AELIUS MODESTUS DEO MARTI); a metal jug and a stone weight at about 24 ft.; next a 'meal stone,' and then a second patera with two handles. Intermixed were fragments of horns, bones, half-burnt sticks and many pieces of leather.

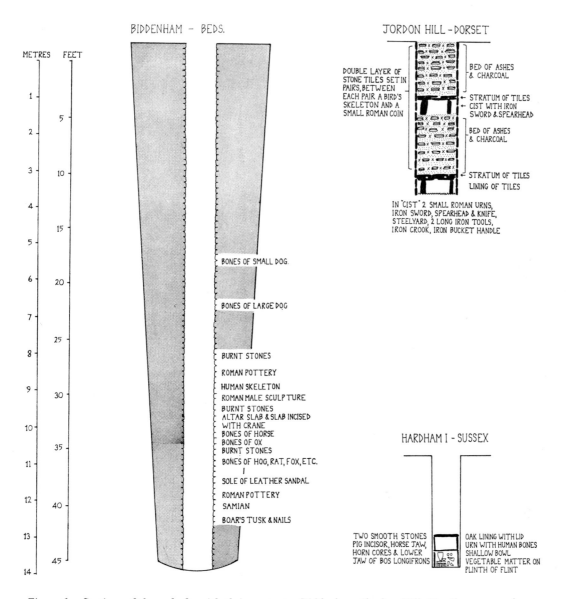

Figure 64. Sections of three shafts with their contents: Biddenham, Jordan Hill, Hardham 1.

BRAMPTON, Cumberland[23]
Situation   Open country.
Diameter   2 ft.
Depth   10 ft.
Character and Contents   Over 60 pieces of ironwork, many of them bent in two, were found in the pit; they included agricultural tools, a plough-share, a hoe, a scythe, etc.; hooks, chains, wheels, buckets and cart fittings, all in a fragmented state.

BRISLINGTON, Bristol[24]
Situation   Roman villa.
Diameter   5 ft.
Depth   38 ft.
Character and Contents   For the first 12 ft., fragments of black pottery and Samian ware were discovered; between 24 ft. and 28 ft. there was a large collection of bones and teeth of various animals, several human skulls, some bones, and nearly perfect metal vessels and pottery. Between 32 ft. and 36 ft., animal bones and pottery fragments; between 36 ft. and 38 ft., small animal bones, pottery fragments, some bronze objects and a wooden comb.

CADBURY CASTLE, Devonshire[25]
Situation   In a presumptive Iron Age hill-fort.
Diameter   8 ft. at the top; 6 ft. at 25 ft.; 3 ft. at 4 ft. from the bottom.
Depth   58 ft.
Character and Contents   In 1847 an indentation near the centre of the fort was opened, and at a depth of some 6 ft. from the surface the presence of a shaft was established. The shaft was lined with puddled clay. Rubble and earth filling gave way to sherds, ashes, fragments of bone, ornaments and beads; 20 metal bracelets and 4 of shale were found. At 30 ft. a bronze ring with a paste intaglio; and thereafter two small rings, a pierced jet button; several glass and enamel beads; horses' teeth, charcoal, clay, rubble, a few fragments of human bones and some ashes. No water was found when bottom was reached; an iron knife blade was found in the lower part of the shaft.

CAERWENT, Monmouthshire[26]
Situation   A Romano-British town. The Caerwent wells, like those of any Roman town of reasonable size, are numerous and extremely difficult to classify. Some would, of course, have been wells of a straightforward domestic kind, but certain others seem to come into the class of structure under present consideration. Only those that seem to be relevant here are discussed, although others may have equal claim to ritual associations at some stage of their existence.
Diameter   *Well 1*, 3 ft. 6 in. at the top, narrowing to 3 ft.; *well 2*, 2 ft. 4 in. at mouth and at bottom, 2 ft. 9 in. to 3 ft. at 8 ft. down.
Depth   *Well 1*, about 27 ft.; *well 2*, 25 ft. 6 in.; *well 3*, 21 ft. 9 in.
Character and Contents   *Well 1*, at House VIII N, was steined; water was found at 20 ft. 3 in. There were many loose stones in the filling. At 20 ft. 1 in. were a fragment of glass, charred oak, cow bones; pottery, stones and the staves and bands of a bucket were found between 23 ft. and 27 ft. Three coins were found, and hazel nuts and twigs.

In *well 2*, to the east of house VI N, were two or three fragments of a human skull, several ox skulls, other bones, pieces of pottery and fragments of a bucket.

In *well 2a*, to the east of House VIII N, there were the skulls of five dogs.

Well 2b, near House IX, contained the skull of a large dog among other things.

Well 3 was situated in the courtyard of House VII N. At the depth of 7 ft. a large sandstone slab was wedged across the well, beneath which a void extended until water level was reached, at 15 ft. The well was steined to 17 ft.; immediately beneath this level flat stones set on edge formed a 'box' in the well. For the next 2 ft. the well was filled with stones, slabs and tile mortar. Between 19 ft. and 20 ft. fragments of several buckets were found; and at 20 ft. another flat slab. Beneath this, at the bottom of the well, were a pewter jug and a pewter plate ornamented with a wheel in a square frame. Pottery, wood, metal fittings and a cow's rib were also found.

Well 4 contained the figure of a seated deity and a collection of iron tools.

A large *pit* found in a small building (Block A) contained amongst other things a sandstone trough, paving slabs, pottery and two human skulls at differing depths.

CALKE WOOD, RICKINGHALL, Suffolk[27]
Situation   Found during clay-digging operations, very close to a four-sided embanked enclosure of uncertain date.
Diameter   No measurement recorded.
Depth   30 ft.
Character and Contents   The shaft was reinforced with a lining of clay which was in turn lined with an organic substance. A few sherds of beaker pottery were found, together with bones, burnt stones and baked lumps of clay. The excavators were unable to carry out as full an investigation as the interest and peculiarities of the site warranted.

The work of the men engaged in cutting clay was constantly hampered by the occurrence of silted-up shafts or pits of a depth of about 15 ft., some of which contained Romano-British sherds and others traces of Iron Age occupation material. It is possibly of some significance that the little bronze Wattisfield boar, now in Ipswich Museum, was ploughed up in a field immediately adjacent to the wood containing this complex of some two dozen shafts.

CARRAWBURGH, Northumberland[28]
Situation   Beside the Roman fort BROCOLITIA.
Diameter   Square-sectioned at the top; 8 ft. 6 in. by 7 ft. 9 in.
Depth   7 ft.
Character and Contents   Although there are many wells which contain deposits of a votive nature in the British Isles which cannot be included here, the well at Carrawburgh, sacred to the Celtic goddess Coventina, cannot be omitted. When excavated towards the end of the nineteenth century it was found to contain an amazing number of objects of a religious character, among them a huge collection of over 13,000 coins dating from between A.D. 41 to 383; 24 undamaged altars, several dedicated to the patron goddess of the well; pins, brooches, a variety of bronze objects including a horse and a dog, shrine bells, vessels, Samian ware and a human skull.

Two of the altars had a ring attached to the *focus*, presumably for suspension over or immersion in the sacred spring.

CRAYFORD, Kent[29]
Situation   Found in a chalk pit.
Diameter   No measurement recorded.
Depth   42 ft. 6 in.
Character and Contents   A dene-hole discovered in a chalk pit at Perry Street, to the north of Crayford, had been excavated through the chalk to the flint to a depth of 42 ft. 6 in. At the bottom was a cone of sandy clay with flint blocks and flakes; then coarser soil and very coarse pottery; above that, a 12-ft. layer of pottery representing about 150 vessels. The lower sherds were probably pre-Roman (see the RAMSGATE shaft); the upper were of Samian, Upchurch and local wares. There were also bits of iron, bones of young animals and oyster shells.

In another shaft nearby the remains of a fire were found.

DANEBURY HILL, NETHER WALLOP, Hampshire[30]
Situation   Within an Iron Age hill-fort.
Diameter   4 ft. 10 in.
Depth   8 ft.
Character and Contents   A cylindrical shaft filled with a mixture of chalk and earth, and containing a few large flints, bones and sherds. Ox bones were also present, and the bones and skulls of goats.

Two other shafts have been reported at this site.

DARENTH, Kent[31]
Situation   In an open field, near Rye Croft Wood.
Diameter   4 ft. 6 in. by 3 ft. 4 in.
Depth   3 ft.
Character and Contents   Packed with large flints, the pit contained a large two-handled buff-coloured urn 32 in. high, an iron lampstand, a Samian saucer and a red goblet.

DUNSTABLE, Bedfordshire[32]
Situation   Found at SEWELL, near MAIDEN BOWER (which are both alternative names for this shaft) in 1859, when the Dunstable–London railway was under construction.
Diameter   3 ft. 6 in. to the depth of 70 ft., thereafter lessening to 2 ft. 7 in. at 110 ft.
Depth   About 120 ft.
Character and Contents   The long, narrow, dry shaft was packed with pottery, human bones, Roman tiles, sandstone slabs, animal bones and charred wood. Coins were also said to have been found.

EWELL, Surrey[33]
Situation   Site of Staneway House (now a plant nursery) in a chalk pit. Ten shafts in all were found.
Diameter   No measurements recorded.
Depth   Between 12 ft. and 37 ft.
Character and Contents   Eight shafts were found in or about 1846, and it is of the first importance to note that the excavators observed an appearance of *orderliness* about the arrangement of the contents of the shafts. They contained, in the following order, large animal bones, including cow, sheep, stag and pig; a layer of Samian ware sherds some of which made up whole vessels; a fine rich mould apparently mixed with animal matter and containing oyster shells; and, in one pit, apple pips and cherry stones, a small bronze ring, the bones of a cock and a hare (Caesar's statement on the sanctity of these creatures is relevant here), and the almost entire skeleton of a large dog – the bones were in a well-preserved state but the head had been severed from the body and placed about one foot from it. In the corresponding layers in other pits bones of dogs, fragments of glass, fibulae and portions of decayed bronze, perhaps horse trappings, were found. In the next layer were amphorae and other vessels, and then vessels of dark-coloured ware several of which were perfect. In every pit was an equal quantity of iron nails. In one, an iron rod was found at the bottom; in another, an iron hammer and two pieces of oak about 18 in. long, sharpened at either end and 'resembling stakes.' Amongst the black ware were a few portions of burnt human bones. All the animal bones were unburnt.

In two more shafts, discovered in about 1859, antlers were found, together with bones of ox, boar, hare and fowl, as well as fragments of iron and iron nails. Numerous sherds included 20 identifiable varieties.

In 1948 a shaft discovered at North Looe, Ewell, was excavated to a depth of 23 ft. 6 in. It apparently contained Iron Age material, but it has not been possible to obtain a satisfactory report of the excavation.

FELIXSTOWE, Suffolk[34]
Situation   On the cliffs about one mile north of Felixstowe.
Section   2 ft. 6 in.
Depth   No measurement recorded.
Character and Contents   In 1873–4 what was described as a hearth with burnt and broken animal bones was found 4 ft. below the surface at the top of the cliff. Under this was a 'floor' about 18 in. thick below which was a square-section shaft the sides of which were lined with wood. In the northeast corner of the bottom of the shaft was a Roman vessel filled with earth in which were acorns.

FRITTENDEN, Kent[35]
Situation   In a marshy wood.
Diameter   No measurement recorded.
Depth   15 ft.
Character and Contents   Two Upchurch urns were found on solid ground at the bottom of a pit filled with decayed vegetable matter. Timberwork was found in the pit (see BEKESBOURNE).

GREAT CHESTERFORD, Essex[36]
Situation   In a Roman station.

Diameter   Various.
Depth   Various.
Character and Contents   Some 45 shafts were found, all of which appeared to have been made with care. Finds included a bone knife-handle portraying a torc-wearing Hercules; a bronze figurine of a river god; the heads of two ravens and a cock; bones of dogs and bullocks, bird bones, pottery and some oyster shells. One shaft was 6 ft. deep, and had been carefully sealed at the top with chalk. In it were 96 objects of iron belonging to a smith's equipment, many of them much worn.

    Neville, who excavated many of these shafts, says 'the presence of so many vessels of pottery in the shafts, deposited entire at intervals, is a strong evidence against their having been used merely as rubbish holes'; and 'the only suggestion as yet offered regarding their use, with any degree of probability, is that they were in some manner connected with funeral or sacrificial rites, and although the facts which have been noticed may point to none in particular, many circumstances will be found on considering them, to denote that they were so.'

GREENHITHE, Kent[37]

Situation   Found in a chalk pit.
Diameter   22 ft. to 23 ft. wide at the broadest.
Depth   35 ft.
Character and Contents   A perpendicular shaft descended to a depth of 35 ft. from a point in the centre of a pear-shaped cavity found in the chalk pit. The filling included sand, gravel and animal bones of horse, ox, pig, deer, together with a few bird bones and a horn of *Bos longifrons*. Sherds of coarse pottery, and a few of Samian; iron nails, an iron key, a fragment of an iron hoop, two carved bone sockets, two 'worked' stones. At the bottom were three human skeletons, placed side by side.

HARDHAM, Sussex[38] (fig. 64)

Situation   Found when a railway was under construction.
Section   About 2 ft. 6 in. square to 6 ft. square.
Depth   About 10 ft.
Character and Contents   *Shaft 1*. The shaft was steined from near the top to the bottom. At the bottom was a lining of oak planks, 2 ft. 8 in. high, which had no bottom but allegedly had a lid. In this 'box' were several fragments of roughly tanned leather and, on a low platform of flints covered with a layer of black vegetable matter, a rudely-fashioned cinerary urn containing burnt human bones and a 'shallow patera', both of a dark ware and both upright. Close to these were three horn cores, a few broken bones and a lower jaw containing teeth, all of *Bos longifrons*. In addition there were one of the incisors of a pig and part of the jaw of a horse; coarse potsherds and a fragment of Samian ware; and two round stones, one of flint and the other of sandstone together with a mass of chalky white substance.

    Shaft 2 was similar to *shaft 1*, but measured 4 ft. square. The wooden 'box' at the bottom contained two vessels on a stone platform covered with vegetation. Three horn cores of *Bos longifrons* were found, a fragment of leather and an iron nail. In addition a pottery wine-funnel, a pear-shaped vase, a fragment of bent iron rod and a bronze pin were found, while the black clay filling mixed with sand contained numerous pieces of pottery and fragments of flint, and was highly charged with carbon.

    Shaft 3 contained one cinerary urn placed upright on a Roman brick, two horn cores of *Bos longifrons* and numerous sherds.

    There were platforms of flints at the bottoms of both *shaft 4* and *shaft 5*. The latter was 6 ft. square, and its angles were strengthened by oak beams.

    Shaft 6 was circular, steined, and contained an amphora measuring 5 ft. 6 in. in circumference, placed mouth downward, together with two Roman coins and a quantity of dark matter.

HEYWOOD, Wiltshire[39]

Situation   At the Westbury Iron Works.
Diameter   No measurement recorded.
Depth   No measurement recorded.
Character and Contents   A well opened in 1879 was found to contain a considerable quantity of broken pottery, a well-preserved and complete skull of *Bos longifrons*, the complete skull of a horse with a hole pierced in the cheek-bone, and, at the bottom, parts of four human skulls.

IPSDEN, Oxfordshire[40]
Situation   No information.
Diameter   'Very narrow' at the mouth.
Depth   No measurement recorded.
Character and Contents   The sides of the well were described as being of rough, ribbed chalk. At some considerable depth from the top three huge logs of wood stood perpendicularly in the well.

IPSWICH, Suffolk[41] (Pl. XI, top)
Situation   The brickfield of Messrs Bolton & Co.
Diameter   *Shaft 1*, 2 ft. 10 in. by 3 ft. 4 in.; *shaft 2*, 6 ft. near the top, 10 ft. lower down, less again lower still.
Depth   *Shaft 1*, more than 29 ft.; *shaft 2*, more than 66 ft.
Character and Contents   *Shaft 1* was lined with clay the surface of which had been smoothed off. At 16 ft. a small piece of Romano-British pottery was found, and at 20 ft. a piece of matted hair judged to be of hare, rabbit or badger had been preserved. Excavations ceased when danger threatened.

Shaft 2 was some 3 yd. west-southwest of *1*. The uppermost 18 ft. had been carefully filled in; and at exactly 20 ft. from the surface there was a similar portion of hair to that found in the other shaft. This lay under a mass of strong clay that had been puddled and formed into the shape of a pillar; and black pebbles had been pressed into its surface. The pillar of clay stood upright centrally in the shaft. When chalk was reached the walls were coated with reddish-brown clay. The soil of the filling was analysed; 'It appears that the material in the shaft is mainly clay which had had some animal matter (the nature of which is very difficult to determine) in contact with it at some time. The brown colour is due to iron compounds.' In this shaft very clear traces of the timbering used in the original excavation are present. At the point where the shaft passed into the chalk two small pieces of silver sheeting were found, and a cylindrical piece of polished marble; and below these, pieces of brick. At a depth of about 45 ft. from the surface there was a pavement of chalk flints.

A *third shaft*, which also seems to have been deliberately filled in, and which seemed to be larger than the others but was not excavated, was situated about 2 yd. west-southwest of *shaft 2*.

ISLE OF THANET, Kent[42]
Situation   Between St Peter's and Reading Street.
Diameter   30 ft. by 40 ft. at the top.
Depth   11 ft.
Character and Contents   All surface trace of the pit was obliterated by a cap of brick earth. When this was removed a small band of chalk delineating the margin of the pit was apparent, and an opening and a 'kind of path' could be traced on the northeast side. It only proved possible to excavate the north half of the pit.

At a depth of 6 ft. 9 in. from the surface, and at a point which seemed to be over the centre of the pit, two lumps of baked clay and 30 small pellets were found. Then an iron nail, a 'well-formed flint spear-head' and a few fragments of charcoal. Flint flakes were found interspersed with the brick earth all through the pit, but chiefly near the bottom. They showed signs of fire. Animal remains, comprising split and fractured bones, were found at various depths, but chiefly near the bottom. The animals represented included *Bos longifrons*, dog (skull and lower jaw), goat, horse, pig and red deer (bones and antler). Only one animal of each kind was present. The pottery, which was entirely Romano-British with no Samian present, consisted of small fragments. The flint, bones and pottery were clearly all deposited at the same time.

JORDON HILL, Somerset[43] (fig. 64)
Situation   Within a Romano-British temple.
Diameter   No measurement recorded.
Depth   14 ft.
Character and Contents   A dry well found in the south corner of the temple had been filled in a very singular fashion. The well was lined with clay in which a layer of used stone tiles was set edgeways. At the bottom of the well, on a bed of clay, there was a rough cist formed of two oblong stones in which there were two Roman urns, a broad iron sword 21 in. long, an iron spearhead, an iron knife, two long pieces of iron, and a steelyard; there were no bones of any kind. Next above the cist was a stratum of thick stone tiles like those which lined the well, and on it a bed of ashes and charcoal. On this was a double layer of stone tiles, arranged in pairs, and between each pair was the skeleton of one bird together with one small Roman coin. There was another bed of ashes above the upper tier of tiles, and thereafter an alternating succession of tiles enclosing bird skeletons

and coins, and beds of ashes. There were sixteen repetitions between the top and the bottom of the well, interrupted at the halfway point by a cist containing an iron sword, a spearhead and urns like those in the cist at the bottom. The birds represented were raven, crow, buzzard and starling, all prognostic birds according to Celtic belief. Bones of hare were also present.

KIDLINGTON, Oxfordshire[44]
Situation   Found in a quarry northeast of the church.
Diameter   No measurement recorded.
Depth   No measurement recorded.
Character and Contents   In 1840 a 'small Roman urn' was found under a stone at the bottom of a steined shaft. The shaft was filled with bones and broken red and white pottery, and an abundance of coins. Traces of 'dwellings and earthen ramparts' were recorded nearby.

LINCOLN, Lincolnshire[45]
Situation   At the rear of the Adam and Eve inn.
Diameter   No measurement recorded.
Depth   40 ft. but bottom not reached.
Character and Contents   A steined shaft was found and briefly recorded in 1961, together with the information that another shaft exists in the garden of 2 Pottergate, Lincoln. In 1848 many pits, all containing bones, fragments of pottery and other objects, were found near the Eastgate, but it has not proved possible to obtain fuller information about these.

LONDON. 1. LOTHBURY[46]
Situation   In Londinium.
Section   About 3 ft. square.
Depth   No measurement recorded.
Character and Contents   The well or shaft was lined with boards until near the bottom; below the level at which the lining ceased the section became oval. Vessels were found, some of which were whole; a coin of Allectus; and two iron implements said to represent respectively a boat-hook and a bucket handle.

LONDON. 2. NEW ROYAL EXCHANGE[47]
Situation   In Londinium.
Diameter   No measurement recorded.
Depth   No measurement recorded.
Character and Contents   Meagre information records that a shaft was found in the last century; and that it contained knives, styli and 'modelling tools in steel.'

MAIDEN CASTLE, Dorset[48]
Situation   Within an Iron Age hill-fort.
Diameter   No measurement recorded.
Depth   Between 4 ft. and 10 ft.
Character and Contents   In 1868 seven pits were found in an area measuring 16 ft. square. They contained animal bones, sherds of pottery and 'other pieces of hardware.'

MOUNT CABURN, Sussex[49]
Situation   In a hill-top enclosure, presumably an Iron Age hill-fort, measuring $3\frac{1}{2}$ acres in extent.
Diameter   Main pit, 35 ft. at top with shaft 12 ft. at top.
Depth   Main shaft 11 ft. deep from bottom of pit.
Character and Contents   One among 147 pits located in this enclosure was singular. On the surface it appeared as a large, shallow depression surrounded by a low bank and measuring 35 ft. in diameter. In the centre there was discovered an almost circular shaft 12 ft. in diameter at the top, narrowing to 7 ft. 6 in. at the depth of 4 ft. below its top and to 5 ft. 3 in. at its bottom, 11 ft. from its top. In the mould in the depression above the shaft there were found bones of ox, pig and rabbit, the leg (with spur) of a fighting cock, and oyster shells. After the first 3 ft. the shaft was filled with clean chalk, the larger blocks at the bottom. At the bottom of the shaft were one piece of the base of a pot, a large iron clinker and a dog bone.

NEWSTEAD, Roxburghshire[50]

Situation   Within Roman fort and annexe. Numerous pits, shafts and wells were found, in many instances of so singular a character that they can only be dealt with here in a cursory manner.

Diameter   Given in individual descriptions.

Depth   Given in individual descriptions.

Character and Contents   Not all the pits are of the same period; but it is noteworthy that in trying to date them Curle says, 'At the same time a considerable number, including those in which the most remarkable finds were made, produced pottery resembling that recovered from the ditch of the early fort, which is approximately of the first century.' He also says, 'It is a curious fact that, with the exception of Pits I, XXIII and XCV, comparatively little was obtained from the later pits.' The extraordinary nature of some of the contents puzzled the excavators by reason both of their value and their complexity; but a solution is surely available in terms of other examples under consideration in this paper. Curle describes the contents of 107 pits, shafts or wells, and his reports are excellent and clear. A selection of the more important pits and their contents are briefly described.

Pit I

Diameter   20 ft. at surface, 6 ft. 6 in. at bottom.

Depth   25 ft. 6 in.

Contents   These include, at 5 ft. down, a piece of twisted silver wire, part of a penannular brooch, two bronze rings, twelve links of a small bronze chain; at 8 ft., a human skeleton, near it a bronze penannular brooch and what was probably part of another; at 12 ft., an altar dedicated to Jupiter and a coin below it; from 14 ft. down, bones of animals, 'frequent' skulls of *Bos longifrons* and horses, also deer antlers. Lower down more pottery and antlers, and at 21 ft. an iron bar. At 22 ft., a complete human skull, with part of another near it. Lower down there were two iron knives, amphorae necks, a terra sigillata cup base, pieces of chain armour, two reliefs in stone of boars, five iron arrowheads, and so on.

Pit VII

Diameter   8 ft. 8 in. at the surface, 3 ft. 10 in. at the bottom.

Depth   17 ft.

Contents   At 7 ft. the black deposit which so often occurs in these shafts. There were many twigs in this pit. Finds include part of a terra sigillata dish, necks of two amphorae, fragments of glass, a spearhead, animal bones, skulls of horses, the leg bone of a crane (a sacred Celtic bird), and oyster shells.

Pit XIV

Diameter   5 ft. at the top, 2 ft. at the bottom.

Depth   16 ft.

Contents   At 3 ft. 6 in., a small piece of Castor ware; at 15 ft., a sword standing upright; also, pottery vessels, two chisels, a hoe, four hub rings for wheels, two nails with large flat heads, an anchor-shaped iron mounting and other objects.

Pit XVI

Diameter   7 ft. at surface, 2 ft. at the bottom.

Depth   22 ft.

Contents   At 20 ft. a collection of 94 pieces of metal which include a sword blade, five spearheads, four axes, five hammers, two pairs of tongs, a smith's 'drift,' a small anvil, two chisels, two gouges, an axe, a mower's anvil, four scythes, a triple link with three chains attached, a linchpin, 24 nave bands for wheels, three hub linings, twenty pieces of wrought iron and so on. Amongst these objects was part of a human skull. Also found were an oak plank and a large urn of black ware.

Pit XVII

Diameter   6 ft. 6 in. at the top, 4 ft. 10 in. at the bottom.

Depth   31 ft. 9 in.

Contents   The top of the pit was 'sealed' with a mass of clay beneath which was dark-coloured matter. Near the surface a small piece of Castor ware was found. In the first 18 ft., the bones of nine horses; at 18 ft. 9 in. the skeleton of a dwarf lay across the pit; below the skeleton the skull of a dog, the skull of an ox, fragments of leather and many oyster shells. Also found were bricks, portions of flue tiles and fragments of terra sigillata; a large iron hammer, a small saw, an iron stylus and a finger ring; oyster shells; and many hazel nuts.

Pit XXII
Diameter   8 ft. 6 in. at the top, 10 ft. at the bottom.
Depth   23 ft.
Contents   'At a depth of 8 ft. the usual black deposit began,' the deposit containing many twigs among which hazel was identified. At 8 ft. a small fragment of terra sigillata was found, and at 10 ft. the skull of a horse; at 14 ft., an iron sickle and a crude iron armlet. There followed the skull of a dog, antlers of red deer and portions of amphorae and, at 17 ft., a well-preserved quern. Between 18 ft. and 20 ft. were two bridle bits of iron, an iron helmet with a visor in the form of a human face, nine bronze discs and other bronze objects, 'a brass helmet and an iron helmet,' the ear-piece of yet another helmet, and pottery.

Pit XXIII
Diameter   8 ft. at the top, 10 ft. at the bottom.
Depth   30 ft.
Contents   At 10 ft., a pair of red deer antlers, a piece of a terra sigillata bowl and part of a quern stone. Then *standing upright* in the pit was a branch of birch 9 ft. long. At 20 ft. the skulls of two horses and some pieces of oak; at 21 ft. two more portions of querns and a large square brick. At 22 ft. two wooden wheels one on top of the other; a little to the south of these a human skull with a cut in it lay beside a bucket with birch branches above. At 23 ft. 9 in., an oak bucket with iron hoops and mountings; thereafter a horse skull, the skulls of five dogs, and a number of red deer antlers. Also found were an axe head and fragments of material.

Pit XXIV
Diameter   10 ft. at the top, 3 ft. at the bottom.
Depth   14 ft.
Contents   Among other items fragments of terra sigillata and black ware; the skull of a dog; a raven's beak; and the leg bone of a cock.

Pit LVI
Diameter   5 ft. at the top, 4 ft. at the bottom.
Depth   16 ft.
Contents   In the pit, which was very full of vegetable matter, were found the skulls of two dogs; the skull of an ox; the skull of a horse, and other bones. Among other finds were the base of a platter and other pottery, two rings of iron, a wooden spindle, and a bone pin terminating in a human bust.

Pit LVII
Diameter   17 ft. by 18 ft. at the top; 8 ft. by 5 ft. 6 in. at the bottom.
Depth   21 ft.
Contents   At 12 ft., a piece of pottery and a human skull, a piece of charred oak beam, a bronze pot and the bronze handle of a tankard. Beneath these a sword bent double and with a bone hilt, a small sword and a bronze mounting. At 15 ft. a bronze helmet mask, an iron lamp, a hub ring, another sword. At 19 ft. 6 in., two bronze pots; at 20 ft., a bronze ewer. Other pottery was found; animal bones were scarce.

Pit LVIII
Diameter   7 ft. at the top, 3 ft. 6 in. at the bottom.
Depth   19 ft. 6 in.
Contents   These include an iron sword the upper part of which was bent over the blade; a piece of brass embossed with a late Celtic [*sic*] design, a bronze terret, part of a much corroded brass coin, a small lead cup, other metal objects, and pottery.

Pit LXV
Section   6 ft. by 7 ft. 6 in. at the top; 3 ft. 6 in. by 4 ft. 3 in. at the bottom.
Depth   17 ft.
Contents   Amongst other items a small horn object, and a coin, a fibula spring, a hinge, a loop and a surgeon's probe, all of brass. At the bottom were an iron hanging lamp, a denarius, fragments of a black urn and other coarse pottery, and a spoke for a small wheel. In one corner of the pit an oaken steering oar 5 ft. 5 in. long stood upright.

Pit LXXXIX
Diameter   9 ft. at the top, 3 ft. 6 in. at the bottom.
Depth   16 ft.
Contents   These included the neck of an amphora and other pottery fragments, a well-made whetstone, an iron hoe, shoes, and pieces of leather, bones of oxen and horses, and the complete, well-preserved skull of a dog.

Pit XCII
Diameter   5 ft. at the top, 2 ft. at the bottom.
Depth   8 ft. 6 in.
Contents   The filling was mostly of sticky yellow clay, with great quantities of animal bones; there was no pottery. A circular disc of bronze was found; and, at the depth of 6 ft. 6 in., the figure of a horse in fine white terracotta.

   Many of the other pits excavated by Curle contained objects of interest to this study, including iron implements, skulls of horse and ox, hazel nuts, and quantities of fragmented pottery. The whole Newstead complex is deserving of a separate treatment, and the above descriptions are concerned only with those structures which appear to be most significant in relation to ritual.

   More pits, found in Well Meadow during the construction of a railway in 1846, clearly belong to the same complex.

NEWSTEAD, WELL MEADOW, Roxburghshire[51]

Character and Contents   Five or six large pits or shafts were found within a space about 30 yd. square. Two were steined, apparently with river stones. Among the large pits were fifteen or sixteen smaller pits, about 3 ft. in both depth and diameter; these were plastered over the sides and bottom with a lining of whitish clay 5 or 6 in. thick. The pits were filled with sherds, large oyster shells, skulls, bones and horns of deer, all mixed with black, foetid earth.

   The skeleton of a man standing up, with a spear beside him, was found in a pit situated southeast of the main group and measuring 3 ft. to 4 ft. in diameter and about 10 ft. in depth.

NORTHFLEET, Kent[52]

Situation   Found at a cement works situated north of New Barn Farm, between Northfleet and Swanscombe, and consisting of an oval chamber which was originally connected to the surface by a shaft that was destroyed by the workings.
Diameter   The oval chamber, 27 ft. 6 in. by 20 ft.
Depth   The oval chamber, 9 ft.; the shaft must have been about 37 ft. deep.
Character and Contents   Pottery was recovered from the infilling of the chamber and a complete, pear-shaped pottery vessel was found on the same level as a horse's skull. Eight groups of sherds were found at varying levels in the western half of the infilling. All the pottery found is of native manufacture and dates between the mid-first and mid-second century A.D. Parts of three roof tiles were also found. On a shelf at the east end of the chamber were 41 manufactured flint flakes, and several more were found in the infilling. Most of the animal bones and teeth recovered were found to have been purposefully placed. The animals seem first to have been dismembered and then put in different parts of the chamber. They were found in the following groups: dog, horse and sheep bones together with the skull of a large dog; the skull of a horse and an ox tooth; most of the skeleton of a fox with the skull missing, and a bird bone; the skull of the above fox, with bones of badger, bird, dog and sheep; the skull of a badger and the jaws of a dog; bones of badger, bird and horse; bones of hornless sheep, and a horse tooth; some bones and two skulls of sheep, some bird bones; horse, ox and sheep bones; bones of badger and horse, skulls of badger and sheep, jaw of ox; horse bones; skull of horse, ox tooth; horse, ox and sheep bones; skull of ox; skull and limb bones of hornless sheep, with the lower jawbone of an ox.

PLUMSTEAD, Kent[53]

Situation   A dene-hole leading to a cavity in the chalk.
Diameter   No measurement recorded.
Depth   Dene-hole 30 ft. deep, cavity in it about 30 ft. deep.
Character and Contents   At the bottom of the cavity were seven or eight Upchurch urns; part of an iron knife and an iron bell; oyster shells and burnt sticks. The remaining part of the shaft was filled with sherds and human and animal bones. No object later than the Romano-British period was found.

PURBERRY SHOT, EWELL, Surrey[54]

Situation   In the grounds of Purberry Shot, a house now demolished.

Diameter   No measurement recorded.

Depth   About 42 ft.

Character and Contents   Discovered and excavated in 1941, the shaft was found to have contained large quantities of pottery. From the top to a depth of 9 ft. the shaft was lined with chalk blocks with a backing of stiff yellow clay. A few almost complete pottery vessels, including a mortarium dating to about A.D. 120, were found in the upper 10 ft. Other objects found in the shaft included part of an iron brooch probably of pre-Roman date; an iron razor and blade, an iron knife and other objects of iron. The lowest few feet of the shaft widened as if to form a small chamber at the bottom.

RAMSGATE, Kent[55]

Situation   A shaft surrounded by seven pits was found in a chalk pit between 1876 and 1888.

Section   2 ft. 6 in. decreasing to 10 in. square.

Depth   115 ft.

Character and Contents   The pits contained potsherds, animal bones, oyster shells and fragments of thin bronze from a bucket-shaped cauldron. Roman sherds and coins were found near, but not in, the pits.

     The shaft, which was provided with footholds, was almost completely filled with flints. The lowest 30 in., however, contained alternate layers of earth, flints and bones, the last including *Bos longifrons*, dog, horse and roebuck, also pieces of iron. Romano-British sherds and a vessel shaped like a deep basin with lug handles. Near the bottom of the shaft were some stone slabs, one nearly circular measuring 2 ft. 6 in. in diameter and having a hole through the centre.

RICHBOROUGH, Kent[56]

Situation   Revealed when a railway was being constructed on the hill a short distance south of the Roman fort.

Diameter   No measurement recorded.

Depth   No measurement recorded.

Character and Contents   Several pits were found, filled with dark, rich mould impregnated with animal and vegetable matter, in which were portions of antlers, bones of boar, goat and sheep, potsherds and other objects.

ROTHERFIELD PEPPARD, Oxfordshire[57]

Situation   Pit discovered in 1675 during cleaning-out operations at the bottom of a pond near Blount's Court.

Diameter   No measurement recorded.

Depth   50 to 60 ft.

Character and Contents   Two broken Romano-British urns were found in the pit, together with a stag's head, fragments of blue and white substance, hazel nuts and many whole oak trunks.

SANDWICH, Kent (also referred to as EASTRY and HAMMILL)[58] (fig. 65; Pl. XII)

Situation   On a hilltop.

Diameter   A circular chamber 8 ft. in diameter in the bottom of which was a shaft 3 ft. in diameter.

Depth   Chamber, 4 ft. 3 in.; shaft, 71 ft.

Character and Contents   The chamber contained large quantities of fragmented Samian and Romano-British sherds. The mouth of the shaft was sealed by a 1 ft. layer of chalk lumps intermixed with similar pottery to that found in the chamber. The part of the shaft that had been sunk through chalk was lined with clay. The bottom of the shaft was saucer-shaped; and here was found a complete Belgic jar broken into small pieces. Near it were pieces of two other large vessels, apparently incomplete when set in position. The first 48 ft. of the shaft yielded sherds and animal remains. The shaft is dated by the excavator to about A.D. 100.

     At a distance of 44 ft. north of the shaft was a saucer-shaped hollow containing sherds, flints, bones of horse, ox, sheep or goat; antler of red deer; a group of horse's teeth; and part of a pipe-clay Venus figurine.

     There was also a small, circular pit, containing pottery, which had been largely dug away by the mechanical excavator prior to the archaeological excavation.

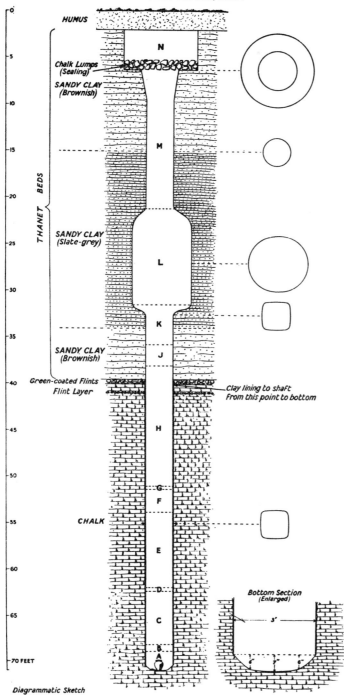

Figure 65. Section of shaft at Eastry, Sandwich, Kent.

SILCHESTER, Hampshire[59]
Situation   In the Roman town several pits and wells seem to show ritual characteristics but, like Caerwent, selection is sometimes problematical.
Diameters and Depths   Various.
Character and Contents   From the part of the town known as Insula I is recorded a pit which was found to contain a sword blade broken in two, and two iron bars, at a depth of 5 ft. from the surface. Below these was a collection of almost 60 iron objects.

In 1900 a second collection of iron objects, numbering over 100 pieces, was found in a well or shaft 21 ft. 7 in. deep.

In 1899 several wells or shafts and pits were found with intact pottery vessels in them. In one instance the well or shaft was completely filled up with clean gravel but had four perfect pottery vessels at the bottom. The excavators remarked upon the evidence for the deliberate placing of vessels in selected positions in shafts.

STONE, Buckinghamshire[60]
Situation   In the grounds of an asylum.
Diameter   No measurement recorded.
Depth   More than 19 ft.
Character and Contents   In about 1851 workmen found a shaft in which, at a depth of 8 ft. from the surface, they came upon 'a stratum of hard stone' through which a circular hole had been cut. Immediately beneath this was 'a chamber in which were many portions of cinerary urns some of which contained human bones,' together with the bones of some large animals and burnt oak and beech. The shaft continued for a further 11 ft. to a second and thicker stratum of rock beneath which was another chamber. This contained similar objects to the other but with the addition of the skull, teeth and one horn of an ox, a piece of skin, and burnt and unburnt wood. Twelve urns of various forms and sizes were found as well as two bronze rings and a bucket with iron hoops.

At about the same time workmen exposed a shaft 27 ft. deep in an adjacent sand pit. The only recorded discovery in this shaft is an urn at a depth of 15 ft. from the surface.

STROOD, Kent[61]
Situation   About a dozen pits were found near the parish church.
Diameter or Section   Some of the pits were square, others round, all 'about 4 ft. wide.'
Depth   About 10 ft.
Character and Contents   The pits were set closely together. Many objects were recovered from them, including several Samian vessels, plain and decorated, three Upchurch beakers, two indented beakers of black ware with granulated surfaces, a vase and fragments of Castor ware, a 'cauldron' of reddish clay, etc.; some coins and a bronze finger ring; iron knives and nails and a link of an iron chain, 'glass,' bone pins, a human skeleton, bones of deer, dog, ox and pig, and some oyster shells.

STURMINSTER MARSHALL, Dorset[62]
Situation   In the 'common field' of the parish.
Diameter   From 6 ft. to 8 ft.
Depth   From 8 ft. to 10 ft.
Character and Contents   Six pits were found in 1842. In one was a pot of coarse black ware broken, together with fragments of another vessel. On the floor of another portions of four or five vessels were found heaped together, with the skull of an ox and the skull of a dog. There were sherds in other pits.

'A pit discovered some few years ago at Littleton near Blandford by Mr Durden was, from the information received, in many respects analogous to those from Sturminster Marshall.'

WELLINGBOROUGH, Northamptonshire[63]
Situation   Found in digging for ironstone.
Diameter   No measurement recorded.
Depth   No measurement recorded.
Character and Contents   The pit, which was neatly lined with limestone, contained deer bones and several 'Roman ollae,' one perfect.

WINCHESTER, Hampshire[64]
Situation In the old parade field at the Barracks.
Diameter No measurement recorded.
Depth At least 130 ft.
Character and Contents During the construction of the railway in 1839–40 a series of pits or shafts was found, amongst them one of the depth recorded. This shaft was found to contain burnt wood, Romano-British pottery, bones and oyster shells.

WINTERBORNE KINGSTON, Dorset[65]
Situation Two shafts, in neighbouring fields.
Diameters *Shaft 1*, 8 ft.; *shaft 2*, 3 ft. 8 in.
Depth *Shaft 1*, bottom not reached at 70 ft.; *shaft 2*, 85 ft.
Character and Contents *Shaft 1*, which was steined to the depth of about 12 ft., contained one small pottery vessel complete and a great many sherds including hard black, grey and brown wares and Samian; several blocks of Kimmeridge shale; many iron nails, and ashes.

Shaft 2 contained a piece of sheet metal with the figure of a hare embossed upon it, a Purbeck marble vase, bronze fibulae and other ornaments, coins, iron nails, pieces of Kimmeridge shale and of glass, a mass of broken pottery, part of a quern, bones of dog, ox, pig and sheep, oyster shells, mould and flints.

At a point about 4 ft. east of *shaft 2*, and at a depth of 18 in. from the surface, an area measuring about 6 ft. in diameter was demarcated by eight burnt tiles of different sizes arranged edgeways at intervals of 10 in. from each other. In the centre was a small, conical sarsen stone, close to which lay an iron knife.

A *pit* measuring 6 ft. by 5 ft., and 4 ft. in depth, was found a few feet northeast of the circle. The pit contained 'about two cartloads' of broken pottery, flints and ashes.

WOLFHAMCOTE, Warwickshire (also called SAWBRIDGE)[66]
Situation Found in 1689.
Section 4 ft. square.
Depth Bottom not reached at 40 ft.
Character and Contents A large square stone with a hole in it, on which stood urns of grey ware, was found at a depth of 20 ft. Twelve of the urns were taken out intact and twelve others were broken by a fall of stone from above. The shaft became narrower as it got deeper, but the bottom was not reached.

WROXETER, Shropshire[67]
Situation Within the Roman town. Again it is difficult to differentiate between those having cult importance and those having none. The following seem to be significant.

Well 1
Diameter No measurement recorded.
Depth About 50 ft.
Character and Contents Recorded by Blakeway as being situated in a field near a smithy, and having 'an accumulation of potsherds and bones above it.'

Well 2
Diameter 2 ft. 3 in. at the top, 3 ft. at the bottom.
Depth 28 ft.
Character and Contents (Atkinson Well I) In the first 5 ft., clay, rough stones and sherds; in the next 5 ft., clay, stones and ox bones; from 20 ft. to 24 ft., large stones, some dressed; from 24 ft. to 28 ft., tiles, a large coarse pot and an iron axe.

Well 3
Diameter 2 ft. 9 in.
Depth 12 ft. 6 in.
Character and Contents Steined, and containing earth, building rubbish and potsherds; two iron knife-blades and some iron nails; a pair of bronze tweezers and a coin; and, at the depth of 8 ft., some animal bones. At the very bottom were three whole pots, with some flat pieces of oak.

WYCHWOOD, Oxfordshire[68]
Situation　On top of a hill near a spring in Slate Pit Copse.
Diameter　No measurement recorded.
Depth　No measurement recorded.
Character and Contents　A stone-lined shaft which narrowed as it deepened. It contained bones of boar and sheep, and bones and horns of *Bos longifrons*; sherds of grey and Samian pottery, iron nails and a billhook, and oyster shells.

This alphabetical list of the shafts, pits and wells in Britain which have a presumptively votive and ritual significance does not claim to be exhaustive, but the remarkable uniformity of features found, irrespective of the depth or form of the shaft in question, gives a firm basis for suggested interpretation and analysis.

The careful lining of shafts, sometimes with elaborate detail such as pebble, flint or tile inlays, the deposits of metal objects, among them the iron knives, the oyster shells, human and animal heads, carefully arranged single or multiple vessels, coins, all these impress by their persistent occurrence. The number of dogs and dog skulls is also noteworthy; the Celtic mallet god Sucellos, 'The Good Striker,' has the dog as his attribute, and Nodons of Lydney is clearly connected with dogs. A bronze votive dog was recovered from Coventina's well at Carrawburgh; and the Irish and Welsh tales, especially the Irish, have numerous examples of dogs in mythological contexts. The ancient Irish custom of giving many of the semi-divine heroes dog epithets (*Cú* Roí, *Cú* Chulainn) also suggests the early veneration of the animal and its role in cult legends.

Bones of hare and cock seem to bear out Caesar's statement as to the sanctity of these animals in Britain.[69] Dio Cassius, moreover, tells us that Boudicca released a hare in honour of her goddess Andrasta.[70] The pieces of matted hair found in two of the shafts at Ipswich, both of an animal such as the hare and both at a depth of 20 ft., are suggestive of the deliberate placing of such a beast in the shafts, and point towards sacrifice.

The presumably ritual bending in two of swords and spears, and the bars of iron and lead, which occur in the shafts, the quantities of worn-out or fragmented iron goods, especially the tools of a smith, the strange smooth stones, often two in number and sometimes subjected to fire, these likewise are all suggestive of cult.

We cannot hope to offer full interpretations or explanations for all the strange and frequently baffling features of these shafts and pits, any more than this can be done for other aspects of archaeology. What we can do is to examine them in the light of known Celtic cult practice; we can then see a certain intelligibility and a reasonable hope of at least a limited interpretation emerging. The human skulls, the dog remains, the heads of ravens, the smooth stones, the smashed pottery, the bronze vessels at the bottom of votive wells, the venerated weapons, the equipment of the divine smith, the votive hazel nuts and acorns, the sacred trees, the full equipment for the otherworld feast, the animals sacrificed for prognostication and other ritual purposes, all these can be found regularly in Celtic religion.[71] An examination of the extant material for the religious cults of the Celts shows striking parallels, and suggests explanations and interpretations for features which are otherwise confused and meaningless.

The problems involved in understanding the great complex of pits at Newstead, so many of which are so clearly of a ritual character, are considerable. It is extraordinary to find the annexe of a Roman fort full of such structures, many of which even the excavators could not dismiss as mere rubbish pits. It may be debated whether the whole adjacent unexcavated area may not also be full of pits; in which case we should have a great complex such as is known to have occurred elsewhere, for example, at Great Chesterford, Essex, or Lossow, Prussia,[72] and other places. Whether these were the work of the Selgovae, whose largest hill-fort was on Eildon Hill North overlooking the site, and whose cult centre (Segloes) this may have been,[73] or whether it was due to a Belgic element either serving in the Roman army at Newstead or having settled in the area prior to the coming of the Romans, we do not know. But it is sufficient to say that, extraordinary although many not only of the deposits, but of the actual groupings in the shafts, may seem, in each instance they can be seen to make sense in terms of native cults. The drama of a spear-bearing warrior standing upright in a shaft at Newstead

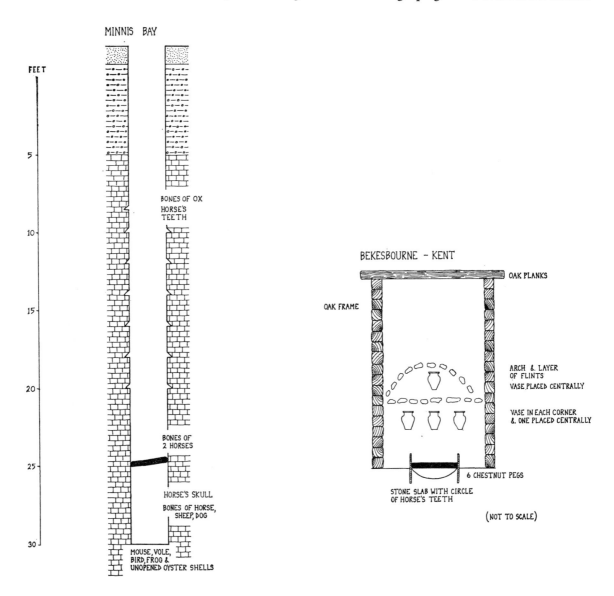

Figure 66. Section of shaft at Minnis Bay (Birchington) and Bekesbourne.

seems to echo the tradition of the Old Irish King Loegaire, son of Niall, whose body was buried standing upright in the ramparts of his own fortress, facing southwards, his spear and shield beside him.[74]

An examination of both structure and content indicates that we are dealing with phenomena and religious attitudes which are as widespread and deep-seated amongst the Celts as are such particular cults as that of the human head, evidence of which is also abundant in these structures. In the above examples we seem to be confronted with a regional development of religious practice in which the shaft, pit or well is the focus of ritual and the recipient of offering. This is paralleled widely in Europe and, over and above a more general evidence for the cult of wells and sacred pools, there is an astonishing identity both of structure and of content in many of the shafts and pits described by Schwarz and others.

The fact that these Iron Age and Roman shafts can be shown to have a widespread ancestry in Europe in general does indeed open up possible lines of inquiry into the origin and development of Celtic cults, and the marked regional peculiarities of such structures in the British Isles would seem to be explicable in terms of tribal settlement and individual religious expression. Like so much else, owing both to the lateness of the written tradition in Ireland and to the fact that since literature was sponsored by the Christian Church, paganism was censored and suppressed, little of direct evidence for the use of structures like these in religious ritual is to be obtained. But the mythological origin of certain literary motifs and characters is from time to time apparent, while it is certainly irrefutable that wells were worshipped, ritual conducted beside them, and heads were severed and flung into them, often magically embuing the waters with extra powers. Fertility, severed heads and sacred waters, then, are regularly associated with each other.[75]

But over and above this general evidence for the veneration of springs and the placing of pottery and heads in them, there are one or two literary instances which appear to be more specific, and suggest that such shafts and pits as those from Britain, with their fertility-ritual connections, were known in some form or other. One particular episode, in a story where the mythological elements are predominant, is worth consideration. It is the account of the entry of the Dagda, the *Good God*, into the camp of the enemy, the Fomorians, to ask for a truce. Upon the granting of the truce a feast is prepared for him. This consists of a huge mess of porridge which is made in the gigantic cauldron of the Fomorian king. The porridge contains four score gallons of fresh milk and a similar amount of meal and fat; goats and pigs and sheep are put into it, and the whole mess is boiled up. There is a hole in the ground into which the contents of the cauldron are poured. 'Then the Dagda took his ladle, and it was big enough for a man and woman to lie on the middle of it.' The Dagda eats every scrap of his huge meal, and 'then at the end he puts his curved finger over the bottom of the hole, among mould and gravel.'[76] This description of a ritual feast eaten from a pit by a well-attested Irish pagan god in a tale containing many mythological features is suggestive of the type of cult legend which may have given rise to the ritual involved in creating the vast shafts and pits into which were thrown whole pigs, goats and sheep, animal fat, cereal and vessels.

There are many other hints in the vernacular literatures of the British Isles about belief in the well, cave or burial mound as entrances to the pagan otherworld, and stories are extant which describe the entry of a god or a hero into the territory of the supernatural beings by jumping down a well shaft, or entering a cave in a hill-side. Seymour,[77] in considering the cave on St Patrick's Purgatory, an island in Lough Derg, Co. Donegal, from the viewpoint of early Irish Christian *vision* literature, makes an interesting comment. He says, 'It seems probable that in pre-Christian, perhaps even in pre-Celtic, times the cave or pit in the little island in Lough Derg was a well-known heathen sanctuary where, it may be, oracles were delivered or communication was established with a world beneath the earth, or a deity worshipped, of which the bird-like demon *Cornu* was but a pale image.'

Continental parallels for the shafts in Britain are numerous and impressive. For our purposes, one or two complexes of shafts and pits are of particular importance in that they seem to cast light on ritual analogous to that which we presume was practised in and about the insular structures. Although the sanctuary recently discovered at Libenice, in Czechoslovakia,[78] for example, does not contain deep shafts, excavations have revealed a great number of pits, filled with smashed pottery and with bones derived from human and animal sacrifices. The ritual nature of the enclosure has been demonstrated conclusively, and the excavators commented on the extremely fragmented nature of the pottery which, they suggest, was smashed for ritual purposes. This is well supported by the insular evidence. At Libenice the skull of an adult human was found, as in so many of the British shafts and pits, and the animal bones include those of bulls, dogs (two), goats, pigs and sheep. In stating that the association of ideas between pits and fertility and funerary rites is clear, the excavators mention that here there is full evidence for sacrifice within a pit or ditch. This is precisely what the evidence from Britain suggests.

A second group of pits which finds close parallels in Britain is that from Trelleborg,[79] Denmark, found underneath houses of the Viking period. Both wells and pits were found, and traces of ritual enclosures beside them, recalling, for example, that at Winterborne Kingston. Nørlund says, 'One can surmise that sacrificial rites took place within these small round enclosures, and that afterwards the sacrificed human beings and animals were brought out of the doorways and thrown into the sacrificial wells nearby.' Nørlund also states that after the construction of the Viking period fortress at Trelleborg, two of the ritual wells appear to have been cleaned out and used as water wells; and this is what we surmise must have been the case in certain instances in Roman Britain, especially in towns such as Caerwent, Silchester and Wroxeter, where much is suggestive of ritual in connection with the pits and wells while other features seem to indicate functional use, probably at a later stage.

Again, at Lossow,[80] in Prussia, many shafts were found, measuring from 15 feet to 24 feet in depth and dating to about 700 B.C. The shafts were filled with clay layers in which were found the remains of human beings, cattle and horses. Some 60 pits were recorded, but Schuchhardt suggests that if the area were completely cleared the total would probably be nearer 500. More parallels could be cited, but in this context one other will serve to underline the widespread and ritual nature of such shafts and pits. In 1880 two small temples were excavated on a hill-top near Poitiers,[81] France. Their resemblance to the Silchester temples includes east-facing entrances. Near the temples a shaft 120 feet deep was found within a walled enclosure. Many objects of the kinds described above were brought up from the shaft, including a bronze vessel bearing a votive inscription to *Mercurius Adsmerius*, a local Celtic deity equated with Mercury. Worship on hill-tops is well known in Celtic contexts, as is the belief that hills led down into the dwellings of the gods. Presumably it was believed that by digging a deep shaft down into a hill the worshippers were brought nearer to divine territory, and invocations were more likely to be observed and accepted by the gods.

It has been suggested recently[82] that the scene on the Gundestrup cauldron in which a deity appears to be thrusting a man into a cauldron shows, in fact, not a cauldron but an offer-shaft; and this interpretation is based on the fact that the soldiers in the scene are carrying a complete tree, with roots intact, towards the sacrificial structure. In view of the numerous examples from Europe and from Britain of the presence of trees and large branches deep in ritual shafts and pits, this indeed seems a possible interpretation; it is strengthened by the representation of a terrier-type dog leaping up at the side of the deity; we have seen that numerous examples of dog remains are recorded in shafts. But we must not forget that there is good evidence both for ritual drowning in cauldrons and for cauldrons of regeneration, belonging to gods, which had the power to restore dead warriors to life. The sacred tree likewise has its own widespread popularity in Celtic cults; so the scene could be interpreted equally well in either of the above ways.

Although there is then nothing from the vernacular literature which points directly and unequivocally to a knowledge of ritual shafts of the kind we are considering, there is sufficient evidence of a general kind to show that in the concept of the sanctity of certain wells, caves, pools, and burial mounds, we have beliefs which are found throughout the Celtic world and which seem to reflect those expressed in the form of offer-shafts. But we also know that an archaism prevailed in many parts of Britain as well as in Ireland, and the very elaborate and sophisticated nature of the deep shafts, the carefully constructed pits and votive wells, is in keeping with what we know of the general differences in material culture between the insular and the Continental Celts, and their relative degrees of sophistication. It is not therefore surprising to find that the distribution of shafts, pits and wells of a presumptively votive character is so markedly in *Belgic* Britain, and that it coincides so strikingly with the distribution of Romano-Celtic temples and that of villas (fig. 67). The fact that the earlier shafts and pits, too, come from this same area suggests that the Belgic Britons were carrying on and elaborating a tradition which had its roots in Bronze Age Britain and, perhaps, in the entire early Indo-European world. The outliers in the north may, as we have seen, be due to the presence of Belgic elements either serving in the Roman army or coming as settlers shortly before the Roman encroachment. There is plenty of evidence to suggest that soldiers in the Roman army, many of whom were Celts, did not spurn the power of local deities and ritual customs, but rather that, after reconciling the strange powers with their own 'official' gods, they carried out ritual in the manner of the natives.

Analysis of the nature, distribution and contents of shafts, pits and wells of an apparent votive and ritual import in Britain leads to the conclusion that they were particularly manifestations of Belgic British religious belief, the underlying mythology being common to the whole Celtic world but receiving individual and striking material expression in the Belgic areas of Britain. These sites, with associated structures, may then be regarded as the true sanctuaries of the Belgic Britons, with possible direct Druidic associations, at which ritual of a powerful and elaborate nature was practised.

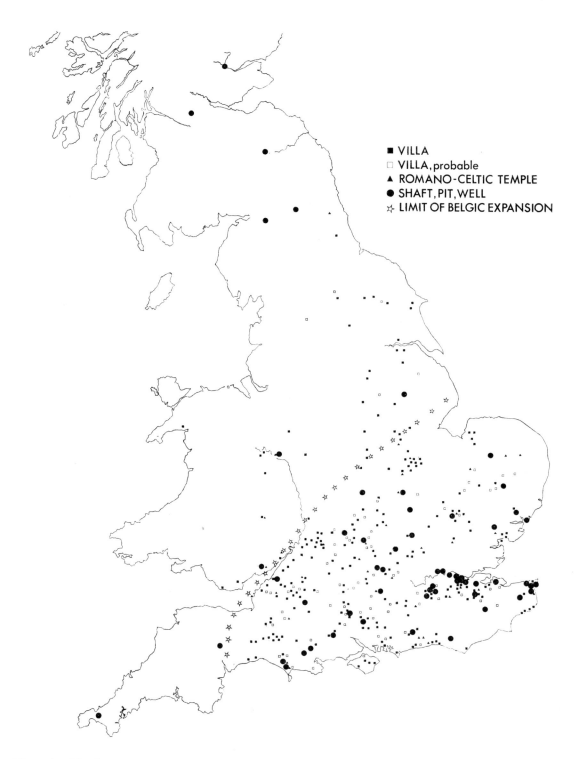

Figure 67. Distribution of shafts, pits and wells, Romano-Celtic temples, and villas.

Acknowledgments: I wish to express my warmest gratitude to Major J. P. T. Burchell, F.S.A., for generously placing at my disposal all his own excavation notes and illustrations, and his notes and references to comparative material; as well as for kind permission to publish the photographs on Pls. XI, bottom and XII, bottom. My especial thanks are also due to my husband, R. W. Feachem, for originals of the line drawings and the map, and for constant help at every stage of the work. Pl. XII, top appears by permission of the British Museum, and Pl. XI, top by permission of the Suffolk Institute of Archaeology and Natural History.

Appendix

	Animal bones, teeth	Ashes	Associated structures	Bars of iron, lead	Bird skulls, bones, etc.	Bronze objects	Buckets, whole or parts	Burnt stone, flints	Clay or chalk lining or packing	Coins	Cult objects	Deer antlers, bones, etc.	Dog skulls, bones, etc.	Goat skulls, bones, etc.	Hare skulls, bones, etc.	Horse skulls, bones, etc.	Human skulls, bones, etc.	Iron knives	Iron nails	Iron objects, bent	Iron objects, various	Metal weapons, helmets, etc.	Organic matter	Ornamental objects, various	Ox skulls, bones, etc.	Oyster shells	Pig skulls, bones, etc.	Pins – bronze, bone	Potsherds	Pottery vessels, whole or almost whole	Quern stones	Sandals, pieces of leather	Smooth stones	Trees, whole or large parts	Twigs, leaves, acorns, nuts, stones, seeds
Ardleigh	×								×		×					×							×						×						×
Armsley	×					×		×		×	×	×				×		×	×		×		×		×				×	×	×	×		×	×
Ashill 1	×		×			×	×				×					×		×			×				×	×			×	×	×			×	×
Ashill 2											×														×							×		×	
Ashill pit	×												×																×						
Ashtead 1	×																												×						
Ashtead 2	×																												×						
Asthall 1	×		×			×					5																		×	×					
Asthall 2			×																										×						
Asthall pit																		×			×							×	×						
Aylesford	×						×		×		×																		×						
Bar Hill	×		×							×	×	×									×				×	×			×	×				×	×
Bedford	×							×																					×						
Bekesbourne 1				'													×												×					×	
Bekesbourne 2																													×						
Bertha		×		×																		×	×						×					×	
Biddenham	×			×						×			×			×													×						
Birchington	×		×											×											×	×			×					×	
Bossens	×		×			×							×												×							×	×		×
Brampton							×																×	×											
Brislington	×		×			×											×												×	×					
Cadbury Castle	×	×	×			×			×								×	×						×					×						×
Caerwent 1	×		×				×		×	×							×																	×	×
Caerwent 2	×		×				×		×								×									×									
Caerwent 2a			×								5																								
Caerwent 2b			×										×																						
Caerwent 3	×						×														×								×	×				×	

	Animal bones, teeth	Ashes	Associated structures	Bars of iron, lead	Bird skulls, bones, etc.	Bronze objects	Buckets, whole or parts	Burnt stone, flints	Clay or chalk lining or packing	Coins	Cult objects	Deer antlers, bones, etc.	Dog skulls, bones, etc.	Goat skulls, bones, etc.	Hare skulls, bones, etc.	Horse skulls, bones, etc.	Human skulls, bones, etc.	Iron knives	Iron nails	Iron objects, bent	Iron objects, various	Metal weapons, helmets, etc.	Organic matter	Ornamental objects, various	Ox skulls, bones, etc.	Oyster shells	Pig skulls, bones, etc.	Pins – bronze, bone	Potsherds	Pottery vessels, whole or almost whole	Quern stones	Sandals, pieces of leather	Smooth stones	Trees, whole or large parts	Twigs, leaves, acorns, nuts, stones, seeds
Caerwent 4											×										×														
Caerwent pit																				×									×						
Calke Wood			×					×	×													×							×						
Carrawburgh	×		×			×				×	×	×					×				×				×		×	×	×	×					
Crayford	×																				×					×			×						
Danebury Hill	×		×											×															×						
Darenth																							×											×	
Dunstable	×									×							×												×					×	
Ewell (8)	×				×	×						×	×		×		×	×			×				×	×	×		×	×				×	×
Felixstowe	×																												×					×	×
Frittenden																													×					×	
Great Chesterford (45)			×		×	×			×		×		×						×		×				×	×			×						
Greenhithe	×				×				×		×								×	×	×								×				×		
Hardham 1												×	×												×		×		×	×		×	×	×	
Hardham 2														×	×								×		×			×	×	×		×			
Hardham 3																									×				×	×					
Hardham 4												×									×								×					×	
Hardham 5												×									×								×					×	
Hardham 6												×									×								×						
Heywood																×	×								×				×						
Ipsden																																			×
Ipswich 1																	×												×						
Ipswich 2							×			×							×				×														
Isle of Thanet	×						×					×	×	×		×		×			×				×		×		×						
Jordon Hill		×	×		×			×		×						×			×		×	×								×					
Kidlington	×		×													×													×	×					
Lincoln	×																												×						
London 1						×				×											×								×	×					
London 2																			×		×														
Maiden Castle (7)	×		×																										×						
Mount Caburn			×	×								×		×							×				×	×	×		×						
Newstead I	×		×	×								×	×	×		×	×	×				×	×	×	×				×						
Newstead VII	×		×		×											×						×	×			×			×						×
Newstead XIV			×								×					×						×	×	×					×	×					
Newstead XVI			×															×	×					×					×	×				×	
Newstead XVII			×						×							×	×				×			×	×	×			×			×			×
Newstead XXII			×			×						×	×			×					×			×	×	×	×		×				×		×
Newstead XXIII			×					×				×	5			×	×				×	×		×					×			×			×
Newstead XXIV			×	×							×										×								×						
Newstead LVI	×		×								×					×					×			×	×					×	×				

	Animal bones, teeth	Ashes	Associated structures	Bars of iron, lead	Bird skulls, bones, etc.	Bronze objects	Buckets, whole or parts	Burnt stone, flints	Clay or chalk lining or packing	Coins	Cult objects	Deer antlers, bones, etc.	Dog skulls, bones, etc.	Goat skulls, bones, etc.	Hare skulls, bones, etc.	Horse skulls, bones, etc.	Human skulls, bones, etc.	Iron knives	Iron nails	Iron objects, bent	Iron objects, various	Metal weapons, helmets, etc.	Organic matter	Ornamental objects, various	Ox skulls, bones, etc.	Oyster shells	Pig skulls, bones, etc.	Pins – bronze, bone	Potsherds	Pottery vessels, whole or almost whole	Quern stones	Sandals, pieces of leather	Smooth stones	Trees, whole or large parts	Twigs, leaves, acorns, nuts, stones, seeds
Newstead LVII	×		×			×											×			×	×	×	×						×	×				×	
Newstead LVIII			×			×				×										×			×						×	×					
Newstead LXV			×			×				×	×										×		×	×					×						
Newstead LXXXIX			×									×				×					×		×		×				×				×		
Newstead XCII	×		×			×		×		×													×												
Newstead, Well Meadow pits	×		×				×			×							×				×	×	×		×				×						
Northfleet	×			×				×				×				×										×			×	×					
Plumstead	×																	×	×		×						×		×	×					×
Purberry Shot								×											×		×			×					×	×					
Ramsgate	×					×	×					×			×											×			×	×					
Richborough	×									×			×										×					×							
Rotherfield Peppard										×																				×				×	×
Sandwich	×						×			×	×		×			×									×				×	×					
Silchester pit				×																×	×														
Silchester 1900 well																					×														
Silchester 1899 wells, pits																														×					
Stone, pit																														×					
Stone, well	×					×	×										×							×	×				×	×				×	
Strood	×					×		×		×	×							×	×	×		×		×	×	×	×	×	×	×					
Sturminster Marshall												×													×				×	×					
Wellingborough	×						×																						×	×					
Winchester	×																									×			×					×	
Winterborne Kingston 1			×															×											×	×					
Winterborne Kingston 2	×		×			×				×	×	×			×			×							×	×	×	×	×	×	×				
Winterborne Kingston circle																	×																		
Winterborne Kingston pit			×					×																						×					
Wolfhamcote																																		×	
Wroxeter 1	×																													×					
Wroxeter 2																					×				×				×	×					
Wroxeter 3	×					×				×								×	×										×	×				×	
Wychwood	×																	×			×					×	×	×		×					

Notes

1. O'Rahilly, *Early Irish History and Mythology* (1946) 117 ff.
2. *Ant. J.* X (1930) 30–3
3. *Arch. J.* XXXVIII (1871) 391–409
4. *W.A.M.* XVIII (1879) 319–59
5. Baudry and Ballereau, *Puits funéraires gallo-romains du Bernard (Vendée)* (1873)
6. *Jahresbericht der bayerischen Bodendenkmalpflege* (1962) 22–7
7. *Ant. J.* XLIII (1963) 286–7
8. *Antiquity* XL (1966) 227–8
9. *A.N.L.* IX (1949) 13
10. *Colchester Archaeology Group Quarterly Bulletin* VIII (1965) 30–8
11. *Proceedings of the Hampshire Field Club and Archaeological Society* X (1931) 56–62
12. *Arch J.* XXXII (1875) 108; XLVI (1889) 352
13. *Sy.A.C.* XLI (1933) 93 ff.
14. *Oxon.* XIX–XX (1954–5) 29 ff.
15. *Arch.* LII (1890) 317 ff.
16. *P.S.A.S.* XL (1905–6) 410 ff.
17. *P.S.A.* (2) III (1864–7) 305
18. *A.C.* II (1859) 43–8
19. Stuart, *Caledonia Romana* (2nd ed. 1852) 205
20. *Bedfordshire Architectural and Archaeological Society* (1857) 283–90
21. *A.N.L.* IX (1949) 52; *A.C.* LI (1940) 191–4
22. Borlase, *Antiquities of the County of Cornwall* (1769) 316
23. *C. & W.* LXVI (1966) 1–36
24. Barker, *An Account of the Remains of a Roman Villa discovered at Brislington, Bristol, 1899*; published by the City Museum, Bristol (1901)
25. *Arch. J.* V (1848) 193–8; *T.D.A.* LXXXIV (1952) 105 ff.
26. *Arch.* LVIII (1902) 133; LIX (1905) 295; LX (1906) 122, 123, 462
27. *P.S.I.* XXVIII (1958–60) 1–28
28. *Arch. Ael.* VIII (1880) 1–39
29. *V.C.H.* Kent III, 146
30. *P.S.A.* (1) IV (1856–9) 241
31. *V.C.H.* Kent III, 146
32. *V.C.H.* Bedfordshire II, 6 ff.
33. *Arch.* XXXII (1847) 451–5
34. *Arch. J.* XXXI (1874) 303
35. *V.C.H.* Kent III, 146
36. *Arch. J.* XII (1855) 109–26; XIII (1856) 1–13; XVII (1860) 117–27
37. *Arch. J.* XXXVII (1880) 193–5
38. *Sx.A.C.* XVI (1864) 52 ff.
39. *V.C.H.* Wiltshire I, 76
40. Price, *Roman Antiquities* (1873) 37
41. *P.S.I.* XXII (1935) 141–9
42. *Journal of the Ethnological Society of London* I (1868–9) 1–12
43. *Abstracts of the Proceedings of the Ashmolean Society* II (1843–52) 55
44. *V.C.H.* Oxfordshire I, 339
45. *L.A.A.S.* IX (1961) 109; *Arch. J.* V (1848) 197; XIX (1862) 169–71
46. Price, *op. cit.* (1873) 31
47. Smith, *Antiquities of Richborough, Reculver and Lymne in Kent* (1850) 55
48. Warne, *Ancient Dorset* (1872) 80
49. *Arch.* XLVI (1881) 423 ff.; *Sx.A.C.* LXVIII (1927) 1 ff.
50. Curle, *A Roman Frontier Post* (1911) 47 ff.
51. *Archaeologia Scotica* IV (1867) 424
52. From J. P. T. Burchell's excavation notes

53. *J.B.A.A.* XLVII (1891) 88; *P.S.A.* (2) XIII (1891) 245; *Arch. Camb.* XXI (1910) xlviii
54. *Sy.A.C.* XLVII (1941) xxv; L (1949) 9–46
55. *V.C.H.* Kent III, 146
56. Smith, *op. cit.* (1850) 55
57. *V.C.H.* Oxfordshire I, 339
58. *A.N.L.* IX (1949) 13; and J. P. T. Burchell's notes
59. *Arch.* LII (1890) 742, 743; LIV (1894) 139–56; LVII (1900) 96 f., 247
60. *Arch.* XXXIV (1852) 21–32
61. *V.C.H.* Kent III, 146
62. Warne, *op. cit.* 330
63. Price, *op. cit.* (1873) 37
64. *V.C.H.* Hampshire and the Isle of Wight I, 287
65. Warne, *op. cit.* 204; *P.D.N.H.* XI (1890) 1–6
66. *V.C.H.* Warwickshire I, 249
67. *V.C.H.* Shropshire I, 239; Blakeway MS. in Bodleian Library, No. 25, fol. 9.14; Wright, *Uriconium* (1872) 219; Bushe-Fox, *Research Reports of the Society of Antiquaries of London* (1912, 1913, 1914)
68. *V.C.H.* Oxfordshire I, 339
69. Caesar, *de Bello Gallico* V, 12
70. Dio Cassius LXII, 2
71. Ross, *Pagan Celtic Britain* (1967)
72. Schuchhardt, *Vorgeschichte von Deutschland* (1939) 165
73. Richmond (ed.), *Roman and Native in North Britain* (1958) 139
74. *Revue Celtique* XV (1894) 280
75. Ross, *Scottish Studies* VI (1962) 31–48
76. Stokes, *Revue Celtique* XII (1891) 87
77. Seymour, *Irish Visions of the Other-world* (1930) 177
78. Rybová and Soudský, *Libenice . . . Sanctuaire celtique en Bohême Centrale* (Praha, 1962)
79. Nørlund, *Trelleborg* (1948)
80. *ibid.*
81. *Memoires Soc. Antiq. de l'Ouest* X (1887) 487–95; *Arch.* LII (1890) 748
82. Kimmig, *Fundberichte aus Schwaben, neue folge* XVII (1965) 135–43

Hanging bowls

Elizabeth Fowler

To present the Abercromby Professor with yet another paper on hanging bowls would be inapposite were it not for the fact that a phrase by him in an article on the Royal Tombs of Alaca Hüyük,[1] 'its [the animal style of the north] influence is still perceptible in the animal art of our own Dark Ages and Early Christian period,' was the initial stimulus for my own interest in Dark Age problems. With the hope therefore that this essay into our barbarian past will fall within his spheres of study, I offer him my appreciation for his teaching, writing, encouragement and friendship.

This reconsideration of what has become, somewhat unnecessarily, one of the more controversial issues of the post-Roman period is an attempt to examine the evidence in a different way from that hitherto tried and to classify the bowls themselves along new lines. The paper is intended to be complementary to an earlier one, on the penannular brooches and associated metalwork,[2] and arguments there presented will not be repeated. The recent discovery, during controlled excavations, of two complete 'hanging bowls,' on St Ninian's Isle, Shetland, and Ford Down, near Salisbury,[3] and the publications of Professor Gunther Haseloff,[4] Dr Françoise Henry,[5] and Leslie Alcock,[6] make such a review of the subject opportune, for it is clear that no propounded solution is entirely satisfactory. I do not propose to make a detailed analysis of each hanging bowl and escutcheon, nor to summarize previous arguments. The former is the function of an illustrated corpus, an Inventaria of Hanging Bowls, which is sadly lacking from our shelves (I am grateful to R. L. S. Bruce-Mitford and Mrs A. Keiller for allowing me to see the list compiled by the British Museum). The latter, with principal references, has been provided by Haseloff.[7]

As most discussions of hanging bowls begin with an argument for their use as decorative hanging vases,[8] lamps,[9] hand-basins[10] or votive chalices,[11] it will be at least conventional to offer the alternative solution, already suggested by Leistol. 'And such was the King's concern for the welfare of his people, that in a number of places where he had noticed clear springs adjacent to the highway, he ordered posts to be erected with brass bowls hanging from them, so that travellers could drink and refresh themselves. And so great was the people's affection for him, and so great the awe in which he was held, that no one presumed to use these bowls for any other purpose.'[12] Bede was writing of the great Northumbrian King Edwin whose reign ended in the disasters of 633. This, presumably, is the reason for the lack of evidence of the wealthy monastic and secular culture that must have existed in Northumbria,[13] and for the few remains of hanging bowls found there. It is not impossible for some of the smaller bowls to have been used secondarily as drinking vessels or indeed as serving bowls, even if their original function was something totally different. The crab-apples and onions in the Ford bowl, and the sets of silver bowls with the St Ninian's Isle bowl and in the Sutton Hoo deposit, suggest both a culinary usage and a ceremonial meal.

While the Very Rev. Monsignor McRoberts' argument[14] that the Continental practice of presenting votive chalices to churches influenced the Celtic Church in the seventh and later centuries is convincing for the later bowls, two caveats need to be made against it. It is generally agreed that the hanging bowls originated in late Roman Britain[15] and that the first bowls could be of fifth- or even late fourth-century date (see below), well before the attested Continental practice of hanging votive chalices in churches. Nor need they necessarily be Christian at this date. Initially, therefore, the bowls must have had some other purpose or purposes. Even if we accept Edwin's order for the use of bowls as public drinking vessels, we should still have to explain why a Northumbrian adopted a British article. Perhaps they were purely utilitarian household objects, like their Romano-British forerunners, capable of adaptation to both ecclesiastical and secular usage, and as decorative or as plain as their makers chose.

Secondly, it is debatable whether these bowls could ever have hung from a height suspended on chains or cords. Examination of those escutcheons still fixed to the bowls shows that the 'mouth' of the animal merely rests on or against the rim of the bowl. The St Ninian's Isle Bowl is one of the few exceptions in that the escutcheons are riveted, not soldered (see below), but even here the boars' mouths are not fixed to the rim. The upward pull which would follow if the bowl were suspended would result in considerable pressure on the weakest part, the junction between animal mouth and rim (fig. 68b). It is worth recalling that the makers of iron- or bronze-bound wooden buckets in both Roman and Saxon times exercised considerable skill in securing the handles to the body of the vessel (fig. 69a), and so presumably could have done likewise with bronze bowls had they been intended for suspension. Furthermore, it is surely curious that, as far as I have been able to ascertain, none of the complete bowls have been found with any remains of chains which, had they existed, must have been substantial. Cords, if used, are unlikely to have survived.

It might, however, be possible to visualize the bowls suspended from three hooks at the top of a tripod (fig. 69b). The pull exerted would then be at an angle to the rim and the rings would rub against the neck of the escutcheon rather than the rim. Obviously every bowl should be examined to see if this is the case, and I have not found it possible to do so yet. I owe this idea to a pupil of Professor C. F. C. Hawkes, Herr Hayo Vierck,[15a] but the elaborations are my own. If the bowl was thus suspended from a tripod, it could be at a convenient height either for hand-washing, or for use as a ceremonial vessel, or even as a lamp, and so the internal decoration becomes understandable. It is arguable that the bronze 'lamp' from Ballinderry I Crannog was similarly suspended from a tripod, using the 'adjusting' hook and the two rings. It would, for one thing, be far easier to adjust the wick with the lamp at a reachable level. The Ballinderry 'lamp,' however, is later than most of the hanging bowls, is different in shape and function from all of them, and is only linked to them by the technique of manufacture and ornament. It cannot, therefore, be used as part of an argument for the use of fifth- and sixth-century bowls. Some do not accept it as a lamp, and McRoberts states that there is no evidence for lamps in Celtic churches.[16]

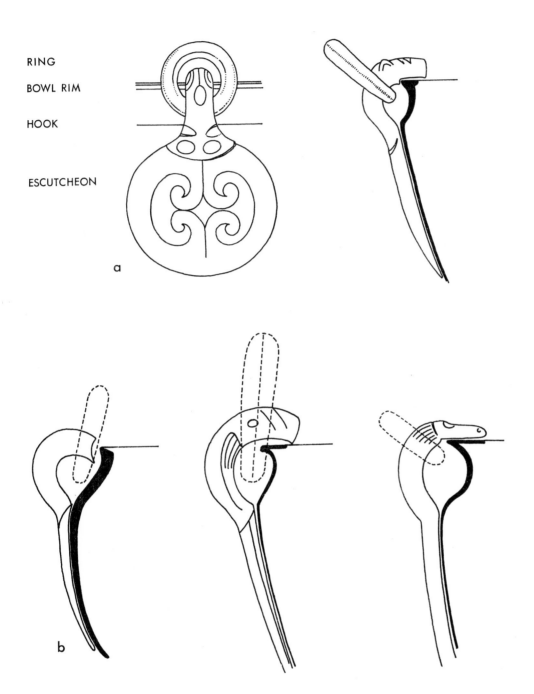

RING

BOWL RIM

HOOK

ESCUTCHEON

a

b

Figure 68. a. Principal parts of a hanging bowl escutcheon.
b. Rim types to illustrate problems of suspension.

The closest analogy to this method of tripod suspension is provided by the bowl and tripods seen on some Roman tombstones and altars and by the known Roman usage of wooden or metal folding tripods and bowls.[17] These folding ones could well have formed part of the religious 'kit' of an emperor or legionary commander on campaign, whence the idea could have passed into civil use. This is only a hypothesis as I have not been able to make a search for sculptural remains, but it accords well with other lines of evidence about borrowings from the Roman army and administration in the fourth and fifth centuries.[18]

Let us suppose that the bowls were used with tripods, but subsequently a new use for them was found which necessitated a strengthening of the rim; and this is precisely what we find on the rims of the much larger bowls deposited in Viking graves in Scandinavia, which are generally considered to be late eighth and ninth century in date. Both Kilbride-Jones and Dr F. Henry noted and carefully illustrated this rim-strengthening tendency (fig. 70) which culminated in the elaborate rims rolled round an iron wire – a trick developed in Ireland, it would seem, since the closest analogies to the escutcheons on the Viking deposited bowls are with Irish eighth-century metalwork.[19] Yet several of these bowls have plain 'archaic' escutcheons, like late Romano-British ones found in England.

Earlier solutions to the problem of the place of origin of the bowls and their makers still seem unsatisfactory. None of the typological series worked out by Kendrick, Kilbride-Jones, Dr Henry and Haseloff will easily accommodate new discoveries, whether their series are based on analysis of bowl shapes, or rim forms, or artistic motifs and techniques. The discovery of the bowls from Loveden Hill, Lincolnshire, suggests that Haseloff's arguments need modification.[20] The St Ninian's Isle silver bowl introduces new elements, combining a unique type of escutcheon with an 'older' rim form. (The existence of the Witham silver bowl, of which only drawings survive in the possession of the Society of Antiquaries, is now seen to be quite plausible, and clearly it and the St Ninian's Isle bowl are curious offshoots from the main run of hanging bowls.) The Ford Down bowl is close to the acknowledged late Romano-British examples, yet its last owner was probably buried in the seventh century.[21] The Hildersham bowl reminds us that it was perfectly possible for one bowl to have dissimilar escutcheons.[22] Two dissimilar escutcheons, like those from Stoke Golding which display allegedly 'early' and 'late' features, could actually belong to the same bowl and maker.[23] The original account of the discovery of these two pieces strongly suggests that there was one burial in the mound, and therefore only one bowl, from which the two escutcheons were removed. There is not even consistency in the techniques of making the bowls, spun and cast ones existing side by side. Escutcheons could either be soldered or riveted to the bowl. The Capheaton bowl has both riveted and soldered escutcheons;[24] the presumed early Wilton bowl and the late St Ninian's Isle one both have riveted escutcheons.[25] Finally, as is well known, the actual motifs used to decorate the escutcheons are a mixed bag, ranging from the late Roman provincial designs noted by Leeds and Kendrick, to the spirals of the Book of Durrow: exactly the mixture of motifs one might expect in the heterogeneous societies of Britain in the fifth and succeeding centuries.

To impose a coherent logical pattern on this mass of material is asking too much, and, one may ask, to what end? Perhaps in trying to construct a sequence, we have been imposing a modern concept of tidiness and order where none existed: obscuring, not clarifying the

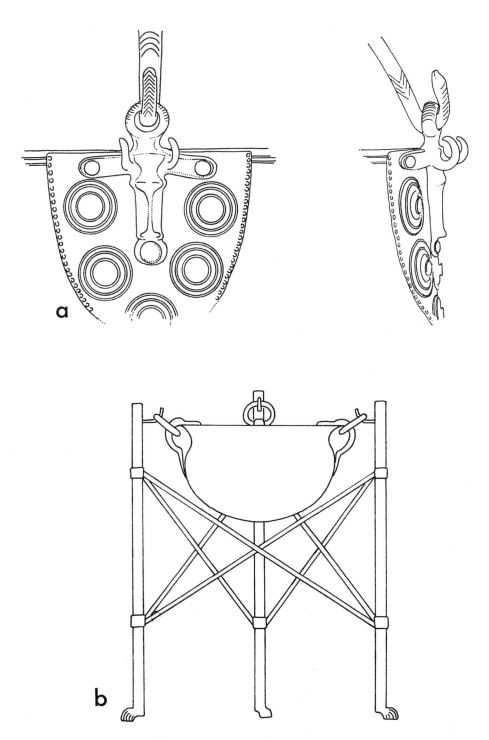

Figure 69. a. Suspension of a bucket handle (Mountsorrel, Leics.; after Hawkes).
b. Hypothetical suspension of a hanging bowl from a tripod.

situation. Leeds long ago made the acute observation that the bowls 'are the one thing found in Anglo-Saxon graves that neither date themselves nor the objects associated with them.' Professor Haseloff in the 1964 Rhind lectures indicated how all work on hanging bowls since 1898 has merely consisted of shuffling dates and bowls around. The time has surely come to consider the bowls themselves; not to prove, or disprove, any particular nationalistic, artistic or typological theories.

Thanks to the invaluable studies of Dr Henry[26] and Kilbride-Jones[27] in particular, it is possible to start any fresh discussion with a number of accepted premises. Professor C. F. C. Hawkes[28] confirmed Dr Henry's arguments for the existence of skilled bronze-smiths well into the fourth century, making both bowls and buckets. He also demonstrated how the use of animal-headed escutcheons was common to both vessels and might therefore be supposed to have influenced the hanging bowl escutcheon. The origin of the hanging bowl lies in these bronze, sometimes silver, vessels of the Roman period. Incidentally, the so-called silver hanging dish in the Traprain Treasure and its swan escutcheons have confused earlier commentators. It is clear that no chains were used but instead a rectangular handle was hooked through the out-bent swans' heads on each side. Curle himself noted this when discussing two of the similar but separate escutcheons in the Treasure.[29] The shell-shaped bowl is so shallow ($2\frac{1}{2}$ inches overall height) as to make its suspension improbable if filled with water, and it has been provided with a foot-ring for standing. The handles are for carrying or are merely decorative.

Late-Roman bowls, like Finningley and Irchester, had rims which were slightly thickened and inclined inwards; the hooks were either cast in the form of birds or animals with triangular or heater-shaped escutcheons. Alternatively the hook was bent outwards and given a more oval escutcheon, often ending in a circular appendage. The number of escutcheons per bowl was either three or four, and decoration on them was limited to the emphasizing of the animal features. Parallel features can be noted on the contemporary pins and penannular brooches. It was this type of bowl which appears both in late fourth-century contexts and in several Anglo-Saxon cemeteries which probably started to be used in the earliest years of the settlement (Sarre, Chessel Down, Twyford). The implications are that these bowls were what the British were using in the fifth century. But one bowl from Grave 103, Sleaford, Lincoln-shire, found with a bronze-bound bucket and a pair of tweezers (not particularly Saxon associations), had a new rim form: one made by folding over and hammering down the rim edge. It has four escutcheons with out-bent hooks. Clearly a craftsman was working on a technically more complicated rim form in the fifth century A.D. Indeed, it is possible to see this development in physical terms (fig. 70, 2–3). The Tummel Bridge, Perth, hoard of metalwork contained, as well as the silver penannular brooches, the fragmentary remains of two bowls and part of an escutcheon from one of them.[30] The bowl rims show a slight thickening of the rim, perhaps a hammering-down, while the one associated with the escutcheon, a circular and open-work one, shows a distinct rim flattening, taken a step further in the Castle Tioram, Moidart, bowl which also has a circular, open-work escutcheon (fig. 68a).

This new rim and escutcheon form is seen in completeness in the Wilton bowl (Pl. XIII, bottom) unfortunately found without any associations in 1860 during drainage works between the main entrance to Wilton House and Kingsbury Square. The bowl has four bird hooks with circular escutcheons, bearing a design of four pelta-shaped openings arranged quadrilaterally, making a Greek cross in bronze in the centre. What is left of the Tummel Bridge escutcheon enables a reconstruction to be made which shows the Wilton pattern in reverse. The other open-work design is that represented by the Castle Tioram piece, and now, by the new find from Eastwell, Leicestershire, of two laterally opposed peltae shapes, incorrectly compared to the Tummel Bridge escutcheon when first published.[31] The hooks of these escutcheons bear two ovals, engraved at the base of the hook, which are presumably elaborations of the faintly discernible markings in a similar position on the Twyford bird-head escutcheons and the Wilton circular ones. In everything bar shape, the escutcheons fit easily into the context of late Roman provincial metalwork. The design can be paralleled, for a late fourth-century source at Richborough[32] yielded a roundel comparable with the Wilton escutcheons (fig. 71, 1). One merely has to make the not very difficult assumption that a late fourth-century smith hit on the idea of 'modernizing' the old-fashioned bowl escutcheons by making them circular and in open-work instead of oval and solid. Again, Mrs Chadwick Hawkes'[33] study of the buckles implies that a taste for open-work designs was prevalent in the fourth and fifth centuries, and the pelta shape had long been in use on items of military wear.[34] It is possible to argue from this that the bowls were made by smiths in some contact with the army in late Roman Britain, and also to explain why fragments of bowls turn up in Scotland. Is this yet another pointer

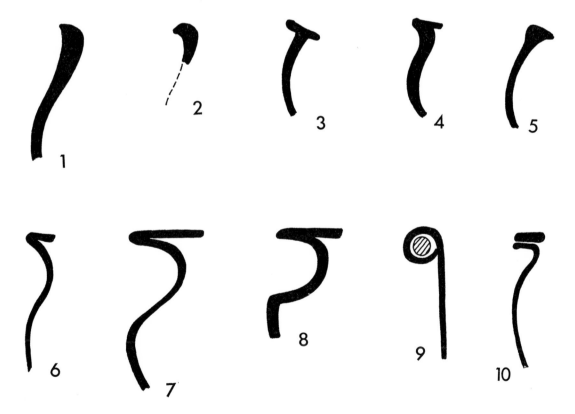

Figure 70. Development of rim types. (After Henry and Kilbride-Jones.) 1. Chessel Down; 2–3. Tummel Bridge; 4. Castle Tioran; 5. Baginton; 6. Wilton; 7. Lowbury; 8. Capheaton; 9. Miklebostad; 10. Ballinderry 2.

to metalworking activity in the Wall area and, as Mrs Chadwick Hawkes demonstrated, in the western and midland parts of Britain? More and more evidence is now accumulating to underline the belief that the end of Roman Britain was not the end of all life. The excavation of Frocester Court Roman Villa, Gloucestershire, has shown a considerable occupation in the late fourth and probably into the fifth century[35] and amongst a mass of bronze objects a complete type F penannular brooch found in an occupation level with a coin of Arcadius, thus neatly confirming the suggested fourth century for the start of the type.[36] The metalworking at, for example, Lydney and Camerton must have been considerable and other sites should exist if only we could recognize them.

While the plain heater and bird-shaped escutcheons continued to be made and attached to both the original in-bent rim as well as the new fold-over rim, the circular ones received new treatment. The unornamented escutcheons and bowls should not be forgotten, however, since they occur in interesting and datable contexts; e.g., the Ballinderry 2 escutcheons and the Ford Down bowl (Pl. XIII, top). Some are ornamented, but with engraved designs, straight on to the bowl, usually with geometric patterns or interlaced knots.

The new treatment which the metalworkers applied to the escutcheons was the use of red champlevé enamel, and an extraordinary variety of patterns. Table 1 is a very schematized list of the pattern groupings: individual bowls are not listed here but will be found in the accompanying table. I have attempted to indicate the possible/probable sources of origin of the patterns, acknowledging that this is at best only a matter of guesswork. For the latter groups, I have not done more than indicate the best current illustrations, since the patterns seem to me to grow out of the experimenting of Groups I–III. It is quite impossible to prove whether the spiral designs on the escutcheons preceded or derived from those in the illuminated MSS. and it is a somewhat sterile argument to pursue. It will become clear which I favour, but I am well aware that it can only be a hypothesis.

There are a few points of importance to stress in considering the first groups. Group I and II escutcheons are linked to the circular, non-ornamented ones because of their open-work, but it is the opposed 'pelta' shape which found favour rather than the 'cross' pattern, probably because the former allowed more room for the design of S-scrolls against red enamel. The Eastwell escutcheon shape leads to the Bann escutcheon. Baginton and Bann are similar but not identical: the former has spirals in thin-line bronze on enamel. This is the technique used on the escutcheons of the Hildersham bowl, though there geometric patterns are employed. It is the thin-line technique which seems significant, and resembles the familiar late Roman provincial use of niello in bronzework and of inlaid silver wire.[37] Notwithstanding Haseloff, fine or thin-line patterns are not necessarily the end product of the 'developed trumpet-pattern.'[38] The Hildersham and Baginton bowls also show some new elements: round discs for the interior and exterior of the base, and, on the Hildersham bowl only, enamelled strips around the top of the bowl and from each escutcheon to the base disc. In each of the divisions thus formed is placed an animal (a boar?), enamelled like the rest of the pieces, but with the dot-and-circle pattern; these animals seem to belong to the same species as those on the Lullingstone bowl, and will be further discussed below. The escutcheons of the Hildersham bowl are set within a frame which is notched all round. The remaining open-work escutcheons, from Fastry and Faversham, are distinctly different from the others, and may represent a separate tradition. The Latin cross of the Faversham examples with their S-dragon supporters[39] and the pelta shape of the Eastry one are enamelled, however, in this fine-line technique.

Group III bowls and escutcheons have in some degree elements from Groups I and II, though new patterns are or can be present every time, for there are no two bowls alike, a fact which makes the construction of a typology inherently impossible. These bowls are not like Beakers or bead-rim pots. But if a great variety of motifs were available to the craftsman, the result would be a series of similar, not identical, bowls. The only element which disappears is the open-work pattern, except that escutcheons like Bekesbourne, Capheaton, Loveden Hill, with a central void sometimes filled with linking patterns, are possibly continuing in the same tradition.

We thus have a number of bowls which show a high degree of experimentation, and if we add to this the fact that circular and heater escutcheons were common there is a strong implication that the craftsmen responsible knew or could recall late-Roman forms and were capable of considerable improvisation from the decorative forms available. Indeed, the three Sutton Hoo bowls, which have still not been satisfactorily published, are the outstanding example of this. The largest Sutton Hoo bowl has an ordinary fold-over hammered rim, red enamel, wiry spirals ending in birds' heads, but also square escutcheons, animal heads with gold-backed garnet eyes and millefiori dots in the enamel, and elaborately engraved frames to the escutcheons (both these latter can be paralleled on the Ballinderry 2 brooch[40]). The second, smaller, bowl also has millefiori patterns, which, whatever the date of the Sutton Hoo deposit, were a feature of Irish work in the sixth and seventh centuries. The problem is therefore to envisage a milieu in which craftsmen were producing objects whose basic outline was derived from fourth-century bronze bowls with animal-headed hooks, but whose decorative elements drew indiscriminately on many sources, at a time when Saxon raiders and settlers could acquire them by some means or other from the late fifth century onwards. The premises advanced by Haseloff[41] are accepted, though it might be possible to argue that one or two escutcheons owe more to Saxon craftsmen than he allows. The Benty Grange disc and the St Ninian's Isle bowl are examples of what might legitimately be called Hiberno-Saxon metalwork.

Table 2 has been drawn up to illustrate some of the more significant facts about hanging bowls which have been ignored in favour of artistic analysis, but which are curious in themselves and may possibly clarify the situation. It is columns 6, 7 and 8 with which we are principally concerned. The seventh-century date of deposition which has been attached to many of the bowls is due to the associations in the graves – coins (once only, at Sutton Hoo), a particularly elaborate brooch (Kingston 205), or weapons (Hildersham, Winchester, Ford Down) and once (Whitby) because of historical associations. But these bowls, eleven in all, do not form a group, nor are the burials concentrated in any one area. They are a most heterogeneous collection with simple and complex rims, and with patterns drawn from all the Groups (Table 3). This can only mean that there were several contemporary centres of manufacture; one group did not supersede another. The hanging bowl story is not a logical progression but a series of parallel developments. One recalls Fox's 'Schools of Celtic Art' coexisting in Britain in the Early Iron Age.[42]

Table 1

Group No.		Patterns and Techniques	Origin and Inspiration	Illustrations
I openwork		red enamel	Embossed bronze brooches	
		Thin line	Hand pins	Leeds, *Celtic Ornament* (1936) fig. 36
		Running scroll	Latchets	Henry, *Irish Art* (1965), Pl. 13
		Bird's head	F2 penannular brooches	*PSAS*, LXXI (1936) figs. 5 and 9
		Hexafoil (Marigold) Rosette	Lydney bone disc (?)	Wheeler, *Lydney Report* (1932) Pl. 31, 151
II openwork		Feather	Late Roman silver-ware	Curle, *Treasure of Traprain* (1923), Pl. 119, 124 *Proc. Camb. Ant. Soc.* (1951) Pl. 9–11
		Zig-zag Dot and Circle Lozenge	Bone combs Bronze bracelets	Kenyon, *Jewry Wall Report* (1948), fig. 22–23 Wheeler, *Lydney Report* (1932), fig. 17
		S-dragon and cross boar and stags	Eurasiatic animal art (?) or Pictish symbols	*JRSAI*, LXVI (1936) Pl. 25, 2–3 *Arch. J.*, CXVIII (1963) 54, fig. 13; 61, fig. 16
III		Foliage	Silverware	De Paor, *Early Christian Ireland* (1958), Pl. 4
		Cross	Christian symbol (?)	*JRSAI*, LXVI (1936) Pl. 27 and 30
		Three limbed pelta Plain pelta	Verulamium disc Escutcheon shape/ mosaics Inscribed stones	Wheeler, *Lydney Report* (1932), Pl. 32a Henry, *Irish Art* (1965) 115

Group No.		Patterns and Techniques	Origin and Inspiration	Illustrations
III—*contd.*		Step pattern	Mosaics/metalwork	Kendrick, *Anglo-Saxon Art* (1938), Pl. 21
		Milled frame	Ribbed bracelets	Wheeler, *Lydney Report* (1932), fig. 17
IIIa		Wiry spirals plus millefiori		Henry, *Irish Art* (1965), Pl. A Leeds, *Celtic Ornament* (1933), Pl. 3
IV		Durrow spiral patterns Red and yellow enamel		*JRSAI*, LXVI (1936), Pl. 32
IVa		Durrow type animals		*Med. Arch.*, VI (1962), fig. 8
IVb		Durrow type spirals plus interlace		*Med. Arch.*, II (1958), Pl. 7 and 8
		Interlace knot	MSS. possibly Mosaic pavements	*Med. Arch.*, II (1958), Pl. 9 Kendrick, *Anglo Saxon Art* (1938), Pl. 20
		Some Group III patterns		
		Geometric patterns	Ardagh chalice Moylough belt	*JRSAI*, LXVI (1936), Pl. 136–8
		Red and yellow enamel Millefiori Human escutcheons		

The extremely cogent arguments of David Wilson[43] on the dating of objects in graves are relevant here. Hanging bowls for the reasons cited above are not susceptible to typological dating for there are not enough similar examples nor a fixed point for beginning and ending. Dating in absolute terms, in the sense that Haseloff wrote of these bowls, is an impossibility at the moment, for the twin pegs of seventh-century chronology, Sutton Hoo and the abandonment of pagan burial practices, seem as debatable as ever. Indeed, calculating the date of deposition of Sutton Hoo is as time-consuming as working out the date of Easter must have been for those Celtic and Roman clergy at the court of King Alchfrith. The presence of coins is no real guarantee of a firm date; dating Sutton Hoo might be a lot easier without the coins and the historical evidence of the genealogies and Bede. Secondly, the evidence of burial practice when Christianity became more widespread is still not fully understood. We simply do not know when the 'custom of making burial deposits' came to an end. If we did not know historically that the body contained in the wooden coffin and furnished with an elaborate jewelled pendant and an ivory comb and silks, amongst other objects, was that of a revered Christian saint,[44] we might well feel that here was a curious pagan burial. Benty Grange and Winchester have recently been claimed as late seventh-century Christian burials.[45] Wilson[46] has succinctly indicated how most of the finest pieces of Anglo-Saxon metalwork were made and buried after the Augustinian Mission. To judge from Bede, the Christianization of the country was an extremely slow and laborious process with the population constantly slipping back into the old ways throughout the seventh century. Hodgkin[47] believed that by the late seventh century Christianity was more or less widespread. Therefore arguments along the lines that the bowls must have been buried 'shortly before' the custom of making burial deposits ended seem entirely fallacious. It would depend on the part of England concerned as much as anything. It may be significant that, for example, of the bowls found in Kent, only three belong to the 'developed trumpet-pattern,' Group IV; if we must use musical terms to describe metalwork patterns, then 'French horn' motif would be more accurate. The majority of the Kentish bowls have Group II or III patterns, the sub-Roman and geometric designs, while two at least bear possible Christian symbols. Since Kent was probably the first part of England to become Christian, though not really effectively so until the mid-seventh century, burial deposits probably ceased there earlier than elsewhere, so one would not expect to find so many bowls there with Durrow type spirals, assuming a late seventh-century date for the MSS. Quite a number of complete bowls have also been found in Kentish contexts, suggesting perhaps manufacture, use and deposit in the same area, the area where the Roman army probably hung on longest.

There is a particular point of interest concerned with the possible Christian symbolism on a few of the bowls. If originally the bowls were used in wealthy secular contexts, to serve drinks or for hand-washing, then a transference to ecclesiastical usage was a simple move, especially if there were still dim memories of bowls functioning in Roman religious rites. Early Christianity borrowed, or assimilated, a good deal from contemporary religions, and Bede himself makes plain that Augustine and his successors were to approach the 'old' worship with care and not seek to destroy it outright. The finding of bowls and fragments on monastic sites is understandable. Dr Henry[48] has suggested a workshop at St Fursey's monastery in Suffolk; if the A.D. 625 date for Sutton Hoo is to be readopted[49] then this disobligingly rules out the view that Fursey's monk-smiths, arriving *c.* 635, influenced, or even made, some of the bowls and jewellery. However, the fact that Fursey apparently made straight for Suffolk suggests that prior contacts existed, perhaps demonstrated by the metal-work. There may have been a workshop at Glastonbury and there was one at Whitby, though since one of the escutcheons from this site was pierced for use as a pendant it is debatable whether the craftsmen produced the hanging bowls there. They would hardly have been made only to be destroyed, so their date does not depend on the foundation of the monastery. Two Irish monastic sites, Ferns and Clonmacnoise, produced complete escutcheons and these and other sites were surely the source of the bowls which the Norsemen carried back to Norway. Dr Henry's attribution to Ireland of the Norse bowls, her Group III, is completely acceptable. They are in rim form and decoration so distinct a group that a new centre of production, using elements from earlier ones, must be postulated. It is the other groups which really pose the problem.

We must now return to the patterns and explain why the Groups are arranged in that particular order. Group I is held to be the earliest because it is closest to the similar open-work but undecorated escutcheons already discussed. The only one of these escutcheons to have associations is the Tummel Bridge one, found with the three silver Type H penannular brooches. These have been dated[50] between the fifth and early eighth centuries. This date is due largely to two external pieces of evidence; the association of many H brooches and E ware, and to the desire to make Tummel Bridge and the Wilton bowl close in date to the fourth-century Richborough roundel (fig. 71, 1 and 2); the disturbed levels on the Jewry Wall site[51] yielded another similar bronze ornament, four peltae arranged round a cross, and decorated with dots and circles. The bowls themselves, whatever the decoration, should follow on from the known late Romano-British series of bowls. The date of E ware and the H brooches has already been laboured at some length and will not here be repeated. A fifth-century date is not impossible, but since the bowl in the Tummel Bridge hoard was already broken, it could be earlier, or the hoard might be a much later deposition. Leeds attributed it to the Pictish raiders, but there were numerous occasions when the people north of the Wall made trouble in the south. The imponderables are many: suffice it here to say that I believe the open-work escutcheons to belong to the fifth century, but this is an entirely subjective and unprovable opinion.

The Group I and II bowls pose a new problem. The patterns are not strange, only em-ployed in a new way, for they can be paralleled on fourth-century Romano-British provincial metalwork. But two of the bowls from these groups are from seventh-century burials. If the decoration and open-work are taken over from, say, fourth- and fifth-century pieces, then these bowls could have been as much as 150 years old when buried. The Hildersham bowl was extremely battered and old-looking when buried but the Baginton bowl is in near-perfect condition, though repaired, and the four escutcheons of this bowl, a feature of Romano-British bowls, increase the probability of a date in the fifth century. It is said that the bowls, because so thin and fragile, could not have lasted very long; the curious thing is that so many of the complete bowls are obviously old, some are patched, and look exactly like long-treasured objects. There are far more escutcheons, forty-five (counting each different design), than complete bowls (twenty-five and seven fragments) which seems to prove the point that the

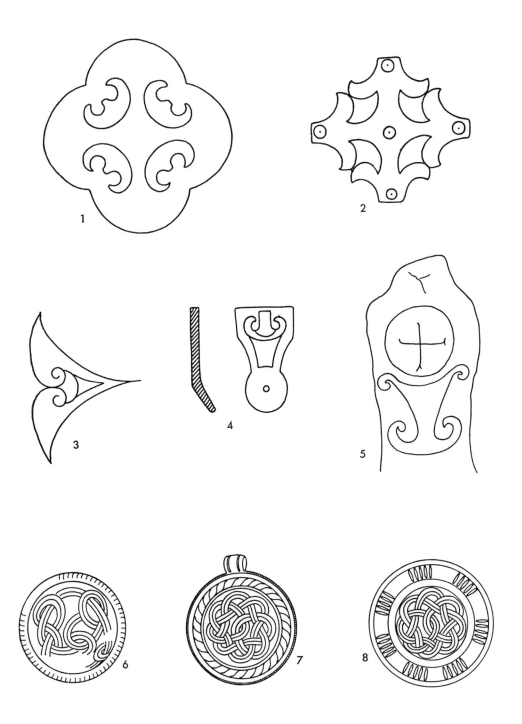

Figure 71. Late Roman openwork mountings from 1. Richborough, 2. Jewry Wall. (After Bushe-Fox and Kenyon.)
Pelta pattern on MSS. 3. Catach of St Columba (after dePaor) : possible hanging bowl escutcheon or shrine mounting. 4. Liddington, Wilts. (published by permission of the Ashmolean Museum) ; 5. memorial stone, Kilfountain Pillar, Kerry ; after Henry.
Bronze discs from 6. Dunadd, Scotland (after P.S.A.S.), 7. a grave in Kent (after Leeds) and 8. Rhenen cemetery, the Netherlands (after Ypey).

bowls disintegrated fairly fast. Those that survived must surely have been heirlooms. There are so few bowls and escutcheons of the open-work, undecorated and decorated, groups that they must have formed a group relatively close in time, if not in space. A distribution map tells us only where these objects were found, and a place of origin cannot be deduced, unless historical evidence of confused conditions, raiding parties from Ireland, Scotland, and the Saxon areas of England, is introduced.

Under these circumstances, and now that Professor O'Kelly,[52] Dr Henry[53] and the de Paors[54] have adequately demonstrated the existence in Ireland of metalworkers and skilled artists, it is possible to envisage separate parallel developments of the bowls and patterns. There was apparently no demand for such bowls in Ireland in the beginning, otherwise some fragments would surely have been found. All the prerequisites for the ornament, even the late-Romanizing, geometric patterns, of Groups II and III exist there, as Dr Henry's cross-slabs and the latchets show. The decorated latchets are frequently quoted, but Smith's original publication[55] devoted as much attention to the non-enamelled examples. These have oblique and transverse hatching on the stem of the latchet, while one has chip-carved triangles. Another has an engraved marigold enclosed within a hexagon on the disc. This engraved ornament is an exact parallel to that on the Type E pins and may well have derived from it. The marigold or rosette pattern is either parallel to, or a foretaste of, the hanging bowl 'marigold,' plain and enamelled, and is of course one of the two principal patterns on the enamelled latchets. The other pattern is that of fine-line spirals on red enamel, like Group I escutcheons. The existence of these latchets, plus a small number of ring-pins with open-work patterns,[56] is the strongest argument that all hanging bowls were made in Ireland. But the actual bowl form and the use of escutcheons are on present evidence foreign to Ireland. Is it possible that these latchets represent a short-lived type of dress ornament emanating from one workshop in the north of Ireland, where the craftsmen were experimenting with various patterns current in fifth-century Britain? In a sense they might be a 'trial run' before the demand for enamelled and decorated escutcheons developed.

There was a demand for the bowls in southern England in the fourth and fifth centuries where the antecedents for the escutcheon shape are present. Dare one suggest that the villa owners, such as were left, had adopted the idea of bowls and tripods from military practice and were using them? It was from these villas, or farms, that the Saxon raiders took some bowls, and having broken up many, using the patterned pieces for dress ornaments, perhaps decided to keep some whole and use them as status symbols. There is really not enough evidence in England to suggest churches on a scale in the fifth century sufficient to account for all the bowls, if all were purely ecclesiastical objects. A secular source is the only answer, though they could have become church vessels later on. Indeed, the Irish smiths may have made bowls for churches and for 'export' to England. Hence the great Sutton Hoo bowl with its exclusively Irish features of engraved frames (Ballinderry 2 brooch), the bird-headed spirals and the millefiori, but with a patch put on by a Saxon smith. There should be places of manufacture in Britain but, apart from the rare excavated sites like Dinas Powis,[57] there is at present insufficient evidence for the existence of metalworkers able to make hanging bowls, though current work in Somerset and Gloucestershire may alter the picture. The lack of early bowls in Ireland may simply be due to the Irish adherence to the monastic vow of poverty; the smiths were perfectly capable of producing other, secular, ornaments. It begins to look as though we are dealing with a convention whereby the hanging bowls of Groups I–III were made by the native inhabitants from the fifth century onwards and decorated in particular styles reserved for the bowls. Later, the bowls were made by men who were aware of the other designs but who elaborated and refined them to such an extent that monkish illuminators were able to adapt them. This line of argument would tie in well with McRoberts' assertion that the votive chalice idea reached England and presumably Ireland and Scotland in the seventh century, and so the bowls become ecclesiastical, particularly in Northumbria. Those still in secular use are buried: the Irish monasteries adapt the idea and evolve a new rim form. One or two odd ones are still made in Britain, Benty Grange, for example, by whom seems hardly to matter now, for the ornament is part of the seventh-century amalgam of styles.

We must briefly consider the bowls which bear not animal patterns, but actual animals: notably the Hildersham and Lullingstone bowls. Long ago Clapham hinted at a Pictish origin for the Lullingstone bowl, but no one took much notice. The recent exposition of the animal art of the Scottish Iron Age by Charles Thomas[58] makes plain that the Pictish animal symbols drew inspiration from the Eurasiatic animal art style and that the Lullingstone creatures (and also the Lion and Calf symbols in the Book of Durrow) are equally to be seen as ultimately deriving from the same source.[59] The Hildersham animals, the Sutton Hoo fish, the Benty Grange boar and even the stag from the Sutton Hoo standard, also come out of this naturalistic Eurasiatic background. I am myself inclined to add the St Ninian's Isle and Steeple Bumpstead 'boars' to the category, since they are essentially recognizable animals, although stylized. Admittedly, the difficulties in assuming the existence of one, or more, craftsmen driven to express themselves in this non-Saxon, and not particularly Irish, manner, are formidable. But however improbable it seems, a look at Thomas' (1963) figs. 11, 15 and 16 is convincing enough. Direct influence from the Pictish material on the hanging bowl animals is not unlikely, accepting an earlier date for the Class I stones.

Kendrick in 1938 made a suggestion that some of the decorative elements (guilloche, even interlace) on the escutcheons could have come from the mosaic pavements of the villas. At the time, this notion was not developed but it now is much more plausible. We know a great deal more about the occupation of towns and villas in the fourth and early fifth centuries, not nearly enough but sufficient to demonstrate a sort of existence and life in certain areas, notably Kent around Canterbury, Norwich, York, St Albans, Silchester, and Somerset/ Gloucester. The Hinton St Mary fourth-century pavement is an indication of not only the presence of Christian believers in Dorset but also the existence of mosaicists with a good repertoire of patterns. Frocester Court Villa is yielding not only strong evidence for a late occupation, but also of a local mosaicist at work in the mid-fourth century, using both classical pattern book designs and his own native British motifs.[60] It is not provable but it seems likely that in certain favoured regions (Somerset/Gloucester was a heavily populated villa area[61] and not occupied by Saxons till the end of the sixth century) a sort of town/farm life persisted into the fifth century at, for example, Chedworth and Cirencester, and therefore late-Roman designs were available.[62]

Geometric and plant motifs (like the Hildersham feathering) were also present on the hoards of late Roman silverware,[63] only a few of which can ever have been buried (Traprain, Balline, Coleraine and Mildenhall). The bulk of the metalwork must have been melted down for reuse by smiths who had therefore an opportunity for absorbing the details into their own repertoire. A cursory examination of some of the hoards supplies several of the hanging bowl patterns. Plate XIX of Curle's Traprain Treasure shows four-leaved rosettes, plant shapes, feathering; plate XXIV of the same shows geometric designs, a quasi-marigold (No. 68) and a running scroll (No. 69). A similar search through the late fourth-century coinage of this country might supply more patterns. Whether or not the earliest Anglo-Saxon coins copied Roman prototypes[64] some must still have been around in the form of trinkets, or lucky charms, to be copied, and the ones in graves prove this. Indeed the curious Barton escutcheons look almost like a bad imitation of a coin with lettering;[65] the 'animal' element is completely unidentifiable.

The argument that the so-called hanging bowl motifs were confined to metalwork, and to whichever part of the British Isles the writer desires to confine the manufacture of the bowls, can be demolished simply by quoting examples from areas far removed from late Romano-British influences. A steatite disc carrying four peltae in an arrangement close to the Tummel Bridge escutcheon was found in the Shetland Isles:[66] a Pictish stone at Dunnichen[67] has a running triple scroll (Group III). Possibly these are arguments for manufacture in the north of Scotland? Surely a more sane approach is to see all these motifs as readily and contemporaneously accessible, rather than as successively developing. Some of the fallacies inherent in the pursuit of the ultimate parallel can be shown by comparing three small bronzes from Scotland, Kent and Holland (fig. 71, 6–8). The Scottish piece[68] comes from Dunadd and is a circular bronze, once gilded, disc, with a ribbed border surrounding a tight triple strand interlace in bronze on red enamel. Exactly similar interlace occurs on a disc pendant from a Kentish grave[69] and on a disc from a grave in the Rhenen cemetery,[70] dated mid to late sixth century. The Kentish pendant has an interlace border; the Rhenen disc is bordered by groups of ribbing separated by plain areas. This type of close interlace is like that distinguished by Haseloff and figures on the Lullingstone bowl, but the Rhenen evidence suggests a much earlier date for the type than that deduced by Haseloff arguing from the MSS. evidence. It only goes to prove that one finds one's evidence where one chooses to look for it, and that depends largely on what one wants to prove.

Archaeologically, the picture of the fifth to seventh centuries is one where several groups of people were living and working each in their own milieu, with a certain amount of exchange of ideas, techniques and designs. Under such circumstances to track down motifs is a fruitless pursuit. The 'pelta' motif (Group III) is a common enough design on F2 penannular brooches, mountings (Liddington (fig. 71, 3–5), Sutton Hoo), hand-pins and stone pillars (Reask).[71] But it is also a motif[72] used in the early MSS., the Catach of St Columba and the Durham A.11.10 fol. 36. If these MSS. are late sixth and early seventh century, do they date the metalwork and the stones? The MSS. and stone pillars show exactly the progression from simple spiral of geometric patterns to complex interlace noted for the metalwork, only, it would seem, slightly later in time. Nordenfalk[73] discussing the pages of Durrow implies that much of the layout derives from 'pagan metalwork.'[74] It should be emphasized firmly that the initial inspiration for the MSS. were Gospel and Mass Books brought from the Mediterranean world, which were then reinterpreted to suit first the Celtic and then the Roman Christian Church, and finally the amalgam of both which dominated society in the eighth century. The stimulus and the market provided by the growth of Christianity, more settled conditions and economic security had a liberating effect on the craftsmen. The small-scale work, pins, brooches, escutcheons, gives way to more elaborate pieces, sometimes still tiny in size, like the Tara brooch, yet more indicative of the general Christianity of the British Isles. The reliquaries, chalices, bowls, even lamps, great stone crosses and illuminated books with gold and jewelled covers, existed, for we have documentary evidence to prove it and, as the colophon in the Book of Lindisfarne tells us, monkish craftsmen to work on them. No one doubts the wealth of this ecclesiastical society, yet there are very few relics because the Viking raids dispersed so much. Yet the same argument, applied a few centuries earlier, is mistrusted, perhaps because the documentary evidence is lacking or suspect.

I do not pretend to have solved the 'problem,' only to have tried to dispel some of the mystique that surrounds the subject. It is largely a problem of our contriving. Either we treat these bowls as archaeological objects which has been the attempt here, using corroboratory evidence from other fields of study where possible; or we see them purely as artistic objects, in which case a picture book is necessary, for discussion of dates, provenance etc. are out of place where there is no certain sequence, no agreed dated associations, and no logical typology. When all is said and done, however, it is salutary to remember how much of any research inevitably builds on and uses the studies of earlier writers. My indebtedness to all, even where I disagree, should be fully acknowledged.

Acknowledgments: I am grateful to Mr J. W. G. Musty for permission to publish the Ford Down bowl (Pl. XIII) in advance of his own publication. Both the Ford Down bowl and the Wilton bowl (Pl. XIII) are in Salisbury and South Wiltshire Museum, and I am grateful to the Curator for allowing photographs to be taken, and to my husband for taking them and for other assistance.

Table 2

Schematic list of hanging bowls and escutcheons, Groups I–IVb and unornamented. (Group V listed by Henry, *op. cit.* (1956) 83–4.)

Key: Col. 1. Site; 2. B: Bowl, D: Disc, E: Escutcheon; 3. Rim form. IB: Inbent, F: Folded over, H: Hammered down; 4. Escutcheon shape and number. O: Open-work, C: Circular, B: Bird-shaped, H: Heater-shaped, V: Circular with void; 5. Ornament patterns by Groups (see Table 1); 6. Associations; 7. Hoard, Burial or single find; 8. Date by centuries.

Col. 1	Col. 2	Col. 3	Col. 4	Col. 5	Col. 6	Col. 7	Col. 8
Beds.							
Totternhoe	E		C	IV	Bone comb, leather purse, knife (linen-bound handle), work box	Burial, F	

Col. 1	Col. 2	Col. 3	Col. 4	Col. 5	Col. 6	Col. 7	Col. 8
Berks.							
Lowbury Hill	B	F	C 3	IV Tinned bronze	Warrior	Burial, M Kilbride–Jones, *P.S.A.S.* LXXI (1936) fig. 11/3 (hereafter Kilbride–Jones 1936)	7
Bucks.							
Oving	E		C	IV	Reused as pendant	Henry, *J.R.S.A.I.* LXVI (1936) pl. 33/8 (hereafter Henry 1936)	
Cambs.							
Barrington A	E		C	IV		Henry 1936 pl. 29/1	
Barrington A or B	E		C	IV		Henry 1936 pl. 33/5	
Barton?	E		B	Plain	Iron and bone objects	Henry 1936 pl. 20/3	
Hildersham	B	H	O 3	II with applied bands and animals	Warrior	Burial, M	7
Derby.							
Benty Grange	E		C Milled frame	IVa	Warrior	Burial, M Ozanne, *Med. Arch.* VI (1962) fig. 8 (hereafter Ozanne 1962)	7
Grindlow	B (frag)	H	V Milled silver frame			Ozanne 1962 fig. 9a	
Middleton Moor	B (frag)		C plus another odd one	IV	Warrior	Burial, M Ozanne 1962 fig. 8	
Co. Down							
River Bann, nr. Coleraine	E		O	I		Henry, *Irish Art* (1955) pl. 3	
Hants.							
Basingstoke	B	F	H 3	III	Warrior	Burial, M Henry 1936 fig. 7/h	
Winchester	B	F	C 3	IV Silvered bronze	Warrior	Henry 1936 pl. 31/2	7
Chessel Down Isle of Wight	B	IB	B 3		Warrior	Burial, M Henry 1936 pl. 22/1	6
Herts.							
Hitchin	E		C	IV		Henry 1936 pl. 32/6	
Inverness							
Castle Tioram, Moidart	B (frag)	H	O	Plain		Fig. 68a	
Kent							
Bekesbourne	E		V	IVb		Haseloff, *Med. Arch.* II (1958), pl. 7	

Col. 1	Col. 2	Col. 3	Col. 4	Col. 5	Col. 6	Col. 7	Col. 8
Dover 1	E		C	III All tinned bronze		Henry 1936 pl. 26/5	
,, 2	E		C	II		Henry 1936 pl. 26/1	
,, 3	E & D		C	II		Henry 1936 pl. 27/3	
Eastry	E		O	II		Henry 1936 pl. 25/3	
Faversham 1	E		O 3	II		Henry 1936 pl. 25/2	
,, 2	B	H	C 3	III with applied bands		Henry 1936 pl. 27/5	
,, 3	E & D		H C	I		Henry 1936 pl. 28/3, 4	
,, 4	D		C 2	IVa		Henry 1936 fig. 9/a, d	
Greenwich	E		C	IV			
Kingston Grave 205	B	F soldered applied rim	C 3 Not true hooks	I & II	Kingston brooch etc.	Burial, F Henry 1936 pl. 27/2	7
Kingston Grave 76	B	F	C Discs only	III	Warrior	Burial, M Henry 1936 pl. 30/1	7
Lullingstone	B	F	C 4 No hooks	II & IVb with applied bands and animals	Warrior	Burial, M Henry 1936 pl. 30/3	7
Sarre	E		B	Plain		Burial Henry 1936 pl. 21/3	
Leics.							
Eastwell	E		O	Plain		*Med. Arch.* (1964), pl. 19/C	
Keythorpe Common	B (frag)		C 3	IV		Burial Now lost	
Stoke Golding	E		C 2, not identical	III & IV		Kilbride-Jones 1936 fig. 8/2, 3	
Twyford	E		B 2, not identical	Plain		Henry 1936 pl. 22/2	
Lincs.							
Barton	B	F	H 3	Plain			
Benniworth	E		H	IV		Kilbride-Jones 1936 fig. 8/8	
Caistor	B		C 3	II with applied band	Warrior	Burial, M	
Loveden Hill 1	B		V 3	IV	Warrior, glass palm cup, sword etc.	Cremation *Med. Arch.* (1960), pl. 24	
,, 2	B		C 3	IV (like Barlaston ?)		Cremation	
,, 3	E		C 2	IV			
Manton Common	B	H	3	IIIa			
Market Rasen	E		C with pelta ends	IV (like Whitby ?)			
			H	IV			
Sleaford Grave 103	B (frag)	H	H 4	Plain	Bucket, tweezers	Burial Henry 1936 pl. 21/4	

Col. 1	Col. 2	Col. 3	Col. 4	Col. 5	Col. 6	Col. 7	Col. 8
Witham	B		Animal escutcheons	Silver		Now lost	
Norfolk							
Thornham	D		C	II		Burial	
Northumb.							
Unlocated	E & D		C 4	IIIa			
Capheaton	B	F	V 3	II not enamelled, but engraved		Burial Henry 1936 pl. 28/9	
Oxford							
Unlocated	E		C	IV	Reused as pendant	Henry 1936 pl. 33/9	
White Horse Hill	D			IVb engraved interlaced knot		Henry 1936 fig. 8	
Perth							
Tummel Bridge	B (frag)		O	Plain	With H brooches	Hoard	5
Shetlands							
St Ninian's Isle	B	F	Animal escutcheons 3	IV Silver disc	Ecclesiastical objects	Hoard, *Antiquity* (1959), pl. 30	
Somerset							
Camerton 1	E		V	IV	Reused as pendant	Burial, child	
„ 2	E		C	IV		Henry 1936 pl. 33/1, 2, 4	
„ 3	E		C	III	Reused as pendant	Burial, F	
Staffs.							
Barlaston	B (frag)	IB	C milled frame	IIIa with applied band	Warrior	Burial, M Ozanne 1962, fig. 96	
Suffolk							
Mildenhall (Barton)	E		C 3 with applied bands, milled frame	II & III		Burial Henry 1936 pl. 34/4	
Needham Market	B		H 2 C disc	I		Burial, now lost Henry 1936 fig. 7/b, g	
Sutton Hoo 1	B	H	C 3 milled frame Square plaques Trout in bottom	IIIa	Ship Burial	Bruce-Mitford, *B.M. Guide*, pl. 9	7
„ 2	B		C details not published	IIIa peltae plus millefiori		Henry 1956 fig. 17b	
„ 3	B		C 2 discs	IVa?			

Col. 1	Col. 2	Col. 3	Col. 4	Col. 5	Col. 6	Col. 7	Col. 8
Surrey							
Morden	D		C	III?			
Warwicks.							
Baginton	B	H	O 4	I	Warrior	Burial Henry 1936 pl. 25/1	7
Chesterton on Fossway	E & D		C 5	III & IV		Henry 1936 pl. 32/3, 7	
Westmorland							
Unlocated	D		C	IV			
Wilts.							
Ford Down	B	F	B 3	II Plain engraved decoration on base	Warrior	Burial pl. XIII	7
Liddington	E		H	III		Fig. 71/4	
Wilton	B		O 4	Plain		Pl. XIII	
Yorks.							
Castle Yard, York	B	H	B 3	Engraved interlace on base		Henry 1936 pl. 30/2	
Finningley	B	IB	B 3	Hippocamp		Kilbride-Jones 1936 fig. 4/1	
Hawnby	B	F	B 3	Punched dots on birds		Henry 1936 pl. 31/1	
Whitby 1	E		H with pelta ends	IVb inter- lace knots around cross		Haseloff 1958 pl. 7/G, F & D	
,, 2	E		H	IVb inter- lace knot			
,, 3	E		V	I			
Unlocated							
Londesborough Coll. B.M.	E		V	I	Reused as pendant	Haseloff 1958 pl. 7/E	
Victoria & Albert Museum	E		C	IV		Henry 1936 pl. 33/7	

Notes

1. *The Listener*, 10 November 1955, 791
2. *Arch. J.* CXX (1964) 98–160
3. *Antiquity* XXXIII (1959) 241–68; *Med. Arch.* IX (1965) 175–6
4. *Med. Arch.* II (1958) 72–103
5. Henry, in (ed.) Harden, *Dark Age Britain, Studies presented to E. T. Leeds* (1956), 71–88; Henry, *Irish Art in the Early Christian Period to A.D. 900* (1965)
6. Alcock, *Dinas Powys* (1963)

7. *Med. Arch.* II (1958) 97–100, n. 141

8. *Arch.* LXXXIX (1943) 27–88

9. *J.R.S.A.I.* LXVI (1936) 211–13

10. *Acta Archaeologica* XXIV (1953) 163

11. *P.S.A.S.* XCIV (1960) 304–5

12. Bede II, 16. (Trans. L. Sherley Price)

13. *ibid.* III, 6 and 24

14. *P.S.A.S.* XCIV (1960) 304–5

15. *J.R.S.A.I.* LXVI (1936) 214–15; Hawkes, in (ed.) Grimes, *Aspects of Archaeology in Britain and Beyond, Essays presented to O. G. S. Crawford* (1951) 172–99

15a. His paper is to be published in *P.R.I.A.* forthcoming.

16. *P.S.A.S.* XCIV (1960) 304

17. Liversidge, *Furniture in Roman Britain* (1955) 35–7 and reference 72; *A.J.A.* LV (1951) 344

18. *P.S.A.S.* LXXXIX (1955–6) 141–2; *Med. Arch.* V (1961) 1–70

19. Henry, *op. cit.* (1956) 83–8

20. *Med. Arch.* IV (1960) 127–8, Pl. 24

21. *Med. Arch.* IX (1965) 176

22. *C.A.S.* XIV (1951) 44–7

23. *Ant. J.* XV (1935) 109–12

24. *Arch. Ael.* VIII (1931) 328–38

25. *Antiquity* XXXIII (1965) 258

26. *J.R.S.A.I.* LXVI (1936) 211–13

27. *P.S.A.S.* LXXI (1936–7) 206–47

28. Hawkes, *op. cit.* (1951) 172–99

29. Curle, *The Treasure of Traprain* (1923) 72–8; *Richborough Second Report* (1928) Pl. 21, fig. 1/45

30. *P.S.A.S.* LXXI (1936–7) fig. 2/2 and 3

31. *Med. Arch.* VIII (1964) 236, Pl. 19/C and D

32. *Richborough Second Report* (1928), Pl. 19/35

33. *Med. Arch.* V (1961) 57–9, fig. 19/c and d

34. Curle, *Newstead : A Roman Frontier Post and its People* (1911) Pl. 76/1 and 3

35. *Proc. Cotteswold Naturalists' Field Club* XXXIV, pt. 3 (1964) 127–32

36. *Arch. J.* CXX (1964) 104

37. *Ant. J.* XXV (1955) 20–44

38. *Med. Arch.* II (1958) 78

39. *Arch. J.* CXVIII (1961) 55, fig. 14

40. *P.R.I.A.* XLVII (C) (1942) 34, fig. 12

41. *Med. Arch.* II (1958) 97

42. Fox, *Pattern and Purpose : Early Celtic Art in Britain* (1958) 22–58

43. *Med. Arch.* III (1959) 115–16; Wilson, *The Anglo-Saxons* (1960) 19–21

44. The relics of St Cuthbert

45. *Med. Arch.* VI–VII (1962–3) 22

46. Wilson, *op. cit.* (1960) 20 and 142

47. Hodgkin, *A History of the Anglo-Saxons* (1935) 268–9 But see Hyslop, *Arch J*, CXX (1963) 191–4.

48. Henry, *op. cit.* (1956) 82

49. *Antiquity* XXXVIII (1964) 252–7

50. *Arch. J.* CXX (1964) 111

51. *Soc. Ant. Lond. Research Committee Report* XV (1948) fig. 84/6

52. *J.C.H.A.S.* LXVI (1961) 1–12; *J.R.S.A.I.* XCV (1965) 149–88

53. Henry, *op. cit.* (1965)

54. de Paor, *Early Christian Ireland* (1958)

55. *P.S.A.* XXX (1917–18) 120–31

56. *Arch. J.* CXX (1964) 131

57. Alcock, *op. cit.*

58. *Arch. J.* CXVIII (1961)

59. *ibid.*, 43–4; *Arch. J.* CXX (1964) 73

60. *Proc. Cotteswold Naturalists' Field Club* XXXIV, pt. 3 (1964), Pl. 1a
61. Stevens, in (ed.) Thomas, *Rural Settlement in Roman Britain*, C.B.A. Research Report VII (1966) 126, fig. 1
62. *Arch.* CXXII (1965) 203–6
63. Curle, *op. cit.*; de Paor, *op. cit.* Pl. 4
64. Sutherland, in (ed.) Harden, *op. cit.* 3–10; *P.S.I.* XXV (1949–51) 14, 33
65. *J.R.S.A.I.* LXVI (1936) 34, Pl. 34, 4
66. *Arch. J.* CXX (1964) 47, fig. 3, 4
67. Anderson and Allen, *The Early Christian Monuments of Scotland* (1903) 207, fig. 223
68. *P.S.A.S.* LXIV (1929–30) 116, fig. 4
69. Leeds, *Early Anglo-Saxon Art and Archaeology* (1936), Pl. 18/f
70. Glazema and Ypey, *Merovingische Ambachtskunst* (1956), Pl. 24
71. de Paor, *op. cit.* fig. 5
72. *Acta Archaeologica* XVIII (1947), figs. 17 and 24
73. *ibid.* 162
74. *Arch. J.* CXVIII (1961) 43–4

Grass-marked pottery in Cornwall

Charles Thomas

The paper which follows is an examination of a little-known class of handmade pottery from Atlantic Britain, the nature of which has only become apparent in the last few years. It is offered in tribute to a friend and colleague who, from his pioneer study of neolithic pottery in 1931 to his most recent reassessment of insular Beakers in 1963, has never ceased to stress the inherent value of this particular form of archaeological evidence. Although this essay is concerned with protohistoric times, the virtual lack of any support from recorded history means that the approach must be the same as that normally employed in dealing with prehistoric topics. As Professor Piggott has long shown himself to be equally at home in the centuries A.D. or B.C., it seems appropriate to choose a theme which combines something of both eras.

The pre-recognition period

In 1887, the Messrs Murray of Hastings (visitors to west Cornwall, described rather tersely as 'gentlemen from a distant shire') enlivened their holiday by digging a ruin known as 'The Sanctuary' on the farm of Bosleven, St Buryan. Their labours were rewarded by the discovery of 'fragments of sun-dried pottery'; the landowner, notified of this activity only at a later stage, tolerantly permitted the work to continue, and when the Murrays had gone home, the Penzance Natural History and Antiquarian Society finished the excavation for them. Thomas Cornish's report is hardly conclusive,[1] but the plan, which shows a complex of rectangular structures and masonry walls, points to a medieval date and in some measure confirms the traditional link with the collegiate church of St Buryan. This, a pre-Conquest foundation of Celtic character, relied for much of its prestige on a supposed charter granted *c.* 930 by king Athelstan.[2]

The sherds, which until 1940 were displayed in a museum in Penzance, were not 'sun-dried,' but merely incompetently fired. They differed little from the harder thin hand-made pottery of Early Iron Age Cornwall, save that one face of the flat basal fragments bore multiple impressions of finely-chopped grass or chaff, incorporated in the surface of the damp clay and burnt out in the process of firing. No one at the time seems to have commented on this novel and curious feature. Nor was this particular discovery repeated before about 1920. A St Ives antiquary (the late R. J. Noall) then laid bare in his garden, with some secrecy, the ruins of a small rectangular hut from which, so he claimed, large numbers of sherds of this kind were recovered.[3]

With the increase of both excavation and systematic fieldwork in Cornwall, further instances of this pottery came to light. A. H. A. Hogg drew attention, in 1930, to the occurrence of bones, shells, slate walls, and sherds in the low sea-cliff at Gunwalloe, in the Lizard peninsula, remarking that the basal sherds showed 'the impression of grass and reeds.'[4] It has now transpired that, by 1939, specimens of this pottery were also found near the site of St Piran's Oratory on Perran Sands, at Constantine Bay, St Merryn, at The Kelsies headland near Newquay, and in the Isles of Scilly. None of these finds was recorded in print.

The 'Viking' attribution

During 1935 the late Professor V. G. Childe was invited to excavate the small promontory fort of Larriban or Larrybane, near Ballintoy on the north coast of Co. Antrim.[5] A re-excavation in 1954, necessitated by a resumption of cliff quarrying, confirmed Childe's original estimate of an occupation in the last few centuries of the first millennium A.D.,[6] mainly on the strength of a specific glass bangle which fortunately accompanied the mass of crude hand-made pottery.

The pottery included many sherds with the impressions of grass, and in his discussion,[7] Childe stated that 'Dr Curle has shown me flat-rimmed sherds with grass temper from Viking houses near Jarlshof, Shetland.' Childe did not state that the Larriban pottery was Viking; on the contrary, he anticipated later opinion by recognizing that similar pottery groups from Ulster (*e.g.*, those from Ballintoy, the Kilbride souterrain, etc.) were broadly datable to the (Irish) Early Christian period, that 'the whole ceramic group is distinctively Ultonian,' and moreover that the flattened rims, despite a superficial resemblance to the rims encountered in Childe's 'Old Keig ware,'[8] had little real cultural significance. Unhappily, Childe failed to make a clear distinction between grass-*tempering*, the purposeful inclusion of vegetable matter in clay and thus in the body of a pot, and grass-*marking*, the result of impressing a newly-made pot upon dried or chopped vegetation, as a statement of his shows.[9] The Larriban sherds are primarily grass-*marked*, and Proudfoot and Wilson could find only six sherds out of a combined total of some thousands which do 'seem to have had a small amount of deliberately added temper of finely chopped . . . grass.'[10]

The reference to the Jarlshof finds becomes less relevant when it is realized that the grass-tempered later Norse pottery of the Northern Isles and northeast Scotland (Freswick Links, etc.) does not appear before the twelfth century, and Curle's sherds from House I at Jarlshof may even be as late as the thirteenth century.[11] The seeds of confusion had nonetheless been sown; grass-marking had been connected with grass-tempering, and both had been connected with Jarlshof and the Norsemen. In 1950 Miss Joan Harding published the results of her careful observation and surface collection on the headland area known as The Kelsies, near Newquay, on the north coast of mid-Cornwall.[12] Her pottery catalogue included a drawing of six rims and two bases with 'crowded imprints of grass,' the caption being 'Potsherds of Viking Date.' The textual descriptions below are headed 'Viking,' and more than one sherd is described as being 'Viking, or of that date.' Her account states, incorrectly, that 'grass-temper' occurred in these Cornish sherds, and that the 'very characteristic north Irish fabric' (*i.e.*, with Antrim limestone grits?) of the Larriban pottery 'has also been found at Viking houses near Jarlshof,' a view for which Childe's cautious paper gave no warrant.

Some of this misunderstanding was due to the late Miss Florence Patchett, a close friend of the present writer, who was responsible for the identification of Miss Harding's finds. Shortly before this time, Miss Patchett had been engaged in examining (at Truro Museum) the mass of pottery from the late R. J. Noall's collection, allegedly but by no means certainly excavated by him from his 'Dark Age house' at Hellesvean, St Ives.[13] The sherds included, besides a great many with grass impressions of the same sort as Miss Harding's from the Kelsies, a number of rims exhibiting the pinched-out lips and inserted internal bars of the type now known as 'bar-lip' or 'bar-lug.'[14] Though in fact there is not, and never has been, any justification for describing bar-lug pottery as Viking,[15] Miss Patchett was well aware of the northwest European background to this particular ceramic device, since it was known to have been found in some quantity at Hedeby or Haithabu in Schleswig-Holstein.

Between 1950 and 1953 R. L. S. Bruce-Mitford conducted a series of excavation seasons for the (then) Ministry of Works at Mawgan Porth, near Newquay, revealing a complex of dwellings inhabited by users of bar-lug pottery, apparently during the ninth and tenth centuries A.D.[16] The bar-lug cooking-pots possessed plain bases, and no trace of any grass impressions was found. But three years earlier, E. M. Jope and R. I. Threlfall, in small-scale excavations at the Gunwalloe cliff-site previously published by Hogg,[17] *had* found bar-lug pottery and grass-marked pottery, identical in fabric, in the one context; a context to which, in their publication,[18] they gave a date of the tenth and eleventh centuries A.D. Together with Childe's Larriban date of A.D. 800, it looked very much as if grass-impressed, grass-tempered, and bar-lug pottery in western Britain were all somehow interconnected, and belonged wholly to the so-called Later Dark Ages, the last few centuries before the Normans.

The sequence at Gwithian, site I

In 1952 the writer, then a student at the Institute of Archaeology under V. G. Childe and F. E. Zeuner, was engaged on some ineffectual research into problems of ancient shore-lines in Cornwall. In the course of a search through the voluminous literature of the area, he found a paper written in 1909 by a Mr Walter Rogers, describing the incidence of bones, shells, and flint along a 'supposed shore-line' in the grass-covered sand-dunes at Gwithian, a property conveniently owned by the present writer's family. Mr Rogers also mentioned a kitchen-midden from which further bones, teeth, and pottery had been thrown out by rabbits,[19] and a photograph which was located in the museum at Truro of some of the sherds proved to have been submitted to the British Museum in 1924 for an opinion. The accompanying letter, which was signed 'R. A. Smith,' positively identified them as 'of neolithic date.'

Mr Rogers' kitchen-midden was soon discovered, and it was obvious that the rabbits had not been idle since 1909; a great deal of pottery lay around, much of it showing grass-impressions, and none of it even vaguely resembling wares of the British neolithic, as that term was understood in 1952. The next spring, a trial section was cut across the mound, encountering immediately a low stone wall and a series of stratified and compacted dark occupation layers. In 1954 a six-week season of excavation took place, and further seasons were conducted in 1955 and 1956,[20] the work being directed jointly by J. V. S. Megaw, Bernard Wailes, and the writer.

Site I, as it was called, is a low mound, mostly composed of wind-blown sand, about 50 yards long. It contained three main levels of occupation, representing three successive phases spread over about six centuries. The sequence may be described in a simplified form. The lowest layer (C) presented traces of huts, almost totally destroyed by stone-robbing, and produced numerous sherds of a fine hard hand-made ware of local origin, subsequently recognized at other sites in Cornwall, which represents a continuation into the fifth and sixth centuries A.D. of the ceramic fashions current during the Roman period. In this sense, it is a true sub-Roman ware, known for a short time as 'Trebarveth' pottery,[21] a term abandoned in favour of 'Gwithian-style' when the products of the Trebarveth (St Keverne) kilns were eventually recognized as somewhat earlier.[22]

Stratified with the Gwithian-style pots, which may have been made on the site (a kiln-flue was found in layer C in 1959), were many pieces of hard wheel-made pottery. Similar fragments were already known from Garranes in Co. Cork[23] and from the north Cornish monastic foundation of Tintagel,[24] and had been regarded as exotic, probably from post-Roman Gaul; only later were they identified,[25] in the case of Class 'A', as Late Roman B and C dishes from north Africa and the Levant respectively, in the case of Class 'B' as amphorae from the Aegean region. These imports, regarded in the 1950s as fifth-century, are now considered to be slightly later. Class 'A' (*sensu* North African Late Roman B) may have reached Britain as early as *c.* 480, but the 'B' ware amphorae belong to the sixth, and perhaps to the early seventh, centuries.

Already present in layer C, together with the imported material and the native Gwithian-style jars, were occasional sherds with impressions of chopped grass on the external bases, and the term *grass-marked* pottery was applied to them.[26] In the next layer, B, the pottery content was dominated by this grass-marked ware, associated with a group of small circular stone-walled huts, also very ruined, and a formidable amount of stone, bone, and iron implements. A limited quantity of both the Class 'A' and 'B' imported pottery and of the sub-Roman Gwithian-style was also found in layer B, but the frequency of rubbish-pits dug from higher levels into lower ones, the occasional compacting of the two layers (otherwise separated by a lens of sterile sand), and the past activities of rabbits, meant that stratigraphical value could only be attached to overall percentages, rather than to individual sherds.

In both layers C and B, sherds of yet another exotic wheel-made type, Class 'E,' were recovered. Whereas nearly all the Class 'A' and 'B' sherds had come from layer C, those of Class 'E' were more evenly divided, 46% in layer C and 54% in layer B. The inference that Class 'E' had a later and longer currency than the 'A' and 'B' wares was obvious, but it seemed just as obvious that they had to be referred to a different origin, were examples of something fired almost at stoneware temperature and hardness, and functionally represented a superior range of kitchen pottery (jars, bowls, beakers) of ultimate Roman ancestry. By 1955 Class 'E' ware was seen to be a wide group found not only in Cornwall but also in south Wales, Ireland, and southwest Scotland, and by 1958 the writer could postulate a source in the region west of the middle Rhineland,[27] describing Class 'E' in such terms as 'Frankish' or 'Merovingian.' Work in this direction has not progressed very much, but the closest *formal* parallels are to be found in published groups from Mainz, Trier, the Dutch, Belgian, and north French cemeteries of the Frankish period, and smaller sites in northwest Germany, mainly during the late sixth and seventh centuries.[28]

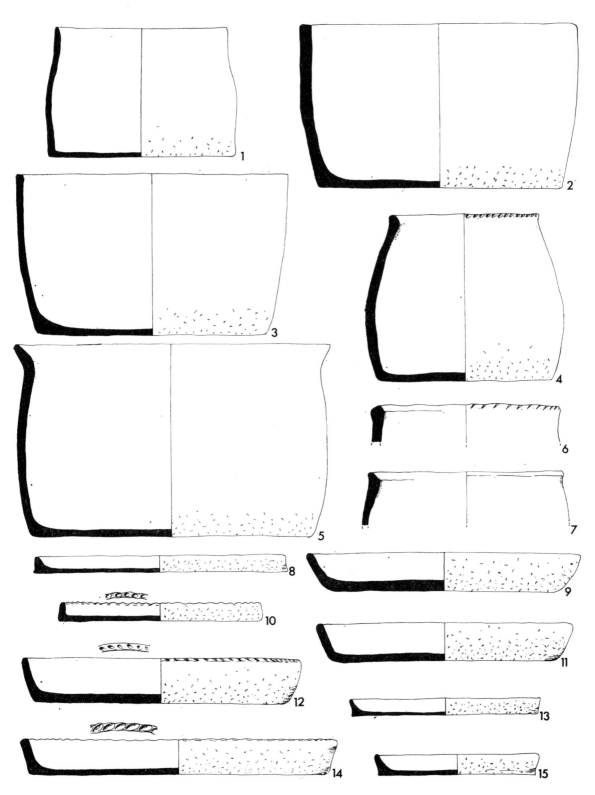

*Figure 72. Early grass-marked pottery. 1–7. Cooking-pots; 8–15. Platters. 1. Chun Castle; 13. Tean (Scilly);
the rest, Gwithian (Site I). (1/4)*

The highest and latest occupation level at Gwithian site I, layer A, yielded an elongated dwelling which, in a crude way, could be regarded as a long-house, in the sense in which the Mawgan Porth dwellings can be described by this imprecise term.[29] The layer yielded no imported wares, apart from a few scraps (obvious intrusions) from rubbish-pit upcasts, and the commonest vessel was a small or medium-sized cooking-pot with two opposed bar-lug handles, similar to those illustrated from Mawgan Porth.[30] Unlike the Mawgan Porth pots, however, the undersides of the Gwithian bar-lug vessels are all heavily grass-marked.

The final date for this site, the orderly abandonment of the layer A homestead, which was being overwhelmed by blown sand, has recently been estimated at c. A.D. 1100.[31] This is in accordance with Mawgan Porth, probably abandoned in the eleventh century, and the depth of occupation represented by layer A suggests that it goes back before A.D. 1000. But bar-lug pottery is also found at Gwithian in the preceding layer B, notably in the upper part of the occupation débris and around a small hut which appears to represent a secondary construction within this phase. The last published assessment of bar-lug pottery within the framework of northwest Europe[32] makes it hard to suppose that this idea could ever have reached Cornwall before c. A.D. 800–50, though it probably did arrive during the ninth century.

Estimates for the three Gwithian site I layers, on a pottery basis, are thus (approximately) as follows. Layer C begins in the fifth century[33] and goes on to the later sixth or early seventh, say c. 600. Layer B begins in the seventh century, and includes the initial phase of bar-lug pottery, say the period 850–900. Layer A covers the tenth and eleventh centuries. The intermissions represented by the lenses of sterile sand between the layers are of course of quite uncertain duration, since sand can both advance and retreat during non-stable phases, but the overall cultural picture suggests that the intervals were of no great length, and represent purely temporary retreats by the inhabitants.

Further work on the problems of grass-marking

The conclusion which must emerge from the foregoing account, a conclusion already perceived by the end of the 1955 season, is that the older date of c. A.D. 800 and later for grass-marked pottery, like its supposed Viking character, would not stand examination; and that grass-marked pottery was being made and used in west Cornwall by the latter part of the sixth century. All subsequent research, on the chronology of the imported wares and on other excavated sites in the southwest, bears this out. A related point, the impact of which is only really given by first-hand inspection, is that the distinction between the sub-Roman Gwithian-style pottery and the later grass-marked pottery is not merely one of the absence or presence of basal grass-impressions. The two differ, in form and fabric, to about the same extent as undecorated Glastonbury ware (Southwestern 2nd B, in Hawkes' terms) and southern British barrel or bucket urns of the former Deverel-Rimbury classification.

There must have been a complete break in traditional methods of preparing the clay, making the pots, and firing them. There is no suggestion that the grass-marked pots found in Cornwall were made elsewhere than in the localities in which their fragments have been found, but it is inconceivable that they were produced by the inheritors of the local Romano-British ceramic tradition, a tradition rooted in the Iron Age B culture-complex and extending over some six centuries. The term 'invasion' is currently out of favour,[34] and rightly so in this case, if it were to imply bands of militant bachelors who would scarcely be interested in pot-production, but an intrusive settlement of grass-marked pottery makers in sixth-century west Cornwall is surely what this evidence indicates.

It was with thoughts of this nature in mind that the excavators of site I at Gwithian under-took a systematic search for further examples of this pottery; in particular, for any site which might yield grass-marked and imported wheel-made pottery directly associated in some domestic context. A small group of sherds, deposited some years beforehand in the Penlee House Museum at Penzance (by the late Rev. H. A. Lewis), and stated to have come from a shore-line midden on the uninhabited island of Tean in the Scillies, seemed to offer the best chance of meeting this aim. In 1956, at the conclusion of the season at Gwithian, Messrs Megaw, Wailes, P. J. Fowler, and the writer, with a small group of friends, moved over to Tean, and camped for some weeks on the island. This expedition was rewarded with the most satisfactory results.[35]

The site proved to be that of a small flat-grave or 'long cist' cemetery of Early Christian type, some of the graves being overlain by a tiny stone oratory which may have been built in the early eighth century. The burials had been inserted into the top of an extensive midden, which adjoined a small oval stone hut, most of which (with some of the midden) had been eroded at high-water mark by the encroaching sea. The abundant finds of all objects sug-gested a broad dating of the third to sixth centuries A.D., and on a number of grounds, it seemed very doubtful whether any secular occupation had persisted later than c. A.D. 600.

The pottery included a good range of the local Romano-British forms, both wheel-made (or wheel-finished) bowls and dishes and coarser hand-made storage jars, a repertoire fairly well known in Scilly from Mr Paul Ashbee's various excavations;[36] some jars with rather devolved or slackened rims, doubtless analogous to the fifth-century Gwithian-style on the west Cornish mainland; imported wheel-made sherds of Classes 'B' and 'E'; and grass-marked pottery.

In this case, the Class 'B' material consisted of pieces of a 'B.ii' amphora, a common type which (it is virtually certain) indicates the sixth century, and fragments of 'B.iv' micaceous water-jars, a variety not represented at Gwithian but present at Tintagel and dating from the late fifth and sixth centuries. There were at least four vessels of Class 'E' ware, most of the fifty-odd sherds belonging to these coming from near the surface of the midden. Grass-marked pots were few in number, a fact which again suggested that occupation here had ceased not long after grass-marked ware was introduced to Scilly.

This short excavation was regarded as confirming the idea raised by the first two seasons at Gwithian; namely, that grass-marked pottery *was* current in west Cornwall and Scilly by the later sixth century. In the same year, the writer published a third, admittedly less cogent, instance of the same association between grass-marked pottery and the imported wares.[37] This was E. T. Leeds' discovery (in 1925 and 1927) of very burnt fragments of Class 'B.i' amphora with a complete grass-marked cooking-pot, from below an internal (and secondary?) structure within Chun Castle.[38]

Early views of distribution
Preliminary distribution lists of grass-marked pottery were given in the first interim report on Gwithian,[39] and four years later in a symposium on the current state of Cornish archaeology,[40]

where an attempt was made to divide the material between 'early' and 'late' sites. Two interesting points emerged. First, the total, and at that time surprising, absence of grass-marked pottery from the extensive excavations at Tintagel,[41] where some form of continuing sub-Roman ware was associated with Classes 'A' and 'B' imported pottery, and where the occupation was considered to extend to at least the eighth century, could only be explained by assuming that grass-marked pottery was in its early stage confined to west Cornwall and Scilly, and that even in its late stage it extended no further east than mid-Cornwall (up to the Camel estuary at Padstow). Secondly, the distribution west of this limit was far from even, most of the finds being coastal, and the bulk of these coming from the northern coast. While some weight must of course be attached to the ease with which surface-finds are made in sand-dune areas, fieldwork and excavation in the non-coastal parishes had nonetheless failed to produce any inland examples of grass-marked pottery.

Early views of origin

In 1954, partly influenced by Childe's work at Larriban, the writer tentatively suggested that the intrusive settlement which was considered responsible for grass-marked pottery had come from Ireland. One facet of this pottery, not yet mentioned, is that the only decoration found on it is confined to the rim, and that the examples of this seen in Cornwall are exactly paralleled, down to the last detail, by those noted at Larriban and other Ulster sites. This, together with the incidence of grass-marking (an uncommon trait at any period) on Irish pottery, and the deceptive similarity between worked bone and iron objects from site I at Gwithian and those found on such major Irish sites as Lagore[42] and Carraig Aille, Lough Gur,[43] naturally prompted the suggestion.

The doubts with which this idea was then received by workers in Ireland followed, inevitably, from the comparatively late date attributed to the appropriate pottery there. Native wares are scarce in Ireland after the local Late Bronze Age. A few sites which must be contemporary with the mainland British Early Iron Age or Roman period, for instance, Freestonehill in Co. Kilkenny,[44] have produced hand-made pottery of uncertain ancestry, and there are even some native Early Christian sherds from Lagore;[45] but only in the province of Ulster, and there mainly in the modern counties of Antrim and Down, does pottery occur in any quantity in the protohistoric period. From its frequent discovery in souterrains, which are among the most frequently revealed types of field-monument in the region, this coarse hand-made pottery with its flat grass-marked bases, finger-tipped or nicked rims, and occasional applied finger-tipped cordons, is generally known as 'souterrain ware,' a useful if misleading term.

While souterrain ware occurs very freely, and is found in almost every rath, souterrain, crannog, or hut-site that anyone may care to explore, it rarely occurs in firm association with any other diagnostic, exotic, or datable artifact. Under these circumstances, any existing estimate of date had to be preferred to none at all. There was, on the one hand, Childe's horizon of *c.* A.D. 800 at Larriban, resting on a glass armlet which could be paralleled at Lagore, where a pseudo-historical chronology buttressed up the dating based on the actual finds. On the other hand was a tenth-century date, derived (on art-historical grounds) from a slate trial-piece found with a developed form of souterrain ware in the rath at Lissue, Co.

Antrim, an excavation by the late Gerhard Bersu.[46] It followed, therefore, that souterrain ware had perforce to be assigned to the end, rather than to the middle, of the first millennium A.D.

This chronology ruled out, at once, any possibility that souterrain ware could have been transferred to Cornwall, by folk-movement, invasion, or missionary activity, as early as A.D. 550–600. Since no one could suppose, on the existing evidence, that grass-marked ware had evolved in Cornwall, to be transferred by a reverse folk-movement to eighth-century Ireland, an impasse was reached. Nor could a source in a third, unidentified, area, external to both Ireland and Cornwall, and early enough to influence both recipients at the appropriate dates, be postulated, since this highly distinctive pottery has not (as far as anyone knows) been found elsewhere in western Europe.

In the last few years, fresh evidence from Ulster suggests the obvious solution; souterrain ware does occur well before A.D. 800, and it must by inference have been present there by the sixth century in some early form. This will be discussed below. It is worth noting that this whole problem throws into relief a constant feature of British protohistory, the yawning gulf between the archaeological evidence and the historic record. It is seldom appreciated that the constant migrations and settlements of the pre-Viking centuries fall into two rough categories; those which are known from some form of written record, contemporary or later, but for which there is yet no corresponding archaeological evidence, and those deducible on archaeological (including epigraphic) grounds, but apparently not reflected in any written record. Linguistic evidence, and especially place-name evidence, is slowly reducing both groups to an acceptable common basis; but the division remains. In the first category, the massive post-Roman migrations to Armorica, which transplanted a language, have apparently left no archaeological record at all,[47] and the establishment of an Irish dynasty in southwest Wales, an event whose reality is not in doubt, is known primarily from late redactions of an Irish minor epic, some genealogies, some inscribed memorial stones, and (most recently) place-name elements in a Welsh dialect.[48] In the second category, one could list the Pictish conquest of northeast Scotland, Orkney, and probably Skye, which has to be inferred from small finds and the incidence of Pictish graphic art,[49] early post-Roman Irish settlements in both the Isle of Man and Galloway, the latter being known imperfectly from recent archaeological work and place-name study,[50] and, it seems, another Irish settlement in west Cornwall.

The final date of grass-marked pottery

A difficulty which faces anyone who tries to sort out large collections of these post-Roman Cornish wares is that the *fabric* of both grass-marked pottery, in the strict sense, and of the bar-lug cooking-pots, is not only the same, but remained much the same for centuries. The bases and lower walls of grass-marked cooking-pots and of bar-lug cooking-pots are identical. For mechanical reasons (the strain imposed on the inserted pottery bars during the suspension of a full vessel) the upper walls of bar-lug pots tend to be thicker than those of grass-marked pots, but plain-rim fragments could be assigned to either type, unless a full rim circuit can be reconstructed. This means that an individual sherd, or even a handful of sherds which do not include a complete profile or an entire rim, cannot legitimately be assigned to the early (pure grass-marked) or middle (bar-lug) phase *per se*, though it is often permissible to do this on the strength of a single diagnostic sherd, like the asymmetrical swelling from the base of a pulled-out bar-lip.

The only certain instances of broad grouping are those where, in a large series, bar-lug pots are wholly absent. In theory, this might indicate either a 'pre-bar-lug' (pre-ninth century) date, or a post-tenth-century date when the bar-lug fashion had expired. In practice, certain distinctive features of the very latest grass-marked pots exclude this element of guesswork.

In the 1957 season work at Gwithian was extended, not only to the Bronze Age sites and the Romano-British homestead at Porth Godrevy, but to the small medieval manor of Crane Godrevy (*CG*) on the high ground to the north of site I. The primary settlement here (apart from the Iron Age 'round' or univallate earthwork[51] within whose enceinte the manor was sited) proved to be a small rectangular stone hut, cut across by the first medieval long-house, and blocked with rubble. A thin occupation found below this blocking, compacted into the slaty floor, included a number of sherds; some were simple rims, others being grass-marked bases.

This was taken at the time as being, and is still held to be, good evidence of continuity between the first-millennium A.D. site I and the medieval settlement, the latter being deserted only in the seventeenth century. Currency of grass-marked pottery in the eleventh or early twelfth century A.D. was, after all, a concept already raised by such sites as Gunwalloe, widely believed to be the Domesday *Winnianton*, and indeed by St Buryan 'Sanctuary.' The Crane Godrevy sherds were quite inadequate for the reconstruction of any shapes or profiles; but this gap in our knowledge was fortunately filled in 1963.

In the January gales of that year, an entirely new complex of sites at Gwithian, on the southwest flank of the beach and close to the 'churchtown' (Gwithian village), was progressively exposed by wind erosion. The main site, Sandy Lane (*SL*), is a linear midden now over 50 yards long, on a buried land-surface capping north-facing dunes; and further to the north, nearer the present shore, lower and older land-surfaces which exhibit the remnants of clearance banks and may include pre-Norman fields are gradually appearing. In August 1963 the Sandy Lane site was dug with some dispatch, regrettably, but necessarily, since it is traversed by a public footpath, and a mass of sherds obtained to augment the hundreds already gathered there during surface collection.

An analysis of this material, published in 1964,[52] confirms what had been suspected; namely, that bar-lug pots went out of fashion some time around A.D. 1000 (at any rate in west Cornwall), but that small grass-marked cooking-pots continued to be produced for at least a century after this time. These later pots, Sandy Lane style 1, are marked by small size, thin walls, and a method of potting in which the final shaping leaves long, oblique, finger-grooves up the inside of the walls.[53] In the successive Sandy Lane style 2, the bodies of the pots are the same, but the rims now show characteristically everted forms common to cooking-pots over most of southern England; one enters, for the first time, the familiar medieval sequence, and in west Cornwall this innovation should be ascribed to the period *c.* 1100–50.[54]

In the last three years, pottery of Sandy Lane styles 1 and 2 has been excavated at four more sites, a chapel site in Scilly,[55] two chapel sites and a secular site in west Cornwall,[56] where independent considerations bear out this dating.

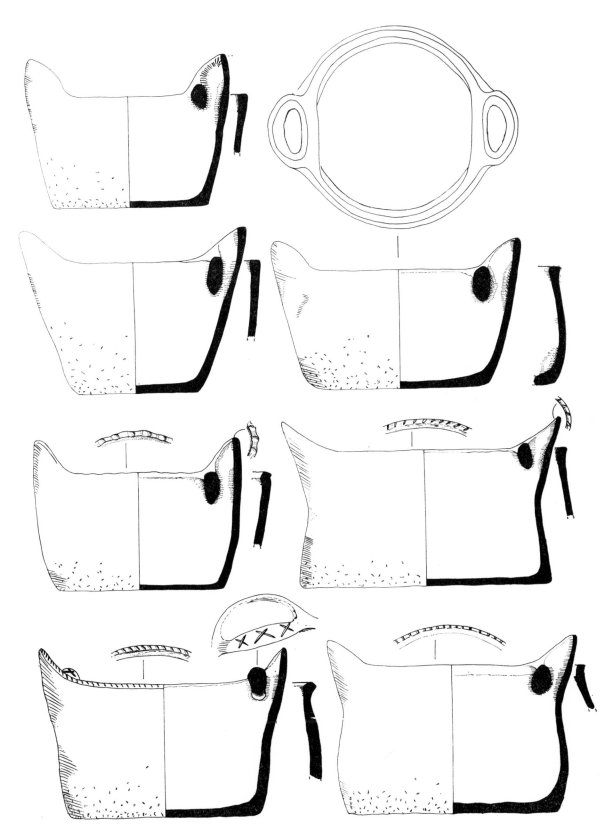

Figure 73. Bar-lug cooking-pots with grass-marked bases, from Gwithian, Site I. (1/4)

Description

Grass-marked pottery is hand-made throughout, the use of a slow wheel or tournette for finishing a pot being detectable only in the very last stage, Sandy Lane style 1, and then perhaps indicating no more than an overlap with Sandy Lane style 2. The fabric is generally thin in proportion to the scale of the vessel, and at all sites where grass-marked pottery has been found, the clay and grits can be supposed to have come from the neighbourhood.

In a few very large vessels, possibly not before the introduction of the bar-lug, the nature of fractures indicates ring-building, but in general the pots must have been coil-built or even pulled up from a lump of clay. Fractures nearly always occur unevenly, making reconstructions difficult. The softness of the core when sherds are found in moist conditions, no less than the frequency with which vessels when in use appear to have been broken even when dropped on nothing more than sand, implies a fairly low firing temperature.

Colours range from dull browns (dark or medium) to grey, a black or greyish-black core being not uncommon. Occasional red patches on the external surface seem to imply the kind of partial oxidization one might expect from casual bonfire firings. Surfaces, when not encrusted with carbon or the remains of carbonized food, are smooth, and sometimes show signs of a crude wash or slip, or of smoothing over with a wet hand.

Two forms consistently occur, the cooking-pot and the platter. The former is shaped rather like a modern saucepan with no handle and with its rim contracted; that is, a flat-based vessel whose height is noticeably less (roughly two-thirds) than its diameter, and whose walls are generally vertical but tend to taper irregularly inwards. These pots are nearly always carbonized externally, the bases flaking as a result of continuous contact with fire, and there is often a crust of carbonized matter (soup or stew?) just over the rim. In use, these pots must have stood directly on a fire. There is, rarely, a slight eversion of the rim, which would permit ease in handling, but normal rim-forms are either flat-topped – so flat that a knife-blade or spatula must have been run around the rim – or else rounded off with only a very faint thickening. In the final Sandy Lane style 1 stage, there is a very characteristic 'burled' profile, where the rim is flat-topped and thickened outwards.

The basal angle varies, but rarely adheres exactly to 90°; it is usually splayed outwards a little, and sags downwards (the result of removal from a slab) giving a small hollow or 'kick' on the underside.

Platters, as a form, seem to have been inherited from the preceding sub-Roman Gwithian-style, a pottery class in which platters identical in shape, but in the superior fabric and finish of this style, are common. They constitute a specifically Cornish sub-Roman type, derived from a low, flat-based, walled dish found in the earlier Roman centuries at such sites as Chysauster and Porthmeor,[57] probably based on a wheel-made Roman coarse-ware model. Grass-marked platters can be up to a foot in diameter, with flat and proportionately rather thick bases, and small vertical or slightly everted walls, the rims being either rounded off or flat-topped. Platters are not found with carbonized exteriors, and were presumably individual eating-plates.

Grass-marking occurs on the exterior bases of both cooking-pots and platters, and in the former, can extend less intensely a short way up the exterior wall. Individual impressions are seldom over 5 mm. long, scattered haphazardly and profusely all over the relevant surface.

Practical experiment at Gwithian has shown that it is quite easy to reproduce grass-marking in a most convincing way, but only by using the fine, short, grasses of the coastal dunes, not meadow-grass or rushes, which have to be plucked, sun-dried, and then chopped very finely. The best explanation is that, like the modern use of sand by some commercial potters, the chopped dried grass was employed to prevent cooking-pots from adhering to the (absorbent) slate slabs on which they were placed to dry green-hard before being fired. Grass would thus be impressed into the undersides of the pots, and transferred sparsely by wet hands, or a breeze, to the lower walls as well. As the pots were probably made in a fairly wet clay (to judge from their commonly 'sagging' look), their bases would have adhered to slate without some such medium as dried grass, and the tensions and cracks resulting from the contractions during the drying process would have led to collapses in the firing.

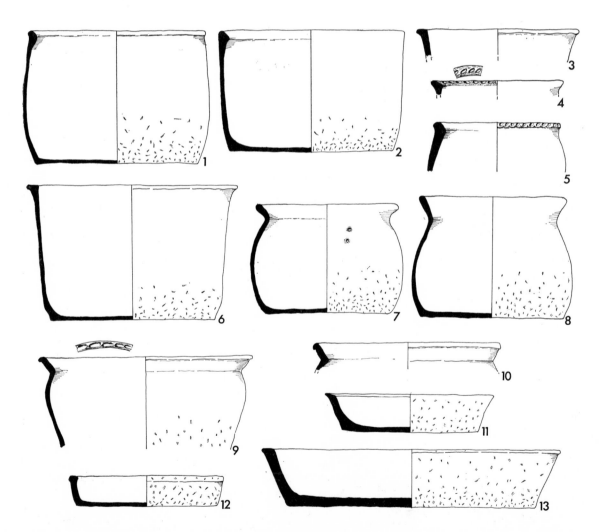

Figure 74. 'Sandy Lane' styles of late grass-marked pottery. Style 1 : 1, 2. Sandy Lane; 3. Lanvean; 4. Gunwalloe; 5. Gwithian (Site I); 6. Crane Godrevy (Gwithian). Style 2 : 7, 8. Chapel Jane (Zennor); 9. Sandy Lane; 10. Crane Godrevy. Platters: 11, 12, 13. Gunwalloe. (1/4)

Though this habit must have had a practical value when first introduced, and even more so with the bar-lug pots, some of which are very thick and heavy, the retention of grass-marking for so long implies pure cultural conservatism. It can never have been really necessary in the case of platters, some of which are no bigger than a modern side-plate, nor indeed with many of the final Sandy Lane grass-marked pots, some of which are tiny, light little vessels holding no more than a pint or so.

Decoration of both cooking-pots and platters is confined to the rim. About a quarter of the platters, and about a third of the cooking-pots, were singled out for enrichment. Finger-tip treatment occurs, as spaced finger-tip (or finger-*nail*) impressions all round the rim; less commonly, one finds the rim has been pinched or crimped, like the edge of a modern Cornish pasty. The only alternative treatment so far noticed is close-set nicking, either with something sharp (like the small post-Roman iron one-edged knives) or with a small bone or the edge of a sheep's rib.

In the bar-lug stage, all that happens is that the *idea* of the bar-lug is added to the extant grass-marked cooking-pot, and certain modifications follow. Bar-lug pots must have been suspended above a fire like a ring-handled cauldron. A practical limit to the size of such pots is imposed by their weight, particularly when filled with liquid, since the adhesive power of fired clay is not all that strong. The two lips which make up the bar-lug handles, diametrically opposed, are first pulled up and outward from the rim in making the pot and then the bars of clay are inserted, and luted horizontally across the insides of these protrusions. The bars form, as it were, internal handles, the protruding lips shielding them, and preventing the flames from the fire beneath from attacking the leather or hay-rope thongs suspending the pot (there is no evidence for iron hooks or chains). In practice, these pots must often have collapsed. Hearths in both layers B and A at Gwithian, site I, yielded numerous pieces of bar-lug pots, and the actual bars which had come away at their roots are found as often as bars which had broken across the middle.

Most reconstructable bar-lug pots from Gwithian have decorated rims (nicked or finger-ornamented), and the decoration is usually carried around the rim of the pot proper and over the rim of the protruding lip. When this happens, the top of the inserted bar – which is normally oval in section, but can also be round, or even roughly rectangular – is also decorated, but not always in the same style as the rim; some bars have slashed saltires or, if they possess flattened tops, nicking on both upper angles.

The present distributional pattern

The picture which this presents today (1967) differs considerably from that current ten years ago. If we define an *early* stage, embracing sites where grass-marked pottery is directly associated with sub-Roman Gwithian style, or with imported wares of the Classes 'A,' 'B,' or 'E,' and where no bar-lug pottery is found, only four certain early sites are known. These are: the lowest layer (C) at Gwithian, site I, the secondary deposit inside Chun Castle, Tean, in the Isles of Scilly, and a new site also in Scilly, Halangy (St Mary's), where grass-marked platters in particular appear to follow on from an occupation in the Roman and fifth centuries.[58]

With the *middle*, or bar-lug, stage, eleven sites are involved. Their distribution is not, as in

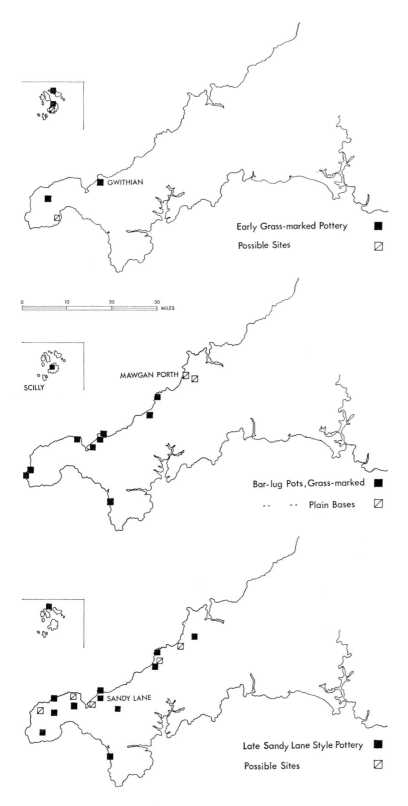

Figure 75. Distributions (March 1967) of the three phases of grass-marked pottery – early grass-marked, bar-lug, and Sandy Lane.

the early stage, confined to west Cornwall, but spreads eastward into the middle of the county; though the two easternmost sites with bar-lug pottery (Mawgan Porth and Lanvean in Mawgan-in-Pydar)[59] clearly mark the limit of the middle-stage range, since between them they have yielded very few grass-marked sherds.

The *final* stage, seen at the type-site of Sandy Lane, has much the same distribution as that of the middle stage. It is worth remarking that though the small Sandy Lane style 1 pots, with their thin walls and distinctive 'burled' rims, did not occur at Mawgan Porth (deserted *c.* A.D. 1000), they were found at Lanvean, about a mile inland, a site probably occupied well into the twelfth century.

A further six sites, none represented in the three groups just outlined, have produced sherds of grass-marked (though not bar-lug) pottery, as chance or casual finds, and it is probable that a number of Cornish sites in the past have also done so; but for lack of information, none of these can be classified yet as of the early, middle, or final stages.

The explanation of the limited distributions in the middle and final stages, emphasized by the relevant maps (fig. 75), is elusive; why the apparent absence in the east of Cornwall? It is true that, due to a fortuitous concentration of archaeological research in the west, rather than in the east, of the county, our knowledge of both northeast and southeast Cornwall is limited, but nothing equivalent to the well-known later Saxon wares of southern England has ever been found in east Cornwall, not even in connection with St Petroc's monastery at Bodmin or the late pre-Norman centre (*Lanstefanton*) at Launceston.[60]

Grass-marked pottery of the early stage can now be seen to be concentrated in Scilly and the very west of Cornwall, and to have spread eastward from there over a period of some centuries. One explanation for its comparatively restricted range may lie in the method of production. In the early phase, and very possibly in the middle, bar-lug period, the pottery appears to have been made *in situ* on a household (or settlement) basis. But the identity in both form and fabric of much of the final-stage Sandy Lane style pots argues a village-industry basis, the products being diffused through local markets or fairs. Whether or not the actual pots at Sandy Lane itself were made in the vicinity of Sandy Lane, and this is likely, since this spot (the historical Conerton) was the paramount manor of Penwith hundred and formed a local focus of settlement,[61] cooking-pots found ten miles to the west at Chapel Jane in Zennor, and five miles southeast at Fenton-Ia in Camborne, appear to be from the same potters, and in sherd form cannot be distinguished as between sites.

The present view as to chronology

Thanks largely to the work (in the Mediterranean and north Africa) of Mr John Hayes, the dating of the Classes 'A' and 'B' imported wares is now on a much more secure basis than it was in 1959, when the present writer offered a chronological scheme for them;[62] and this confirms the postulated sixth-century introduction of grass-marked pottery. But the date at which the idea of the bar-lug, which initiates the middle stage described above, first appears in Cornwall, is still very vague. Students of the period have reached general agreement that Frisian or Frankish traders may have been responsible for its dissemination from some such centre as the Low Countries; it has been suggested that such traders may have come to Cornwall in search of alluvially-won tin, but it must be stressed that this is only a cautious guess within the framework of pure history, with no factual basis in archaeological know-ledge. Moreover, the widespread adoption of the bar-lug idea might be taken as pointing to settlers rather than occasional traders. The initial bar-lug date cannot be very early. It is clear from the wide distribution of the sixth–seventh-century Class 'E' ware, which may also have been disseminated by Frankish or Frisian traders from Channel emporia like Quentovic or Dorestad, that bar-lug pottery was not being exported, either as an idea or in the guise of actual pots, at that date; and the trend of the combined Gwithian and Mawgan Porth evidence points to a rather later period, probably after A.D. 800. The date of the disappearance of the Cornish bar-lug pottery rests partly on the writer's estimate from the Sandy Lane sequence, *c.* 1000, and partly on the coin (of Aethelred II, from the Lydford mint, 990–5) from Mawgan Porth, where, so the excavator thought, 'the site was abandoned not far from the Norman age.'[63] If this horizon leaves a clear field for the final Sandy Lane style pots, *their* disappear-ance is not much later, as is clear from the overlap with the southern English everted-rim cooking-pot tradition. The arguments for dating this overlap to *c.* 1100–50[64] have been independently set out by Mr G. C. Dunning.[65]

The origin and introduction of grass-marked pottery
A welcome innovation over the last few years in Irish archaeology has been the discovery, on a number of sites in northern Ireland, of sherds of the imported Class 'E' pottery, associated with souterrain ware.[66] Without going into tedious detail, these associations do permit an estimate of a slightly earlier age for certain forms of souterrain ware, not necessarily the developed varieties seen at Lissue, Co. Antrim, the long-awaited publication of which is now imminent, but forms which could be the postulated prototypes of the simple Cornish grass-marked cooking-pot, with its flat base, low walls, and grass-marked underside. Whether it will be possible to demonstrate beyond reasonable doubt that such simple forms of souterrain ware were being made in northern Ireland in the sixth century A.D. depends, of course, largely upon the recovery of something suitable from an Ulster rath or crannog; something whose inherent chronology is more acceptable than that of Class 'E' ware, the close dating of which has yet to be worked out. In the meantime, a radiocarbon estimate (D66) of A.D. 480±120, understood to embrace souterrain ware, from Larne, Co. Antrim, may be taken as a pointer in this direction.[67]

    The plain idea of a small-scale Irish settlement in west Cornwall in the sixth century, with settlers who introduced their own souterrain ware, is perfectly acceptable in the broader picture of what was happening in western Britain at this time; the more so, now that our estimate of the part played by widespread Irish migration and conquest is in process of enlargement.[68] The difficulty arises when one turns, as one must, to the limited evidence derived from history (*sensu* annalistic dates, or records of independently-confirmable happen-ings) or 'pseudo-history' (*sensu* the traditions embodied in primarily non-historical writings). Whether or not one chooses to believe that parts of the southern half of Atlantic Britain (west and south Wales, and the great peninsula of Somerset, Devon, and Cornwall) were settled by Irish groups from the fourth (or even the third) century A.D., and most students are now prepared to credit this,[69] the settlers can only be connected with the southernmost Irish regions, and it is useless to look to these regions, counties Cork and Kerry in particular, for prototype grass-marked pottery. Sites which, whatever their absolute dates, cover the sixth century A.D. have been excavated there, and the only pottery they produce is imported pottery of the familiar 'A,' 'B,' and 'E' grouping.[70] It is possible, and within the limited evidence, permissible, to suggest that the presence of inscribed memorial stones with Irish (as opposed to British) personal names, or with actual ogam inscriptions, in east Cornwall and parts of Devon reflect a secondary migration from the established Irish colonies in south Wales.[71] But the part of Cornwall so affected is precisely that part in which grass-marked pottery, early, middle, or late, seems never to occur, and in addition, it can be argued that this limited settlement took place before rather than after A.D. 500.

The grass-marked pottery, as far as its early-stage distribution is concerned, seems to imply a secondary Irish settlement centred on Scilly and the Land's End peninsula; sea-borne colonists coming direct from the souterrain-ware province of northeast Ireland. That souterrain-ware *was* transferred from the homeland to the colonies is suggested by the discovery of some grass-marked sherds in what are presumably primary levels and contexts at Iona, off the west Scottish coast;[72] these must be connected culturally with the Irish settlement of Dalriada from the later fifth century,[73] and chronologically with the establishment of Columcille's monastery at Iona in A.D. 563. In this case, we have direct historical evidence of a sixth-century religious colony, and acceptable historical evidence of a contemporary secular one in the same area. In the case of west Cornwall, there is no evidence for secular settlement from Ulster, or from Ireland in general, beyond late and vague hints as to Irish conquests in the southwest;[74] and unless certain enigmatic and seemingly non-Cornish place-name elements in west Cornwall can be shown to be ultimately Irish in origin, the position is unlikely to improve. There is some very limited evidence for Irish religious activity, evidence which, since it comes from medieval *vitae* and popular tradition, must be regarded as not even secondary but tertiary. Interestingly, this is confined to the initial grass-marked area of west Cornwall, and in so far as the Irish persons named (now the patron saints of various parishes and chapels) are located at all precisely in Ireland, they are connected with the North rather than, as in south Wales, with Munster.[75]

Conclusion

In summary, then, grass-marked pottery can best be regarded as an offshoot of the souterrain ware of Ulster. It was transferred to the extreme west of Cornwall in the sixth century A.D. by settlers coming directly from Ulster, a settlement not historically recorded and thus presumably on a small scale and a family or sub-tribal basis. Grass-marked pottery replaced, as the normal ceramic equipment of peasant households, the older local sub-Roman style, but was never current over a greater area than (approximately) the Isles of Scilly and the western half of Cornwall. Developing in isolation from the parent stock, it never evolved such details as the finger-printed cordons of later Irish souterrain ware (as at, *e.g.*, Lissue) though it retained rim ornament which closely parallels that found in Ulster. In the ninth century, an independent pottery device, the bar-lug handle, reached Cornwall, presumably, on the evidence of its European distribution, through the activities of traders or mercantile settlers from some part of northwest Europe; and over the area in which grass-marked pottery was then current, hybrid cooking-pots with grass-marked bases and bar-lug handles were used until the late tenth or early eleventh centuries. Like the small platters which had been taken over into the grass-marked pottery repertoire from the preceding sub-Roman style, normal but rather small grass-marked cooking-pots continued alongside those with bar-lugs, and as the final or 'Sandy Lane' style, these continued to be used in both Scilly and the western half of Cornwall until the early twelfth century, when they were abandoned in favour of everted-rim cooking-pots of the familiar medieval patterns.

If the failure to provide any historical basis for this argument is bound to mar the picture, there is a brighter and purely archaeological side. The concentrated work of Cornish archaeologists during the last decade has produced a most valuable pottery sequence, one so far unique in the Atlantic province; for it now runs from the pre-Roman Iron Age, through the entire first millennium A.D., and well into the full Middle Ages. Whilst the bulk of this sequence rests on the large and extraordinarily productive sites in the Gwithian area, it is supported by shorter sequences drawn from some thirty other sites in west Cornwall, and rests on a tolerably secure foundation. Pure pottery evidence, like a pure pottery lecture, can be tedious, but a long line of British workers (and the names of Pitt-Rivers, John Abercromby, and Stuart Piggott come to mind at once) has demonstrated its irreplaceable rôle in the syntheses which must follow the mere collection of examples. Slight as the foregoing essay is, it is offered as an exercise of the prehistorian's approach to a pottery group of the historic period, an approach which might be extended with profit to other classes of artefacts in the post-Roman British Isles.

Notes

1. *P.Z.N.H.A.S.* (n.s.) II (1888–8) 337: III (1888–92) 37, 41
2. Finberg, *Early Charters of Cornwall and Devon* (1953) 17 (No. 78)
3. *P.W.C.F.C.* I.2 (1954) 73; *P.W.C.F.C.* II.4 (1960) 151
4. *J.R.I.C.* XXXII.2 (1930) 325
5. *Ant. J.* XVI (1936) 179–98
6. *U.J.A.* XXIV–XXV (1961–2) 91–115
7. *Ant. J.* XVI (1936) 197
8. Most conveniently, summary in Childe, *Prehistoric Communities of the British Isles* (3rd ed., 1949) 210–11
9. *Ant. J.* XVI (1936) 188–90
10. *U.J.A.* XXIV–XXV (1961–2) 97
11. Hamilton, *Excavations at Jarlshof, Shetland* (1956) 187–8
12. *Ant. J.* XXX (1950) 156–69
13. *P.W.C.F.C.* I.2 (1954) 73; *P.W.C.F.C.* II.4 (1960) 151
14. *Med. Arch.* III (1959) 48–9, with map; cf. *Kuml* (1959) 28–52
15. (ed.) Bruce-Mitford, *Recent Archaeological Excavations in Britain* (1956), 190
16. Bruce-Mitford, *op. cit.*; chronology, 195–6
17. *P.W.C.F.C.* I.4 (1956) 136–40
18. *op. cit.* 139
19. *J.R.I.C.* XVIII.1 (1910) 238–40
20. *P.W.C.F.C.* I.2 (1954) 59–72; *P.W.C.F.C.* I, appendix (1956)
21. *P.W.C.F.C.* I.2 (1954) 66–7
22. *Ant. J.* XXIX (1949) 169–82; *The Lizard* (n.s.) I.2 (1958) 15–17
23. *P.P.I.A.* XLVII (C) 2 (1942) 125–34

24. *Ant. J.* XV (1935) 401–19 ('a southern origin, possibly in southern Gaul'); *J.R.I.C.* XXV, appendix (1942) ('foreign wares . . . imported from Visigothic France'); and Radford, *Tintagel Castle, Cornwall* (2nd ed., 1939)

25. *P.W.C.F.C.* II.1 (1957) 15–22 (for class 'A'); *Med. Arch.* III (1959) 89–111 (for class 'B')

26. *P.W.C.F.C.* I.2 (1954) 59

27. Circulated work-notes, December 1958; see *Med. Arch.* III (1959), 96–9

28. *Cf. Trierer Zeitschrift* XI (1936) 75 ff.; Böhner, *Die Fränkischen Altertümer des Trierer Landes* (1958) bd. 2, Taf. 4–6; and Stamm, *Spätrömische und frühmittelalterliche Keramik der Altstadt Frankfurt am Main* ('Schriften des Frankfurter Museums, 1,' 1962), his groups 8 and 9. See now however Peacock and Thomas, 'A Suggested Origin for Class E Imported Pottery,' *C.A.* VI (1967)

29. Thomas, *Gwithian; Ten Years' Work, 1949–1958* (1958) fig. 10

30. Bruce-Mitford, *op. cit.* Pl. xxxvi.a

31. *C.A.* III (1964) 50–1

32. *Med. Arch.* III (1959) 48–9, 'from the 9th century' (Dunning), *Kuml* (1959) 28–52, 'in die Zeit zwischen dem 9. und 11. Jahrh. datiert werden kann' (Becker, summary)

33. *Cf. C.A.* I (1962) 41–2

34. *Antiquity* XL (1966) 172–89

35. Report forthcoming, *C.A.*; *cf. P.W.C.F.C.* II.1 (1957) 33–5

36. Porthcressa Bay, St Mary's (*Arch. J.* CXI (1954) 1 ff.); Halangy Down, St Mary's (*Ant. J.* XXXV (1955) 187 ff.); re-excavation of Halangy Down, interim reports, *C.A.* IV (1965) 36; *C.A.* V (1966) 20

37. *Ant. J.* XXXVI (1956) 75–8

38. *Cf.* now *C.A.* V (1966) 10, suggesting that the amphora sherds are pre-Roman

39. *P.W.C.F.C.* I.2 (1954) 59–72

40. *P.W.C.F.C.* II.2 (1958) 59–72

41. *Ant. J.* XV (1935) 401–19; *J.R.I.C.* XXV, appendix (1942); Radford, *op. cit.*

42. *P.R.I.A.* LIII (C) 1 (1950)

43. *P.R.I.A.* LII (C) 3 (1949)

44. Forthcoming report of G. Bersu's excavations by B. Raftery

45. *P.R.I.A.* LIII (C) 1 (1950) 126, material in N.M.I., Dublin

46. *U.J.A.* X (1947) 30, and final report forthcoming (Belfast)

47. Unless Breton 'ceramique sericitique' (*Annales de Bretagne* LXII (1955) 202–13; *ibid.* LXV (1958), 33–5) is derived in part from Gwithian-style sub-Roman pottery

48. *Cf.* Alcock, *Dinas Powys* (1963) 56–60, with refs.

49. *Arch. J.* CXX (1964) espec. 44–8; (ed.) Wainwright, *The Problem of the Picts* (1955) map 3, 100

50. *T.D.G.N.H.A.S.* XLII (1965), 99–113: XLIII (1966) 112–16; *Scottish Studies* IX (1965) 91 ff.

51. Thomas, *op. cit.* (1958) 28, fig. 13, corrected in *C.A.* III (1964) 42, fig. 13

52. *C.A.* III (1964) espec. 46–51

53. *ibid.* fig. 17 and Pl. I

54. *ibid.* 50

55. St Helen's Isle (*Arch. J.* CXXI (1964) 40 ff.)

56. Chapel Jane, Zennor (noted, *C.A.* IV (1965), 66); Fenton-Ia, Camborne (Thomas, *Christian Antiquities of Camborne* (1967) chapter IV); Lanyon in Madron (interim report, *C.A.* IV (1965) 44–5)

57. Chysauster; *Arch.* LXXXIII (1933) 237 ff.: Porthmeor; *J.R.I.C.* XXIV (1936) appendix

58. *Cf. C.A.* V (1966) 26

59. *P.W.C.F.C.* I.4 (1956) 141–6

60. Coinage; see *J.R.I.C.* XVII.1 (1907) 52–62

61. Thomas, *Gwithian; notes on the church, parish, etc.* (1964) 3–4 and map, fig. 1

62. *Med. Arch.* III (1959) 104–5

63. Bruce-Mitford, *op. cit.* 196

64. *Cf. C.A.* III (1964) 46–51

65. In *Arch. J.* CXXI (1964) 59

66. Cathedral Hill, Downpatrick (*U.J.A.* XVII (1954) 100); Lough Faughan crannog, Co. Down (*U.J.A.* XVIII (1955) 55 and Pl. viii); Ballyfounder rath, Co. Down (*U.J.A.* XXI (1958) 46 and fig. 5); Spittal Ballee, Co. Down (*ibid.* 62); Langford Lodge, Co. Antrim (*U.J.A.* XXVI (1963) 51 and Pl. ix.A); Nendrum, Co. Down (*Med. Arch.* III (1959) 109, catalogue)

67. *Radiocarbon* III (1961) 36; *cf. Archaeological Survey of Northern Ireland : County Down* (1966), 133–5

68. *Cf.* (ed.) Talbot Rice, *The Dark Ages* (1965) 261–2, with map

69. *Cf.* Alcock, *op. cit.*, and Chadwick, *Celtic Britain* (1963) 41–2

70. *e.g.* Garranes, Co. Cork (*P.R.I.A.* XLVII (C) 2 (1942)), and Garryduff, Co. Cork (*P.R.I.A.* LXIII (C) 2 (1962))

71. *P.W.C.F.C.* II.2 (1958) 59–72, with refs. and distribution map

72. *Discovery and Excavation : Scotland* (1959) 10; *Med. Arch.* IV (1960) 138

73. Chadwick, *op. cit.* chapter iii and refs.

74. Cf. *Sanas Chormaic*, ed. Stokes (1868), s.v. *Mug-eime*, 110; ogams and apparent Irish names, Jackson, *Language and History in Early Britain* (1953) 155–6; Taylor, *The Celtic Christianity of Cornwall* (1916) *passim*; Fox, *South West England* (1964) chapter ix

75. Discussion, with map, in Thomas, *Christian Antiquities of Camborne* (1967), chapter iii

Problems and non–problems in palaeo-organology: a musical miscellany

J. V. S. Megaw

Until the rapid development of recording techniques starting in the latter part of the last century, the sound of music had of all the finer arts suffered most from the accidental and intentional ravages of past time. Now with the invasion of science into not only archaeological but musicological research, an increase in the study of both ancient instruments and the sound they may have produced is opening up new areas of investigation. Palaeo-organology, or to borrow the less sonorously pedantic and more immediately meaningful 'musical archaeology' of a recent popular article,[1] is by no means a new study. Already in 1869 François Fétis, then Director of the Brussels Conservatoire, observed that a pipe made of antler found in a megalithic gallery grave near Poitiers was capable of producing four notes of a diatonic scale,[2] and the first bibliography of musical archaeology was published in 1912.[3] The real roots of palaeo-organology lie in the pioneering theoretical and historical research of such men as Curt Sachs[4] and the late Canon F. W. Galpin.[5] Also influential was the movement towards the restoration and actual performance on, particularly, ancient keyboard and stringed instruments in which Galpin was also in the van as the Society which bears his name witnesses. Arnold Dolmetsch's attempts in 1948 at reconstructing the remains of a presumed miniature harp from the early seventh-century Anglo-Saxon ship-burial at Sutton Hoo, with fragments from Taplow, the earliest extant in northern Europe, is a lesser known and perhaps more contentious product of this great family's interest in practical music-making[6] (Pl. XVI, d). In more recent times we have not only the musically-minded archaeologist turning to general,[7] as well as brief regional studies particularly in central and eastern Europe,[8] but the archaeo-logically aware musicologist is also assisting attempts to extend our knowledge of European organology.[9] In the field of modern folk studies ethnomusicologists such as A. L. Lloyd working in the Balkans have suggested a continuity of musical traditions reaching back to the first neolithic farmers if not beyond. Indeed the use of such studies for building up 'a prehis-tory of occidental music' was first suggested by Sachs 30 years ago.[10]

Despite these seemingly encouraging signs of active interest and experimentation it is vital to remember that palaeo-organology, like all basically archaeological studies, must be strictly referred to the very limitations of archaeological evidence and inferences based thereon. In other words, musical archaeology cannot, or should not, be stretched beyond the range of extant material objects as still available to us in the collections of the world's museums or as a last resort, as recognized in the pages of past published accounts of archaeological discoveries, seemingly obvious remarks which must be applied all the more vigorously when reconstructing not just the form but the musical potential of prehistoric instruments.

To particularize, Sir Leonard Woolley's discoveries in the Royal Tombs of Ur not only included a unique range of iconographic material for third-millennium Sumeria but also remains of the actual instruments depicted.[11] On the other hand, the earliest illustration which has been claimed to be that of a musical performer, one of the composite figures sketched on the walls of the Trois Frères cave in the Ariège presumed to be Magdalenian in date,[12] has been equally claimed as showing a primitive end-blown pipe[13] and a musical bow.[14] That archaeological evidence supports the contemporary existence of the former but not the latter is no argument for the non-existence in the Palaeolithic of the musical bow whose natural manufacture from wood or bone and animal sinew would require exceptional physical circumstances to allow of its survival to the present day. Again, that the Australian Aborigine of our own era is to be numbered amongst what have been termed the 'flute-less advance-guards of mankind,'[15] cannot be held as conclusive evidence that the pipe was never known on Antipodean shores any more than the also now absent bow-and-arrow although neither is likely. With these caveats in mind we may proceed to an examination of some on the whole more recent evidence for the main departments of the prehistoric orchestra of Ancient Europe.

Percussion : the 'kitchen department'

The modern musician's slang for the percussion section is not inappropriate since the sense of rhythm is hardly less basic to man than his need for food. As Sachs has put it, 'once man has become fully conscious of the comfort and stimulus that regular pulsation gives he seldom sings without clapping his hands, stamping the ground, or slapping his abdomen, chest, legs or buttocks,'[16] a behaviour pattern which one may also observe amongst the higher apes. Wooden clappers are a natural extension to manual percussion and complex rhythmic patterns are represented among even those communities generally considered the most primitive from the point of view of instrumental music; the Australian Aborigine produces rhythms of up to 320 beats to the minute using a pair of boomerangs.[17]

In the Palaeolithic of Europe, let alone later periods, such utilization of common objects is to be expected if not proven; on the other hand there is the well-known association of bone whistles and notched scrapers of the type still an integral part of kindergarten bands.[18] Enclosed rattles of clay generally assumed to be skeuomorphs of gourds have a long life, neolithic examples coming from the eastern end of the *Linearbandkeramik*[19] province and children's graves of the Usatovo culture contemporary with late Tripolye.[20] Other rattles from northern and western Europe date to the Late Bronze and Early Iron Ages while the bronze 'crotals' found with horns of the later Irish Bronze Age and recently interpreted as part of a local bull cult, whatever their ritual significance, emphasize the continuity of interest in aids to the production of rhythmic sound.[21]

The clearest material evidence for the importance of rhythm in western prehistory is of course offered by the usually double open-ended hour-glass pottery drums of the late neolithic T.R.B. and related regional groups of the north European plain and central Europe.[22] The assumption that the drums developed from wooden prototypes somewhere in the contact zone between the northern and Danubian cultures is supported at least as far as form goes by ethnographic parallels from a wide area ranging from North Africa to Oceania; there seems to be a common and prime interest in the drum amongst many simple agricultural communities which today reaches its height in the wheel-turned pottery instruments of the *virtuosi* drummers of the Upper Nile.[23] The practicability of the European neolithic drum has been proved on careful hand-made copies with 'heads' or vibrating membranes of uncured leather based on T.R.B. drums from Bohemia[24] (Pl. XV). The use of the knobs or pierced lugs visible on all these drums to stretch the head seems even more clearly demonstrated by the carefully shaped horizontally protruding lip above pierced lugs on a veritable bass drum some 60 cm. high found in a late neolithic grave at Egeln, Kr. Stassfurt (Pl. XV, a; fig. 76, 6).[25] The existence of varying sized drums tempts one to conceive of a neolithic concern with pitch as much as rhythm but it is one of the many frustrating features of musical archaeology that the all-important rhythmic no less than tonal patterns – endorsed with who knows what magical powers[26] – which must have been the *raison d'être* for the productions of such prehistoric instruments cannot profitably be the subject even of conjecture.

Piping down the valleys wild : simple end-blown flageolets

The general range of the end-blown or whistle type of instruments known in prehistory only from bone examples is already well documented;[27] however, contrary to the view that pierced phalanges mainly from upper palaeolithic occupation sites represent simple signal or decoy whistles is a recent theory that such objects are part of a long-lived and widespread tradition of schematized human bone idols.[28] It is important though to make a distinction between phalanges pierced just below the articular condyles by a single hole and those with a double hole capable of a pure sound only if one is blocked. Of the former class the largest series are known from the Gravettian open stations of central Moravia. From the most recent excavations at Pavlov are some six examples, five of which produce a clear tone.[29] Single-holed, and therefore at least to the present writer probably whistle, phalanges occur as late as the Otomani phase of the Únětice culture as found in a ritual well at Gánovce near Poprad in Czechoslovakia.[30] Whatever the real use of the perforated phalange it should be noted that neither palaeolithic toe-bones nor indisputable end-blown pipes have been found outside domestic contexts despite the hint offered by Les Trois Frères. This is in contrast to the find conditions of most pipes of the Neolithic, particularly in south Russia, such as pipes from 'Pit grave' culture burials at Bereznovka II,[31] and Bronze Ages or of the presumed pan-pipes to be discussed in the next section.

By the beginning of the upper palaeolithic we have undoubted evidence of man's ability – and concern – to produce comparatively sophisticated instruments. The fragmentary bird-bone pipe from the Aurignacian III levels of the Isturitz cave in the Basses-Pyrénées, only one of eight from this site, has at least three well-cut finger holes[32] and differs little in form from pipes of many millennia later (Pl. XVI, a–b). There is still no hint of 'ritual' use nor, perhaps more important, as yet of musical potential in the three most complex bones of the late Pleistocene which have been claimed as pipes. These are one of elk bone from the late Magdalenian levels and two of slightly later date at Molodova in the Ukraine. The first of

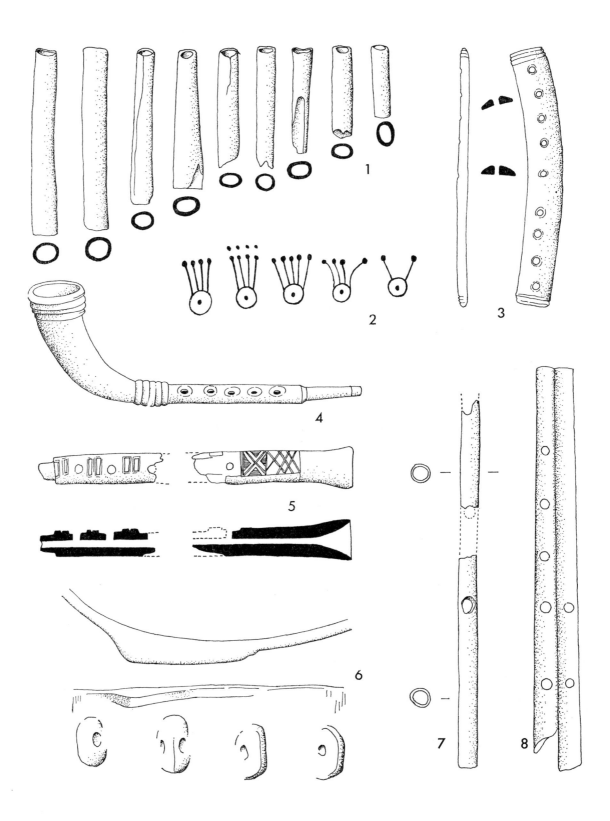

these bones has what might be considered four finger holes and two rear thumb holes and is unfortunately broken at what one would assume to be the upper end.[33] However, the extreme narrowness of the internal bore of the bone and the small size of the 'finger holes' (the largest measures only 6×3 mm.) casts certain doubts as to its feasibility as a musical instrument. A more recent find from Molodova is that of two other bones with pierced holes, one of antler with seven holes on one side and two on the rear; these also have been claimed as pipes but again the holes are of extremely small size (c. 2 mm. in diameter).[34] Two other additions to the listing of more definite bone pipes filling the gap between the mesolithic and the later neolithic period are a long bone with single blow hole and a possible notched or vertical flute without modifications from a *Linearbandkeramik* site at Vederovice, Moravia; from Rumania we have pipes associated with Gumelniţa material.[35] Also from a domestic rather than ritual context is a pipe made from a dog's tibia found in a Bronze Age *terremare* settlement at Montalo, Modena.[36]

For completeness' sake attention should be drawn to a small group of whistles datable to the early centuries of our era and cut from the terminal portion of antler tines; these have well-cut voicing lips but no finger holes. One comes from the Celtic oppidum of Staré Hradisko in Moravia,[37] one from Roman Canterbury[38] and a series of five from various sites in Poland, one with a well-fitted block or fipple.[39] It is unfortunate that this last example cannot be securely dated since such preserved fipples as are known with bone pipes are all fairly late or poorly dated. The four-holed bone pipe with wooden fipple from Paarup now in the Nationalmuseet, Copenhagen, was found under the floor of a farmhouse built in 1869 while nothing at all is known of the date of the pig bone with hardwood fipple in the Musikhistoriska Museet, Stockholm.[40]

None of these additions to the general whistle family offer much hope for further experimentation to test for preferred tonal ranges in ancient bone pipes, experimentation which as so far published has proved entirely inconclusive. In 1963 with the co-operation of Mr G. Elzinga, Dr W. A. van Es and Dr J. D. van der Waals further investigations were made into the largest series of bone pipes known, those from the *terpen* sites of the northwestern Netherlands preserved in the Gemeente Museum, Groningen, and the Fries Museum, Leeuwarden. Dating and study of bone material from the Dutch *terpen* is notoriously difficult since the majority of finds have been made as the result of agricultural work. In view of the general lack of definite pre-Roman bone finds it is usually assumed that most of the pipes are to be dated from the fifth or sixth to the twelfth century A.D.[41] Nonetheless, traditions die hard in regional instrument- no less than music-making and it would seem a fair assumption to

Figure 76. 1. Przeczyce, Poland. Bone pan-pipes, Lausitz culture (1/2).
2. Various localities. Possible lyres as represented on Continental Celtic coinage (not to scale).
3. Dinorben, Denbighshire. Third century B.C. antler ? wrest plank (1/2).
4. Volga region. Reconstruction of eighth-century Late Bronze/Early Iron Age pipe with bronze horn (1/4).
5. Hungate, York. Wooden pipe from Anglo-Norman levels (1/2).
6. Egeln, kr. Stassfurt. Late Neolithic pottery drum. Detail of rim and upper binding lugs (1/4).
7. Wilsford barrow G. 23. Bone pipe, Wessex culture (1/2).
8. Jánoshida, Hungary. Parallel bone pipes from Avar grave (1/2).

regard the *terpen* pipes as a unit and any consistent pattern observed in manufacture or performance valid for the group as a whole. Only bones whose form was complete or capable of accurate reconstruction were included in the sample, 12 from the collections at Groningen and 27 from Leeuwarden. The number of finger holes ranged from none (that is, with only a blow hole provided) to six, the largest group being nineteen with three finger holes on the anterior surface with occasionally a thumb hole on the posterior. This prevalence of three-hole pipes from earliest times I have previously commented on as being the maximum number which may be utilized while holding the instrument with one hand.[42] The distance between voicing lip and the uppermost finger hole follows no constant, being furthest on tubes of greatest length where the finger holes are placed so as to gain the maximum range of tonal variation and thus being always grouped from the lower opening upwards. Distances between individual finger holes ranged from 8 mm. to 22·5 mm., the mean being 16·5 mm., a factor governed doubtless as much by practical considerations, spacing at a finger's-breadth interval for example, as musical. Sheep's tibia, utilized in western Europe since at least the Iron Age,[43] predominate as the raw material.

Seven pipes from the Groningen collections were acoustically tested and the results are recorded in Table 1. It should be clear at a glance that there is little consistency to be noted, even keeping in mind the possibility, or rather probability, of additional tonal variations resulting from partial fingering and over-blowing.

Table 1

Provenance	Inv. No.	Type	Tonal range*	Remarks
Rottum, gem. Kantens	1921/I 52	3 finger holes	f″g″ab″b++″	non-modal
Saxumhuizen, gem. Baflo	1887/VI 62	3 finger holes	b‴c⁗e⁗a♯⁗	non-modal
Westerwijtwerd, gem. Middelstum	1890/VI 11	4 finger holes	bb‴c⁗d‴″e‴″a‴″	
Feerwerd, gem. Ezinge	1890/VI 12	5 finger holes	d♯‴″e‴″f‴″g++‴″ab‴″c⁗	
De Wierhuizen, gem. Appingdam	1917/VIII 8	3 finger, 1 thumb holes	f″f♯″ a″bb″(c‴)	
Warffum, gem. Warffum	1884/I 82	3 finger holes	bb″c‴d‴e‴	
Warffum	1884	3 finger, 1 thumb holes	gb″ab″b″db‴eb‴	pentatonic (Lydian mode)

*In all musical examples here quoted 'middle' c = c′, c below the bottom line of the bass stave = C, a′ = 440 c.p.s. etc.; + and − indicate variations of less than a quarter tone.

Further experimental work on four pipes in the Fries Museum, Leeuwarden, was published while this paper was in the press.[43a] The results of acoustic tests are appended in Table 2. It should be observed that the apparently more extensive range of the Leeuwarden pipes as compared with those shown in Table 1 is the result of extensive use of cross-fingering avoided in my own experiments in view of the impossibility of judging the past use of this expansion of a pipe's natural range:

Table 2

Provenance	Inv. No.	Type	Tonal range	Remarks
Huizum, gem. Leeuwarden	15^A–139	2 finger, 1 thumb holes	d‴e♭‴f‴g‴	diatonic
Hiaure, gem. Westdongeradeel	32–104	3 finger, 1 thumb holes	e♯‴f♯‴g♯‴a♯‴b‴c♯⁗	diatonic
Wetzens, gem. Oostdongeradeel	34^B–42	3 finger, 1 thumb holes	g‴a‴b‴c⁗d⁗	diatonic
Jouswier, gem. Oostdongeradeel	34^D–1	3 finger, 1 thumb holes	e‴f‴f♯‴g‴ g♯‴a‴a♯‴b‴	chromatic

There is little support in these results for the common belief in the world-wide predominance of the pentatonic scale; the only exception in fact is the pipe from Warffum listed in Table 1 under inv. no. 1884. The supposed exception to the priority of the pentatonic system is the 'cultivated' Western style where the diatonic scale combining whole and semitones prevails.[44] Indeed if one were to examine prehistoric pipes in Europe as the sole evidence for the development of tonal systems in the West, the diatonic scale would appear to be of extreme antiquity and in fact have priority over modal or whole-tone scales.[45] Much has been made of the modal scale of the Iron Age pipe from a burial at Malham Tarn in Yorkshire (c⁗c♯⁗d♯⁗f⁗)[46] and the modal nature of all primitive pipes argued,[47] but from our European sample there seems little to support this. Even with well-dated and late examples the twelfth-century A.D. pipe from White Castle, Monmouthshire, having a diatonic range encompassing the popular key of modern primitive vocal accompaniment, B♭ major,[48] may be contrasted with a contemporary bird-bone pipe from the Medieval levels of Canterbury with, once more, three finger holes and a range of b″d‴e‴f♯‴ which could equally be regarded as pentatonic.[49] Obviously the prehistoric penny whistle does not hold the key to the development of early tonal systems.

One class of simple whistle which shows an extension of some of the construction principles of the end-blown pipe into much less convenient material than bone is a group of pottery enclosed resinators, prehistoric *ocarinas*. Earliest of these globular whistles is a late neolithic example with a single blow hole associated with pottery of the Vučedol type from Hochberg, Perchtoldsdorf in Lower Austria; a variation of notes is possible: a′b♭′b′c″.[50] A rather more sophisticated lugged form some 8 cm. long with a single finger hole was found with Tószeg encrusted ware at Vörösmart, Kom. Baranya and gives a♯⁗, the stopping of the finger hole making the difference of less than a quarter tone.[51] Two other Hungarian Bronze Age whistles of this type apparently now lost are that in the form of a bird, as noted by Seewald in such distant settings as the Indus Valley civilization, from a Tószeg B cemetery at Pilín, Kom. Néograd and one from Tószeg itself.[52]

The pipes of Pan

It was Kathleen Schlesinger who observed that from apparently earliest times notched flutes have been concentrated in southeast Asia and the Americas, and pipes fitted with a fipple in Europe.[53] The notched or vertical flute, already briefly attended to, is in fact a difficult instrument to play; the player's breath must be directed against the edge of the open tube instead of being channelled by an inserted block or fipple.[54] The vertical flute which continues today as the Arabian *nay* and in the Balkans and Greek Islands[55] may go back to the Istallóskő pipe of Aurignacian II date with its (diatonic!) range of a‴b♭‴b‴c⁗.[56] However, the notched pipe is certainly not conspicuous against later bone pipes; one or two possibles from the *terpen* material are capable of an alternative explanation (see below).[57] On the other hand, in view of more definite evidence from the Mesolithic onwards, it is not unlikely that the bone tubes from the prewar excavations at Dolní Věstonice, including one with a plug of resin still in place at one end of a red deer metacarpal,[58] represent the first example of a long series of multiple stopped or pan-pipes. All these upper palaeolithic tubes are of varying lengths and all produce different tonal values when blown. The association of four unequal bone tubes found with Aurignacian/Magdalenian polished scrapers in the Le Placard cave in the Charente lends strong support to this theory.[59]

In contrast with the first fipple flutes, most of the evidence for early pan-pipes is from burials. Earliest are the seven or eight sections of bird-bone from grave 8 of the late third-millennium 'Ochre grave' Mariupol cemetery near Kiev[60] while the Kitoi culture hunter-fisher burial on Zhiloi Ostrov in Lake Baikal produced evidence of a four-tube pipe.[61] Finally from this eastern region is the seven-tube pipe from a Pit-grave culture barrow, grave 5/3 at Sakatova, Saratov on the Volga, on which tonal experiments have been made but unfortunately are as yet unpublished (Pl. XIV, a).[62]

For some indication of the musical potential of such primitive pan-pipes one must move to a later period of time. In inhumation grave 89 of a large Lausitz cemetery at Przeczyce, Zawiercie, from beneath a stone cairn were recovered the bones of an old man of about 60 years of age, pottery, bronze bracelets and a pin dating to Montelius V (=Ha.C), two pierced boar's teeth and an amulet in the form of a disc cut from a cow's horn.[63] Scattered in the grave of what the excavators considered could be regarded as a local wise man or *shaman* were nine varying length sections of sheep or goat metapoidals (fig. 76, 1). A subsequent reconstruction aided by stain marks suggesting the position of the original binding gave a range of c‴d‴e‴g‴a‴c⁗d⁗e⁗g⁗. This range is not only unmatched by any other instrument of the Bronze Age but fits so precisely into a two-octave pentatonic scale that one can but be amazed, if not incredulous, at the implications for music in eighth-century B.C. Poland, an area where certainly Sachs gives primacy to the pentatonic system on the basis of folk studies. Incidentally, the scattering of the various sections of the Przeczyce pipes may be due to a similar desire to 'kill' the instrument as encountered with bronze horns of a closely similar date (see below).

It is from a slightly later period that we have the largest body of iconographical evidence for the pan-pipes.[64] These are on decorated bronze buckets of the Iron Age metalworking centres of northern Italy and the head of the Adriatic. The occurrence of pan-pipes in this so-called '*Situla* art' is listed in Table 3, the catalogue numbers being those allotted in the recent publication of the *situla* now in the School of Design, Providence (Rhode Island).[65]

Detailing on the bronze buckets is not always clear (Pl. XIV, b); for example on the Vače *situla* the pan-pipes appear to have six tubes below the horizontal binding and only five above[66] and the Welzelach *situla* is reconstructed from fragments, although on this bucket there are clearly more than the two pan-pipes as noted by Seewald.[67] In view of the highly stylized nature of the *situla* style as a whole and the restricted nature of its subject matter of whatever period, little can or should be made of the variations in individual pipe form. The earliest Greek illustrations of the pan-pipes or *syrinx* date to much the same period as the earliest *situla* representations.[68] The most famous of the former is that of the muse Kaliope with a 9-reed pipe on the early sixth-century François vase, a Greek export found in an Etruscan tomb at Chiusi. For what it is worth, attention has been drawn to the similar variation in the number of tubes on the *syrinx* to the strings of the contemporary lyre, a range of five to thirteen with a preference for between seven and nine.[69] The lack of apparent consistency in the number of individual tubes should arouse no more surprise than variations in finger holes on fipple pipes and is discernible on presentday ethnographic examples.[70]

Table 3

Cat. No.	Provenance	No. of instruments	No. of tubes	Date (B.C.)
21	Magdalenska Gora I, Jugoslavia, tomb XIIID, gr. 55	1	5	6th/5th century
33	Vače, Jugoslavia	1	?5/6	6th/5th
4	Certosa di Bologna, Italy	1	6	early 5th
1	Italy (= the Providence *situla*)	3	7	early 5th
44	Welzelach, Tyrol, Austria	?5	5,4,4,4,?	early 5th

Whether or not the Adriatic region learnt of the pan-pipes through Greece, which had established a colony there as early as *c.* 600 B.C.,[71] or whether this marks a continuity of barbarian musical traditions, it seems probable that later extant pan-pipes in western Europe are due to Mediterranean influence. From a La Tène III cemetery at Klein-Kühnau, Kr. Dessau, is a five-reed instrument, the ends stopped with resin.[72] The fragmentary bone pipes from the Garonne at Agen are assumed to be Gallo-Roman[73] while of clearly more sophisticated form are two closely comparable pan-pipes cut from solid box-wood. One of these is the eight-note instrument from a well at Alesia,[74] the second, also from a Roman well containing second/third-century A.D. pottery, at Barbing-Kreuzhof, Ldkr. Regensburg with four pipes bored in the solid wood.[75] On the former instrument only the third pipe would voice (f♯′). The range which can be obtained from the Alesia *syrinx*, d′e′f♯′g′b′c″d″, is definitely not a modal scale, but whether this is indicative of the establishment of western 'cultivated' music as some have regarded the introduction of our modern system of sharps and flats is not so certain.

The oaten reed

Brief mention has already been made of the vertical flute; the transverse flute, that is one played in the manner of the modern orchestral flute, does not affect our present discussions although it has a longer history in Greece and Italy than generally recognized.[76] It is however possible in view of the apparent rarity of the vertical flute in western Europe, that some bone pipes with no apparent voicing lip may represent the surviving part of an instrument originally fitted with a simple split straw or 'beating reed,' working on the same principle as the old children's trick of blowing on a blade of grass held upright between the palms of the hands. The work of ethnomusicologists in the Balkans tends to suggest a long history for the reed pipe and A. L. Lloyd's recordings of an old Rumanian peasant playing literally on 'oaten reeds,' barley stalks with up-cut split lips, offer the archaeologist a tantalizing hint of the doubtless irrevocably lost evidence for the music of prehistoric Balkan farming communities extending back into the fifth millennium B.C. In Egypt, the single reed pipe has a history dating at least from the third millennium[77] and in Greece from the ninth century B.C.[78]

This is no place to become involved in the complexities of current theories as to the development of music in ancient Greece. Suffice it for our present purposes that the *aulos*,[79] apparently a generic term for all types of reed instruments but not, as constantly mistranslated, flutes, was cylindrical in internal bore, related therefore to the modern clarinet and having the acoustic properties of the so-called 'stopped pipe' with in its most primitive form a maximum compass of approximately an octave; only with a quickly vibrating reed have such pipes the ability to produce a harmonic, the harmonic of the twelfth. The development of the more sophisticated conical pipe, the form of the oboe family, followed only in the third century A.D., although there is a Jewish coin of the time of the Emperor Hadrian which Sachs claims as showing a conical reed instrument.[80] With the invention of the conical pipe comes the ability to produce the harmonic of the octave and a range of two diatonic octaves.[81] Practical as opposed to theoretical studies have as yet done little to further our knowledge of Greek scales and certainly offer no evidence for Kathleen Schlesinger's theory of equidistant finger holes on cylindrical pipes, something which our bone flutes come closer to. The earliest extant fragment of an *aulos* is a bone tube with five finger holes and one thumb hole found in a late sixth-century B.C. level at Brauron.[82] A reconstruction of the complete instrument compares with copies made of the fifth-century Elgin *auloi* found in a tomb near Athens and now in the British Museum; these last have been shown to be capable of an octave range and a pentatonic scale;[83] another fifth-century pipe in two sections with five unequally spaced finger holes comes from Corinth.[84] The scale produced on the Brauron pipe divides at the centre and may point to the use of Ptolemy's tetrachords. On the other hand, if the reconstruction is correct, experiments based on a Hellenistic model *aulos* from the Temple of Apollo at Pergamon give a range of sixteen tones of the key of C major from c to d″.[85] Disagreement as to the type of reed used with the classical pipe continues; recent practical tests have been made with modern broad bassoon reeds or near-equivalents. A final point which experimentation has made clear is the need to match the performance of the mouth-piece and/or reed with the theoretical pitch of the pipe; the low pitch in relation to their length which one can observe on all playable *auloi* is characteristic of cylindrical pipes as a whole.

Returning to the pre- and protohistory of Europe, it can only be guesswork but the swan's ulna from the Wessex Bronze Age bowl barrow Wilsford G.23, far from having a 'carefully shaped mouth-piece' or even a definite voicing lip,[86] might have once been provided with a simple split-straw reed (fig. 76, 7). From fourth/third-century B.C. contexts in the Greek colonies of Histria and Kallatis in Rumania come bone pipes with three, four and six finger holes recently regarded as the remains of crude *auloi* but whether these are locally evolved instruments or made by the Dacians following the more sophisticated Greek models is hard to say.[87] Two apparently matching bone pipes with six finger holes from Mook on the Maas south of Nijmegen were found near a Roman villa and cemetery and could be similarly interpreted[88] as could another bone also with six finger holes from the Hatsum, gem. Menaldumadeel *terp*.[89]

The earliest extant pipe in northern Europe which one may claim with any real certainty as originally utilizing a reed is a wooden instrument from the tenth/eleventh-century Anglo-Danish levels at the Hungate, York (fig. 76, 5).[90] Now in two sections with only three obvious finger holes, there may have been as many as five, the wood bells out towards the bottom while in place of a mouth-piece there is the male half of a tapered joint. The bone is cylindrical and far too narrow for use as a flute but could easily have taken a straw beating-reed and perhaps a mouth-horn or chamber to assist channelling the player's breath. The presence of a separate mouth-piece covering the reed and matched by a bell of horn is the key feature of the Welsh *pibgorn*, three extant examples of which date back to the eighteenth century A.D., but the simple combination of reed-pipe and horn bell has a much more widespread distribution;[91] the Anglo-Saxon *swegel horn* ('shin-bone and horn') indicates just such a use of natural materials as has been postulated for non-reed and hornless bone pipes. From prehistoric times we have Dr J. M. Coles' suggestion that parts of his two-piece Class II Irish Bronze Age 'horns' to be discussed in the next section might have formed the metal bells of such reed instruments[92]; a similar claim has been made for a Late Bronze/Iron Age find from the Volga region (fig. 76, 4) where today the Russian hornpipe or *jaleika* is to be compared with the Scottish 'stock-and-horn.'[93] The second-century A.D. Greek writer, Julius Pollux, teacher of the Emperor Commodus, not only notes that 'the Scythians . . . for their pipe (*aulos*)-playing blow into the bones of eagles and vultures'[94] but also mentions the twin horn bells of the so-called 'Phrygian' or unequal divergent double pipes which were probably introduced to Rome at the close of the third century B.C. together with the cult of Cybele.[95] Anthony Baines has also drawn attention to apparent horn bells on divergent pipes – perhaps introduced from the eastern Mediterranean – depicted on Iberian pottery of not earlier than third-century B.C. date from the Levantine settlement of San Miguel de Liria (fig. 77, 1). There are several depictions of male and female players on both the single and double pipes, one of the former looking for all the world like a shawm; the Liria vases also appear to represent horns.[96] In parenthesis we may note that the only double hornpipe from the British Isles, dated 1701 and found in north Wales, may represent the single extant fragment of a Welsh bagpipe known otherwise only from a sixteenth-century A.D. manuscript.[97]

With utilization of the double pipes naturally follows a considerable extension in the potential of the single performer.[98] He (with the Liria pots and one other exception to be noted later, never 'she' as far as one can tell from the musical iconography of prehistoric Europe) may play the same tune on each pipe, a melody plus a 'drone' or holding ground note, or two-part music. As has been remarked 'it is across the old Greek area, from the Black Sea to Italy and Sardinia, that a living double-pipe tradition today exhibits an intricate mixture of drone and polyphony that is approached nowhere else in the world of folk-music.'[99] The earliest double pipes depicted belong once more to the eastern Mediterranean.

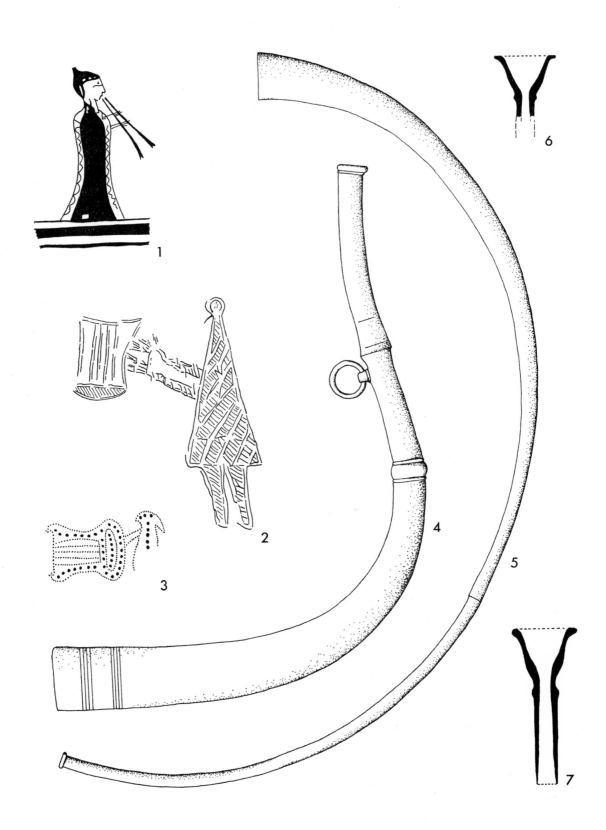

From Egypt there is an Old Kingdom statuette probably of the III Dynasty (with V Dynasty parallels from Saqqarah and Gizeh)[100] while there is the well-known Early Cycladic marble figurine from a grave on Keros, all of at least third-millennium date.[101] On the side of the Hagia Triada sarcophagus from Crete (Late Minoan III) is painted a player on the double pipes, one of which clearly has a funnel-shape bell but whether of horn or not one cannot of course say.[102] A few centuries later than this last example the double pipes also appear in Sardinia; an ithyphallic bronze figurine from Ittiri, Sassari of the Nuraghic culture (*c.* 900–500 B.C.) (Pl. XV, f),[103] underlines the fertility aspect of the reed pipe which continues in the Balkans today. Other Nuraghic figurines who are apparently playing on the triple pipes suggest a considerable antiquity for the still extant tradition of playing on the *launedda*, a word which may be a corrupt dialect diminutive of '*aulos.*' The modern Sardinian performer on the *launedda* uses a technique of continuous playing without the aid of a mouth-horn or bag to produce two-part music plus a drone,[104] a fantastic orchestral sound which has to be heard to be believed.

Turning to continental Europe the earliest evidence for double pipes is a late Ha.D figurine in bronze from Százhalombatta south of Budapest playing what its original publisher regards as a double trumpet[105] but what Seewald plausibly suggests as a reed instrument (Pl. XV, e).[106] The flat crescentic terminals to these divergent pipes seemingly following the Balkan and Mediterranean tradition, may be intended to represent bell-ends. Other and much later Iron Age evidence is limited to the strange hybrid, part helmeted Celt, part Roman centaur, on a British coin of Tasciovanus (Pl. XV, d);[107] this may be the result of copying classical prototypes but in view of the accurate representations of other clearly Celtic instruments, could represent a local survival of the southern form. Later still and perhaps showing in contrast a continuation of the nomadic interest in the reed pipe is the unique discovery in a seventh/eighth-century A.D. grave at Jánoshida in Hungary of two crane's bones originally bound together and found clutched in the hand of an Avar warrior (fig. 76, 8). Although without any sign of a mouthpiece or horn bell, the Jánoshida pipes are of extreme interest in being the earliest extant example of unequal-holed paralleled pipes, since the right pipe has five finger holes and the left two, hinting at the use of simple two-part melody as still employed by the bagpipe players of Finnish extraction in the Volga district.[108]

But we are still far from being certain about the origin and spread of the first reed pipes. The most obvious hypothesis is to relate their evolution to the development and expansion from the Balkans and east Mediterranean of the first agricultural communities together with the resultant availability of the simplest raw materials, the long bones of domestic animals and the stalks of cultivated seed crops.

Figure 77. 1. San Miguel de Liria. Spain. First Century B.C. Iberian painted vase. Detail showing player on double pipes with apparent horn bells (1/2).
2. Sopron, barrow 27, Hungary. Ha.C. pottery urn. Detail showing lyre player (1/2).
3. Klein-Glein, Steiermark. Seventh century B.C. bronze bucket. Detail showing lyre player (1/2).
4. Drumbest, Co. Antrim. Late Bronze Age end-blow horn (1/4).
5. Ardbrin, Co. Down. Iron Age bronze horn (1/8).
6. Brudevaelte II, Denmark. Montelius V Lur mouthpiece (1/2).
7. Modern trombone mouthpiece (1/2).

The lowing horn

We must now consider the organology of the brass section and once more assume that the chances of non-survival have robbed us of the evidence for the earliest stages in the development of this class, the basic essentials of which are a resonating tube into which the player blows, his lips vibrating as he does so. Performance on the Australian Aborigine's *didjeridoo*, which is nothing more than a long hollow tube of wood, is a telling example of virtuosity producing a remarkable range on an instrument simple to the point of crudity.[109] It is however another matter to claim as primitive horns such unrefined hollowed-out bones as that from the Bronze Age burial of Wilsford barrow G.58; probably the earliest representation of a horn is that being played by a Nuraghic figurine from Santu Pedru, Genoni. Here however the instrument looks like a cousin of the Irish end-blow horns now to be discussed.[110]

Of the two main classes of metal wind instruments, the horn of conical bore and the trumpet of cylindrical bore, both are known in the later prehistory of Europe, but only the former in a playable state. Although strictly outside the main regional scope of our survey, it would be improper not to mention, however briefly, the most famous of all ancient trumpets, one of bronze and one of silver, found in the XVIII Dynasty tomb of Tut-ankh-amen, since it was the experiments carried out in 1939 by one Bandsman James Tappern of the 11th Hussars for the British Broadcasting Corporation which in many ways may be said to have laid the foundations of modern practical palaeo-organology.[111] However, the often published statements that the Tut-ankh-amen trumpets and their pendants are capable of producing the main notes of the harmonic series, no less than a claim for Verdi's unconscious archaeological hindsight in his orchestration of the triumphal march from *Aida*,[112] are based on Tappern's recorded performance which made use of a modern trumpet mouthpiece on instruments later demonstrated never to have had such. Indeed, to anticipate, truly functional mouthpieces properly cusped so that the lips of the player may vibrate more freely and with a tapered shank which by restricting the diameter of the main instrument assists extension of the natural scale, are not vouched for until Roman times. The true range of the Egyptian trumpets is effectively restricted to two notes, a rather poorly sounding fundamental and a clearer note between a ninth and tenth above; the bronze trumpet produces c⁺′e♭″, the silver b♭-c-″.[113] The tenth is a curious interval since the natural harmonic of a cylindrical tube is the twelfth as contrasted with a conical tube which sounds the octave, which is in fact voiced on the Egyptian trumpets with the greatest of difficulty. A similar phenomenon is noted with the *didjeridoo* probably due to both classes of instruments in fact being slightly, if irregularly, conical. The limited range of what have been shown to be Egyptian military instruments and their comparative lack of sophistication has been explained by their ancestry in simple cane or wooden pipes, ancient *didjeridoos* in fact, developing in an area lacking the conical and curved natural animal horns; these last are generally acknowledged as the ancestors of all instruments of the true horn family. On the other hand, even the latter, at least in the advanced Bronze Age of ancient Europe dating from about the eighth century onwards, can hardly be regarded as capable of throwing much light on problems of tonal systems in prehistoric times.

Two main groups of Bronze Age horns are known from northwestern Europe and both have been more thoroughly studied in recent years than any single class of prehistoric instruments with the exception of the simple bone flute. In the British Isles upwards of a hundred are known from Irish sites – there is one lost Sussex example – divisible musically into end- and side-blow types[114] and about half that number from Scandinavia, the *lurer*.[115] The second group are found isolated and usually at least in pairs suggesting ritual deposition while the associations of the Irish horns, although these are also found in multiples, are more varied. Both groups, as already noted, suggest skeuomorphs of animal horn prototypes, the Irish the small curved (but not twisted) horn of *Bos longifrons*, the larger more spectacular Scandinavian instruments the upswept, curved, and at the tip, inward-twisted horns of *Bos primigenius*, both prehistoric ancestors of modern breeds of domestic cattle – a point which has contributed to the already mentioned theory of a common veneration of the bull in Late Bronze Age Europe.[116] It is perhaps a pair of actual cow horns which are being played in the scenes incised on the slabs of the long cist of Kivik, Skåne which is probably to be dated about as early as the presumed date of the first *lurer* (Montelius III/IV).

The simpler Irish horns of the two types, those with the slightly oval hole (in lieu of a mouthpiece) set in the side of the tube, are only capable of one tone as are most of the ethnographic forms of side-blow horns of either shell or actual animal horn. On thirteen examples of Irish side-blow instruments the fundamentals range between g and d♯', nine lying between g and b. It was in fact, as Dr Coles has remarked, in the earliest musicological study of the Irish horns, during an attempt to test a side-blow horn that palaeo-organology suffered its first, and it is to be hoped, only martyr. A Dr Robert Ball of Dublin, convinced of the horns' musical nature, tried out their potential for himself. A contemporary account records that:

'It is a melancholy fact, that the loss of this gentleman's life was occasioned by a subsequent experiment of the same kind. In the act of attempting to produce a distinct sound on a large trumpet . . . he burst a blood vessel and died a few days after.'[117]

Noticeable on the castings which constitute the surviving parts of the Irish horns of both types is the lack of internal finishing suggesting no great degree of contemporary interest in their performance capabilities in view of the resultant variations in pitch. This lack of attention to practical points may be regarded as extending to the apparent lack of efficient mouthpieces on the end-blow horns. Many of the latter are incomplete and it is conceivable that wooden mouthpieces might have been used as on African and Brazilian specimens or the Dutch *midwinterhoorn* to be discussed further in the next paragraph. An end-blow horn from Drumbest, Co. Antrim (found with its cast-on tube and another end-blow and two side-blow horns), has a simple slightly splayed terminal much as on the Tut-ankh-amen trumpets (fig. 77, 4). This horn has a range of f d♯ 'c''f'', the second end-blow almost matching this (f d♯'c''), the broken mouthpiece preventing voicing of f''. Two of the two-piece end-blow horns found at Chute Hall, Co. Kerry, with at least two other end-blow and two side-blow horns, though lacking any true mouthpieces can be made to sound bf♯'b'd♯''. There seems yet again little tonal consistency to be observed from the performance of the Irish horns, although it is not necessary to assume that they should have to fit in to any modern pattern.[118] The association of the one-note side-blow instruments with the certainly more versatile end-blow, up to ten of the former and nine of the latter as found in the Dowris, Co. Offaly, hoard, might suggest their use in providing a 'drone' to simple melody on a second instrument; though this is rare in modern folk-music it is not in fact unknown,[119] but however this may be, the Irish series does not exhibit any concrete evidence for primitive 'orchestration.'

The same conclusions may be applied almost equally to the Scandinavian *lurer*. The Irish horns with their short and relatively wide tubes favour production of the fundamental or base tone and the lower partials of the harmonic series. The *lurer*, with a maximum range of sixteen partials (but only in the hands of twentieth-century Danish orchestral players!), in effect are limited to between nine and seven notes. When one approaches the point of over-blowing, a series of notes commencing with the octave followed by the harmonic of the fifth, fourth and so on to the seventh partial or harmonic produces a more or less coherent scale. The upper partials are however very difficult to produce and apart from the natural harmonics of the horn necessitating the large gaps in the lower register other breaks in what would otherwise be a true diatonic scale are due once more to imperfections in manufacture. Cup-shaped mouthpieces of a sort are in fact provided on most of the *lurer*, seen at their simplest on the presumed oldest example, Gullåkra, which has one not unlike the extant Irish mouth-piece of Drumbest. Since such cusped mouthpieces aid performance particularly on conical tubes as has already been noted, one would expect their association with the *lurer* to indicate a considerable degree of musical sophistication especially in view of their superficial resem-blances to modern mouthpieces (figs. 77, 6–7). In fact the form of mouthpieces on the *lurer* seems wholly arbitrary and the two basic types the result of individual casting whim rather than instrument maker's skill.[120] One incidental point about mouthpieces: Coles in com-menting on the common lack or breakage of the mouthpiece ends of the Irish end-blow horns suggests possible intentional 'killing' of the instruments pointing out survival of such practices in the Dutch *midwinterhoorn* of the province of Twente.[121] Even clearer evidence of inten-tional destruction is given by the Brudevælte *lurer* which when found in 1797 had all their six mouthpieces broken off and deposited separately, tied together. The *midwinterhoorn* is actually a wooden end-blow horn with tube mouthpiece cut at an angle something like the now lost Iron Age *carnyx* from the River Witham (see below) and a tonal range of (b♭)f′b♭′d″f″, the lowest note only being played with difficulty. In the context of wooden horns one should finally recall that there is a reference to a single wooden horn of presumed Bronze Age date from Diamond Hill, Killashandra, Ireland.[122]

Returning to the *lurer*, as we have observed earlier there is no need to expect a diatonic scale as a prerequisite for prehistoric music,[123] but examining the range of fundamentals for those *lurer* which have been acoustically examined, there is once more a disappointing lack of consistency (Table 4).

The comparatively restricted variation in fundamentals with the exception of the somewhat simpler and presumed earlier Swedish example may, as with the Irish side-blow horns, be a factor of manufacturing methods rather than musical selection. On the other hand since each group of *lurer* tested share the same fundamental, they could clearly, and by the law of averages would have produced simple harmony if only accidentally. Such casual harmony, so-called 'heterophony,' is common to all primitive groups.[124] The making and final deposi-tion of both Irish and Danish horns in identical forms would also seem to assume the playing of more than one instrument at one and the same time. In conclusion, however, Dr Coles' comment at the end of his study of the Irish horns would seem to go as far as we can at the moment:

'The *lurer* and Irish horns must be considered on the evidence available, as a northwestern European phenomenon of animal-horn wind-instruments translated into metal in areas where bronze casting techniques had already reached a degree of perfection unsurpassed elsewhere.'[125]

For horns and trumpets of the Iron Age one has to rely almost entirely on iconographic evidence. Brief mention has already been made of possible horns on Iberian pottery (p. 343 above), while two of the later series of Italian *situlae* show simple short curved horns: the Benvenuti *situla* from Este and the Arnoaldi *situla* from Bologna. A fifth-century mirror also from the Arnoaldi cemetery depicts a warrior blowing a similar horn.[126] A reflection of Etruscan forms has been claimed several times for the *situla* instruments and in view of what is known of Iron Age horns north of the Alps, the earliest of such instruments in Etruscan Italy are of considerable interest. The earliest extant Etruscan trumpet, of bronze but having basically the cylindrical form with added horn-shaped bell of our presumed wooden prototypes and present folk instruments such as the Swiss *Alpenhorn*,[127] is that from a fifth-century grave at Caere with an estimated range of seven partials or harmonics of the note G.[128] A small Etruscan bronze figurine from Torre Annunziatta (now in the British Museum) of about 470 B.C. shows a naked youth playing a trumpet but with the mug- rather than cup-shaped bell parallel to the main line of the instrument instead of turning out at an angle or back upon itself.[129] The figure holds the trumpet tilted down at an angle across the body suggesting an eccentrically placed mouthpiece like that of the *midwinterhoorn* or the Celtic trumpets. Another early representation of the straight-bored trumpet with horn-shaped bell is on part of a wall painting in the early fifth-century 'Tomba della Scimmia,' Chuisi.[130] The large tightly curved form of conical horn rather than trumpet which was to evolve into the Roman *bucina* is known from much the same period.[131] All this material is however too late to be regarded as influencing the forms of our Bronze Age horns.

Table 4

Provenance	Phase of Montelius B.A.	No. of instruments	Length in cm.	Fundamental
Gullåkra, Sweden	?III (probably later)	1	110	A♭
Maltbæk, Denmark	IV	2	188	E
Brudevælte I*	V	2	223, 224	C
Brudevælte II	V	3	192, 196, 197	E♭
Telerup	V	2	206, 208	D
Revheim	V	1	163	F♯
Folvisdam	VI	2	149	G

* A third instrument of this group was presented in 1845 to the now State Hermitage, Leningrad.

It is the Iron Age Celts, who directly or indirectly borrowed so much from Italy, who took over from there both main types of wind-instrument as well as their predominantly military or ceremonial use. It is nevertheless not until the second century at the earliest that we have evidence of the Celtic *carnyx* or war trumpet with its bell decorated with the totemic boar and known best from the three figures on the Gundestrup cauldron. In view of the now generally agreed Dacian origin of the last piece it is interesting to note a reference to two fragments of a 'Dacian' silver trumpet unfortunately lost during the First World War from Islaz in Rumania.[132] For the *carnyx* itself the basic study is Professor Piggott's own;[133] earliest are those shown amongst the accurately depicted Middle Le Tène booty on the Pergamene frieze probably executed by order of Eumenes II before 181 B.C.[134] Representations on Continental and British Celtic coinage and the Arch of Orange, the Deskford, Banff, boar's head, and the destroyed Tattershall Ferry, River Witham, fragments, depicted in extant drawings with angled mouthpiece, show the popularity of the war trumpet the length and breadth of the late Celtic world while Trajan's Column shows its use amongst the Dacians. Coins of Cunobelin seem to show animal horns and an ithyphallic figurine from the Hradiště *oppidum* (not generally recognized for what it is) the continuity of the simple end-blow horn with curved bell[135] (Pl. XVI, c) while the Late La Tène Durnau fragment looks closest to the form of the bell on such presumed prototypes as the Caere *lituus* but there is still a time lag of at least two centuries to account for. One other addition to the European lists may be made here: from the cemetery at Idria near Bača in the old eastern Hallstatt region comes a bronze figurine of a warrior with Illyrian tunic and ridged helmet.[136] The upraised right arm and pursed lips clearly represent a trumpeter in action, his separately made instrument now lost, while the grave-goods and style of the figurine[137] indicate a date probably in the fourth century, the helmet and other details suggesting Etruscan influences.

At the present time while one cannot deny the artistic genius of the La Tène period there is little evidence save ambiguous references to stringed instruments (see below) to show its musical qualities; such fine pieces as the Gaulish 'herald trumpet' from the Neuvy-en-Sullias sanctuary with its well-formed mouthpiece can only represent the direct influence of Rome,[138] while for the curved-horn type most of the native material evidence comes from the British Isles. The Gaulish horn from Nizza now in the Prähistorisches Staatssammlung in Munich, made in three sections,[139] is close to the presumed original form of the first-century B.C. fragment from the Llyn Cerrig Bach hoard.[140] This last is claimed as an Irish export in view of the only other extant horns of this curved type. Lough-na-Shade, Co. Antrim, found in 1794 allegedly with three other horns now lost, is considered of the third century B.C. on the basis of the design of the decorative disc taking the place of the bell[141] and the 240 cm.-long two-piece Ardbrin, Co. Down, horn has a simple rolled-over mouthpiece of precisely the same pattern as the Tut-ankh-amen trumpets (fig. 77, 5); there is also a published reference to another fragmentary horn of the Ardbrin type having been found near Loughbrickland also in Co. Down.[142] Both existing Irish horns have been tested to estimate their musical range[143] though neither is in a particularly good condition owing to the slackness of the riveted seams, and Lough-na-Shade will not in fact sound. Ardbrin at present gives only three notes – B♭++ f b♭+ – approaching for what it is worth the range of one of the Dowris end-blow horns. This however is the limit of our knowledge of the acoustic potentials of the Golden Age of the pre-Roman Celts.

Apollo's lyre, legacy of Greece?

The last group of instruments to be discussed in any detail, the multiple-stringed asymmetrical harp and symmetrical lyre, is really the most advanced musically speaking since not only do the individual strings indicate an obvious interest in a range of notes with the possibility of producing quite complex harmony on the one instrument but in the very existence of tuning methods, however primitive, a concern not just for a certain pitch but for maintaining that pitch.

In the ancient Near East the earliest evidence for stringed instruments dates once more to the third millennium B.C., in Egypt the bow harp,[144] in Sumeria the frame harp.[145] The famous Early Cycladic harp-playing figurine from Keros[146] must represent the western spread of the latter innovation. In central Europe however we have to wait once more until the Iron Age for positive evidence.[147] On the unique series of incised urns from the Ha.C cemetery at Sopron in Hungary are no less than six separate representations of primitive lyres being played, the strings, if one can correctly interpret the fairly crude drawing, being mainly four in number (fig. 77, 2).[148] Of much the same period, that is the seventh century B.C., is the late Kurd type bucket with repousse ornament from the Krollhugel *Fürstengrab* at Klein-Glein in Steiermark (fig. 77, 3). Here one figure is seen holding a four-string lyre while there is what appears to be the sound-board of a second.[149] Seewald regards all these representations as products not so much of the Celtic as the North Illyrian world while suggesting a different background for the lyres shown on three of the bronze *situlae*, Magdalenska Gora II (with strings not clearly defined), the Providence *situla* (? nine strings), and Certosa (five strings; Pl. XIV, b).[150] Friedrich Behn, observing the asymmetry of the lyre yokes as shown on the *situlae*, tentatively suggests links with Egypt, an unlikely theory which has not met with support. Indeed this asymmetry may be due to nothing more than an unskilled attempt at perspective. As with the pan-pipes, the influence of Greece in the eastern Hallstatt region is much more probable. The four-string lyre, the lyre of Homer's day, contemporary with the early Hallstatt Iron Age, has a long vogue in the Greek world.[151] Yet although there is a gradual increase in the number of strings from three to twelve by the fifth century B.C., the Hagia Triada sarcophagus of *c.* 1100 B.C. clearly shows a *seven*-string lyre.[152] Here the lyre's association with a death cult recalls that, on the Sopron vases, despite the seeming gaiety of many of the scenes, is included a funeral cortège. Despite detailed contemporary illustration, actual surviving examples of Greek lyres themselves are very rare though late finds in the British Museum allow close comparison with the modern five-string Uganda lyre and allow one to gain some idea of their far from brilliant timbre.[153] The existence of tuning bulges rather than keys and the relationship of the number of strings to the assumed pentatonic tuning of the lyre have been noted more than once.[154] Equally it should be remembered that a continual need for retuning would have been the price to pay for the absence of proper keys or pegs.

Seewald has put forward the settlement, *c.* 400 B.C., of La Tène Celts in the northern Balkans and Adriatic area as one reason why the lyre seems to disappear from this area after this date. There is some evidence to counter this view of the Celts' lack of interest in the lyre; beneath the rampart of the Dinorben, Denbighshire, hill-fort from the third-century B.C. occupation of a hut floor comes a curved antler plaque with nine perforations, suggested as part of the wrest-plank of a stringed instrument with at least eight of the holes being for pegs or other string fastenings (fig. 76, 3).[155] The antler is about 13·5 cm. long and the distance between the 'peg holes' *c.* 1 cm. which seems very little, the Sutton Hoo harp as reconstructed measuring about twice this and a modern Irish harp 1·25 cm. between strings. If the Dinorben fragment is indeed part of a musical instrument, then, *pace* Dr Carl Dolmetsch, in view of the evidence we have been discussing it is more likely to have come from a lyre rather than a member of the harp or psaltery family. As Dr Savory points out, there is once more the evidence of Celtic coins, and once more the difficulty of deciding to what a degree lyres on coins represent mere copyings or a living and local musical tradition; Mr Allen sees as schematic representations of lyres the rayed symbols found on many coins as far east as Germany, though in Britain the form is rare (fig. 76, 2).[156] Still, in the first century B.C. Diodorus Siculus was commenting on Gaulish 'lyric poets called *bardoi*' singing to the accompaniment of a stringed instrument[157] while Professor Kenneth Jackson has suggested that the Irish hero tales of the first millennium A.D. with their frequent reference to skilled harp-players reflect the society of the pre-Roman Iron Age.[158] It may seem strange then, that for the Irish harp, the instrument *par excellence* of the Celtic Far West, there is no representation of earlier than the tenth century A.D.[159]

In the non-Celtic regions of the early centuries A.D. the miniature Sutton Hoo harp reconstructed with six strings mainly on the basis of twelfth-century illustrations (Pl. XVI, d)[160] and its contemporary from the Taplow barrow[161] are hardly earlier than the first pictures in England of the so-called 'Nordic lyre,' the *gusle* or *gęśle* of Slav folk music.[162] On the Nordic lyre, which is related to the Welsh *crwth*, the yoke and sound-box are constructed as one solid oval with a circular opening across which the fan of the strings contracts down to the heel. The earliest actual lyres of this type date to about the eighth century, two being found as long ago as 1846 in Alemanic graves at Oberflacht in Württemberg. On the basis of the fragments now in the Museum für Vor- und Frühgeschichte, Berlin, and the Württembergisches Landesmuseum, Stuttgart, one six- and one eight-stringed instrument have been reconstructed.[163] Also with six strings is the lyre in the Römisch-Germanisches Museum, Cologne, from remains in the 'Grab des Sangers' beneath the St Severin Church; this too is dated to the eighth century (Pl. XVI, e).[164] Since the excavations of medieval Gdańsk in 1959 revealed a five-string *gęśle* of the later thirteenth century,[165] several others of much the same period have come to light in Poland and no less than fourteen from the major excavations of Old Novgorod.[166] Miss Alicia Simon in her summary of the Gdańsk finds notes that the seventh-century Byzantine writer Theophylaktes Simokattes gives an account of Slav prisoners with '*kitharai*' being brought from the Baltic to Thrace in A.D. 591 while Behn discussing the Oberflacht lyres quotes a verse from the early seventh-century Venatius Fortunatus which indicates the barbarian use of the *harpa*.[167] Clearly instruments of the harp/lyre family were well established in the northern Celtic and non-Celtic regions by the early centuries A.D. and it would be interesting to be able to have more evidence to support Otto Schrader's more than forty-year-old theory for an original diffusion of the lyre into Free Germany from Greece via the south of France, let alone Illyria. For the moment, as far as the musical archaeology of the early post-Roman period in Ancient Europe is concerned, we are still very much in the Dark Ages.

Here a term must be put to these random jottings in which I have attempted to deal only with the main classes of musical instruments for which we have archaeological evidence. Continued excavation in museum collections will doubtless bring more and perhaps revolutionary facts to light. For example, the Jew's harp with its open-ended metal frame and vibrating tongue producing the natural harmonic scale has, since Sachs, been regarded as originating in India and arriving in Europe as late as the fourteenth century A.D.[168] Now however it has been recognized that there are examples dating certainly to the Roman period and perhaps even to Late La Tène.[169] Palaeo-organology is not only a young but still virtually untried if not unrecognized study whose sole contributions at the moment may seem to be unduly pessimistic. If it has indicated that many problems are unlikely ever to be capable of solution – the invention of recording techniques was made perhaps three millennia too late – it has also helped to point up certain wrong attitudes, certain posings of non-problems, in our musical thinking.

To take one last example; to argue that the notes produced on a primitive bone pipe correspond with certain tonal values now used, thus indicating an accuracy of tuning and concern for absolute pitch on the part of the ancient instrument maker, is to start from a wholly false premise. Rather, a long series of pipes tending to conform to such a pattern for accidental reasons of manufacture may have led to the fixing of certain basic scales or modes. Even today when our Western equal temperment scale offers only one artificial solution to the 'problem' of standard pitch, it may be noted that many folk singers are less concerned with pitch fluctuations than, for example, the common blackbird; the lack of what one might term 'professionalism' is noticeable in most primitive music. Again, bagpipe chanter scales do not fall strictly within the principles of equal temperment; that the fifth and fourth almost invariably can be sounded could however be the chance result of equal spaces between the piercing of the finger holes;[170] certainly the fifth is a common interval to be noted from our experiments with early pipes (Table I). Sachs' theory of scale development based on certain instinctive principles following the simple notes of the harmonic series, chiefly the octave, fourth and fifth, is considered to lead to the use of diatonic scales close to our own and those of modern primitive melody. With this must be compared the apparent coexistence of non-modal and pentatonic scales as presented here. Though 'there can be no doubt that vocal music antedated instrumental music by an infinitely long period,'[171] instrumental techniques must have developed from the first side by side with the growing patterns of vocal performances. It is not impossible that the continued researches of palaeo-organology and ethnomusicology may yet further the systematization of these patterns. In his *Ancient Europe*, Stuart Piggott has indicated the preservation and transmission of accustomed modes in the barbarian society of prehistory through even to our times.[172] With the aid of musical archaeology we may glimpse another aspect of this broader picture.

Acknowledgments: My first debt is to Professor Stuart Piggott since it was he who, ten years ago, first suggested this topic as an antidote to what seemed at the time more arduous studies. In an essay which is no more than a culling of other men's flowers, more particular acknowledgments are owed to many colleagues, prehistorians, musicologists or both. Chief amongst these are: Mr D. F. Allen (London), Mr Anthony Baines (Uppingham School, Glos.), Dr J. M. Coles (University of Cambridge), Professor Frederick Crane (Louisiana State University, Baton Rouge), Dr A. Häusler (Martin-Luther-Universität, Halle-Wittenberg), Dr R. I. Jack

(University of Sydney), Professor T. A. Jones (Monash University, Melbourne), Dr J. G. Landels (University of Reading), Dr F. Ll. Harrison (University of Oxford), Mr James MacGillivray (London), Miss Joan Rimmer (Littlemore, Oxon.), Dr Otto Seewald (Vienna), Mr I. W. A. Spink (University of Sydney), and Professor Kurt Willvonseder (Salzburger Museum Carolino Augusteum, Salzburg). Aspects of my work in palaeo-organology have been materially assisted by grants from the University of Sydney Research Committee for which I am duly grateful.

Notes

1. *HiFi/Stereo Review* 13: 6 (1964) 43–9
2. Fétis, *Histoire générale de la musique* (1869) 25–6 and figs. 3–4
3. Schlesinger, *A bibliography of musical instruments and archaeology* (1912)
4. Sachs, *Geist und Werden der Musikinstrumente* (1929); *id.*, *The history of musical instruments* (1940); *id.*, *The rise of music in the ancient world, East and West* (1943)
5. Galpin, *Old English instruments of Music* (3rd ed., 1932); *id.*, *The music of the Sumerians, Babylonians and Assyrians* (1937)
6. *q.v. A.N.L.* I (1948) 11–13; see also n. 160.
7. Behn, *Musikleben in Altertum und frühen Mittelalter* (1954); (ed.) Besseler and Schneider, *Musikgeschichte in Bildern* II (1963–)
8. *e.g.* Austria: *Oberösterr. Heimatblättern* XIV (1960) 186–7; Hungary: Banner, 'Prehistoric musical instruments in the Carpathian Basin,' *Magyar Múzeum* II (1947); Rumania: *Beiträge zur Musikwissenschaft* VIII (1966) 3–14; Poland: *Archaeologia Polona* VIII (1965) 132 and n. 1; Belgium: *Bull. Inst. arch. liègeois* 67 (1949–50) 21–8
9. *e.g.* (ed.) Baines, *Musical instruments through the ages* (2nd ed., 1965); Harrison and Rimmer, *European musical instruments* (1964)
10. *Musical Quarterly* 24 (1938), 147–52; in general see Kunst, *Ethno-musicology* (3rd ed., 1959); for folk music of the Balkans and Asia Minor and related complex rhythmic patterns see *Antiquity and Survival* II: 4 (1958) 387–404 on which see also n. 55 below
11. Galpin, *op. cit.* (1937) 126–37
12. Harrison and Rimmer, *op. cit.* ill. 1; Leroi-Gourhan, *Préhistoire de l'art occidental* (1965), esp. 308–10 and fig. 57
13. Seewald, *Beiträge zur Kenntnis der steinzeitlichen Musikinstrumente Europas* (1934) 42–3
14. *New Scientist* XVI (1962) 511–14
15. Baines, *Woodwind instruments and their history* (2nd ed., 1962) 171
16. Sachs, *op. cit.* (1943) 45
17. *Oceania* XXVIII (1957) 7–8
18. Seewald, *op. cit.* (1934) 13 and Taf. I: 3–4; Buchner, *Musical instruments through the ages* (n.d.) Pls. 1–5
19. Seewald, *op. cit.* (1934) 128 and Taf. VIII: 11
20. *W.Z.M.L.U.* IX: 3 (1959) 326 and Taf. V: 1
21. *Antiquity* XXXIX (1965) 217–19; *Antiquity* XL (1966) 56–7
22. Seewald, *op. cit.* (1934) 59–126; *Mitt. d. Anthrop. Gesellschaft Wien* XCII (1962) 259–65; Buchner, *op. cit.* Pl. 6–7
23. (ed.) Baines, *op. cit.* (1965) 34–5; Collaer, *Musikgeschichte in Bildern* I: 1 (1964) 142–3 and ill.
24. Harrison and Rimmer, *op. cit.* (1964) 3 and ill. 8. The reconstruction was arranged by Miss Rimmer at the writer's suggestion; the co-operation of Dr Jiří Neustupný, Národní Muzeum, Prague and the British Leather Manufacturers' Research Association is gratefully acknowledged.
25. *Ausgrabungen und Funde* VIII (1963) 24–6 and Taf. 4a
26. *Cf. Arctic Institute of N. America : Anthropology of the North : Trans. from Russian Sources* IV (1963) 101–5
27. Seewald, *op. cit.* (1934) 22–58; *Ethnos* XIV (1949) 140–8; (ed.) Blume, *Musik in Geschichte und Gegenwart* IV (1955) col. 330–5; *Antiquity* XXXIV (1960) 6–13; *Antiquity* XXXV (1961) 55–7; *Galpin Soc. J.* XVI (1963) 85–94; *Galpin Soc. J.* XVII (1964) 116–17
28. *42. B.R.-G.K. 1961* (1962) 174–305 esp. 235 ff. and Abb. 5

29. I am indebted to Dr Bohuslav Klíma, A.Ú.ČSAV (Brno) for allowing me to examine in 1964 the unpublished material from Dolní Věstonice and Pavlov. The following notes were recorded for the Pavlov phalange whistles: a'''' (inv. no. 359360), c'''' (369657), f#'''' (561360), g'''' (432761). On earlier finds see *Congrès préhistorique de France : XIIe sess. 1936* (1937) 770–84

30. (ed.) Genovés, *A Pedro Bosch-Gimpera* (1963) 427–39 and fig. 7: 8

31. *M.I.A.SSSR.* LX (1959) 184 and fig. 56: 6

32. *Archives de l'Institut de Paléontologie humaine* XXV (1952) 59; *Antiquity* XXXIV (1960) 8 and Pl. II: 7

33. *K.S.I.I.M.K.* LIX (1955) 129–30 and fig. 54; *W.Z.M.L.U.* IX: 3 (1959) 321 and Taf. I: 4

34. *K.S.I.I.M.K.* LXIII (1956) 150–2 and fig. 70

35. Moravia: Moravské Muzeum, Brno inv. no. ve. 62.530 (unpublished). I am grateful to Dr K. Valoch for showing me this piece. Rumania: *Beiträge zur Musikwissenschaft* VIII (1966) 3

36. *Strena Helbigiana* (1900), 232 f.; Montelius, *La civilisation primitive en Italie* sér. B (1895), 120 f. and Pl. 19, fig. 18

37. Meduna, *Staré Hradisko : Katalog der Funde in Museum der Stadt Boskovice* (1961) Taf. 13: 11

38. inv. no. CXIV M III 10 (unpublished); information courtesy Professor S. S. Frere, University of Oxford

39. *Wiadomości arch.* XVI (1939) 348–56 and Tab. LXVI: 8, 10–13

40. Paarup: *Kuml* (1951) 148–9 and fig. 6: *Antiquity* XXXIV (1960) 11 and Pl. II: 1; Stockholm: information from Professor Frederick Crane

41. Roes, *Bone and antler objects from the Frisian terp-mounds* (1963) 59–62 and Pl. XLVIII ff.

42. *Antiquity* XXXIV (1960) 12; *Galpin Soc. J.* XVI (1963) 87

43. *Antiquity* XXXIV (1960) 10

43a. *Tijdschr. v.d. Vereeniging voor Nederlandse Muziek Geschiedenis* XX: 3 (1966) 178–85

44. Nettle, *Music in primitive culture* (1956) 48

45. *Galpin Soc. J.* XVI (1963) 91, Table I

46. *Galpin Soc. J.* V (1952) 34–8

47. Schlesinger, *The Greek aulos* (1939), *passim*

48. *Med. Arch.* V (1961) 176–80 and Pl. XXIX

49. inv. no. CXX B III 5 (unpublished): Professor Frere granted facilities for study

50. *Acta Praehistorica* (Buenos Aires) V–VII (1961–3) 176–82

51. *Acta Praehistorica* II (1958) 111–21

52. Hampel, *Antiquités préhistoriques de la Hongrie* (1876) Pl. XIII, figs. 29 and 31

53. Schlesinger, *op. cit.* (1939) 261

54. *Congrès préhistorique de France : XIIe sess. 1936* (1937) 773 and figs. 1 and 8

55. Harrison and Rimmer, *op. cit.* (1964) 2–3 and ill. 5–6; Bessaraboff, *Ancient European musical instruments* (reprinted, New York, 1964) 47–8

56. *Acta Arch. Hung.* V (1955) 133–45

57. Stiens, gem. Leeuwarderadeel (inv. no. 21–53): four finger holes and one possible thumb hole; Hantum, gem. Westdongeradeel (inv. no. 31–18): three finger holes

58. *Galpin Soc. J.* XVI (1963) 90

59. *Comptes rendus de l'Academie des Sciences* LXXIX (1874), 1277; see also Piggott, *Ancient Europe* (1965) 35

60. *W.Z.M.L.U.* IX: 3 (1959) 323; *Antiquity* XXXV (1961) 56

61. *Trans. American Phil. Soc.* XLVIII (1958) 69–70 and fig. 66; *W.Z.M.L.U.* IX: 3 (1959) 326–7 and Taf. III: 3. Three tubes only are mentioned in error in *Antiquity* XXXIV (1960) 56

62. *M.I.A.SSSR.* LX (1959) 159 ff.; *W.Z.M.L.U.* IX: 3 (1959) 325 and Taf. V: 2

63. *Archaeologia Polana* VIII (1965) 131–48; *Inventaria Arch. : Pologne* XVI (1966) PL 96, 1–2

64. (ed.) Federhofer, *Festschrift Alfred Orel* (1960), 166 and n. 28

65. *Römisch-Germanische Forschungen* XXVI (1962)

66. Compare the somewhat simplified drawing in Lucke and Frey, *op. cit.* Taf. 73 with Kastelic *et al.*, *Situla Art* (1965) Pl. 4

67. *Oberösterr. Heimatblättern* XIV (1960) 187

68. Wegner, *Musikgeschichte in Bildern* II: 4 (1963) 58; Fleischhauer, *Musikgeschichte in Bildern* II: 5 (1964) 22–3

69. Behn, *op. cit.* (1954) 110 and Abb. 145

70. e.g. *Musikgeschichte in Bildern* I: 1 (1964) 166–7 and ill.

71. Boardman, *The Greeks overseas* (1964) 232–6

72. *Zeitschrift für Ethnologie* XXXIV (1907) 190–1; Behn, *op. cit.* (1954) 111, 147 and Abb. 193
73. Behn, *loc. cit.*
74. *Pro Alesia* I (1906–7) 161 ff. and Pl. 21; Behn, *op. cit.* (1954) 146–7 noting seven not eight tubes
75. *Bayerische Vorgeschichtsblätter* XXVI (1961) 48–60 and Taf. 1–2
76. *Acta Musicologica* XXIV (1952) 108–12
77. Hickmann, *Musicologie pharaonique; études sur l'evolution de l'art musical dans L'Egypte ancienne* (reprint, 1956) 32–4; *id., Musikgeschichte in Bildern* II: 1 (1961) 24–7, 114 and 118–19
78. Schlesinger, *op. cit.* (1939); *A.J.A.* L (1948) 217–40; Aign, *Die Geschichte der Musikinstrumente des ägäischen Raumes bis um 700 b. Chr.* (1963)
80. Sachs, *op. cit.* (1940) 120
81. (ed.) Sherrington and Oldham, *Music, Librarians and instruments* (1961) 218–20
82. *Annual of the British School of Archaeology, Athens* LVIII (1963) 116–19
83. Harrison and Rimmer, *op. cit.* (1964) 7 and ill. 19
84. *Musikgeschichte in Bildern* II: 4 (1963) 30 and Abb. 9
85. Behn, *op. cit.* (1954) 101–3 and Abb. 134
86. *W.A.M.* LV (1954) 323; *Antiquity* XXXIV (1960) 9 and Pl. II: 6; *Antiquity* XXXV (1961) 56; Annable and Simpson, *Guide Catalogue of the Neolithic and Bronze Age collections in Devizes Museum* (1964) 26 and 45 = No. 167
87. *Beiträge zur Musikwissenschaft* VIII (1966) 8–9
88. Rijksmuseum Kam, Nijmegen cat. no. 62 (unpublished); information from Professor Crane
89. Fries Museum, Leeuwarden inv. no. 49ᴬ–153; for site see van Giffen in *5–6. Jaarverslag van de Vereeniging voor Terpenonderzoek* (1921–2); *7–8. Jaarverslag . . .* (1923–4)
90. *Arch. J.* CXVI (1959) 63, 85 and fig. 19: 20; *Medieval Arch.* V (1961) 179, n. 17. I am grateful to Mr Anthony Baines for his confirming remarks on the Hungate pipe.
91. Baines, 'Bagpipes,' *Pitt-Rivers Mus. Occ. Papers on Technology* 9 (1960) 30–2; *Scottish Studies* X: 1 (1966) 114–16
92. *P.P.S.* XXIX (1963) 342
93. *M.I.A.SSSR.* CX (1963) 107–8 and fig. 18
94. *Onomasticon* IV 74
95. Harrison and Rimmer, *op. cit.* (1964) 8 and ill. 22; Fleischhauer, *op. cit.* (1964) 84 and Abb. 47
96. Salazar, *La Música en España* (1955), Pl. 2; Baines, *op. cit.* (1960) 57–8 and fig. 30. For the Liria pottery in general see Piggott, *op. cit.* (1965) 223 and fig. 128 following Arribas, *The Iberians* (n.d., but 1963) 170 ff.; for representations of musicians *id.* 64 and figs. 4 (= Baines, *loc. cit.*), 6 (with ?horn player), and 13 (= Clark, *Archaeology and Society* (rev. ed., 1960) 224 and fig. 46 – 'San Miguel de Lina' [*sic*])
97. Baines, *op. cit.* (1960) 40–1; B.M. Add. MS. 15036
98. Harrison and Rimmer, *op. cit.* (1964)
99. Baines, *op. cit.* (1962) 201
100. *Galpin Soc. J.* IV (1951) 25–7, and figs. 1–2
101. Bossert, *Altkreta* (1923) Abb. 18 and 20; Zervos, *L'Art des Cyclades* (1957) fig. 302
102. *Antiquity* XXXIV (1960) 140–1
103. Zervos, *La Civilisation de la Sardaigne* (1954) 314–15 and fig. 389
104. Baines, *op. cit.* (1962) 195, 204 and fig. 44c; *id. op. cit.* (1960) 101; cf. *P.P.S.* XXIX (1963) 342, n. 2
105. *Archaeologia Értésitő* LXXXI (1954) 165–7 and Taf. XLII: 3a–b
106. (ed.) Federhofer, *op. cit.* 170, n. 47
107. *P.P.S.* XXIV (1958) 60 and No. 53
108. *Archaeologia Hungarica* XIV (1934); Baines, *op. cit.* (1960) 51–3 and fig. 24
109. *Oceania* XXVIII (1957) 8–10
110. *W.A.M.* LV (1954) 321 and fig. 3 ('Wilsford Barrow 18'); Annable and Simpson, *op. cit.* No. 212, Santu Pedru: Zervos, *op. cit.* (1957) fig. 388
111. *Ann. du Service des Antiquités de L'Egypte* suppl. 1 (1946); *J.R.A.I.* LXXVII (1946–7) 33–45
112. Hussey, *Verdi* (1940) 188–9
113. *J.R.A.I.* LXXVII (1946–7) 35 gives b♭ d″ and a♭ c″ respectively
114. *P.P.S.* XXIX (1963) 326–43
115. Broholm *et al.*, *The Lures of the Bronze Age* (1948) esp. chaps. V–VI; Broholm, *Bronzelurene i National-museet: en arkæologisk undersøgalse* (1958)

116. *Antiquity* XXXIX (1965) 217–19
117. *U.J.A.* VIII (1860) 101
118. *P.P.S.* XXIX (1963) 343
119. Baines, *op. cit.* (1960) 25–6
120. Broholm *et al.*, *op. cit.* 100–6
121. *Antiquity and Survival* II: 5–6 (1959) 292–6; *P.P.S.* XXIX (1963) 340
122. Evans, *Ancient Bronze implements* (1881) 360
123. *cf. P.P.S.* XXIX (1963) 346
124. Broholm *et al.*, *op. cit.* 96–7
125. *P.P.S.* XXIX (1963) 349
126. *Situlae :* Behn, *op. cit.* (1954) 129 and Abb. 160; Lucke and Frey, *op. cit.* (1962) cat. nos. 7 and 3; Federhofer, *op. cit.* 166–7; mirror: (ed.) Pallotino, *Mostra dell'arte delle situla del Po al Danubio* (1961) cat. no. 22
127. *Antiquity and Survival* II: 5–6 (1959) 295 and fig. 5
128. *J.R.S.A.I.* LXXXI (1951) 6 and 58; Behn, *op. cit.* (1954) 131; *P.P.S.* XXIX (1963) 348
129. Walters, *B.M. Catalogue of bronzes : Greek, Roman and Etruscan* (1899) no. 223 – information from Dr D. A. Strong
130. Fleischhauer, *op. cit.* (1964) 44, Abb. 18–19
131. *ibid.*
132. *Beiträge zur Musikwissenschaft* VIII (1966) 9
133. *Ant. J.* XXXIX (1959) 19, 32; review in *Galpin Soc. J.* XIII (1960) 108–11
134. Powell, *The Celts* (1957) 266 and Pl. 48–9; *40. B. R-G.K. 1958* (1959) 115, n. 136
135. Coins: *P.P.S.* XXIV (1958) 60 and nos. 52 and 79; Stradonice: Forman and Poulík, *Prehistoric Art* (n.d.) ill. 138 – 'carrying unidentified object'; Filip, *Keltové ve Střední Evropě* (1956), Tab. CXXV: 7, *id.*, *Celtic civilization and its heritage* (1962), 178 and Pl. XXXV – 'a man carrying a club'; only Buchner, *op. cit.*, Pl. 15 and Déchelette, *Manuel d'Archéologie* IV (2nd ed., 1927) 686 call it a trumpet
136. *Mitt. d. Prähist. Komm. d. Kaiser. Akad. d. Wiss.* I (1903) 291–363; Déchelette, *op. cit.*, fig. 452
137. I am indebted to Drs Lore and O.-H. Frey for their comments on this piece; see *Jahrb. d. Hist. Ver. f. das Fürstentum Liechtenstein* 33 (1933) 27 ff. and (for helmets) *Situla* 8 (1965) 177–86
138. Behn, *op. cit.* (1954) 144 and Abb. 186
139. Behn *op. cit.* (1954) 143 and Abb. 186
140. Fox, *A find of the Early Iron Age from Llyn Cerrig Bach, Anglesey* (1947) 34, 44–5, 86–7 and Pl. XII
141. In *Trans. Royal Irish Acad.* VIII (1802) 11; *U.J.A.* VIII (1860) 103 ff.; Fox, *loc. cit.*; Behn, *op. cit.* (1954) 150 and Abb. 186; *Arch.* XCVI (1955) 215 ff. and Pl. LXXXVa
142. *Archaeological Survey of N. Ireland : An archaeological survey of Co. Down* (1966) 54–6, fig. 33: 107 and Pl. 22
143. Information from Dr Coles and Dr Joseph Raftery, National Museum of Ireland. Comments on the tonal range are based on a recording made available by Radio Éireann
144. Behn, *op. cit.* (1954) 34–43 and Abb. 39–57; Hickmann, *op. cit.* (1961) 20 ff.
145. Galpin, *op. cit.* (1937) 26–37; Stander, *Die Harfen u. Leiern Vorderasiens in babylonischer u. assyrischer Zeit* (1961)
146. Zervos, *op. cit.* (1957) fig. 316–17; see also *ibid.* fig. 333–4 and Behn, *op. cit.* (1954) 90 and Abb. 122 – wrongly titled 'Amorgos' for a pair from Thera; all three figures play bow harps
147. Federhofer, *op. cit.* 159–71
148. *Archaeologia Hungarica* XIII (1934); Piggott, *op. cit.* (1965) 181, 199 and fig. 111
149. *Praehistorische Zeitschrift* XXIV (1933) 219–82; (ed.) Pallotino, *op. cit.* (1961) cat. no. 5
150. Federhofer, *op. cit.* 106–7 and n. 30; Lucke and Frey, *op. cit.* cat. nos. 22 (sixth/fifth century), 1 (early fifth), 4 (early fifth)
151. *Mitt. Deutsch. Arch. Inst. (Athen. Mitt.)* XIV (1929) 194–200
152. Behn, *op. cit.* (1954) 80 and Abb. 108; Marinatos, *Crete and Mycenae* (1960) 151–2 and Pl. XXIXA
153. Hickmann in *Musik in Geschichte und Gegenwart* V (1956) cols. 1541–4; (ed.) Baines, *op. cit.* (1965) 44–5; Harrison and Rimmer, *op. cit.* 6–7
154. Sachs, *op. cit.* (1940) 134–5; *Class. Quarterly* XLIX (1956) 169–86; Harrison and Rimmer, *loc. cit.*
155. Gardner and Savory, *Dinorben* (1964) 169–70, fig. 26: 3 and Pl. XXXIV 6: 2

156. *P.P.S.* XXIV (1958) 58 and 60; additional comments *in litt.* See also Forrer, *Keltishe Numismatik* (1908) figs. 447–9; Lengyel, *L'art gaulois dans les médailles* (1954), Pl. XVII, 197 (= most realistic, a coin of the Redones)

157. *Bibliotheke Historike* V 31

158. Jackson, *The oldest Irish tradition : a window on the Iron Age* (1964) 24 ff.

159. Bessaraboff, *op. cit.* (1964) 214–17; Harrison and Rimmer, *op. cit.* 13 and ill. 34

160. *Proc. Royal Institute G.B.* XXIV (1947–50) 440–9 and Pl. II; *Nature* CLXI (1950) 339–41; *P.S.I.* XXV (1950) 63; C. L. Wrenn reprinted in (ed.) Nicholson, *An anthology of Beowulf criticism* (1963) 321–5

161. *P.S.I.* XXV (1950) Pl. XV

162. Harrison and Rimmer, *op. cit.* ill. 32; in general see Werner in *Aus Verfassungs- und Landesgesch. : Festschr. f. Theodor Mayer* I (1954) 9–15

163. Niemeyer in *Musik in Geschichte und Gegenwart* (4th ed. 1816–17); Bessaraboff, *op. cit.* 211 and Pl. VIII: cat. no. 225

164. *I.P.E.K.* XV–XVI (1941–2) 124–39

165. *Galpin Soc. J.* X (1957) 63–5

166. Poland: *Prace i materiały Muz. Arch. i Etnograficzego w Łódzi* ser. arch. 12 (1966) 7–35; Novgorod: *K.S.I.I.M.K.* XCIX (1964) 5–6 and ris. 9; Thompson, *Novgorod the Great* (1967) 101 and fig. 103

167. Behn, *op. cit.* (1954) 152 ff. and Abb. 197

168. Sachs, *Reallexikon der Musikinstrumente* (reprint, 1964) 255; see for example *M.I.A. SSSR.* LXV (1959) 117 and ris. 103; Thompson, *op. cit.*, 76 and 101 with fig. 78 = Old Novgorod (? sixteenth century A.D.)

169. Information from Proffessor Crane: Roman: Rijksmuseum Kam, Nijmegen, cat. no. 75a; La Tène: *Revue du Berry et du Centre* LXI (1935) 101–5 and LXII (1936) 6–11

170. Bessaraboff, *op. cit.* (1964) 86; Baines, *op. cit.* (1960) 22–4

171. *Oceania* XXVIII (1957) 6

172. Piggott, *op. cit.* (1965) 259–60

Index